Marriages
and
Related Items
Abstracted from the

MENDON
DISPATCH

of
Mendon, Adams County
Illinois

1877–1905

Mrs. Joseph J. Beals, Sr.
&
Sandy Kirchner

HERITAGE BOOKS
2015

HERITAGE BOOKS

AN IMPRINT OF HERITAGE BOOKS, INC.

Books, CDs, and more—Worldwide

For our listing of thousands of titles see our website
at
www.HeritageBooks.com

Published 2015 by
HERITAGE BOOKS, INC.
Publishing Division
5810 Ruatan Street
Berwyn Heights, Md. 20740

Copyright © 1997
Mrs. Joseph J. Beals, Sr. and Sandy Kirchner

International Standard Book Numbers
Paperbound: 978-0-7884-0749-9
Clothbound: 978-0-7884-6203-0

Contents

-Note to Reader-

Pages 273 and 274 are identical. Since this book was manually
typed and the error could not be easily corrected, we chose to print the
manuscript in its original form. We appologize for the mistake.

INTRODUCTION

The death related items in this book were abstracted from the *Mendon Dispatch* newspapers of Mendon, Illinois. These papers were dated from 1877 through 1905. In the early 1960s, while doing research on our own genealogy in the *Mendon Dispatch*, we found so much other valuable information that we decided to start writing it all on 3 x 5" index cards. We wrote down any items that mentioned a family name. Although this book consists of death related announcements, our collection of index cards includes information from advertisements, jury lists, criminal courts, and letters remaining at the post office. We hope to prepare these remaining items for publication as time permits. An appendix in this book contains an additional list of names.

The Rosebud was the first printed newspaper; it was first published July 3, 1857. The first privately owned newspaper was established in 1877 and known as the *Mendon Enterprise*. In 1878 the ownership and name were changed. The new name for the newspaper was the *Mendon Dispatch*.

Mendon Township was originally part of the military tract called "Bear Creek Country," since its northern boundary was Bear Creek and the southern was Rock Creek. Mendon became a township in 1851. In 1829 the records show the first settler in the county to be Ebenezer Riddle. Many of the earliest settlers were from Kentucky and Connecticut. Many of these settlers brought their families with them.

The Mendon prairie was originally settled in 1829. This area was to be the location for the village of Fairfield, which was laid out in 1833. In 1839 the name of Fairfield was changed to Mendon when it was discovered that a town of Fairfield already existed.

In 1832 the 160 acre site, which was to become the village of Mendon, was purchased for $200.00. The $1.25 per acre was the going price for land. The first sale of lots was in the fall of 1833. The first building was a blacksmith shop.

In 1867 Mendon was incorporated as a town, its boundaries embracing one square mile. Feed and flour mills were the leading enterprises of the early days.

Mrs. Joseph J. Beals, Sr.
Mrs. Sandy Kirchner
Box 279
Cherokee, IA 51012

ADAMS COUNTY

Illinois

1872

	R5W	R6W	R7W	R8W	R9W	R10W
T2N	Northeast	Houston	Keene		Lima	
T1N	Clayton	Camp Point	Honey Creek	Mendon	Ursa	
T1S	Concord	Columbus	Gilmer	Ellington		
T2S	McKee	Liberty	Burton	Melrose		
T3S	Beverly	Richfield	Payson	Fall Creek		

1

Aaron, Charles N.   "Big Neck"   Apr 28, 1892
    Charles N. Aaron of Chiola, who was murdered by a "big negro" was a
nephew of Caleb Aaron of this community. Mr and Mrs A. attended the funeral
there.

Abrames, Wm A.   "Lima"   May 17, 1883
    Rev. J.W. Madison red'd his commission as a notary public in the place
of Wm A. Abrames deceased. Mr A. died May 2nd at his home in Lima.

Abrams. Mrs Ellen   Set 22, 1898
    see Rawlings-------son of Mrs V. K. Rawlings

Abrams, Mrs Ellen C.   Mar 14, 1901
    see Rawlings, John H.

Abrams, William A.   "Probate"   May 31, 1883
    3rd Monday of July 1883   Ellen C. Abrams, Ex.

Achese, Wesley   "Coatsburg"   Jan 22, 1891
    Died Jan 12th at the home of his uncle, Perry Barlow, Wesley Achese in
his 35th yr. Services at the Christian church. Body taken to Columbus for
burial.

Ackerman, Miss Mary   "Coatsburg"   Nov 20, 1884
    Miss Mary Ackerman was buried here Nov 13th

Adair,   "Local"   Apr 19, 1900
    The 5 month old baby of Mr and Mrs Charles Adair of York Neck was buried
in Coatsburg cemetery Sat.

Adair,   "Local"   Sep 4, 1890
    3 yr old son of Mr and Mrs J. M. Adair of York Neck fell into a well and
drowned Sept 2nd.

Adair, -----   "Marcelline"   Aug 22, 1901
    died, the yuongest child of Mr and Mrs Frank Adair. Buried Franklin
cemetery Thursday morning at 10.

Adair, Charles F.   "died"   Nov 4, 1880
    Died, in Quincy Oct 30th of typhoid fever, Charles F. Adair. He was 3rd
child of Jas. Adair of Mendon twp. 27 yrs old. Funeral was held at his father
home by Rev Pershire.

Adair, Mrs Elizabeth   "Obituary"   Jun 9, 1898
    Died, at her home in Honey Creek twp June 3rd, Elizabeth Adair, wife of
J. R. Adair. Elizabeth Anne Hudson was born in Jefferson Co. Tenn. March 18th
1839. was 59 yrs 2 mo's 16 days old. Moved with parents to Adams Co. May 1868
Lived York Neck then Big Neck. Married J. R. Adair Jan 9, 1872. They had 3
sons and 2 daughters all survive her. Joined the Christian church 1872-
Services by Elder Shoptaugh and Rev Reed in Christain church at Coatsburg.
Buried in village cemetery. Leaves husband and 5 children, 3 brothers, and
2 sisters.

Adair, Horatio Thomas   "Obituary"   Nov 24, 1898
    Died- Horatio Thomas Adair of <u>paraltsis</u> Nov 17th at his home near
    Marcelline. Age 69 yrs 4 mo's 6 days. Born Boone Co. Mo. Mar 23, 1829
    Came to Adams Co. with his parents Jan 1, 1832. Married F. M. Randolph
    Apr 18, 18<u>84</u> who survives him. Buried Keith cemetery Sat. at noon.
    Services by Rev E. K. Crews of Mendon at Mr A's home.

Adair, James   "Probate"   Apr 28, 1892
    1st Monday of June 1892 Emily J. Adair, Adm.

Adair, Mr Jas.   "Local"   Mar 17, 1892
    Mr Jas. Adair died Sunday A. M. 70 yrs old. Buried in Franklin cemetery
    He was a brother of Mrs Tarr recently deceased.

Adair, Mr Jas. F.   "Died"   Mar 11, 1880
    Died- Mr Jas. F. Adair at his hime 1½ miles E. of Marcelline last
    Monday. He was one of the oldest persons in this part of the Co.
    Born in state of Delaware Oct 22, 1786. Married in Bourban Co. Ky.
    in 1811. Moved to Boone Co. Mo. in 1823 and on to Adams Co. Ill.
    in 1832. Father of 11 children, 9 still living. All at funeral except
    Mrs M. James who lives in Colorado.

Adair, Mr James   "Marcelline"   Mar 17, 1892
    Died- Mr James Adair Sunday at his home 2 miles N. E. of here. Born
    Bourban Co. Ky. April 4, 1822. Came with parents to Adams Co. in 1831.
    Married 2 times and father of 8 children- 4 by 1st wife 2 survive him.
    Also his last wife and 4 small children survive him. Services at
    Franklin church by Rev M. L. Schmuker.

Adair, John   "Probate"   Jan 23, 1890
    1st Monday of April 1890   George A. Cornaga, Adm.

Adair, John   "Loraine"   Aug 1, 1889
    Died- word of the death of John Adair, formerly of this place,
    reached here from Colo. Sat. His wife is daughter of Thomas Lowry, of
    Houston twp.

Adair, John R.   "Probate"   Jan 9, 1902
    1st Monday of March 1902   Anderson E. Adair, Adm.

Adair, Mrs M. A.   "Died"   Mar 16, 1899
    Last Friday Mrs M. A. Adair was called to attend funeral of her
    brother at or near Elvaston. He had been an invalid 13 yrs. Buried Sun.

Adair, Martha   "Died"   Dec 26, 1878
    Died- our grandmother Martha Adair. Born Aug 22, 1794 in Bourban Co. Ky
    where she lived until 1823 when she moved to Boone Co. Mo. with her
    husband James F. Adair whom she married at age 16 yrs. They lived in
    Boone Co. for 9 yrs and then to Adams Co. She had 11 children. All
    living except Richard and Robert who died 2 or 3 yrs ago. Grandmother
    of 50- gr. grandmother of 53. She had 10 sisters and brothers. James F.
    Adair was born Oct 22, 1786 in Delaware. Moved to Ky. also leaves
    husband.

Adair, Mrs Martha — May 3, 1905
 see McKinney, J. W.

Adair, Nancy Jane   "Obituary"   Apr 27, 1904
 Nancy Jane Adair was born Dec 30, 1817 and died Apr 22, 1904 was 86 yrs
 3 mo's 23 days old. Married Wm M. Wade in 1834 and had 3 children, 2 sons
 1 daughter. She was left a widow in 1842 with 3 children and married 2nd
 Nov 17, 1844 to James A. Goodwin and had 1 daughter. Mr G. died in
 Sept 1881. She joined M. E. church 1847. Moved to Loraine 1882. Leaves 1
 daughter, 4 grandchildren and 4 gr. grandchildren. Funeral Sun. 9 A. M.
 Apr 24th from the house. Buried Keath cemetery.

Adair, Ray   "York Neck"   Sep 11, 1890
 Ray, son of Mr and Mrs J. M. Adair age 16 mo's fell into a slough Tues.
 and broke his neck. Buried York Neck. An older brother mentioned, but
 no name given for him.

Adair, Richard A.   "Probate"   Feb 9, 1888
 1st Monday of April 1888   John Pratt, Adm.

Adair, Richard   "Loraine"   Feb 2, 1888
 Funeral of the late Richard Adair was well attended last Monday under the
 auspices of the G. A. R. post of Loraine. Services by Elder Rice Harris
 of Basco. Buried in our cemetery. Leaves a wife and daughter, 2 sons,
 an aged mother, brother and sister.

Adair, R. A.   "Loraine"   Jan 26, 1888
 Died- R. A. Adair Sun. 2 A. M. of pneumonia. Funeral 1 P. M. today.

Adair, Sallie   Oct 17, 1895
 see Stone, Mr Micajah

Adair, Mr Taylor   "Lima"   Mar 17, 1892
 Mr Taylor Adair went to see his father Mr James Adair Sun. and found
 him dead. He having died in the early morning.

Adair, Wilson   "Local"   Jul 20, 1904
 Died- Wilson Adair, age 70 yrs at his home at Marcelline early Sun. A. M
 Buried Mon. P. M. Son Charles of Nebr. failed to arrive before his
 father's death. Leaves widow and several children. "Whig"

Adams,   "Camp Point"   Aug 25, 1881
 Died- baby of William J. Adams Aug 20th
 same paper says- Born to Will Adams, a boy

Adams, Rev G. F.   Jun 26, 1884
 Rev G. F. Adams of Blandenville was shot while hunting Jun 11th.
 He was 35 yrs old.

Addis, Charles   Apr 14, 1892
   see Wible, Sarah

Addis, Cora Bell   Apr 14, 1892
   see Wible, Sarah

Agard, Mrs   "Local"   Nov 11, 1897
   Died- Mrs Agard of Marcelline Monday of rupture of a blood vessel.
   Was about 60 yrs old. "Herald"

Agard, Bert   "Local   Aug 11, 1898
   Died- Bert, son of widow Agard of Marcelline last Thursday, age 13
   yrs, 8 mo's. Buried the next day in Keith graveyard.

Agard, Bert   "Local Ursa Aug 6th"   Aug 18, 1898
   Died- Bert, youngest child of Mrs Jennie Agard of Marcelline. Born
   Dec 3, 1884 and died Aug 4th. Age 13 yrs 8 mo's. Leaves mother,
   5 brothers and 2 sisters. Mr W. I. Agard his father died 3 yrs ago.

Agard, Irving   "Indian Grave"   Jun 13, 1895
   Died, Mr Irving Agard Sunday night. Buried today at 11.

Agers, Freddie   "Coatsburg"   May 2, 1889
   Died- at his home in Coatsburg Sunday Apr 20th little Freddie, son
   of Charles and Sophia Agers, Age 3 yrs 8 mo's 4 days.

Agey, Mrs Mary   Feb 4, 1892
   see Groves, Mrs Amanda

Ahalt, Grandma   "Ursa"   Apr 18, 1901
   Died, Grandma Ahalt of near Rock Creek last Friday. Buried in Denson
   cemetery Sun. Funeral at the M. P. church.

Ahalt, Mrs   "Marcelline"   Apr 18, 1901
   A large number of people of this vicinity attended the funeral of
   Mrs Ahalt at Ursa Sunday.

Ahland, Wm   "Local"   Mar 16, 1904
   Wm Ahland, who formerly lived in Mendon twp, but late of near Palmyra,
   died of pneumonia Sat. P. M. Buried in cemetery at Palmyra, Mo.
   He visited here a short while ago.

Aikens, Minta   "Loraine"   Mar 2, 1882
   Died, Miss Minta, oldest daughter of Dr Jas. S. Aikens and wife
   on Feb 22nd.

Akers, Mrs   Dec 8, 1886
   see Nichols, Mrs H. C.

Akin, Capt Wm B.   Mar 13, 1884
   Capt Wm B. Akin of Co. K. 78th Ill. Inf., brother of Dr Akin of
   Loraine and of Mrs Dr Coffield of Mendon died at Lewiston, Idaho
   Feb 25th.

Akins, ___   "Loraine"   Jan 29, 1880
    Died- Friday A.M. , daughter of Dr Jas. Akins. Age 18 mo's

Akins, Mrs Dr   Jan 23, 1890
    see McFarland, John

Akins, Dr   Feb 9, 1899
    see Coffield, Dr James

Akins, Dr and Mrs   Mar 30, 1899
    see Brown, Mrs Lillie

Akins, Miss Alice   Mar 30, 1899
    see Brown, Mrs Lillie

Akins, Miss Bessie   Mar 30, 1899
    see Brown, Mrs Lillie

Akins, Miss Emma   "Local"   Jun 1, 1904
    Miss Emma, 2 nd eldest daughter of Mr and Mrs Wm Akins of Loraine,
    died Sunday at 5 A.M. of measles. Buried Franklin cemetery Tuesday.

Akins, Harry D.   Mar 30, 1899
    see Brown, Mrs Lillie

Akins, Homer   "Loraine"   Sep 6, 1888
    Died- Homer Akins, youngest son of Dr and Mrs J.S. Akins. Buried
    in the wheat at Mr Lemmon's elevator. Was 13 yrs old. Services by Rev
    C.F. McKown of Clayton, assissted by Rev R.P. Droke of Mendon at the
    Dunkard church at 2 P.M. Saturday. Buried in our cemetery.

Akins, Jesse   "Loraine"   Oct 23, 1890
    Little Jesse Akins, youngest son of Dr and Mrs M.J. Akins died
    October 23rd.

Akins, Lillie   Mar 30, 1899
    see Brown, Mrs Lillie

Akins, Mary Arvilla B.   Feb 9, 1899
    see Coffield, Dr James

Akins, Wm B.   Mar 30, 1899
    see Brown, Mrs Lillie

Akins, Mrs Wm   "Big Neck"   Apr 5, 1888
    Mr Steven Groves recently rec'd word of the death of his sister,
    Mrs Wm Akins of Missouri. She was well known here.

Alexander, Mrs J.C.   "Loraine"   May 12, 1881
    Mrs J.C. Alexander died May 10th. Was buried at the old Reese burying
    ground.

Alexander, Perry   "Local"   Jul 16, 1891
    death of Perry Alexander of Adams Co. at his home the latter part of
    the week. Funeral Sunday July 12th by Rev John Ruddell of Marcelline.
    Father was Samuel Alexander. Sister is Mrs James Thornton of Mt Hebron.

Allen, _____   "Ursa"   Jul 16, 1891
    a boy named Allen age 15 yrs living west of Ursa died of Cholera
    July 10th.

Allen, _____   "Tioga"   Jul 23, 1891
    the burial of a son of Mr Gideon Allen age 16 yrs took place in the
    Tioga cemetery Sunday.

Allen, Old Grandma   "Loraine"   Jul 28, 1886
    Old Grandma Allen died Tuesday and buried Thursday at Tioga. Mr and
    Mrs Allen came to this country in an early day.

Allen, _____   "Ursa"   May 28, 1903
    C.C. Allen (Bud) rec'd word this A.M. that his father had just died.

Allen, Andrew   "Tioga"   Dec 28, 1893
    Andrew Allen, age 10 yrs whose father lives in the bottoms was buried
    at this place Wed.

Allen, Mrs Elizabeth   "Tioga"   Jul 28, 1886
    died, Mrs Elizabeth Allen age 60 yrs. husband was John Allen-- They
    had lived in this twp over 40 yrs. Buried in Tioga cemetery July 21st.
    Leave husband and several children.

Allen, R.H.   "deaths Adam Co. Quincy"   Mar 16, 1899
    died R.H. Allen Friday A.M. of grip and pneumonia, born Illinois
    leaves wife and three daughters.

Allison, Mrs Elizabeth   Mar 17, 1898
    see Nedrow, Mrs Eliza

Alphine, Mrs M.J.   "Payson"   Aug 19, 1880
    Mrs M.J. Alphine daughter of S. Hendricks died on Monday Aug 16th of
    consumption.

Alsman, Mrs Emma   "Fall Creek"   Mar 17, 1886
    Mrs Emma Alsman died last Sunday of Consumption and buried at the
    Fall Creek M.P. church Monday. Her husband was buried at the same
    place about a yr ago, she leaves one child a little over a yr old.

Altenhein, John F.   "Local"   May 23, 1895
    died, John F. Altenhein formerly if Ellington twp died at the old home-
    stead Monday eve. born Oct 8, 1861 in Melrose twp Adams Co. Was a
    farmer until about 5 yrs ago when he went into the commission business
    at 1221 Broadway, Quincy. Leaves a wife and 1 son. Buried in Woodland
    cemetery.

7

Altheide, Peter   "Local"   Jul 10, 1890
    Peter Altheide of Melrose died last Monday morning. He was killed in a
    mower accident on his farm. No age given.

Altheide, Roy   "Tioga"   May 31, 1900
    Last Tuesday afternoon Roy Altheide, age 17 yrs of Sutter vicinity was
    killed by lightning when working in a field in his aunt's farm, Mrs
    Mary Altheide. Funeral Thursday at Evangelical church by Rev P. Ott--
    buried in German cemetery.

Althouse, Mrs Anna Isabelle   "Obituary"   Mar 2, 1904
    Mrs Anna Isabelle Althouse, who has lived in St. Louis since 1833
    died at her home Sun 9 P.M. Feb 21st 1904--was nearly 91 yrs old--
    born at Bremen, Germany where her father was a miller. In 1833 she
    came to U.S. and went directly to St.Louis--in 1840 she married
    Henry Althouse, they celebrated their 50th wedding anniversary in 1890-
    two yrs later Mr A. died--three children survive her, August of
    Washington D.C. and Misses Nettie and Anna Althouse--had 9 grand-
    children.
    (deceased was Mrs Charles Shupe's grandmother, Ed.)

Alverson, Miss Sarah   Oct 2, 1879
    see Wood, Mr Henry

Amburn, Bertram   "deaths in Adams Co., Quincy"   Apr 20, 1899
    died--Bertram Monday A.M. of typhoid pneumonia-- lived in Quincy since
    Sept 13, 1874--was a pressman by trade.

Ammerman, _____   "Payson"   Aug 4, 1881
    died a one yr old child of T.V. Ammerman. Buried July 30th, 1881

Ammerman, Mrs   "Center"   Apr 14, 1881
    died Mrs Ammerman, a sister of Mrs J. Funk at hre home in Quincy
    last Sat., Apr 9th.

Anderson, _____   "Local"   Nov 11, 1897
    died--infant child of Mr and Mrs Riley Anderson from convulsions
    Monday night--buried following day in village cemetery.

Anderson, Capt.   "Local"   Mar 12, 1885
    died, Capt Anderson of Marcelline March 7th. He had passed the alloted
    age of mortals by several yrs. Services by S.H. Bradley, D.D.G.M.

Anderson, _____   "Local"   Sep 27, 1894
    died--the 3 month old child of Mr and Mrs Riley Anderson on Tuesday
    eve. Buried in Mnedon cemetery.

Anderson, _____   "Personal"   Apr 12, 1883
    Mr and Mrs Edward Anderson lost an infant daughter last week, about
    three months old.

Anderson, _____ Mrs   "Obituary"   Apr 13, 1899
    see Hill, Mrs DeWitt

Anderson, Eddie   "Obituary"   Mar 21, 1889
  see Higbie, Mrs Edmund

Anderson, Mrs G. A.   "Obituary"   Dec 6, 1900
  see Slonigar, Joshua

Anderson, Mrs. Capt. J.C. "Local"   Oct. 26, 1887
  Mrs. Anderson, widow of the late Capt. J.C. Anderson and mother of
  Mrs. W.E. Miller died at her home in Marcelline last week.

Anderson, Katie   "Obituary"   Mar. 21, 1889
  see Higbie, Mrs. Edmund

Anderson, Oscar   "Ursa"   Sep. 22, 1898
  died--Oscar Anderson, age 29 yrs. last Sunday S.W. of this place of
  typhoid fever, buried in Keith cemetery on Monday.

Anderson, Mrs. T.B.   Jun. 30, 1898
  see McAdams, Charles

Anderson, Thos. B.   "Obituary"   Jul. 9, 1903
  Thos. B. Anderson born Dec. 13, 1865, at Marcelline, Ill. died at his
  home in Ursa July 5th--age 37 yrs 6 mo's 22 days. Married Mrs. Mattie
  McAdams, June 6, 1886--leaves wife and 2 children, Ruby and Lossa, his
  mother of Wheatland, Calif. was a member of Christian church at Marcelline.
  Services at the home by Rev. S.R. Reno of Mendon and buried Keith
  cemetery.

Anderson, Mr. Thos. B.   "Local"   Jul. 9, 1903
  Mr. Thos. B. Anderson, age 37 yrs died at his home in Ursa Sunday after
  a lingering illness from lung trouble. Leaves a widow and 2 children.
  Buried Tuesday A.M. in Keith Cemetery.

Anderson, Tommy   "Ursa"   Jul. 9, 1903
  Tommy Anderson died of consumption Sunday afternoon--buried Keith
  Cemetery today.

Andrew, Euphemia Virginia   Mar. 9, 1904
  see Huston, Mrs. James

Andrew, J.M.   Mar. 9, 1904
  see Huston, Mrs. James

Andrew, Mr. and Mrs.   "Obituary"   Feb. 25, 1892
  see Halsey, Wiley

Andrew, Miss Patience   "Probate"   Mar. 3, 1892
  see Halsey, Wiley

Andrews, Mrs.____   Jan. 17, 1895
  see Walker, John C.

Andrews, Adela Drusilla   "Obituary"   Dec. 22, 1898
  see Nedrow, Mrs. Adela (Andrews)

Andrews, George M.   "Local"   Oct. 2, 1902
    George M. Andrews of Denver, Colo., one of the engineers on the Denver
    and Rio Grande R.R. was killed Tuesday Sept. 23rd near Monument, Colo.
    by the explosion of the boiler. Had worked for the co. since 1885--
    1st as a fireman--before that he had lived Mendon and worked for his
    uncle, Mr. Jas. Andrew. Mr. Myers Andrew of Denver is a cousin of the
    deceased.

Andrew, Mrs. J.M.   "Obituary"   Dec. 2, 1897
    see Gilmer, Frederick A.

Andrews, J.W.   "Carthage Gazette"   Mar. 5, 1885
    The suicide of J.W. Andrews on the 21st of Feb. he was 38 years old--
    born and raised in Warsaw, Ill., moved to Washington territory about
    2 yrs ago, but returned to Warsaw about a week ago. He shot himself
    through the temple. Buried Monday. Had relatives in Carthage and Warsaw.

Andrew, James   "Death"   Aug. 27, 1903
    James Andrew died last Sunday P.M., August 23rd, at his farm home 4 miles
    N.E. of Mendon-- came to Adams Co. 50 years ago and farmed along Bear
    Creek (40 acres). His older son James Myers Andrews came from Denver,
    Colo. to see his father who was attended by another son, John, who lived
    with his dad. Was born Adams Co. Penn. Dec. 1, 1823 and there married
    Miss Margaret L. Seabrooks in 1840--they had 5 children--wife died 6 yrs
    ago--and eldest son, William, about 8 yrs ago. Surviving children are
    Mrs. Wiley Halsey, of Keene Twp., John and Mrs. James Huston both of here
    and Jas. M. of Denver, Colo. He was a Republican and Lutheran.
    Services at Lutheran Church Tuesday 3 P.M. by Rev. A.M. Reitzel.
    Buried Mendon Cemetery.

Andrew, James   "Local"   Oct. 1, 1903
    The bond of James Huston, executor of the estate of James Andrew was
    filed and approved last Sat.

Andrew, James   "Probate"   Oct. 1, 1903
    James Andrew, deceased, 1st Monday of Dec. 1903, James Huston, Ex.

Aneal, Mr. and Mrs. Will   "Fowler"   Aug. 1, 1889
    Mr. and Mrs. Will Aneal buried their youngest son, 16 mo's last week.

Antweiler, Phillip   "Fatal Accident"   Oct. 11, 1883
    Phillip Antweiler proprieter of the beer shop known as the Cedar Creek
    House was found lying under his wagon near his house with his neck
    broken.

Arent, Mrs. Martha Ann   "Deaths in Adams Co. Quincy"   Apr. 6, 1899
    Died, Mrs. Martha Ann Arent of grip and old age--74 yrs old.

Armour, Joshua F.   "Local"   Sep. 26, 1901
    Joshua F. Armour, the veteran auctioneer died at his home 1 mile N
    of the city limits of Quincy at noon last Sunday. 76 yrs old resident
    of Quincy 61 yrs--leave a wife, 2 daughters and 4 sons.

Arnold, Charles Rockwell   "Obituary"   Jan. 26, 1893
    Died--Mr. Charles Rockwell Arnold at his home in Hamilton, Hancock
    Co. early in the morning of Jan. 11th--was son of Rev. J.R. Arnold,
    a Cong. minister and one of 12 children--10 boys, 2 girls-- Mr. S. S.
    Arnold of Mendon is only surviving brother. He was born in Waterbury,
    Conn. Nov. 22, 1832. Came west to Keokuk and attended Medical
    College. Was a member of A.O.O.W. and organizer of the Hamilton
    Lodge #204, was president of the Quincy, Keokuk and Chicago R.R.
    at the time of his death. Married Miss Marion C. Atwood, Oct. 4, 1860
    at Edwardsville, Ill., who survives him. They had no children, had 2
    adopted children, Ernest and Miss Rita Arnold. Ernest is engaged in
    the banking business in Chicago and Rita is quite prominent in musical
    circles.

Arnold, Eddie   "Big Neck"   Jun 27, 1889
    Died- Wed. eve little Eddie, oldest son of Solomn and Lucy Arnold of
    spasm of the throat. Age 2 yrs 4 mo's. Buried in Curless cemetery Thurs.

Arnold, Mrs Elizabeth A.   "Obituary"   Dec 1, 1892
    Died- Mrs Elizabeth A. Arnold (nee Bradley) was born in East Haven,
    Conn. Sept 12, 1811. Came here with her parents in March of "32" and
    died Wed. Nov 23rd. Age 75 yrs 2 mo's 11 days. Joined Cong. church at
    age 17 yrs. married Jan 15, 1849 to John L. Arnold also of Mendon who
    died many yrs ago. 1 child, Miss Julia Arnold survives. Funeral Fri. P.M
    at her home by Rev Wm Burgess pastor of the Cong. church. Distant
    mourners were, her sister, Mrs Harrison of Chicago, her nephew, Rev Hy
    Harrison of Chicago, editor of the Advance, her niece, Mrs Kimball of
    Galesburg and her brother in law Mr S.S. Arnold from Whitehall, Ill.
    Mrs H. is staying with her niece and surviving sister, Miss Sarah
    Bradley and Mrs K. with her mother, Mrs Dan'l Bradley.

Arnold, Mrs Fleming   "Big Neck"   Dec 15, 1886
    Died- at her home in Big Neck, Mrs Fleming Arnold on Dec 6th. Mrs A.
    was 63 yrs 6 mo's 4 days old. Leaves a husband and 7 children.

Arnold, Frances   "Obituary"   Jan 23, 1902
    see Clark, Mrs Sadie

Arnold, Frank   "Local"   Feb 16, 1888
    Frank Arnold the C.B. and Q. brakeman injured at West Point Jan 17th
    died at St Mary's hospital in Quincy Friday night.

Arnold, John   Mar 15, 1877
    From "Rose Bud" a paper published by the students of Enion School in
    Mendon on July 3, 1857, the death of Mr John Arnold is recorded.

Arnold, John L.   Jun 5, 1902
    List of Mexican war soldiers buried in Mendon cemetery is John L.
    Arnold.

Arnold, Luther H.   "Local"   Oct 9, 1884
 Remains of Mr Luther H. Arnold arrived from Chicago and buried in
 Mendon. Was accompanied by his brother S.S. Arnold of Mendon, W.W.
 Arnold of Whitehall and Dr C. Arnold of Hamilton. He was 49 yrs
 9 mo's 17 days old. Leaves a wife and 2 children.

Arnold, S.S.   "Funeral"   Feb 17, 1886
 see Leggatt, A.J.

Arnold, Mr S.S.   "Death"   Jan 18, 1900
 Died- Mr S.S. Arnold Jan 11th at 4 P.M. Services at the house at 2 P.M.
 by Rev Bayne. Buried in Mendon cemetery. Seth Shairlor Arnold came
 from an old New England family. Born Chester, N.H. Mar 12, 1830
 His father was a Cong. minister when S.S. was young the family moved
 to Westminister, Vt. and his boyhood was spent on Colchester and
 Waterbury, Conn. He went west to Baltimore when young to learn the
 machinist trade, building and testing one of the engines of the B&O
 railroad. At 24 he Came west and stopped at St Louis and then Keokuk
 where his older brother was Prof. in the Medical college. He soon came
 to Mendon where his brother John was. In 1858 he went to Calif. and
 returned in 1865 and started a tile and sewer pipe factory at
 Whitehall, Ill. Married Dec 31, 1869 to Miss Sarah J. Benton, eldest
 daughter of the late Abram Benton. Moved back to Mendon 1870. Had 2
 daughters Miss Sarah L. and Francis B.The Arnold family were among the
 founders of Hadden, Conn. early in the 17th century. Both of S.S.'s
 grandfathers were revolutionary officers.

Arnold, Sadie   "Obituary"   Jan 23, 1902
 see Clark, Mrs Sadie

Arnold, Mrs Sarah J.   "Obituary"   Jan 23, 1902
 see Clark, Mrs Sadie

Arnold, W.W.   "Obitaury"   Sep 27, 1888
 Died- Mr W. W. Arnold of Whitehall, Greene Co. died Friday A.M.
Buried next day in the Whitehall cemetery by the side of his children. Wm
 Arnold was the son of a Congregational preacher who preached in New
 England 40 yrs. Born Colchester, Conn. April 4, 1837 and attended
 Tuffts college, Munson Mass. Came to Ill. in 1861. First to Jersey-
 ville and in 1863 to Whitehall where he lived since. On May 22, 1862
 at Keokuk, Iowa he married Miss Harriet Josephine Atwood. They had 4
 children. 3 are buried in Whitehall cemetery. Miss Fannie Esther
 Arnold is still living. He was one of a family of 10 brothers and 2
 sisters of whom 2 brothers survive. S.S. Arnold of Mendon, Ill and
 C.R. Arnold of Chicago.

Arnold, mr W. W.   "Local"   Sep 27, 1888
 Mrs S. S. Arnold and Miss Julia Arnold left to attend the funeral on
 Sat. for Mr W.W. Arnold at Whitehall.

Arnold, Willie   "Local"   Oct 23, 1890
 Willie, oldest son of Scot Arnold of Big Neck died Oct 21st.

12

Aron, Mrs John   "Local"   Jul 20, 1893
    Mrs John Aron, mother of Charles Aron who was murdered died at her
    home in Quincy Sat. morning from a complication of blood poisoning
    neurolgia and cancer.

Aron, Wm P.   "Obituary"   Apr 14, 1881
    see Powell, Mrs L. M.

Arras, Mrs J.N. Arras died Sunday at 6 P.M. Age 74 yrs 8 days. Leaves
    husband and 7 children. Services by Rev Ott and buried in Mendon
    cemetery Tuesday A.M.

Arras, John Nichilas   "Obituary"   Jul 20, 1904
    John Nicholas Arras was born at Kleingumben, Hesse Darmstadt, Germany
    June 2, 1815 and baptizes at age 14 yrs by Rev Lindenbaum at the
    Lutheran church of his native place. Came to U.S. 1832 landing at
    Baltimore and settled Chambersburg, Penn and moved to Massillon, O.
    in 1836. Married 1841 to Christine Rau and had 7 children- 4 survive
    him, Caroline, Anna, May and Margaret. Family came to Ill. in 1853.
    The mother died in 1892 and 3 yrs later Mr A. moved to Fowler where
    he died July 7, 1904. Age 89 yrs 1 mo. 5 days.

Artaburne, Mr   Mar 31, 1881
    Died, Mr Artaburne of Quincy March 25th and brought to Ursa for
    burial in a neighboring cemetery by his friends.

Ashbaugh, Mrs   "Loraine"   Feb 28, 1884
    Feb 16th Mrs Ashbaugh died. Funeral at church Sunday 4 P.M. by Rev Mr
    Bean. Buried in Graveyard N.E. of town.

Ashbaugh, Mr   Mar 13, 1884
    Mr Ashbaugh died last Thursday or Friday. His wife died Mar 6th or 7th

Ashbaugh, Miss Mary   "Loraine"   Jul 2, 1885
    Miss Mary Ashbaugh died June 24th. Buried June 26th. Services by
    Rev T. M. Johnson.

Ashbaugh, Miss Mary   "Loraine"   Jul 2, 1885
    Miss Mary Ashbaugh died Wed. night of consumption and was buried
    Thursday. Services by Rev T. M. Johnson.

Ashenfelter, Emma M.   "Local"   Sep 28, 1887
    "San Francisco Chronical" Died, in this city Sept 3rd Emma M.
    widow of the late Capt Benjamin F. Ashenfelter, beloved mother of
    Andrew Ashenfelter, a native of Dauphin Co. Penn. Age 41 yrs
    3 mo's 19 days.

Asher, Lettitia Adaline   "Obituary"   Feb 17, 1904
    see Hastings, Thomas Gilbert

Asher, Miss Mary   "Obituary"   Feb 12, 1891
    see Furry, David

13

Asher, Mrs Warren   "Elm Grove"   Feb 3, 1898
    Died, Mrs Warren Asher last Sunday night of consumption. This makes
    2 children that Mr and Mrs Wm Hastings have lost within a yr.

Asher, Mrs Warren   "Obitaury"   Feb 10, 1898
    see Hastings, Letitia Adeline

Aspey, Mr   "Lima"   May 9, 1895
    Funerals of Mr Aspey was at Ebenezer on Monday of last week. Mr A. was
    a resident of the Neck where he farmed until moving to Golden.

Aten, Major John   "Payson"   Oct 23, 1879
    Died- on Oct 18th Major John Aten. Services at 3 P.M. Sunday by Rev.
    Wallace at the Congregational church.

Aton, Mrs Major   "Payson"   Mar 23, 1882
    Mrs Major Aton was buried here last week.

Atwater, Mrs   "Obituary"   Dec 13, 1883
    see Harrison, Nathan

Atwater, Mrs Almeria F.   "Gone to Rest"   Jul 28, 1892
    Died- Mrs Almeria F. Atwater, widow of the late Edward Atwater died at
    the home of her daughter, Mrs J. R. Copelin at 7:30 Friday July 22nd
    She was born in North Guilford, Conn Sept 6, 1813. Was nearly 79 yrs
    old. When she was 18 her parents made their first movement wesr to
    Penn. where in 1843 she married Edward Atwater, of Plymouth, Conn.
    and in the company of her parents came to Mendon in the fall of 1849.
    Was a member of the Episcopal church of the Good Shepherd in Quincy.
    Buried Mendon cemetery. A small wreath or sheaf of wheat was placed
    upon the casket and buried with the deceased. It was the gift of the
    late Mrs Edward Fowler of Chicago and was used at the funeral of Mrs A's
    brother, the late Nathan Harrison of Chicago and afterwards at Mrs
    Fowler's own funeral- both of whom are buried in Mendon cemetery.

Atwood, Miss Harriet Josephine "Obituary"   Sep 27, 1888
    see Arnold, W.W.

Atwood, Miss Marion C.   "Obituary"   Jan 26, 1893
    see Arnold, Charles Rockwell

Aumann, Chris   "Local"   Jul 27, 1887
    Mr Chris Aumann of Quincy died at Siloan Springs on Sat. A.M. Was
    buried in Woodland cemetery Sun P.M. Death caused from Bright's
    disease. Leaves a wife and 2 daughters. The elder married to Fred
    Bernard, the photographer.

Ausmus, Mrs Ann   Death in Adams Co."   Mar30, 1899
    Died, Mrs Ann Ausmus age 91 yrs at the home of her daughter, Mrs
    Frank Hogan in Concord twp Monday night March 20th.

14

Ausmus, Mabel M.   "Obituary"   Mar 14, 1901
    Died- Mabel M. Ausmus born in Spring Co. Kan. June 21, 1880. Joined
    M.E. church at Paloma Feb 1894 and transferred to Loraine. Married
    in 1900 to Joseph F. Hardy and died March 6, 1901 at age 20 yrs 9 mo's
    15 days. Services at the home of her parents March 8th at 10 A.M. by
    Rev F. P. Bonnefon her pastor and Rev S. N. Wakefield of Mendon. Buried
    in Curless cemetery.

Austin, Dr Adelbert   "Uncle's death"   May 17, 1905
    see Wilcox, Morton

Austin, Mrs Caroline E.   "Local"   Mar 15, 1900
    Died- Mrs Caroline E. Austin died Tuesday morning at 5 from an attack
    of grip. 80 yrs old.

Austin, Mrs Catherine   "Obituary"   Mar 15, 1900
    see Barclay, Caroline E.

Austin, Charles Henry   "Died"   Oct 28, 1880
    Died- on Monday Oct 18th of diptheria, Charles Henry, 2nd son of Wm
    and Mary Austin. Age 3 yrs 1 mo. 12 days.

Austin, Cornelius   "Obituary"   Mar 15, 1900
    see Barclay, Caroline E.

Austin, Daniel W.   "Obituary"   Mar 15, 1900
    see Barclay, Caroline E.

Austin, Harry Clinton   "Died"   May 11, 1882
    May 4th death of Harry Clinton Austin age 4 yrs 7 mo's 25 days. Only son
    of Cornelius and Marietta S. Austin. Cause, Scarlet fever.

Austin, John C.   "Obituary"   Mar 15, 1900
    see Barclay, Caroline E.

Austin, John C.   "Obituary"   Jul 31, 1879
    Died- Mr John C. Austin at his home 3½ miles N.E. of Mendon on Friday
    July 25th. Services held at the home on Sunday the 26th. Born in
    Logan, Wayne Co. N. Y. in 1814. Came to Mendon in 1842 where he lived
    since. Member of M. E. Church. Leaves sons.

Austin, John C.   "Probate"   Aug 21, 1879
    1st Monday of October 1879   Cornelius Austin, Adm.

Austin, Lewis E.   "Local"   Aug 31, 1887
    Died- Wed night Aug 24th at age 22 yrs 5 mo's 28 days at his home N.E.
    of town, Lewis E. Austin only son of Mr and Mrs Peter Austin. Services
    at the M. E. church by Rev E. P. Droke, assisted by Rev E. W. Souders
    of the Lutheran church. Buried Mendon cemetery

Austin, Mrs Phaebe   "Obituary"   Dec 8, 1898
    see McFarland, Mrs Debora

Austin, Wm   "Obituary"   Mar 15, 1900
    see Barclay, Caroline E.

15

Austin, Wm   Died"   Oct 21, 1880
    Died- a son of Wm Austin on Monday of diptheria age 3 yrs.

Austin, Mrs Wm B.   "Obituary"   Dec 22, 1898
    see Wilcox, Mrs Jane

Austin, Mrs William   "Death"   May 17, 1905
    see Wilcox, Morton Robert

Austin, Winnie May   Feb 2, 1882
    Died- Feb 1st 1882 Winnie May Austin age 1 yr 11 mo's 20 days. Was
    daughter of Daniel and Maria.

Avise, Mr W. M.   "Obituary"   Dec 13, 1888
    Died- Sunday eve Mr W. M. Avise of Quincy. Mr A's wife died June 22,
    1886. He was the father of 7 children, 3 of whom, George, Walter and
    Cora survive him. Funeral held at his home at 817 N. 6th St.

Awerkamp, Mrs Catherine A.   "Deaths in Adams Co."   Apr 20, 1899
    Died- Mrs Catherine A. Awerkamp of heart failure Friday. She was born
    in Germany in 1825. Lived Quincy 32 yrs. Leaves 1 daughter and 1 son.

Aydelotte, Dan   "Obituary"   Jul 5, 1900
    see Lewis, Mrs J. W.

Babb, Mrs   "Payson"   Sep 11, 1879
    Died- recently of consumption, Mrs Babb.

Babcock, Chester A.   "Local"   Aug, 1899
    Died- Chester A. Babcock Monday A.M. He was a lawyer.

Bachmann, Fred   "Ursa"   Mar 6, 1890
    Died, Fred Bachmann March 3rd.

Bachman, Fred   "Probate Notice"   Mar 13, 1890
    Fred Bachman 1st Monday of May 1890 Annie Bachman, Adm.

Bade, Mr   Obituary"   May 2, 1889
    see Margaret J. Wible (Mrs Charles A.)

Baggerly, Miss Ella   "Obituary"   Feb 26, 1902
    see Mrs Fannie Thompson

Bagley, Charley   "Died"   Jul 24, 1879
    Died- Little Charley, son of Frank and Jennie Bagley at the home of
    his grandfather, Mr Wm Witts. Was only a few mo's old. Died from
    mumps. He was an only child.

Bagley, David   "Paloma"   Feb 15, 1900
    Died- Feb 7th at the home of Mr and Mrs Wm C. Bagley, their infant
    son David, nearly 5 mo's old. Services by Rev Babbs Friday. Buried
    in Headley graveyard W. of town.

Bagley, Jennie S.   "Obituary"   Mar 2, 1893
    see James,Mary F.

Bailey, A.K.   "Edgings"   May 25, 1877
    A.K. Bailey's fine horse "Greely" died Tuesday.

Bailey, Father   "Loraine"   Mar 13, 1879
    Father Bailey, father of A. K. Bailey died Wed. Mar 15th at his
    home in Honey Creek twp.

Bailey, Honora   Sep 14, 1887
    Sale of real estate of Honora Bailey, deceased by J.E. McMurry, Adm.

Bailey, Rebecca   "York Neck"   Feb 13, 1890
    Died- Rebecca Bailey of Camp Point formerly of York Neck. Going to
    bury grandma were Mr T. Beer and Mr A.K. Turner families and Miss
Etta Turner.

Bailey, Thomas   "Obituary"   Dec 1882
    see Kelly, Mrs Eleanor B.

Baird, Fred   Death in Adams Co."   Mar 30, 1899
    Died- Fred Baird of Camp Point Thursday of spinal meningitis. 20 yrs
    old and a painter by trade.

Baird, Mrs James   "Camp Point"   Jul 26, 1900
    see Denny, Mr

Baker, Esq.   "Funeral"   Mar 9, 1887
    see Hutchinson, Mrs

Baker, Grandma   "Payson"   Jun 16, 1886
    Grandma Baker was buried here last Monday.

Baker, Mrs   "Green Grove"   Jan 12, 1899
    Died- Mrs Baker an old resident of this community at her home 1½
    miles S. of Hickory Ridge. Cause, old age.

Baker, Mrs   "Obituary"   Apr 5, 1888
    see Ownings, J.R.

Baker, Squire   "Burial"   Apr 28, 1886
    see Thompson, Mrs

Baker, Cal   "Obituary"   Mar 21, 1895
    see Brown, John A.

Baker, J.   Burial list"   Jun 4, 1885
    see Crane, Rev. E.C.

Baker, J.O.   "List of C war burials"   Jun 5, 1902
    see Battell, Richard

Baker, James O.   Obituary"   Nov 19, 1903
    see Inman, Lavina J.

Baker, Jas. T.   "Local"   Dec 7, 1904
    Jas. T. Baker of Quincy and for many yrs in charge of the stamp
    dept. in the post office died of pleurisy Monday 9P.M. Was 90 yrs old
    last Sept. Yrs ago he kept a grocery store on the corner of 5th and
    Maine.

Baker, Mrs Katie (Dick)   "Tioga"   Sep 12, 1901
    Died- last Sat. night August 24th Mrs Katie Baker, wife of Dick Baker.
    age 28 yrs. Leaves husband and 3 children. Services Monday P.M. at
    the M.E. church. Buried in Fletcher cemetery.

Baker, Mrs Lavina J.   "Obituary"   Nov 19, 1903
    see Inman, Lavina J..

Baker, Margaret C.   "Commissioner's Sale"   Jul 10, 1884
    see Owings, Howard W.

Baker, May   "Tioga"   Nov 10, 1898
    Funeral of May Baker, Age 6 yrs, daughter of Mr and Mrs Isaac Baker
    near Sutter on Monday.

Baker, Mrs Seth M.   "Obituary"   Mar 1, 1901
    see Mitchell, David

Baldwin, Ben   "Obituary"   Jan 28, 1892
   see Sloan, Arthur D.

Baldwin, Benjamin   "Died"   Oct 8, 1891
   Benjamin Baldwin and son were shot by Mr B's step-son in Omaha, Nebr.
Mr B. lived 14 miles West of Blair, Nebr. Step-son's name was Long.
Baldwin was father of 2 sons and a daughter.Mr B's brother G. D.
Baldwin lived in Mendon. (in another acct of this same paper the
step-son's name was given as Arthur Sloan.)

Baldwin, Mr E. C.   "Obituary"   Aug 3, 1882
   Death of Mr E.C. Baldwin on August 1st. .r B. came to this state with
his father in 1837. Leaves a wife, but no children.

Baldwin, E. G.   "Obituary"   Feb 11, 1892
   see Tanner, Dr.

Baldwin, G. H.   "Obituary"   Frb 11, 1892
   see Tanner, Dr.

Baldwin, Mrs G. H.   "Obituary"   Dec 29, 1898
   see Hewitt, Thomas

Baldwin, George D.   "Local"   Mar 29, 1905
   the will of the late George D. Baldwin of Mendon was yesterday
admitted to probate. Anna V. Baldwin, wife of deceased is executrix
and rec's all the property with exception of 500.00 which is divided
equal among his 5 children. "Quincy Whig"

Baldwin, Geo. D.   "Local"   Aug 16, 1905
   The inventory of Geo. D. Baldwin's estate shows- Real estate 2,800.00
Chattels 100.00 Notes and accts 140.00

Baldwin, George D.   "Probate"   Apr 19, 1905
   George D. Baldwin, deceased- 1st Monday of June 1905 Anna V. Baldwin,
Ex.

Baldwin, George Dutton   "Obituary"   Mar 22, 1905
   George Dutton Baldwin was born at Watertown, Conn. 1828 and came to
Ill. with his parents at age 10 yrs and located in Mendon twp, Adams
Co. where he lived since. Owned a farm 1 mile W. of Mendon where he
lived until 11 yrs ago when he moved into town. Joined the Cong'l
church at age 20 yrs. Married Maria A Smith of Chardon, Ohio in 1856.
She died in 1862. They had 1 son and 2 daughters, Charles A. of Newhall,
Mo. Mary A. Tallcott of Rothville, Mo. and Jennie S. Krieger of
Peoria, Ill. Married second in 1863 to Anna V. Copp of Denmark, Iowa
They had 2 children, Nettie A. Scott of Emmetsburg, Iowa and Lucy
A. Tumbleson, of Rock Falls, Ill. Cause of death was dropsical heart
failure at the home of his daughter, Lucy A, Tumbleson of Rock Falls
with whom he and his wife spent the winter. Leaves wife and 5
children, a sister, Mrs Lucy A. Ray of Portland, Oregon. Funeral at
Cong'l church by Rev J. E. Bacon.

19

Baldwin, Gilbert   May 29, 1884
    Died- Little Gilbert, son of Mr and Mrs G. H. Baldwin died May 22nd.
    He was 5½ yrs old. He leaves his parents and 1 brother.

Baldwin, Mrs H.   "Obituary"   Mar 15, 1888
    see Bauchmann, Mr

Baldwin, H.B.   "Obituary"   Nov 21, 1889
    see Palmer, Mrs J. C.

Baldwin, H. B.   "Probate Notice"   Apr 28, 1881
    see Dailey, Amanda

Baldwin, Harry D.   "In Memoriam"   Dec 1, 1898
    Died- Harry D. Baldwin one of the earliest settlers of this prairie
    and until the last 6 yrs a resident of this village died at his home
    at 704 N. 5th Street, Quincy. Sunday at 12:20 P.M. at age 85 yrs.
    Born North Guilford, Conn. Dec 5, 1813. His father was Col. Benjamin
    Baldwin and mother was Betsey Chittenden, daughter of Abraham
    Chittenden and ½ sister of Col. John B. Chittenden. Came with parents
    to Ill. when he was 20 yrs old. Reached Quincy in 1833and settled
    in Sect 18 of Honey Creek twp about 1½ mils E. of Mendon on goverment
    land. Married 1841 to Melinda Hubbard whose parents also came from
    Conn.and settled at Plymouth 1835. He remained on the Hubbard farm
    5 yrs and moved to his fathers farm in Honey Creek where his only
    son and child now lives with his family. Mrs B. died in 1872. and on
    April 30, 1874 he married his 2nd wife, the widow of ____ Miller
    of Quincy. Her maiden name was Susannah Barr who survives him.
    Buried village cemetery after services Tuesday A.M. at the Cong'l
    church by Rev Bayne.

Baldwin, Henry   "Obituary"   Feb 27, 1890
    see Palmer, J.C.

Baldwin, Henry   "Local"   Jan 14, 1892
    Died- Henry, eldest son of Mr G. H. Baldwin in North Guilford, Conn.
    on New Yrs day where he was spending his college vacation with his
    uncle Mr Ed Bartlett. His father left for the East to bring the body
    back. Funeral will be in the morning at the Cong'l church at 2P.M.
    by Bishop Burgess of the Episcopal church. Pall-bearers were;
    Rev Herbert A. Grantham, Wm F. Mayo of Quincy, J.M.D. Davidson of
    Burlington, Iowa, R.W. Hewitt of Moline, Ill. Buried Mendon cemetery.

Baldwin, Mrs Henry   "Obituary"   Apr 10, 1890
    see Searle, Deacon S.

Baldwin, Henry B.   "Probate Notice"   Dec 29, 1898
    Henry B. Baldwin- 1st Monday of March 1899-- Geo. H. Baldwin, Adm.

Baldwin, Mrs Susan B.   "Local"   Dec 18, 1902
    Died- Mrs Susan B. Baldwin, one of Quincy's pioneer residents at her
    home at 704 N. 5th Street early Sunday A.M. Lived Quincy 63 yrs.
    Mr B. died some 4 yrs ago. She was born in Penn. and came to Quincy
    when a young girl from her native state by wagon. Survived by Newto Barr
    of Monmouth, a brother and Mrs E.C. Barstow, a sister of Quincy. "Whig"
    (ED. Mrs B. was the widow of our late townsman, Mr Henry B. Baldwin.)

Ball, Mr Thos D.   "Local"   Mar 20, 1902
    Mrs T. D. Ball of Winters, Calif. renews her Mendon Dispatch and
tells of the death of her husband, Mr Thos. D. Ball on Feb 27, 1902
    he was 76 yrs old. Buried in Sacramento, Calif March 3rd by
    Sacremento Lodge #40 F.&A.M. of which he was a member.

Ballard, Wm Sr.   Local"   Dec 11, 1890
    Wm Ballard Sr. of Emporia, Kansas died Dec 3rd. He was 68 yrs old and
    lived around Fowler. He had 1 son, Wm Ballard and 1 daughter, Mrs
    Crawford of Decatur. He belonged to the Methodist Episcopal church
    Services by Rev. F.C. Read.

Ballew, Mrs Mollie   "Obituary"   Nov 1898
    see Berrier, Mrs Hannah Mason

Banks, Eli   "Death"   Oct 31, 1901
    Died- Oct 23rd 1901, Eli Banks age 86 yrs 11 mo's. Funeral from his
    home 1119 W. Adams St Friday the 25th inst. Burial private. "Chicago
    Tribune" ED: Mr B. was one of the earlist settlers of Mendon. Came
    here about 1837 and was in partnership with the late C.E. Betts
    in the mfg'er of wagons before retiring:of Mr Betts. He was a devout
    Episcopalin. He left here about 25 yrs ago and moved to Chicago
    and with his son was in the agricultural business and at whose home
    he died.

Banks, Mrs Eli   "Local"   Nov 18, 1885
    Mrs Eli Banks of Chicago and a former resident and old settler of
    Mendon died at her home in Chicago Monday night a week ago.

Banks, Fernando   "Loraine"   May 19, 1892
    Died- Fernando Banks living 1½ miles from Loraine was killed when he
    was kicked by a horse at 9:30 A.M. Wed. Dr Christie of Quincy was
    called. He was 34 yrs old. Leaves a wife and 2 small children. Funeral
    by Rev Miller of this place on Friday morning. Buried in our cemetery.

Banks, J.J.   "Obituary"   Nov 30, 1893
    see Ketchum, Mrs Clara

Banks, Mrs J.J.   "Local"   Dec 8, 1886
    Died- Mrs J.J. Banks of Loraine died yesterday evening. Buried in
    Loraine cemetery today. Leaves a husband and family.

Banks, John C.   "Local"   Jun 25, 1903
    Died- June 4th John C. Banks. Age 56 yrs. Funeral from the home at
    200 S. Ashland Ave. La Grange, Ill. Sunday 7th inst at 12:45
    Burial private.

Banks, Mr.   "Loraine"   Aug 14, 1879
    Died- Mr Banks of Dallas city, father of John J. Banks of this place
    died Fri. eve Aug 8th at his home. He was an aged man.

Banks, Russell   Jun 19, 1890
    June 14th death of Russell infant son of Fernando and Belle Banks. Age
    10 mo's. Died from whooping cough.

Barber, Wm   "Local"   May 8, 1895
    Died- Wm Barber, formerly of Honey Creek. Died at Skidmore, Mo. on
    April 26th. Age 82 yrs 5 days. died from cancer and had been blind
    for yrs. Born in England in 1813. Moved from this neighborhood to Mo.
    in 1873.

Barclay, Mrs Ann E.   "Obitaury"   Feb 5, 1885
    see Clark, Mary

Barclay, Ann Elizabeth   "Probate Notice"   May 18, 1882
    3rd Monday in July 1882   J.H. Wright, Ex.

Barclay, Caroline E.   "Obituary"   Mar 15, 1900
    Died- Caroline E. Barclay born near Lyons Co. N.Y. Nov 21, 1820 and
    died Mendon March 13th. She was oldest of 11 children. Married John C.
    Austin at Xmas time 1839. In June of 1842 they settled on a farm a few
    miles N.E. of Mendon and in May of 1888 she moved to town of Mendon. Mr
    A. died July 25, 1879. They had 6 children, 3 died in infancy. 3 sons
    survive her, Daniel W. of Mendon, Mo. , Cornelius and Wm of this place.
    She joined the Baptist church in N.Y. and in Mendon in 1854. 2 sisters
    and 3 brothers survive her, namely Mrs Catherine Austin of Lyons, N.Y.
    Mrs Abram Chittenden of this twp, John of Kalamozoo, Mich., Ira of
    Hurdland and Wallace of Brownong, Mo. Services yesterday at 2 P.M. at the
    M.E. Church by Rev S.N. Wakefield. Buried beside her husband in village
    cemetery. Pallbearers were, Chalres French, D.L. Dickerman, S.H. Bradley
    W.T. Nutt, D.W. Dickerman and C.B. Garrett.

Barclay, Daniel   "Probate Notice"   May 24, 1888
    1st Monday of August 1888   Abraham Chittenden, Adm

Barclay, Dan'l   "Local"   May 3, 1888
    Died- News reached us today of the death the night before of Mr
    Dan'l Barclay in his 97th yr. Services at the house this A.M.
    Buried Mendon cemetery.

Barclay, Daniel   "Obituary"   May 10, 1888
    Mr Daniel Barclay was born in New York City Oct 8, 1792 and in early
    life moved to Lyons, N.Y. where he married Miss Phebe Perine. They had
    11 children of whom 6 are still living. 3 sons and 3 daughters. In 1851
    they came to Ill. and settled near Mendon and raised their family. Mr
    B. died May 1st at age 95 yrs 5 mo's 22 days. He was a member of the
    Methodist Epicopal church. Services held at his home by Rev R.P. Droke.
    Buried Mendon cemetery.

Barclay, Mrs David   "Died"   Mar 8, 1883
    Mrs David Barclay died Feb 26th. Was born Aug 6, 1799 in New York state
    Married David Barclay Feb 1819 and cmae to Ill. in 1851. Mother of 11
    children, 6 survive her, 3 sons 3 daughters.

Barclay, Mrs Elizabeth   "Died"   Apr 27, 1882
    Mrs Elizabeth Barclay died of cancer Sunday April 23rd. Age 66 yrs.
    Services at M.E. church by Rev J.K. Miller of Beardstown. She was born
    Lyons, Wayne Co. N.Y. and married to W. P. Barclay in 1846. They at
    once moved to Mendon prairie. Leaves a very aged mother.

Barclay, Mrs Foster   "Personal"   Apr 22, 1880
    Mrs Foster Barclay of Lyons, N.Y. a daughter of Mrs McGibbons of our
    village died of paralysis on April 12, 1880. Had been sick several yrs.

Barker, Ann   "Obituary"   Jan 26, 1899
    see Chittenden, S.R.

Barker, Judge Ebenezer   "Local"   Jan 12, 1887
    Died- Judge Ebenezer Barker og Quincy Friday night. He married Miss
    Frisbie of Mendon. He was 63 yrs old. Funeral held at his home on the
    corner of Hampshire and 14th St. Services by Rev Dana. Buried in
    Mendon cemetery on the Lyman Frisbie lot. Pall-bearers were all his
    nephews on the mothers side of Mrs Barker., S. F. Chittenden, G.R.
    Chittenden, C.A. Chittenden, Joseph Frisbie Jr. and Harry Frisbie and
    John R. Chittenden. He leaves a wife and 2 daughters, the youngest
    being married and living in N.J. The oldest living at Quincy.

Barker, Mrs Mary   Obituary"   Jun 18, 1903
    see Chittenden, Mrs Caroline Frisbie

Barker, Mrs Mary A.   "Obituary"   May 16, 1901
    see Frisbie, Morris E.

Barlow, John   "Lima"   Apr 22, 1880
    John Barlow, son in law of Joe Harness died last week.

Barlow, Mrs Joseph Jr.   "Obituary"   May 9, 1895
    see Berry, Col. W.W.

Barlow, Joseph C.   "Local"   Jun 6, 1895
    Died- last Thursday A.M. Mr Joseph C. Barlow of Quincy. Age 59 yrs.
    Funeral Sat. P.M.

Barlow, Mr and Mrs Patrick   "Local"   Dec 1, 1886
    The 18 yr old son of Mr and Mrs Patrick Barlow was run over by a
    switch engine in the R.R. yards at Quincy and killed instantly.

Barlow, Perry   "Obituary"   Jan 22, 1891
    see Achese, Wesley

Barnett, Mr Davis   "Local"   Nov 17, 1886
    Died- at his home in Camp Point on Sun. Nov 14th at 8:30 P.M. 86 yrs
    old. Mr Davis Barnett, formerly of this place. Born in Nelson Co. Ky.
    Dec 28, 1800. Moved to Ralls Co. Mo. in 1823 and on to Adams Co. 1836.
    Married 3 times. Leaves a wife and 6 children. Buried Mendon cemetery
    with Masonic rites. Services by Rev Droke of the M.E. church.

Barnett, Mrs Minnie Bell Wait "Local"   Dec 14, 1887
    Died- Wed. Dec 7th at Marcelline age 19 yrs 8 mo's 5 days, Mrs
    Minnie Bell Wait Barnett, wife of James Barnett and daughter of
    John and Phebe Wait of Marcelline. Married only 16 mo's. Buried in
    Keith cemetery east of Marcelline on Thursday P.M. Services by Rev.
    E.P. Droke. Leaves husband and parents.

Barr, Miss Mary E.   Jan 13, 1881
    Miss Mary E. Barr died at the home of her brother, Dr George Barr.
    Funeral will be Jan 15th.1881

Barr, Newton   "Death"   Dec 18, 1902
    see Baldwin, Mrs Susan B.

Barr, Susannah   "Obituary"   Dec 1, 1898
    see Baldwin, Harry D.

Barr, Mrs W.W.   "Obituary"   Nov 21, 1889
    see Palmer, Mrs J.C.

Barr, Wm   "Ellington"   Dec 18, 1884
    Mr Wm Barr who left this neighborhood to go to California lost a
    little boy lately. Cause of death not known.

Barrow, Levia   "Payson"   Dec 20, 1883
    The remains of Mrs Levia Barrow was brought here for burial Dec 18th.
    She was a sister of Mrs J. Mann.

Barry, Mrs   "Plug Run"   Feb 21, 1895
    Mrs Barry living S.W. of here is very low having been stricken down
    with paralysis some 5 weeks ago. LATER:Died- Mrs Barry died this A.M.
    (Wed.) at 4 o'clock.

Barry, Cassander V.   "Obituary"   Feb 17, 1904
    see Hastings, Thomas Gilbert

Barry, Green B.   "Obituary"   Feb 28, 1895
    see Ried, Minerva A.

Barry, Green B.   "Probate Notice"   Mar 16, 1882
    C. H. Woods named Adm.

Barry, Green B.   "Public Sale"   Dec 13, 1883
    Public Sale of real estate in Circuit court of Adams Co. Nov 2, 1883
    Green B. Barry, deceased #3467
    names mentioned are- Minerva A. Barry, Josephine Worman, DeWitt Worman
    Clinton F. Barry, Sarah Barry, Delena Tomlin, John W. Tomlin,
    Rosina F. Harwood, Cassius M. Harwood, Jacob G. Barry, Cora M. Barry,
    John F. Barry, James A. Barry, Rufus Barry, Mary E. Barry, and
    Charles H. Wood Adm of estate of Green B. Barry, deceased.
    Quincy, Ill. Nov 14, 1883   William A. Richardson master in Chancery
    as foresaid.   Bonney and Woods Solicitors for Comp.

Barry, Henrietta (Mrs John)   "Fowler & Oakland"   Oct 13, 1898
    Died- Henrietta, wife of John Barry, living about a mile E. of Oakland
    last Tuesday at her home of heart disease and dropsey. Buried next
    day in Coatsburg cemetery.

Barry, Jacob   "Plug Run"   Nov 29, 1894
    Died- Tuesday Nov 20th Jacob Barry, living about 2 miles S.E. of here.
    28 yrs old. Had been doctoring for 2 yrs for a sore throat. Buried in
    Wesley cemetery.

Barry, Jacob G.   "Elm Grove"   Nov 29, 1894
    Funeral services for the late Jacob G. Barry were held at the
    Elm Grove church Thursday A.M. Nov 22nd. Buried Wesley chapel.

Barry, James   "Coatsburg"   Jan 18, 1894
    Little James Barry, only son of Mr and Mrs James Barry, died at this
    place Wed. eve Jan 10th. 13 yrs old. Funeral by Elder Dilly of Camp
    Point.

Barry, Michael J.   "Local"   Aug 2, 1905
    Michael J. Barry, second Sergeant of the Quincy police force
    committed suicide Monday at noon by shooting himself in the head.

Barstow, Mrs E.C.   "Death"   Dec 18, 1902
    see Baldwin, Mrs Susan B.

Bartholomew, Henry L. (M.D.)   "Local"   Nov 1, 1888
    Died- rec'd word Sat. morning of the death of Henry L. Bartholomew, M.D.
    age 48 yrs at Warren, Penn his home for the past 25 yrs. He attended school
    in Mendon as his parents were among the early settlers of Mendon
    locating on the farm now owned by Mr Leighty. Funeral Monday Oct 29th.

Bartlett, Mr Ed   "Obituary"   Jan 7, 1892
    see Baldwin, Henry

Bartlett, Harry   "Death"   Feb 9, 1899
    see Doran, Elmer N.

Bartlett, Mrs S.P.   "Death"   Jan 24, 1901
    see Duncan, Ferdinand M.

Batchy, Casper   "Camp Point Journal"   Jan 29, 1885
    On Tuesday the community was shocked by the death of Casper Batchy.

Bates, Mr and Mrs Lee   "Camp Point Journal"   Oct 25, 1900
    The infant child of Mr and Mrs Lee Bates was buried here last week.

Bates, Horace N.   Clayton Enterprise"   Feb 12, 1885
    Horace N. Bates, a resident of Mount Sterling since 1847 died Wed.
    Mr B. was a native of Mass. and 72 yrs old.

Bates, Horace N.   Feb 12, 1885
    Horace N. Bates a resident of Mt Sterling since 1847 died at his home
    Feb 6th. Mr B. was a native of Mass. 72 yrs old.

25

Bates, Horace N.   "Clayton"   Feb 12, 1885
    Horace N. Bates a resident of Mt Pleasant since 1847 died at his
    home last Wed. He was 72 yrs old and a native of Mass.

Bates, Myra Josephine   "Obituary"   Aug 24, 1899
    see Guthrie, Mrs Myra Josephine

Bates, W.S.   "Obituary"   Aug 24, 1899
    see Guthrie, Mrs Myra Josephine

Batley, Mrs Alice   "Obituary"   Dec 29, 1898
    see Tharpe, John W.

Battell, Mrs F.W.   "Local"   Dec 28, 1899
    see Wright, Milton

Battell, F.W.   "Obituary"   May 31, 1888
    see Wible, Mrs Clara Alice

Battell, George S.   "Death"   Mar 6, 1902
    Sunday A.M. Mrs H.S. Battell rec'd news that her son, George died
    at his home in Kansas City, Mo. Sat. eve Was sick 2 wks.. Death caused
    by an attack of grip and heart disease. He was born in Mendon, Ill.
    and 45 yrs old. Learned the tinners trade in Wm Thompson's shop in 1882
    he went to K.C. He is survived by wife, son, mother, 2 sister's
    and 3 brother's. Mother left here for Quincy to be joined by her daught-
    er Mrs Ann Gibbs of Quincy and her 2 sons F.W. and R.L. and their
    wives of Gelesburg and will go to Kansas City.

Battell, Cornelia   "Local"   Dec 21, 1893
    see Weister, Wm

Battell, Richard   "Soldier list"   Jun 5, 1902
    Civil war Soldier s buried in Mendon cemetery

Battell, Richard   "Probate Notice"   Mar 4, .880
    3 rd Monday of April 1880-- Hanna Battell, Adm

Battell, Richard   Adm Sale"   Jun 17, 1880
    Hannah Battell, Adm of the estate of Richard Battell deceased,
    vs. Anna E. Gibbs, Edward S. Battell, French W. Battell, Hannah M.
    Poling, George S. Battell, Richard L. Battell, Cornelia S. Battell,
    and Wm Reece. Petition to sell land to pay debts #372 Wed. July 21st
    1880 Dated Mendon, Ill. June 14, 1880   Hannah Battell, Adm.

Bauchmann, Mr   "Local"   Mar 15, 1888
    Mrs H. Baldwin was called to Quincy by the death of a near relative
    Mr Bauchmann, of Lancaster, Penn who had been visiting in Calif. for
    his health. He only got as far as Quincy where he died on Friday. His
    remains were taken East for burial.

Bauman, Mrs Theresa (Mrs Will) "Coatsburg"   Nov 15, 1894
    Died- Tuesday Nov 6th Theresa Bauman (nee Hammer) widow of Will
    Buman who died about a month ago. She died of consumption. Leaves
    3 children and 2 brothers. Services at the German church by Rev Klemm.

Bavery, Victor   "Local"   Oct 26, 1893
    Victor Bavery of Elvaston near Indian Grave lake and J.L. Ross went
    hunting. Their horses become frightened and a gun went off hitting
    Mr B. in the stomach. He died shortly. Buried at Elvaston.

Bayne, Dr   "Camp Point"   Jun 27, 1901
    Mrs Jas. Jacobs was called to the bedside of her brother, Dr Bayne
    of Macomb. He died Sat. and buried Monday..

Beal, Mrs Albina (Mrs Elijah) "Obituary"   Jan 10, 1889
    Died- Albina Beal (nee Thayer) eldest child of Mrs and the late
    F.M. Thayer of this town died at her home in Clarinda, Iowa Sat. A.M.
    Jan 5, 1889 Age 40 yrs 3 mo's 8 days. Born Adams Co. Ill. Sept 28,
    1848. Married Oct 18, 1868 to Elijah Beal of Terre Haute, Ill. and
    moved with husband in 1881 to Iowa.Services at her home in
    Clarinda Jan 7th by Rev T.C. Smith her pastor for the past 2 yrs.
    Buried Mendon Ill. in Franklin Church burying ground by the side
    of her father.

Bean, Mr   "Loraine"   Apr 13, 1893
    Died- Old Mr Bean, who lived many yrs near Green Grove, died at his
    home Friday eve and buried Sunday.

Bean, Mrs   "Payson"   Jan 1, 1880
    Died- Mrs Bean formerly of this place died last Monday in Quincy. Was
    brought to Fall Creek on Dec 24th 1879 for burial. Her husband and some
    grandchildren are buried there. She was a sister of Mrs J.C. Tibbets.

Bean, A.J. (Jud)   Died"   Jun 21, 1888
    Died- June 12th at Gunnison, Colo. A.J. Bean (Jud) formerly of this
    place and brother of Mrs Wm Benson. Remains were taken to Denver
    where 2 sisters reside for burial. Mr B. was the only son of the late
    Asa Bean and Jane D. Bean, now Mrs David Barnett. Leaves a wife and
    1 daughter by his 1st wife, widowed mother and 4 sisters. He was one
    of "the boys" of Co. A. 119th Regt Ill. Vol.

Bean, Arthur   "Obituary"   Oct 17, 1895
    see Frisbie, Harry

Bean, Mrs Clarence   "Obituary"   Oct 17, 1895
    see Frisbie, Harry

Bean, Mrs Georgeia   "Death"   May 14, 1903
    see Fitzgerald, Millie

Beam, Walter   Dec 20, 1881
    died- Walter Beam age 11 yrs, son of Phillip Beam formerly of Ursa,
    now of Sherman Texas.

Beatly, Mrs Alie C.   May 15, 1884
    Death of Mrs Alie C. Beatly of New Haven, Fayette Co. Penn. April 18,
    1884. 24 yrs old. Was youngest sister of Mrs Eli Wilkins of Mendon.

Beatty, Mrs   "Obituary"   Jan 28, 1892
    see Fletcher, Mrs Wm

Beatty, Mrs G.   "Obituary"   Mar 10, 1886
    see Heberling, Mrs

Beatty, Mrs Georgiana   "Death"   Mar 20, 1902
    see Workman, Thomas

Beatty, Thomas   "Big Neck"   Mar 12, 1891
    Sarah Campbell rec'd a telegram last week notifing her of the death
    of Thomas Beatty, an uncle who lived in Quincy.

Beatty, Wm   "Obituary"   Aug 21, 1890
    see McCormack, Mrs Maggie

Beaty, George   "Probate Notice"   Nov 2, 1887
    1st Monday of Dec. 1887   Wm Beaty, Adm.

Bebee, Mrs Anna   "Obituary"   May 18, 1887
    see Morehead, Daniel

Becherer, Mrs Sarah E.   "Death"   Jan 11, 1905
    see Cochran, Thomas W.

Beck, Emma   "Obituary"   Jul 14, 1898
    see Sprankle, Wm

Beck, John Q.   "Obituary"   Jul 14, 1898

    see Sprankle, Wm

Beckerer, Mrs Sarah E.   "Obituary"   Mar 2, 1899
    Cochran, Mrs Nancy Nevins

Becking, Frank   Quincy"   Mar 9, 1899
    Died- Mr Frank Becking age 35 yrs died Sunday eve at St Mary's
    hospital of pneumonia. Leaves wife and 1 child.

Bedale, Francis Elizabeth   "Obituary"   Jun 26, 1902
    see Hillman, Joseph

Bedale, Mrs Jane   "Obituary"   Jun 26, 1902
    see Hillman, Joseph

Beebe, Albert   "Personal"   Oct 9, 1879
    Albert Beebe of Quincy died Sunday A.M. He was a member of the firm
    Harris and beebe, tobacconists.

Beeler, Mr J.   "Tioga"   Feb 18, 1892
    Died- Feb 10th Mr J. Beeler of LaGrippe. Leaves a wife and 4 children.

Beer, Claude   "York Neck"   Aug 17, 1899
    Died- Sunday at 6 A. M. little Claude Beer, only son of Mr and Mrs
    Warren Beer of spinal meniiitis. Was 2 yrs old. Services at Ebenezer
    church and buried in Ebenezer cemetery.

Beer, Mr T.   "Obituary"   Feb 13, 1890
    see Bailey, Rebecca

Beerer, Mrs Sabie   "Funeral"   May 24, 1888
    see Worman, Moses G.

Bell, J.T.   "Loraine"   Sep 29, 1881
    Died youngest child of Mr and Mrs J. T. Bell Sept 26th. Was scalded
    to death.

Benjamin, Jemima   Quincy"   Nov 20, 1884
    Death of Jemima Benjamin (colored lady) last night Nov 19th at her
    home at 9th and Lind St's. She was over 100 yrs old. A brother who is
    113 yrs old testified she was 115 yrs old.

Benneson, Miss Tabitha   Deaths in Adams Co."   Feb 16, 1899
    Died- Miss Tabitha Benneson, Quincy died Monday. Was 84 yrs old and
    a sister of the late Hon. W.H. Benneson.

Bennet, W.H.   Estate"   Dec 14, 1899
    Mr B. was named Adm. of Charles Gilmer estate

Bennit, Miss Mary   "Payson"   Apr 17, 1879
    Died- in Kansas April 9th of consumption, far from home save for a
    fond mother who was with her in her last moments. Miss Mary, daughter
    of Wesley Bennit who lives S. of Payson. She was 23 yrs old and a
    christian. Her remains were brought home Friday for burial on Sat.
    Services by Rev. H.E. Adams.

Benson, Mr   Death"   Mar 22, 1883
    see McDonald, Miss Sallie

Benson, Mr   "Death"   Jun 11, 1885
    Mr Benson was called to Elvaston by the illness of his daughter
    Mrs Smith. He was accompanied by his son Tom. Mrs Smith died Monday eve.
    CORRECTION: June 18, 1885 The daughters name was Mrs Urton, not Smith.

Benson, Eliza   "Death"   Mar 29, 1905
    see Rust, charles W.

Benson, Eliza   "Death"   Mar 29, 1905
    see Rust, Mrs Eliza Benson

Benson, Mr Tom   "Death"   Jun 11, 1885
   see Mrs Smith

Benson, Mrs Wm   "Obituary"   Jun 21, 1888
   see Bean, A.J. (Jud)

Bentel, Mr Wm   "Local"   Jul 28, 1886
Died- Mr Wm Bentel of Columbus twp. Leaves a wife and 5 children.
It is presumed he will be buried in Camp Point cemetery beside his
parents and children.

Benton, Mr   "Local"   Aug 17, 1887
Mr __ Benton, from Minnesota, a grandson of Mr Abram Benton's
oldest brother who was killed at the battle of Antieham, has been
visiting relatives here.

Benton, Mrs A.   "Death"   Feb 20, 1890
   see Chittenden, David

Benton, Mr A.   "Obituary"   Feb 17, 1886
   see Leggatt, Mr A.J.

Benton, Abram   "Death"   Jan 18, 1900
   see Arnold, S.S.

Benton, Mrs Cecelia (Mrs Joel) ""Local"   Aug 10, 1904
Remains of Mrs Cecelia Benton, widow of the late Joel Benton
arrived Friday A.M. from North Guilford, Conn. where she has lived
since the death of her husband several yrs ago. Services held at the
Zion Episcopal church by Rev Robert Hewitt. Buried beside her husband
in the private burial lot North of town. Was over 90 yrs old.

Benton, D.C.   "News"   Jul 5, 1883
Son of Mr D.C. Benton of Melrose was drowned Sunday July 1st.
He was 10 yrs old.

Benton, Joel   "Probate Notice"   June 1, 1882
Wm W. Benton named Ex.

Benton, Mr Joel   "Died"   May 4, 1882
Mr Joel Benton died May 1st age 71 yrs. Born North Guilford, Conn.
Camr to Mendon 1834. Services by Rev D. Davidson of the Quincy
cathedral at his home in Mendon. Buried in Mendon cemetery.

Benton, Joel   "Will"   May 25, 1882
To his wife Celia W. Benton he leaves the homestead during her life
time, the household goods, a horse and carriage and 10,000 dollars
in any notes or certificates of any bank in the hands of the executor.
To Joel B. his grandson a farm in Mendon twp of 160 acres and the notes
of James Betts remaining unpaid. To Celia B. his grandaughter 1,000
to Dudley B. Cooke his nephew 100.00 to his Ex. 1,000 in trust for
the American Missionary Assoc. of New York City. To W. W. Benton his
son all the remaining of his personal and real estate.

Benton, Julia   "Obituary"   May 17, 1900
  see Cooke, Dudley Benton

Benton, Julia   Death"   Jan 6, 1881
  Died the wife of Mr A.D. Cooke born Feb 7th 1801. Married Mr C. when
he was about 27 yrs old. She is sister of Joel and Abraham Benton of
Mendon. Children still living Jan 6, 1881, Mr D.B. Cooke, Mrs C.
Hoffman, Mrs S.M. Boyer. They moved to Atwater, Portage Co. Ohio
and resided there for 11 yrs before moving to Mendon.

Benton, W.W.   "Local"   Aug 3, 1904
  Mr W.W. Banton yesterday rec'd word that his aged mother, who had
been making her home at North Guilford, Conn. died Tuesday A.M.
Remains will be brought here for burial probably Thursday. Services at
Zion Epicopal church. She was over 90 yrs old.

Benton, William W.   Adm of Estate"   Apr 17, 1902
  see Hoffman, Charles H.

Benz, Henry   "Deaths in Adams Co."   Aug 9, 1899
  Died- Henry, 13 yr old son of Mr and Mrs George Benz of Burton twp.
Sat A.M.

Berer, Mrs J. S.   "Obituary"   Nov 1, 1900
  see Worman, Mrs Nancy

Berlin, August   "Obituary"   Jan 10, 1889
  see Giffy, Aug.

Berline, August   "Ursa"   Nov 23, 1882
  Buried, a small child of August Berline Nov 16th at Denson's cemetery.

Bernard, Albert   Oct 27, 1881
  Died- Albert Bernard at his father's home in Mo.

Bernard, Mrs Fred   "Obituary"   Jan 27, 1887
  see Aumann, Chris

Bernard, Mrs Lou   "Payson"   Apr 6, 1882
  Mrs Lou Bernard who lately lost her husband is at her mother's.

Berrian, Wm   "Local"   Oct 4, 1894
  Judge Berrian returned from Brooklyn, N.Y. Sat. where he went to
attend the funeral of his brother, Wm.

31

Berrier, Mrs Hannah Mason   "Obituary"   Nov 17, 1898
Died- Mrs Hannah Mason Berrier who was born in N. Y. state Feb 5, 1822
and died in Honey Creek, Adams Co. Nov 14th. Age 76 yrs 9 mo's 9 days.
Leaves a husband, 4 daughters and 3 sons. Hannah Mason married Wm
Berrier in 1840 and moved to Ill. in 1847 and lived here since. Had 8
children, all living except Wm. who died a few yrs ago. Others are;
Mrs Jane Laughrey of Mendon, Mrs Mollow Ballew of Wichita Kansas, John and
James of Camp Point, Mrs Mina Kincade of Shelbina, Mo., David of
Kirksville, Mo., Mrs Lottie Guise of Quincy. All at funeral except
Mrs Ballew and David. Services at the house Wed. at 9 A.M. by Rev
E.K. Crews of Mendon. Buried Mendon cemetery.

Berrier, Wm   "Local"   Jan 5, 1899
Died- Wm Berrier, an aged resident of Honey Creek died suddenly in his
chair last Thursday at noon and buried Mendon cemetery on Sat. Last
Nov 14th his wife died, now he rests by her side.

Berry, Mr Green   "News"   Feb 9, 1882
Mr Green Berry living 3 miles S. of Mendon died Feb 3rd. He was an old
resident of Mendon.

Berry, Ida   Mar 17, 1881
Ida Berry died March 15th at the home of her father, Green Berry of
Mendon twp.

Berry, Jake   "Local"   Nov 22, 1894
Died- "Jake" Berry died at his home about 3½ miles S. of town of
consumption on Tuesday afternoon and buried this A.M. at the Wesley
Chapel.

Berry, Minnie   "Coatsburg"   May 18, 1893
Died- Minnie Berry, wife of J.V. Bogart at her home in Coatsburg
May 13th age 17yrs 8 mo's 14 days. Was member of Christian church.
Leaves a husband, father, mother, brother and sister. Services at the
Christian church by Elder W.S. Lowe. Buried in village cemetery.

Berry, Col. W.W.   Death"   May 9, 1895
Died- Col. W.W. Berry of Quincy from apaplexy at his home at
1451 Hampshire St at 2 P.M. Monday. Was born Hanford Co. Maryland
58 yrs ago. Come to Quincy in 1873. Was in the Civil War and carries
a rebel bullet in his neck to this day. After the war he settled at
Winchester, Scott Co. Ill. and practiced law several yrs. Then to
Quincy for several yrs,He was a Republican and was commander of the
Louisville Legion all thru the war. Leaves a wife and 7 children,
Mrs Mary McKee, Edith, Ethel and a son Will Berry an electrician in
Chicago, Mrs A.B. Kingsbury of New York, Miss Florence and Mrs Joseph
Barlow Jr.

Best, John H.   Apr 13, 1882
Mr John H. Best a 45 yr resident of Quincy died last Sunday.

Betts, Mrs   "Death"   Jul 1898
  see Spencer, Rev Seymour

Betts, Almira S.   "Local"   Sep 24, 1903
  A report was filed Tuesday by A.H. Scranton, Adm. of the estate of
  Almira S. Betts, showing 177.69 rec'd and 183.45 paid out, leaving a
  balance due the Adm. of 5.76 "Whig"

Betts, Almyra S.   "Probate Notice"   Jun 20, 1901
  1st Monday of August 1901 Amos H. Scranton, Adm.

Betts, Coley C.   "Obituary"   Apr 4, 1901
  see Spencer, Miss Elmira

Betts, Mr Coley E.   "Obituary"   May 12, 1886
  Died- An old settler on the Mendon prairie, Mr Coley E. Betts at the
  age of 77 yrs 7 mo's 5 days. Born in Wilton, Conn. Oct 3, 1808. Came
  to St Louis in 1835 and on to Adams Co. in June of 1837 where he lived
  since. Married May 6, 1841 to Miss Almira Spencer of Payson. They had
  8 children (6 daughter's and 2 son's) Leaves a widow and 5 children,
  Mrs Harriet E. Hewitt, tje eldest lives at East Nodaway, Iowa, Jas. A.,
  Wm S., and Ellen S. are at home and Mary A. is living in Payson. Their
  45th wedding anniversary was 2 days before his death. Services at the
  Cong'l church Monday by Rev E. W. Souders and buried in Mendon Cemetery.

Betts, Ellen   "Obituary"   Apr 4, 1901
  see Spencer, Miss Elmira

Betts, Miss Ellen   "Death"   Apr 23, 1903
  see Scarborough, Mrs Hattie and Mr Joel K.

Betts, Mrs Elmira   "Obituary"   Apr 4, 1901
  see Spencer, Miss Elmira

Betts, Harriet   "Obituary"   Apr 4, 1901
  see Spencer, Miss Elmira

Betts, James   "Obituary"   Apr 4, 1901
  see Spencer, Miss Elmira

Betts, James A.   June 5, 1902
  He was listed as a civil war veteran buried in Mendon cemetery.

Betts, James A.   Jun 1, 1904
  in Civil war veteran list as buried in Mendon cemetery.

Betts, James A.   "Death"   Nov 7, 1901
  James A. Betts was born in Mendon, Ill. Apr 29, 1842 and died Nov 5,
  1901 at age 59 yrs 6 mo's 6 days. Entered U.S. Service in Co. a. 119th
  Reg Ill Vol Inf at Quincy Ill. Sept 12, 1862 and discharged Aug 21,
  1865 at Mobile, Ala. Services at Cong'l church Thurs. 2 P.M. Survived by
  3 sister's, Mrs Hattie Hewitt of College Springs, Iowa, Mrs Mary
  Scranton of Payson and Miss Ellen, and 1 brother, William.

33

Betts, William   "Death"   Apr 23, 1903
   see Scarborough, Mrs Hattie and Mr Joel K.

Betts, William   "Obituary"   Apr 4, 1901
   see Spencer, Miss Elmira

Bills, Mary Elizabeth   "Obituary"   Sep 8, 1892
   see Hyatt, Mrs Mary Elizabeth

Bimson, Mrs Robert   "Deaths in Adams Co."   Apr 20, 1899
   Died- Mrs Robert Bimson Sat. A.M. Was born Gretna Green Scotland 1829.
   Came to Quincy 1848. Leaves 3 daughters and 2 sons.

Bingaman, Anna M.   "Deaths"   May 31, 1905
   see Seifert, Daniel D.

Bingamann, Miss Jane   "Death"   Jun 7, 1894
   see Davis, Levi

Bingaman, Margaret A.   "Obituary"   Feb 3, 1904
   see Nedrow, Mrs Margaret A.

Bingamon, Sarah B.   "Obituary"   May 19, 1898
   see Gibbs, Alexander

Bingeman, Miss Margaret A. "Obituary"   Apr 17, 1902
   see Nedrow, Eli

Binson, Mrs Frank   "Obituary"   Dec 22, 1898
   see Nedrow, Mrs Adela (Andrews)

Birch, Wm   Deaths"   Nov 20, 1890
   Death of 3 pioneer citizens Noc 2nd in Selma, Iowa. Wm Birch Age 83 yrs
   J. Walker age 81 yrs and Jacob Lefevie age 104 yrs. The 3 came to Iowa
   when the indians and bears made their homes in the holls around
   Burlington and have lived there since. Their deaths occured within
   a few minutes of one another.

Birdsall, Mr Pleasant   "Payson"   Apr 17, 1879
   Died- April 8th a child of Mr Pleasant Birdsall, who lives E. of Payson.

Bishop, Mr Jas. M.   "Local"   Mar 17, 1892
   Mr Jas. M. Bishop former mayor of Quincy died at his home at Omaha, Neb.
   Remains were brought to Quincy.

Bishop, Margaret   "Obituary"   Jan 3, 1901
   see Wilson, Darby

Bissel, Mr and Mrs Wm   "Local"   Dec 20, 1900
   The 4 yr old child of Mr and Mrs Wm Bissel of Marcelline was buried in
   Keith cemetery Monday.

34

Bissell, Mr and Mrs Wm   "Ursa"   Dec 27, 1900
    Born to Mr and Mrs Wm Bissell, a son on Dec 16th. The same day, their
    1st born age 3 died.

Bittle, Christ   "Local"   Nov 6, 1884
    Died Oct 24th at his hime at Paloma, Christ Bittle in his 54th yr.
    Buried graveyard at Fowler.

Bittle, Christ   "Local"   Nov 13, 1884
    Christ Bittle died at his home at Paloma Oct 24th. 54 yrs old.
    Buried Fowler cemetery.

Bittleson, Mrs Charles   "Ursa"   Jun 23, 1881
    Died, Mrs Charles Bittleson, wife of Charles Bittleson on June 15th.

Bittleson, Mrs John   "Death"   Dec 28, 1899
    see Thompson, Mrs Lewis

Bittleson, Mrs John   "Obituary"   Jan 21, 1892
    see McAdams, William

Bittleson, Mrs John   "Ursa   Oct 26, 1899
    Died, Mondat at 11 A.M. Mrs John Bittleson. Leaves a husband and 3 sons.

Bittleson, Mrs John   "Ursa"   Oct 26, 1899
    Died Mrs John Bittleson Monday. Funeral at Christian church Tuesday
    A.M.

Bittner, Mrs Frank   "Obituary"   Feb 15, 1900
    see Smith, Patrick

Bixby, Mrs   "Fowler"   Jan 27, 1904
    Remains of Mrs Bixby, formerly of this place was brought here from
    Missouri yesterday for burial in the Law cemetery in Honey Creek twp.
    She was a sister of Mrs John Olson.

Black, Dr J.N.   "Local"   Jun 14, 1905
    Dr J.N. Black, of Clayton died Thursday night from an overdose of
    hypodermic injection of morphine which he administered to himself to
    produce sleep. Was 45 yrs old. Leaves a wife.

Blackford, Mr and Mrs A.W.   "Local"   May 26, 1886
    Mr and Mrs A.W. Blackford lost their 3 mo. old baby Sat. Buried in
    Mendon cemetery Sunday. Services by Rev Souders at the grave.

Blackman, Charles   "Death"   Mar 29, 1905
    see Stillamn, Samuel Osgood

Blackman, James   "Loraine"   Aug 28, 1884
    James Blackman buried a child here Aug 23rd.

Blackman, Mr James   "Loraine"   Mar 29, 1894
    Died- Mr James Blackman died Friday 9 A.M. of typhoid pneumonia.
    Buried here Sunday according to the ancient order United Workmen of
    which he was a member. Funeral at M.E. church at 11 A.M. by Rev.
    W.E. Rose. Leaves a wife and children. 40 workmen on horseback followed
    the hearse to the church.

Blackman, Kate   "Death"   Jan 31, 1901
    see Linn, Mrs Kate

Blackman, Maudie   "Pryer"   Sep 4, 1884
    Died- Maudie, daughter of Mr and Mrs Blackman. Age 23 mo's. Services
    by F. L. Wilson.

Blackwell, Mrs Minnie   "Fowler"   Mar 27, 1884
    The remains of Mrs Minnie Blackwell of Great Bend, Kansas was
    buried in the cemetery north of town Sat. She was a daughter of
    Mr G.W. Stranakan. Mr B. will remain a few days.

Blaisdall, Mr   "Ursa"   Apr 11, 1889
    Died- Mr Blaisdall, died last Friday night and buried in Denson
    cemetery Sunday. He lived several miles W. of here and was about
    75 yrs old.

Blakesly, Mrs A. W.   "Obituary"   Jul 6, 1899
    see Watson, Geo. W.

Blakesly, Asa W.   "Deaths in Adams Co."   Apr 6, 1899
    Died- Squire Asa W. Blakesly last Thursday of heart failure. Born
    Madison Co. New York 1818. Came west 1841 and lived Quincy since.
    1846. He was a prominent Mason. Leaves a wife, 1 son and 1 daughter.

Blatter, Geo. W.   "Deaths in Adams Co."   Mar 23, 1899
    Died- Geo. W. Blatter Monday. Age 47 yrs. Leaves a wife and 8 children.

Blazer, Mrs Hannah   "Local"   Dec 20, 1888
    Died- Mrs Hannah Blazer, sister of Mrs W.L. McClung. Funeral today
    at Big Neck.

Blazer, Hannah   "Obituary"   Dec 27, 1888
    Died- Hannah Blazer died Wednesday Dec 19th. She was born Germany
    about the yr 1818. Her parents came to this country when she was 1 yr
    old and settled near Lancaster, Ohio. She joined the Methodist church
    in Ohio about 40 yrs ago. She came to Illinois in 1853. She was never
    married. Buried Dec 20th at the Reece cemetery in Big Neck. Services
    by Rev. R. P. Droke pastor of the M. E. Church at Mendon.

36

Blazer, Rachel Louise   Death"   Mar 9, 1904
    Rachel Louise Blazer- McClung was born in Fairfield Co. Ohio
    april 18, 1821 and died at her home in Mendon March 6th. She was
    82 yrs 10 mo's 18 days old. Married in Ohio 1844 to William L. McClung
    They had 6 children. (4 sons 2 daughters) Samuel H., Charity H.,
    William Allen, Louis Cass, James Brooks and Clara Belle. William and
    Louis died in infancy. Samuel lives in Mendon. Charity H.(Smith) lives
    4½ miles N.E. of Mendon and Clara Belle (Zern) lives near Colusa,
    Hancock Co Ill Wm L. deceased husband died 8 yrs before her on Jan 21,
    1896. She came to Ill. 1854 from Ohio with her husband and settled 4½
    miles N.E. of Mendon and stayed there till 1892. Funeral at the M.E.
    church Monday by Rev S.R. Reno and Rev A.M. Reitzel of the Lutjeran
    church. Buried beside her husband in Mendon cemetery.

Bliven, S.G.   "Camp Point Journal"   Jul 16, 1891
    S. G. Bliven of Burton who has passes his 4 score and 4 died on
    June 30th. Mr B. Came from N.Y. a a very poor man and at death was
    one of the richest in Adams Co. He leaves a large family and all are
    married.

Bloom, Mr L.H.   "Local"   Jul 3, 1884
    Mr J.H. Bloom of Quincy was found in the loft of his stable with a
    rope around his neck and life extinct.

Blouser, Ms   "Payson"   Mar 9, 1882
    Old lady Blouser was buried in Payson last week.

Blutgut, Joseph   Jul 3, 1884
    Mr Joseph W. Blutgut of Quincy died July 1st. Buried in Woodland Cem.

Blutgut, Joseph W.   "Local"   Jul 3, 1884
    Mr Joseph W. Blutgut of Quincy cut his throat and died. Buried in
    Woodland cemetery.

Blyler, Mrs Ben   "Obituary"   Aug 15, 1895
    see Lawber, Mr Geo.

Bockenfeld, Herman   "Obituary"   Mar 30, 1899
    see Holtschlag, Mrs Elizabeth

Bodine, Mrs   "Obituary"   Aug 26, 1880
    see Pecare, Ike

Bogart, Mrs J.V.   "Obituary"   May 18, 1893
    see Berry, Minnie

Boge, Mr and Mrs A.   "Tioga"   Sep 7, 1893
    Died- infant child of Mr and Mrs A. Boge Sat. Sept 2nd.

Boge, Mr and Mrs G.   "Tioga"   Apr 11, 1895
    Died- the infant of Mr and Mrs G. Boge.

Boge, Mrs G.   "Tioga"   May 2, 1895
Died- on Friday April 19th Mrs G. Boge. Age 34 yrs. Buried in the
German cemetery at Tioga Apr 21st. Leaves a husband and 1 son.

Boger, Mrs Fred   "Obituary"   Aug 9, 1900
see Kobel, Jacob

Boger, Mrs Gertie   "Death"   Jan 4, 1900
see Roth, Mrs John W.

Bolt, Miss Annie   Death"   Jan 18, 1905
see Selby, Lewis V.

Bolt, Miss Annie   Death"   Sep 9, 1880
see Crenshaw, Annie

Bolt, Geo. Lincoln   Death"   Mar 22, 1900
Died- Geo. Lincoln Bolt died March 6th at 4:30 P.M. Born Oct 14, 1867
in Adams Co. Ill. near Mendon. Parents were Jacob and Lizzie Bolt and
with them in 1877 moved to Americus, Lyon Co. Kansas and in 1888
moved to Missouri. Married Carrie Harness of Lima, Ill Feb 1, 1893.
Services at the M.P. Church at Lima Thursday March 8th at 11 A.M.
by Rev Ringland. Leaves a wife and 2 children, a father, 4 brothers
and 4 sisters.

Bolt, Jacob Esq.   Death"   Sep 9, 1880
see Crenshaw, Annie

Bolt, Mr John   "Lima"   Mar 17, 1892
Died= March 8th Mr John Bolt who was born in Penn. 1827 and came
west as a young man and settled on a farm in Mendon twp, but soon
moved to Lima until his death. Leaves a wife, 2 sons and 2 daughters.
Funeral Friday P.M. by Rev Johnson of LaPrairie. 1 daughter is
Mrs Minnie McLaughlin of Wichita, Kansas.

Bolt, John   "Probate Notice"   May 5, 1892
1st Monday of June 1892   Flora N. Bolt, Adm.

Bolt, John   "Local"   Mar 17, 1892
Died, John Bolt of Lima.

Bond, George   "Edgings"   Aug 24, 1877
Died- George Bond an old citizen of Quincy died in that city Wednesday.
Moved to Quincy about 1834.

Bone, Hewitt   Exchange from Herald"   Aug 4, 1892
Hewitt Bone an engineer on the "Q" was killed between Galsburg and
Chicago Friday morning. Lived in Galesburg. Leaves a wife and
2 children.

Booher, Mrs J.E.   "Local"   Oct 17, 1901
see Swaney, Mrs E.

38

Booker, Goerge "Loraine" Mar 22, 1905
 Mrs John Reece of Carthage was called here Thursday by the death of
 her brother, George Booker
 Sam and John Booker of Carthage was here Thursday on acct of the death
 of their father.

Booker, George W. "Obituary" Mar 22, 1905
 George W. Booker was born March 24, 1831 at Scottdale, Westmoreland
 Co. Penn and died March 16th at his home on Loraine. Age 73 yrs 11 mo's
 20 days. Came to Ill. in 1850 and settled near Mendon. Married
 Nancy A. Whittelsey August 4, 1852. They had 5 children, 3 daughters
 and 2 sons all living. He enlisted in the Army Oct of 1864 and
 stayed till end of war. Joined M.E. church 1852 and later the Christian
 church. Leaves wife, 3 daughters and 2 sons, 1 sister, Mrs Mary
 Reece of Carthage, Ill. 28 grandchildren and 5 gr. grandchildren.
 Services at the home Friday at 2 P.M. by Rev Barringer. Buried in
 Loraine cemetery.

Booth, Elizabeth Death" Aug 23, 1894
 see Colvin, Davis P.

Booth, Miss Louise "Obituary" Feb 14, 1889
 see Powell, John Thomas

Booth, Stephen "Fowler" May 8, 1884
 Remains of Stephen Booth of Gilmer were buried norht of Fowler.

Booth, Mrs Stephen "Fowler" Jan 23, 1902
 Funeral of Mrs Stephen Booth was held at Paloma Tuesday. Buried
 Stahl cemetery north of Fowler.

Booth, Mr W. Aug 7, 1890
 Mr W. Booth on of the pioneers of Adams Co. died at Barry of Cancer.
 Buried at Ursa. Leaves a wife and a number of children.

Booth, Mrs Wm "Local" Dec 13, 1888
 Died- Mrs Wm Booth, nee Jeffery, died Sat. A.M. and was buried in
 Columbus cemetery. Born near London, England in 1825. Married Mr B.
 in 1846. 8 children and husband left to mourn her loss. Was a
 member of Methodist church.

Boquet, Harry Accident" Jun 2, 1898
 Harry, 12 yr old son of the late Louis Boquet was electrocuted
 Tuesday P.M. on his way home from school when he climbed a 35 ft
 pole and came into contact with 2 wires.

Borger, Mr and Mrs Wm "Loraine" Jun 30, 1886
 An infant of Mr and Mrs Wm Borger died Sunday morning.

Borgholthaus, Mrs   "Local"   Nov 1, 1894
   Died- Mrs Borgholthaus, mother of our townsman Mr J. F. Borgholthaus
   died at the home of her daughter, Mrs Dr Vowles in Fowler Friday
   night after a few hours illness. She was one of the oldest residents
   of Fowler. Funeral Monday at 3 P.M. Buried in village cemetery.

Borgholthaus, Fred   Death"   Apr 19, 1900
   see, Inghram, Berdie

Borgholthaus, George W.   "Obituary"   Dec 1, 1886
   Died- at his home in Fowler, Adams Co. Ill at 1:40 P.M. Wednesday
   Nov 24th Mr George W. Borgholthaus. Born in York Co. Penn Dec 3, 1817
   Came with parents to Bloomfield, Adams Co. in summer of 1838. Both
   parents died in Bloomfield. Lived 48 yrs in Adams Co. and about 18
   yrs at Fowler. Married Miss Sarah A. Richey ofAdams Co. Sept 24, 1840
   He was 68 yrs 11 mo's 21 days old. Leaves a wife and 5 children
   (2 daughter's and 3 son's) grown and at his funeral. Son Albion lives
   in Moberly, Mo. oldest son Rufus lives Minneapolis, Minn. Oldest
daughter, Mrs Katie Butler lives at Terre Haute, Ind. sone Fredrick lives
   Fowler and youngest daughter, Mattie (now Mrs Vowels) lives Fowler.

Bortz, Mr and Mrs   "Obituary"   Jan 19, 1888
   see Siple, John

Bortz, Mrs J.M.   "Obituary"   May 19, 1881
   see Burke, Mrs

Bortz, John   "Local"   Aug 18, 1886
   Died- infant child of Mr and Mrs John Bortz . It was about 12 days
   old. Services by Rev E.W. Souders. Buried in Mendon cemetery.

Boscow, Mrs Alice   "Local"   Jul 27, 1887
   Last weeks Carthage paper carried the obituary of Mrs Alice Boscow,
   a highly honored "Mother of Isreal" 92 yrs 24 days old. Her maiden
   name was Newall and was born in Liverpool, England. Also married there.
   Came to U.S. in 1842 and settled in Warsaw.

Bouns, Charley   "Indian Grave"   Jan 10, 1895
   Mr charley Bouns was buried last Sunday.

Bounds, Mrs   "Marcelline"   Mar 1, 1883
   Mrs Bounds, wife of Joseph Bounds died Feb 22nd of consumption. She
   had been an invalid several yrs. She leaves a husband and 8 small
   children.

Bourne, Mrs Jane   "Marcelline"   Dec 25, 1884
   Died- Dec 9th at her home in Marcelline Mrs Jane Bourne. 37 yrs old.
   Services by Rev Stodgel. Leaves a husband and 4 children.

Bowles, Gus   "Payson"   Sep 11, 1879
    Died- recently, Mr Gus Bowles of consumption.

Bowles, Jesse   "Obituary"   Jan 29, 1891
    see Nichols, James

Bowles, Miss Mourning   "Obituary"   Jan 29, 1891
    see Nichols, James

Bowles, Wm A.   Nov 3, 1881
    Suicide, Mr Wm A. Bowles in Brooklyn, N.Y. He was a son of A.C. Bowles.

Bowman, Ethal   "Marcelline"   Oct 15, 1903
    Died- Sept 23rd at the home of her parents Frank O. Bowman at
Los Gatos, Calif. Ethel, 10 yrs 7 mo's old. She with her mother, brother
    and sister left here last March to join her father who had been there
    about a yr. Died from appendicitis and inflamation of the bowels.

Bowman, John   "Marcelline"   Nov 9, 1893
    Funeral services of Mr John Bowman was last Friday at the M.E. Church.
    He was a member of the A.O.U.W. Buried in the Keath cemetery.

Boyce, Mrs Nancy   "Obituary"   Nov 23, 1887
    see Kuhn, Isaac

Boyd, Miss Annie   "Obituary"   Feb 25, 1892
    see Halsey, Wiley

Boyer, Mrs   "Local"   Feb 26, 1885
    News has reached Mendon of the death of Mrs Boyer, mother of our
    former townsman, Mr S.M. Boyer at her home in Kansas.

Boyer, Mrs Hannah C.   "Obituary"   Feb 23, 1887
    "Richmond, Mo. Conservater"
    Sudden death of Mrs Hannah C. Boyer, wife of Prof S.M. Boyer of our
    city. Leaves her husband and 4 children. Eldest child is 11 yrs old.
    Youngest an infant only 3 weeks old. Member of M.E. church. Moved to
    our city from Mendon, Ill. only a few yrs ago. She was cared for by
    her sister, Mrs C.H. Hoffman of Mendon, Ill. Funeral at the M.E.
    church. Services by Rev H.D. Groves.

Boyer, S.M.   "Local"   Feb 26, 1885
    Died- mother of S.M. Boyer died at her home in Kansas.

Boyer, Mrs S.M.   "Obituary"   Jan 6, 1881
    see Cooke, A.D.

Boyle, Mrs John   "Camp Point"   Dec 11, 1879
    Died- Mrs John Boyle Saturday from inflamation of the bowels. Services
    at the Christian church Sunday. Leaves a husband and 5 children. The
    youngest only a baby of a few weeks.

Boyles, Mrs A.   "Obituary"   Oct 29, 1891
   see Ross, Mrs Caroline

Brackensick, Miss Anna   "Tioga"   Mar 2, 1899
   Died- Miss Anna Brackensick, daughter of Mr and Mrs Lewis Brackensick
   Funeral at the Evangelical church Wednesday Feb 22nd by Rev Mr Peter
   Wemhoner and Rev P. Ott.

Brackensick, Harry   "Tioga"   Sep 27, 1900
   Died- Wednesday Sept 19th Harry, son of Mr and Mrs Lewis Brackensick
   age 16 yrs. Services by Rev Ott. Buried in German cemetery Thursday
   afternoon.

Bradbury, Mrs Ann   Nov 24, 1886
   "Clip fron Quincy Journal"
   Died- Mrs Ann Bradbury, one of the oldest and best known citizens of
   Ellington twp Thursday. She was 70 yrs old and a sister of Mrs John T.
   Turner. Had lived Ellington twp 52 yrs. Buried in Woodland cemetery.
   She was also an aunt to Mt F.C. Turner.

Bradfield, Samuel   "Payson"   Jan 25, 1883
   see McIntyre, Mrs

Bradford, Mrs Jennie   "Deaths in Adams Co."   Apr 6, 1899
   Died- Mrs Jennie Bradford at Clayton Friday March 24th. Born Cincinnati,
   Ohio 1832. Lived Clayton over 30 yrs.

Bradford, John K.   "Probate Notice"   Dec 11, 1879
   1st Monday of April, 1880 Abram Benton, Adm.

Bradley, Mrs D.   Jun 22, 1899
   Grave decorated at Mendon cemetery Memorial day.

Bradley, D.A.   Aug 9, 1905
   Funeral of Mr Daniel A. Bradley was last Thursday P.M. at the home of
   his wife's mother, Mrs V.C. Young by Rev Jos. F. Bacon and Rev Marvin
   Harrieson of Scribner, Nebr. Pall-bearers were, W.J. Nutt, C.W. Pepple,
   H.F. Chittenden, S.F. Chittenden, Wm S. Betts, and J.R. Urech.

Bradley, Mrs D.A.   "Obituary"   Jan 8, 1891
   see Young, Dr Peter

Bradley, Daniel   June 22, 1899
   Grave decorated at Mendon cemetery on Memorial day.

Bradley, Mrs Daniel   "Obituary"   Dec 1, 1892
   see Arnold, Mrs Elizabeth A.

Bradley, Daniel A.   "Obituary"   Aug 2, 1905
    News rec'd here Monday A.M. of the death of Daniel A. Bradley at his
    home in McPherson, Kansas. He spent 35 yrs of his life in this
    community and his family almost 75 yrs here. Word came to his brother
    Samuel H. and brother in law Charles A. Chittenden saying he had died
    Monday A.M. at 5. from heart failure it is thought. Remains shipped
    back to Mendon for burial. Daniel Arthur Bradley was essentially a
    Mendon man. His grandfather and grandmother, Samuel and Elizabeth
    Bradley were members of the first 35 persons which came overland from
    East Haven, Conn in 1831. Son of these Daniel was about 21 yrs old
    when he with the family settled in Adams Co. He Married Josephine Brown
    of Quincy and to them were born 7 children of whom Daniel A. was the
    youngest being born in Mendon Feb 26, 1855. Remaining in his family is
    Samuel H., Miss Ellen of Mendon and Mrs Josephine Kimball, wife of E.S.
    Kimball of Galesburg. The partner and helpmate of Mr B. for almost 29
    yrs was Laura Young, daughter of Dr Peter and Virginia C. Young of
    Mendon to whom he was married Nov 29, 1876. They had 3 children all
    of whom died in infancy and are buried in Mendon cemetery. He was a member
    of Cong'l church of Mendon.

Bradley, Daniel Young   "Obituary"   Aug 9, 1888
    Died in Mendon, Ill. August 6th age 5 mo's, Daniel Young, only child
    of D. A. and Laura A. Bradley of Leoti, Kansas. Services held at the
    home of Dr and Mrs Young, Mrs B's parents by Rev Stephen D. Peet.
    Buried in Mendon cemetery in the Young's family burying place.

Bradley, Elizabeth A.   "Obituary"   Dec 1, 1892
    see Arnold, Mrs Elizabeth A.

Bradley, Frank Armstrong   Sep 24, 1891
    Frank Armstrong, infant son of Mr and Mrs D.A. Bradley of Abilene,
    Kansas was buried Mendon Sept 17th by the side of his little brother.
    Services held in the home of Mrs Bradley Sr. by Rev M.L. Schmucker.
    He was a nephew of Mrs C.A. Chittenden.

Bradley, S.H.   Funeral"   Nov 22, 1894
    see Harrison, Rev Henry

Bradley, Mr S.H.   "Obituary"   Nov 22, 1894
    see Harrison, Rev. Henry

Bradley, Miss Sarah   "Obituary"   Dec 1, 1892
    see Arnold, Mrs Elizabeth A.

Bradley, Miss Sarah Hemmingway   Mar 26, 1903
The remains of Miss Sarah Hemmingway Bradley who died at Scribner, Neb. March 20th arrived Tuesday for burial which took place immediately on arrival of the trian from Burlington. Funeral held at Scribner and body buried in Bradley family plot in Mendon cemetery. Services by Rev. J.S. Bayne. She was born in East Haven, Conn Jan 15, 1815 and came to Ill. with father's family in 1831 and lived Mendon till fall of 1866 when with her sister, Mrs G.A. Harrison with whom she lived moved to Chicago. In 1894 she moved to Scribner, Nebr. where she lived with her nephew, Rev M.B. Harrison till her death. She was an aunt of S.H. Bradley, Miss Ellen Bradley and Mrs Julia L. Bray.

Bradley, Mrs William H.   "Local"   Feb 19, 1903
Died- Mrs William H. Bradley of Chicago, mother of Mrs Victor F. Lawson died Sunday night after a long illness. Lived Mendon in 1836 and later moved to Galena where she married W. H. Bradley in 1842. He died in 1892. 2 other children besides Mrs Lawson survive her, they are, William Harrison Bradley now living in England and Miss Anna M. Bradley.

Brady, John   "Local"   Jul 23, 1903
John Brady of Quincy, son of Mr and Mrs Matthew Brady of Honey Creek who was stabbed by D. Gates Seybold during a quarrel Thursday died Monday afternoon. Was employed past 6 yrs as helper in the carpenter gang of the C.B.&Q. railroad. Leaves wife and 3 children. He was 52 yrs old. Also leaves father, mother and several brothers and sisters.

Brady, Mrs Pat   "Local"   Aug 25, 1892
Died- Mrs Pat Brady of Honey Creek died Saturday from an injur to the spine gotten some 1 yr ago. Buried Monday morning in the Catholic cemetery at Bloomfield. Leaves a husband and 2 small children.

Bragg, Mrs Anna   "Tioga"   Jun 9, 1898
Died- Mrs Anna Bragg wife of Ben Bragg died Wednesday afternoon. Was 26 yrs old. Buried German cemetery at Tioga Friday afternoon. Services by Rev P. Ott.

Bragg, Mr and Mrs Syl   "Tioga"   Oct 17, 1889
Died, Sunday morning at 3 A.M. The infant child of Mr and Mrs Syl Bragg. Funeral today. (Monday)

Braggebos, Mrs   "Ursa"   Oct 5, 1893
Died- Mrs Braggebos on Saturday Sept 30th at her home. She was a native of Germany. Was 56 yrs old. Buried at Baptist cemetery after services in the German church. Leaves husband and 2 daughters, Mrs Emma Shriver and Miss Rosa Braggebos .

Brapy, Miss Bessie   Death"   May 3, 1905
see Sigsbee, Miss Rose (Agness)

Bratton, Thos and Wife   "Loraine"   Mar 20, 1902
3 month old baby of Mr and Mrs Thos. Bratton died Saturday of spinal trouble. Buried yesterday.

Brawley,   "Payson"   Jan 26, 1882
    Died- -- a family by the name of Brawley living on the bottoms buried
    a child last Saturday. The mother on Sunday and another child on Monday.

Bray, Mr and Mrs A.D.   Apr 3, 1884
    Died- March 31st the infant son of Mr and Mrs A.D. Bray. Mrs Bray
    is the daughter of Mr and Mrs Miller. Charles Miller and wife Elizabeth
    of Elvaston, Hancock Co. were at the funeral.

Bray, Charley   "Local"   Aug 7, 1890
    Charley Bray of Crestline, Kansas died July 28th. He was 16 yrs old. He
    was formerly of the Mendon area and the son of O.W. Bray. Charley's
    mother died last winter.

Bray, David C.   Apr 16, 1891
    David C. Bray (Known as Deacon Bray) died April 9th. Was 74 yrs old.
    He was born July 12, 1817 at Guilford, Conn. Came to Mendon, Ill with
    his parents in 1838. In 1844 he married Miss Amelia R. Webster in Conn.
    bringing her to Ill. Mrs B. died Dec 17, 1869 leaving 3 children. They are,
    Mrs John Spencer of Payson, Mr A.D. Bray living on the home farm. and
    Mr Oliver Bray of Crestline, Kansas. Married 2nd to Miss Mary J. Noyes
    on Jan 16, 1872. Mary was eldest daughter of Mrs J. Fowler, by whom he
    leaves 1 daughter, Miss Mary C. Bray. Services in the Cong'l church
    in Mendon by Rev Dr S.D. Peet. Buried Mendon cemetery.

Bray, David C.   "Probate Notice"   Jun 11, 1891
    1st Monday of August 1891   Alfred Bray, Adm.

Bray, David C.   "Obituary"   Nov 19, 1891
    see Dudley, Mrs E.B.

Bray, Eliza   "Obituary"   Sep 12, 1901
    see Dudley, James H.

Bray, Eliza B.   "Obituary"   Nov 19, 1891
    see Dudley, Mrs E.B.

Bray, Mr J.H.   "Obituary"   Nov 16, 1887
    see Wright, John

Bray, James Evans   "Local"   Jan 17, 1889
    Died- in Los Angeles, Calif. Jan 3rd James Evans Bray, son of R.L. and
    Josephine Bray age 4 yrs 3 mo's 20 days from diptheria complicated with
    Quinsy.

Bray, Jimmie   "Letter"   Jan 17, 1889
    Letter from D.W. Wise of Los Angeles, Calif Jan 8th
    R.L. Bray and wife lost their little boy Jimmie. He was buried in this
    city Jan 4th in the P.M. Died from diptheria.

45

Bray, John H.   "Obituary"   Nov 19, 1891
    see Dudley, Mrs E.B.

Bray, John Henry   "Death"   Sept 13, 1905
    John Henry Bray was born in N. Guilford, Conn. Oct 18, 1828 and died
    in Kansas City, Mo. at the home of his daughter, Mrs Lunbeck on
    Sept 8th. He was 76 yrs 10 mo's 21 days old. Came west with his parents
    in early childhood. 1st settled in Ohio for 2 yrs and then in Mendon, Ill.
    He was youngest and last surviving of a family of 6 children (4 sons
    2 daughters), all having lived in or about Mendon. Married Laura Amanda
    Durfee on Dec 25, 1854. She died in Kansas city, Mo also on Aug 1, 1897.
    They had 4 children, Robinson L. who died in Los Angles Calif. Feb 1888,
    Mrs Gertrude Lunbeck, John E. and Mary Evelyn now of Kansas city, Mo.
    He attended school in Mendon and later in Academy at Waverly, Ill. and
    Knox college at Galesburg, Ill. He was in the mercantile business in
    Mendon many yrs. Was post master of Mendon during the civil war. Joined
    Cong'l church in Mendon early in life. Services at the home of Oliver
    Bray by Rev S.R. Reno of the Methodist church. Buried in Mendon cemetery.

Bray, Mrs Julia L.   "Obituary"   Mar 26, 1903
    see Bradley, Miss Sarah Hemmingway

Bray, Mary J.   May 18, 1904
    see Moore, Annice S. partion #1689 of Jeannette Fowler, deceased.

Bray, Mrs Lucinda   "Paloma"   Mar 21, 1889
    Died- Mrs Lucinda Bray, nee Whitney, died here Friday eve. Born at
    Chesterville, Maine in 1811. Came to Illinois in 1832 and married Mr B.
    in 1840. Her husband died yrs ago.

Bray, Mrs Mary   Obituary"   Sep 11, 1902
    see Fowler, Mrs Jeanette

Bray, O.W.   "Local"   Jan 3, 1901
    The youngest son of O. W. Bray of Crestline, Kansas died Friday of
    typhoid fever.

Bray, Robert & Josie   "Died"   Feb 26, 1880
    Died- on Friday A.M. Feb 20th of brain fever, Gilbert Edwin, only
    child of Robert and Josie Bray. Age 1 yr 10 mo's 8 days.

Bray, Robinson (R.L.)   "Local"   Feb 14, 1889
    Mr D.C. Bray rec'd a card from his brother, Mr J.H. Bray from
    Los Angles, Calif. telling of the death of his son R.L. Bray 3 days
    before from internal hemorrhage, the result of a fever. Robinson was
    33 yrs 10 mo's old. Attended school in Mendon, Ill. Leaves a widow and
    1 child.

Bray, Mrs Sarah   "Obituary"   Nov 19, 1891
    see Dudley, Mrs E.B.

Bray, Miss Sarah   "Local"   Jun 29, 1893
Died- Wednesday Miss Sarah Bray at 2 P.M. Funeral today.

Bray, Miss Sarah C.   Jul 13, 1893
Died- an early settler of Adams Co. Miss Sarah C. Bray on June 27th.
Born in North Guilford, Conn. July 31, 1808 being 84 yrs 10 mo's 27 days.
Came here as a child with her parents in 1837. Was a member of the Cong'l
church. Surviving her are 1 brother, Mr J. H. Bray of Leoti, Kansas
and 1 sister, Mrs Jas. Dudley of this twp.

Bray, Wells   Jan 23, 1879
Died- Mr Wells Bray of Paloma, a former resident of this place this A.M.
His remains will probably be brought here for burial tomorrow.

Brayman, Mrs   "Obituary"   Feb 7, 1884
see Warren, Ansel

Brelsford, Robert   "Local"   Aug 9, 1900
Robert Brelsford, father of Mrs Melvin Shaffer returned home from Mo.
where he had been to attend the funeral of his son.

Bremmelmeyer, Mrs Louisa   "Deaths in Adams Co."   Mar 23, 1899
Quincy- Died, Mrs Louisa Bremmelmeyer last Friday A.M. Suffered from
rheumatism 12 yrs. Was born Germany Nov 2, 1835.

Breniman, Laverna   "Obituary"   May 23, 1895
see Guseman, Mrs Laverna

Breniman, W. and Wm H.   "Obituary"   May 23, 1895
see Guseman, Mrs Laverna

Brenneman, Mr   "Loraine"   Aug 9, 1905
Mr Brenneman, of Stillwell is dead. Funeral today.

Brewer, A.J.   "Payson"   Apr 5, 1883
Mr A.J. Brewer was buried this week.

Bricker, Mrs   "Local"   Dec 3, 1903
Mr and Mrs W. Morrison attended the funeral of Mrs Bricker at Mallard,
Hancock Co. Thursday last.

Bridgeman, Mrs   "Payson"   May 12, 1886
Died- last Monday night, Mrs Bridgeman. She was a sister of Mrs
Comstock of Quincy who died a few yrs ago and an aunt of Charles Comstock
of the stone works. Buried in Quincy.

Briggs, Richard   "Fowler"   Jul 3, 1902
Funeral of Mr Richard Briggs was at the Methodist church here Monday
P.M. at 1:30 by Rev Parker Shields. Mr B. lived in Quincy, but had
been living with Mrs Meyers near Cliola the past 3 yrs. Died Sat. A.M.

Bringer, Mr and Mrs Henry   "Tioga"   Feb 14, 1901
    Mr and Mrs Henry Bringer recently buried their twin daughter.

Brinkman, J.W.   "Deaths in Adams Co.   Feb 29, 1899
    Quincy, Mr J.W. Brinkman, a native of Germany died Friday A.M. Age 79
    yrs. Leaves a wife and 3 sons and 2 daughters.

Brinton, Mrs   "Obituary"   Aug 17, 1882
    see Horn, Mr Adam

Brinton, Mrs   "Obituary"   Oct 26, 1887
    see Horn, Mr Peter G.

Brinton, Wm P.   "Died"   Nov 26, 1891
    Died, Mr Wm P. Brinton of 16th and Hampshire Sts. Quincy Sunday eve
    of heart failure. His daughter was at the Cong'l church when she rec'd
    the word. He was born Jan 27, 1827 in Penn. Came to Illinois in 1866 and
    moved to Quincy 10 yrs ago. Leaves a wife and 2 daughters, Mrs Anna
    Chittenden of Mendon and Miss Cora, of Quincy. He was raised a
    Quaker. Services at the home Tuesday afternoon at 3:30. Private burial
    at Fowler tomorrow at 9 "Whig"

Bristow, Mr Geo.   "Lima"   Sep 25, 1884
    We learn from Joel Clark of the death of Mr Geo. Bristow and Wm Crank
    of Bitter Creek, Kansas while digging a well they were overcome by
    fowl air.

Broniski, Nettie   "Died in fire"   Mar 30, 1904
    see McDonald, Rose

Brooker, Thomas W.   "Personal"   Oct 9, 1879
    Thomas W. Brooker of Quincy died Saturday afternoon.

Brooks, Mr James   "Payson"   Jun 17, 1880
    Mr James Brooks had a child buried on June 10th, an infant of a few wks.

Brooks, Mrs James   "Payson"   Jun 10, 1880
    Died- Mrs James Brooks died of consumption June 4th. Leaves husband
    and 5 children.

Brophy, Mrs   "Local"   Jun 15, 1893
    Died- Mrs Brophy, wife of circuit clerk Brophy died Wednesday June 8th
    and was buried from St Peters Catholic church on Friday June 9th.
    Was 58 yrs old and born in Co. Kilkenny, Ireland. daughter died short
    time before her.

Brothers, Geo.   "Obituary"   Jan 3, 1895
    see Shipe, Elizabeth

Brothers, John   "Lima"   Mar 2, 1893
    Died, Uncle John Brothers, who until 5 yrs ago was a resident of Lima
    died at Lemoore, Calif on Feb 8th. Was 59 yrs old. Leaves a wife
    3 sons and 2 daughters. Lived in Lima 35 yrs.

Brothers, John Finley   "Obituary"   Feb 23, 1893
    Died- at his home in this place Friday morning Feb 8th, John Finley
    Brothers. Age 69 yrs. He had gone to Lemoore, Calif in 1888 to be
    near his son's and daughter. Born in Ohio, but moved to Penn at an early
    age where he grew up and married. In 1851 he moved to Adams Co., Ill.
    where he lived until going to Calif in "88". Leaves 3 sons all of
    Lemoore and 1 daughter, Mrs H.E. Doyal who resides in Hanford. Also
    leaves an aged wife. Funeral today at 1 P.M. at the family home.
    Burial in Grangeville cemetery. Born near Frederickburg, Holmes Co.
    Ohio April 5, 1824. Married Mary A. Abrams of Westmoreland Co. Penn.
    Dec 9, 1847. Lived Lima 35 yrs.

Brown, Mrs   "Ellington"   Feb 13, 1890
    Died Feb 3rd Mrs Brown. She lived with her daughter, Mrs James Hedges.

Brown, Mrs A.L.   "Death"   Mar 9, 1899
    see Sigsworth, Mrs Sarah

Brown, Anna C.   "Quincy Optic"   Nov 9, 1893
    The will of the late Anna C. Brown left her wealth to charitable and
    humane institions.

Brown, Mrs Bob   "Local"   Apr 14, 1898
    News has been rec'd by Capt Brown that his brother Bob's wife was
    killed in a runaway at Salt Lake City Saturday.

Brown, Chas.   Jun 1, 1899
    Grave decorated in Mendon cemetery Memorial day.

Brown, Chas. C.   Jun 1, 1904
    His was one of the civil war soldiers graves decorated Memorial day
    in Mendon cemetery.

Brown, Mrs Claude   "Death"   Sep 17, 1903
    see Murphy, John

Brown, Mrs E.   "Local"   May 29, 1902
    Mrs E. Brown rec'd word Tuesday of the death of her sisters husband
    at Baton Rouge, La.

Brown, Mrs F.   "Local"   Mar 30, 1899
    Chas McColm of Barry came up to attend the funeral of his sister in law,
    Mrs F. Brown.

Brown, Dr George Lafayette   "Death"   Aug 24, 1904
   Died of tuberculosis, Dr George Lafayette Brown who graduated from
   Keokuk Medical college last yr and had lived in Keokuk for the past
   several yrs Friday afternoon at the home of his parents, Dr and Mrs
   Lafayette Brown about midway between Hamilton and Warsaw. Born in
   Richland Center, Wisc. on Nov 23, 1871. Leaves parents 2 brothers and
   2 sisters, Miss Eleanor Brown at home, Charles M. of Chicago, Mrs
   William Wright of same city and Arthur at home. "Daily Gate City,
   Keokuk, Iowa August 13th" -- Funeral held from St Titus Episcopal
   church at Hamilton Monday A.M. Aug 15th at 10:30 by Rev R.C. Mollwain.
   Buried Oakland cemetery.

Brown, Harry   Death"   Oct 18, 1894
   Died- Little Harry Brown, youngest son of Capt and Mrs Wm Brown on
   Friday Oct 12th at 8 P.M. age 16 yrs. 8 yrs ago he was stricken with
   some mysterious cerebral or spinal affection. Buried Sunday P.M.
   in the family lot. Services at the house and the graveside by Rev Wm
   Burgess.

Brown, John A.   "Local"   Mar 21, 1895
   Died, Mr John A. Brown, bookeeper for Reidinger and Oertle at the
   home of his brother in law, Mr Cal Baker. He placed a gun to his
   mouth and shot himself. Mr B. left a note saying he thought he was
   losing his mind and did not want to be a burden on anyone as a insane
   man. He was about 40 yrs old and worth about 30,000.00 was not married.

Brown, Josephine   "Obituary"   Aug 2, 1905
   see Bradley, Daniel A.

Brown, Mrs Lillie   "Obituary"   Mar 30, 1899
   Died- Lillie, wife of Frank Brown of Loraine and the daughter of Dr and
   Mrs Akins of this village at the parental home of consumption Tuesday
   at 11 A.M. Age 26 yrs. Leaves husband and 2 girls, 3 and 4 yrs old, 3
   sisters and 2 brothers, Mrs Alice Lemmon of Augusta, Mrs Arvilla McColm
   of Barry, Bessie at home, Wm B. Akins of Mendon and Harry D. of
   Lewisburg, Kansas. She joined the M.E. church when 16 yrs old. Funeral
   today at the house at 10 A.M. and then at the M.E. church at Loraine at
   1 P.M. Buried in family lot in Loraine cemetery.

Brown, Lizzie Lunn   "Local"   May 11, 1887
   J.F. Joseph of Camp Point rec'd a telegram last week from Jas. H. Lunn
   of Salem, Oregon announcing the death of Lizzie Lunn Brown. Mrs Lunn's
   daughter by a former marriage. We regret to learn of her early death.

Brown, Mary   "Payson"   Dec 7, 1882
   Buried Dec 6th, Mrs Mary Brown daughter of Eli Seehorn in Fall Creek
   cemetery.

Brown, Mrs Mary   "Death"   Jan 20,1904
   see Dickson, Rev Dr Alexander and wife

Brown, Mary Francis Dickson   "Obituary"   Sep 14, 1899
    Died- Mary Francis Dickson. Born Ireland 1816 and died Clinton, Iowa
    Sept 8th. Came to U.S. with her parents 1824 to Lansingburgh, near
    Troy, New York state. Married Dr W. J. Brown of Rochester, N.Y. 1839.
    Came west 1845 on the Ohio river to Louisville, Ky. Moved to LaGrange,
    Mo. Keokuk, Iowa and Quincy, Ill. Settled Mendon 1850. Had 7 sons, W.J.,
    Charles C., Alexander, Ed S., Thomas J., Frank P. and Robert C. all
    living except Alexander who died in infancy. Charles C. died here in
    1872. The father died in Mendon in 1873. 7 yrs ago they went to Clinton
    to live with sons Thomas and Frank. Member of the Cong'l church of
    Mendon. Services here at her old home Sunday afternoon by Rev J.S.
    Bayne after which she was buried beside her husband.

Brown, Mr and Mrs S.   "Obituary"   Feb 16, 1899
    see Galloway, Mrs Nancy

Brown, Mr Sample   "Death in Adams Co.   Mar 9, 1899
    Died- Mr Sample Brown at his home in Clayton Feb 26th. Was nearly 80
    yrs old. Leaves a wife and 6 children.

Brown, Mrs Tilly   "News"   Jun 4, 1885
    Died at her home in Quincy May 20th in her 28th yr, Tilly wife of
    Robert C. Brown formerly of Mendon. Buried Woodland cemetery. Mr Wm
    and Thomas Brown, their mother and Mrs Wm Brown was present.

Brown, Mrs Tilly   "Local"   Jun 4, 1885
    Died- at her home in Quincy Wednesday last of consumption in her 28th
    yr. Tilly was the wife of Robert C. Brown formerly of Mendon. Buried
    Woodland cemetery on Friday. Mr Wm and Thomas Brown, their mother and
    Mrs Wm Brown were at the funeral.

Brown, W.H.   "Local"   Jun 8, 1887
    W. H. Brown, an employe of the Whig, is supposed to have been
    drowned yesterday, while bathing.

Brown, W.H.   "Local"   Jun 8, 1887
    The body of W.H. Brown, the Whig Compositor, who drowned while
    bathing, was found in the river Thursday evening ans buried the next
    day in the Woodland cemetery.

Brown, W.J.   Jun 5, 1902
    in list of Civil war soldiers buried in Mendon cemetery.

Brown, Mrs W.J.   "Death"   Jan 20, 1904
    see Dickson, Rev Dr Alexander and wife.

Brown, Wm Sr.   "News"   Jul 15, 1880
    Wm Brown Sr. of Quincy, the father of the Brown Bros bakers. a well
    known citizen started out to visit his native place, Paisley, Scotland
    and died some 2 days before the steamer reached port.

Brown, Capt and Mrs Wm   "Obituary"   Sep 8, 1892
    see Hyatt, Mrs Mary Elizabeth

Brown, Wm J.   "Probate Notice"   May 31, 1900
    1st Monday of August 1900   Elizabeth Brown, Ex.

Brown, Wm J.   Jun 1, 1904
    in list of Civil War soldiers buried in Mendon cemetery.

Brown, Wm   "Local"   May 3, 1900
    Thos. J. Brown of Clinton, Iowa was called here by the illness of his
    brother Wm, but did not arrive in time to see him alive.

Brown, Capt William J.   "Death"   May 3, 1900
    Died- Capt William J. Brown of paralysis at his home Thursday at
    3 P.M. He was the oldest son of Dr W.J. Brown and Mary F. (Dickson)
    Brown Born Rochester, N.Y. Aug 20, 1840. Came to Mendon when 11 yrs old
    with parents. Entered Co. E. 10th Ill. Inf. at the outbreak of the
    war. Discharged 1861 and reinlisted in the 118th Ill. Inf. and
    mustered out 1865. In 1867 he married in Memphis, Tenn to Miss
    Elizabeth Hyatt whom he met at Baton Rouge during the war. Leaves 4
    brothers and a wife. Had 7 children of whom 4 survive him, Mrs Geo. Rust
    of Lima, Miss Beuiah B., Alex S. and Clarence S. of Mendon. Services at
    the house by Rev Wakefield. Buried in Mendon cemetery.

Browning, Hon O.H.   Aug 18, 1881
    Died- Aug 10th Hon O.H. Browning of Quincy age 75 yrs.

Browning, Mrs O.H.   "Local"   Jan 29, 1885
    Mrs O.H. Browning of Quincy died.

Browning, Mrs O.H.   "Local"   Jan 29, 1885
    Since our last issue Mrs O.H. Browning of Quincy has followed lamented
    husband to that "Bourne" from which no traveler returns.

Brownrigg,Mrs   "Columbus"   Nov 5, 1885
    Mrs Brownrigg age67 yrs was buried in the Columbus cemetery Sunday.

Brownsfield, Thomas   "Obituary"   Apr 3, 1884
    see Wells, Mr

Bruggebos, Conrad Julius   "Death"   Aug 27, 1903
    Died- Conrad Julius Bruggebos Monday at 3 P.M. at the home of his
    son in law, Louis Shriver, 2 miles S. of Ursa from infirmities incident
    to old age. Born Germany 88 yrs ago. Came to U.S. 1846 going 1st to
    New Orleans, 2 yrs later to this county. His wife died about 10 yrs
    ago. He leaves only 2 daughters, Mrs Louis Shriver and Miss Rosa.
    Services yesterday at 2 P.M. in the Ursa Lutheran church of which he
    was a member.

Brumby, Grandma   "West Point"   Mar 16, 1893
    Died- Grandma Brumby age 78 yrs at the home of her son 2 miles N.E.
    of town March 7th.

Brumfield, Mrs H.F.   "Big Neck"   Jan 27, 1898
    Mrs H.F. Brumfield has returned to her old home after being in Calif.
    for 2 yrs. where she lost her husband.

Bryant, Rev.   "West Point"   Mar 16, 1893
    Mr and Mrs Dr Bryant went to Versatilies last week to attend the
    funeral of Dr's father, Rev Bryant

Bryant, Mrs Ike   "Ellington"   Jul 24, 1884
    Miss Sarah Wire formerly of Tioga, but late of Ellington was called to
    the bottoms Friday by the death of her sister Mrs Ike Bryant.

Bryson, Geo.   "Obituary"   Dec 31, 1891
    see Hendrickson, Elizabeth

Buckingham, Miss   "Death"   Mar 9, 1904
    see Witt, Philip W.

Buckingham, Witt   "Big Neck"   Aug 9, 1888
    Died- Little Witt, infant son of Mr and Mrs C. A. Buckingham Wed.
    He was nearly 3 yrs old. Born Sept 1, 1885 and buried in Curless
    cemetery.

Buckley, Edward H.   Jan 16, 1890
    Edward H. Buckley, lawyer from Quincy died at the age of 75 yrs on
    Jan. 13th.

Bugg, Eldry   "Loraine"   Dec 12, 1901
    Mrs G. T. Kennedy is visiting friends in Macomb where she went last
    Friday to attend the funeral of Eldry Bugg.

Bull, Catherine R.   "Obituary"   Aug 8, 1901
    see Lunn, John

Bull, Mrs Lorenzo   "Local"   Nov 26, 1903
    Died, Mrs Lorenzo Bull of Quincy Tuesday night. She was the wife of
    the venerable banker.

Buman, Will   "Coatsburg"   Oct 25, 1894
    Died- Will Buman at his home in Coatsburg Oct 13th after a brief
    illness. Leaves a wife who is suffering from consumption and 2 small
    children. Services by the Lutheran minister.

Bunger, Wm   "West Point"   Jan 31, 1884
    Wm Bunger the old mail agent on this branch of the "Q" died Jan 26th
    The funeral took place Sat A.M. with Masonic honors. The cause of death
    was blood poisonong from a wound rec"d during Vicksburg during the
    civil war.

Bunje, Mr and Mrs Henry   "Coatsburg"   Oct 13, 1886
    Infant child of Henry Bunje was buried here last Monday.

53

Bunje, Mrs Henry   "Coatsburg"   Oct 6, 1886
    Died- at Coatsburg Oct 1st Mrs Henry Bunje. Leaves husband and 3 small
    children.

Burall, Mrs Solmon   "Ursa"   Apr 19, 1883
    Died- at her home a few miles S. of Ursa, Mrs Solomon Burall. Leaves
    husband and 3 small children.

Burke, Mr   "Marcelline"   Sep 28, 1882
    Mr Burke an old citizen of this community died at the home of his son
    Leander Sept 26th. Was 82 yrs old.

Burke, Mrs   May 19, 1881
    Died- May 11th at Mendon Mrs Burke of West of Ursa. She was the mother
    of Mrs J.M. Borts. Buried Mendon cemetery.

Burleigh, Dr H.O.   "Local"   Jan 12, 1888
    "A special to the Kansas City Sunday Journal dated, Wichta, Kansas
    Dec 31, 1887"
    Tuesday afternoon Dr H.O. Burleigh dropped dead at the bedside of his
    dying wife. The Dr was a one time resident of Mendon.

Burnett, Mrs Frank T.   Local"   Jun 22, 1899
    Died- Mrs Frank T. Burnett, daughter of Rev E.W. Souders former pastor
    of the Lutheran church died of consumption at the parental home in
    Clinton, Iowa June 7th.

Burnham, Geo.   "Local"   Mar 23, 1899
    C.F. Burnham attended the funeral of his little nephew, son of Geo.
    Burnham in Quincy Sat.

Burnham, Mrs C. F.   "Local"   Aug 29, 1901
    see Cromer, Mrs Ida

Burnahm, Mrs W. H.   "Local"   Dec 5, 1901
    Died- Mrs W.H. Burnham, mother of our druggist, C.F. Burnham at her
    home in Quincy Tuesday A.M. of pneumonia. Born Penn. 63 yrs ago. lived
    Quincy 40 yrs Leaves 3 sons and 1 daughter. Funeral today.

Burns, Mrs Ann   "Death in Adams Co".   Apr 13, 1899
    Died- Mrs Ann Burns at St Vincents hospital Tuesday of old age.
    Was a former resident of Palmyra, Mo.

Burrall, Mrs Lydia   "Ellington"   Apr 10, 1884
    Mrs Lydia Burrall died March 30th. Services by Rev Stodgel at
    Pleasant Grove cuurch.

Burress, Mr   "Obituary"   May 12, 1892
    see Mullins, Mrs Pierce

54

Burrows, Mr   "Ursa"   May 19, 1892
    Mr Burrows died Saturday May 7th at 10 P.M. Services by Rev Ward at
    the house on Sunday at 2 P.M. Buried in Denson cemetery. He was an old
    resident of Adams Co.. 70 yrs old Leaves a wife and several married
    children.

Burrows, Charlotte   Dec 26, 1889
    Charlotte Burrows, wife of J. Burrows of Marcelline died Dec 18th.
    She was born Oct 16, 1825 in Butler co. Ohio and died at age 64 yrs
    1 mo. 2 days. Married 43 yrs 9 mo's and the mother of 8 children. 4 of
    whom are living. She lived in Ursa twp 30 yrs.

Burrows, Mrs George   "Mallard"   Nov 30, 1887
    Mrs Burrows, wife of George Burrows died Nov 17th.

Burrows, Robert   "Ursa"   Mar 14, 1889
    Died- infant son of Mr and Mrs Robert Burrows. Buried in the Denson
    cemetery Saturday.

Burton, Miss Rebecca   "Obituary"   Apr 27, 1887
    see Weed, Deacon L.A.

Burtsell, Meriah   "Obituary"   Dec 29, 1898
    see Tharpe, John W.

Buschman, John Edgar   "Local"   May 22, 1902
    John Edgar Buschman 17 yrs old committed suicide at the home of his
    parents in Quincy Tuesday afternoon by taking strychnine. His brother
    died last yr and he has grieved since.

Bush, Mrs Ed   "Payson"   Aug 3, 1882
    A sister of Mrs Ed Bush of Marblehead was buried near Richfield last
    Sunday.

Bushman, Susan   "Death"   Mar 3, 1892
    see Scranton, Miss Kate

Butler, Mrs Hanna   "Obituary"   Aug 13, 1891
    see Kells, Richard

Butler, Hannah   "Died"   July 20, 1904
    Aunt Hannah Butler died at her home in Mendon Tuesday 8:30 A.M. Was
    about 80 yrs old Born County Caven, Ireland and with 2 sisters came to
    U.S. in 1850 and settled Mendon to stay till she died except the time
    she lived on the farm occupied by D.W. Worman. Few yrs after coming here
    she married John Butler who died April 1872. They had 2 children, both
    dying in infancy. Leaves 3 sisters, Mrs Wm Hewitt of Honey Creek,
    Mrs Thos. Hewitt of Mendon and Mrs Martha Franch who still lives in
    the old counry. Funeral at the Zion Episcopal church at 3 P.M. today
    by Rev Robert Hewitt. Buried beside her husband in Mendon cemetery.

Butler, Hammah   "Probate Notice"   Oct 19, 1904
    1st Monday of December 1904   Anna Mealiff, Adm.

Butler, Mrs Hannah   "Local"   Jul 27, 1904
    Will of the late Mrs Hannah Butler was filed for probate in the Co.
    court Thursday. It provides that after payment of 100.00 to a sister,
    Mrs Sarah Hewitt, the reminder of the estate shall go to Mrs Anna
    Mealiff, a niece.

Butler, Hannah   Probate of Will"   Aug 3, 1904
    "Notice for Probate of Will" Estate of Hannah Butler, deceased to
    Anna Mealiff, Sarah Hewitt, Bessie Hewitt, Hannah Kells, Mamie Kells,
    William Kells, Robert G. Kells, Martha French and unknown heirs,
    legatees and devisees of said Martha French. Fanny Fee and unknown
    heirs of said Fanny Fee, Ann Seweel and unknown heirs legatees and
    devisees of said Ann Seweel, David Kells and unknown heirs, legatees
    and devisees of said David Kells and Jane Fife and unknown heirs,
    legatees and heirs of said deceased and Mrs Sarah Hewitt and Mrs Anna
    Mealiff, legatees and devisses of said deceased.

Butler, Mrs J.H.   Nov 8, 1894
    see Borgholthaus,Mrs
    Mrs J.H. Butler and ____ of Councill Grove, Kansas were called home by
    the funeral of their mother, Mrs Borgholthaus. They were guests of
    Mrs Dr. Vowles.

Butler, Mrs Katie   "Obituary"   Dec 1, 1886
    see Borgholthaus, George W.

Butler, Mrs Neva Grimes   "Obituary"   Aug 16, 1894
    "Sunday School Supplement"
    Died- Mrs Neva Grimes Butler a member of the Presbyterian church at
    Camp Point. Died in March of 1894

Byler, Mrs   "Local"   May 31, 1894
    Mrs Byler an old resident of Honey Creek twp died last week and buried
    in the family burying ground.

Byler, Mrs Harriet   May 31, 1894
    "Coatsburg corner of Quincy Herald"
    The remains of Mrs Harriet Byler was buried in Coatsburg last Sat.
    Died at her home in Honey Creek twp on Thursday May 24th at 1 P.M.
    She was 72 or 73 yrs old.

Byrd, Dr   "Local"   Aug 17, 1887
    Death of Dr Byrd, the eminent surgeon of Quincy. He died at his home at
    Slater, Mo. Buried in Quincy in the Woodland cemetery. Services at
    St John's Cathedral by Rev Corbyn.

Byrd, Dr W.A.   "Obituary"   Feb 21, 1884
    see Smith, Mrs Susan

Cabe, Harry   Jun 1, 1904
    Included in list of Civil was soldiers buried in Mendon cemetery.

Cadogan, Mrs Catherine   "Deaths in Adams Co."   Feb 23, 1899
    Died- Mrs Catherine Cadogan at St Mary's hospital Wednesday Feb 15th.
    Age 48 yrs.

Cadogan, John P.   "Local"   May 11, 1887
    Quincy lost another of her best citizens, John P. Cadogan, the
    oldest newspaper publisher in the city. Died at his home on Vermont St.
    Thursday May 5th in his 63rd yr. Buried Woodland cemetery on Sunday.

Cain, Mr Bennett   "Local"   Jul 26, 1894
    Died- Mr Bennett Cain, of Loranie last Wednesday. Buried Friday.

Cain, Ellen J.   "Probate Notice"   Nov   1890
    1st Monday of Dec 1890   John Pratt, Adm.

Cain, Ellen   Sep 25, 1890
    Ellen Cain died in Jacksonville and was brought home Sept 18th for
    burial by her son James B. and son in law E.F. Thomas. Buried Mendon.

Cain, Mr Jas.   Feb 13, 1890
    Died- Feb 9th, Mr Jas. Cain of Loraine. Age 64 yrs. Buried Feb 10th.

Cain, James   "Probate Notice"   Dec 4, 1890
    1st Monday of January 1891   John Pratt, Adm.

Cain, Jesse   "Local"   Apr 10, 1890
    Died- Jesse Cain about 22 yrs old on the 4th. Was the son of Laban Cain
    of Golden.

Cain, Jno.   "Obituary"   Nov 1, 1900
    see Kincheloe, Isaac Newton

Cain, John W.   Mar 10, 1881
    Mr John W. Cain died of erysipelas Friday March 4th. Age 26 yrs. He
    was born about 7½ miles north of Loraine, Ill. March 26, 1855 where
    he has lived since his birth. He married Miss Laura Cubbage, daughter
    of Mr and Mrs Wm Cubbage. Leaves wife and parents. Buried in Loraine
    cemetery by IOOF lodge last Sunday.

Cain, Roe Anna   "Obituary"   Sep 14, 1877
    see Grimm, Christopher

Cake, Harry   Jun 5, 1902
    Included in list of Civil war soldiers buried in Mendon cemetery.

Caldwell, Mr and Mrs Curtis   "Death"   Mar 23, 1899
    see Green, Mrs John L.

Caldwell, Margaret A.   "Local"   Mar 1, 1894
    Mrs Henry Francis was called to Knoxville, Knox Co. by the illness
    of her aunt, Mrs Caldwell. (The last surviving sister of Mr Ben Gilmer)
    Later- Died at Knoxville, Ill. Feb 26th Margaret A. wife of William P.
    Caldwell age 61 yrs.

Calhoun, Mr   "Payson"   Sep 11, 1879
    Died recently a child of Mr Calhoun.

Calwell, Mrs Belle   "Mt Pleasant"   Nov 5, 1903
    Funeral services of Mrs Belle Calwell was Oct 14th at the Stone
    church cemetery. She died about a yr ago at her home in Kansas City
    Her body was placed in a vault temporarily until it could be
    convenietly arrenged for burial here. She was eldest daughter of
    the late David P. Colvin.

Camerer, Mrs J. E.   "Paloma"   Feb 21, 1889
    Mrs J.E. Camerer died Wednesday at 9 P.M. of paralysis. Mr J.E. is the
    only surviver of the older circle.

Cameron, Frank   May 4, 1877
    Died- Frank Cameron, a former resident of this place died near
    Jacksonville, Ill last Friday.

Cameron, Mrs John   "Loraine"   Jun 2, 1881
    Mrs John Cameron died Mat 28th and was buried in Reece cemetery.

Campbell, Judge   "Local"   Apr 20, 1887
    Died Saturday April 16th Judge Campbell of Marcelline from dropsy. He
    was a large man standing 6 ft 3 inches tall and weighing 340 pounds.
    He was a well known character among the older residents of this part.

Campbell, Squire   "Ursa"   Oct 20, 1898
    Died- Squire Campbell of this place Sunday A.M. of typhoid fever. He
    was no doubt the largest man in the Co. weighing near 400 pounds.
    Leaves a wife and 7 children. Funeral at the Christian church today.
    Buried in the Stone church cemetery.

Campbell, Mrs   "Paloma"   Apr 21, 1886
    Mrs Campbell, nee Gooding, was buried Sunday. Services by Rev Wolforth

Campbell, Mrs   "Death"   Mar 10, 1886
    see Heberling, Mrs

Campbell, Rev A.B.   Mar 9, 1882
    Died- Rev A.B. Campbell at Dallas City. Services by Rev Wallace of
    Payson. He was a resident here for 25 yrs or more.

Campbell, Rev A.B.   Mar 16, 1882
   Rev A.B. Campbell of Dallas funeral was on March 9th and attended by
   Mrs Campbell and her sons Wm R. and John G. and Mary the only daughter
   George Campbell being at Laredo, Texas and Alex at Oberlin, Ohio were
neither present. Rev S. A. Wallace of Payson preached the services. Rev A.B.
   was the son of William and Mary G. Campbell and the youngest of 8
   children. 3 of whom are still living. He was born at Rensselaerville,
   Albany Co. N.Y. Sept 11, 1824 later moving to Oak Hill in the adj. Co.
   of Greene. Graduated 1846 from Union College. First settled at
   Rushville, Ill in the autumn of 1850. He was orsained in Quincy 1851
   and the same yr married Miss Anna M. Hollister of Manchester Vt.
   In 1855 he was called to the Cong'l church at Mendon, Ill. serving 26
   yrs, resigned in March 1881. Age 57 yrs 5 mo's 25 days. His oldest
   son is pastor at Boston, Mass. 2nd son George is with the railroad at
   Laredo, Teaxas and John G. is asst editor of Litchfield, Ill Monitor.
   Alexander is in college and Mary is at home with her mother.

Campbell, Miss Alice   "Local"   May 22, 1902
   Miss Alice Campbell died at her home in Big Neck Monday May 19th
   after an illness of several months.

Campbell, Mrs Elizabeth   "Obituary"   Jun 4, 1885
   see Nichols, Mr J.P.

Campbell, Frank   "Payson"   Apr 20, 1882
   Frank Campbell died April 17th.

Campbell, James   "Ursa"   Feb 1, 1905
   Died, Wednesday Jan 25th at 6 A.M. at the home of Mrs Nancy Campbell
   1 mile W. of Ursa, James Campbell who had been sick 2 yrs and had
   just recently returned from Jacksonville. Services at Christian church.
   Buried Stone cemetery. Leaves a divorced wife and 1 daughter and
   3 sons.

Campbell, Mr Lee R.   "Ursa"   Apr 20, 1887
   Mr Lee R. Campbell of Marcelline died Saturday P.M. Remains were
   taken to Quincy on Monday.

Campbell, Lewis   "Ursa"   Apr 24, 1884
   a 3 yr old child of Lewis Campbell of Quincy was buried here a few
   days ago.

Campbell, Mrs Lucy   "Death"   Apr 26, 1894
   see Golden, Thankful

Campbell, Mrs Malinda   "Local"   Aug 17, 1899
   Died- Mrs Malinda Campbell of Ursa. Age 74 yrs Saturday morning. Buried
   in the Stone church cemetery. Services at the Christian church where
   she was a member by Rev G.F. Knight. Her husband died about 25 yrs ago.

59

Campbell, Mrs Mary   "Obituary"   Oct 31, 1889
    Died- Mrs Mary Campbell of Ursa Sept 28th. She was the mother of the
    first white child born in Adams Co. and was the daughter of Samuel
    Groshong. Born in Lincoln Co. Mo. May 1811 and came to Adams Co. with
    her father in 1823 where her father built the first log cabin in Ursa
    twp. She married George Campbell in Aug 1825 by Willard Keyes J.P.
    This was the first marriage in the history of the Co. Gave birth to the
    first white child, A.J. Campbell on Aug 11, 1827. Her husband died
    Dec 24, 1864 in his 74th yr. Services by J.M. Ruddle.

Campbell, Miss Nora   "Obituary"   Jul 20, 1887
    see Lawrence, Jas.

Campbell, Sarah   "Obituary"   Mar 12, 1891
    see Beatty, Thomas

Campbell, Thomas   "Ursa"   Nov 1, 1888
    Died- Thomas Campbell an old resident of this twp at his home on
    Rock Creek at 6 A.M. Friday. Buried in the old Stone church cemetery
    Saturday.

Cannel, Mrs Robert   Nov 10, 1881
    Died- November 6th, Mrs Robert Cannel. Leaves we believe 4 children,
    from a few weeks old to 14 yrs.

Cannell,Miss Mollie   "Local"   Jan 25, 1900
    Died- Miss Mollie Cannel, daughter of Robert Cannell,living N.W. of here
    at the St Mary's hospital Quincy Sunday morning from pneumonia. 31 yrs
    old Leaves her father, 1 sister and 2 brothers. Buried Tuesday morning
    in Franklin cemetery.

Cantiell, Jackson   "Coatsburg"   Sept 13, 1894
    The remains of Jackson Cantiell was brought here Thursday eve from
    Corning, Ark. where he was killed by a train. It was accompanied by
    a number of relatives. Buried in village cemetery. Services by Elder
    Dilly of Camp Point.

Cantrell, Thomas   "Coatsburg"   Jan 12, 1887
    Died- Thomas Cantrell at his home 4 miles north of Coatsburg Saturday
    morning Jan 8th of paralyis. Buried in Coatsburg cemetery Sunday.

Card, David   "Loraine"   Jul 31, 1890
    Saturday morning at the residence 1 3/4 miles N.W. of Loraine, David
    Card age 29 yrs 9 mo's 14 days died. Services by Rev R. Crank at the
    Dunkard church. Leaves a wife and 1 child.

Card, David   "Probate Notice"   Aug 14, 1890
    1st Monday of October 1890   H.W. Strickler, Adm.

Carey, Dr   Sep 18, 1884
    "Clip from Quincy Journal"
    Dr Carey of West Point, Hancock Co. died last week. He was well known
    in Adams Co. and Hancock Co. Having lived in West Point 26 yrs.

Carl, Mrs John B.   "Camp Point"   Feb 27, 1879
     Mrs Carl, relic of the late John B. Carl who was a well known citizen
     here 25 yrs ago and mimister of the Christian church died Sunday morning
     Ago 86 yrs.

Carley, Mrs C.E.   "Death"
     see Wilcox, Chester A.   Aug 3, 1899

Carlin, Mr   "Quincy Optic"   Jul 28, 1898
     Died- Mr Carlin, father of Mrs Dr Lambert of Coatsburg at his home
     in West Point, Ill. Thursday afternoon.

Carlin, Margaret   "Obituary"   Aug 10, 1893
     see Smith, Mrs Patrick

Carlin, William   "Camp Point"   Nov 30, 1882
     Died- baby of William Carlin on November 25th. Buried at Hebron cemetery

Carlisle, Mary   "Obituary"   Feb 26, 1903
     see McClelland, Dr Cochran

Carlock, Archie   "Estate"   Apr 12, 1894
     see McAdams, Clifton

Carlock, George   "Lima"   May 20, 1880
     George Carlock died of consumption at the home of his parents in this
     place May 2nd at age 22 yrs.

Carlock, Jas. A.   "Obituary"   Jan 17, 1895
     see Shipe, Arthur W.

Carlock, Lee H.   "estate"   Apr 12, 1894
     see McAdams, Clifton

Carlock, Wm W.   "Estate"   Apr 12, 1894
     see McAdams, Clifton

Carmean, R.O.   "Ursa"   Jul 6, 1887
     Miss Emma Carmean, now of Burlington is visiting with friends since
     the funeral of her brother, R.O. Carmean.

Carmean, Rowe   "Local"   Jun 29, 1887
     Died- Rowe Carmean age 25 yrs. Leaves a wife whom he married a yr ago.

Carney, Mr and Mrs   "Lima"   May 14, 1885
     Mr and Mrs Carney lost a child while it was asleep when their home
     burned.

Carolin, Andrew   "Will"   Oct 1, 1885
     see McGovern, Patrick

Carpenter, Miss Mary   "Lima"   Jul 4, 1895
    Died- last Sunday about noon at the home of T.F. Leeper, living a mile
    or 2 W. of town, Miss Mary Carpenter, a young lady who had been working
    for them the past 3 mo's. Leaves a father, mother, several brothers and
    sisters. Buried Tioga cemetery.

Carpenter, Mrs Sarah   "Local"   Dec 28, 1904
    The death of Sarah Carpenter (nee Leach) age 58 yrs occured at Keokuk,
    Iowa Monday afternoon. Born in Mendon April 2, 1846 Married Isaac
    Carpenter in Quincy 39 yrs ago. Leaves a son and a daughter, Frank and
    Sadie, a brother D.W. Leach and 2 sisters, Mrs Deliah Daley and Mrs
    Emma Daley, all of Keokuk.

Carr, Mrs   "Coatsburg"   Jan 28, 1892
    Died- Mrs Carr. She had just returned from Burdoff where her sick
    daughter lives. She died Tuesday at 4 A.M.

Carr, Nathaniel   "Payson"   Nov 16, 1887
    Old uncle Nathaniel Carr of Fall Creek had a train hit his wagon
    between Bluff Hall and Fall Creek. Was taken to Hannibalby the train
    where he died. Funeral will be at Craigtown at 2 P.M. today.
    "Article dated Nov 14th"

Carroll, Andy   Sep 1, 1892
    Died- Andy, 8 yr old son of Phil Carroll of Ellington after finding
    some whiskey and drinking it.

Carroll, Mr John   "Local"   Sep 13, 1894
    Died at his home near Bloomfield, Adams Co. on Friday night Sept 7th
    after an illness of over a yr. Age 37 yrs. Mr John Carroll, a well
    known farmer. Leaves a wife and 4 children. Funeral Sunday was a mile
    in length.

Carroll, John   "Probate Notice"   Oct 25, 1894
    1st Monday of January 1895   Lena Carroll, Ex.

Carr, Mr and Mrs Alvin   "Loraine"   Sep 25, 1890
    Infant child of Mr and Mrs Alvin Carr died Sept 20th. Buried at
    Breckenridge.

Carter, Adolph   "Local"   Dec 22, 1886
    Adolph Carter, a poor waek minded boy, son of Mr John Carter of Quincy
    was found frozen stiff and dead Thursday A.M.

Carter, J.   "Mendon"   Feb 23, 1882
    Died- February 17th Mr J. Carter age 39 yrs. He has been a resident of
    our village only a few months and leaves a wife and 3 children.

Carter, Mrs V.   "Tioga"   Jun 13, 1895
    Died- on Friday June 7th at 11 P.M. Leaves a husband and 4 children.
    Buried in the village cemetery Sunday P.M. Services by Rev B.F.
    Macmanama.

Carver, Thomas and Elizabeth   "Local"   Jul 7, 1898
    Died- on Thursday P.M. June 30th, son of Thomas and Elizabeth Carver,
    of Clayton. Age 24 yrs. Deceased was a very diminutive stature, about
    30 inches we are told. Buried Mendon on Saturday.

Cary, Mr Edward   "Lima"   Jan 14, 1892
    Mr Edward Cary, wife and daughter Edith went to Tama, Iowa to attend
    the funeral of his mother who died Dec 27th of LaGrippe. Age 83 yrs.

Casley, B. J.   Card of Thanks"   Oct 3, 1889
    From B.J. Casley to those who assisted in any way during the illness
    and death of his wife.

Casley, B.J.   "Obituary"   Sep 12, 1889
    see Dunbar, Josephine

Casley, Mrs Jacob   "Local"   Aug 14, 1902
    Mrs Jacob Casley died at 6 A.M. yesterday. Funeral Friday A.M. at 9.

Casley, Mr and Mrs J.C.   "Local"   Jun 23, 1898
    Died- 5 yr old daughter of Mr and Mrs J.C. Casley Saturday at 8 P.M. of
    inflammation of the bowels. Funeral at the house this P.M. at 5.

Casley, Mrs J.C.   "Death"   Jan 7, 1892
    see Hendrickson, Mrs

Casley, Rebecca   "Probate Notice"   Sep 21, 1899
    1st Monday of Nov 1899 Lucy Casley, Ex.

Casley, Mrs Rebecca   "Obituary"   Jun 1, 1899
    Died- Mrs Rebecca Casley at her home in Mendon of paralysis of the
    heart Saturday May 27th at 1 P.M. Age 72 yrs 2 mo's 11 days. Born
    Fairfield, Penn March 15, 1827. Her husband died several yrs ago.
    They had 7 children 5 sons 2 daughters all living, namely
    Alex of Hamilton, Beniah of Quincy, John and Charles of Kansas Jacob C.,
    Lucy and Sarah of Mendon. Services at the Lutheran church of which
    she was a member by Rev J.S. Bayne.

Casley, Mrs Susan Kayler   "Obituary"   Aug 21, 1902
    Funeral of Mrs Susan Kayler was at the home of her husband, Mr Jacob
    Casley Friday A.M. Aug 15th at 9 A.M. by Rev J.S. Bayne. She was born
    July 11, 1838 at Mount Pleasant, Penn (Westmoreland Co.) and married
    Jacob Casley Oct 9, 1856 and came to Mendon in Nov. of the same yr.
    Was a member of the United Brethern church. Leaves husband and daughter
    Cora. Pallbearers were- L.D. Nichols, C.A. Chittenden, August
    Stockhecke, Wm Thompson, C. Austin and S.H. McClung.

Casteel, Mr and Mrs Alex   "Local"   Sep 14, 1904
    Mr and Mrs Alex Casteel of Quincy mourn the death of 2 of their
    children ages 9 and 11 yrs. They were starting a fire with coal oil
    when it took fire causing an explosion and they were fatally burned.

Castle, Dr E.G.   "Personal"   Sep 23, 1880
Died- Dr E.G. Castle a well known and popular physican of Quincy died Monday morning.

Castle, Mr Timothy H.   "Personal"   Jun 24, 1880
Died- Mr Timothy H. Castle, one of Quincy's oldest citizens died Tuesday P.M. Was one of the leading partners of Comstock and Castle Co.

Cates, Rosa   "Death?"   Dec 6, 1900
see Powell, Mrs Rosa

Caterlin, Margaret   "Death"   Mar 1, 1883
see Thomas, Benj. J.

Cathers, Mr John   "Coatsburg"   Sep 17, 1885
Mr John Cathers of Peoria was called home by the death of his brother.

Cathers, Mr Will   "Coatsburg"   Sep 17, 1885
Mr Will Cathers died of typhoid fever last Wednesday Sept 9th and was buried in Coatsburg cemetery on Thursday.

Cecil, Teresa   "Obituary"   Nov 13, 1902
Teresa Cecil, born May 10, 1823 in Kentucky During her youth her family came to Illinois. 1841 she married Wm L. Cubbage of Knox Co. Ill. and 1848 they came to Adams Co. where they lived since in Keene twp. Converted in 1857, member of M.E. church for many yrs. Leaves husband of 61 yrs, several brothers and sisters, 4 children, 3 sons, and 1 daughter, a number of grandchildren and several great grandchildren. Services by Rev J.H. Jones at Loraine M.E. church Monday A.M. Buried Curless cemetery.

Chambers, Mary Elizabeth   "Obituary"   Aug 1, 1901
see Leckbie, Joseph Griffith

Chandler, Charles   "Loraine"   May 19, 1881
Born and died a child of Charles Chandler.

Chandler, Frankie   "west Point"   Jul 12, 1894
Died- Frankie Chandler July 8th at 5 o'clock. Age 13 yrs 1 mo. 2 days from spinal trouble. Leaves a father, mother, 1 sister and 2 brothers.

Chant, Mrs   May 1,1890
Died- Mrs Chant of Port Jarvis N.Y. aged over 80 yrs. She was from West of England. Had lived in this country about 18 yrs. She was the mother of Mr Joseph Chant of Mendon.

Chant, Geo. T.   "Obituary"   Dec 29, 1898
see Hewitt, Thomas

Chant, Mrs Joseph   "Obituary"   Dec 4, 1890
see Jennings, Thomas W.

Chant, Joseph   "Obituary"   Jul 15, 1900
    Died- July 11th at 3 P.M. Joseph Chant, born at Stoke Somersetshire,
    England August 13, 1830. Left England at age 18 yrs and came to New York
    Traveled thru N.Y., Canada and Penn. finally settling in Missouri where
    in 1858 he married Miss Susan A. Jennings. 1861 they came to Mendon, Ill
    Had 10 children all living- Geo. T. of Stronghurst, Ill. William and
    Charles of Mendon, Joseph of LaPlata, Mo. , Herbert of Burlington, Iowa
    Freeman of Fulton, Mo., Elizabeth (Mrs Wesley Clair), Myrtle, Amy
    and Florence all of Mendon. He was baptised in the Episcopalian church
    before leaving England. Services will be at the Zion Epis. church at
    2:30 P.M. Thursday by Rev T. A. Waterman.

Chant, Joseph Sr.   "Local"   Jul 19, 1900
    At the funeral of Joseph Chant Sr. last Thursday his 6 sons acted as
    pallbearers. The 4 who reside away from Mendon are, Geo., Joseph, Herbert
    and Freeman.

Chant, Mrs Wm   "Obituary"   Dec 22, 1898
    see Nedrow, Mrs Adela (Andrews)

Chapman, Mr Lish   "Payson"   Aug 18, 1886
    Mr Lish Chapman buried their child yesterday. (about a yr old)

Chase, Mrs   "Death"   Aug 20, 1891
    see Tittle, Mrs Hamilton

Chase, Abner   "Jotting by Hundes"   Sep 22, 1881
    Abner Chase along with the Chase family moved from Penn. to near
    Fowler around 1830. I rememberfrom 1838 as being a very generous man
    died in his prime Abram Chase Jr. was a tinner and died quite young.
    Father Chase lived to see his childrens children. a Wonderful man.

Chase, Mrs Charles   May 22, 1884
    Mrs Charles Chase age 75 yrs died May 14th. Services by Rev Janes.
    Burialin cemetery at Wesley Chapel.

Chase, Mr Charlie   "Ellington"   Jan 26, 1887
    Mr Charlie Chase of Canon City, Colo formerly of Ellington died at his
    home Jan 14th of lung trouble. His remains were brought back here for
    burial in the cemetery at Wesley Chapel Jan 19th. Leaves a wife and 1
    child.

Chase, Col. E.B.C.   "News"   Jul 8, 1880
    see Shannon, Col W.M.

Chase, Mrs George   "Fowler"   Aug 4, 1886
    Died- Mrs George Chase on last Thursday eve.

Chase, Kitty   "Ellington"   Jan 22, 1885
    Aunt Kitty Chase died at her home in Fowler Wednesday and buried Thurs.

Chase, Kitty   "Ellington"   Jan 22, 1885
    Aunt Kitty Chase died at her home in Fowler Jan 14th and buried on the
    15th.

Chatten, Mrs W.I. "Death in Adams Co." Mar 16, 1899
    Died- Mrs W.I. Chatten, the mother of Enoch, Harvey and Charles Chatten
    Monday afternoon at the home of her daughter, Mrs R.I. McIntyre in
    Chicago. 78 yrs old. Went to Chicago last fall to visit her daughter
    Leaves another daughter, Mrs Z.S. Pratt of Rockford.

Cherill, Miss Grace "News" Sep 23, 1880
    Died- Miss Grace Cherrill of Carthage. She was a graduate of
    Carthage college and was teaching school.

Cherry, Elizabeth "Obituary" Sep 14, 1899
    see Wyatt, Thomas

Cherry, Mary "Obituary" Aug 11, 1881
    see Simmons, John K.

Cherry, Wm "Obituary" Jan 24, 1889
    see Wyatt, Mrs Thomas

Cherry, Wm Dec 7, 1877
    Died- in Hancock Co. Ill. November 28th, Mr Wm Cherry age 75 yrs
    6 mo's. Leaves a wife, son and daughter.

Chidsey, Miss Frances "obituary" Jul 20, 1893
    see Taft, Mrs Samuel

Childers, Mrs Charles "Payson" Feb 24, 1886
    Mrs Charles Childers who has been very poorly with consumption for
    some time was buried last week. Leaves a husband.

Chittenden, Abraham "Obituary" Dec 1, 1898
    see Baldwin, Harry D.

Chittenden, Abraham "Obituary" Jun 1, 1904
    Died- last Friday Abraham Chittenden. He came with his parents over-
    land from Guilford, Conn. in the fall of 1831 and in spring of 1832 the
    colony selected the present site of Mendon twp for their homes and a
    town and built cabins. He was born in Guilford, Conn Dec 1824. was
    almost 80 yrs old at time of his death. Married Miss Letitia Barclay
    1852. They had 3 children, Harry F. who lives on the old home place
    N.E. of town, Mrs Geo. W. Shupe of San Antonio, Texas, and Abraham
    of Wichita, Kansas. Funeral Sunday at 2:30 P.M. at the home by Rev
    Joseph F. Bacon and later at the church.

Chittenden, Abraham "Probate Notice" Jul 20, 1904
    1st Monday of Sept 1904 Lettitia S. Chittenden, Ex.

Chittenden, Abraham "Local" Jun 15, 1904
    The will of the late Abraham Chittenden was filed Friday for probate.
    leaves son's Henry F. and Abraham and daughter, Mrs Sarah E. Shupe
    1.00 each- remainder of estate to go to the widow, Letitia S.
    Chittenden.

Chittenden, Mrs Abram "Obituary" Mar 15, 1900
    see Barclay, Caroline E.

Chittenden, Betsey   "obituary"   Dec 1, 1898
    see Baldwin, Harry D.

Chittenden, C.A.   "Obituary"   Jan 12, 1887
    see Barker, Judge Ebenezer

Chittenden, Charles A.   "Obituary"   Aug 2, 1905
    see Bradley, Daniel A.

Chittenden, C.A.   "Obituary"   Apr 21, 1892
    see Bradley, Frank Armstrong

Chittenden, Mrs Caroline B. "Obituary"   May 16, 1901
    see Frisbie, Morris E.

Chittenden, Mrs Caroline   "Died"   Jun 18, 1903
    Died- Mrs Caroline Frisbie Chittenden at 2:15 A.M. Thursday June 11th
    Born in Branford, Conn April 19, 1821 Came to Illinois with her father's
    family 1837. Married Jan 2, 1845 to the late Samuel R. Chittenden who
    died 4 yrs ago. Survived by 3 sons, John R., Samuel F. and George R.
    Chittenden, 2 grandsons, William B. and S.R. Chittenden, also 1 older
    brother, Joseph B. Frisbie and 3 sisters, Mrs Mary Barker of New York
    city, Mrs E.F. Rea of St Louis and Mrs Elizabeth Chittenden of Mendon
    and a number of nieces and nephews. Funeral at the family home at 2 P.M.
    Friday by Rev J.S. Bayne and Rev S.R. Reno. Buried in family lot in the
    village cemetery.

Chittenden, David   Feb 20, 1890
    Died- David Chittenden in his home near North Guilford, Conn Feb 7th
    buried Feb 9th. age 72 yrs. His daughter was Mrs A. Benton.

Chittenden, Mrs Elizabeth P. "Obituary"   May 16, 1901
    see Frisbie, Morris E.

Chittenden, G.R.   "Obituary"   Jan 12, 1887
    see Barker, Judge Ebenezer

Chittenden, Mrs Harry   "Obituary"   Apr 25, 1889
    see James, Mrs E.B.

Chittenden, Mr and Mrs Harry   Sep 25, 1890
    Frank, only son of Mr and Mrs Harry Chittenden died Sept 24th.

Chittenden, Henry   "Local"   Nov 24, 1892
    Mr Henry Chittenden of Warsaw, a brother of Hon. S.R. and A. Chittenden
    of Mendon died at Keokuk, Iowa hospital Saturday eve. Buried at Warsaw
    Monday by the side of his wife. He was 71 yrs old.

Chittenden, Mrs Hy   Feb 12, 1891
    Mrs Hy Chittenden died suddenly while her husband was in Springfield.

Chittenden, Mr and Mrs Harry "Obituary"   May 9, 1901
    see Norris, Mrs Nellie

Chittenden, J.R.   "Died"   Sep 28, 1904
    died- Friday 1 A.M. J.R. Chittenden of bronchial pneumonia and a weak
    heart. Born in Mendon Sept 14, 1847 and lived here since. He was the
    oldest son of the late Senator Samuel R. and Caroline B. Chittenden.
    Married Oct 21, 1875 to Miss Anna S. Brinton and had 2 sons, William B.
    of Springfield, Ill. and Samuel R. of Mendon who with their mother
    and 2 brothers, Samuel F. and George R. survive him. He was a member of
    the Cong'l church. Services at the late home Sunday P.M. by Rev Joseph
    F. Bacon. Buried Mendon cemetery in the family plot.

Chittenden, Mrs J.R.   "Local"   Nov 26, 1891
    Mrs J.R. Chittenden's father, Mr Brinton of Quincy died last night.

Chittenden, John R.   "Obituary"   Jan 12, 1887
    see Barker, Judge Ebenezer

Chittenden, Col. John B.   "Obituary"   Dec 1, 1898
    see Baldwin, Harry D.

Chittenden, Miss Nellie   "Obituary"   May 9, 1901
    see Norris, Mrs Nellie

Chittenden, S.F.   "Obituary"   Jan 12, 1887
    see Barker, Judge Ebenezer

Chittenden, Mrs S.F.   "Obituary"   Jan 3, 1895
    see McCormick, Mrs Leah

Chittenden, Mrs S.F.   "Obituary"   Jan 28, 1894
    see McCormick, John

Chittenden, Mrs S.F.   "Death"   Mar 1, 1905
    see Rust, Mrs Michael

Chittenden, Hon. S.R.   "Death"   Jan 26, 1899
    Died- Hon. S.R. Chittenden Sunday night from heart failure. Nephew C.A.
    Chittenden spent part of afternoon with him, also his wife and son George
    R. Samuel Robinson Chittenden born Guilford, Conn Oct 2, 1817 the oldest
    son of Col John B. Chittenden of Guilford. Mother was daughter of Col.
    Samuel Robinson of the same place. Parents married Jan 12, 1814. Lived
    Conn. till 1831 when Mr C. Sr moved his family to Ill. spent winter of
    1831 in Quincythen settled on S.W. ¼ of sect 11 near the present site of
    Mendon. Feb 1833 he bought the N.E.¼ of sect 11 laid out and plotted the
    village of Fairfield, (now Mendon) built a home where they lived 3 yrs.
    Mr C's wife died near Mendon Oct 30, 1862 and Mr C. died 3 mo'slater on
    Jan 23, 1863 Samuel was 14 when his parents settled on the prairie and
    the oldest child. Lived at home until 22 yrs old when he married in
    Mendon Jan 2, 1844 to Caroline B. daughter of Lyman and Ann (Barker)
    Frisbie, natives of Branford, Conn where Caroline was also born. She was
    educated in New Haven- they had 3 sons John R., Samuel F. and George R.
    all living and in business in Mendon. S.R. was 1 of 7 born to Col C. and
    only 1 survives now, Deacon Abraham C. of this twp. Was originally a
    whig but now a Democrat since 1856. Was J.P. for 20 yrs Funeral from the
    house yesterday bt Rev Bayne of the Cong'l church. Buried village
    cemetery on the family plot.

Chittenden, Mr and Mrs S.R.   "Funeral"   Dec 29, 1886
   see Rae, Mr

Chittenden, Samuel R.   "Probate Notice"   Jun 8, 1899
   1st Monday of August 1899   George R. Chittenden, Adm.

Christopher, Mrs Senior   May 7, 1891
"From Walnut Valley Times, El Dorado, Kansas"
   Died at the family home in Riverside on May 2nd of heart failure.
   69 yrs old, Mrs Senior Christopher.

Chuning, Mrs Wm   "Coatsburg"   Apr 24, 1890
   Died while helping her husband put out a fire, Mrs Wm Chuning, living
   3 miles north of Coatsburg April 22nd.

Circles, Caroline   "Obituary"   Dec 16, 1897
   see Simmons, Elias

Clair, Mrs   "Local"   Nov 24, 1898
   Old Mrs Clair is sinking, her sons Frank and George are here from
   Carrolton, Mo. and her grandson Orton Walker and wife are here from
   Quincy.

Clair, Mrs Albert   Feb 19, 1891
   Mrs Albert Clair died Feb 17th at the home of her parents, Mr and Mrs
   Wm Hastings. Buried Mendon cemetery.

Clair, Mrs Albert   Feb 26, 1891
   Annie (Hastings) Clair age 22 yrs 9 mo's 7 days died. She was born
   May 10, 1968 and married August 24, 1890 to Albert Clair. Buried
   Saturday afternoon Feb 21st in Mendon cemetery. Services bt Rev M.L.
   Schmucker.

Clair, Benjamin   "Local"   Feb 22, 1900
   Died- Benjamin Clair of Honey Creek died Sunday evening at 5. Buried
   Mendon cemetery Tuesday P.M.

Clair, Benjamin   "Obituary"   Mar 1, 1900
   Died Benjamin Clair, born Westmoreland Co. Penn March 1820. Married
   1846 to Mary Ann Smith of same Co. and state who survives him. Had
   12 children. Came to Adams Co. from Penn 1857 and settled on the farm
   where he died. Joined U.B. church at age 22 yrs. Died Feb 18th at 5 P.M.
   Children from a distance for funeral were, John. Geo. Clark, Nathan of
   Chariton Co. Mo. Services Tuesday Feb 20th at the farm home 2 miles
   E. of Mendon by Rev S.N. Wakefield pastor of the M.E. church. Buried in
   Mendon cemetery.

Clair, Benjamin   "Probate Notice"   Mar 29, 1900
   1st Monday of June 1900   Benjamin F. Clair, Ex.
   Inghram and Crewdson, Attorneys.

Clair, Mrs Clark   "death"   Feb 14, 1889
   see Woods, Mrs

Clair, David   "Obituary"   May 16, 1901
   see Davis, Isabella

Clair Elijah   Jun 1, 1904
   included in list of civil war soldiers buried in Mendon cemetery.

Clair, Harvey W.   "Local"   Jun 4, 1891
   Died at Jacksonville, Ill insane asylum after 6 mo's confinement
   April 1891. Better known as Harvey Hatton age 16 yrs. insanity caused
   by reading to much.

Clair, Henry   "Local"   Jan 24, 1901
   Henry Clair, brother of our townsman, Geo. Clair died Sunday of
   consumption at St Mary's hospital, Quincy.

Clair, Isabella Davis   "Obituary"   May 16, 1901
   Died Isabella Davis, born Cumberland Co. Penn Feb 13, 1822 died this
   village May 8th. Married David Clair Sept 20, 1849 had 8 children.
   5 still living are, Lizzie and Charles of Mendon, Agnes Dunham of
   Fort Collins, Colo. Frank D. of Carrolton, Mo. and George of Ottumwa,
   Iowa. She had been sick 3 yrs. Was a member of the Mendon M. E. church.
   Services at the house Thursday P.M. by Rev S.N. Wakefield. Buried
   Mendon cemetery. Pallbearers were, J.P. Nichols, J.A. Harrieson,
   S.F. Chittenden, Wm Thompson, Wm McFarland and F.O. Dickerman.

Clair, John   "Died"   Jun 21, 1905
   Died- John Clair, born Westmoreland Co. Penn Jan 1, 1819. Married
   Margaret Shupe in Penn Feb 13, 1845 at home of brides uncle, Daniel
   Worman by Rev Ritler. Came to Ill in 1856 and farmed. Retired in 1887
   and moved into Mendon where he lived since. Was a former member of the
   Episcopal church in Mendon. Died June 14th from paralysis. He was one
   of a family of 10 children, but one remains, Mrs Smith of Payson.
   She was too feeble to attend the funeral. Leaves an aged wife and 7
   children, 28 grandchildren. Children are, Wesley, Mrs Wm Thompson,
   Mrs Albert Wible, Mrs William McIntyre all of Mendon, Ill. John of
   Loraine, Mrs James Kincaid of Bellingham, Washington and Mrs E.E.
   Cramer of Callao, Mo. Services at the home in Mendon by Rev S.R. Reno
   and Rev A.M. Reitzel. Buried in Mendon Cemetery.

Clair, John   "Probate Notice"   Jun 28, 1905
   1st Monday of Sept 1905   Wesley Clair, Adm.

Clair, Miss Lizzie   "Obituary"   Oct 13, 1892
   see O'Dear, Mrs Lizzie

Clair, Miss Martha   "Obituary"   Aug 13, 1891
   see Kells, Mr Richard

Clair, Nancy Ann   "Obituary"   Feb 17, 1904
   see Hastings, Thomas Gilbert

Clair, Mrs Wesley   "Obituary"   Mar 7, 1895
Died- Mrs Wesley Clair Saturday A.M. Sick 9 days. Funeral Monday P.M.
Services at the house and at the grave side by her former pastor, Rev.
A.B. Peck, now of Bowen. Mary H. Talcott was born near Mendon, Ill.
Nov 11, 1850. Married Wesley Clair Nov 6, 1875 and died at their home
1 mile W. of Mendon March 2nd Leaves a widowed mother, 2 sisters,
4 brothers, husband and 5 children. Joined the M.E. church in 1876.
One brother is Mr Asa W. Talcott of Hollenburg, Kansas.

Clair, Mrs Wesley   "Obituary"   Jul 15, 1900
see Chant, Joseph

Clapper, Mr A.   "Tioga"   Nov 19, 1891
Died- on Nov 14th at 8 P.M. Mr A. Clapper. Will be buried in Tioga
cemetery Nov 16th.

Clapper, Alexander   "Probate Notice"   Feb 4, 1892
1st Monday of April 1892 Catherine Clapper, Adm.

Clapper, Mr and Mrs James   "Marcelline"   Jun 4, 1903
The infant child of Mr and Mrs James Clapper died early this A.M.
Buried this eve at 8 P.M. Hooping cough the cause of death.

Clapper, Philip   "Tioga"   Dec 25, 1902
The remains of Philip Clapper of Lima Twp was buried in the town
cemetery last Wednesday.

Clapper, Mr and Mrs Jas.   "Marcelline"   Jan 31, 1895
died- The infant son of Mr and Mrs Jas. Clapper was buried at the
Keath cemetery last Sunday afternoon. It lived less than 3 weeks.

Clark, Abraham P.   "Obituary"   Jun 21, 1888
see Lowery, John

Clark, Mr Alex   "Lima"   Apr 4, 1895
Joseph Clark rec'd a telegram telling of the death of his father,
Mr Alex Clark at Wichita, Kansas recently. Mr C. was a former resident
of Lima for many yrs.

Clark, Arthur   Dec 19, 1878
Died- Tuesday Dec 17th of consumption at the home of his uncle
Vincent Francis Esq. 1 mile S. of Mendon. Arthur Clark in his 21st yr.
Body was taken to St Louis on Wednesday for burial.

Clark, B.F.   Nov 15, 1883
Died- Mr B.F. Clark formerly of Mendon now of Greenborough, N.C.
Died Sept 15th age 40 yrs 9 mo's.

Clark, Miss Charlotte   "Death"   Mar 29, 1905
see Stillman, Samuel Osgood

Clark, Chas D.   "Obituary"   Feb 19, 1903
    see Denson, William

Clark, Mrs F.   "Tioga"   Mar 7, 1889
    Rev J.D. Crooks, elder of the South M.E. church here was called to
    Breckenridge the 1st of the week to preach the funerals of Mrs F. Clark
    and daughter Rosa. Services held Monday eve.

Clark, Freddie   Jan 16, 1879
    Died- Saturday January 11th of pneumonia, Freddie, son of John and
    Jennie Clark. Age 4 yrs.

Clark, Herschel   "Loraine"   Jul 23, 1903
    Master Chester Clark rec'd word last Saturday that his brother Herschel,
    had been drowned while visiting in Oklahoma.

Clark, J.H.   "Local"   Oct 12, 1899
    Killed- J.H. Clark, a lineman of the electric light co. in Quincy
    fell 30 ft from a pole on Hampshire St. Tuesday and was killed. Leaves a
    wife and a 2 yr old child.

Clark, James   "Death in Adams Co."   Apr 13, 1899
    Died- James Clark, nearly 100 yrs old Friday A.M. at the home of his
    daughter, Mrs E.C. Follansbee. Born near Wilksbarre, Penn July 29, 1799
    Moved to Quincy 1863. Joined the Masons 1820

Clark, Mrs Jennie   "Elm Grove"   May 23, 1901
    Mrs Jennie Clark of the old peoples home in Quincy was buried in
    Bloomfield cemetery a short time ago.

Clark, John   "Local"   Apr 6, 1877
    Infant child of John Clark died Wednesday night.

Clark, Mrs Laura V.   "Obituary"   Feb 19, 1903
    see Dendon, William

Clark, Mary   "Obituary"   Feb 5, 1885
    Mary Clark was born New Jersey July 1795 and died January 29, 1885
    She married Aaron Gibbs in 1811 in Lyons, N.Y. where they raised 10
    children. 3 of whom preceded her in death. She was left a widow some
    30 yrs ago and lived with a daughter, Mrs Ann E. Barclay of Mendon
    until the death of the latter some 2 or more yrs ago. Since then she
    has lived with her son Aaron of Fall Creek, Ill. Services by Rev J.G.
    Bonnell of Chaddock college, Quincy in the Methodist church of Mendon.

Clark, Mrs Mary   Mt Hebron"   Sep 12, 1895
    DiedTuesday A.M. Mrs Mary Clark, now of Quincy, but formerly of here.

Clark, Mrs Nona   "Obituary   Aug 13, 1891
    see Selby, James

Clark, Mrs Nona   "Obituary"   Apr 4, 1895
    see Selby, Mrs Louisa

Clark, Mr S.P.   "Personal"   Oct 5, 1882
     Mr S.P. Clark was taken sick while on jury duty and died. was 45 yrs old.

Clark, Mrs Sadie   "Death"   Jan 23, 1902
     Funeral of Mrs Sadie Clark was at her mother's home, Mrs Sarah J. Arnold,
     last Saturday at 2:30 P.M. by Rev J.S. Bayne. She was born Mendon, Ill.
     Oct 1, 1878 and died in Quincy January 15th at 7:20 P.M. She married
     R. Vernon Clark Sept 5, 1900. Attended Monticello Seminary 1894-98
     Joined Cong'l church March 19, 1893. Leaves husband and child, mother,
     and sister. Funeral at her late home in Quincy 204 S. 12th Street last
     Friday afternoon at 2 P.M. by Dr S.H. Dana. Her father died several yrs
     ago. She was eldest daughter. Leaves sister Frances and husband and 6 mo
     old babe. Lived Whitehall, Ill after her marriage for a time and had only
     just recently moved to this city.

Clark, Sally Ann   "Death"
     see Francis, Mrs Sally Ann   Aug 30, 1905

Clark, Sarah O.   "Obituary"   Oct 11, 1888
     Died- at her home in Walker twp, Hancock Co. Ill. Oct 1st Sarah O.
     Clark wife of F. M. Clark. She was born Dec 20, 1841 in Adams Co. Came
     to this twp with her parents, Mr James S. and Sarah Rankin in Jan 1848
     and lived here till time of her death. Married Nov 24, 1861 to F.M. Clark
     who survives her. They had 7 children 4 sons and 3 daughters. Sons,
     Benjamin F., Joseph Mc and Lafayette Cary and 1 daughter Rosa Josephine
     Victotia 10 yrs old survuve her. Member of Christain church.

Clark, Rosa   "Tioga"   Mar 7, 1889
     Rev J. D. Crooks, elder of the South M.E. Church here was called to
     Breckenridge the firdt of the week to preach the funerals of Mrs F.
     Clark and daughter Rosa. Services held Monday eve.

Clark, Thomas   "Personal"   Jul 29, 1880
     Mr Vincent Francis left for St Louis yesterday, in charge of the body
     of the late Thomas Clark.

Clark, Thomas   "Died"   Jul 29, 1880
     Died- on July 28th at the residence of Vincent Francis Esq. Thomas
     Clark, of St Louis, Mo. in his 51st yr.

Clark, William   "Obituary"
     see Denson, William   Feb 19, 1903

Clarke, Charles   "Camp Point"   Jul 12, 1900
     Died- Charles Clarke died of consumption Saturday July 7th at 3 at the
     home of his brother Fred. Was member of the M.E. Church and president of
     the Epworth League at Chicago last yr. 28 yrs old. Services by Rev R.L.
     McNabb and buried in the cemetery south of town.

Claypool, Mrs Amelia C.   "Local"   Jun 27, 1889
     "From Nickerson Kansas "Industry"
     Died- Mrs Amelia C. Claypool, wife of the editor of the Industry and
     daughter of Mr and Mrs A. Wipprecht of Sedalia, Mo. (formerly of Mendon,
     Ill.) died Sunday eve June 9th at her home in Nickerson, Kansas. 22 yrs
     9 mo's 23 days old. Married at her home in Sedalia on May 10, 1888 and
     buried in Wildmead cemetery.

73

Clayton, Miss Bertha A.   Nov 20, 1879
    Died- Tuesday A.M. at the residence of Prof. Griffin, Miss Berthe A.
    Clayton of Bowen, Hancock Co. Ill. Age 20 yrs. She was attending school
    here. died from an attack of diptheria. Remains taken to Bowen for
    burial. A memorial service will be at the M.E. church at 11 A.M. Sunday.

Cline, Mrs   "Local"   Sep 8, 1886
    Mrs Cline living N. of town died last week and was buried in Mendon
    cemetery.

Cline, Mrs Tom   "MtHebron"   Sep 8, 1886
    Mrs tom Cline died Sept 1st. Buried Mendon cemetery Sept 2nd. Leaves
    a husband and 3 children.

Coburn, Mr Geo. Ames   "Local"   Jan 28, 1892
    Died- Mr Geo. Ames Coburn, of the firm Watson and Coburn, boot and shoe
    dealer was struck in the head by a piece of falling ice from a roof of a
    bldg at 515 Maine St. died within 2 hours. Leaves aged parents and wife.
    remains taken to Haverhill, Mass where repose the bodies of all the
    deceased members of his family.

Cochran, Mrs Nancy Nevins   "Obituary"   Mar 2, 1899
    Died- Mrs Nancy Nevins Cochran at her home in Grove twp Taylor Co.
    Iowa. Married Thomas Cochran. Born Anticlave, Londonderry, Ireland
    Oct 25, 1832 and died Feb 15, 1899. Was 66 yrs 3 mo's 20 days old. Came
    to America with her parents at age 3 yrs and lived Canada for a time.
    parents finally located in Camp Point where she met T. W. Cochran and
    married Oct 17, 1856. Lived Adams Co. till 1879 when they moved to Iowa
    near Grinnell where they lived until the fall of "82" when they moved to
    the farm where she died in 1899 Mother of 9 (5 died young) 4 surviving
    are, Henry A., Thomas A., Mrs Sarah E. Beckerer all of Grove twp and
    Mrs Maggie E. Richney of Sharps. Member of Ellington Presbyterian church
    and rhe Presbyterian church of Lennox. Services at the Prairie Chapel
    Friday 10 A.M. by Rev S. Alexander of Lennox.

Cochran, Thomas W.   "Obituary"   Jan 11, 1905
    Thomas W. Cochran born March 30, 1833 in Parish of Dunboa county
    Londonderry, Ireland died at the home of his son, Henry A. near Lennox,
    Iowa Jan 2, 1905 of heart failure. Came to U.S. at age 17 yrs coming to
    Quincy, Ill. Married Oct 17, 1856 to Miss Nancy Nevins. Lived Adams Co.
    till 1879when they went to Iowa near Grinnell till fall of 1882 when they
    moved to Taylor Co. near Lenox where his wife died Feb 15, 1899. Had 9
    children, 5 died in early childhood. 4 surviving are, Mrs Sarah E.
    Becherer, Henry A., Mrs Maggie A. Richey and Thomas A. all of Lenox, Iowa
    Funeral by Rev Samuel Wiley and buried in cemetery at Blue Grove.

Coe, Ira   "Local"   Aug 17, 1899
    Died- Ira Coe, the fruit grower of Melrose twp. He was thrown from a
    wagon in Quincy Tuesday A.M. and hurled against a tree breaking his neck
    causing almost instant death.

Coffield, Mrs Dr.   "Death"   Mar 13, 1884
    see Akin, Capt Wm B.

Coffield, Harold   "Local"   Nov 13, 1902
    Mr and Mrs H.B. Coffield of Quincy buried their infant son in Mendon
cemetery Sunday Nov 9th. Services by Rev S.R. Reno of the Mendon M.E.
church. Little Harold was about 5 mo's old. Sick 2 days.

Coffield, Henry   Sep 20, 1883
    Henry Coffield living near Clayton was found dead Sept 17th apparently
suicide.

Coffield, James   Jun 22, 1899
    included in list of graves decorated Memorial day of soldiers buried
in Mendon cemetery.

Coffield, Dr James   "York Neck"   Feb 9, 1899
    Mr J. F. Irvin and family attended the funeral of his cousin, Dr James
Coffield in Mendon on Monday.

Coffield, James   Dec 11, 1902
    see Myers, C.C.

Coffield, Dr James   "Obituary"   Feb 9, 1899
    Died- Dr James Coffield Saturday A.M. 61 yrs old from disease of the
liver and complications of right lung. Was eldest son of John and
Sarah Coffield who were married in Washington Co. Penn Nov 9, 1837 and
moved to Adams Co. Ill. Sect 6 Camp Point twp Jan 1, 1838 where they
raised 2 boys, James and Thomas. Thomas only living member of the family
lives Lincoln, Nebr. Dr. was born Camp Point August 21, 1838 and died
Mendon Feb 4th age 60 yrs 5 mo's 13 days. Married May 4, 1865 to
Arvilla B. Akins, a sister of Dr Akins. They had 4 sons, Joel Irving
died Nov 26, 1871, John died Feb 25, 1871. Mother and Harry B. and
Glenn A. survive him. Dr attended medical school at Keokuk, Iowa and
medical college at St Louis. March 1, 1874 he located in Loraine. April
26, 1881 he moved to Mendon. Funeral Monday P.M. at the houes by Rev
E.K. Crews. Burial in village cemetery.

Coffield, James   "Probate Notice"   Mar 2, 1899
    1st Monday of April 1899   Harry B. Coffield, Adm. Coffield and
McCory, attorneys.

Coffield, John   Sept 24, 1891
    John Coffield died in Mendon at home Sept 19th. 78 yrs 10 mo's 15 days
old. Born Washington Co. Penn. Nov 4, 1812. Came to Ill. in 1835 to look
for a location and returned east for awhile. The following yr he
settled in York Neck, Camp Point twp on the farm where he lived until 6
yrs ago when he moved to Mendon near his son the Dr. In November 1837
he married Miss Sarah Irvin also from Penn who survives him and has
just had her 80th birthday. 2 children were born to them, Dr Jas. Coffield
of Mendon and Thomas of Lincoln, Nebr. Funeral in the M.E. church by Rev.
M.L. Schmucker of the Lutheran church. Buried in Mendon cemetery.

Coffield, John   "Probate Notice"   Sep 1, 1892
    1st Monday of November 1892   James Coffield, Adm.

Coger, Eddie Howard   "Died"   Nov 27, 1879
    Died Tuesday, November 25th of croup and diptheria, Eddie Howard, son
    of E.B. Coger of this village. Age between 2 and 3 yrs.

Coil, John   "Marcelline"   Dec 15, 1892
    Died, old uncle John Coil yesterday.

Cole, John   "Deaths in Adams co.   Feb 23, 1899
    Died, Mr John Cole, a native of Maryland. Age 67 yrs died last Friday.
    Leaves a wife and several children.

Cole, Mr Joshua   "Payson"   Mar 26, 1885
    Died March 15th Mr Joshua Cole. He lived here and Pike Co/ for 54½ yrs
    except 5 weeks of his life. He leaves a wife and 4 children.

Collier, Mrs   "Payson"   Mar 20, 1884
    Death has taken one of our oldest citizens Mrs Collier. She leaves
    several children.

Colliers, Mrs Geo.   "Payson"   Dec 25, 1884
    Mrs Geo. Colliers formerly of this twp, but lately of Hannibal was
    buried at Fall Creek church last Saturday.

Colliers, Mr George   "Payson"   Dec 9, 1885
    Mr George Colliers, a resident of Fall Creek several yrs was buried
    at the Fall Creek church yesterday. Mr C. dropped dead without and
    warning. Dr says of heart disease.

Collins, Prof.   "Death"   Dec 15, 1898
    see Pond, Mr Geo. P.

Collins, Alexander   "Paloma"   May 17, 1888
    Alexander Collins (Deceased) real estate was appraised last week. Some
    400 acres of land will be sold soon.

Collins, Charles   "Ursa"   Sep 20, 1905
    Charles Collins, principal of our school was called to Payson last
    week by the death of his mother.

Collins, Mrs D.H.   "Local"   Jan 19, 1888
    Mrs D.H. Collins, of Payson died Saturday. Leaves her husband, 3 sons,
    and 1 daughter. All married.

Collins, Miss Fanny C.   "Death"   May 31, 1894
    The tragic death of Mrs Kendall from the Herald of May 28th
    Community was shocked last evening by the sudden death of Mrs W. H.
    Kendall. Death was the result of fright and heart trouble. While out
    riding with Mrs Mary A. Torrence a dog frightened the horse coming down
    the hill. Mrs K. was driving and Mrs T. seeing she could not manage the
    horse also took hold of the reins, horse almost turned the buggy over
    and was finally stopped when it ran into a fence. Neither was hurt, but
    Mrs K. could not get her breath. A moment later her head fell back and
    she was dead. Remains were taken to the city by undertaker Daugherty.
    Mrs K. was born Miss Fanny C. Collins in Liberty, Adams Co. April 8, 1840
    Had lived in this co. all her life. Member of the Cong'l church. Leaves
                              -cont-

a husband, Dr H. W. Kendall, 1 son, L.W. Kendall of Chicago and a
daughter Mrs J.H. Wheeler of Minneapolis. She was a cousin of Hon. W.H.
Collins and Oliver Collins of Liberty.

Collins, Frank   "Big Neck"   Feb 12, 1891
   Feb 4th Frank Collins died. Age 4 yrs 8 mo's 5 days. He was the son of
   Mr and Mrs C.W. Collins. Buried Camp Point cemetery. Services by Elder
   Groves from the Christain church.

Collins, George   Jul 14, 1881
   Died- 2 children of George Collins who moved from Payson to Hannibal
   last spring. 1 male and 1 female

Collins, Mr H.W.   "Local"   Apr 2, 1903
   News rec'd here yesterday A.M. of the death of Mr H.W. Collins, Tuesday
   at St Louis. Mr C. was formerly princapal of Mendon High School. He
   would have graduated this spring from his chosen profession of dentistry.

Collins, H.W.   "Local"   Apr 9, 1903
   Funeral at Liberty Friday for H. W. Collins was postponed till next
   day because of the storm. Mr C. died in St Louis.

Collins, Harry Wilmer   "Died"   Apr 16, 1903
   Harry Wilmer Collins was born 3 miles N.W. of Liberty, Ill. March 25, 1876
   Died from typhoid fever at Jewish hospital in St Louis Mo. March 31st.
   Was 27 yrs 6 days old. Had planned to marry Miss Jessie Cramer of
   Mendon in May. Died Tuesday at 6 P.M. Graduated from school at Liberty
   and attended college at Jacksonville. Came to Mendon at age 19 yrs and
   taught 1 yr and was principal 2 yrs. Entered dental university St Louis
   in 1900. Remains reached Quincy at 6 P.M. Wednesday and was taken to
   Daughtery's that night and to the home at Liberty the next eve. Funeral
   was to be held Friday but was postponed because of the storm. Services by
   Rev Dusenberry at Presbyterianchurch 2 P.M. Leaves mother, father,
   1 brother Morris Collins of Great Bend, Kansas ans a sister Mrs Wagner
   of Liberty.

Collusion, Mrs Nannie (Wm)   "Death in Adams Co Quincy"   Mar 23, 1899
   Died, Mrs Nannie Collusion of cancer Friday March 17th. Wife of Wm
   Collusion. an inmate of the soldiers home.

Colt, Mrs Ellen   "Death"
   see Kuhn,Isaac   Nov 23, 1887

Colvin, Mr   "Payson"   Apr 8, 1880
   Last Sunday Mr Colvin of Kenderhook was buried by Masonic rites. 150
   Masons were present.

Colvin, Miss Bernice   "Ursa"   Nov 1, 1900
   Died- Friday Oct 26th at 10 A.M., Miss Bernice Colvin. Services at
   the M.P. church by Rev Ringland. 7 of her school mates from Hamilton,
   Ill. drove down to attend the funeral. 6 girls were pall-bearers.

Colvin, Mr D.P.   "Obituary"   Aug 23, 1894
     Died- at his residence in Ursa twp August 21st at 7 P.M. Mr D.P. Colvin
     in his 80 th yr. Was an old settler of this twp. Has lived in the same
     home he died in for the past 50 yrs. Born in Kentucky. Leaves a wife and
     7 children, 4 daughters and 3 sons. Services at the family home Thursday
     at 10 A.M. Buried in Stone church cemetery.

Colvin, David P.   "Obituary"   Nov 5, 1903
     see Calwell, Mrs Belle

Colvin, Davis P.   "Local"   Aug 23, 1894
     Died- Mr Davis P. Colvin, an old resident of Ursa twp Tuesday A.M.
     He was a well to do farmer living about 2 miles this side of Ursa. Born
     in Pendleton, Co. Kentucky on Feb 24, 1815 and came to Adams Co. 1838.
     He was married 3 times. 1st wife was Elizabeth Booth of Bourbon Co. Ky.
     They had 5 children. 2nd wife was Caroline Kirkpatrick, born in this Co.
     they had 2 children. 3rd wife was Mary E. Hedges whom he married in 1870.

Colvin, Rodney   "Ursa"   Jan 16, 1902
     2 P.M. Thursday was the funeral of Rodney, son of Mr and Mrs James
     Colvin. Burial was at the Stone church on Friday A.M.

Colwell, Wm P.   "Local"   Dec 23, 1897
     Died, Mr Wm P. Colwell of Knoxville, Ill. a former resident and brother-
     in-law of Mr Ben Gilmer died of consumption Sunday Dec 19th. Funeral
     the following day.

Combs, Lydia   Oct 30, 1890
     Died- Oct 13th at the age of 50 yrs, Lydia Combs, wife of Milton R.
     Combs. Was the oldest daughter of Mr and Mrs P.R. McGrew and lived in
     Raymond, Nebr. Leaves husband and 8 children.

Comer, Mrs Ida   "Local"   Jul 18, 1895
     Mrs Ida Comer, of Kansas is here visiting her parents, Mr and Mrs McCarl.
     she came to attend the funeral of her nephew, Emmett.

Comstock, Mrs   "Obituary"   May 12, 1886
     see Bridgeman, Mrs

Comstock, Agetta   "Payson"   Jun 24, 1880
     Died- in Quincy June 18th, Agetta, only daughter of Mrs Comstock, of
     the firm Comstock, Castle and Co.

Comstock, Charles   "Obituary"   May 12, 1886
     see Bridgeman, Mrs

Conger, Jasper   "Elm Grove"   Jan 23, 1890
     Died- January 25th Jasper Conger Age 40 yrs 2 mo's 23 days. Buried
     January 27th at Wesley Chapel. Mr R.B. Starr made appropriate remarks.
     No Minister.

Conger, Mr R.   "Obituary"   Feb 27, 1890
     see Seward, Julia Ann

78

Conger, Mr Wm A.   "Fowler"   Apr 27, 1893
    Died- Mr Wm A. Conger died in Missouri a few days ago. Formerly a
    resident of Elm Grove. Buried in Wesley Chapel cemetery N. of Quincy.
    age 78 yrs.

Conklin, Elizabeth   "Deaths"   Jul 5, 1905
    see Smith, Hamilton

Conover, Mrs   "Obituary"   Oct 6, 1881
    see Steward, Mrs Leve

Conover, David H.   "Adm. Sale"   Dec 30, 1880
    Administors sale to be held Feb 12, 1881
    Sale of real estate of David H. Conover of Lima subject to homestead
    rights of Mary H. Conover, widow and William J. Conover, Charles J.
    Conover, John J. Conover and Roxa Conover, as widow and children. Includes
    40 acres in N.W. corner of S.W. ¼ Section 11 in twp 2 N. Range 9 West
    of the 4th Meridian, Adams Co.

Conover, George   "Lima"   Apr 23, 1885
    George Conover died at Tioga April 10th and buried Lima cemetery April
    12th. He was a teacher of Music.

Conover, George   "Probate Notice"   May 21, 1885
    3rd Monday of July 1885 M. Dazey and E. Cory Adm's.

Connover, John and Sallie   "Lima"   Feb 24, 1886
    The infant daughter of John and Sallie Connover died last Tuesday eve
    of pulmonary disease.

Conover, Mrs Lola   "Obituary"   Mar 8, 1894
    see Fawbush, Mrs Sarah

Conrey, Miss Lou   "Deaths in Adams Co.   Feb 16, 1899
    Died- Miss Lou Conrey, the only daughter of Mr and Mrs John Conrey of
    Camp Point Friday afternoon after an illness of 2 mo's.

Cook, Mrs   "Payson"   Nov 3, 1886
    Mrs Cook of Richfield who had reached the age of 95 yrs was buried
    last week.

Cook, Chauncey   "Obituary"   May 10, 1900
    Died- Chauncey Cook born Payson July 20, 1850. Married Sept 6, 1871
    to Miss Orena Tyler of Richfield, Ill. Had 6 children. 3 sons survive
    along with their mother. Was a member of the Cong'l church of Adams, Ill.
    Masonic lodge of Payson also. Died May 3rd at 11:30 A.M. 49 yrs old.
    Leaves a wife, 3 sons, an aged mother, 5 brothers and 2 sisters. Services
    at his home in Quincy May 5th by Rev Wm J. Spire.

Cook, Lucian   "Coatsburg"   Aug 4, 1892
    Lucian Cook of LaGrange, Mo. formerly of Big Neck was buried in
    Coatsburg July 23rd.

Coon, Mrs Ida   "Death"   Sep 17, 1903
    see Murphy, John

Cooke, A.D.   Jan 6, 1881
    Mr A.D. Cooke died in his 80th yr. Born Feb 7, 1801. When he was about
    27 yrs old he married Miss Julia Benton who was a sister of Joel and
    Abraham Benton of Mendon. Moved to Atwater, Portage Co. Ohio. lived there
    11 yrs before coming to Mendon. Has lived in or about Mendon since. He
    joined the Cong'l church at about 21 yrs of age until coming to Mendon
    then he joined the Episcopal church. Mr C. was the last left of 7 children.
    He leaves Mr D.B. Cooke and 2 daughters, Mrs C.H. Hoffman and Mrs S.M.
    Boyer to mourn.

Cooke, A.D.   "Obituary"   Jan 23, 1902
    see Hoffman, Charles Henry

Cooke, Aaron D.   "Probate Notice"   Feb 24, 1881
    D.B. Cooke, Adm

Cooke, Mrs C.B.   "Obituary"   Dec 4, 1902
    see Felgar, Simon S.

Cooke, Mrs C.B.   "Obituary"   Oct 15, 1891
    see Morehead, Cordelia

Cooke, D.B.   Jun 12, 1902
    Notice of final settlement to the heirs of the estate of D.B. Cooke.
    July term of Co. court Adams Co. dated July 8, 1902
    Parthenia Cooke, Adm.

Cooke, D.B.   "Probate Notice"   Jul 12, 1900
    1st Monday of August 1900   Parthenia Cooke Adm.

Cooke, D.B.   June 1, 1904
    included in list of Civil war soldiers buried in Mendon cemetery.

Cooke, Mrs D.B.   "Obituary"   May 18, 1887
    see Morehead, Daniel

Cooke, Mrs D.B.   "Obituary"   Sep 26, 1895
    see Smith, Mrs Rodney

Cooke, Mrs D.B.   "Death"   Jun 2, 1886
    see Reynolds, Charles T.

Cooke, Mrs D.B.   "Death"   Mar 9, 1904
    see Morehead, thomas M.

Cooke, Dudley Benton   "Obituary"   May 17, 1900
    Died- Dudley Benton Cooke - born Aug 7, 1843 on the farm owned by F.O.
    Dickerman 1½ miles N. of Mendon. Died May 13th at 1:30 P.M. Was only
    son of Aaron Dudley and Julia Benton Cooke. Family moved to the village
    in spring of 1855 where they lived except for the 1 yr in Quincy Summer
    of 1864 he enlisted in the 137th Reg C.A. Ill. Vol. Inf. Feb 7, 1866
    he married Parthenia Morehead of Quincy had 4 children, the oldest son,
    Albertie Dudley died at age 7 yrs. Leaves wife, 3 children, Frank Elmer,
    Ora Belle and Charles Breckenridge, a grandaughter, little Martha, 1
    sister, Mrs C.H. Hoffman. Services at the house by Rev J. S. Bayne of the
    Cong'l church.
                -Cont-

80

Pallbearers were, C.A. Chittenden, G.H. Baldwin, F.F. Dudley,
A.L. Bray, B.A. VanDyke and W.R. Cramer.

Cooke, Miss Elizabeth A.   "Obituary"   Jan 23, 1902
    see Hoffman, Charles Henry

Cooke, Mrs Julia   "Obituary"   Aug 11, 1881
    Mrs Julia Cooke 76 yrs old died Aug 8th at her daughters, Mrs C.H. Hoffman
    Born North Guilford, Conn May 16, 1806 and moved to near Mendon in 1838.
    Married A.D. Cooke Sept 26, 1827. Her husband died last January. She
    leaves a son and 2 daughters.

Cooper, Mr John   " Ursa"   Nov 19, 1891
    Mr John Cooper died Monday at 10 P.M. Funeral from the Methodist church
    by Rev Ward Wednesday at 11 A.M. (Mr C. was a former Mendon resident)

Cooper, John   "Local"   Nov 19, 1891
    The death of John Cooper, a former resident of Mendon is reported in
    the Ursa news.

Cooper, Miss Lydia   "Payson"   May 9, 1889
    Died- Miss Lydia Cooper, a 14 yr old daughter of Charles Cooper was
    buried here yesterday. She had had the measles some mo's ago and never
    fully recovered.

Copeland, Mrs Thomas   "West Point"   Apr 12, 1894
    Died- Mrs Thomas Copeland died at the home of her grandaughter, Mrs
    Dean Frey, March 27th. Age 83 yrs. Funeral Thursday P.M. at the Baptist
    church 4 miles N.E. of town.

Copelin, Mrs Eunice Atheda   "Died"   Feb 24, 1904
    Died on Friday Feb 19th, Mrs Eunice Atheda Copelin in her 56th yr.
    Eunice Atwater was born in Penn Dec 5, 1848 and in 1850 with her parents
    came to Mendon. Married J. R. Copelin August 1, 1889. Services at the
    Zion church Monday A.M. by Rev Dean Moore of Quincy. Buried Mendon
    Cemetery. Coming from a distance were, Mrs R.R. McIntyre, deceased
    daughter and her husband and daughter Mirah of Hannibal, John Copelin
    son of deceased. Telegram rec'd from Nathan I. Harrison a cousin of
    Mrs C. of Denver, Colo. Also leaves a husband.

Copelin, Eunice Altheada   "Probate Notice"   May 4, 1904
    1st Monday of June 1904   James R. Copelin, Ex.

Copelin, Eunice Altheada   "Local"   May 4, 1904
    An inventory has been filed in the estate of Eunice Altheada Copelin
    and also an appraisement bill. Real estate amt 2,500.00 Notes 8700.00
    and Chattels valued 38.25

Copelin, Mrs J.R.   "Funeral   Nov 29, 1894
    see Harrison, Rev Henry

Copelin, Josie   "Obituary"   May 21, 1885
    see McNay, Gertie

81

Copp, Anna V.   "Death"   Mar 22, 1905
    see Baldwin, George Dutton

Corder, Rovilla   "Obituary"   Jan 22, 1891
    see Judy, Wm Winepark

Cormany, Mrs George   "Payson"   Feb 2, 1888
    Buried last Monday Mrs George Cormany. She was an old settler and
    approx. 76 yrs old.

Corn, Mrs Maria   "Fowler"   Nov 30, 1893
    Last Friday the remains of Mrs Maria Corn, Asa Corn's mother was
    buried in the North cemetery. She was about 90 yrs old and had been
    in slavery until emancipated.

Cornelius, Albert   Aug 4, 1881
    Drowned on Saturday Albert Cornelius July 30th. Lived Quincy

Corrill, Mrs M.   "Local"   Nov 13, 1884
    Mr Charles McVay and wife accompanied by their daughter Mrs Charles
    French went to Quincy Saturday November 7th to attend the funeral of
    Mrs M. Corrill which took place at Woodland cemetery the following day.
    She was 92 yrs old.

Corse, Mrs Ed   "Coatsburg"   Jun 6, 1889
    Died- Mrs Ed Corse was buried in the cemetery here last Tuesday.
    Remains were brought here from Quincy. Leaves a husband and a little
    girl, father,sisters and brothers.

Cort, Miss Aggie A.(Agnes) "Local"   Feb 19, 1885
    Miss Aggie A. Cort daughter of Peter Cort died Saturday Feb 14th.
    Services from the Lutheran church and buried Marcelline in the family
    burying ground. She was 25 yrs 10 mo's 21 days old. Agnes as she was
    more familiarly called had been a sufferer for some time.

Cort, Miss Aggie   Mar 5, 1885
    Mr and Mrs John Wible were called here by the death of Miss Aggie Cort,
    Mrs Wible's sister.

Cort, Hester   "Obituary"   Dec 15, 1892
    see VanDyde, Wm

Cort, Peter   "Death"   Mar 1, 1878
    see Wilson, Mrs Sophia

Cort, Mr Peter   Oct 29, 1891
    Mr Peter Cort had the remains of 7 members of his family removed last
    Friday from the Keith burying ground near Marcelline to the Mendon
    cemetery. They consist of his father, wife, his daughter Mrs Mary S.
    Wilson, Mrs J.A. Wible, Miss Aggie Cort and the infant child of Mr and
    Mrs Charles Wright.

Cort, Peter   "Death"   Nov 10, 1892
Died- Mr Peter Cort died Friday Nov 4th at 1 P.M. Age 72 yrs 4 mo's
10 days. Born Westmoreland Co. Penn. June 24, 1820 and came to Illinois
in 1855 and settled in Mendon where he has lived since. His wife and 3
children died before him and 5 children survive him, 1 son and 4 daughters.
Mr C's youngest and only surviving brother, Mr J.B. Cort of Philadelphia
Mo. and his grandson, Mr Herbert Wilson of Malta Bend, Mo. were here
for the funeral. Services at the Lutheran church by Rev M.L. Schmucker.
He joined the Lutheran church in 1856. Buried Mendon cemetery.

Cort, Peter   "Probate Notice"   Nov 24, 1892
1st Monday of January 1893 J.K. Martin, Adm.

Cory, Mr and Mrs A.K.   "Lima"   Aug 3, 1893
Infant son of Mr and Mrs A.K. Cory was buried last Monday.

Coughlin, Wm   Aug 6, 1881
Died August 6th at the age of 26 yrs, Wm Coughlin Quincy switchman
in a railroad accident.

Councilman, Mary   Nov 10, 1881
Died, Miss Mary Councilman Ocyober 22nd in Bushnell. Age 100 yrs 3 mo's
4 days. Probably the oldest person in the military tract.

Count, Mrs   "Payson"   Nov 29, 1883
The funeral of Mrs Count will be preached today at 2

Count, Mrs   "Payson"   Nov 29, 1883
Funeral of Mrs Count will be November 29th at the M.E. church.

Cowles, Mrs H.P.   "death"   Mar 2, 1904
see Dickerman, Mrs Laura

Cox, Mrs John   "Big Neck"   Jun 27, 1889
Died- Mrs John Cox Wednesday. Her sister, Mrs Tuxford was called from
Camp Point, but did not arrive before she died.

Cox, Mary Jane   "Obituary"   Nov 11, 1897
see Miller, Mrs Mary Jane

Cox, Nellie   "Loraine"   May 5, 1898
Died- last Thursday at 9. Old aunt Nellei Cox at the home of her daughter,
Mrs Albert Hartman. Services at the house by Bro. Collins. Buried in the
Chili cemetery.

Cox, Shep   "Local"   Mar 14, 1895
Judge Epler has appointed J.W. Miller as conservator of Shep Cox and he
will qualify at once. The estate is valued at 30,000.00 or more.

Crabby, Mr and Mrs John   "Obituary"   Nov 28, 1901
see Lemmon, Mrs Ashel

Crabtree, William   "Woodbine"   Jan 31, 1889
William Crabtree lost his fine imported gander. He died for the want of
a new suit of clothes.

83

Craig, Mr Henry   "Local"   Sep 22, 1898
    Died- Mr Henry Craig at his home at Clayton Tuesday afternoon. Age 80 yrs
    He was active in politics in Adams Co. in earlier yrs.

Crail, Mr and Mrs A.L.   "Loraine"   Sep 26, 1895
    Died- The little babe of Mr and Mrs A.L. Crail last Friday.

Cramer, Blance   Apr 30, 1891
    Blance Cramer little daughter of Mr and Mrs W.R. Cramer died April 25th
    od diptheria. Funeral by Rev F.C. Read. She had a brother LeRoy.

Cramer, Mrs E.E.   "Death"   Jun 21, 1905
    see Clair, John

Cramer, Capt H.P.W.   "Local"   Dec 28, 1899
    Died- Capt H.P.W. Cramer.

Cramer, Capt H.P.W.   "Local"   May 4, 1887
    Capt H.P.W. Cramer is the subject of a somewhat remarkable experience.
    Within the past 3 mo's he has lost by death a sister, a brother- in-
    law and 3 cousins who have all passed their 3 score and 10. His sister
    died in Marshall Co. Virginia, his brother-in-law and 1 cousin in
    Penn and the other 2 cousins in Carroll Co. Ill. The Capt and his
    widowed sister is all thats left of a family of 11 children.

Cramer, Capt H.P.W.   "Obituary"   Jan 11, 1900
    Died- Capt H.P.W. Cramer Born Feb 1, 1824 near Centerville, Somerset Co.
    Penn. April 22, 1844 he married Jane A. Dean and had 7 children. 4 still
    living. Came to Illinois in spring of 1852 landing at Quincy June 14th.
    Came right to Mendon where they lived till August 1899 when they went to
    St Paul, Minn to their daughter's, Mrs A.H. Taft. He died in St Paul
    near midnight Dec 26th. Leaves a wife and 4 children and 1 sister, Mrs
    Catherine Imel of Draketown, Penn Buried from his daughter's home
    Dec 29th. Services by Rev Soper of Plymouth Cong'l church. He was a
    member of the 50th Ill. Inf. Buried in the vault beneath the chapel
    at Oakland cemetery as they do not inter in the north during the winter
    months. Final burial will be in the spring.

Cramer, Capt H.P.W.   "Obituary"   Mar 29, 1900
    see Dean, Jane A.

Cramer, Miss Jessie   "Death"   Apr 16, 1903
    see Collins, Harry Wilmer

Cramer, Mr and Mrs W.R.   "Died"   Oct 21, 1880
    Died- on Tuesday morning the only daughter of Mr and Mrs W.R. Cramer
    of croup. Age 2 yrs.

Cramer, W.R.   "Local"   Mar 15, 1900
    Telegram rec'd announcing the death of W.R. Cramer's mother in St
    Paul, Minn.

Crandal, Mr Silas   "Obituary"   May 18, 1893
    see Groves, Mrs

84

Crandel, Miss Maggie   "Death"   Feb 23, 1882
   see Thompson, Miss Minnie

Crane, Mrs   "Loraine"   Jun 28, 1903
   Gracie Spicer went to Carmen to attned the funeral of Mrs Crane.

Crane, Addie   "Obituary"   May 15, 1902
   see Whelden, Mary Crane

Crane, Alice M.   "Obituary"   May 15, 1902
   see Whelden, Mary Crane

Crane, Charles E.   "Obituary"   May 15, 1902
   see Whelden, Mary Crane

Crane, Rev. E.C.   "Local"   Jul 13, 1887
   News of the death at Manchester, N.H. from cholera infantum the infant
   child of Rev E.C. Crane age 6 mo's 14 days.

Crane, Rev E.C.   "Death"   Jun 29, 1893
   "Vermont Tribune"
   Died- Wednesday eve June 14th Rev E.C. Crane. Funeral at the Cong'l
   church Friday at 1:30 Remains taken to Manchester, N.H. for burial.

Crane, Nr E.C.   "Local"   Jun 29 1893
   Died- Mr E.C. Crane, a one time pastor of our Cong'l church, but
   recently of the Vermont Tribune, published at Ludlow, Vermont. Leaves
   a wife and children.

Crane, Rev E.C.   "Obituary"   May 15, 1902
   see Wheldon, Mrs Mary

Crane, Mrs E.C.   "Obituary   May 15, 1902
   see Wheldon, Mrs Mary

Crane, Edward C.   "Obituary"   May 15, 1902
   see Wheldon, Mary Crane

Crane, Ephraim H.   "Obituary"   May 15, 1902
   see Wheldon, Mary Crane

Crane, Lizzie A.   "Obituary"   May 15, 1902
   see Wheldon, Mary Crane

Crank, Sheriff   "Obituary"   Aug 16, 1888
   From Savannah, Mo. "Democrat of August 3rd
   Died Sheriff Crank of Andrew Co. accidently shot himself Monday July 30th
   Died the next day. Born in Adams Co. Ill. May 24, 1845. was 43 yrs 2 mo's
   7 days old. Served with the 5th Ill. Reg. during the war and in 1867
   moved to Henry Co. Mo. and in 1876 moved to Andrew Co.. In 1884 he was
   elected sheriff and again in 1886. He was member of Christain church.
   Leaves a wife and 2 children, Albert, the deputy sheriff and Gertie
   15 yrs old.
   <u>CORRECTED</u> in August 23rd paper. He served in the 50th Ill. Reg A. not
   the 5th.

Crank, C.O.   "Obituary"   Frb 9, 1899
    see Shepherd, Mrs Samuel

Crank, Jane   "Obituary"   Feb 9, 1899
    see Shepherd, Mrs Samuel

Crank, Mrs Jas. A.(Lizzie)   Jul 28, 1881
    Died- Mrs Lizzie Crank age 28 yrs. Wife of Jas. A. Crank. Daughter of
    Aaron Kelly on July 21, 1881. Leaves a husband.

Crank, Mr Jesse   "Died"   Feb 5, 1880
    Died- on last Wednesday Feb 4th, Mr Jesse Crank. 74 yrs old.

Crank, Jesse   "Probate Notice"   Mar 4, 1880
    1st Monday of April 1880   James A. Crank, Ex.

Crank, Mr and Mrs Jesse (Eliza)   Feb 3, 1881
    Mrs Eliza Crank wodow of the late Jesse Crank died Jan 27th of pneumonia
    age 70 yrs.

Crank, Mary Jane   "Obituary"   Feb 9, 1899
    Died- Mary Jane Crank, daughter of Jesse and Eliza Crank. Born Adams Co.
    January 22, 1833. Married Samuel Shepherd Nov 13, 1853 and since lived
    in Adams Co.. They had 10 children, 6 sons and 4 daughters, all survive
    her but 1 son. Joined Christain church 1858 under Elder John Harris
    and was a charter member of Mt Hebron church. Died Feb 1st age 66yrs
    10 days old. Buried in Baptist cemetery on Friday.

Crank, Mrs Riley   "Obituary"   Sep 10, 1885
    see Spicer, James

Crawford, Genevieve   "Local"   Oct 17, 1895
    Died- Genevieve, 2 yr old daughter of Mr and Mrs John Crawford Tuesday A.M.
    of tonsilitis and laryngitis. Buried yesterday P.M. Services at the
    house by Rev R.M. Hartrick and Rev Waterman. Their 2 little boys, Marvin
    and Cecil have been suffering from same trouble.

Crawford, Miss Jane   "Obituary"   Jun 11, 1903
    see Davis, George W.

Crawford, John   "Obituary"   Nov 3, 1881
    see Hedges, Mary

Crawford, Mrs John Jr.   "Local"   Oct 24, 1895
    Mrs Daniels, mother of Mrs John Crawford Jr. came here to attend the
    funeral of her little grandaughter. Leaves for her home in Triplett, Mo.
    today.

Crawford, Paul   "Local"   Oct 6, 1892
    Died- Little Paul, son of Mr and Mrs John Crawford. Buried Saturday
    afternoon after services at the house by Rev A.A. White. 5 yrs old.

Crawford, Mr and Mrs Will   "Loraine"   Dec 6, 1900
    A little child of Mr and Mrs Will Crawford was buried here Monday eve.

Crays, Mrs Julia   "Loraine"   Nov 23, 1893
    Died- Mrs Julia Crays, wife of H.H. Crays died Friday eve of typhoid
    fever. She was the daughter of Mr and Mrs Martin Klatt and married
    Mr C. some 9 yrs ago. She being his 2nd wife. Services by Elder Rose
    at the house Sunday at 10 A.M. Buried in Woodville cemetery. Leaves a
    husband and 2 small children, 1 brother, 1 sister, father and mother.

Cray, Wm   "Big Neck"   Feb 12, 1885
    Wm Cray died Feb 6th. He was a Vol in the 78th Ill. Inf. and was
    wounded at the battle of Jonesbourough. Leaves a wife and 6 children.

Crayton, P.L.   "Coatsburg"   May 16, 1889
    Died, at his home in Coatsburg May 4th of malarial fever, P.L. Crayton
    76 yrs old. Leaves a wife who is blind and 3 daughters. Services at
    the house by Rev Groves. Buried in the village cemetery.

Crenshaw, Mrs Annie   "Lima"   Sep 9, 1880
    Died- at the home of Richard Harness Esq. near Lima on Saturday eve
    August 21st, Mrs Annie Crenshaw, formerly Annie Bolt, daughter of
    Jacob Bolt,Esq. of Emporia, Kansas. She was here visiting friends and
    relatives.

Crenshaw, Mr and Mrs J.O.   "Lima"   Sep 25, 1890
    The infant baby of Mr and Mrs J.O. Crenshaw died last Sept 18th. Buried
    in Lima cemetery.

Crenshaw, Mrs Martha   "Death"   Aug 3, 1904
    Died- Mrs Martha Crenshaw of Lima very suddenly Friday A.M. while at
    the breakfast table from heart disease. Born this county 68 yrs ago and
    has always lived here. Leaves husband , 2 daughters and 3 sons.

Crenshaw, Mrs Martha   "Lima"   Nov 29, 1894
    Died- Mrs Martha Crenshaw, at the home of her daughter, Mrs James I.
    Frazier last Sunday eve. Her husband died some 4 yrs ago. Leaves 2
    daughters, Mrs Frazier and Mrs Frank Jacobs. Buried beside her husband
    in the Crenshaw cemetery. Services by Rev McNamara of the M.E. Church
    South at the Hebron church.

Crenshaw, Mr and Mrs Perry   "Tioga"   Feb 25, 1892
    Died- Feb 15th the infant child of Mr and Mrs Perry Crenshaw.

Crenshaw, Mr Theophilus   "Lima"   Jun 4, 1891
    Died- at his home near Lima May 26th, Mr Theophilus Crenshaw. 76 yrs old.
    Buried Crenshaw cemetery near Hebron church.

Crippen, Sam'l   "Local"   Feb 21, 1889
    Died- News rec'd Friday of the death of Sam'l Crippen, a farmer and
    stock raiser living S. of Camp Point died of rheumatism that attacked
    the heart. Born in Virginia in 1833. Came to Adams Co. with his parents
    when he was 10 yrs old and lived near Camp Point since then. Leaves a
    wife and 6 children.

Criswell, Mrs Wm   "Obituary"   Mar 2, 1899
    see Judy, Mrs Nancy

Cromer, Mrs Ida   "Local"   Aug 29, 1901
    Mrs C.F. Burnham left for Rantoul, Kansas to see her sister Ida who
    died Friday night. Mrs Cromer has been bedfast several mo's.

Cromer, Ida J.   "Local"   Aug 29, 1901
    Died- Ida J. Cromer, daughter of D.M. McCarl Born Sept 12, 1856 died
    August 23rd at age 44 yrs 11 mo's 11 days. Leaves a husband and 4 children
    (3 boys 1 girl) besides her father, mother, 2 brothers and 3 sisters.

Cromwell, Hattie   "Camp Point"   Jan 19, 1882
    Died- Hattie Cromwell, daughter of Joseph Cromwell, age 16 yrs. Buried
    in our cemetery. Joseph Cromwell is from La Prairie.

Crook, Miss   "Burton"   Nov 20, 1879
    Quiet funeral at our village churchyard yesterday. Sunday a Miss Crook from
    McKee twp who died Saturday was brought here to be buried by the side
    of her peparted friends.

Crooks, Miss Mary   "Obituary"   Dec 27, 1900
    see McClyment, William H.

Crotts, John   "Probate Notice"   Jun 21, 1894
    1st Monday of August 1894   James B. Hatton, Adm.

Crow, Austin   "Lima"   Feb 4, 1892
    Mr and Mrs Daniel Crow and son Wm went to LaBelle, Mo. Wednesday to
    attend the funeral of their son and brother, Austin Crow, formerly
    of this place.

Crow, Daniel   "Obituary"   Dec 28, 1893
    see Pilcher, Eliza A.

Crow, Parkerson   "Lima"   Jun 1, 1882
    Died on May 31st, Parkerson, 3rd son of Daniel and Mary Crow.

Crow, Medford   "Ellington"   Nov 29, 1888
    Died- Mr Medford Crow one of our old citizens at his home Monday A.M.
    November 19th. Buried at the Presbyterian church in Ellington the next
    day. Services by Rev Droke of Mendon. Heart disease and stomach trouble
    was the cause of death. Leaves only a wife.

Crowe, Mr Daniel   "Local"   Oct 6, 1892
    Mr Daniel Crowe an old settler of Adams Co. died at his home 2 miles
    north of Fowler on Friday night. Age 82 yrs. Buried Fowler cemetery.

Crowson, Mr   "Payson"   Sep 11, 1879
    Died recently of consumption, Mr Crowson.

Cupp, George   "Payson"   Jul 1, 1880
    Mr George Cupp's babe was buried last Thursday.

Curless, Mrs Addison (Allie)   "Loraine"   Oct 4, 1894
    Died- Saturday A.M. Sept 29th, Mrs Allie Curless, wife of Addison
    Curless age 22 yrs. Funeral Sunday at 11 A.M. by Elder Hollawell assisted
    by Rev Rose at the Christain church of which she was a member. Buried in
    our cemetery beside her father. Leaves a husband, mother, 2 brothers,
    2 children. One an infant.

Curless, Mrs Emma   "Obituary"   Feb 26, 1902
    see Thompson, Mrs Fannie

Curless, John   "Loraine"   Nov 8, 1888
    Died- John Curless

Curless, John   "Local"   Oct 18, 1888
    Died- Mr John Curless of Loraine suddenly in his wagon Monday eve.

Curless, John   "Loraine"   Oct 25, 1888
    Died - Monday about 4 P.M. Mr John Curless (Uncle John) 65 yrs old.
    Member of the M.E. church for 30 yrs. Services at the M.E church by Rev
    Johnson of Lima. Buried in Reece cemetery. Procession of 65 wagons
    beside the hearse and brother Odd Fellows on Horse back. Leaves wife
    4 sons snd 4 daughters.

Curless, John   "Obituary"   Aug 15, 1901
    see Seals, Rachel

Curless, Johnnie   "Obituary"   Apr 12, 1900
    Johnnie Curless, son of Mr and Mrs Millard Curless born near Loraine
    June 7, 1889 died April 8th. Services at the family home 2 miles S. of
    Loraine by Rev S.N. Wakefield. Buried in Curless cemetery about 2½
    miles S.E. of Loraine.

Curless, Mrs Millard   "Local"   Oct 17, 1895
    Died- Mrs Millard Curless, a sister of Mrs Wm Gilmer at her home about
    2 miles S. of Loraine. Burial to be in Reece burying ground.

Curless, Mrs Rachel   "Loraine"   Aug 8, 1901
    Mrs Rachel Curless is very sick. Dr James Curless of Ursa was called.
    All her children are home now, Mrs Crawford of Bowen, Mrs Trammel and
    Mrs Rose Ruffcorn of Breckenridge. The other children are S.M. Millard,
    Addison Curless and Mrs Belle Ruffcorn all live within 2 miles of town.

Curless, Mrs S.M.   "Loraine"   Mar 22, 1900
    Mrs S.M. Curless returned Monday from LaGrange where she accompanied the
    remains of her father for burial.

Curless, Mr Samuel   "Loraine"   Feb 23, 1887
    Died- Mr Samuel Curless formerly of this twp, but several yrs ago moved
    to Camp Point died at his home there last Thursday. Buried Loriane in
    the cemetery on his farm.

89

Curliss, Johnny   "Loraine"   Apr 12, 1900
    Died- Johnny Curliss at the home of his parents Mr and Mrs Millard
    Curless on Sunday afternoon. Funeral Monday by Rev Wakefield. Buried
    in Curliss cemetery. Leaves mother, father, brother and sister.

Curry, Mrs   "Camp Point"   Oct 11, 1900
    The funeral of Mrs Curry was Sunday afternoon. Services by O. Dilley.
    Buried in the cemetery.

Curry, Mrs Alma   Aug 16, 1894
    "Sundayschool supplement" List of deaths in Clayton twp included
    Mrs Alma Curry.

Curry, Mrs Catharine   Quincy"   Mar 30, 1899
    Died- Mrs Catharine Curry, a native of Ireland. Age 65 yrs. Died at
    St Mary's hospital Wednesday eve March 22nd. Leaves 3 children.

Curry, Miss Letitia   "Obituary"   Sep 11, 1890
    see Gilliland, Mrs W.P.

Cuyler, Mrs W.F.   "Obituary"   May 19, 1886
    see Ellis, Horatio T.

Cuyler, Walter   "Local"   Aug 14, 1890
    Walter Cuyler died at the family residence August 2nd at the age of
    52 yrs. Formerly proprieter of the English Kitchen in Quincy.

Cyrus, Geo. W.   "Obituary"   Apr 4, 1895
    see Strickler, Clark

Dabney, Mrs Sarah   Oct 4, 1894
    Died- Mrs Sarah Dabney at her home in Barry, Pike Co. a few mo's ago.
    Was in her 96th yr. Born Kentucky. Her husband servrd in the Rev. war.
    These facts given to us by her grandson, Mr W.E. Dabney, of Barry.

Dailey, Amanda   "Probate Notice"
    H.B. Baldwin, Adm.   Apr 28, 1881

Daily, Mrs   "Personal"   Aug 19, 1880
    Mrs Daily who had moved to the Co. house died there last Saturday and
    was buried Monday in Mendon cemetery. She was 73 yrs old. Lost 2 sons
    in the war of the Rebellion, one of whom was killed at the battle
    of Shiloh.

Daily, Mrs Amanda   "News"   Feb 12, 1880
    Mr Henry B. Baldwin has been appointed by the court as conservator for
    Mrs Amanda Daily who is adjudged a distracted person and sent to the
    Co. home.

Daily, Jacob   "Camp Point"   Feb 27, 1879
    Jacob Daily of Bowen, formerly a resident of this vicinity was buried
    in Hebron cemetery Monday. Age 67 yrs. Came to this Co. in 1840.

Daily, James   Jun 1, 1904
    Included in list of Civil war soldiers buried in Mendon cemetery.

Daily, Robert   Jun 1, 1904
    Included in list of Civil war soldiers buried in Mendon cemetery.

Dalby, Mr Joseph   "Ursa"   Mar 23, 1893
    Died- Mr Joseph Dalby of Quincy from typhoid fever. Buried in Woodland
    cemetery yesterday. He was brother of Mrs Maria Leachman who went to
    Quincy to take care of him.

Daley, Mrs Deliah   "Death"
    see Carpenter, Mrs Sarah   Dec 28, 1904

Daley, Mrs Emma   "Death"
    see Carpenter, Mrs Sarah   Dec 28, 1904

Daley, Robert   June 1, 1899
    Included in list of Soldiers graves decorated on Memorial Day in
    Mendon cemetery.

Dalton, Miss Josie   "Bowen"   Feb 27, 1879
    Funeral services of Miss Josie Dalton was preached at the M.E.
    church last Saturday by Rev P.L. Turner. Died on the night of Feb 20th.
    age 16 yrs.

Damerell, Mr   "Stillwell"   Aug 18, 1881
    Mr Damerell about 66 yrs old died recently.

Damesell, Mrs M.   "Death"   Mar 2, 1899
    see Kelly, John S.

Daniels, Mrs   "Funeral"   Oct 24, 1895
    see Crawford, Mrs John Jr.

Daniels, Mary Ann   "Obituary"   Oct 28, 1897
    see Swan, Mrs Mary Ann

Danley, Mrs   Oct 14, 1880
    see McDonal, Mrs Samuel

Darby, D.H.   "Funeral"   Feb 14, 1889
    see Hendrickson, Jas. H.

Darby, D.H.   Jun 1, 1904
    Included in list of Civil war soldiers buried in Mendon cemetery.

Darby, Mrs D.H.   "Obituary"   Apr 24, 1884
    see Hill, Mrs E.S.

Darby, Mrs D.H. (Dan'l)   "Obituary"   Jan 3, 1895
    Died- Mrs D.H. Darby Sunday A.M. December 30th. Funeral Tuesday A.M.
    at the M.E. church by Rev R.A. Hartick and Rev Wm Burgess. Buried
    Mendon cemetery by the side of her husband who died nearly 6 yrs ago.
    Born Mary A. Hendrickson at Middletown, Ohio July 23, 1832. Came with
    parents, John and Mary Hendrickson to Illinois at an early age. Lived
    Mendon most of her life. Married Dan'l H. Darby Sept 27, 1862. They
    had 5 children, 1 boy died in infancy, others still living.

Darby, Daniel H.   "Obituary"   Feb 14, 1889
    Died- Mr D.H. Darby Monday at 8:15 P.M. He had lived in Mendon 27 yrs.
    He was a skillful and ingenious mechanic and was editor of the Mendon
    Dispatch when it was started un 1878 until 1883. Born Catskill, Green Co.
    New York July 19, 1821. Located in Mendon in July 1861. Married Mary A.
    Hendrickson Sept 27, 1861. She was born in Middletown, Ohio July 23, 1833.
    He enlisted in the 119th Regt Ill. Inf. August 9, 1862 and served 3 yrs .
    Was one of Pap Smith's guerillas. His early yrs were spent in Ohio to
    which he moved as a boy with his parents. Leaves a widow and 4 children
    (3 girls 1 boy) all now at home and 1 boy is buried in Mendon cemetery.
    Also 3 children by a former marriage, 2 sons and 1 daughter. 1 son lives
    in St Louis Mo. and the other one with his sister in Minnesota. Funeral
Wednesday at 2 P.M. at the M.E. church by Rev R.P. Droke assisted by Elder
    T.M. Johnson of the Christain church and the Rev S.D. Peet of the Cong'l
    church. G.A.R. post #380 Of Loraine of which he was a member was in
    charge of the funeral. Buried Mendon cemetery.

Darnell, Miss Laura   "Lima"   Nov 13, 1879
    Miss Laura Darnell who is teaching at the Occidental, 2 miles west of
    Lima was called home to Hamilton to see a sick sister who died the day
    after her arrival home.

Daugherty, Annie see Wood, Mrs Sarah	"Death"	Mar 22, 1905
Daugherty, Edward see Wood, Mrs Sarah	"Death"	Mar 22, 1905
Daugherty, Francis see Wood, Mrs Sarah	"Death"	Mar 22, 1905
Daugherty, Frank see Wood, Mrs Sarah	"Death"	Mar 22, 1905

Daugherty, Mr and Mrs Geo.　　"Local"　　　　　　　　　　　Feb 16, 1893
Infant child of Mr and Mrs Geo. Daugherty died last Friday and buried
at Fowler on Sunday.

Daugherty, George see Myers, Mrs Mary A.	"Death"	Nov 23, 1904
Daugherty, Mrs J. see Thomas, Benj, L.	"Obituary"	Mar 1, 1883
Daugherty, James see Myers, Mrs Mary A.	"Death"	Nov 23, 1904
Daugherty, James see Wood, Mrs Sarah	"Death"	Mar 22, 1905

Daugherty, Mrs Jane　　　　　"Obituary"　　　　　　　　　Sep 11, 1902
Mrs Jane Daugherty died suddenly of heart failure in her chair at her
home Friday afternoon. Her son William's wife was upstairs. Services at
the house Sunday P.M. by Rev J.S. Bayne. Buried Fowler cemetery.
Mrs Jane Aiken Daugherty was born Jan 1, 1829 in Calerlin Co. Derry,
Ireland and died Sept 5th 1902. Age 73 yrs 8 mo's 5 days. Came to U.S.
at age 16 yrs and was married in Philadelphia, Penn to John Daugherty
Moved to Illinois 1859 and transferred to Presbyterian church fromthe
Presby church of Philadelphia. Then to the United Brethern at Elm Grove
Had 7 children, 5 sons 2 daughters, 6 living are James, George, Thomas,
William, Mrs Martha Shriver and Mrs Mary Myers.

Daugherty, John　　　　　　　"Probate Notice"　　　　　　Jan 17, 1895
1st Monday of March 1895　　Geo. and Wm Daugherty, Ex's

Daugherty, John　　　　　　　"Local"　　　　　　　　　　　Dec 27, 1894
Died- at his home 3½ miles S.W. of Mendon yesterday A.M. Mr John Daugherty
age 78 yrs and 1 day. Services at the house Friday at 10 A.M. Burial will
be in the Fowler cemetery. Leaves a wife and 6 children. 4 boys and
2 girls.

Daugherty, Leo see Wood, Mrs Sarah	"Death"	Mar 22, 1905
Daugherty, Maggie see Wood, Mrs Sarah	"Death"	Mar 22, 1905

Daugherty, Mary   "Death"   Mar 22, 1905
    see Wood, Mrs Sarah

Daugherty, Mrs Mary   "Local"   Feb 9, 1899
    Mrs W.G. Morris accompanied by her daughter, Mrs Ott left for their
    home at Council Bluffs, Iowa. Mrs M. was called here by the death of
    her mother, Mrs Mary Daugherty.

Daugherty, Mary A.   "Death"   Nov 23, 1904
    see Myers, Mrs Mary A.

Daugherty, Michael   "Ursa"   Sep 1, 1892
    Died- on Saturday August 27th at 3 P.M. Mr Michael Daugherty 82 yrs old.
    Born in Westmoreland Co. Penn in 1810. Married Elizabeth Funk Dec 10, 1830
    lived Adams Co. 40 yrs. Leaves an aged wife and 2 daughters and 5 sons.
    Member of Pleasant Grove M.P. church. Services by Rev. Ward. Buried
    at Wesley Chapel cemetery.

Daugherty, Mrs Phoebe E.   "Death"   Feb 1, 1905
    Funeral of Mrs Phoebe E. Daugherty, wife of James W. Daugherty was at
    the Lutheran church Sunday 3 .PM. by Rev A.M. Reitzel. Phoebe E. Furry
    was born near Mendon Sept 9, 1856 and died at their home 3 miles S.W.
    of Mendon Jan 27th. Age 48 yrs 4 mo's 18 days. Married James W. Daugherty
    Feb 15, 1877 and had 5 children, Elmer, Clifford, Nettie, Celestia and
    willie who survive her also surviving her is her husband. She joined
    the Lutheran church of Mendon Jan 31, 1875. Died Friday at 2 P.M.
    Pall-bearers were, Henry Racket, August Stockhecke Jr., Frank Evans,
    L.C. Myers, Wm Rowbotham Jr. and James Rowbotham.

Daugherty, Miss Sarah   "Death"   Mar 22, 1905
    see Wood, Mrs Sarah

Daugherty, Thomas   "Death"   Nov 23, 1904
    see Myers, Mrs Mary A.

Daugherty, Tom   "Death"   Mar 22, 1905
    see Wood, Mrs Sarah

Daugherty, Mr and Mrs Thos.   "Local"   Dec 7, 1893
    died- infant son of Mr and Mrs Thos. Daugherty on Saturday afternoon
    of pneunonia. Buried Monday in the Stahl cemetery at Fowler.

Daugherty, Thomas   "Death"   Nov 23, 1904
    see Myers, Mrs Mary A.

Davidson, Mrs Elizabeth   "Local"   Jan 3, 1901
    Mrs Elizabeth Davidson, wife of Rev. J.M. Davidson, formerly of the
    Zion Episcopal church died at Edwater, a Chicago suburb.

Davis, Esq.   "News"   May   1880
     The oldest son of Esq. Davis of Lima twp died Saturday of pneumonia,
     following an atteck of measles.

Davis, Squire   "Marcelline"   Jun 7, 1894
     Funeral services of Squire Davis were by Rev S.F. Walton at the
     Christain church last Friday A.M. under direction of lodge #127
     I.O.O.F. He had gone to Quincy for medical treatment where he died a
     few days later. Buried in Denson cemetery near Ursa.

Davis, Mr and Mrs Allen   "Fowler"   Aug 6, 1891
     Mr and Mrs Allen Davis of LaGrange, Missouri buried a child in the
     cemetery north of the village today.

Davis, Miss Annie   "Camp Point"   Apr 28, 1881
     Miss Annie Davis died April 24th.

Davis, Mrs G.H.   "Deaths in Adams Co."   Feb 16, 1899
     Died- Mrs G.H. Davis, wife of the stock agent of the C.B.&Q. railroad
     at her home between Broadway and Spring, Quincy Saturday night.

Davis, George   "Death"   Jul 2, 1903
     see McFarland, William

Davis, Mr and Mrs Geo.   "Funeral"   Nov 12, 1893
     see Perry, James

Davis, George W.   "Obituary"   Jun 11, 1903
     George W. Davis born in Mt Pleasant, Westmoreland Co. Penn June 14, 1837
     and died on his home at Mendon, Ill. June 7, 1903. Was 65 yrs 11 mo's
     23 days old. Lived first few yrs at Payson, Ill and was a cooper by
     trade. Married Miss Jane Crawford Oct 23, 1867 and lived Mendon since.
     Had 5 children, John, Emery, Lillie, George and Lawrence, all living.
     Services from the family home by Rev S.R. Reno, pastor of the Methodist
     church. Buried Mendon cemetery.

Davis, Mrs Hattie   "Obituary"   Jan 29, 1899
     see Devore, Andrew

Davis, John C.   "Ursa"   May 20, 1880
     Funeral services of John C. Davis, eldest son of Esq. Davis of Lima
     twp was held at the Christain church at Ursa Monday May 10th by Rev.
     Yates. Remains were buried with due cermony at the cemetery ½ mile N.
     of here.

Davis, Joseph S.   "CampPoint"   Jan 27, 1881
     Joseph S. Davis died Jan 24th of consumption. He leaves a wife and
     infant child.

Davis, Levi   "Death"   Jun 7, 1894
    Died- Mr Davis last Thursday A.M. at the Franklin house in Quincy
    from pneumonia. His wife and 2 sons were with him. He had gone to Quincy
    for medical treatment. Body taken to Messicks undertaking establishment
    and then to his home in Lima twp. Levi Davis was born in Cumberland Co.
    Penn Feb 18, 1828, went to Franklin Co. Penn when quite young with parents.
    In 1851 he moved and settled in Adams Co,.Ill. In 1852 he went to Calif.
    on a gold hunting exp. and returned in 1854. Married Miss Jane Bingaman
    in 1854. Miss B. is a native of Adams Co. Penn.born July 1834. They
    had 6 children, 3 sons 3 daughters. 2 of the daughters are married,
    1 lives near Palmyra. Mr D. owned 280 acres of the most valuable land
    in Lima twp. Was a Democrat. In 1867 he was elected Justice of Peace
    and served 9 yrs.

Davis, Levi   "Probate Notice"   Jul 12, 1894
    1st Monday of Sept 1894   Jane Davis, Adm.

Davis, Levi   "Quincy Herald"   May 31, 1894
    Squire Levi Davis, of Lima is ill with pneumonia at the Franklin House.
    Mr D. is 60 yrs old. LATER: He died May 29th.

Davis, Margaret   "Paloma"   Nov 29, 1888
    Died- Margaret Davis, 2½ miles S. of our village suddenly Saturday morning.

Day, Samuel J.   "Local"   Sep 7, 1899
    Died- Samuel J. Day formerly of Mendon in Sioux City, Iowa August 29th
    from an overdose of morphine. Mr D. taught shool here about 1859 and 60
    and in 61. Gave up his school to enlist under the 1st call for volunteers

Day, Mrs Sarah Scranton   "Local"   Oct 11, 1894
    Died- at Great Bend, Kansas Oct 4th, Mrs Sarah Scranton Day. She
    formerly lived in Mendon.

Dazey, Emily   "Obituary"   Jan 7, 1892
    see Selby, Mr and Mrs Milton

Dazey, Mrs Ishmeal (Stacey)   "Obituary"   Sep 17, 1885
    Died Sept 8th at her home near Lima, Mrs Stacey Dazey in her 89th yr.
    Born Millersburg, Bourbon Co. Ky. where her brother still resides. Her
    maiden name was Turner. At age 15 yrs she married Ishmeal Dazey and a
    few yrs later moved to Adams Co. Ill. They had 11 children.

Dazey, Miss Milly   "Death"   Jan 18, 1905
    see Selby, Lewis V.

Deaderick, D.F. (Frank)   "Local"   Feb 23, 1899
    Died- Saturday eve D.F. (Frank) Deaderick of Quincy, Supt of Water wks.
    Funeral Tuesday.

Dean, Miss   "Local"   Aug 31, 1887
    Mrs Hunter of Dakota, only sister of the late Miss Dean is here in hope
    of securing possession of the small estate left by the deceased.

Dean, Jane A.   "Obituary"   Jan 11, 1900
    see Cramer, Capt H.P.W.

Dean, Jane A.   "Obituary"   Mar 29, 1900
    Died- Jane A. Dean. Born Bedford, Penn Oct 11, 1825. Married 1844 to
    Capt H.P.W. Cramer and came to Mendon 1852 being induced to come by
    Mrs C's uncle Daniel Dean who at that time owned the old Quigg farm.
    They lived Mendon till last August when they moved to their daughter's
    in St Paul. She died 7:30 A.M. March 13th. Had been helpless invalid
    last 4 yrs. Her husband died December 26th and they now lie in the
    vault at Oakland cemetery awaiting burial when spring comes.

Dean, Ruth   "Probate Notice"   Nov 9, 1887
    1st Monday of December 1887   Mary Dean Hunter, Adm.

Dearing, Miss Matilda   "Death"   Apr 26, 1905
    see French, Mrs Matilda

Dearwester, Mr and Mrs Jas.   "Death"   Dec 24, 1903
    see Potter, Mrs Sarah

Dearwester, Miss Sarah   "Death"   Dec 24, 1903
    see Potter, Mrs Sarah

Decker, Miss Kate   "Honey Creek"   Jan 5, 1887
    Died- at her home north of Coatsburg December 30th, Miss Kate Decker
    of typhoid fever. Buried Camp Point cemetery.

Dedert, Mr and Mrs   "Bloomfield"   Mar 13, 1902
    Mr and Mrs Dedert rec'd word that Mrs D's mother died in Quincy last wk.

Dedert, Christian   "Quincy Whig"   May 23, 1895
    Died- Christian Dedert about 11 yrs old of Mendon twp. died at 610 S.
    14th St. here after being brought to the city for treatment about 2
    weeks ago. Died of rheumatism of the heart.

Demaree, Albert   "Local"   Jul 20, 1899
    Died- Albert Demaree, a resident of Quincy died there Saturday A.M.
    He was a Mason and past sec'y of Bodley lodge #1.

Demont, August   Dec 8, 1881
    Suicide at Quincy of August Demont.

Demoss, Callie   "Coatsburg"   Mar 1, 1894
    Died- at his home Friday A.M. Feb. 23rd Callie Demoss, youngest son of
    Mr and Mrs Calvin Demoss. He had been a patient sufferer for some time
    with the dread disease of consumption. Leaves a father, mother, 4
    sisters and 1 brother. He was 30 yrs old at the time of his death.
    Services at the Christain church Subday P.M. by Elder Dilly assisted by
    Rev Booth and Rev Kline of Camp Point.

Dempsey, Mrs Annie E.   "Local"   Aug 8, 1895
  Mrs Annie E. Dempsey, widow of Edward Dempsey died at her home in Quincy
  Sunday of Catarrhal fever. Until 3 years ago she was a resident of
  Fowler. Age 49 yrs.

Dempsy, Mr E.   "Fowler"   Feb 10, 1881
  Mr E. Dempsy died Feb 3rd while returning from Quincy. He is survived
  by his wife and a half a dozen small children.

Dempsey, Jimmy   "Death"   Mar 16, 1899
  Died- Uncle Jimmy Dempsey, one of the pioneers od Adams Co. at his
  home near Fowler Sunday at 1 from heart disease. He was 77 yrs old.
  He leaves 3 sons and 1 daughter, Mrs Charles Scheufele, whose
  husband is a butcher, C.E. Dempsey operator at the depot is a nephew
  as are, Ed Nolan and Lwarence Lawler by marriage.

Dempsey, Mark Sr.   "Ellington"   Aug 21, 1884
  Mark Dempsey Sr. died Saturday and was buried Monday.

Dempsey, Miss Rozella   "Fowler"   Mar 28, 1901
  Several persons from here attended the funeral of Miss Rozella Dempsey
  at Quincy Saturday.

Dempsey, Miss Susie   "Local"   Jan 17, 1889
  Died- Saturday evening January 12th at 6:30 P.M. Miss Susie Dempsey of
  Bloomfield. Age about 27 yrs. She was buried Monday the 14th in the
  Catholic cemetery at Bloomfield by Rev Father Gassenhues.

Denny, Mr   "Camp Point"   Jul 26, 1900
  Mrs James Baird was called home from visiting relatives in St Louis
  by the death of her brother, Mr Denny of Quincy. Services at the
  Christian church of this city and buried in Camp Point cemetery.

Denson, Mrs E.A.   "Local"   Apr 23, 1903
  Died- Mrs E.A. Denson of near Ursa died about noon Thursday April 16th
  at the age of 86 yrs 16 days. Funeral hekd at the Ursa Christian
  church Saturday A.M.

Denson, Mr and Mrs J.T.   "Ursa"   Jul 9, 1891
  July 3rd Mrs J.T. Denson died. She was born Fannie W. Randolph in 1860.
  Married J.T. Denson Dec 21, 1880. Buried in the Denson cemetery. Leaves
  husband and 2 sons, Chester and Wayne. Services in Christian church by Rev.
  Henry Blancke of Liberty.

Denson, Mr John   "Local"   Jul 31, 1884
  Mr John Denson of Ursa died. Age 73 yrs. He was one of the earlest
  settlers of this vicinity.

Denson, John   "Ursa"   Jul 31, 1884
  John Denson died July 23rd. Born 1807 in North Carolina. Came to Ill.
  in 1828 and in 1830 settled on the farm where he lived until death.
  His oldest son is deceased. Samuel Denson of Calif. arrived this A.M.

Denson, John   "Probate Notice"   Aug 21, 1884
  1st Monday of Oct. 1884   J.T. Denson, Adm.

Denson, John   "Probate Notice"   Aug 21, 1884
    1st Monday of October 1884   J.T. Denson, Adm.

Denson, Mrs John   "Local"   Jul 9, 1891
    The death of Mrs John Denson of Ursa is reported.

Denson, Mr and Mrs John   "Obituary"   Feb 14, 1884
    see Payne, Mrs Mary

Denson, Miss Melissa   "Local"   Jan 4, 1900
    Lee Thompson and wife attended the funeral Monday at Ursa of Miss
    Melissa Denson, who died of consumption Saturday night.

Denson, William   "Death"   Feb 19, 1903
    Died- William Denson of Quincy, Ill. at his home 214 Chestnut St.
    Saturday Feb 14th at 2:30 P.M. of heart failure and Brights disease.
    Born Ursa, Ill. 61 yrs ago. During his life in Ursa he farmed and
    taught school. After moving to Mendon he was in mercantile business and
    later moved to Quincy where he was in real estate, loan and insurance
    business. Married Mrs Laura V. Clark 1879 and had 3 sons, 2 living
    Homer of Quincy, Ill. and Harry of Hot Springs, Ark. Also 2 step sons
    Chas, D. Clark of Los Angles, Calif and William of Arizona, wife and
    mother also survive him. Mother is 87 yrs old. 3 brothers, Judge S.C.
    of San Francisco, Calif., Robert of Ursa survive him. Services at the
    home Monday P.M. by Rev Parker Shields. Buried Ursa in Denson cemetery
    with Masonic rites.

Denson, Wm   "Death"   Apr 18, 1895
    see Varnier, Miss Vinnie

Denson, Wm   "Ursa"   Feb 19, 1903
    Body of Wm Denson who died Saturday P.M. in Quincy accompanied by
    12 of his brother masons was brought here yesterday for burial. Burial in
    Denson cemetery.

Dempsey, Mrs Annie E.   "Local"   Aug 8, 1895
    Mrs Annie E. Dempsey, widow of Edward Dempsey, till 3 yrs ago a resident
    of Fowler died at her home in Quincy Sunday of Catarrhal fever.
    Age 49 yrs.

Detert, Mr and Mrs Wm   "Local"   Jan 4, 1900
    Died- 3 yrs old son of Mr and Mrs Wm Detert Monday morning.

Devore, Mrs A.   Jul 21, 1881
    Died- Mrs A. Devore on Wednesday July 20th. Age 53 yrs.

Devore, Mrs Alex   "Obituary"   Aug 11, 1886
    see Woodruff, Mrs

Devore, Mr and Mrs Alex   "Died"   Nov 5, 1885
    Died on November 3rd a young daughter of Mr and Mrs Alex Devore.
    Another daughter 5 or 6 yrs old lies dangerously ill.

Devore, Mr Andrew   "Obituary"   Jan 29, 1899
   Died- Mr Andrew Devore at his home in Honey Creek twp 2½ miles E.
   of Mendon Sunday A.M. January 22nd. 80 yrs old from heart failure.
   His daughter, Mrs Hitchcock and his grandaughter, Miss Ella Johnson
   of St Louis has been caring for him. Born near Dunningsville,
   Washington Co. Penn. May 4, 1819. At age 20 in Washington Co. he married
   Miss Eleanor Jones and had 8 children. Came to Ill. in 1846 with
   his family and settled in Quincy where he worked in the mills for 9 yrs.
   6 in the old Eagle mills. 1857 moved to Mendon and joined the late
   Peter Wible in the Milling business for 2 yrs. Stayed on as head miller
   until 1872. His wife died in 1858 leaving him with 5 children, Wm.,
   Sarah, Josephine, Elmira S., George and Alexander. Married 2nd on
   Feb 1, 1860 to Miss Harriet K. Foulk of Connelsville, Fayette Co. Penn.
   She died July 20, 1881. They had 5 children, only the oldest and youngest
   survive him. His surviving children are, Mrs S.J. Hitchcock of
   St Louis, Mrs Elmira Weinberger of Omaha, Nebr., Mrs Hattie Davis of
   Los Angles, Calif., Alexander of Coatsburg,and Enoch of Kellogg, Iowa
   Mr D. owned a farm of 240 acres in Sect 8 and 9 in Honey Creek where
   they lived since 1862. Buried in Mendon cemetery Monday afternoon,
   but at his own request without religous rites.

Devore, Mrs Cordelia   "Obituary"   Sep 7, 1904
   see Woodruff, Charles Edwin

Dewey, Miss Adeline   "Death"   Feb 5, 1891
   see McVay, Charles

Dewey, Lorenzo D.   "Obituary"   Nov 8, 1888
   Died- Lorenzo D. Dewey, born in Chautauqua Co. N.Y. August 14, 1827
   died at Cheney, Kansas November 2, 1888 at age 61 yrs 2 mp's 18 days.
   Came to Clermont Co. Ohio when 18 yrs old and married Amanda Fletcher
   there at age 19 yrs. They had 6 children 3 sons and 3 daughters. 4 of
   whom survive him. Wm F. Alvina A. Arthur E. and Jessie B. wife of Elder
   R.A. Omer of Camp Point. He came to Adams Co. In 1848 and settled E.
   of Mendon where he farmed until 1867 except for 1 yr when he went to
   Quincy. He was head miller of Casco Mills, Camp Point and soon moved
   his family there. In 1884 he moved to Cheney, Kansas because of
   declining health and engaged in Mercantile business. Was a member of the
   Baptist church 30 yrs and more recently the M.E. church of Cheney.
   Remains arrived in Mendon on the evening train. Services from the
   Methodist church by Rev. R.P. Droke. Masonic brothers were in charge
   and escorted hime to the Mendon cemetery for burial. W. Bro. and
   Geor. W. Cyrus of Camp Point preformed services at the grave.

Dexter, Mrs Kate   "Settlement"   Sep 7, 1904
   see Jacobs, James C.

Dick, Mrs   "Local"   Dec 14, 1893
   Mrs McCarl was called to Chicago by the message that her sister,
   Mrs Dick (nee Wible) had died.

Dick, J. Fowler   "Obituary"   Mar 20, 1890
   see Fowler, Mrs E.H.

```
Dick, Jesse                 "Obituary"              Jan 31, 1901
    Died- Jesse Dick, born in Westmoreland Co. Penn. November 13, 1829
    died at Knox Co. Missouri Jan 21st. Age 71 yrs 2 mo's 8 days. Married
    Katerine Furry and they had 7 children, 5 boys 2 girls. 1 son and 1
    daughter are dead. Living are his wife, Jesse, Charles, John, David and
    Emma. Remains brought to Mendon for burial. He lived Mendon many yrs.
    Services by Rev S.N. Wakefield of the Methodist church at the grave-
    side. Sons Jesse and Charles accompanied the remains here. All others
    were to ill to come.

Dick, Mrs Jesse             "Obituary"              Feb 28, 1889
    see Furry, Henry

Dick, Mrs Jesse             "Obituary"              Sep 24, 1885
    see Furry, Lewis

Dick, Mr and Mrs Jesse      "Obituary"              Jun 7, 1894
    see Wright, Mrs Rufus

Dick, Mr Matthew            "Local"                 Sep 24, 1885
    Mr Matthew Dick, head of Dick Bros of Quincy died September 19th of
    asphyxia at his residence on State between 11th and 12th St. Funeral
    Tuesday.

Dick, Matthew               Suicide"                Dec 11, 1884
    see Libbet, Christ

Dickerman, Mrs D.L.         "Obituary"              Sep 11, 1902
    see Fowler, Mrs Jeanette

Dickerman, Mrs D.W.         "Death"                 Mar 1, 1905
    see Rust, Mrs Michael

Dickerman, Mrs D.W.         "Obituary"              Jun 28, 1894
    see McCormick, John

Dickerman, Mrs DeWitt       "Obituary"              Jan 3, 1895
    see McCormick, Mrs Leah

Dickerman, Estella I.       "Estate"                May 18, 1904
    see Moore, Annice S.

Dickerman, I.R.(Ira Rice)   "Death"                 Apr 10, 1902
    I.R. Dickerman, another of Mendon's early settlers died April 4th. Ira
    Rice Dickerman was born Wallingford, Conn. August 7, 1814 where he spent
    his childhood. Later went west stopping at Burton, Ohio a few yrs. Aug 13,
    1838 he married Miss Laura E. Smith, oldest daughter of Deacon Lorin
    Smith of Chardon, O. Spring of 1839 leaving wife in Burton he came west
    to Mendon and worked for Edward H. Fowler for the summer. Fall of 1839
    he went back for his wife. They started west in a 2 horse wagon with all
    their belongings arriving in Mendon Nov 5, 1839. He leaves his aged wife
    3 sons, D.L., D.W., F.O. and 1 daughter died when she was about 5 yrs old.
    7 grandchildren, 5 gr grandchildren. He was 87 yrs 7 mo's 27 days old.
    Pallbearers were the 3 sons and John Dickerman, Chas. A. Nutt and F.M.
    Ralph a grandson. John Dickerman and Chas. Nutt are husbands of grand-
    daughters. Funeral Sunday A.M. April 6th by Rev S.N. Wakefield. Buried
    Mendon cemetery.
```

101

Dickerman, Mrs I.R.   "Local"   Mar 2, 1904
    Mrs W.H. Flemming and daughter, Viola and Alta and her sister, Miss
    Jessie Dickerman of West Chicago arrived Tuesday A.M. called here by
    the death of their grandmother, Mrs I. R. Dickerman.

Dickerman, Ira R.   "Probate Notice"   Apr 17, 1902
    1st Monday of June 1902 D.L. Dickerman, Adm.

Dickerman, Mrs John   "Local"   Apr 5, 1905
    Died- Mrs John Dickerman Sunday 1 P.M. Services were held at the Zion
    Episcopal church Tuesday P.M. by Dean Moore of Quincy.

Dickerman, Mrs Julia   "Death"   Jul 5, 1905
    see Smith, Hamilton

Dickerman, Mrs Laura   "Died"   Mar 2, 1904
    Died- Mrs Laura Dickerman Monday evening of this week from pneumonia
    and old age. Maiden name was Laura E. Smith, born May 28, 1819 near
    Chardon, Geouga Co. Ohio. The oldest of a family of 12 children.
    Married Ira R. Dickerman August 13, 1838 and they came to Mendon in
    fall of 1839 driving overland in a 2 horse wagon arriving here Nov 5th
    and lived here since.Joined the Cong'l church soon after arriving.
    Leaves 3 sons, D.L., D.W. and F.O. Dickerman of this place. 7 grand-
    children, 5 of these in Mendon 1 in Nebraska and 1 in West Chicago.
    7 Gr grandchildren, 1 sister, Mrs H.P. Cowles of Winnebago, Ill.
    Funeral today at 2 P.M. at the Cong'l church by Rev Joseph F. Bacon,
    pastor of the Cong'l church and Rev S.R. Reno of the M.E. Church and
    Rev A.M. Reitzel of the Lutheran church. Her sons and a grandson were
    pallbearers by her request.

Dickerman, Sarah J.   "Obituary"   Apr 12, 1905
    Died- April 2nd, Sarah J., wife of John F. Dickerman, age 27 yrs 27 days.
    Buried from the Zion church of Mendon April 4th. She was daughter of
    James Mealiff and was born March 5, 1878. Married John F. Dickerman
    Feb 3, 1902. Leaves husband and little daughter. Died from consumption.

Dickhut, Mrs Adolph   "Fowler"   Oct 1, 1885
    Mrs Adolph Dickhut died Sept 29th.

Dickhut, Mrs Adolph   "Fowler"   Oct 1, 1885
    Mrs Adolph Dickhut died Oct 1st. Funeral on Oct 2nd.

Dickhut, Andrew   "Local"   Feb 29, 1899
    Died- Mr Andrew Dickhut of Fowler died last night.

Dickinson, Oscar   "Death"   Jun 21, 1905
    see Felt, George O.

Dickman, Mr   "Indian Grave"   Jul 25, 1895
    Died- Mr Dickman died last wednesday P.M. and buried at Ursa Stone church
    cemetery.

Dickman, Mr and Mrs   "Indian Grave"   May 23, 1895
    Died- a little child of Mr and Mrs Dickman last Saturday.

Dickman, Mr and Mrs Adolph   "Indian Grave"   Aug 8, 1895
    Died- Young son of Mr and Mrs Adolph Dickman Monday evening at 7 .
    Age 4 mo's 21 days of brain fever.

Dickson, Rev Dr. Alexander and wife   Jan 20, 1904
    Died- the ending of the old yr and the begining of the new marked the
    deaths of Rev Dr. Alexander Dickson and his wife. The latter died
    Thursday eve about 8:30 and exactly 12 hours later at 8:30 A.M. Friday
    Mr Dickson died. He was 76 yrs old and she was 70 yrs old. Married 50
    yrs. Both died from pneumonia. They lived with Mrs D's brother, Edward
    Lansing, at Lansings grove in the town of Schaghicoke, Troy, N.Y.
    Dr D. was a brother of the late Mrs Mary Brown, widow of Dr W.J. Brown
    former residents of Mendon.

Dickson, Mary F.   "Obituary"
    see Brown, Capt. William J.   May 3, 1900

Dickson, Mrs Mary Francis   "Obituary"
    see Brown, Mary Francos Dickson   Sep 14, 1899

Dilley, Miss Lottie   "Camp Point"   Jan 24, 1901
    Miss Lottie Dilley went to Roseville last week to attend the funeral of
    her grandmother.

Dillon, Mrs   "Payson"   Nov 1, 1883
    Wife of Dr Dillon died in Decatur October 25th. Moved from here a
    short time ago.

Dillon, Dr F. and Geo.   "Marblehead"   Nov 1, 1883
    Dr F. Dillon and brother Geo. have gone to Decatur to visit their
    mother who is sick. She has since died.

Dillon, Mrs Lew   "Payson"   Jun 20, 1889
    Died- Mrs Lew Dillon died of consumption, she was a daughter of R.F.
    Edmonds. 30 yrs old. Leaves a husband and 3 children. Next day after
    the funeral Mr D. rec'd word from Quincy that his father, Dr Dillon
    was near death.

Dills, Miss Annie   "Funeral"
    see Scranton, Mary   Jan 17, 1895

Dise, Mrs   "Camp Point"   May 10, 1900
    The funeral of Mrs Dise will be at the M.E. Church on Tuesday of this wk.

Ditmer, Mr and Mrs Albert   "Elm Grove"   Aug 7, 1890
    Infant child of Mr and Mrs Albert Ditmer of Quincy died last Thursday.
    Buried Mendon cemetery.

Dittmer, Mrs Pauline   "Death"
    see Rolf, Mrs Theresia   Mar 30, 1904

Dix, Mr and Mrs Charles   "Tioga"   Jan 14, 1892
    Died- Mr and Mrs Charles Diz's 9 month old babe on Jan 4th. Buried
    Tioga cemetery.

Dix, Mr and Mrs G.   "Tioga"   Feb 21, 1895
    Died- The infant child of Mr and Mrs G. Dix died Saturday. Buried
    in village cemetery Sunday P.M.

Dix, Mrs H.   "Tioga"   Aug 15, 1895
    Died- on August 10th at her home N.E. of this place, Mrs H. Dix 70 yrs
    old. Leaves 7 children, husband preceded her in death. Buried in
    German cemetery Monday afternoon. Services by Rev P. Ott.

Dix, Mrs Viola   "Tioga"   Mar 1, 1894
    Died- Mrs Viola Dix last Sunday night at 12 at the home of her parents
    Mr and Mrs W. Karns. Services by Rev Wheeler. Buried in Tioga cemetery
    Tuesday.

Dixon, Mrs H.   "News"   Jul 16, 1885
    Died at Ursa on July 9th following child birth, Mrs H. Dixon age 30 yrs.
    Buried Ursa cemetery. She was sister of Mrs Sam Nedrow of Mendon and
    had been married 11 mo's. Infant daughter lives.

Dobbs, Mrs A.M.   "Local"   Jan 27, 1886
    Died- December 21st at Perrysburg N.Y. Age 41 yrs, Mrs A. M. Dobbs,
    wife of the Rev Dr A.S. Dobbs. Dr delivered a series of lectures in
    Mendon last Feb. They were married shortly after leaving here.

Dobler, Susan   "Obituary"   Oct 18, 1894
    see Funk, Samuel

Dodge, Dr   "Local"   Oct 3, 1895
    Died- Dr Dodge of the Baldwin Park Sanitarium, Quincy died Tuesday
    afternoon of blood poisoning caused from trimming his corn 2 yrs
    ago. was 61 yrs old. Leaves a widow and 11 children. Taken to Hamilton for
    burial.

Doering, Mr   "Coatsburg"   Mar 13, 1890
    Mr Doering died March 2nd in his 73 rd yr. Buried March 4th at Coatburg.

Dogherty. James   "Local"   Feb 5, 1885
    Died at his home in Honey Creek Mr James Dogherty age 73 yrs. Funeral
    will be held in the Episcopal church on Thursday.

Donaldson, Jack   "Payson"   Apr 17, 1879
    Died- on April 8th of pneumonia Mr Jack Donaldson. He was sick 2 wks.
    Funeral services by Rev H.C. Adams pastor of the M.E. Church. Mr D's
    wife was buried 4 months ago.

Donaldson, Mrs Mary   "Payson"   Dec 19, 1878
    Died- on Wednesday December 9th, Mrs Mary, wife of Jackson Donaldson.
    Buried Wednesday Decmeber 11th. Services by Rev H.C. Admas at the
    M.E. church.

Donichan, James   "Local"   Mar 29, 1894
    died- James Donichan (Mary Ann Hillman's husband) died last Friday
    of consumption. Buried Sunday in Bloomfield Catholic cemetery.

Donley, Miss Eliza   "Loraine"   Aug 17, 1904
    Died, Miss Eliza Donley

Donley, Mr Henry   "York Neck"   Jul 27, 1893
    Mr Henry Donley, after a long illness died Friday July 21st. He was
born in Ireland in 1830. Married his 1st wife in Ireland and emigrated
to this country. His wife died in 1884 and was buried in MtHebron
cemetery. He married 2nd wife, who survives him in 1890. Had 8 children by
his 1st wife who suvive him. He was buried beside his wife in MtHebron
Cemetery on Sunday.

Donley, Henry   "Local"   July 27, 1893
    An account of the death of Henry Donley will be found in our York Neck
correspondence. Buried Reece cemetery on Monday. Mr Pearce was also
buried there the same day.

Donley, Mrs Sarah J.   "Payson"   Nov 30, 1887
    Died- on the night of Nov 25th, Mrs Sarah J. Donley, wife of Hugh Donley.
Services by Rev McFadden at the M.E. church.

Donnelly,   "Jotting by Hundes"   Sep 22, 1881
    Donnelly was an odd genius. He lived alone for many years till his
family came from kentucky. Killed at an old age by a train a few yrs ago.

Donnelly, Henry   Sep 21, 1893
    Jacob Groves is appointed adm of the estate of Henry Donnelly.

Donnelly, Mrs Jane   "Local"   Oct 6, 1892
    Mrs Jane Donnelly, an old lady of 90 yrs and well known in the Fowler
area died suddenly just after entering the train for Quincy Saturday
morning. She was the mother of Mrs Jas. Smith and on her way to St Louis
to join the family now settled there. Funeral took place in Quincy.

Donohue, Mrs   "Local"   Oct 19, 1887
    Mrs Donohue about 78 yrs old died at her home in Honey Creek on
Thursday night and was buried Saturday at Bloomfield according to the
rites of the Roman catholic church. We think she was born in Ireland.

Doran, Elmer N.   "Local"   Feb 9, 1899
    According to the press dispatcher, Harry Bartlett, of Clayton, Ill.
is the nearest relative of Private Elmer N. Doran, of Co. 1 1st Colo.
Reg. who was killed at Manila last Sunday.

Doran, Samuel   "Ursa"   Apr 20, 1887
    Samuel Doran, who assisted his mother in keeping the poor farm was
killed in a farm accident last week.

Dorsey, Dr A.W.   "Local"   Aug 3, 1887
    Died- Dr A.W. Dorsey of Marcelline. Funeral today.

Doty, Mrs   "Obituary"   Aug 15, 1895
    see Lawber, Mr Geo.

Doty, Mrs Esther E.   "Quincy"   Mar 23, 1899
    Died- Mrs Esther E. Doty, a widow of age 65 yrs Thursday night March
    16th of pneumonia.

Dougherty, Addie C.   "Obituary"   Feb 16, 1893
    Died- Addied C. Dougherty, infant daughter if George and Julia Dougherty.
    She was born November 18th 1892 and died Feb 10th 1893. Age 2 mo's 22 days.
    Services at the house by J.B. Carbough. Buried in Fowler cemetery.

Dougherty, Arthur   "Obituary"   Jan 29, 1899
    see Edmonds, Mary

Dougherty, Mrs Geo.   "Obituary"   Feb 28, 1889
    see Furry, Henry

Dougherty, Jackson   "Obituary"   Jan 29, 1899
    see Edmonds, Mary

Dougherty, Mrs Jas.   "Obituary"   Feb 28, 1889
    see Furry, Henry

Dougherty, John   "Obituary"   Jan 3, 1895
    Died- John Daugherty, born Coleraline Co. Derry Ireland Dec 25, 1816.
    Died at his home in Mendon twp December 26, 1894 at age 78 yrs 1 day.
    Married Miss Jane Aikens May 10, 1854 had 7 children. 6 still living.
    Came to U.S. early in life. His parents, brothers and sisters remained
    in Ireland, but later came to U.S. He died from cancer. 4 children are
    married and 2 left at home with their mother. Services at the house
    by Rev H.F. Kline pastor of the U.B. church in Quincy. Buried in Fowler
    cemetery.

Dougherty, Matt   Jun 22, 1899
    Included in graves decorated in Mendon cemetery on Memorial Day services.

Dougherty, Mathew   "Local"   Feb 12, 1885
    Funeral of Mathew Dougherty was on Thursday. He was born in 1812 in
    Coleraine, County Derry, Ireland and was about 8 yrs employed by the
    British Coast Guard and Revenue Service. Leaves a widow and 3 sons.
    Only 1 son is married. Services from the Zion church by Rev Crockett.

Dougherty, Matthew   "Obituary"   Jan 29, 1899
    see Edmonds, Mary

Dougherty, Theodore   "Obituary"   Jan 29, 1899
    see Edmonds, Mary

Dougherty, Cpl. Thomas H.   "Relic of War"   Sep 26, 1889
    Mr A.J. Dougherty rec'd a bible by mail from Capt Robert W. Patrick of
    Philadelphia, Penn. The bible belonged to Mr D's brother Corporal Thomas H.
    Dougherty, of Co. E. 82nd Penn Vol. who was killed in the battle of
    Cold Harbor, Va. June 4, 1864. It was picked up on the battle field at
    the battle of Harrisonburgh, Va. while in action by Cpl. J.L. Currier,
    Co. D. 3rd Regt Vermont Vol. It was lying near a dead soldier whose name
    is on the 1st page. In regard to the death of Thomas it occurred on
    June 3rd 1863 "Some discrepancies will be noticed in dates and places
    which we have no means of reconciling or explaining.

Douglas, Mrs   "Local"   July 21, 1898
    Died- an old lady, Mrs Douglas of 706 N. 9th St. died in Quincy the
    other day. Supposed to be over 104 yrs old.

Downing, Albert   "Will"   Jul 5, 1894
    see Witt, Samuel R.

Downing, Mrs E.Y.   "Death"   Mar 2, 1899
    see Kelly, John S.

Downing, Ebon C.   "Quincy News"   June 5, 1884
    Death of Ebon C. Downing at his home in Camp Point. 66 yrs old.

Downing, J.E.   Aug 25, 1881
    Died the infant daughter of J.E. Downing's August 19th.

Downing, James E.   "Local"   Jul 7, 1898
    Died- Hon James E. Downing, one of the most prominent citizens of
    Adams Co. died at 2 A.M. yesterday about 2½ miles north of Camp Point.

Downing, Mrs Martha   "Died"   Nov 28, 1878
    Died- November 21st at her home in Chariton Co. Missouri, Mrs Martha
    wife of Wm Downing in her 38th yr. She was the daughter of Elijah Hewitt
    and for many yrs was a resident of this place. Married Mr D. in 1859 and
    lived here until 5 yrs ago when they moved to Mo. She was a kind mother
    and wife.

Downing, Mrs Rezin   "Camp Point"   Dec 9, 1880
    Died- Mrs Rezin Downing, age 97 yrs

Downing, Wm M.   "Died"   Aug 12, 1880
    Died- July 15th at his home near Basco, Ill. of congestion, Wm M.
    Downing in his 48 th yr. Born in Penn November 29, 1832 and came to
    Illinois with his mother when young. Married Martha J. Hewitt November
    16, 1859 and lived near Mendon until about 10 yrs ago when they moved
    to Mo. His wife died in 1878 leaving hime with 4 children. In July
    1879 he returned to Illinois and married Nancy Shourer. He was a member
    of the U.B. church. Served 3 yrs as a soldier in the last war.

Doyal, Mrs H.E.   "Obituary"   Feb 23, 1893
    see Brothers, John Finley

Doyle, Mrs Harry   "Local"   Nov 13, 1902
    Sad news of the death of Mrs Harry Doyle of Telluride, Colo. was rec'd
    last week.

Doyle, John   Sep 4, 1884
    Infant daughter of John Doyle's died Sept 3rd of typhoid fever and
    was buried Lima cemetery.

Doyle, John   "Probate Notice"   Oct 24, 1895
    1st Monday of Jan 1896   Elizabeth Doyle, Adm.

Doyle, Miss Mamie   "Death"   Aug 28, 1902
    see Hadley, Nelson D.

Doyle, Mary A.   "Death"   Aug 28, 1902
   see Hadley, Nelson D.

Doyle, Mrs Purl   "Local"   Mar 10, 1898
   "Tulluride, Colo. Daily Journal March 4th"
   Harry Doyle rec'd word of the death of his sister in law, Mrs Purl Doyle
   at Cripple Creek. Mrs D. died as a result of a critical surgical
   operation for an intestinal trouble.

Doyle, Mrs W.H. jr.   "Death"   Nov 20, 1902
   Mrs W. H. Doyle Jr. died at her home on West Maine St. Saturday November
   8th 1902 3 days after an operation. Born Syracuse, N.Y. Feb 1865.
   Was a German Lutheran parentage. Came to Telluride 13 yrs ago and 11 yrs
   ago in June was married to W.H. Doyle Jr. in Telluride. Leaves husband in
   Telluride, 3 brothers in the East and 1 in N.J. Funeral Monday at 2 P.M.
   at the Cong'l church. Buried in Lone Tree Cemetery.(Telluride Colo.
   Journal) Ed: Husband is eldest son of Mr and Mrs W.H. Doyle of our town.

Draper, Esq.   Jul 14, 1881
   Died a few days ago Esq Draper, lawyer of Carthage in Leadville, Colo.
   while on business there.

Dressback, Mrs Frank   "Local"   Dec 6, 1900
   Mrs Frank Dressback, known here as Flora Swan, died at Sacramento, Calif.
   November 4th. She was formerly a resident of this village.

Drummond, Mrs John   "Indian Grave"   Jan 17, 1895
   It is repaortd that Mrs John Drummond of Minnesots is dead. She was
   formerly of this vicinity.
   CORRECTION: Jan 24, 1895 "Ursa" Mrs Drummond of Minnesota is not dead.

Drucitta, Lillie   "Obituary"   Feb 17, 1904
   see Hastings, Thomas Gilbert.

Dubarr, Jas.   "Stillwell"   Nov 17, 1881
   Died- 2 children of Jas. Dubarr.

Dudley, Mrs E.B.   "Obituary"   Nov 19, 1891
   Mrs E.B. Dudley died Tuesday P.M. Born Eliza B. Bray at North Guilford,
   Conn. Aug 2, 1814 and married James H. Dudley Oct 1836. Shortly after
   they came to Illinois and settles on a farm on this prairie hwere they
   lived until 16 yrs ago when they moved to town. They belonged to the
   Cong'l church. Her brother was the late Deacon David C. Bray. She
   leaves an aged husband, 3 sons and 1 daughter, F.F. Dudley, E.H. Dudley
   and Mrs C.C. Myers of this twp and J.C. Dudley of Conway Springs, Kansas
   besides a sister, Mrs Sarah Bray of Mendon and Mr John H. Bray of
   Denver, Colo. Funeral at the Cong'l church by Rev M.L. Schmucker of
   the Lutheran church.

Dudley, Mrs F.F.   "Death"   Apr 20, 1899
   see Myers, Mrs Anna Tinsman

Dudley, Mrs Herman   "Death"   Jan 4, 1904
   see Strickler, David W.

Dudley, Mrs Jas.   "Obituary"   Jul 13, 1893
   see Bray, Miss Sarah C.

Dudley, Jas. H.   "Obituary"   Apr 25, 1889
   see Worman, Mary E.

Dudley, Jas. H.   "Obituary"   Nov 14, 1901
   see Worman, Michael

Dudley, James   "Local"   Sep 12, 1901
   The funeral services of James Dudley will be at the residence of his
   daughter, Mrs Sarah Myers Thursday at 2 P.M.

Dudley, James H.   "Obituary"   Sep 12, 1901
   Died- James H. Dudley, born in North Guilford, Conn. Nov 4, 1811. He
   was eldest son and 3rd child in a family of 10 children 5 girls 5 boys.
   His father lived to be over 98 yrs old. 1 brother and 1 sister survive
   him in Conn. He came west in 1835 and 1 yr later went back and married
   Eliza Bray. They had 5 children 2 girls and 3 boys. The eldest, Mary,
   Mrs Michael Worman died about 10 yrs ago, Mrs Sarah Myers, F.F. Dudley,
   E. Dudley and J.C. Dudley of Conway Springs, Kansas susvive their
   father. When he came west he settled on the farm occupied by E.H. Dudley
   now. 26 yrs ago he moved into Mendon. His wife died 10 yrs ago and he
   has lived with son Frank and daughter, Mrs Myers. Joined the church in
   Conn. and was a member of the Cong'l church in Mendon 65 yrs. Leaves
   11 grandchildren, 19 gr grandchildren. Funeral at the home of Mrs Sarah
   Myers 2½ miles N.W. of Mendon at 2 P.M. today. Services by Rev J.S.
   Bayne. Buried in Mendon cemetery beside his wife.

Dudley, James H.   "Probate Notice"   Sep 26, 1901
   1st Monday of December 1901   Franklin F. Dudley, Ex.

Dudley, Mary E.   "Obituary"   Apr 25, 1889
   see Worman, Mary E.

Dudley, Michael   "Obituary"   Nov 14, 1901
   see Worman, Michael

Duffin, Mrs   "Died"   Feb 8, 1883
   Mrs Duffin died Feb 4th at the age of 80 yrs. She was a native of
   England. Her husband died several yrs ago.

Duffy, Mrs B.F.   "Obituary"   Nov 23, 1887
   see Kuhn, Isaac

Duffy, Mr and Mrs B.F.   "Death"   Jan 17, 1895
   see Walker, John C.

Duffy, Mrs Ben   "Accident"   Nov 9, 1887
   see Kuhn, Isaac

Duffy, Mrs Grace   "Death"   Apr 11, 1889
   see Ingersoll, Ralph A.

Duffy, John   "Local"   Jun 25, 1903
   Mr B.F. Duffy of Albia, Iowa was called to Kansas by the death of his
   eldest brother, John

Duffy, Joseph B.   "Local"   Jul 30, 1891
   "The review of Dallas City, Hancock Co."
   Records the death of Joseph B. Duffy of Dallas City, July 17th. Age
   66 yrs. Mr D. was the father of A.N. and B.F. Duffy of Mendon, but now
   of Burlington, Iowa

Duffy, Lilian Ingersoll   "Died   Jun 24, 1880
   Died- on Tuesday afternoon June 22nd, Lilian Ingersoll, infant daughter
   of Albert and Grace Duffy of Cholera infantum.

Duker, J.H.   "Local"   Nov 19, 1903
   J.H. Duker, president of the Quincy National Bank died very suddenly
   Saturday eve at his home from the rupture of a blood vessel.

Dumbauld, Arthur   "Obituary"   Jul 11, 1901
   see Lint, Catherine

Dumbauld, Ausburn   "Local"   Jan 26, 1899
   Died- in Rock Island, Uriah Dumbauld's brother, Ausburn of typhoid
   fever. Age 41 yrs.

Dumbauld, Catherine   "Probate Notice"   Oct 24, 1901
   1st Monday of December 1901   Urie Dumbauld, Adm with will to be
   annexed.

Dumbauld, Eldon   "Obituary"   Jul 11, 1901
   see Lint, Catherine

Dumbauld, Hugh   "Probate Notice"   Dec 19, 1878
   3rd Monday of Feb 1879   Uriah Dumbauld Adm.

Dumbauld, Janie   "Obituary"   Jul 11, 1901
   see Lint, Catherine

Dumbauld, Lennie   "Obituary"   Jul 11, 1901
   see Lint, Catherine

Dumbauld, Osborn   "Death"   Feb 2, 1899
   "From the Rock Island papers"
   Died- Osborn Dumbauld at 4:45 P.M. yesterday at his home at 737-14½ St
   He had been working for the Rock Island police force 7 yrs. died from
   typhoid fever. Born Mendon June 27, 1857. Moved to Quincy and to Rock
   Island in 1880. Worked as a motorman and hack driver in charge of the
   Harper House bus. In 1892 Mayor McConochie appointed him to the police
   force as a guide of the patrol team. Leaves a wife and 2 daughters,
   Miss Laura and Mona, 4 brothers and 3 sisters. Member of Camp #29
   Modern Woodman of America.

Dumbauld, Uriah   "Obituary"   Jul 11, 1901
   see Lint, Catherine

Dumbauld, Edward   "Local"   Mar 22, 1900
    Uriah Dumbauld rec'd word of the death of his brother Edward at Orange,
    California on March 12th of consumption. He formerly lived here.

Dumbauld, Wm   "Obituary"   Jul 11, 1901
    see Lint, Catherine

Dunbar, Josephine   "Obituary"   Sep 12, 1889
    Died- Josephine Dunbar. Born Feb 9, 1855 near Stillwell, Hancock, Co.
    Married B.J. Casley May 17, 1873. Died Mendon, Ill September 6 th
    leaving husband and 5 children.

Dunbar, Pearly   "Loraine"   Mar 27, 1902
    Died- Pearly Dunbar, grandaughter of Mrs Wilson who died last week.
    Her mother was here at Mrs W's and couldn't take her back home after
    the funeral as she was tooo sick. She was taken to Webster for burial
    last Monday. Mrs D's daughter is the 16th near relative that has died
    in the past 3 yrs. She was 9 yrs old.

Duncan, Ferdinand M.   "Whig"   Jan 24, 1901
    Died Ferdinand M. Duncan Saturday night at his home at 122 N. 11th St.
    Born Ellington twp Feb 24, 1837. He was almost 64 yrs old. Leaves his
    widow, (his 2nd wife) 2 daughters, 3 brothers, 1 sister and 5 grand-
    children, his daughter are, Mrs H.M. Frisbie of Mendon twp, Mrs Mary
    Simmons who lives on the Ellington farm. Brothers are W.F. Duncan of
    Quincy, Hubbard of Hutchinson, Kansas and M.A. of Bakerfield, Calif.
    Sister is Mrs S.P. Bartlett, wife of the Supt of the Illinois Fish
    Commission. He was a member of the Lutheran Memorial church of Quincy.

Duncan, John   "Ursa"   Mar 6, 1890
    Died John Duncan on March 2nd.

Duncan, Miss Nannie   "Mt Pleasant"   Apr 23, 1903
    Several neighbors were at the depot to meet the body of Miss Nannie
    Duncan and attend burial at Stone church cemetery. She formerly lived
    in this neighborhood. Was 65 yrs old. She was a faithful member of the
    Christian church many yrs.

Duncan, Mrs Wm   "Obituary"   Jul 18, 1895
    see Grover, Mrs P.B.

Dunham, Mrs Agnes   "Obituary"   May 16, 1901
    see Clair, Isabella Davis

Dunlap, David   "Local"   Feb 14, 1889
    Died- at West Line, Cass Co. Missouri Feb 2nd, David Dunlap. Age 82
    yrs 11 mo's 15 days. Born in Mercer Co. Ky. Feb 18, 1806. Moved to
    Calloway Co. Mo. in 1826 and on to Adams Co. Ill. in 1830. Then to
    Cass Co. Mo. in 1867 where he died. Mr D. lived on what is known as
    Uncle Johnnie Wible's place. Mr D. was the step father of Mr M.C.
    Varnier, of Ursa.

Dunlap, Dr W.B.   "Camp Point"   Apr 19, 1883
    Dr W.B. Dunlap formerly of Liberty died at Lincoln, Nebr on the 8th
    of April. Buried in Hebron cemetery.

Dunsworth, J.H.   "Local"   May 12, 1892
    Died- J.H. Dunsworth of the "Plymouth Enterprise"

Durant, Mrs   "Bowensburg"   Mar 2, 1882
    Mrs Durant died Feb 22nd. She lived 1½ miles N.W. of Bowensburg.

Durant, Thomas E.   "obituary"   Sep 6, 1888
    Died- Mr Thomas E. Durant, an old resident of this Co. died in Quincy
    Tuesday A.M. He was 66 yrs old. Born in Carthage, Tenn August 14, 1822
    Came to this Co. in 1837. Leaves a wife and married daughter.
    (the writer of this "Mr Urech" learned the harness trade under Mr D.
    28 yrs ago)

Durfee, Laura Amanda   "Deaths"   Sep 13, 1905
    see Bray, John Henry

Durheit, Mr   "Fowler & Oakland"   Jan 12, 1899
    Died- Mr Durheit, an aged citizen of Fowler last Thursday at 2.
    Funeral at Evangelical Lutheran church in Fowler Sunday A.M. Buried
    in Stahl cemetery.

Durholt, Henry C.   "Local"   Dec 11, 1902
    Henry C. Durholt, of Quincy died Sunday A.M. Age 77 yrs. Lived
    Quincy 47 yrs. He was a member of the Board of Supervisors from 1878
    to 1901.

Dutton, Mrs Sarah Marie   "Obituary"   Mar 9, 1893
    As rec'd from deceased daughter Miss S.A. Dutton.
    Mrs Sarah Marie Dutton died at her home in Durant, Iowa Feb 21st. She
    was the widow of Rev Thos. Dutton 77 yrs old. She was born Sarah Marie
    Whitney in Reading, Conn Oct 27, 1816. Both parents died within a few
    months of each other when she was 15 yrs old. From 1831 to 39 she attended
    school at the young ladies Seminary in Litchfield, Conn. and with
    relatives in New York City, New Haven and New Milford, Conn. In
    1839 she married Rev Thomas Dutton in Guilford, Conn. Moved with her
    husband and family to Mendon. Ill. in 1844. In 1855 they returned to
    New England and stayed until the fall of 1866 when the family came
    to Durant, Iowa.

Dutton, Rev Thomas   "Local"   Mar 26, 1885
    Died in Durant, Iowa March 8th Rev Thomas Dutton, formerly of Mendon.
    He was 73 yrs old.

Dyer, Simon   "Death"   Oct 13, 1881
    see Smith, Granville

Dyke, Mrs   "Obituary"   Dec 1, 1886
    see Smith, Nathaniel

Dykes, Mrs Sarah   "Death"   Jul 5, 1905
    see Smith, Hamilton

Dyler, Catherine Sophia   "Death"   Aug 3, 1893
    see Pepple, John H.

Earel, Mrs   "Columbus"   Jan 6, 1886
    Mrs Earel died at her son's, Barzilla of old age. She was buried on the
    farm beside her husband.

Earele, Mrs J.J.   "Funeral"   Sep 3, 1900
    see Mull, Mr

Eaton, Mr   "LaGrange, Mo."   Jun 24, 1880
    Mr Eaton was buried here Monday at 11 P.M. The first burial at night
    we ever witnessed.

Eaton, David   "Payson"   Oct 5, 1887
    Died- David Eaton last Tuesday night. Leaves a wife and 5 children.
    (Children are all grown)

Eaton, Isaac Mrs   "Payson"   Feb 22, 1883
    Mrs Isaac Eaton died Feb 15th. Leaves a husband.

Ebert, Louis   "Suicide"   Jan 12, 1899
    see Richter, Miss Kate

Echert, Delia   "Obituary"   Sep 14, 1899
    see Mitchell, Mrs Estella

Echon, Mr Perry   Apr 12, 1883
    Died at his residence near Lima on April 9th, Mr Perry Echon.

Eckhoff, Heye   "Local"   Dec 31, 1903
    Heye Eckhoff, age 83 yrs was found frozen to death at the home of
    his son, 6 miles W. of Golden Xmas afteroon. His son and family were
    attending the Xmas services at the German Lutheran church in Golden
    and returned home to find him in the yard.

Eckles, Lizzie   "Obituary"   Mar 2, 1893
    see James, Mary F.

Eckles, Martha A.   "Obituary"   Feb 26, 1903
    see Hunter, John

Eckles, Wm   "Big Neck"   Oct 15, 1891
    Wm Eckles died of consumption October 11th.

Eckles, William F.   "Local"   Oct 22, 1891
    An unknown correspondent sends from Golden an obituary notice of the
    late William F. Eckles of Houston twp. The notice is unobjectonable
    and we have returned it to the postmaster in Golden.

Eckman, Mrs W.W.   "Death"   Jan 24, 1901
    see Sinnock, George

Eddy, Miss   "Obituary"   Dec 14, 1899
Died- at her home in South Los Angles, Calif. nee Eddy, 43 yrs old.
She was a former resident of Adams Co., Ill. Moved to Calif 13 yrs ago.
Leaves her husband, mother, Mrs Esther Eddy of Loraine, 1 brother,
Dr C.M. Eddy of Plymouth and 1 sister, Mrs B.H. Strickler of Loraine.

Eddy, Al   "Mt Hebron"   Apr 27, 1899
Funeral of Al Eddy was held by Rev Hill at the Chrisyian church at
Loraine and at the home of Mrs Rogers on Friday. Buried Loraine
cemetery. Died April 20th.

Eddy, Allen   "Loraine"   Apr 27, 1899
Died- Allen Eddy. Mrs Leta Eddy and 2 children left for Plymouth. She
remained here for the funeral of Allen Eddy on Friday. Charlie her
husband was also present.

Eddy, Mrs E.A.   "Death"   Oct 29, 1891
see Ross, Mrs Caroline

Eddy, Esther A.   "Death"   Apr 27, 1899
see Thacker, Allen A.

Edmond, George   "Payson"   Aug 17, 1882
George Edmond buried a 10 month old child August 10th.

Edmonds, Miss Emma   "Payson"   Feb 10, 1886
Miss Emma, daughter of Mr R.F. Edmonds died last night.

Edmonds, Mary   "Obituary"   Jan 29, 1899
Died- Mary Edmonds. Born Timby, Pembrokeshire, South Wales June 23, 1816
Died Jan 23, 1899 at her home in Honey Creek twp. Age 82 yrs 6 mo's
29 days. At age 14 she moved with parents to Ireland where she married
Matthew Dougherty in 1833. She joined the Episcopal church at age 16 yrs.
Came to America at age 25 yrs. Landing at St Johns, lower Canada. Moved
to Summit Hill, Carbon Co. Penn in 1842. Lived there till spring of
1867 when they moved to near Mendon. Husband died Feb 3, 1885. She
leaves 3 sons and 6 daughters, sons are Theodore, Arthur and Jackson,
daughters are, Mrs Joseph Nevins of Reading, Penn.,Mrs W.D.L. Gibson
of Nesquehoning, Penn., Mrs Wm McElmoyle of Summit Hill, Penn.,
Mrs W.G. Morris of Council Bluffs, Iowa, Mrs A.M. Mullen of Big Neck, Ill.
Mrs Thomas Fleming of Mendon, Ill. Funeral at the Zion church by Rev
N.M. Purce. Buried in the village cemetery.

Edmonds, R.F.   "Death"   June 20, 1889
see Dillon, Mrs Lew

Edmonds, R.F.   "Death"   Feb 16, 1887
see Montgomery, Estella

Edwards, Mrs   "Obituary"   Aug 16, 1894
Died- Mrs Edwards of the Highland S.S. of Quincy. A teacher for many
yrs and for the past 3 yrs an invalid. Died last June

Edwards, Wm   "Wanted"   Sep 26, 1895
Wm Edwards is wanted- Owensboro, Ky Sept 21
Dear Sir; If you can give me any information concerning the present

continued from last page.
    address of the heirs of Wm Edwards, brother of Miles S. Edwards, grand
    nephew of Robert Edwards, it will be greatly appreciated. Recent
    developments in a long contested case in New York have made it very
    important to locate the living heirs at once. Wm Edwards is supposed
    to have settled somewhere in Illinois about 1833 or 40.
                        A.D. Powers

Eicharn, Charlie   "Indian Grave"   Jul 11, 1895
    Died- little Charlie Eicharn Saturday evening. His mother is in
    Quincy hospital not expected to live.

Eisle, W.F.   "Local"   Apr 18, 1901
    Died- the news of the death of W.F. Eisle March 23rd at Omaha, Nebr.
    He was a former tailor in Mendon.

Elderbrook, Miss   "Ursa"   Apr 14, 1898
    Died- today, Miss Elderbrook near Marcelline from consumption.

Elerbrook, Henry and wife   "Marcelline"   Feb 7, 1901
    Born to Mr and Mrs Henry Elerbrook a daughter, but only lived a short
    time.

Elfers, J.H.   "Local"   Jan 5, 1899
    Drowned, Mr J.H. Elfers, a stone cutter employed by C.D. Van Frank in
    cutting ice was drowned in the bay Tuesday evening.

Elick, Martin   Oct 23, 1890
    October 16th Martin Elick died at his home in Scotland, Co. Missouri
    He was 75 yrs old. Lived Scotland 15 yrs. Came to Lima and Adams Co.
    in 1850

Elick, Mrs Mary   "Local"   Mar 31, 1898
    Rec'd word of the death of Mrs Mary Elick of LaBelle, Missouri
    which occured yesterday. She was a former resident of this Co for 30 yrs.

Ellerbrook, Mrs C.   "Tioga"   Apr 11, 1895
    Died at her home near Marcelline Thursday April 4th at 3 P.M.
    Mrs C. Ellerbrook. Was 45 yrs old. Buried German cemetery at Tioga
    Saturday P.M.

Ellerbrook, Peter   "Quincy"   Mar 2, 1899
    Died- Peter Ellerbrook of grip and a liver complaint. Leaves a wife
    and a brother.

Elliot, Mr Will   "Coatsburg"   Jul 9, 1885
    Mr Will <u>Elliot</u> and sister attended the funeral of their uncle at
    Chili last week.

Elliott, Miss   "Obituary"   Jan 29, 1891
    see Whitlock, Derrick

Elliott, Miss Amelia   "Coatsburg"   Jun 16, 1886
    Miss Amelia Elliott has returned from Ohio hwere she attended the
    funeral of her grandfather.

Elliott, Mrs Joseph   "Payson"   Dec 21, 1887
    Buried on Dec 6th, Mrs Joseph Elliott. 84 yrs old. Leaves her husband.
    She was a sister of Dr Sturgis of Quincy.

Elliott, Mrs Wm   "Payson"   Jul 15, 1880
    Died- on the 9th at the residence of Mr J. Elliott, Mrs Wm Elliott of
    Hannibal, having come here for her health. Cause dropsey.

Elliott, Lizzie   "Will Contest"   Jun 15, 1893
    see Snodgrass, T.C.

Ellis, Eugene   "Marcelline"   Sep 25, 1902
    Eugene Ellis died last Friday at his sister's on the Trimble farm,
    east of town.

Ellis, George   "Local"   Jan 15, 1885
    Died at the residence of his son in law, L.C. Verner on Friday the 26th,
    George Ellis in his 69th yr. Leaves 4 grown children.

Ellis, Jas.   Jul 28, 1881
    Died Jas. Ellis an old citizen of Lima twp on July 24th.

Ellis, Mr Horatio T.   "Local"   May 19, 1886
    Mr Horatio T. Ellis died Friday at his home at 132 N. 5th St Quincy
    At the age of 75 yrs. Came from Ky. in 1834. In 1836 he married Miss
    Eubanks after whose father Eubanks station was named. 2 weeks before
    Mr E. died he and his wife celebrated their golden wedding. He leaves
    a wife, 2 sons and 3 daughters, Jas. T. Ellis of St Louis, H.T. Ellis
    Jr. of St Joe, Mrs John Lennox, Mrs W.F. Cuyler and Mrs A.R. Pippitt
    all of Quincy. Funeral from his residence.

Ellis, Mr O.T.   "Quincy"   Dec 9, 1880
    Died December 5th Mr O.T. Ellis, proprieter of the Ballard House.

Ellis, Tom   Dec 19, 1889
    Tom Ellis died November 4th.

Ely, Mr   "Local"   Aug 3, 1893
    Mr Wm McFarland rec'd the following telegram- Colorado Springs,
    Co?? , 93   Mr Ely died at 5:45 P.M. notify relatives, Dr Rice.

Ely, Miss Debora   "Obituary"   Dec 8, 1898
    see McFarland, Mrs Debora

Ely, Ernest   "Mendon"   Dec 15, 1881
    Died- Dec 13th Ernest second son of Jared and Sally Ely. Age 5 yrs
    10 months.

Ely, Jared   "Obituary"   Aug 10, 1893
Died- Mr Jared Ely at Colorado Springs, Colo. August 1st 1893. Friday
night his remains were brought to Mendon for burial in Mendon cemetery.
Services at the house by Rev Wm Burgess. He was born in Ohio Oct 6, 1830
Came with his father to Mendon 55 yrs ago (at the age of 8 yrs) On
November 3, 1870 he married Sarah McFarland of Mendon. They had 4
children, 2 sons 2 daughters. Both sons are dead. Joined the Lutheran
church 13 yrs ago on April 9, 1882. Leaves a wife and 2 daughters.

Ely, Jared   "Will"   Aug 31, 1893
The will of the late Jared Ely of Mendon who died August 1st was
admitted to Probate yesterday. The instrument was executed July 16, 1891
and the signature of the testator was wittnessed by Edmund Higbee,
F. W. Battell, Albert Wible a-nd Wm McFarland. He leaves his wife,
Sarah Ely property in Mendon and also all the furniture. To his oldest
daughter, Olive, he leaves 40 acres of land and $7,000. To his
youngest daughter, Esther, several tracts of land. Everything else to his
wife. She is named executor. Mrs Ely was appointed guardian of her
2 daughters, Olive age 14 yrs and Esther age 9 yrs.

Ely, Jared   "Probate Notice"   Aug 31, 1893
1st Monday of November 1893 Sarah Ely, Ex.

Ely, Mrs Ralph   Jan 25, 1883
Mrs Ralph Ely died January 20th. 74 yrs old. She was an old settler
having lived here 45 yrs. Leaves a husband 4 yrs older than herself and
1 son and 3 daughters. Services by Rev McKown at the Methodist church.
Her youngest daughter is Mrs Adam McFarland.

Ely, Ralph   "Died"   Mar 1, 1883
Mr Ralph Ely died Feb 25th in his 80th yr. Born Deerfield, Ohio
August 1803. He moved to Mendon 1838. Mrs Ely died 5 weeks ago. They
celebrated their 50th wedding some few yrs ago. Leaves 1 son and 3
daughters. Buried Mendon cemetery.

Ely, Wallace   Dec 29, 1881
Died- Decmeber 23rd, Wallace, the oldest son of Mr and Mrs Jared Ely.
Rev Kunkelman will officiate.

Emery, Mr and Mrs Thomas "Local"   Jan 27, 1886
Infant child of Mr and Mrs Thomas Emery of Honey Creek was found dead
in bed. Funeral will be Sunday afternoon in Mendon cemetery.

Emmen, Mrs Belle   "Lima"   Mar 30, 1882
Mrs Belle Emmen of Quincy died March 26th at the home of her mother.

Emmons, Mr and Mrs   "Loraine"   Oct 6, 1886
An infant child of Mr and Mrs Emmons died Friday evening. Buried
Tioga cemetery.

Emmons, George   "Local"   Mar 23, 1887
Mr George Emmons who was shot a week ago by assassins died at his home
in Breckenridge, Hancock, Co. Sunday P.M.

Emmons, George   "Tioga"   Apr 6, 1887
   George Emmons who was shot at Breckenridge about a month ago died at
   his mother's residence in Rocky Run April 1st. Leaves a child, 2
   brothers and 2 sisters.

Emory, Mr Thomas   "News"   Oct 12, 1882
   Mr Thomas Emory who was so seriously injured by a reaper some months
   ago died Friday October 6th. He was buried October 7th SEE EMERY

Enlow, Dr W.G.   "Death in Adams Co."   Apr 6, 1899
   Died- Dr W.G. Enlow of Liberty. He was sick 4 to 5 wks. 45 yrs old.

Ensminger, Capt.   Mar 2, 1882
   Editor Jacob R. Urech noted the death of Capt Ensminger of Lima, an
   old service buddy.

Ensminger, Mrs   "Mt Hebron"   Mar 15, 1894
   Died- Mrs Ensminger, mother of Mrs Henry Linnenburger of this vicinity
   died March 7th and buried Tioga March 9th.

Ensminger, John   "Tioga"   May 24, 1900
   Last Thursday afternoon an 18 month old child of John Ensminger was
   buried in our village cemetery.

Epperson, Mrs Harry   "Payson"   Aug 3, 1882
   Mrs Harry Epperson rec'd word yesterday that her sister living in
   Ottumwa lost a child by death.

Epping, Mrs Bernard   "Death in Adams Co."   Mar 2, 1899
   Died- Mrs Bernard Epping Sunday of old age and grip. She was born
   Germany November 21, 1820. Leaves husband and 3 children.

Epping, Henry   May 10, 1883
   Henry Epping employed by Collins Plow Co. was badly hurt Friday May 4th
   when a emery wheel burst while he was running it. He died May 5th.

Erdman, Mr Henry   "Fowler"   Nov 27, 1884
   Mr Henry Erdman buried a son November 20th. his death caused by
   diptheria.

Erke, August   "Fowler & Oakland"   Mar 1, 1900
   Funeral of August Erke was at the Lutheran church last Wednesday by
   Rev Laatch. He was over 70 yrs old.

Ernst, Christ   "Death"   Nov 11, 1880
   Died- Christ Ernst, an old citizen of Quincy Sunday A.M.

Ertel, Daniel   "Obituary"   Feb 9, 1899
   Died- Mr Daniel Ertel, aged father of F.G. Ertel formerly principal of
   our school at the home of a daughter, Mrs Nicholas Hafer of pneumonia
   Thursday Feb 2nd. Born Neuberg, Bavaria, Germany Jan 7, 1815. About 62
   yrs ago he came direct to Quincy & lived there until 1861 when he moved
   to Coatsburg where he lived until 1 yr ago and returned to Quincy. His
   wife died about 18 yrs ago. Buried in Woodland cemetery Saturday P.M.
   Services by Rev Kramer of the Salem church.

118

Ertel, Mr F.G.   "Death"   Nov 11, 1897
    see Tieken, Mrs Dr J.D.

Ertel, Mrs F.G.   "Death"   Aug 7, 1890
    see Kauder, Conrad

Ertz, Frederick   "Camp Point"   Jul 22, 1880
    Frederick Ertz, a German farmer of Columbus twp was killed Monday when
    he was thrown from his wagon when his team ran away.

Ertz, Leno   "Columbus"   Mar 15, 1888
    Leno Ertz died at his home.

Eshom, Mr Andrew   "Local"   Feb 2, 1888
    Mr Andrew Eshom died January 26th at his home in Lima twp. Buried
    next day at the Stone church cmeetery between Marcelline and Ursa.
    58 yrs old.

Eshom, Andrew   "Probate Notice"   Feb 23, 1888
    1st Monday of April 1888   Eliza Eshom, Adm.

Eshom, Mrs Effie   "Marcelline"   Jun 16, 1892
    The funeral of Mrs Effie Eshom was the largest we have seen in this place.

Eshom, Mrs Lydia   "Ursa"   May 8, 1884
    Young son of Mrs Lydia Eshom of Lima died. Buried at the Stone Chapel
    cemetery.

Eshom, Perry L.   "Probate Notice"   Jun 7, 1883
    3rd Monday of July 1883   Lydia E. Eshom, Adm.

Eshom, Mrs Willis   "Local"   Oct 5, 1899
    John Francis left for Gibbs, Missouri Monday night. Called there by
    the death of his sister, Mrs Willis Eshom.

Eshorn, Mrs Sallie   "Lima"   Mar 23, 1882
    We regret to announce the death of Mrs Sallie Eshorn. She died at the
    residence of her son in law, Mr Savil Orr on March 17th.

Estus, Mr   "Payson"   Mar 20, 1879
    Died- Tuesday March 11th at the residence of his son in law, John
    Kidder, Mr Estus. 80 yrs old. Services at the house.

Eull, Prof John M.   "Local"   Nov 16, 1887
    Died- last week in Quincy, Prof John M. Eull.

Evans, Anna   "Masters Sale"   Jan 20, 1898
    see Worman, Geo. M.

Evans, George E.   "Probate Notice"   Sep 7, 1904
    see Evans, Mary Ann

Evans, Mrs Frank   "Obituary"   Jun 26, 1902
 see Hillman, Joseph

Evans, George   Deaths"   Jul 6, 1904
 see Green, Mary Ann

Evans, Mr George   "Local"   Dec 2, 1885
 Died- at his home near Fowler Thursday morning. Age 72 yrs, Mr George Evans
 Services by Rev E.C. Crane. Buried Fowler cemetery. General Morgan
 (brother in law) and 2 other comrades of the Mexican war were present
 to pay the last tribute to the memory of the deceased.

Evans, George   "Probate Notice"   Jan 13, 1886
 3rd Monday of March 1886 James Evans, Ex.

Evans, Ida   "Death"   Jul 6, 1904
 see Green, Mary Ann

Evans, Mrs James   "Obituary"   Apr 20, 1899
 see Myers, Mrs Anna Tinsman

Evans, Mary   Local"   Jul 6, 1904
 Grandma Mary Evans who we mentioned last wk as being very low, died
 Sunday night. Funeral at the Elm Grove church yesterday afternoon by
 Rev J.B. Carbough of Good Hope, Ill. Buried Fowler cemetery.
 see Green, Mary Ann obituary

Evans, Mary Ann   "Probate Notice"   Sep 7, 1904
 1st Monday of November 1904 George E. Evans and Frank Evans, ??

Everett, Capt J.W.   "Local"   Aug 17, 1899
 Died- Capt J.W. Everett of Quincy there Tuesday A.M.

Everson, Wm   "Edgings"   Jun 15, 1877
 We learn the the daughter of Wm Everston who resides near Coatsburg
 committed suicide, by hanging last Wednesday night.

Ewing, Mr A.J.   "Tioga"   Sep 29, 1886
 Died- September 19th at 7:15 A.M. Mr A.J. Ewing in his 48th yr. Born
 in Brown Co. Ohio October 28, 1838 the son of Jackson and Catherine
 Ewing who moved to Ky in 1841 and to this Co. in 1846 where A.J. farmed
 until 1870 when he began a mercantile business in Tioga. He was a
 member of the M.E. church for 10 yrs. Married Feb 8, 1863 to Miss
 Minerva Gray. They had 3 children of whom 2 are still living. Buried in
 Tioga cemetery September 20th with Masonic honors. Services by Rev
 J.D. Crooks. Leaves a wife, 2 daughters, 2 brothers and 3 sisters.

Exon, Mrs James   "Mallard"   Mar 28, 1889
 Died- last Tuesday, Mrs James Exon of consumption.

Fahey, J.W.   "Local"   Jul 2, 1903
    Died- Mr J.W. Fahey, formerly station agent at Ursa died from apendicitis
    June 18th at Springfield, Mo. Age 34 yrs. Remains brought back to
    Augusta, Ill. for burial. Had been employed temporaily at Okmulges, I.T.
    for the Frisco R.R. co. Was taken ill June 6th and on the 16th was
    taken to the Co. hospital at Springfiled, Mo. where he underwent an
    operation which afterwards proved fatal.

Farlow, Sam Jr.   "Died"   Feb 16, 1899
    Died- Sam Farlow Jr., eldest son of J. Farlow of Augusta. He had his
    right leg amputated at the hip Wednesday. died at St Mary's hospital
    Quincy Friday A.M. He was mail clerk running from Galesburg to Kansas
    city. Born Camp Point August 1864. Leaves a wife and 3 children. Was a
    member of the Modern Woodman.

Farlow, Mr and Mrs Wm   "Death"   Jun 5, 1884
    see Owen, Mrs Nellie

Farmer, Mary Jane   "Obituary"   Jun 20, 1901
    see Seals, Dennis

Farner, Dr W.H.   "Obituary"   Dec 19, 1878
    Died- Dr W.H. Farner at his residence near Loraine. Age 60 yrs on the
    14 of December. Born Cincinnati, Ohio and came to Keene twp when a
    boy with his step father, Mr George Rust. Married daughter of Dr. Smith
    of Montpelier and moved to Wisconsin for 2 or 3 yrs, then to Keokuk,
    Iowa. He established the first wholesale drug store in Keokuk. Leaves
    a wife, 1 son and 2 daughters. Buried Monday 1 P.M. at Loraine.

Farrell, Mrs Edward   "Fowler"   Feb 2, 1893
    Died- Saturday A.M. at the home of her son, Henry, Mrs Farrlell, relict
    of Edward Farrell 72 yrs old. Had been a helpless lady about 5 yrs
    having had a stroke of paralysis, but died of typhoid pneumonia.
    Funeral at the house after which she was buried in the family grave-
    yard.

Farrell, Mr Michael   "Local"   Nov 9, 1893
    Died- Mr Michael Farrell, police magistrate of Quincy died Wednesday
    night of last week. Born Ireland. A resident of Quincy many yrs.

Farrell, Mrs Michael   "Local"   Dec 22, 1886
    Died- Mrs Farrell, wife of Michael Farrell deputy post master at Quincy
    died Friday night and was buried Monday A.M.

Fawbush, Mrs Sarah   "Lima"   Mar 8, 1894
    Died- at her home here, Mrs Sarah Fawbush 59 yrs old. Leaves 2 children,
    Mrs Lola Conover and Walter, both of whom were here during her sickness.
    Services by Rev Hathaway. Buried Lima Cemetery.

Fawbush, Wm   "Local"   Jun 22, 1887
    News rec'd from Kansas of the death of Mr Wm Fawbush, formerly of Lima.

Fearson, Mrs   "Obituary"   Sep 8, 1892
    see Hyatt, Mrs Mary Elizabeth

Featheringill, Mrs Louisa   "Local"   Jun 18, 1903
     Died- Mrs Louisa Featheringill of Marcelline Sunday eve June 14th at 8.
     She was 69 yrs old and lived Marcelline a good many yrs. Was mother of
     Mrs Samuel Nedrow of Mendon. Buried Monday P.M. in the cemetery at the
     Stone church.

Featheringill, Miss May Luella   "Obituary"   Mar 9, 1904
     see Nedrow, Samuel C.

Fees, Frank   "Local"   Oct 3, 1895
     Frank Fees, a switchman on the C.B. & Q. railroad at Quincy was killed
     by an incoming Hannibal and St Joe train early Saturday A.M.

Felgar, Mrs David   "Obituary"   May 10, 1900
     see Huston, Mrs Susan

Felgar, Gracie   "Local"   Apr 14, 1886
     Died- From diptheria, little Gracie, daughter of Mr and Mrs David
     Felgar at her home in Newton, Kansas. Her maternal grandmother, Mrs
     Huston and her aunt, Miss Della Felgar have left to attend the funeral.

Felgar, John   "Obituary"   Apr 4, 1895
     Died- Mr John Felgar Wednesday A.M. March 27th of heart trouble.
     Funeral at the Lutheran church by Reb Whitehill of Kansas City, former
     pastor of the church. Born Westmoreland Co. Penn 1818. Married 1840
     and came to Adams Co. in spring of 1851. He was a farmer. Member of
     Lutheran church. Leaves a wife and 6 children, 4 sons and 2 daughters.

Felgar, John   "Quincy Whig"   Apr 25, 1895
     An inventory of the estate of the late John Felgar was filed in Co.
     court yesterday (Tuesday). Real estate is valued at 13,480.00 and he
     had 1000.00 in notes and chattels besides.

Felgar, John   "Probate Notice"   Apr 18, 1895
     1st Monday of June 1895   Simon S. Felgar, Ex.

Felgar, John   "Probate Notice"   Jan 8, 1903
     William H. Felgar was Friday appointed Adm. of the estate of the late
     John Felgar. "Whig"

Felgar, Mrs Mary   "Obituary"   Nov 30, 1899
     see Hardy, Joseph Patterson

Felgar, Mrs S.S.   "Obituary"   May 10, 1900
     see Huston, Mrs Susan

Felgar, Simon S.   "Obituary"   Dec 4, 1902
     Simon S. Felgar of Honey Creek died Monday A.M. of typhoid fever at his
     home 3 miles N.E. of Mendon. Services at his home Tuesday 1 P.M. Dec. 2nd
     by Rev J.S. Bayne. Born Pleasant Unity, Westmoreland Co. Penn. 1848. and
     came with parents to Mendon, Ill. 1851 where he lived since. Married
     Annie J. Huston Dec. 7, 1875. Leaves a wife, 1 daughter, Mrs C.B. Cooke,
     mother, 3 brothers, William, David and W.I., 2 sisters, Mrs Robert
     McClelland and Mrs Della Rohrbaugh. Member of the Mendon camp of M.W.A.
     #751.

Felgar, Simon S.   "Probate Notice"   Dec 18, 1902
    1st Monday of Feb. 1903   Annie J. Felgar, Adm.

Felgar, Simon   "Local"   Dec 25, 1902
    An inventory of the estate of the late Simon Felgar was filed in Co.
    Court Friday. Real estate was valued at 9500.00 and personal property
    1000.00   "Whig"

Felgar, Mrs Simon   " News"   May 21, 1891
    see Huston, Miss Sarah

Feldman, Mrs Catherine   "Quincy"   Apr 20, 1899
    Died- Mrs Catherine Feldman on April 12th of old age. Resident of
    Quincy 53 yrs. Leaves husband and 3 daughters.

Fellows, Mrs Sallie   "Payson"   Sep 11, 1879
    Died recently, Mrs Sallie Fellows.

Felsman, Miss   "Obituary"   Sep 21, 1887
    see Metz, Joe

Felt, George O.   "1st victim of war"   Jun 21, 1905
    recalls the facts that in Riverside cemetery along the river above
    Hamilton lies the resting place of George O. Felt who was 19 yrs old
    when he was bushwacked and killed August 16, 1861 near Palmyra, Mo.
    He was a member of Co. D. 16th Ill. Vol. Inf. under Col. Robert Smith.
    Oscar Dickinson was wounded and died a week or 2 later. The body of
    Felt was brought back home and buried. "Nauvoo Independent"

Fendrich, Edward   "Burton"   Mar 6, 1879
    Died- Edward, son of Mr Fendrich, in Quincy where he was attending
    school.

Fenton, Mr and Mrs John   "Marcelline"   Oct 3, 1895
    Died- a little daughter of Mr and Mrs John Fenton last Thursday.
    Buried Friday at the Keath cemetery.

Ferguson, George   Apr 20, 1882
    Five little children of Mr George Ferguson who occupies Dr. Callihans
    farm west of Carthage were taken with diptheria on Tuesday night of
    last week and 4 of them have died since.

Ferree, Charlie   "Loraine"   Jul 14, 1881
    Died, Charlie, the youngest child of Jas. W. Ferree on July 12th.

Ferree, John E.   "Local"   Feb 16, 1888
    Died- last Friday in Quincy John E. Ferree of the C.B.&Q. railroad.
    Cause dropsy. Born at Ursa January 23, 1847. Some 18 yrs ago he married
    Miss Lizzie Robbins of Quincy by whom he leaves 1 child, a son 16 yrs
    old. Mr F. was a nephew of Mrs Van Dien of this place.

Ferris, Mr   Jul 24, 1879
    a child of Mr Ferris died on July 18th.

Ferris, Mrs   "Loraine"   Feb 23, 1888
    Mrs Ferris's little babe died Sunday A.M. and will be buried here today.

Ferris, Mrs   "Loraine"   Sep 5, 1889
    Elder Biggs preached the funeral services of the late Mrs Ferris at the
    M.E. Church Sunday.

Ferris, Mrs Susan   "Loraine"   Aug 1, 1885
    Died- Mrs Susan Ferris, oldest daughter of Mr and Mrs Wm Cubbage died
    at the home of her parents Sunday night of consumption. Buried in our
    cemetery. Leaves several children, an aged father and mother, brothers
    and sister.

Ferwicke, Mrs Louis   "Death in Adams Co."   Feb 16, 1899
    Died- Mrs Louis Ferwicke of Quincy of dropsy Sunday A.M. Was 53 yrs old.
    Leaves husband and 1 daughter.

Fichet, John   "Payson"   Mar 6, 1879
    Died- Monday Feb 24th, a child of John Fichet. Age 8 mo's.

Fields, Joseph   "Fowler"   Mar 20, 1890
    Joseph Fields died Friday. Buried Sunday. 70 yrs old.

Fields, Joseph   Mar 20, 1890
    Mr Joseph Fields of Fowler died March 14th. Age 71 yrs. He was born
    in Philadelphia. Came west quite young. Funeral in Methodist church
    in Fowler. Leaves a wife and several children.

Fifer, John   "Obituary"   Sep 4, 1890
    see McGrew, Paul R.

Fifer, Mr and Mrs John   "Obituary"   Feb 23, .893
    see McGrew, Mrs Hannah C.

Finch, John B.   "Lima"   Dec 7, 1887
    Memorial services for the late John B. Finch was held at the M.E. church
    Sunday by Rev Johnson.

Finkle, Os.   "Local"   Jul 3, 1884
    The remains of Os Finkle a member of Mr Mankins traveling show whose
    death occured last week from an accident while preforming some where
    in Michigan was brought home to Quincy and buried there Monday P.M.
    July 1st.

Finlay, Mr M.B.   "Mendon"   Mar 30, 1882
    Died, Mr M.B. Finlay of Quincy.

Finley, Lycurguus E.   "Obituary"   Mar 2, 1899
    see Judy, Mrs Nancy

124

Finley, Mrs W.   "Obituary"   Mar 2, 1899
    see Judy, Mrs Nancy

Finley, Mrs Xantippe   "Obituary"   Mar 2, 1899
    see Judy, Mrs Nancy

Finney, Mr and Mrs   "Lima"   Sep 15, 1892
    The youngest child of Mr and Mrs Finney was buried last Sunday afternoon.

Finney, John   "Funeral"   Jan 28, 1892
    see Selby, Mr and Mrs Ernest

Finney, Mrs Laura   "Death"   Jan 18, 1905
    see Selby, Lewis V.

Fisher, Johnny   Dec 23, 1880
    Johnny Fisher died in Bloomington where he has been living. He leaves
    a wife.

Fisher, Julia F.   "Estate Sale"   Apr 12, 1894
    see McAdams, Clifton

Fisher, Wm H.   "Sale of Real Estate by Ex."   May 3, 1894
    see Johnson, John H.

Fitch, Mrs   "Local"   Frb 19, 1885
    Mrs Fitch of Chicago is staying with her brother, Mr R.B. Starr. She
    is here for the funeral of her little nephew, Willis Starr.

Fitzgerald, Mrs Millie   "Local"   May 14, 1903
    Mr and Mrs E. Hewitt of Hutchinson, Kansas has lost 2 daughters in the
    past 3 weeks, Mrs Millie Fitzgerald died of blood poisoning 3 weeks
    ago and Mrs Georgia Bean died of smallpox last Friday, both leaving
    small children.

Flack, Mr John   Mar 6, 1884
    Mr John Flack of Honey Creek died Feb 29th of pneumonia.

Flack, John V.   "Probate Notice"   Mar 20, 1884
    3rd Monday of May 1884   Charles W. Cammerer, Adm.

Flack, Richard,   "Local"   Aug 31, 1887
    Died- Mr Richard Flack an old settler of the prairie died on Saturday
    A.M. at the home of his daughter near Breckenridge, Hancock, Co. and
    buried the next day. 85 or 86 yrs old.

Flack, Mr and Mrs Richard   "Death"   Aug 28, 1902
    see Simmons, James

Flack, Richard Sr.   "Probate Notice"   May 10, 1888
    1st Monday of July 1888   Richard Flack Jr. Adm.

Flaherty, John   "Local"   Mar 20, 1902
    John Flaherty, an old inmate of the Soldier's home had both legs
    severed by being run over by a trolley car Tuesday eve near the home
    On 8th St. Died shortly after being taken to the hospital.

Fleming, Mrs Elizabeth A.   "Local"   Jan 4, 1888
    Died- Mrs Elizabeth A. Fleming (nee Heine) wife of George S. Fleming
    of Honey Creek twp Adams Co. Ill. died on Sunday A.M. January 1st at
    7 A.M. Age 37 yrs 8 mo's 2 days. Buried in Mendon cemetery. Born April
    29, 1850 in Northampton Co. Penn and married Dec 26, 1868. She and her
    husband came to Illinois on April 14th the following yr and settled on the
    farm where they have continued to live. Leaves husband and 6 children.
    4 boys and 2 girls.

Fleming, Mrs Geo. F.   "York Neck"   Jan 12, 1888
    Died- New yrs day, Mrs Geo. F. Fleming. Leaves husband and children.

Fleming, Mr and Mrs George   "Local"   Feb 9, 1887
    A male child born to Mr and Mrs George Fleming of Honey Creek on
    Monday 31st ulto. Died at the age of 3 days. Buried Mendon cemetery.

Fleming, Mrs Thomas   "Obituary"   Jan 29, 1899
    see Edmonds, Mary

Fleming, Mr George S.   "Local"   Jul 31, 1890
    Mr George S. Flemming had a handsome marble monument erected over the
    remains of his wife in the Mendon cemetery. She was a good wife and
    mother and a good christian woman.

Flemming, Viola   "Death"   Mar 2, 1904
    see Dickerman, Mrs I.R.

Flemming, Mrs W.H.   "Death"   Mar 2, 1904
    see Dickerman, Mrs I.R.

Fletcher, Dr and Mrs   "Death"   May 19, 1892
    see Kells, Mrs Wm

Fletcher, Senator   "Carthage"   Jan 10, 1884
    The mother of Senator Fletcher who lives several miles east of town was
    buried in Carthage cemetery.

Fletcher, Rev A.H.   "Died"   Feb 26, 1880
    Died- Rev A.H. Fletcher former pastor of the Cong"l church of Mendon
    died in Armada, Michigan Feb 8th.

Fletcher, Adin H.   "Obituary"   Sep 29, 1881
    see Safford, Elizabeth W.

Fletcher, Amanda   "Obituary"   Nov 8, 1888
    see Dewey, Lorenzo D.

Fletcher, Charles   Oct 13, 1881
    Died- October 4th, Charles Fletcher son of Ephraim Fletcher formerly
    of Mendon vicinity now at Pueblo, Colo.

126

Fletcher, Chas. Wolvertine   "Obituary"   Apr 24, 1902
     Died- Thursday April 10th Chas Wolvertine Fletcher. Age 89 yrs 5 mo's
     9 days. Born in Clermont Co. Ohio Nov 1, 1812 and there married Miss
     Evaline Moore Feb 28, 1833. Had 8 children 4 sons 4 daughters. 3 sons and
     1 daughter preceded their parents in death. Surviving are, Dr Joseph
     Fletcher, Warren Fletcher of Mendon, Mrs Hannah Shriver of Grand Junction,
     Colo., Mrs George Van Valer of Hamilton and Miss Alvina Fletcher of
     Warsaw. Mrs F. died January 25, 1892. Miss F. was the stay and comfort
     for her father in his old age. Family moved to Adams Co. Ill. from
     Ohio in 1842 and stayed till 1873 when they moved to Minnesota. After 5
     yrs they returned to Ill. and settled in Warsaw to stay. Funeral Sat.
     afternoon from the home by Rev J.M. Thompson. Buried Oakland cemetery.

Fletcher, Mr E.S.   "Death"   Nov 21, 1901
     "Copied from Great Bend, Kansas Beacon"
     Mr E.S. Fletcher died at his home at 8:50 November 13, 1901. Born in
     Clarmont Co. Ohio November 3, 1824. Married March 31, 1848 to Miss Sarah
     Meek of Lancaster, Ohio. Moved to Illinois same yr. 1878 he moved to
     Pratt Co. Kansas and to Barton Co. in March 1882. His parents were
     Methodists, but Mr F. himself never united with any church but was in
     sympathy with the christian church of which his wife is a devoted
     member. Leaves wife, 4 sons and 2 daughters.

Fletcher, Mrs Elizabeth   "Obituary"   Nov 30, 1899
     qee Hardy, Joseph Patterson

Fletcher, Hannah   "Probate"   Dec 4, 1879
     1st Monday Feb. 1880 Wm Fletcher, Adm.

Fletcher, Mrs Hannah   "Died"   Nov 27, 1879
     Died- Mrs Hannah Fletcher in Quincy Friday November 21st. Age 86 yrs.
     Buried in our cemetery Sunday P.M. Born near the town of Salem, N.J.
     October 13, 1793 and at the age of 7 yrs moved to Clemont Co. Ohio.
     Married Mr F. October 10, 1811. (Mr F. died 14 yrs ago) They came to
     Adams Co. Illinois in November 1849. She was the mother of 9 children.
     8 are still living. Had 56 grandchildren and 50 gr grandchildren and
     2 gr gr grandchildren.

Fletcher, Dr J.W.   "Local"   Dec 29, 1898
     Died- Dr J.W. Fletcher of Ursa of typhoid fever on Xmas A.M. Was 39
     yrs old. Services at the M.P. church of which he was a member under
     the auspices of Oddfellows and Modern Woodman. Buried in Stone church
     cemetery N. of the village. Leaves a widow and 2 children and his aged
     parents, Dr and Mrs Fletcher of this village.

Fletcher, Jesse   "Probate Notice"   Jan 15, 1880
     Executor's and Adm. sale Jesse Fletcher, deceased Wm Fletcher, Adm and
     Ex.

Fletcher, Miss Louise   "Local"   Nov 22, 1900
    Died- Miss Louise Fletcher, daughter of Mrs Mary J. Fletcher and a
    sister of Mrs Mary E. Turner of Ursa died at her home in Galesburg last
    week. Born in Mendon twp September 29, 1849 and lived here until 1864
    when she and her mother and a sister moved to Galesburg. Buried Monday
    at the Woodland cemetery in Quincy.

Fletcher, Lucetta   "Obituary"   Mar 13, 1890
    see Nicholson, John

Fletcher, Sarah Elizabeth   "Obituary"   May 19, 1892
    see Kells, Mrs Wm

Fletcher, Mrs Warren   "Obituary"   Jan 23, 1890
    see McFarland, John

Fletcher, Mr and Mrs Wm   "Obituary"   Jan 28, 1892
    From Wichita, Kansas, Died- Mrs Wm Fletcher at the family home in the
    Fletcher block. 58 yrs old. Leaves a husband and 5 grown children.
    2 children are in this city and 1 in Guthrie, 2 daughters, Mrs Beatty
    and Mrs Hybarker both of this city. Death caused by complication of
    la grippe and lung fever. Services at the family residence at 2 P.M.
    Sunday.

Flint, James   May 15, 1884
    James Flint, probably the oldest man in Illinois died Monday of last
    week at the home of his son James Flint Jr. in Salem twp Was 108 yrs old.

Flynn, Lewis   "Deaths in Adams Co."   Feb 23, 1899
    Died- Mr Lewis Flynn, an old citizen of McKee died Friday Feb. 17th.
    Age 70 yrs.

Follansbee, Mrs E.C.   "Death"   Apr 13, 1899
    see Clark, James

Follum, Mr   "Ursa"   Dec 31, 1903
    The remains of a young man named Follum was brought here and buried
    near the Stone church Saturday.

Follum, Mrs John   "Indian Grave"   Mar 28, 1895
    Died, Mrs John Follum last Friday at 7 P.M. of cancer of the breast.
    Leaves husband and children.

Folum, James   "Local"   Jan 19, 1899
    Died- Mr James Folum of Elm Grove Monday night.

Foltz, Mr   "Loraine"   Nov 20,1879
    Mr Foltz of Houston twp died last week.

Foltz, Arthur   "Fowler"   Jan 12, 1888
    The remains of Arthur Foltz of Big Neck were buried in the cemetery N.
    of town today.

Foltz, Martha C.   "Obituary"   May 31, 1900
    Died- Martha C. (Pierce) Foltz. Born May 1, 1869 died at her home in
    Chicago May 24th. Age 31 yrs 24 days. Married September 10, 1889 to
    Wm E. Foltz. Had 1 child, Edna who with her father survive her. She was
    the daughter of E.O. & N.M. Pierce of Big Neck. Also leaves a mother,
    2 sisters and 3 brothers. Remains arrived from Chicago Sunday and
    brought to the York Neck church. Services by Rev Bonefon after which
    she was laid to rest beside her father.

Foltz, Mrs Mary   "Local"   Feb 9, 1888
    Mrs Mary Foltz, aunt of our townsman, Mr C.S. Horn, died at her home in
    Fowler Monday.

Foltz, Mrs Mary   "Fowler"   Feb 16, 1888
    This forenoon Mrs Mary Foltz died. Leaves a son and a daughter. Funeral
    Wednesday.

Foltz, Mr Quil   "Big Neck"   Nov 23, 1887
    Died- at his home in Big Neck Nov 11th, Mr Quil Foltz from typhoid
    fever. Age 37 yrs 3 mo's 21 days. Leaves a wife and 4 children. Buried
    in Fowler cemetery Monday.

Foot, Rev Horatio   "Local"   May 12, 1886
    Rev Horatio Foot died yesterday at 3 at the "Pines". The home of his
    son in Ellington twp. He was 90 yrs 3 mo's old. Services will be held
    at the home of Mr Thomas Foot by Rev S.H. Dana of the 1st Cong'l
    church at Quincy. Buried Woodland cemetery.

Ford, Arthur   "Camp Point"   Jul 4, 1901
    The funeral of the brakeman Arthur Ford who was crushed to death at
    Minneapolis was here Saturday A.M. Knights and Pythias conducted it.
    Buried in Camp Point cemetery.

Ford, Rhoda M.   Apr 23, 1885
    Obituary sent in by an old friend, Mrs C. Cherry of Tioga.
    Rhoda M. Ford born Goshen, Mass June 1817 and moved to N.Y.. Moved in
    1844 to Illinois where she married. Came to Iowa City in 1861 where she
    lived since except 5 yrs spent at her sons in Georgetown, Colo. She
    had 3 children, Mrs Thomas, Mrs Grekee and Mr Ford of Colorado.
    Services here. Died of Cancer Feb. 14th. Buried Iowa City cemetery.

Forga, Mr   "Payson"   Apr 3, 1879
    A child of Mr Forga, living 3 miles N. of Payson died March 28th.

Forsee, Dr B.W.   "Lima"   Aug 24, 1882
    Died- August 21st Dr B.W. Forsee. Services by the Masonic order of which
    he was a member.

Forsee, B.W.   "Probate Notice"   Sep 7, 1882
    3rd Monday of November   Levi Davis, Adm.

Forsyth, Miss Lucy   "Death"   Sep 4, 1884
    see Nelson, Mrs

Forsyth, Mrs Mary   "Ursa"   Jul 31, 1890
    July 25th Mrs Mary Forsyth died. Age 89 yrs 9 mo's 29 days. Born in
                                 -Cont-

Forsyth,Cont-
    Kentucky and at the age of 18 married Robert Forsyth. Came to Illinois
    in 1830 where he died in 1875. Had 11 children. Services by Rev T.B.
    Ausmus July 27th in the old Stone church.

Forsythe, Mrs   "Local"   Aug 18, 1892
    The remains of an old lady from West Point, we believe a Mrs Forsythe
    was buried here Saturday.

Forsythe, Alphia   "Big Neck"   Sep 10, 1891
    Alphia Forsythe died September 4th. Buried family cemetery September
    6th. He had been married twice and father of 4 children, 2 sons 2
    daughters. All by his first wife, the 2 sons and 1st wife are dead,
    but 2nd wife and daughters survive him.

Forsythe, Berry   "Death"   Feb 17, 1898
    "Denver Republican Feb 8th"
    Died- Berry Forsythe, rental agent of the Steele block at 16th and
    Stout St. Was found dead in room 27 of the bldg last night about 8:30
    death due to strangulation. Was dead about 12 hrs. Sunday he had visited
    his mother who lives with his married sister, Mrs Sherlock at 1427- 28th
    Street. His youngest daughter also lives there, his wife being an invalid
    and compelled to live in Salt Lake where she is now with her eldest
    daughter. 48 yrs old. Had lived Denver over 20 yrs. Born in Mendon, Ill.
    Had lived with the late Vincent Francis a number of yrs when he was
    farming S. of town.

Forsythe, Cyrus   "Edgings"   Jun 15, 1877
    Cyrus Forsythe, an old colored gentleman residing in the S. part of
    town died suddenly Tuesday eve.

Forsythe, Cyrus   Jun 5, 1902
    Included in list of Civil War soldiers buried in Mendon cemetery.

Forscyhte, Daniel W.   "Mendon Missouri"
    Daniel W. Forscythe died July 4th of congestion of the stomach.

Forsythe, Johnny   "Died"   Feb 22, 1882
    Died- Johnny Forsythe, youngest son of Mrs Forsythe(now Hawkins)
    age 11 yrs.

Forsythe, Miss Lucy   "local"   Apr 2, 1885
    Mrs Nelson, nee Miss Lucy Forsythe, died March 26th and was buried
    March 27th. Services by Rev E.C. Crane.

Forsyhte, Mrs Madison   "York Neck"   Aug 25, 1892
    Mr M.M. McMullen and Sidney McGill from Bowen, Hancock Co. passed
    thru the Neck August 12th enroute to the Stone graveyard near
    Marcelline to dig the grave of Mrs Madison Forsythe (nee Laughlin)
    an old lady of Hancock Co.

Forsythe, Miss Martha   "Death"   Jan 22, 1903
    see Metcalf, Mrs Sarah

Forsythe, Mary H.   "Obituary"   Jun 29, 1887
 see Hatton, L.B.

Forsythe, Sarah   Nov 30, 1882
 Died- Miss Sarah Forsythe November 27th at the home of her mother
 Mrs Hawkins. Services at the home November 28th by Rev McKown.

Foster, Mrs Eliza Ann   "Death"   Aug 24, 1904
 Mrs Eliza Ann Foster died, age 56 yrs at 10:20 Tuesday A.M. from the
 effects of a tumor operation early Tuesday A.M. and never rallied.
 Came to Illinois with her parents when 2 yrs old and from this state
 to Ohio and returning to Illinois after a few yrs settling in this co in
 1887. Joined Christian church at age 11 yrs and later her husbands
 choice, Lutheran Evangelical church. when she moved to Pleasant Grove
 neighborhood she joined M.E. church. Married Edward Heaney December 24,
 1867 and had 10 children, living are, Samuel and Walter, Mrs Frank Robinson and Mrs Will Pierce. 1st husband died and in 1889 she married
 Sylvanus Foster and had 1 child, Bertha. Funeral at 1st M.E. church
 in this city Wednesday 1 P.M. Buried Pleasant Grove cemetery.
 "Mt Vernon Daily Register August 16th"

Foster, Sylvanus   "Obituary"   Aug 24, 1904
 see Foster, Mrs Eliza Ann

Foulk, Miss Harriet K. "Obituary"   Jan 29, 1899
 see Devore, Andrew

Fountain, Thomas J.   "Local"   Jun 7, 1888
 "From Quincy Paper" Death of Mr Thomas J. Fountain, the resturant
 keeper of Hampshire St in his 41st yr. on June 4th. Services held at
 St Peters church.

Fowler, Mrs   "Obituary"   Sep 18, 1890
 see Hayes, Mrs Wm B.

Fowler, Mrs E.H.   "Obituary"   Mar 20, 1890
 Mrs Fowler died March 16th. She was the widow of the late Edward
 Fowler formerly of Mendon. Buried March 18th. Leaves daughters, Emma
 L. Fowler and Mrs Symonds of Quincy and 2 sons, Henry Strong and
 Harvey W. Fowler and an adopted son, J. Fowler Dick. She came to Mendon
 in 1836, they were among the founders of the town of Mendon and among
 the 1st members of the Cong'l church. In 1857 they established the town
 of Fowler. Mr E. H. Fowler died in 1875. Both buried in Mendon.

Fowler, Mrs J.   "Local"   Sep 11, 1902
 Arthur Garrett, wife and daughter of Quincy came up Tuesday to attend
 the funeral of his grandmother, Mrs J. Fowler.

Fowler, Jeanette   "Local"   Sep 18, 1902
   Will of the late Jeanette Fowler of Mendon was filed for probate
   Monday. It was executed Oct 17, 1891. She leaves 200.00 to each of
   her grandchildren, leaves the homestead in Mendon to her daughter, Mary
   J. Bray and Frances A. Garrett, the rest devided between the 3 daughters,
   the 2 named and Estella Dickerman.

Fowler, Mrs Jeannette   "Obituary"   Sep 11, 1902
   Funeral of Mrs Jeannette Fowler of Mendon who died at her home Sunday
   2 P.M. was at the Cong'l church Tuesday Sept 9th at 10 A.M. by Rev J.S.
   Bayne. Buried beside her husband in Mendon cemetery. Born August 22, 1811
   in New Haven, the City of the Elms under the shadow of Yale University
   Joined church at age 15 yrs. Married April 16, 1834 to Henry E. Fowler
   by Dr Leonard Bacon. Before her marriage she taught school in New Haven
   and after her husbands death taught school in Mendon. Came with husband
   to Illinois in 1834 and the 1st night was spent on the very spot where
   her grandaughter, Mrs Dudley Myers now resides. She had a general
   store in Mendon 1855 to 1864. Was member of the Cong'l church at Mendon
   68 yrs. 3 daughters survive her, Mrs Mary Bray, Mrs C.B. Garrett and Mrs
   D.L. Dickerman and 6 great grandchildren (no mention of Grandchildren)

Fowler, Jeannette   "Probate Notice"   Oct 16, 1902
   1st Monday of December 1902   C.B. Garrett, Adm.

Fowler, Jeanette   "Local"   Oct 16, 1902
   An inventory of the estate of the late Jeannette Fowler was filed
   in Co. court yesterday. Real estate is worth 1,900.00, notes 10,061.08
   and there is 651.95 cash on hand.   "Whig"   C.B. Garrett, Adm.

Fowler, Jeannette   "partition #1689   May 18, 1904
   see Moore, Annice S.

Fox, J.B.   "Death"   May 8, 1888
   see McDade, Mamie

Foxwell, Mary J.   "Obituary"   Jan 3, 1901
   see Wilson, Darby

Francis,   "Local"   Dec 20, 1883
   The Francis estate was sold Saturday. The sons bought the entire farm
   at 50.00 per acre.

Francis, Asaph   "Commissioners land sale"   Dec 13, 1883
   Saturday the 15th day of December the estate sale of Asaph Francis
   deceased. Sale will take place at the residence of Sarah Ann Francis.

Francis, Asaph   "Deaths"   Aug 30, 1905
   see Francis, Mrs Sally ann

Francis, George   "Death"   Feb 21, 1884
   see Whitbred

Francis, Heman   "Local"   Oct 19, 1899
   Died- Heman Francis, son of Mrs S. A. Francis living 3 miles N. of
   town Thursday October 12th. Age 45 yrs 7 mo's 7 days. Buried next day
   in Mendon cemetery. Services by Rev J.S. Bayne.

Francis, Mr and Mrs Henry   "Local"   Aug 8, 1889
   Died- Rumor tells us that Mr and Mrs Henry Francis have lost their only
   child, a girl between 2 and 3 yrs.

Francis, John   "Death"   Oct 5, 1899
   see Eshom, Mrs Willis

Francis, Mrs John T.   "Camp Point"   Jul 28, 1881
   Death of Mrs John T. Francis bride of a few months. Daughter of the
   late John A. Roth. Buried July 17th.
                               "Camp Point"   Aug 18, 1881
   Mrs John T. Francis's brother, John W. Roth returned here from Denver
   for her funeral a few weeks ago.

Francis, Joseph   "Local"   Nov 27, 1884
   Died November 23rd Joseph Francis. 36 yrs old. Buried Mendon. Services
   by Rev E.C. Crane.

Francis, Miss Sallie   "Obituary"   Jan 29, 1903
   see Robertson, James F.

Francis, Mrs Sally ann   "Died"   Aug 30, 1905
   Funeral of Mrs Sally Ann Francis was at the home of Henry Francis
   Saturday 10 A.M. by Rev A.M. Reitzel of the Lutheran church. Buried Mendon
   cemetery. Sally Ann Clark was born in Falmouth, Pendleton Co. Ky.
   May 12, 1817 Died August 24, 1905 at hte age of 88 yrs 3 mo's 12 days.
   Married Asaph Francis August 16, 1838 at Carthage, Ill. Had 11 children
   6 sons and 5 daughters of whom 2 sons and 4 daughters survive her.
   Mr F. died 1861. She came with parents to Quincy 1830 floating down
   the Ohio on a flat boat then by steamer to Quincy. 1838 she came as
   a bride to the farm where she died. a period of 67 yrs 8 days. United
   with Christian church yrs ago.

Francis, Mr Samuel   "Camp Point"   Sep 12, 1901
   Funeral of Mr Samuel Francis was held here Monday. He was 84 yrs old and
   lived here several yrs.

Francis, Mrs Sarah   May 3, 1883
   Died- April 30th Mrs Sarah Francis wife of Vincent Francis. Maiden
   name was Hatchett. Born in Berkhamstead, England in 1823. Married
   Mr Francis 1849. Came to Mendon Jan 6, 1850. Leaves 1 daughter, Mrs
   R.S. Townsend of Chicago and 3 orphan children who have been under her
   care for several yrs. Services by Rev. McKown.

Francis, Vincent   "Death"   Jul 29, 1880
   see Clark, Thomas

Francis, Vincent   "death"   Dec 19, 1878
   see Clark, Arthur

Frank, Mr P.M.   "Death in Adams Co."   Mar 2, 1899
Died- Mr P.M. Frank in Kansas City Sunday P.M. while on his way to
Fort Scott. Remains brought to Quincy for burial.

Franks, Mrs   Sep 4, 1884
Mrs Franks of West Point commited suicide Tuesday September 2nd.

Frazer, Mr Lemuel   "Center"   Oct 7, 1880
Mr Lemuel Frazer, an old citizen of Ursa twp died yesterday.

Frazier, Miss Ada   "Ursa"   Apr 13, 1899
Died- Miss Ada Frazier living a short distance S. of Ursa last week
and was buried in Frazier's cemetery. Services by Rev. T.B. Wadliegh.
She was the daughter of Mr and Mrs Joe Frazier. 23 yrs old. leaves her
parents, 3 brothers and 1 sister.

Frazier, Alex and Bros.   "Mt Pleasant"   Apr 23, 1903
The Frazier Bros. had the body of their father who was buried in a
family burying ground removed to the Stone church cemetery and laid
beside their mother, who died last winter. Alex Frazier had his Children
removed also at the same time to the same lot.

Frazier, Alex   "Ursa"   Apr 6, 1887
Died- infant child of Mr and Mrs Alex Frazier.

Frazier, Mr and Mrs Alex   "Center"   Apr 6, 1887
Died- A small child of Mr and Mrs Alex Frazier, age 7 mo's and 11 days.

Frazier, Mrs Lemuel (Eva) "Ursa"   Dec 11, 1902
Died- Mrs Lemuel Frazier, widow of the late Lemuel Frazier at her home
3 miles S.E. of here at 5 P.M. Sunday. Services at the Christian
church at 2:30 P.M. Tuesday. Buried near her folks at Stone church
cemetery.

Frazier, Mrs Eva J.   "Obituary"   Dec 11, 1902
Died, Mrs Eva J. Frazier, one of the pioneers of Adams Co. suddenly
Sunday eve Dec 7th at her home in Ursa twp. Born 1829 in Maryland.
She was 73 yrs old. Came west with her parents when 7 yrs old. Making
the journey from Maryland to St Louis in Wagons. They came to Adams Co.
the same yr and lived here since. Married Lemuel Frazier over 50 yrs
ago and died in the same homestead as she entered as a bride. Husband
died a score of yrs ago. Leaves 9 children, Alexander R., Thomas J.,
John E. and George of Adams Co., Charles of Nebraska, Mrs Tom B. Smith
of Ursa, Mrs Ida Rumbaugh of Nebraska, Mrs Rose Ford of Illiopolis, Ill.
and Mrs Etta Wilderman of East St Louis. "Whig"

Frazier, G.M.   "Fowler"   Feb 27, 1879
We understand that G.M. Frazier, son of Geo. Frazier who was reported
drowned some time age is now floating in New Orleans.

Frazier, Mrs James   "Ellington"   Sep 17, 1885
    Mrs James Frazier died and was buried in the Frazier cemetery. Services
    by Mr Ruddle.

                            "News"   Sep 10, 1885
    Died- August 29th, Mrs Frazier wife of James Frazier of Ursa. Age
    73 yrs. Buried in family burying ground.

Frazier, James Sr.   Nov 21, 1889
    James Frazier Sr. known as Uncle Jimmie died at his home in the south
    part of this twp on November 18th at the age of 83 yrs. Funeral on
    Thursday November 21st at his home by Uncle John Ruddell (Uncle of
    decedent) He was buried at the Frazier burying ground 2 miles southeast
    of Ursa, Ill.

Frazier, Mrs James I.   "Death"
    see Crenshaw, Mrs Martha   Nov 29, 1894

Frazier, Joel   "Ursa"   Jul 26, 1905
    Funeral of Joel Frazier was at the Christian church last Sunday by
    Rev W.O. Livingston. Buried New Providence cemetery.

Frazier, L.G.   "Personal"   Oct 7, 1880
    Died- L.G. Frazier an old citizen of Ursa Twp on October 5th.

Frazier, Mr Lafayette   "Tioga"   Feb 3, 1886
    Died- Mr Lafayette Frazier who has been confinded to his bed for
    nearly 2 yrs died at the residence of his son George Frazier at 3 A.M.
    in his 68th yr. Services by Rev J.D. Cooke. Body was laid to rest in
    the Fletcher graveyard.

Frazier, Mrs M.B.   "Death"
    see Taylor, Mrs Barbara   Mar 2, 1899

Frazier, W.   "News"   Dec 12, 1878
    Mr W. Frazier, a son of the late Geo. Frazier of Mendon twp is
    supposed to have drowned accidently near Belmont, Mo. in the early
    part of the month.

Frederick,   "a Sad Fatality"   Aug 24, 1887
    News reached here Wednesday of the death by burning that morning in
    Honey Creek of a young man named Frederick, age 18 yrs. He and his
    brother's were cleaning brush and tried burning a bee's nest and fire
    got out of control. Their father was not at home.

Frederick,   "York Neck"   Aug 31, 1887
    CORRECTION:Young Frederick that died was 19 yrs old.

Frederick, Mrs Harriet   "Mallard"   Mar 28, 1889
    Died- Mrs Harriet Frederick died from typhoid pneumonia.

Frederick, Jake   "Loraine"   Feb 5, 1903
    Mr Jake Frederick died at his home near Woodville Sunday A.M.

    Mrs J.M. Fry attended the funeral of Jake Frederick at Woodville
    Monday.

Frederick, Willie   "Glenwood"   Aug 24, 1887
    Willie Frederick was burned to death by fire in the granary.

Fredrick, Miss Mary   "Obituary"   Aug 17, 1899
    see Hardy, George

Free, Mrs Dr   "Death"   Feb 2, 1887
    see Wilcox, Dr Luman H.

Freeman, James   "Marcelline"   Mar 1, 1883
    5 yr old son of James Freeman died Feb 28th.

French, Mrs Charles   "Obituary"   Feb 5, 1891
    see McVay, Mr Charles

French, James   "Coatsburg"   Dec 8, 1886
    James French and wife of Monmouth were called home last week by the
    death of his mother.

French, Mrs Jos.   "Coatsburg"   Dec 8, 1886
    Died- on Wednesday A.M. Mrs Jos. French age 58 yrs. Funeral by Rev R.A.
    Omer. Her remains were followed to the cemetery by a large number of
    friends.

French, Mrs Jos.   "Coatsburg"   Dec 8, 1886
    Mrs Akers, mother of Mrs H.C. Nichols of Quincy attended the funeral of
    her sister, Mrs Jos. French.

French, Mrs Martha   "Death"   Jul 20, 1904
    see Butler, Hannah

French, Matilda   "Probate Notice"   Aug 2, 1905
    1st Monday of October 1905   Frank French, Ex.

French, Mrs Matilda   "Death"   Apr 26, 1905
    Funeral of Mrs Matilda French was at the house Saturday at 2:30 P.M.
    by Rev A.M. Reitzel. Miss Matilda Dearing was born in Atterbury, England
    August 24, 1833, died at her home in Mendon Settled Mendon 1845. Married
    1849 to Thomas French who died 10 yrs ago. 3 sons, 6 daughters, 6
    grandchildren survive her. Baptized in Episcopal church of England
    and on coming to U.S. never united with the church.

French, Matilda   "Notice of Probate of Will" Jun 28, 1905
    Estate of Matilda French, deceased to Charles French, Mary French, Sarah
    French, Frank French, Lizzie Siple, Lucy French, Henry French, Lillie
    Smith and Annie Nichols, heirs of said deceased to said Sarah French
    sole legatee and devisee of said deceased.

French, Thomas   "Local"   Feb 14, 1895
    Died- at his home in Mendon last Friday Feb 8th of dropsy, Mr Thomas
    French age 77 yrs 2 mo's 16 days. Born in Deddington Oxfordshire,
    England. Came to U.S. 1845. Was a mason by trade. Married 2 times.
    Leaves a widow and 9 children, 3 sons and 6 daughters. Buried Mendon
    cemetery Sunday P.M. after services at the house by Rev R.A. Hartaick
    of the M.E. church.

French, Thomas   "Probate Notice"   Feb 21, 1895
    1st Monday of April 1895   Charles E. and Francis French, Adms.

Frey, Mrs Dean   "Obituary"   Apr 12, 1894
    see Copeland, Mrs Thomas

Frick, Mrs Mary   "Obituary"   Jun 8, 1899
    see Leckbee, Julia Anna Rhodes

Fricke, Frederick Sr.   "Fowler"   Jan 29, 1891
    Frederick Fricke Sr died January 29th. Age 74 yrs. Leaves a wife and
    5 children.

Frike, Mrs Anna   "Fowler"   Jan 27, 1904
    Died- Mrs Anna Frike an old resident of this place on January 9th.
    age 76 yrs. Leaves 2 sons, 3 daughters and 6 grandchildren and 1 great-
    grandchild. Husband and 6 children died several yrs ago.

Frike, Mrs Anna   "Local"   Jan 27, 1904
    Will of the late Mrs Anna Frike, of Fowler was filed for probate
    Saturday. Leaves her 2 sons, Fredercik G. and Thomas E. 2.00 each,
    her daughters 2000.00 each and a daughter-in-law 200.00.
    Daughters Mrs Dorothy Hubert and Celia J. Robinson named executrixes.
    "Whig"

Frike, Mr and Mrs Fred (Anna)   "Death"   Jan 9, 1890
    see Robertson, Anna

Frisbie, Miss   "Obituary"   Jan 12, 1887
    see Barker, Judge Ebenezer

Frisbie, Ann   "Obituary"   Jan 26, 1899
    see Chittenden, S.R.

Frisbie, Carleton   "Local"   Mar 15, 1905
    Died- Carleton Frisbie, youngest son of Mr and Mrs Joseph Frisbie Jr.
    Born June 14, 1904. Funeral at 3 P.M. Monday by Rev J.F. Bacon.

Frisbie, Mrs Caroline   "Obituary"   Mar 8, 1905
Funeral of Mrs Caroline Frisbie was at the home of Harry M. Frisbie
Sunday at 2:30 P.M. by Rev J.F. Bacon of the Cong'l church. Died March
1st. Was sick about 3 yrs. Son Harry and wife took care of her. Maiden
name was Caroline McMillen, born at Pleasant Unity, Westmoreland Co.
Penn. January 27, 1834. Came to Mendon at age 19 yrs to visit a brother
and met Morris Frisbie and they were married 1858. Had 2 sons, Lyman B.
of San Diego, Calif. and Harry M. of Mendon. Mr F. died May 13, 1901.
She lived with Harry since. Was a member of the Cong'l church of Mendon.
Present from abroad at funeral were- a niece Mrs James Machesney of
Goff, Penn, Mrs S.P. Bartlett and Mr and Mrs Wm Duncan of Quincy, Mr
and Mrs H.J. Vickers of Adams Ill., son Lyman B. did not arrive from
San Diego until Sunday A.M.

Frisbie, Mrs Caroline   "Local: Mar 1, 1905
Mrs Caroline Frisbie has lain unconscious for the past 36 hrs.
Later; She died at 11:30 Wednesday A.M.

Frisbie, Caroline B.   "Obituary"
see Chittenden, S.R.   Jan 26, 1899

Frisbie, Flora May   "Local"   Jan 11, 1894
Died- Flora May, daughter of Mr and Mrs Joseph Frisbie Jr. died
Tuesday A.M. January 9th. Age 2 yrs 7 mo's. Buried in Mendon cemetery
Wednesday P.M.

Frisbie, Mrs H.M.   "Death"
see Duncan, Ferdinand M.   Jan 24, 1901

Frisbie, Mrs H.M.   "death"
see Metcalf, Mrs Sarah   Jan 22, 1903

Frisbie, Harry   "Fatal Shooting"   Oct 17, 1895
Mr and Mrs J.B. Frisbie rec'd a telegram from Rockford Sunday that
their little grandson Harry had been accidently shot and killed the
day before at the home of Mrs Clarence Bean, on S. Main St. Harry was
the son of Will Frisbie, a well known farmer. He was 11 yrs old. He
and a friend, Arthur Bean were playing with the gun and a sword. He was
Will Frisbie's 2nd youngest son.

Frisbie, Harry   "Obituary"
see Barker, Judge Ebenezer   Jan 12, 1887

Frisbie, J.B.   "Death"
see Rea, Mrs Emeline Frisbie   Feb 22, 1905

Frisbie, Mr and Mrs J.B. Jr.   "Local"   Nov 23, 1899
Died- the youngest child of Mr and Mrs J.B. Frisbie Jr.

Frisbie, James G.   "Obituary"
see Frisbie, Sarah A. (Lay)   Nov 2, 1904

Frisbie, Mr and Mrs Jos.   "Death"   Apr 30, 1885
   see Rohr, Mrs Dr

Frisbie, Joseph B.   "Obituary"   Jun 8, 1903
   see Chittenden, Mrs Caroline Frisbie

Frisbie, Joseph Jr.   "Obituary"   Jan 12, 1887
   see Barker, Judge Ebenezer

Frisbie, Mrs L.B.   "Obituary"   May 2, 1901
   see Reese, Frederick

Frisbie, Lyman   "Obituary"   Jan 26, 1899
   see Chittenden, S.R.

Frisbie, Lyman   "Obituary"   Jan 12, 1887
   see Barker, Judge Ebenezer

Frisbie, Mrs Lyman   "Death"   Oct 29, 1891
   see Parker, Rev Henry

Frisbie, Mr and Mrs Lyman   "Local"   Feb 16, 1887
News has been rec'd of the death from pneumonia, of Mr and Mrs Lyman
Frisbie's little girl, at the age of 5 mo's 22 days on Feb 10th in
San Diego, Calif.

Frisbie, Mrs M.E.   "Death"   Sep 20, 1888
   see Wigans, Mrs C.

Frisbie, Morris E.   "Dead"   May 16, 1901
Died- pioneer resident of Mendon twp, Morris E. Frisbie at his home
2 miles west of Mendon Monday May 13th about 1 P.M. 71 yrs old. Lived
in Mendon 64 yrs. Born Branford, Conn January 31, 1830. Came west with
parents, brothers and sisters at age 7 yrs. Coming overland to
Wheeling, then down the Ohio and up the Mississippi to Quincy. Married
1858 to Caroline McMillen who with his 2 sons survive him. Lyman B.
of San Diego, Calif and Harry M. of Mendon. He was next to youngest in a
family of 8 children, 2 of whom died in infancy. Of the surviving 6
children there are 2 brothers and 4 sisters. the eldest J.B. Frisbie Sr.
almost 82 yrs old and the youngest Mrs Elizabeth P. Chittenden age
69 yrs. others are Mrs Caroline B. Chittenden Mrs Emeline F. Rea of
St Louis, Mo. and Mrs Mary A. Barker of Brooklyn, N.Y. Funeral today
at 2 from the house 2 miles west of town.

Frisbie, Morris E.   "Probate Notice"   Sep 26, 1901
   1st Monday of November 1901   Harry M. Frisbie, Adm.

Frisbie, Roger G.   "Local"   Nov 23, 1899
Died- Roger G. Frisbie, infant son of J.B. and Myrta Frisbie Sunday
A.M. November 19th. Buried the following day. Death caused by whooping
cough. Born July 7, 1898.

Frisbie, Mr S.   Mar 23, 1877
    Mr S. Frisbie mentioned in history of Mendon, death given as May 7, 1868

Frisbie, Sarah A. (Lay)   "Died"   Nov 2, 1904
    Sarah A. Lay Frisbie born in Branford, Conn Jan 29, 1823 and died at her
    home in Mendon Illinois October 24th. She was 81 yrs 8 mo's 28 days old.
    Married Joseph B. Frisbie May 5, 1845 and came west next month and
    settled in Mendon where she lived since except 4 yrs spent in Rockford,
    Illinois for the purpose of educating her children. Leaves husband and
    5 children, Louise, Willoughby L., Mary P., Joseph B. jr. and James G.
    12 grandchildren and 1 gr grandchild, 1 sister, Mrs Cornelia Parker of
    New Haven, Conn. She was the daughter of Dr Willoughby Lynde Lay. Comes
    from pure english ancestry settling in New England in Colonoal times.
    Buried Mendon cemetery.
    In the rest of this item it lists other relatives on both sided of the
    family back as far as 1346   A must to see!

Frisbie, Mr Wm   "Local"   Dec 23, 1885
    News of the death of Mr Wm Frisbie in New Orleans. He was agent of the
    Mississippi transportation Co. Mr F.'s father was a cousin of our towns-
    men Joseph and Morris Frisbie. On the death of Wm's father he was taken
    and raised by Mr and Mrs Rea of St Louis.

Frost, Mrs Dinah   "Paloma"   May 4, 1899
    Died- Mrs Dinah Frost at her home N. of Paloma last Wednesday eve.
    She was 84 yrs old. Had lived near Paloma for many yrs with her son
    Worthy. Services by Rev Mr Coates of Macomb at the Free Will Methodist
    church. Buried in Family cemetery.

Frost, Mrs Kate   "Funeral"   May 24, 1884
    see Worman, Moses G.

Frost, Mrs Tenie   "Obituary"   Mar 16, 1904
    see Thayer, Charles

Frost, Mrs Tenie   "Obituary"   Oct 29, 1903
    see Tomlinson, Alice Jane

Frost, Mr Worthy   "Local"   Jun 2, 1886
    Died- Saturday May 29th at his home near Fowler, Mr Worthy Frost,
    an old and well known settler in his 70th yr. Born in Athens Co. Ohio
    March 20, 1817 and came to Illinois in 1835. Leaves a wife and 4
    children. Buried in Stahl cemetery Monday. Services by Rev Howard
    Miller of the M.E. church of Mendon.

Fry, Jacob J.   Feb 20, 1879
    In Memorium- our friend and neighbor, Jacob J. Fry.
    J.J. Fry born Pike Co. Mo. Feb 17, 1844. He enlisted in the 78th Reg.
    Co. D. in 1864 at Quincy and was wounded at Jonesborough, Ga. losing
    1 leg, was discharged May 3, 1865. Married Caroline Seward March 17, 1869
    Services by Rev Tanner. He was 35 yrs old, died from dropsy Feb 8, 1879
    Leaves a widow and 3 children. Buried at Loraine Sunday Feb 9th at 4 P.M.

Frye, Charles J.   "Obituary"   May 18, 1904
Deid, Charles J. son of J.J. and Caroline Frye. Born Loraine, Illinois
Feb 19, 1875 and died May 16, 1904 age 27 yrs 2 mo's 26 days. Leaves
mother and 10 sisters, Mrs Albert Murphy of Quincy and Miss Minnie
of Loraine. Funeral at the house 3 P.M. Tuesday by Rev C.S. Bunghman and
buried in Loraine cemetery.

Fryer, John   "Payson"   Jun 4, 1880
A child of John Fryer, of Craigtown was buried on the 27th of last
month. Age 10 months.

Fulmer, Mr F.L.   "West Point"   Apr 14, 1881
Mr F. L. Fulmer rec'd word of his father's death at Sheboyan, Wisc.

Fulton, Mrs Wm   "Obituary"   Feb 27, 1890
see Mann, Isabella

Funk, Mrs   "Local"   May 21, 1891
Louis A. Rupp and one of his men came up and put a handsome monument
in the west addition to the cemetery to the memory of the late Mrs Funk.

Funk, Elizabeth   "Obituary"   Sep 1, 1892
see Daugherty, Michael

Funk, Mrs George   "Obituary"   Feb 28, 1889
see Furry, Henry

Funk, Mrs J.   "Death"   Apr 14, 1881
see Ammerman, Mrs

Funk, Mr and Mrs Jacob   "Obituary"   Mar 24, 1886
see McClelland, Mrs Susie

Funk, Samuel   "Local"   Oct 18, 1894
Died- Mr Samuel Funk at Jacksonville Monday eve in his 83rd yr. He
was a resident of this twp over 40 yrs. Born June 1812 in Westmoreland
Co. Penn. and came to Mendon twp in 1853. Married in 1837 to Mrs
Susan Staffey (nee Dobler). They had 2 children, a daughter who died
in infancy and 1 son Mr Jacob Funk who is living on the old homestead.
Mrs F. died nearly 4 yrs ago. Buried in Mendon cemetery after services
in the M.E. church at Mendon by Rev Wm Burgess in the absence of the
pastor. Buried beside his wife.

Funk, Samuel   "Probate Notice"   Nov 15, 1894
1st Monday of January 1895   Jacob Funk, Adm.

Funk, Susan (nee Dobler)   "Died"   Jan 8, 1891
Susan (Dobler) Funk was born June 18, 1815 in Lancaster Penn. Married
in Westmoreland Co. Penn to Samuel Funk in spring of 1853. The 2 with
their son Jacob moved to Illinois. They lived S.W. of Mendon 4 miles.
Also had a daughter who died in infancy. Services from the M.E. church
in Mendon.

141

Furney, Mrs Mary   May 10, 1883
    Suicide- Mrs Mary Furney of Liberty twp on May 2nd. Wife of Lewis
    Furney. She cut her throat in the barn. Leaves a husband and 3 children.

Furry, Catherine   "Obituary"   Jan 30, 1902
    Catherine Furry, born Westmoreland Co. Penn August 8, 1829 died at her
    home in Knox City, Mo. January 27th. Married Jesse Dick October 25, 1852
    had 7 children. Husband and 2 children died before her. Leaves 5 children
    2 brothers. Services held ar her home in Knox City, Mo. and remains
    were placed on the train to be conveyed here. Remains reached here
    Tuesday eve and buried beside her husband in Mendon Cemetery. Mr and Mrs
    Dick were residentes here many yrs, living 1½ miles S.W. of Mendon. From
    here they moved to Liberty, this Co. and then to Knox City, Mo. where
    several of their children still reside.

Furry, Cora   Dec 7, 1877
    Died Sunday eve last, Cora, daughter of David and Mary Furry. Age
    7 yrs.

Furry, David   Feb 12, 1891
    David Furry died at his home in Quincy Feb 8th. Buried Mendon from the
    M.E. church by Rev Mr Wheat of the Trinity M.E. church. He was born
    Westmoreland Co. Penn July 19, 1831. Came to Adams Co. Ill in 1851 or
    52. Married twice. 1st wife no name, he had 3 children 1 died in infancy
    Charles died early manhood and Mrs Edward Sproat of Emmett, Calif, daugh-
    ter   2nd wife was Miss Mary Asher who he married on September 15, 1869
    they had 9 children. No names.

Furry, Mr and Mrs David   "Obituary"   Feb 28, 1901
    see Sproat, Edward

Furry, Elizabeth   "Obituary"   Feb 28, 1901
    see Sproat, Edward

Furry, Mrs Georgia A.   "Local"   May 4, 1893
    The remains of Georgia A. Furry, widow of the late Louis M. Furry who
    died in Texas 5 yrs ago was brought to Quincy Friday eve for burial. She
    died at Jacksonville the day before. Age 41 yrs. Body accompanied by her
    sister and husband. Mrs F. (nee Wilcox) was a former resident of this twp.

Furry, Henry   "Obituary"   Feb 28, 1889
    Died- Mr Henry Furry on Friday Feb 22nd at noon. Was 55 yrs and 6 days
    old. Funeral was Sunday at the house by Rev Thomas pastor of the
    Lutheran church. Buried in Mendon cemetery. Born Westmoreland Co. Penn
    Feb 16, 1834 Came to Illinois with his parents in "51" being the 4th born
    of 8 children, 4 brothers and an only sister survive him, Leonard, living
    in California, Mrs Jesse Dick of Liberty, Adams Co., David living here,
    Isaac and Jesse in Missouri. John died in California about 2 yrs ago
    and Lewis in Texas. Married Miss Susan Wright January 1856, they had
    7 children 4 girls and 3 boys. all living. 3 boys and 1 girl still at home
    3 married daughters, Mrs Jas. Dougherty, Mrs Geo. Dougherty and Mrs
    Geo. Funk.

Furry, Jesse   Aug 4, 1881
    Died, little son of Jesse Fury last Friday July 29th

Furry, John   "Local"   Mar 23, 1887
    "From Stockton, California Daily Independent"
    Died in Modesto March 13th John Furry, a native of Penn. (A brother
    of David and Henry Furry) Age 50 yrs 8 mo's 4 days.

Furry, Katherine   "Obituary"   Jan 31, 1901
    see Dick, Jesse

Furry, Mr Isaac   "Star"   Sep 24, 1885
    Mr Isaac Furry of Carrollton, Mo. was here to attend the funeral of
    his brother, Lewis who died at Marshall, Texas.

Furry, Lewis   "News"   Sep 24, 1885
    News reached Mendon on September 17 of the death of Mr Lewis Furry
    at Marshall, Texas. Remains were brought to Quincy and funeral took place
    at family home at 1414 State St. He died from typhoid fever. Leaves a
    wife, the daughter of George W. Wilcox of Quincy, 6 brothers, Henry,
    and David of Mendon, Isaac and Jesse of Missouri, Leonard and John of
    California and 1 sister, Mrs Jesse Dick of Liberty.

Furry, Mary   "Probate Notice"   Mar 6, 1879
    3rd Monday of May 1879 David and Henry Furry Adms.

Furry, Mrs Mary   "Obituary"   Feb 27, 1879
    Mrs Mary Furry was born in Lancaster Co. Penn November 1805 and died
    Feb 22nd 1879 at age 73 yrs 2 mo's 22 days. Married David Furry Sr. in
    Mt Pleasant, Westmoreland Co. Penn. Mr Furry died about 6 yrs ago.
    She was mother of 9 children, 8 still living. Member of U.B. church for
    30 yrs or more. Services by Rev V.C. Randolph at her home on Feb 25th

                                                     Feb 27, 1879
    Died- at her residence near Mendon, Illinois Saturday Feb 22nd, Mrs
    Mary Furry, age 73 yrs 2 mo's 22 days.

Furry, Mrs Mary   "death"   Mar 22, 1905
    see Wood, Mrs Sarah

Furry, Miss Phoebe E.   "Death"   Feb 1, 1905
    see Daugherty, Mrs Phoebe E.

Fusselman, Mr and Mrs C.B.   "Life and Death"   Jun 13, 1889
    Born Tuesday night of last week, a son to Mr and Mrs C.B. Fusselman of
    Honey Creek and on Thursday their 22 month old boy drowned in the
    creek nearby. Buried in Mendon cemetery.

Gahan, Mr   "Local"   Jun 27, 1895
    A man named Gahan, an inmate of the poor house either fell or was
    thrown out a window and killed last week.

Gallaher, Mr James   "Local"   Mar 22, 1894
    Died- Mr James Gallaher, librarian of the Quincy library died last
    Thursday A.M. Funeral on Sunday P.M. at the Vermont Baptist church and
    buried at the Woodlawn cemetery with Masonic rites.

Gallimore, Mrs Tillie   "Death"   Aug 23, 1905
    see Lynum, Clyde

Galloway, Mrs Nancy   "Death in Adams Co."   Feb 16, 1899
    Died- Mrs Nancy Galloway at the home of her son in law and daughter,
    Mr and Mrs S. Brown in Concord twp Monday A.M. Feb 6th. Was 83 yrs old.

Gardner, Mrs Julia   "Local"   Mar 30, 1893
    Remains of Mrs Julia Gardner of Quincy, youngest daughter of Mr and Mrs
    Nehemiah Wright of Marion Co. Missouri (Formerly of Mendon) was
    brought here for burial Tuesday P.M. Services at the Cong'l church.
    Died from consumption. 17 yrs old. Mrs Wright and son Wallace
    accompanied the body.

Garmer, Mrs B.F.   "Obituary"   Mar 16, 1903
    see Johnson, George W.

Garmer, Mrs Ben   "Petition"   May 18, 1904
    see Moore, Annice S. Petition #1689

Garner, Luetta   Aug 21, 1890
    August 13 Miss Luetta Garner died of cholera morbus at the home of
    her grandparents, Mr and Mrs Wm and Susan Seals of Big Neck. She was
    eldest daughter of James and Manda Garner of Quincy. Age 23 yrs 7 mo's
    26 days. Services by Elder H.W. Strickler.

Garner, Mr Wm   "West Point"   Dec 21, 1893
    Died- Mr Wm Garner this afternoon at his son's home, Mr Fletcher
    Garner of Quincy. His son Geo. Garner of Red Cloud, Nebr and his daughter,
    Mrs Walker were called by the his illness. Leaves a wife and 5 children.

Garner, Mr Wm   "West Point"   Dec 28, 1893
    Died- in our community, Mr Wm Garner. Born Clark Co. December 2, 1815
    Died December 16, 1893. Age 78 yrs 14 days. Leaves a wife and 5 children,
    4 sons and 1 daughter. Services Monday at 11 A.M. at the M.E. church
    of which he was a member. Buried in West Point cemetery.

Garnett, Frederic   "Obituary"   Mar 6, 1902
    see Guthrie, Margaret Susan

Garnett, Joseph   "Obituary"   Mar 6, 1902
    see Guthrie, Margaret Susan

Garnett, Sarah   "Obituary"   Mar 6, 1902
    see Guthrie, Margaret Susan

Garnett, William H.   "Obituary"   Mar 6, 1902
     see Guthrie, Margaret Susan

Garrett, Mrs Alvin   "Camp Point"   Jan 10, 1901
     Died- Mrs Alvin Garrett died at her home east of town Wednesday at 11
     A.M.. Funeral at the house on Friday at 2 P.M. by Orrin Dilley. Buried
     in our village cemetery. Leaves husband , 2 grown daughters and a
     little son 4 yrs old.

Garrett, Arthur and wife   "Funeral"   Sep 11, 1902
     see Fowler, Mrs J.

Garrett, Ben   "Quincy Items"   Dec 9, 1880
     Ben Garrett was killed December 4th. Was run over by a locomotive.
     Leaves wife and 1 child.

Garrett, Bert   "Local"   Feb 2, 1888
     Bert Garrett died last night.

Garrett, C.B.   "Petition # 1689"   May 18, 1904
     see Moore, Annice S.

Garrett, Mrs C.B.   "Obituary"   Sep 11, 1902
     see Fowler, Mrs Jeanette

Garrett, Frances A.   Petition #1689   May 18, 1904
     see Moore, Annice S.

Garrett, Herbert C. (Bert)   "Obituary"   Feb 9, 1888
     Herbert C. Garrett, 2nd son of Mr and Mrs C.B. Garrett of this place
     came home from Moody junction a few miles below Quincy Saturday Jan 21st
     suffering from pneumonia and was buried in Mendon cemetery 2 weeks later.
     (Known as Bert) Bert died on Thursday Morning Feb 2nd at 5 A.M. and
     buried Saturday A.M. in Mendon cemetery. Burial held up for arrival of
     elder brother Arthur to arrive from Kansas. He was 21 yrs 8 mo's 29 days
     old. Services by Rev S.D. Peet.

Garrity, Maggie   "Local"   Mar 17, 1886
     Died- on Sunday afternoon of consumption, Maggie, only daughter of
     Mr and Mrs Jas. Garrity. Age 19 yrs 4 mo's 22 days. Services at the house
     by Rev E.W. Souders. Buried in the Stone church burying ground, north
     of Ursa.

Gates, Mrs Lucy Tanner   "Local"   Jun 23, 1886
     Died- Mrs Lucy Tanner Gates, wife of our station agent, Mr A.L. Gates
     at the age of 25 yrs. Services held at her home by Rev E.W. Souders.
     Buried in Basco, her former home.

Gaushell, Mr Frank   "Local"   May 9, 1889
     Died- Mr Frank Gaushell, for nearly 15 yrs connected with the Quincy
     News and the last 1½ yrs editor and publisher died at San Antonio, Texas
     on Monday A.M. of consumption. his mother tried to join him before his
     death, but did not arrive in time. Buried Quincy.

Gay, Mr and Mrs Arthur   "Camp Point"   May 24, 1900
    Died- the 7 yr old son of Mr and Mrs Arthur Gay Monday night of
    diabetes.

Gay, Chas.   "Funeral"   Apr 4, 1895
    see Strickler, Clark

Gay, Mrs Charles   "Local"   May 24, 1900
    Died- Mrs Charles Gay of Camp Point yesterday.

Gay, Mrs Charles V.   "Camp Point"   May 31, 1900
    The funeral of Mrs Charles V. Gay was last Thursday afternoon. She was
    the mother of Arthur Gay, whose son was buried the day before. Services
    by Rec Laycox.

Gay, Rex   "Camp Point"   May 31, 1900
    The funeral of Mr and Mrs Arthur Gay's little son, Rex was last
    Wednesday. He was 8 yrs old and their only child.

Gay, Rex   "Local"   May 24, 1900
    W.G. Gay, our banker, attended the funeral of Rex, son of Mr and Mrs
    Arthur Gay, at Camp Point yesterday.

Gebert,
    see Geibert

Gebert, Mr John   "York Neck"   Feb 10, 1898
    Mrs Etta Gebert will have a public sale Feb 17th. She is Adm. for
    John Gebert, deceased.

Gehring, Mrs John   "Quincy"   Apr 20, 1899
    Died- Mrs John Gehring, Wednesday April 12th. Was 76 yrs old. Leaves
    husband, 2 daughters and 1 son.

Geibert,
    See Gebert

Geibert, Clarence Albert   "Obituary"   Mar 16, 1904
    Clarence Albert Geibert, son of Mrs D.E. Geibert, born September 3, 1895
    died March 8th. Age 8 yrs 6 mo's 5 days. His father died more than 6 yrs
    ago. Leaves his mother. Funeral at the M.E. church at Coatsburg Wednesday
    March 9th by Rev C.S. Baughman of Loraine. This leaves Mrs G. alone.

Geibert, John   "Obituary"   Jan 20, 1898
    Died- of typhoid fever Sunday January 17th, Mr John Geibert. Was sick
    14 weeks. Born October 15, 1866. Was 31 yrs 3 mo's 1 day old. Married
    Miss Etta Turner October 3, 1894. They had 1 son, Clarence. Leaves a
    wife, 1 son, father, 4 brothers and 5 sisters.

Geibert, Mrs L.E.   "Local"   Mar 9, 1904
    The son of Mrs L.E. Geibert living about 5 miles N.E. of Mendon died
    of consumption Monday eve.

146

Geise, Henry A.   "Quincy"   Dec 9, 1880
    Died- Mr Henry A. Geise on December 6th. He was a well known citizen
    of Quincy.

George, Anderson   "Payson"   Oct 13, 1886
    Funeral of Anderson George was preached yesterday at the Cong'l church
    by Rev Alliban. Mr George died of consumption in his 35th yr. Buried
    in Barry.

George, Harry   "Died"   Feb 20, 1879
    Died, the youngest child of Mr Harry George last week.

George, Henry   "Died"   Apr 5, 1883
    The body of Henry George was brought to Mendon by train on April 3rd
    accompanied by his daughter, Mrs Wilson of Greensburg, Penn and Rev
    King of Lomax and Mr Morehead of Mt Pleasant, Iowa He was born in
    Westmoreland Co. Penn April 2, 1805 and died at the home of his son in law
    Mr Morehead April 2nd. He came to Adams Co. in 1865. Buried Fowler.

Gerard, Sam   "Death"   Mar 21, 1895
    see "Old Lady Patterson"

Gerber, Mrs Joseph   "Death"   Mar 2, 1899
    see Schauf, Henry

Gerhardt, Mrs George   "Loraine"   Dec 18, 1890
    Mrs George Gerhardt died December 12th and was buried in Tioga. She
    lived a few miles northwest of Loraine. Leaves a husband and an infant.

Gerhart, Charles and wife   "Loraine"   Dec 27, 1894
    Died- the small infant son of Mr and Mrs Charles Gerhart Sunday. At birth
    it weighed 1½ pounds. It was 3 months old and weighed 4 pounds at death.
    Buried in our cemetery yesterday.

Gerhart, Charley and Addie   "White Oak Ridge"   Dec 27, 1894
    Died- Mary, youngest child of Charley and Addie Gerhart Sunday at
    3 A.M. Age 4 months. Buried at Loraine cemetery.

Gerisch, Dr and Mrs W.T.   "Local"   Apr 21, 1886
    In the absence of her parents, the little daughter of Dr and Mrs W.T.
    Gerisch of LaMars, Iowa got hold of some merphine pills and ate several
    of them. She died the following day. Was 2 yrs 5 months old.

Gibbs, Mrs A.   "Local"   Apr 26, 1900
    Mrs A. Gibbs left for Peoria, Ill to live with her grandaughter, Mrs
    C.H. Goldstein, nee Gertie Tibbett. Her husband is buried in Mendon
    cemetery.

Gibbs, Aaron   "Obituary"   Feb 5, 1885
    see Clark, Mary

Gibbs, Alex   "Death"   Mar 20, 1879
    see Thompson, Mary E.

147

Gibbs, Alex   "Obituary"   Oct 7, 1880
    see Shambaugh, Mrs Emma J.

Gibbs, Alexander   "Obituary"   May 19, 1898
    Died- Alexander Gibbs Friday night May 13th at the home of his son,
    Wm Gibbs in his 84th yr. Born December 1814 at Middletown, Adams Co.
    Penn. Married Sarah B. Bingamon March 16, 1845 at Cashtown, Penn.
    They had 5 children all but one son is buried in Mendon cemetery.
    Joined U.B. church at Mt Pleasant, Westmoreland Co. Penn 1854. Came to
    Mendon 1857 and joined the Lutheran church. Services by Rev Crews of
    the M.E. church at the Lutheran church Sunday afternoon. Buried village
    cemetery. Leaves wife and 1 son.

Gibbs, Mrs Anna E.   "Adm Sale"   Jun 17, 1880
    see Battell, Richard

Gibbs, Delbert A. "Bert"   "Killed"   Jan 14, 1905
    Delbert A. Gibbs, a Burlington Route switchman was run over and killed
    at 4 A.M. last Wednesday at Walton Heoghts, Quincy. He lost his balance
    and fell off of a coal car. Bert was unmarried, leaves a widowed mother,
    7 brothers and 1 sister. Would have been 36 yrs old next Feb. Lived with
    his mother, Mrs Annie Gibbs at 903 N. 4th Street. "Quincy Herald"

Gibbs, Mrs Elizabeth   "Death"   May 24, 1883
    see McGibbons, John

Gibbs, Mr Harry Coleman   Jul 22, 1882
    Died July 20th, Harry Coleman Gibbs, eldest son of W.H. and Lucinda
    Gibbs of this village. Age 13 yrs.

Gibbs, Ida May   "Edgings"   Aug 24, 1877
    Died- Sunday August 19,th Ida May Gibbs, 6th child of J.C. and E.J.
    Gibbs. Age 2 yrs 2 days. Services from the M.E. church on Monday August
    20th by Rev Randolph.

Gibbs, John   "Local"   Feb 5, 1885
    John Gibbs of Mendon, Mo. and his brother Swain Gibbs of Fall Creek
    are here for the funeral of their mother.

Gibbs, John B.   "Death"   Aug 21, 1884
    see Hobbs, Thomas

Gibbs, Swain   "Local"   Feb 5, 1885
    John Gibbs of Mendon Mo. and his brother Swain Gibbs of Fall Creek
    are here for the funeral of their mother.

Gibbs, Mrs Swain   "Local"   Mar 26, 1891
    Mrs Swain Gibbs of Fall Creek came to attend the funeral of her sister,
    Mrs Wm A. Poling, but arrived to late for it.

Gibbs, William E.   "Coatsburg"   Aug 22, 1889
    Died- Mr William E. Gibbs. He leaves a wife and 5 children, 1 brother
    C.M. Gibbs of here. Services by Rev King Friday morning at 10. Burial
    in our village cemetery.

148

Gibson, Charles S.   Heirs"   Apr 14, 1892
    see Wible, Sarah

Gibson, James   "Obituary"   Dec 24, 1891
    see Reynolds, Mr

Gibson, Mrs James   "Big Neck"   Nov 2, 1887
    Died- at her home in Big Neck on October 21st, Mrs James Gibson,
    age 38 yrs. Leaves husband and 7 children.

Gibson, Joseph   "Local"   Jan 3, 1901
    Joseph Gibson, of Big Neck died Friday night December 21st.

Gibson, Lizzie   "Obituary"   Dec 4, 1890
    see Woods, Mr and Mrs Leander

Gibson, Mrs Maria   "Obituary"   Jun 26, 1890
    see Wible, Andrew

Gibson, Mrs Maria   "Death"   May 31, 1888
    see Wible, Mrs John

Gibson, Maria D.   "Estate Suit"   Apr 14, 1892
    see Wible, Sarah

Gibson, Miss Mary   "Obituary"   Feb 9, 1893
    Died- Tuesday morning about 4 A.M. Miss Mary Gibson (McIntyre)
    Buried Mendon cemetery. She was youngest of 4 children 3 boys and 1 girl
    all of whom were born in Ulverston, Lancashire, England. The oldest John
    McIntyre was killed in battle near Grand Ecore on the banks of the
    Red River, Louisiana on April 9, 1864. The second died when young and is
    buried in the churchyard of Ulverston parish church, the father lies in
    Kirk Bradden cemetery Isle of Man, and the mother in Mendon cemetery
    where only daughter is to be buried. The writer of this is only
    survivor of the family. She was born March 4, 1833 (60 yrs old) Came to
    this country with the writer in the fall of 1876 and resided in Mendon
    since. Services at the Zion church at 10 A.M. according to the rites
    of Protestant Episcopal church by Rev Grantham, priest in charge.

Gibson, Mrs W.D.L.   "Obituary"   Jan 29, 1899
    see Edmonds, Mary

Gifford, Mr Edward A.   "Local"   Mar 10, 1886
    Death in California on the 3rd, Mr Edward A. Gifford. a one time
    conductor on the Carthage branch of the C.B.&Q. He went to California
    3 yrs ago in poor health.

Giffy, Aug.   "Ursa"   Jan 10, 1889
    Died- Dec 31, 1888 Aug Giffy, a mute drowned in a well. He lived
    with his brother in law, Mr August Berlin.

Gilasbie, Mrs James   "News"   Jul 16, 1885
    Mrs James Gilasbie of Payson died July 11th.

Gilasbie, Mrs James   "Local"   Jul 16, 1885
    Mrs James Gilasbie of Payson died last Saturday.

Gilbert, Mrs M.M.   "death"   Jul 16, 1885
    see Hudnall, Mrs W.T.

Gill, Mrs Stella   "Obituary"   Jul 13, 1899
    see Worman, Mrs Mary

Gillett, Mr Eli   "York Neck"   Mar 8, 1894
    Thos. Beer went to Augusta Wednesday to attend the funeral of Mr
    Eli Gillett, an old comrade of the 78th Ill. Reg. who died of heart
    disease. He was a member of A.O.U.W. and the G.A.R. Buried by G.A.R.

Gilliland, Mrs Dr   "Obituary"   Apr 20, 1899
    see Myers, Mrs Anna Tinsman

Gilliland, Mrs Caroline   "death"   Jul 5, 1905
    see Smith, Hamilton

Gilliland, Mrs Mary   "Death"   Jul 5, 1905
    see Smith, Hamilton

Gilliland, Mildred   "Obituary"   Jun 18, 1891
    see Lieghty, Mrs John

Gilliland, Mildred Ann   "Obituary"   Jul 6, 1899
    see Leighty, John

Gilliland, Thomas   "Local"   Sep 28, 1904
    Two funerals Sunday in Mendon in the A.M. Thomas Gilliland nearly
    21 yrs old and John R. Chittenden in the prime of life in the P.M.

Gilliland, Thomas Bayard   "Death"   Sep 28, 1904
    Funeral of Thomas Bayard Gilliland, son of Thomas J. and Mary E.
    Gilliland was held at the Lutheran church Sunday at 10 A.M. by pastor
    Rev A.M. Reitzel. He was born December 21, 1883 and died Sept 22, 1904
    Leaves father, mother, 4 brothers and 4 sisters.

Gilliland, Dr W.E.   Feb 17, 1881
    Died, a son of Dr W.E. Gilliland last week in Pueblo, Colorado.

Gilliland, Mrs W.P.   "Local"   Sep 4, 1890
    Mrs Gilliland the aged partner of Squire W.P. Gilliland died Sept 2nd.
    Was buried in the family burying ground.

Gilliland, Mrs W.P.   Sep 11, 1890
    Letitia Curry was born December 20, 1808 in Shelby Co. Ky. and married
    W.P. Gilliland March 9, 1827. Died September 3rd. They had 5 sons and
    4 daughters. Eldest son is 62 yrs old. Buried in family burying ground.

Gilliland, Wm P.   "Probate Notice"   Oct 3, 1901
    1st Monday of December 1901   William E. Gilliland, Adm.

150

Gilmer,Mr and Mrs B.   "Funeral"   Nov 5, 1885
    see Stewart. Mr V.V.

Gilmer, Ben   "death"   Dec 23, 1897
    see Colwell, Wm P.

Gilmer, Mr Ben   "Death"   Mar 1, 1894
    see Caldwell, Margaet A. or Calwell

Gilmer, Benjamin   "Died"   Jan 11, 1905
    Benjamin Gilmer was found dead in bed Monday A.M. after retiring in
    usual health. Coroner verdict of cause was heart failure night of
    January 8th Born Alleghany Co. Penn. September 22, 1825 died Mendon
    Illinois January 9th 1905. Was 79 yrs 3 mo's 17 days old. Came to Adams
    Co November 1847. Married Miss Leah D. Wilhelm October 1848 had 6
    children, Frederick A. died a few yrs ago, others are W.H. of Mendon,
    Mrs J.M. Andrew of Denver Colo., Mrs Eva Stewart of Shreveport. La.
    Frank of Pueblo, Colo and Miss Ella of Mendon. For nearly a ½ century
    Mr Gilmer was in the horse-shoeing and blacksmithing business. Services
    at the Lutheran church Wednesday by Rev A.M. Reitzel. Buried Mendon
    cemetery. Wife also survives him.

Gilmer, Benjamin   "Probate Notice"   Feb 1, 1905
    1st Monday of April 1905   B.A. Van Dyke, Adm.

Gilmer, Charles M.   Dec 14, 1899
    Judge Epler appoints W.H. Bennett as Adm. for the estate of M. Gilmer.

Gilmer, Mrs Frank   "Local"   Mar 22, 1894
    News reached us of the death of Frank Gilmer's wife at her home in
    Denver, Col. Saturday A.M. Leaves a baby son only a few days old and
    her husband. Buried at Grand Pass, Mo.

Gilmer, Mr Frederick A.   "Local"   Dec 2, 1897
    Died- Tuesday at 6 A.M. Mr Frederick A. Gilmer of acute pneumonia
    brought on by exposure. Was 2nd son of Benjamin and Leah Gilmer. Born
    August 6, 1851. Never married. Was a member of McFarland and Gilmer
    butchers and Grocers in Mendon many yrs. Was a J.P. and a police
    magistrate mant yrs. Leaves his aged parents, 2 brothers, Wm of here and
    Frank of Springfield, Mo., 3 sisters, Mrs J.M. Andrew of Denver, Colo.,
    Mrs Vinet Stewart of Sulphyr Springs, Ark and Ella who lives at home.
    Funeral in charge of Masonic lodge and buried in village cemetery.

Gilmer, Frederick A.   "Probate Notice"   Dec 9, 1897
    1st Monday of Feb. 1898   Benjamin Gilmer, Adm.

Gilmer, John T.   "Jottings by Hundes"   Sept 22, 1881
    John T. Gilmer was a virginian , lived there 20 yrs and then 20 yrs on
    Georgia, 20 in Kentucky and 22 in Adams Co. Ill. He died at his
    daughters, Mrs Wilson. John T. Gilmer Jr. died in peace.

Gilmer, Mrs Mary   Jun 30, 1898
    Died- Grandma Gilmer, Mendon's oldest inhabitant Saturday at 2 P.M.
    of old age. Was 96 yrs 24 days old. Mary Stone was born near Morgantown,
    Virginia June 1, 1802 and died June 25th 1898. She was one of 12 children
    born to Rev William and Margaret Augustine Stone. Marreid in 1823 to
    Benjamin Gilmer and came to Mendon in 1850 with her husband. They had
    6 children, William deceased, Benjamin, living in Mendon, Sarah who died
    in infancy, Margaret Colwell, deceased, Chanty Barclay of Novelty, Mo.
    and Rhoda Wible, deceased. 25 grandchildren 15 of whom are living. 39
    gr grandchildren, 32 of whom are living. She was a member of the Methodist
    church in Mendon. She and her husband would ride miles on horseback
    with their children in Penn. to attend church. Mr Gilmer died May 17, 1864
    Her father Rev Stone was one of the ones who held the famous Campbell
    Stone debate. Services Sunday A.M. at the M.E.church by Rev E.K. Crews.
    Buried in the village cemetery.

Gilmer, Miss Mary   "Obituary"   Feb 6, 1902
    see Seger. Charles E.

Gilmer, Mrs Wm   "Death"   Oct 17, 1895
    see Curless, Mrs Millard

Girard, Mrs   "West Point"   May 18, 1893
    Misses Maggie Cavanaugh and Ethel Gordon attended the funeral of
    Mrs Girard at Basco one day last week.

Glance, Miss Effie   "Suicide"   Jun 21, 1905
    see Pyles, Josh

Glance, Wm   "Tioga"   Aug 31, 1887
    Died- August 23rd at 4 A.M. Mr Wm Glance in his 32nd yr. Born Kentucky
    July 17, 1855. Came to Illinois with his parents in 1859 and settled
    in Lima twp where the continued to live. Leaves a wife, 3 children, a
    father, several brothers and sisters. Services on Wednesday August 24th
    by Rev Crooks and Kerns. Mr C.speaking in English and Rev K. in German.

Glaser, Henry   "Death in Adams Co. Quincy"   Mar 16, 1899
    Died- Mr Henry Glaser Friday A.M. Was born Germany and lived Quincy
    since 1852. Leaves 3 sons and 1 daughter.

Glay, Henry   "Local"   Jun 15, 1893
    Died- Mr Henry Glay, tenant on Mr P. Quigs farm died at his mothers home
    near Fowler Monday night. Buried yesterday P.M. in the Fowler cemetery.
    Leaves a widow and infant child.

Glazier, Mrs   "Fowler"   Apr 24, 1902
    Several from here attended the funeral of Mrs Glazier near Cliola
    Sunday.

Glenn, Mrs   "Funeral"   Mar 29, 1900
    see Gooding, Edward

Glenn, Mrs Ella   "Death"   Apr 5, 1900
    see Gooding, Mr and Mrs D.W.

Gnuse, Mr   "Marcelline"   Mar 16, 1904
Fred Holtman and son August attended the funeral of Mr Gnuse in Quincy.

Gnuse, Mrs   "Ursa"   May 24, 1894
Mrs Gnuse who lived 2 miles south of Ursa was buried in Quincy last
Friday.

Gnuse, August   "Ursa   Nov 17, 1898
Died- Mr August Gnuse died yesterday at his home south of here with
typhoid fever.

Goebel, Anna C.   "Obituary"   May 12, 1898
see Steiner, Mrs Anna C.

Goetz, Mrs Jessie   "Death"   Dec 14, 1904
see Morgan, Joseph L.

Gohrman, John   "Burton"   Mar 6, 1879
Mr John Gohrman, member of A.F.& A.M. died at Liberty, Illinois.
Buried near there on Feb 25th by members of the order.

Golden, Mrs Elizabeth   "Local"   Aug 21, 1890
Died- Mrs Elizabeth Golden wife of the late J.W. Golden in her 71st yr
at Derry, Oregon. Buried beside her husband in Seward, Nebr. Leaves
1 daughter, Mrs Jacob Rust and a son John Golden. They formerly lived
in Mt Hebron district 6 miles N.W. of Mendon.

Golden, Mrs J.W.   Sep 4, 1890
Mrs J.W. Golden of Staplehurst, Nebr. formerly of Mendon died. Sister
Golden died in Derry Oregon August 16th. Was 70 yrs 1 mo 4 days old. Born
in Bourbon Co. Ky. July 11, 1820 Moved with parents to McDonough Co. Ill.
where she married Brother J.W. Golden in Sept 1840. They had 3 sons and
8 daughters. Moved to Nebraska in 1882. Husband died 2 yrs ago. Buried
in Seward Nebr. beside her husband.

Golden, J. W. Sr.   "Obituary"   Sep 6, 1888
Died- J.W. Golden Sr. of Staplehurst, Nebr. Sunday August 26th, 1888
Born Pendleton Co. Ky. March 20, 1819. Came to this Co with his father
in 1837. Lived for a time near Columbus and moved to Mendon twp where he
lived during the winter of "37 anf "38". He then moved to Marcelline in
March of "38" married Sept 1840 to Elizabeth StClair of McDonough Co.
They had 11 children 8 daughters and 3 sons all but 2 survive him.
They moved to Mendon twp in 1844 where he lived till Feb 1883 when
he moved to Staplehurst, Nebr. Leaves a wife and 9 children. Services on
the 27th at 9 A.M. by Elder T.J. Burton of the Christian church of which
he was a member for more than 20 yrs.

Golden, Mrs Stephen   "Local"   Jan 18, 1900
Died- The wife of Mr Stephen Golden of Marcelline yesterday morning.
Will be buried Thursday P.M. in the Keith graveyard.

Golden, Stephen   "Marcelline"   Dec 4, 1902
Mr Stephen Golden was buried at Keith graveyard Thursday.

Golden, Stephen M.   "Local"   Dec 4, 1902
    Stephen M. Golden, age 71 yrs, one of the pioneers of Adams Co. died
    at Jacksonville Wednesday November 26th and was buried in Keilh graveyard
    near Marcelline on Thanksgiving day. Was taken to the asylum 2 weeks ago.
    Wife died 3 yrs ago and since that time his nephew, Harry StClair and
    family have been living with him.

Golden, Mrs Thankful   "Paloma"   Apr 26, 1894
    Died- suddenly at the home of her daughter, Mrs Lucy Cambell in Quincy,
    Illinois. Mrs Thanful Golden, nee whitney died at the age of 85 yrs. Was
    brought here for burial. Services by Rev A.A. White at the F.W.B. church
    Buried in Gooding cemetery.

Goodapple, Mrs Geo.   "Quincy"   Mar 23, 1899
    Died- Mrs Geo. Goodapple in going down the stairs at her daughter's,
    Mrs Louise Lambur she fell down the stairs hitting her head and was
    killed. Age 77 yrs. Born Germany. Lived Quincy 50 yrs. Leaves husband
    in very poor health.

Gooding, Miss   "death"   Apr 21, 1886
    see Campbell, Mrs

Gooding, Mr D.W.   "News"   Jun 4, 1880
    Mr D.W. Gooding an old citizen of Honey Creek twp died at his home near
    Paloma Wednesday of last week from pneumonia.

Gooding, Mr and Mrs D.W.   "Local"   Apr 5, 1900
    Mr and Mrs D.W. Gooding were called to Bowen Tuesday by the sudden
    death of Mrs g's sister, Mrs Ella Glenn. They will remain until after
    the funeral.

Gooding, Mr and Mrs Howard "Local"   May 23, 1889
    Died- the infant child of Mr and Mrs Howard Gooding living east of town
    died Sunday A.M. and was buried next day at Fowler. Services held at the
    house by Rev S.D. Peet.

Gooding, Jabez   "Local"   Aug 2, 1888
    Jabez Gooding age 74 yrs living north of Bloomfield was found dead
    in a field yesterday at noon. He was killed by a sun stroke while shock-
    ing oats.

Gooding, Mrs Keziah   "Paloma"   Apr 26, 1888
    Mrs Keziah Gooding died at 11 P.M. April 19th at the residence of her
    daughter, Mrs Addie White. She was an old settler of this Co. Born in
    Athens Co. Ohio March 5, 1815 and married D.W. Gooding in 1833. In 1837
    they came to this twp and settled near Quincy and after a few yrs they
    moved to this twp. Husband died in 1880 and since she has lived with her
    son, Webster Gooding. They had 12 children, 6 sons and 6 daughters of
    whom 8 are still livinig. Was a member of the Missionary Baptist church,
    but attended the Freewill Baptist church here where the funeral was held
    Friday by Rev Steward of the 4th Street Baptist church of Quincy.

Gooding, Nelson J.   "Local"   Aug 14, 1902
    Rev S.N. Wakefield was called to the home of Mr and Mrs Wm H. Gooding
    Tuesday to conduct funeral of their youngest child, Nelson J. who was
    born May 15, 1901 and died August 11, 1902. Funeral at the home and was
    buried at cemetery near by.

Gooding, Mrs W.M.   "death"   Mar 15, 1905
    see Hewes, Samuel E.

Goodnow, Hy   "Died"   Oct 15, 1891
    Death of Hy Goodnow of Loraine from typhoid fever last week.

Goodnow, Henry   "Probate Notice"   Oct 22, 1891
    1st Monday of December 1891   John Pratt, Adm with the will annexed.

Goodwin, A. Esq.   "Obituary"   Nov 11, 1885
    see Stafford, Mrs Wm

Goodwin, Alexander   "Lima"   Oct 22, 1885
    Alexander Goodwin Esq. an old citizen of Rocky Run twp living near this
    place died of typhoid fever a short time ago. He was a member of the
    Christian church and a Republican.

Goodwin, Alexander Esq.   "Columbus"   Oct 22, 1885
    Alexander Goodwin Esq. and old citizen of Rocky Run twp died of typhoid
    fever.

Goodwin, Miss Dorah   "Death"   Nov 11, 1885
    see Stafford, Mr Wm R.

Goodwin, James A.   "Obituary"   Apr 27, 1904
    see Adair, Nancy Jane

Goodwin, Mrs Lydia   "Tioga"   Aug 25, 1886
    Died- August 20th Mrs Lydia Goodwin in her 66th yr. Born in Indiana
    June 29, 1820. Came west with her husband Alexander Goodwin about 1839
    and settled in Rocky Run twp about 2 miles west of Tioga. Husband died
    last fall. Leaves 8 children and several grandchildren. Buried Fletcher
    graveyard August 23rd.

Goodwin, Nancy Jane   "Obituary"   Apr 27, 1904
    see Adair, Nancy Jane

Graff, Peter   "Local"   Dec 29, 1894
    Died- Mr Peter Graff of Quincy, father of our Matt Graff at his home in
    the city Thursday eve of dropsy. 75 yrs old. Buried Monday in the
    German catholic cemetery. Leaves a wife and _ children.

Graff, Peter F. Jr   "Died"   May 6, 1890
    Died- at the residence of his fathers on Friday April 30th Peter F.
    Graff Jr. Age 24 yrs.

Graham, Miss   "death"   Feb 16, 1893
    see Kinney, Mrs Joseph

155

Graham, Mrs Eliza A.   "Obituary"   Sep 9, 1880
    see Thompson, Wm

Graham, James   "Coatsburg"   Nov 2, 1887
    News reached us of the death of James Graham's mother. He was called
    east nearly a yr ago. Mr G. and family will return here in the spring.

Grahm, Bruce   "News"   Jul 15, 1880
    Bruce Grahm a baggageman on the Burlington and Southwestern railroad
    was killed Saturday. He was about 23 yrs old and resided at Milan, Mo.
    where his parents and 2 sisters live.

Grammer, Charles M.   "Local"   Nov 28, 1901
    Charles M. Graham an old citizen of Beverly twp died last week. Age
    74 yrs. Was stricken with paralysis about 8 months ago. Was a member
    of the board of supervisors for 25 yrs. Leaves a wife and 15 children.

Grant, Richard   "Local"   May 25, 1899
    Died- Richard Grant at his home in Bloomfield Friday at 10:30 P.M.
    Born Ireland 1811. Came to U.S. in 1840. Served under Capt Kelly during
    the Mexican war. Married Mary Gorman of Quincy 1849 and in 1854 they
    moved to a farm near Bloomfiled where he lived till 3 yrs ago when he
    retired and settled in Bloomfiled. Leaves 1 son, Patrick Grant of
    Bloomfield and 3 daughters who are in the West. Buried Monday A.M.

Grant, Mrs Richard   "Elm Grove"   Mar 8, 1900
    Mrs Grant of Bloomfield was buried last Tuesday Feb 27th in the Bloom-
    field cemetery. She was the wife of Richard Grant, deceased.

Gray, James   "Tioga"   Jun 16, 1886
    Died- June 7th James Gray age 23 yrs 7 mo's. He was born and raised
    in this neighborhood. Died of consumption. Buried in Fletcher graveyard
    June 8th. Services by Rev Crooks.

Gray, Mary   "Estate"   Jun 15, 1893
    see Snograss, T.C.

Gray, Miss Minerva   "Obituary"   Sep 29, 1886
    see Ewing, A.J.

Gray, Mr and Mrs W.S.   "Coatsburg"   Aug 10, 1893
    Died- Sunday morning at age 1 yr 9 mo's, the youngest son of Mr and
    Mrs W.S. Gray. Russell was a bright child loved by all. Services by Rev
    White of Paloma at the U.B. Church Monday. Buried in village cemetery.

Green, Mr   "Payson"   Sep 11, 1879
    Died recently a child of Mr Green's

Green, Mr   "Ursa"   Mar 26, 1891
    Funeral of Mr Green was March 25th from the Methodist church. 61 yrs
    old. Leaves a wife, 2 daughters, aged mother, 9 brothers and 1 sister.

Green, Mrs B.F.   "Petition"   May 18, 1904
    see Moore, Annice S.

Green, Mrs B.F.   "Obituary"   Mar 16, 1904
    see Johnson, George W.

Green, Mr Amos   "Local"   Oct 31, 1901
    Mr Amos Green, an old citizen of Quincy died at his home in that city
    last Friday. Buried Woodland cemetery Sunday. Was nearly 86 yrs old and
    is survived by 1 son and 3 daughters.

Green, Mrs Amos   "Obituary"   Oct 10, 1895
    see Riddle, Mr Orville E.

Green, Francis A.   "Will"   Feb 8, 1883
    see Smith, Caleb

Green, Mrs John   "Ellington"   Oct 18, 1888
    Funeral of Mrs John Green of Riversidae who died on Thursday Oct. 11th
    was buried at Pleasant Grove October 13th. Services by Rev Droke of
    Mendon.

Green, Mrs John L.   "Quincy"   Mar 23, 1899
    Died- Mrs John L. Green at Blessings hospital Thursday March 15th.
    Was 45 yrs old and daughter of Mr and Mrs Curtis Caldwell of Payson twp.

Green, Mary Ann   "Obituary"   Jul 6, 1904
    Mary Ann Green was born Maysville, Ky. December 18, 1830 and died
    at her home in Mendon twp July .4th 1904 at age 73 yrs 6 mo's 10 days
    Came with parents to Quincy, Ill. 1838. Married George Evans Feb 22, 1848
    had 7 children, 6 survive her. 3 sons and 3 daughters. 1 daughter, Ida
    Worman died Feb 10, 1872 and the father and husband November 25, 1885.
    Joined the Elm Grove U.B. church 1890 under the preaching of Bro. Andy
    Winsett. Leaves a brother and 6 children. Spent over 3 score yrs in
    Adams Co. the first few in Quincy.

Green, Mrs Susan F,   "Local"   Jan 17, 1901
    Died- Mrs Susan F. Green, wife of Amos Green at the family residence
    in Quincy Tuesday afternoon. She was the daughter of Ebenzier Riddle
    who came with his family to Mendon in 1829 from Kentucky. She was 63 yrs
    old. Leaves her husband and an only daughter, Mrs Herbert Mills.

Greenstreet, James   "Probate Notice"   Feb 19, 1880
    3rd Monday of April 1880   Thomas J. Hunter, Adm.

Grekee, Mrs   "Obituary"   Apr 23, 1885
    see Ford, Rhoda M.

Griffin, Mrs Eunice Kimball   Jan 22, 1891
    Mrs Eunice Kimball Griffin, mother of conductor G.A. Griffin died
    early this morning at the age of 83 yrs. She moved to Galesburg from
    Mendon in 1853. Her husband died 12 yrs ago.

157

Griffin, Mrs Eunice Kimball   "Obituary"   Jan 22, 1891
   "Galesburg Republican Register"
   Mrs Eunice Kimball Griffin, mother of conductor G.A. Griffin died this
   A.M. at the residence on Duffield Ave Age 83 yrs. She moved to Galesburg
   in 1853 from Mendon, Ill. and lived there since. Her husband died 12 yrs
   ago. She is survived by a brother living in the East, said to be nearly
   100 yrs old. Conductor G. is her only son.

Griffin, H.   "Obituary"   Mar 2, 1882
   see Reynors, _____

Griffith, Capt.   "Camp Point"   Oct 18, 1900
   Funeral of Capt Griffith was Monday A.M. He lived in the country
south of here and was as well as usual only a few days before his death.

Griggs, Dave   "Lima"   Apr 29, 1880
   A young man named Dave Griggs died at the home of Jas. Higgins last wk.

Grigsby, Mrs Irene   Jun 5, 1884
   Mrs Irene Grigsby died in Coatsburg on May 18th at age 72 yrs. She was
   a resident of Adams Co. for 35 yrs. She was the mother of John Grigsby
   and Mrs Phirman of Coatsburg.

Grimes, Abraham   "Obituary"   Jan 12, 1887
   Died- at his home December 31st Abraham Grimes, born in Oldham Co. Ky.
   Jan 1, 1800. Came to Illinois in 1838. Leaves 7 children. Was a member
   of the Baptist church.

Grimes, Mr Abram   "Local"   Jan 5, 1887
   Mr Abram Grimes of Ursa twp died Friday Dec 31st. He was born Jan , 1800

Grimes, Mr Abe Sr.   " Ursa"   Jan 5, 1887
   Mr Abe Grimes Sr. died at his home Dec 30th. Buried Denson's cemetery
   on New Yrs day which was his 88th birthday.

Grimes, Elizabeth   "Ursa"   May 21, 1903
   Last week Elizabeth, wife of Uncle Jacob Grimes died of congestion
   of the lungs.

Grimes, Henry   "Ursa"   Feb 20, 1890
   Died- Feb 19th, Mr Henry Grimes of Ursa. Age 55 yrs.

Grimes, Michael   "Bloomfield"   Jun 6, 1901
   Michael Grimes, the oldest resident of our village died last week and
   was buried in Bloomfield cemetery. Age 84 yrs.

Grimes, Mrs S.R.   "Death"   Mar 22, 1900
   Died- Mrs S.R.Grimes of Dixie, Washington, as taken from a letter from
   S.W. Grimes dated March 12th. He found his mother dead in her bed. She
   was born and raised around Adams Co. Born Dec 21, 1834. Her husband died
   April 12, 1899

Grimes, Mr S.S.   "Ursa"   Jun 16, 1897
   Died- Mr S.S. Grimes of this place last Wednesday A.M. Age 77yrs 10 mo's
   Buried in Stine church cemetery last Friday. Leaves many relatives.

158

Grimes, Mrs Samuel   "Ursa"   Feb 10, 1898
    Died yesterday, Mrs Samuel Grimes at 4 P.M. Funeral at 2 P.M. tomorrow.

Grimes, Mr and Mrs Wm   "Ursa"   Nov 24, 1881
    Died, Mr and Mrs Wm Grimes of typhoid fever. He died November 14th and
    she died November 18th. They had been married 3 months.

Grimmer, Henry A.   "Quincy"   Mar 23, 1899
    Died- Henry A. Grimmer, the expert accountant of consumption in Melrose
    twp. Age 40 yrs. Leaves a wife.

Grisson, Miss Effie   "Rumor of her death"   May 6, 1880
    see Potter, Mrs Charles

Grosh, Mr   "Camp Point"   Apr 19, 1900
    The funeral of Mr Grosh's son was Sunday at the Ebenezer church north
    of here.

Grosh, Mrs A.R.   "Local"   Jan 17, 1889
    Died, Mrs A.R. Grosh yesterday morning at her home in Big Neck.

Grosh, Mrs A.R.   "Loraine"   Jan 24, 1889
    Died- Mrs A.R. Grosh at her home in Big Neck Tuesday morning of lung
    fever. Services at her residence by Rev Wilson of Camp Point. Buried
    in Big Neck cemetery beside her husband. Was 63 yrs old. Leaves 1 son
    and 1 daughter, Mr E.L. Grosh and Mrs I.W. Randles plus grandchildren.

Grosh, Mrs America R.   "Obituary"   Jan 24, 1889
    Died- Mrs America R. Grosh, widow of the late E.L. Grosh at her home in
    Big Neck Keene twp on January 15th age 63 yrs. She and her husband
    were pioneers of that neighborhood. Mother of 5 children. 3 are daed.
    Services held at her late residence on the 16th.. Signed D.W. Wilson.

Grosh, Jude   "Loraine"   Apr 12, 1900
    Quite a number from this place attended the funeral of Jude Grosh
    Sunday at the Union church. The oldest son of E.L. Grosh.

Groshong, Mary   "Obituary"   Oct 31, 1889
    see Campbell, Mrs Mary

Groshong, Mary   "Obituary"   Oct 31, 1889
    see Campbell, Mrs Mary

Gross, B.J.   "Payson"   Aug 17, 1882
    A child of B.J. Gross died yesterday.

Grove, Mrs Rebecca   "Payson"   Mar 25, 1880
    Died- March 20th at the residence of her son, Mrs Rebecca Grove. Age
    76 yrs 14 days. Services by Dr Murphy at the M.E. church.

Grover, Ella W.   "Probate Notice"   Dec 18, 1890
    1st Monday of Feb 1891   John C. Grover, Adm.

159

Grover, Mrs J.   "Ellington"   May 21, 1885
    Mrs J. Grover died this morning May 14th. buried in the cemetery at
    Wesley Chapel Thursday.

Grover, Mrs J.   "Ellington"   May 21, 1885
    Mrs J.Grover died May 12th. Buried in the cemetery at Wesley Chapel
    May 14th.

Grover, Mr and Mrs J.C.   Oct 30, 1890
    Week old infant of Mr and Mrs J.C. Grover died October 24th.

Grover, Mrs J.C.   "Obituary"   May 10, 1900
    see Huston, Mrs Susan

Grover, Mrs J.C.   "Obituary"   Mar 12, 1903
    see Huston, William

Grover, Jhon   "Local"   May 18, 1887
    The youngest child of Mr John Grover of Ellington died on Sunday and
    was buried next day.

Grover, Mrs P.B.   "Local"   Jul 18, 1895
    Died- Mrs P.B. Grover at her home at 906- N. 5th St Quincy Monday eve.
    Was 85 yrs old. Spent most of her life in Ellington twp. 15 yrs ago her
    family moved to Quincy. Leaves her husband and 3 children, Mrs Wm Duncan,
    John Grover and Miss Mattie Grover. Buried in family burying ground at
    Ellington.

Groves, Mrs   "Ursa"   Feb 4, 1892
    Mrs Groves was buried at the Stone church cemetery this A.M. at 10.

Groves, Mrs   "Mt Hebron"   May 18, 1893
    Mr Silas Crandal of Sidney, Iowa was called to attend the funeral of
    his niece, Mrs Groves at Fall Creek.

Groves, Mrs Amanda   "Local"   Feb 4, 1892
    Died- Mrs Amanda Groves of Marcelline on Sunday at the home of her
    daughter, Mrs Mary Agey, Canton, Mo. She was the mother of Dr Groves,
    also of Marcelline.

Groves, Mrs George   "Death"   Mar 15, 1905
    see Shepherd, Mrs Susan

Groves, Mr John   "Ursa"   Apr 7, 1881
    Mr John Groves died of heart disease Tuesday March 29th.

Groves, Steven   "Death"   Apr 5, 1888
    see Akins, Mrs Wm

Groves, Stephen   "Local"   Apr 6, 1904
    Stephen Groves, father of our ex- repres. Jacob Groves died suddenly at
    his home near Big Neck from infirmities incident to old age. He was born
    in Cabell Co. West Virginia Feb 22, 1818.

Groves, Vesta   "Local"   Nov 11, 1897
    Died- infant child, Vesta, from diptheria Tuesday night, daughter of
    Mr and Mrs Geo. Groves living 3 miles N.W. of town. Buried in Franklin
    church burying ground.

Grubb, Henry   "Payson"   Oct 26, 1882
    Henry Grubb buried one of his children last week.

Grubb, Mrs Samuel   "Death"   Feb 2, 1887
    see Wilcox, Dr Luman H.

Guard, Mr and Mrs Jasper   "Tioga"   Dec 28, 1893
    Double funeral at this place last Sunday. Mr Jasper Guard who recently
    moved to the bottoms, and his wife were both buried in the same grave.

Gunlack, Roy   "Loraine"   Jul 30, 1903
    Remains of Roy, son of Mr and Mrs Wm Gunlock of Lima was buried in
    the cemetery here Monday. Died from whooping cough and pneumonia.

Gunn, Alice   "Obituary"   Dec 26, 1901
    see Morris, Mrs Charles

Gunn, Ella   Apr 21, 1898
    Died- Ella Gunn last Thursday A.M. at 7 at her home in Honey Creek twp
    of consumption. Buried Saturday April 16th in St Joseph Catholic
    church yard at Bloomfield. Leaves her mother, 5 brothers and 3 sisters.
    born January 20, 1870 died at at age 28 yrs 2 mo's 19 days.

Gunn, Miss Ellen   "York Neck"   Apr 14, 1898
    Died- Miss Ellen Gunn this morning.

Gunn, Mrs Ellen   "Local"   Apr 6, 1904
    Died- Mrs Ellen Gunn, living on the place formerly owned by Geo. S.
    Flemming died last night. Her son and wife of Kansas City, Mo. arrived
    this A.M.

Gunn, Miss Sarah   Jan 25, 1883
    Miss Sarah Gunn of Honey Creek died January 21st. She lived with the
    Harry Henderson family.

Guseman, Cyrene C.   "Obituary"   Nov 1, 1900
    see Kincheloe, Isaac Newton

Guseman, D.E.   "Death"   Apr 11, 1889
    see Prather, Mrs

Guseman, D.E.   "Obituary"   Nov 1, 1900
    Kincheloe, Isaac Newton

Guseman, Mrs Laverna   "Loraine"   May 23, 1895
    Died- of cancer of the breast at her home 1½ miles N.W. of Loraine on
    Friday at 4 A.M. May 17th, Mrs Laverna Guseman (nee Breiman) wife of
    Wm A. Guseman. Age 56 yrs. Was a member of the M.E. church. Services by
    Rev Rose st the Green Grove church Saturday at 11 A.M. Buried in
    Breniman graveyard. Relatives from a distance was, W. and Wm H.
    Breniman of Iowa brothers of the deceased, also D.E. Guseman of
    Mt Pleasant, Iowa brother in law of deceased. Leaves her husband and
    2 sons, both young men.

Guseman, Orville   "Loraine"   Feb 22, 1905
    The remains of little Orville, son of James and Mrs Guseman of Aurora,
    Illinois were shipped here for burial last Tuesday.

Guseman, W.A.   "Death"   Apr 11, 1889
    see Prather, Mrs

Guthrie, J.P.   "Center"   Oct 23, 1884
    Parties from here attended the funeral of J.P. Guthrie of West Point
    October 18th. Services by Rev H. Blancke. Age 82 yrs. Lived this
    vicinity nearly 30 yrs.

Guthrie, Mr L.   "Local"   Oct 23, 1884
    Mr L. Guthrie of West Point died on October 21st of typhoid fever.

Guthrie, L.   "Local"   Oct 23, 1884
    L. Guthrie the youthful and respected station agent at West Point died
    October 21st of typhoid pneumonia.

Guthrie, Margaret Susan   "Obituary"   Mar 6, 1902
    Margaret Susan Guthrie, born in Adams Co. Illinois December 30, 1843 and
    died at her home near Taylor Ridge at 8 P.M. Monday Feb 10, 1902. Joined
    Lutheran church at age 16 yrs. Married March 7, 1867 to William G.
    Garnett and joined the Episcopal church. Leaves husband, 3 children,
    Frederic E., Sarah and Joseph, 2 sisters and 2 brothers. Funeral at the
    home by Rev E. Mc Omber at 1 P.M. Wednesday. Buried Andalusia cemetery.
    "The Reynolds, Ill. Press"

Guthrie, Mrs Myra Josephine   "Local"   Aug 24, 1899
    Mrs Myra Josephine Guthrie, wife of James Guthrie and a daughter of W.S.
    Bates died at her home 1 mile N. of Camp Point Saturday. Buried Monday.
    Was 41 yrs old.

Guthrie, Mrs Sarah   In Memoriam"   Mar 13, 1879
    Read at the funeral of Mrs Sarah Guthrie on March 4, 1879 who died
    March 2nd at age 73 yrs. (Poem follows this, but not copied)

Guyman, A.   "Loraine"   Apr 21, 1881
    Died- the youngest child of the A. Guyman's.

Guymon, Alonzo   "Loraine"   Feb 26, 1885
    Alonzo Guymon died Feb 23rd. Leaves wife and 2 children.

Guymon, Alonzo   "Loraine"   Feb 26, 1885
   Alonzo Guymon died Monday night. Leaves wife and 2 small children.

Guymon, Alonzo   "Death"   Nov 30, 1893
   see Ketchum, Mrs Clara

Guymon, Carl   "Loraine"   Jan 19, 1899
   Died- Carl Guymon, a former Loraine boy died at Hamilton, Illinois
   Friday A.M. Buried here Saturday at 3 P.M. Was a step son of S. A.
   Ketchum.

Guymon, Mr J.   "Mallard"   Nov 9, 1887
   Died- Mr J. Guymon October 27th from consumption. Leaves a wife and
   3 children.

163

Habel, Mr George   "Tioga"   Dec 7, 1887
    Died- December 1st in Quincy, Mr George Habel age 60 yrs. Mr H. was
    a farmer living 3 miles S. of here. Leaves a wife and several children.

Habighorst, Mr   "Payson"   Mar 25, 1880
    Died- Mr Habighorst's child on March 15th. Buried Tuesday.

Habighorst. Mrs W   "Payson"   Apr 28, 1886
    see Jenners, Mrs

Habighorst, Mrs Wm   "Payson"   Sep 14, 1887
    Died- Mrs Wm Habighorst Wednesday at 8:30 A.M. Leaves a husband and
    4 children.

Habighorst, Mr and Mrs Wm   "Payson"   Dec 9, 1885
    An infant son of Wm Habighorst was buried yesterday.

Hadley, Dr D.H.   "Obituary"   Feb 16, 1899
    see Hale, Caleb B.

Hadley, Mr N.D.   "Funeral"   Sep 4, 1902
    see Saunders, Frank

Hadley, Nelson D.   "Death"   Aug 28, 1902
    Yesterday A.M. Nelson D. Hadley died. Mr and Mrs H. were touring the
South when he became sick. (Mrs H. is former Mamie Doyle) and they came home
    Monday eve. He died Tuesday. Leaves a wife. He was born Canandaiqua, N.Y.
    October 9, 1859 and died at the home of wife's paretns in Mendon August
    27th at age 42 yrs 10 mo's 18 days. Married Miss Mamie Doyle in
New York City April 13, 1887. Funeral Friday at 11 A.M. by Rev S.N. Wakefield.
    Buried Mendon cemetery. He was a genius as he designed most of the
    instruments they used in their profession, that of "Novelty Instrumental
    and Bell Ringers" They traveled under the name of Hadley and Hart.

Hafner, Mrs Nicholas   "Obituary"   Feb 9, 1899
    see Ertel, Daniel

Hagerbaumer, Mrs Anna   "Death in Adams Co."   Feb 16, 1899
    Died- Mrs Anna Hagerbaumer an old resident of the county Monday P.M.
    at the home of her son in law Fred Brinkoetter in Melrose twp. Was a
    native of Eikum, Harfort, Germany. Age 76 yrs.

Hagerty, John T.   "Camp Point"   Mar 3, 1881
    John T. Hagerty formerly of Camp Point died Feb 27th at Stansberry, Mo.
    Had wife and 3 grown children. Buried Camp Point by the Odd Fellows.

Hagmeyer, Mrs   "Death in Adams Co."   Feb 16, 1899
    Died- Mrs Hagmeyer of Fowler at the home of her daughter, Mrs Henning
    last Thursday.

Hagmeyer, Wesley   "Fowler"   Jan 4, 1888
    Wesley Hagmeyer, youngest son of Jacob Hagmeyer died of inflammation of
    the stomach and bowels last week. 16 yrs old.

Hahn, Mrs Lucy Ellen   "Local"   Aug 15, 1889
    Died- Mrs Lucy Ellen Hahn, mother of Mr C.C. Hahn the able writer died
    last week at her home in Medicine Lodge, Kansas. Age 66 yrs.

Haines, John   "Lima"   Jan 10, 1895
    Died- at his home east of Lima from pneumonia, John Haines.

Hains, Thomas   "Loraine"   Aug 31, 1887
    Thomas Hains, a grandson of uncle Tommy Hudson died Friday eve from
    typhoid fever.

Hair, Mrs Clem   "Coatsburg"   Apr 21, 1886
    Funeral of Mrs Clem Hair took place at her home near Columbus. She died
    last Thursday evening.

Hair, Mary Elizabeth   "Columbus"   Apr 28, 1886
    Died- April 15th Mary Elizabeth Hair, wife of Clement Hair of
    consumption. Age 26 yrs. Services by Rev Wohfarth assisted by Elder
    R.A. Omer. Leaves a husband and 2 small children.

Hale, Caleb B.   "Death in Adams Co."   Feb 16, 1899
    Died- Caleb B. Hale in Quincy Saturday night at the home of his
    brother in law, Dr D.H. Hadley. Was a native of Michigan. 54 yrs old.

Haley, Jesse   "Camp Point Journal"   Feb 19, 1885
    Jesse Haley died Saturday afternoon from exposure the night before. He
    laid out about 2 miles west of town and was broght home Saturday morning
    unconscious. He was about 43 yrs old and had no family except 1 boy
    about 18 yrs old who had joined him only last week. He made his home with
    his father Coleman Haley and was widely known as an expert brick man.

Haley, Mrs Kate   "Died"   Feb 19, 1880
    Died- on Monday Feb 16th, Mrs Kate Haley, wife of Jesse Haley. 19 yrs
    old. Was daughter of Meshach Wilcox of Camp Point, but formerly of
    this village. Been ill since the birth of her child a few months ago.
    Buried in Mendon cemetery beside her mother and sister.

Hall, Mr   "Marblehead"   Mar 17, 1881
    Died, a man named Hall shot by man named Hinnes. In March 24th paper
    the mens names are reversed.

Hall, Prof   "Camp Point"   Aug 5, 1880
    Died- the infant child of Prof Hall's Sunday and was buried Monday.

Hall, John   "Payson"   Jun 10, 1880
    A child of John Hall was buried at the Fall Creek church last Saturday.
    Age 19 months.

Hall, Prof S.F.   "Local"   Apr 16, 1903
    Prof S.F. Hall, who taught school at Maplewood High School at Camp
    Point many yrs, died at his home in that city Saturday evening from
    cancer of the stomach. Born Oswego, N.Y. November 14, 1838. Leaves a
    wife and 1 son, Louis A. Hall of Camp Point, 4 daughters, Mrs Nina B.
    Gabriel of Payson, Mrs Bessie A. Dunn and Miss Edith Hall of Quincy (3)

Halsey, Maggie May   "Died"   Aug 10, 1882
    Died- August 4th of scarlet fever, Maggie May Halsey, eldest daughter
    of Wiley and Patience Halsey. Age 7 yrs 23 days.

Halsey, Wiley   "Death"   Feb 25, 1892
    Died- Mr Wiley Halsey Feb 20th. 71 yrs old. Born in Meigs Co. Ohio
    September 17, 1821. Came to Adams Co. in 1846 settling on a farm
    near Loraine where he lived since. Leaves a wife and 3 children, 2
    brothers, 1 living in Canton, Illinois the other in Ohio. He married
    twice, 1st to Miss Annie Boyd in 1848 she died November 11, 1872
    His 2nd wife was Miss Patience Andrew who he married on August 23, 1873.
    He was buried at the Mendon cemetery Monday Feb 22nd. Services by Rev M.
    L. Schmucker of the Lutheran church. Among the mourners was his
    brother, James of Canton, Illinois.

Halsey, Wiley   "Loraine"   Feb 25, 1892
    Died- Wiley Halsey at his home at 12 Saturday the 20th of paralysis
    of the bowels. 72 yrs old. Lived on the farm where he died 47 yrs.
    His 1st wife died in 1872 and he married 2nd in 1874 to daughter of
    Mr and Mrs James Andrew. They had 3 children. He was buried in Mendon
    cemetery on Monday the 22nd.

Halsey, Wiley   "Probate Notice"   Mar 3, 1892
    1st Monday of May 1892   Patience E. Halsey, Adm.
    Gilmer and Moore, attorneys.

Ham, Mrs   "Coatsburg"   Jan 4, 1888
    Died- a young child of Mrs Ham Monday A.M. Buried Tuesday P.M.

Hamilton, Gen E.B.   "Local"   Mar 27, 1902
    Capt John D. Rosenbrook and C.A. Chittenden attended the funeral of
    Gen E.B. Hamilton in Quincy Saturday.

Hamilton, Rev John   "Obituary"   Mar 24, 1886
    see Vandersall, Elizabeth

Hammer, A.   "Honey Creek"   Nov 10, 1886
    A. Hammer, an old resident of Coatsburg died November 2nd of dropsy.

Hammer, Theresa   "Obituary"   Nov 15, 1894
    see Bauman, Theresa

Hammond, Julius S.   "Died"   Feb 1, 1878
    Mr Julius S. Hammond, an old citizen of Mendon died in Ellington, Conn.
    January 23rd. Age 78 yrs 7 months. He lived Mendon for 15 yrs 1840-55

Hamp, Grandma   "Lima"   Oct 6, 1886
    The remains of Grnadma Hamp were buried at the Stone church, south of
    Marcelline on Friday the 1st. Age 87 yrs. Had lived Lima for over
    50 yrs. She was the oldest settler in the north part of the Co.

Hampsmeier, Charles   "Killed"   Oct 26, 1904

Hampsmeier, Charles   "Killed"   Oct 26, 1904
    Charles Hampsmeier, 16 yr old son of Henry Hampsmeier of Payson was
    instantly killed by a bolt of lightning about 11 A.M. Thursday while
    driving a team and wagon. His father was walking behind.

Hampton, Mrs Nelson   "Payson"   Apr 27, 1882
    Mrs Nelson Hampton died April 24th of cancer.

Haner, Daniel   "Probate Notice"   Nov 29, 1894
    Daniel Haner, 1st Monday of Feb. 1895 S.M. Wallace, Adm.
    Wallace and Peters, attorneys.

Haner, Mr and Mrs Gus   "Tioga"   Oct 10, 1901
    Mr and Mrs Gus Haner living about 2 miles S.W. of town lost an infant
    child, Lawrence, last Thursday. Buried in the German cemetery.

Haner, Mrs Hannah   "Tioga"   Jun 29, 1887
    Died June 18th, Mrs Hannah Haner in her 56th yr. Was a member of the
    Evangelical church. Leaves a husband and serverl children.

Haney, Mrs D.   "Tioga"   Mar 3, 1898
    Died- Tuesday Feb 22nd, Mr D. Haney, age 69 yrs. Funeral Friday.
    Buried in the German cemetery at Tioga.

Hansen, Nettie V.   "Estate Suit"   Apr 12, 1894
    see McAdams, Clifton

Harbin, Mr   "Camp Point"   Nov 7, 1901
    Mr Harbin, a colored man living in the West part of town last Thursday
    at 4:30 P.M. Buried Friday. This is the 6th one of the family inside
    of 2 yrs.

Harding, Miss Etta   Feb 8, 1883
    Died January 28th at the home of her mother, Miss Etta Harding.
    Age 24 yrs. Services at M.E. church by Rev J.W. Madison of Lima.

Harding, Mark   Nov 7, 1889
    Mark Harding, age 16 yrs died November 1st. Buried in Lima November 3rd
    Funeral services by Rev Kane at the M.E. church.

Hardy, Mr and Mrs Bap   "Loraine"   Feb 19, 1901
    Mr and Mrs Bap Hardy were called to Adrian Wednesday on acct of the
    illness of Mrs H.'s father. He died Monday.

Hardy, Baptist   "Loraine"   Mar 8, 1905
    Baptist Hardy was called to Adrain Friday by the death of his sister.

Hardy, Mrs Ben   "Local"   Jan 1891
    Mr and Mrs Henry Pittman have returned from Topeka, Kansas in
    consequence of the death of their niece, Mrs Ben Hardy and will settle
    down once more on the home farm.

Hardy, Calphurnia E.   "Estate Sale"   Apr 5, 1888
    see Owings, Howard W.

Hardy, Carl James   "Obituary"   Dec 24, 1903
    Carl James, infant son of Mr and Mrs James Hardy born November 28, 1903
    and died December 19, 1903. Age 3 weeks. Funeral at Loraine by C.D.
    Haskell. Buried Reece cemetery.

Hardy, Mrs Catherine   Dec 25, 1890
    Died at her home in Big Neck December 16th, Mrs Catherine Wartick Hardy.
    (nee Wartick) Born York Neck December 24, 1864. Married Benjamin Hardy
    Feb 19, 1889. Was 26 yrs old less 8 days. Baby preceeded her in death
    6 days before. Services at the home by Elder W.H. Strickler. Buried in
    Big Neck Cemetery.

Hardy, Mrs Elizabeth   "Obituary"   Mar 1, 1900
    see Shriver, Appollo

Hardy, Mrs Emma   "Local"   Apr 25, 1895
    Died- at her home in Hurdland, Mo. Friday P.M. April 19th of consumption
    Emma, wife of B.M. Hardy, age 34 yrs 6 mo's 6 days. Buried Marcelline
    Sunday A.M. at Stone's church burying ground. Maiden name was Potter.
    Born Hancock Co.Brother, Mr S.M. Potter lives in Marcelline. Married
    November 16, 1887. Leaves a husband and a boy 6 yrs old.

Hardy, Mrs Frank   "Local"   May 8, 1902
    Mr and Mrs S.H. McClung attended the funeral of Mrs Frank Hardy at
    Breckenridge last Thursday.

Hardy, George   "Death"   May 24, 1888
    see Moore, Sam

Hardy, Mr and Mrs Henry   "Loraine"   Oct 17, 1901
    An infant child of Mr and Mrs Henry Hardy died Monday and was buried
    in Reece cemetery Tuesday P.M.

Hardy, J.C.   Jan 19, 1882
    J.C. Hardy was buried Sunday January 15th, 1882

Hardy, J.C.   "Ursa"   Jan 19, 1882
    The remains of J.C. Hardy were buried in the cemetery near Stone
    church Sunday.

Hardy, J.C.   "Local"   Jan 9, 1902
    Mrs Casandra Hardy, as Adm. of the estate of J.P. Hardy, deceased will
    sell at her home 3 3/4 miles north-east of Mendon on Thursday January
    23rd all personal property of deceased, consisting of mules, horses,
    cows, cattle, sheep, hogs, grain, hay and agriculturial impl's.

Hardy, Mrs J.P.   "Obituary"   Jul 24, 1884
    see McClung, Mrs Elizabeth

Hardy, Jessie   "Loraine"   Oct 12, 1899
    Died- little Jessie Hardy, oldest daughter of Samuel and Mary Hardy
    a week ago last Thursday. Buried at the Curless graveyard on Friday.
    Age 3 yrs 9 mo's 5 days.

Hardy, Joe   "Funeral"   Feb 26, 1903
    see Stowe, Mr

Hardy, John   "Obituary"   Jun 21, 1888
     see Lowery, John

Hardy, Mrs John   "Mendon"   Jan 5, 1882
     Died- January 3rd, Mrs John Hardy. Buried January 5th at the old
     Stone church near Ursa.

Hardy, John C.   Jan 19, 1882
     Died January 13th, Mr John Hardy. His wife died Tuesday of last week.

Hardy, John C.   Feb 16, 1882
     Notice to all persons indebted to the estate of John C. Hardy please
     pay Levi Davis, Adm.

Hardy, Mr and Mrs Jos.   "Death"   Jun 12, 1890
     see Stewart, Robert

Hardy, Joseph P.   "Probate Notice"   Dec 21, 1899
     1st Monday of March 1900   Casandra Hardy, Adm.

Hardy, Joseph Patterson   "Obituary"   Nov 30, 1899
     Died- Joseph Patterson Hardy at his home 4 miles north-east of Mendon
     Wednesday eve November 22nd. Was 63 yrs old Born January 6, 1837 on
     the farm where he died and grew up. 1858 he married Casandria McClung
     They had 7 children. His wife and 4 children survive him, Joel D.,
     of Lowery City, Mo., Mrs Emma Tolbert of Pleasant Retreat, Mo., Matthew
     of Hurdland, Mo. and William living on the home place. 2 died in infancy
     and Bessie died Dec 14, 1895. His father died near Hickory Ridge
     July 22, 1873. He had 4 brothers and 4 sisters, the youngest 49 yrs old
     and the oldest 70 yrs, their names are Thomas of Bentley, F.M. of
     Hickory Ridge, Bap of Loraine, Mrs Sarah Witt of Chili, Mrs Elizabeth
     Fletcher of Mendon, Mrs Nancy J. Strickler of Loraine, Mrs Louise Harris
     of Ferris and Mrs Mary Felgar of West Point, All Illinois. Their father
     died at age 65 and their mother died 3 yrs later than their father at
     the age of 66 yrs. Took up their homestead 1830. Was a Democrat.
     Services at the Stone church near Ursa Friday November 24th by Rev Dr
     Harris of Ferris, Ill., a nephew of the deceased. Buried Stone church
     cemetery.

Hardy, Mrs Mabel   "Loraine"   Mar 14, 1901
     Died- about 11 P.M. Wednesday March 6th Mrs Mabel Hardy, wife of Mr
     Joe Hardy of this place. Funeral at her father's residence about 2
     miles south of town by Rev S.N. Wakefield of Mendon and Rev F.P. Bonnefon
     She was the 3rd daughter of Mr and Mrs J.A. Ausmus. 21 yrs old, born
     June 21, 1880. Buried in Reece cemetery Friday March 8th.

Hardy, Thomas   "Obituary"   Mar 8, 1900
     Died- Thomas Hardy at his home near Bentley, Hancock Co. Ill. March
     2nd of heart failure. 67 yrs old. was oldest son and 3rd child of
     Baptist Sr. and Tamer Hardy. Born 4 miles north-east of Mendon, Ill.
     Taught school in Mendon vicinity in the "50's" Married 1858 to Margaret
     S. Rogers who died 2 yrs ago. Settled on the farm where he died in 1860
     2½ miles north-east of Bentley. They had 10 children

Hardy, Mrs Thos.   "Local"   Feb 10, 1898
    Died- Mrs Thos. Hardy at her home near Bentley, Hancock Co. Sunday
    after a few days illness.

Harford, Geo.   "Estate Sale"   Jul 10, 1884
    see Owings, Howard W.

Harness, Miss Carrie   "Obituary"   Mar 22, 1900
    see Bolt, Geo. Lincoln

Harness, Mrs Jane Alice Meltabarger   "Obituary"   Sep 3, 1903
    Died- Mrs Jane Alice Meltabarger Harness born December 10, 1862 and
    died Aug 26, 1903 at age 41 yrs 8 mo's 16 days. Married Montville
    Harness September 20, 1883. They had 2 sons, Bertram and Daniel. leaves
    her father, mother, 3 sisters, 1 brother and 2 sons. United with
    Christian church at age 15 yrs. Services at Franklin Baptist church
    5 miles northwest of Mendon by Rev S.R. Reno of Mendon. Buried Franklin
    cemetery.

Harness, Jennie   "Probate Notice"   Nov 5, 1903
    1st Monday of Januray 1904   W.H. Oller, Adm.
    David F. Strickler, attorney for the estate.

Harness, Joe   "Died"   Apr 22, 1880
    see Barlow, John

Harness, Jos.   "Ursa"   Dec 1, 1881
    Jos. Harness was buried at Stone church cemetery November 27th. He
    lived at Lima.

Harris, Rev Dr.   Funeral"   Nov 30, 1899
    see Hardy, Joseph Patterson

Harris, Mrs   "Obituary"   Jan 9, 1890
    see Hill, Martha

Harris, A.B.   "Quincy"   Apr 13, 1899
    Died- A.B. Harris Sunday A.M. from pneumonia. Leaves a wife and 4
    children.

Harris, Dr D.M.   "Local"   Jan 23, 1902
    Executor's sale of personal property of the late Dr D.M. Harris at
    Tioga, Illinois Tuesday Feb 11th. J.N. Harris, Ex.

Harris, Mrs Elizabeth Ann   "Quincy"   Mar 30, 1899
    Died- Mrs Elizabeth Ann Harris Friday March 24th. Lived Quincy 30 yrs.
    Born Feb 28, 1831 near Vandalia, Illinois. Leaves a husband & 7 children.

Harris, George   "Obituary"   Apr 27, 1887
    see Turner, Mary H.

Harris, Mrs Jacob   "Payson"   Dec 25, 1879
    Died- Mrs Jacob Harris died Friday at 12:30 P.M. Services Sunday at
    2:30 by Rev Wallace. Born in Penn. in 1818 and came to Illinois in
    1852. Was 61 yrs 9 mo's 10 days old.

Harris, Mrs Louisa   "Obituary"   Nov 30, 1899
    see Hardy, Joseph Patterson

Harris, Mrs Richard   "Death"   Jan 4, 1901
    see Sinnock, George

Harris, Wm   "Big Neck"   Aug 6, 1891
    The remains of Wm Harris who lived northwest of Loraine was taken
    through our village Saturday enroute for Ebenezer cemetery.

Harris, Wm   "Loraine"   Oct 1, 1885
    Wm Harris who lived in Lima twp died.

Harris, William   "Probate Notice"   Oct 8, 1885
    3rd Monday of November 1885   Clarissa Harris, Ex.

Harrison, Mayor   "death"   Mar 30, 1899
    see Koch, Mrs Susie

Harrison, Almeria F.   "Obituary"   Jul 28, 1892
    see Atwater, Mrs Almeria

Harrison, F. Burgess   "Local"   Dec 14, 1893
    News of the death of Mr F. Burgess Harrison, eldest son of the late
    Nathan B. Harrison, of Chicago, of heart failure at Chadrom, Nebr.
    on December 10th. Buried at Chicago.

Harrison, Mr and Mrs Frank   "Tioga"   Mar 29, 1900
    Died- the infant child of Mr and Mrs Frank Harrison of Hamilton was
    buried in our village cemetery Thursday.

Harrison, Mrs G.A.   "Obituary"   Mar 26, 1903
    see Bradley, Miss Sarah Hemmingway

Harrison, Rev Henry   "Local"   Nov 29, 1894
    Mr S.H. Bradley, Miss Julia Arnold and Mrs J.R. Copelin went to
    Chicago to attend the funeral of their relative, the Rev Henry Harrison.
    Buried in Graceland cemetery.

Harrison, Rev Henry   Nov 22, 1894
    Death of Rev Henry Harrison of Chicago.
    Editor of the Advance
    Mr S. H. Bradley rec'd the following telegram;
    LaGrange, Ill 7:15 P.M
    Mr Harrison fatally injured by train this P.M.. Wire later as to funeral.
    signed, M.J. Carpenter

Harrison, Henry S.   "In Memoriam"   Dec 6, 1894
Memorial services for Henry S. Harrison was held last Sunday A.M. at
the Cong'l church. Pulpit was draped in black and displayed a protrait
of the deceased. Services by Rev W. Burgess.

Harrison, Rev Hy.   Apr 11, 1895
The remains of the late Rev Hy Harrison whose untimely taking off in
Chicago last November is still fresh in the memories of the people of
Mendon arrived here yesterday A.M. accompanied by his widow, his brother,
the Rev Marvin Harrison of Scribner, Nebr. and Mrs Kimball of Galesburg
and were laid to rest in the family lot. Services were simple by Rev
Wm Burgess and a brief address by Mr Harrieson and all was over.

Harrison, Rev Hy   "Death"   Dec 1, 1892
see Arnold, Mrs Elizabeth A.

Harrison, J.A.   "Local"   Dec 16, 1897
Mr J.A. Harrison rec'd news last week from Michigan of the death on
November 23rd of an elder brother.

Harrison, Mr and Mrs Joseph   "Obituary"   May 2, 1889
see Shumate, Mrs

Harrison, Rev M.B.   "Obituary"   Mar 26, 1903
see Bradley, Miss Sarah Hemmingway

Harrison, Natha I.   "Death"   Feb 24, 1904
see Copelin, Mrs Eunice Atheda

Harrison, Nathan   "Obituary"   Jul 28, 1892
see Atwater, Mrs Almeria F.

Harrison, Nathan   Dec 13, 1883
The remains of Mr Nathan Harrison were brought to Mendon from Chicago
December 7th and placed in the village yard. He was a brother of Mrs
Atwater of Mendon. He formerly lived Mendon. In recent yrs he lived
Chicago.

Harrison, Nathan   "News"   Dec 13, 1883
The remains of Nathan Harrison was brought here from Chicago and buried
in Mendon cemetery. He was a brother of Mrs Atwater of Mendon.

Harrison, Wm Glenville   Oct 23, 1890
October 3rd Wm Glenville Harrison died. He was born October 12, 1869
in Mendon. Was the oldest son of Mr and Mrs Joseph Harrison. Buried
in Mendon cemetery from the Zion Episcopal church by friend Dr Lloyd
of Cedar Falls, Iowa.

Harry, Mrs Alvina   "York Neck"   Mar 31, 1892
CORRECTION: Died at 1A.M. Tuesday at her home in York Neck Mrs Alvina
Harry, wife of Jasper Harry of blood poisoning. Age 29 yrs. Services by
Rev W. McPheeters of Camp Point at her home in York Neck. Remains taken
to Quincy her former home. Funeral at the Lutheran church. Leaves husband
and a babe.   SEE MRS ALVINA JASPER CARD ALSO.

Harshbarger, Mrs W.A.　　　　"Death"　　　　　　　　　　　　Mar 5, 1903
　　　see Platt, Rev H.D.

Hart, Mrs　　　　　　　　　"Loraine"　　　　　　　　　　　Sep 29, 1881
　　　Mrs Hart died September 20th at the home of her son H.D. Hart.

Hart, Amos　　　　　　　　"Edgings"　　　　　　　　　　　Feb 15, 1878
　　　Mr Amos Hart of Big Neck was burned to death Sunday night when his
　　　residence burned to the ground. He lived by himself.

Hart, Mrs F.W.　　　　　　"Death"　　　　　　　　　　　　Jan 18, 1905
　　　see Lemmon, William Daniel

Hart, Frank　　　　　　　　"Payson"　　　　　　　　　　　Feb 16, 1887
　　　Frank Hart died since last week. Age 19 yrs.

Hart, Mr Gay　　　　　　　"Loraine"　　　　　　　　　　　Oct 18, 1900
　　　The infant child of Mr Gay Hart was buried here Monday.

Hart, Grace　　　　　　　　"Local"　　　　　　　　　　　Mar 8, 1894
　　　Mr and Mrs G.G. Lohr was called to Quincy last week to attend the
　　　funeral of her niece Grace, infant daughter of Dr and Mrs Hart whose
　　　death was caused by membranous croup.

Hart, H.D.　　　　　　　　"Loraine"　　　　　　　　　　　Jul 20, 1899
　　　Died- The body that was found in the river below Quincy proved to be
　　　H.D. Hart of this place. Buried Tuesday at York Neck by a few of the
　　　Odd Fellows.

Hart, Hiram David　　　　　"Whig"　　　　　　　　　　　　Jul 20, 1899
　　　Body found in the river last week and buried near Whipple's ice house
　　　last Thursday was identified as Hiram David Hart of Loraine and taken to
　　　that village last night. was 45 yrs old. Lived Loraine all his life.
　　　Never married. His sister kept house for him. He owned a small farm
　　　½ mile south of Loraine and several lots in Loraine. Left all his proper-
　　　ty to his sister. Was a member of the Loraine lodge of Odd Fellows.

Hart, Mr Isaac　　　　　　"West Point"　　　　　　　　　Apr 12, 1894
　　　Died- Mr Isaac Hart, brother of Dr and W.T. Hart on Aptil 5th at 4 A.M.
　　　in Quincy. 82 yrs old and a former resident of Ottumwa where he was a
　　　fireman in the B.& M. round house for 25 yrs. Remains brought here
　　　from Quincy Friday eve. Services at the home of W.T. Hart and buried
　　　in West Point cemetery.

Hart R.E.　　　　　　　　　　　　　　　　　　　　　　　Dec 13, 1889
　　　Mr R.E. Hart died in Greenley, Colo. on December 4th. He lived in
　　　Mendon, Illinois from 1840 to 1845 and worked as a harness maker.

Hart, Mr W.T.　　　　　　"West Point"　　　　　　　　　Oct 30, 1879
　　　Mr W.T. Hart rec'd word from Clayton of the death of Solomon Wigle,
　　　a brother of Mrs Hart.

Hart, W.W.　　　　　　　　"Local"　　　　　　　　　　　Nov 30, 1887
　　　Died- Mr W.W. Hart, Quincy. He was assistant P.M. at Quincy.

Hartman, Mrs Albert   "Death"   May 5, 1898
   see Cox, Nellie

Hartman, Betsy   "Loraine"   Jan 20, 1898
   Died- old aunt Betsy Hartman. Had she lived until next June she would
   have been 81 yrs old. Leaves 5 sons and 3 daughters.

Hartman, Miss Clara   "Local"   Feb 3, 1898
   10 days from the time the Hartman brothers and sisters buried their
   mother they buried their youngest sister, Miss Clara.

Hartman, Edmund   "Woodville"   Apr 18, 1889
   Died- Edmund Hartman (oldest of the Hartman children) He was 51 yrs 4 mo'
   old. Leaves a widow, aged mother, brothers and sisters.

Hartman, Elizabeth   "Local"   Feb 17, 1898
   Messrs Albert and George Hartman, Adm's will have a sale of personal
   property of the late Elizabeth Hartman on the premises 3½ miles northeast of Loraine March 5th. At the same time Mr Joe Hartman, Adm.
   will sell the personal property of Miss Clara Hartman, deceased.

Hartman, Jos.   "Exchange clip"   Sep 18, 1884
   Mr Jos. Hartman of Loraine has contracted with Jos. DeLess our marble
   man for a handsome Cap monument to be erected in memory of his parents
   in Woodville cemeyerty.

Hartman, Nancy E.   "Obituary"   May 12, 1898
   see Steiner, Mrs Anna C.

Hartman, Peter   Feb 7, 1884
   Mr Peter Hartman died January 30th at his home in Loraine in Keene twp
   He was one of the early settlers of this Co. Was 72 yrs old. His remains
   were laid to rest in the cemetery near the family home on Feb 1st.

Hartman, Peter   "Probate Notice"   Feb 14, 1884
   3rd Monday of April 1884   Alexander Hartman, Adm.

Hartrick, Mr   "Payson"   Aug 5, 1880
   Mr Hartrick of Plainville was buried on August 4th. His wife is sick
   at this writing.

Harwood, Cassius   "Sale of real Estate"   Dec 13, 1883
   see Barry, Green B.

Harwood, Rosina F.   "Sale of Real Estate"   Dec 13, 1883
   see Barry, Green B.

Haselwood, John W.   "Payson"   Jan 22, 1885
   Mr John Haselwood was buried here on the 12th. Leaves a wife and 3
   children.

Haselwood, Miss Lucy   "News"   Jul 23, 1885
    Miss Lucy Haselwood, daughter of Mr and Mrs Willis Haselwood of Quincy
    died July 16th. Was 25 yrs old. She died 1 yr 3 mo's after her brother.

Haskins, Mrs Emily   Feb 8, 1883
    Mrs Emily Haskins died Feb 2nd at the residence of her daughter, Mrs
    G.H. Henderson of Mendon. She was born in Northampton, Mass November
    8, 1811. Moved to New York in 1817. Services at the home of daughter by
    Rev McKown. She married David Haskins in 1833. Was a member of the
    Baptist church. Leaves 2 brothers.

Hastings, Mr and Mrs Alonzo   "Local"   May 11, 1904
    The 7 month old twins of Mr and Mrs Alonzo Hastings, living near Bear
    Creek were buried here Monday P.M.

Hastings, Miss Annie   "Death"   Feb 26, 1891
    see Clair, Mrs Albert

Hastings, Miss Elizabeth   "Death"   Feb 24, 1904
    see Odear, Mrs Elizabeth

Hastings, Letitia Adeline   "Obituary"   Feb 10, 1898
    Died- Letitia Adeline Hastings, born January 25, 1862 and died
    January 30, 1898. Married Warren Asher October 21, 1885. They had 5
    children 2 girls and 3 boys. Husband and 5 children survive her, also
    father, mother, 5 brothers and 4 sisters. 3 of her sisters are dead.

Hastings, Mrs O.C.   "Death"   Mar 8, 1905
    see Odear, Joshua

Hastings, Mr and Mrs Oliver   "Death"   Feb 24, 1904
    see Odear, Mrs Elizabeth

Hastings, Thomas Gilbert   "Obituary"   Feb 17, 1904
    Thomas Gilbert Hastings born December 17, 1882 died at the home of
    his parents, William and Eliza Hastings 3½ miles southeast of Mendon
    Feb 12th. He was 21 yrs 1 month 25 days old. Was attending Mendon
    Public school. 4 sisters died before him, they are Nancy Ann Clair,
    Cassander V. Barry, Lillie Drucitta and Lettitia Adaline Asher. Leaves
    father, mother, 4 brothers, John C., William P., Robert N., James F. and
    4 sisters, Mary E. Lohr, Cora E. Slonigar, Mildred Emma Hendreicks and
    Wilheimina Shay. All present but Mrs Lohr and Mrs Hendricks. Services
    by pastor of Methodist Episcopal church in Mendon by Rev S.R. Reno.
    Buried in Mendon cemetery.

Hastings, Thomas Gilbert   "Local"   Feb 17, 1904
    Funeral Sunday at the Mendon Cong'l church of Thomas Gilbert Hastings.
    School children attended in mass, their former classmate.

Hastings, Mr and Mrs Wm   "Death"   Feb 3, 1898
    see Asher, Mrs Warren

Hastings, Mr and Mrs Wm   "Death"   Feb 19, 1891
    see Clair, Mrs Albert

Hastings, Mr Wm Sr.   "Local"   Nov 16, 1893
   Died- Mr Wm Hastings Sr. a former resident of this vicinity, but the
   last 14 yrs a resident of Grundy Co. Mo. died at his home October 13th
   Leaves a wife and 7 sons.

Hatch, Dr Henry   "Local"   Jul 26, 1905
   Died- Dr Henry Hatch, business partner of Dr J.H. Rice at Blessing
   Hospital Monday at 6 A.M. Was one of Quincy's foremost Dr's. Buried
   at Griggsville.

Hatton, L.B.   "Obituary"   Jun 29, 1887
   Died- L.B. Hatton on June 19th. Born in Melrose twp Adams Co. April
   1837. Married Miss Mary H. Forsyth on January 8, 1861. They had 1 son
   and 2 daughters. Services held at the Baptist church just north of
   Ursa June 21st at 10:00 A.M. by Rev L.S. Hitchens of Ursa. Buried in
   Cemetery close to the church..

Hatton, Mitchell   "Local"   Jul 7, 1886
   Mr L.B. Hatton has been told of the illness of "Uncle Mitchell Hatton"
   of Chariton Co. Mo. who is on a visit to his son James Hatton 2 miles
   east of Loraine. He is not expected to live. (Later information is
   that he died)

Hatton, Mitchel   "Loraine"   Jul 14, 1886
   Uncle Mitchel Hatton was buried in our cemetery last week.

Hatton, N.P.   Jun 5, 1902
   N.P. Hatton included in list of civil war soldiers buried in Mendon
   cemetery.

Hatton, Nicholas P.   "Probate Notice"   Sep 4, 1884
   3rd Monday of November 1884   Rebecca Hatton, Adm.

Hatton, Nicholas Parker   "Died"   Jun 12, 1884
   Nicholas Parker Hatton born Feb 14, 1836 died June 6th. Age 48 yrs
   3 mo's 21 days. Married Rebecca Tuxford December 12, 1859. They had
   2 sons and 3 daughters.

Hatton, S.P.   "Loraine"   Jul 28, 1881
   Death of a child of S.P. Hatton this week.

Hatton, Mrs S.P.   Sep 1, 1881
   Died- August 26,1881, Mrs S.P. Hatton of Loraine. Born Pike Co. Mo.
   December 21, 1845. Leaves husband and 5 children.

Hauke, Mrs Joseph   "Ellington"   Apr 9, 1885
   Mr Joseph Hauke lately returned from California where he went to visit
   his sick wife. She only lived a short time after his arrival.

Hauptner, Francis   Nov 10, 1881
   Died- Mr Francis Hauptner of Columbus, November 4th. He broke his back
   on the way home from Coatsburg.

Hauserman, Philip   Aug 25, 1881
    Committed suicide, Philip Hauserman, age 45 yrs of Quincy. Was single.

Havener, Norrin   "Local"   Aug 14, 1902
    Norrin Havener, a well known farmer of Loraine twp died at his home
    2 miles west of Lima Friday night. Age 71 yrs.

Havens, James Joshua   "Death List"   Dec 11, 1902
    see Myers, C.C.

Havens, Joshua   "Ursa"   Jan 24, 1901
    Died- Joshua Havens of Missouri died. He was the brother of Geo. Havens
    of here.

Hauke, Mr Joseph   "Ellington"   Apr 9, 1885
    Mr Joseph Hauke returned from California where he went to see his wife
    who died shortly after his arrival there.

Hawe, Christopher T.   "Local"   Mar 24, 1898
    "Chicage Record March 21st"
    Died- Christopher T. Hawe, a plumber living at 4813 Langley Ave was
    drowned in the Calumet river yesterday. His body has not been found.
    He and his brother D.J. Hawe and Capt Vance of 2328 Indiana had gone
    to shoot ducks. He was 29 yrs old. Married 9 mo's ago. Was son of Mr
    Daniel Hawe of Honey Creek twp Adams Co. Ill.

Hawe, Daniel   "Fowler & Oakland"   Apr 6, 1899
    Mr Daniel Hawe who was here to attend the funeral of his mother has
    returned to his home in Chicago.

Hawe, Daniel   "Death"   Mar 16, 1904
    Daniel Hawe of Honey Creek twp died at the home of his son, Wm Hawe
    4 miles north of here Sunday A.M. of heart trouble. Was sick past 2
    yrs. Born in county Cork, Ireland 71 yrs ago. Came to Quincy with Gen
    James Singleton and was his trusted friend and servant several yrs.
    Located in Honey Creek twp some 40 yrs ago where he reared his family
of 8 children. 6 children survive him. He was a member of St Edwards Catholic
    church at Bloomfield where he was buried beside his wife at 11 today.

Hawe, Sadie   "Local"   Aug 15, 1895
    Died- Sadie Hawe, infant child of Wm L. and Mary J. Hawe of Mt Hebron
    Tuesday and buried next day at 4 P.M. in Mendin cemetery. Services by
    Charles Crank.

Hawe,Will   "Mt Hebron"   Mar 23, 1899
    The family of Will Hawe were called to Honey Creek by the death of
    his mother.

Hawe, Wm   Death"   Mar 16, 1904
    see Hawe, Daniel

Hawkins, Mrs   "Death"   Feb 22, 1882
    see Forsythe, Johnny

177

Haxel, Mrs   "Death"   Nov 5, 1903
  see Michels, Miss Ada

Hayes, Dan   Jun 7, 1905
  "Diver held under water 24 hrs"
  A diver named Dan Hayes, weighing over 200 lbs, age 45 yrs, married and
  living in a house boat on Bay Island on the shores of Quincy Bay was
  caught while investigating why the large sluice doors didn't close in
  the outlet gates of Lima Lake slough. He was taken to Canton, Mo. alive,
  but died there Monday at 9 P.M.

Hayes, Mrs Wm B.   Sep 18, 1890
  Mrs Wm B. Hayes of New Haven Conn. died September 8th. She was the only
  sister of Mrs Fowler of this town. Age 72 yrs.

Hayne, Isaac   "Loraine"   Apr 10, 1902
  Isaac Hayne's baby died last Tuesday, 18 mo's old.

Haynes, Miss Mary   "Obituary"   Mar 1, 1900
  see Shriver, Apollo

Hazelwood, Alfred   "Local"   Jul 17, 1884
  Alfred Hazelwood, son of county clerk Willis Hazelwood died on Sunday
  night July 13th at the early age of 15 from Brights disease.

Head, Mr Henry   "Local"   Mar 22, 1888
  Died- Mr Henry Head of Quincy died in Washington D.C. of pneumonia
  on Friday A.M. Age 69 yrs. Born in England and came to Quincy 40 yrs
  ago. Leaves 5 children, 3 sons and 2 daughters. Buried in Quincy.

Heaney,   "Mendon"   Dec 8, 1881
  Died December 3rd, a child of 4 yrs of Edward Heaney.

Heaney, Clyde   "Local"   Mar 28, 1901
  Clyde Heaney, son of Mr and Mrs Ashbury Heaney, who recently moved
  from Quincy to Mendon was born July 29, 1899 and died March 23, 1901
  Services at the house by Rev Wakefield March 25th at 4:30 P.M. Buried
  in Mendon cemetery.

Heaney, Ed   "Local"   Feb 2, 1888
  Ed Heaney died at his new home in Mt Vernon, Ill Tuesday A.M. Remains
  brought to Mendon cemetery for burial with Masonic honors.

Heaney, Edward   "Obituary"   Nov 30, 1899
  Died- Edward Heaney, 2nd son of Mr and Mrs Richard Heaney. Born October 1,
  1862 in Mendon and died November 22nd at age 37 yrs 1 mo 21 days. Lived
  7 yrs in Washington D.C. in the employ of Senator Stockbridge. The
  last 6 yrs he traveled as agent for W.P. Engleman of Kalamazoo, Mich.
  Buried Mendon Leaves 6 brothers, Wm of Topeka, Kansas, Asbury and
  Charles of Quincy, Samuel of La Belle, Mo., Richard and Harry and 1
  sister, Mrs Henry Smith and his parents. Services at the M.E. church
  by Rev S.N. Wakefield. Buried Mendon.

Heaney, Edward   "Obituary"   Feb 9, 1888
Remains of the late Edward Heaney arrived in Mendon and buried ther Thurs.
Services by Rev J.W. Thomas at the Lutheran church where he was a member.
He was the oldest son of Mr and Mrs Samuel Heaney and was born Sept 4,
1845 in the parish of Killashandra, county Cavan, Ireland. come with his
parents to this country in the spring of 1849 and lived Mendon vicinity
since that tome till he moved to Mount Vernon last September. Died of
pneumonia January 31st. Leaves a widow and 5 children, 3 boys and 2 girls.

Heaney, Edward   "Obituary"   Aug 24, 1904
see Foster, Mrs Eliza Ann

Heaney, Edward   "Local"   Nov 23, 1899
Died- Edward Heaney of Kalamazoo, Michigan. Was 2nd son of Mr and Mrs
Richard Heaney. Died in Quincy last night. His brother Charley went to
Michigan and brought him back.

Heaney, Edward   Mar 3, 1881
Edward Heaney's child of 8 months died Feb 22nd.

Heaney, James   "Local"   Apr 12, 1894
News rec'd in Quincy Monday of the death at Mt Vernon, Ill. of James,
son of the late Edward Heaney at the age of 23 yrs. When Mrs Heaney
(his grandmother) died last week James was telegramed and the answer came
he was not expected to live. Mr Samuel M. Heaney (his uncle) was there
when he died.

Heaney, Mrs Mary A.   "In Memoriam"   Apr 12, 1894
Died- Mrs Mary A. Heaney at 2 A.M. last Thursday at the home of her son
S.W. Heaney at 931 Hampshire St Quincy. Age 82 yrs. Mary A. Hewitt was
born in the Parish of Killashandra county Cavan Ireland. Married Samuel
Heaney December 2, 1844. Came to U.S. with husband in spring of 1849
Stopped in St Louis about 2 months where Mr H's mother was stricken
down in the cholera epidenic. Lived Mendon till about 2½ yrs ago when
they moved to Quincy with their 2 sons. Leaves husband and 2 sons, Samuel
W. and Noble M. Heaney of Quincy, 1 sister, Mrs Thos Wilcox of Loraine
and a brother, Thomas Hewitt of Mendon besides nieces and nephews and
grandchildren. Buried in Mendon cemetery after services at the Zion
church by Rev R.W. Hewitt of Kewanee, a nephew of deceased.

Heaney, Mrs Mary A.   "Obituary"   Apr 12, 1894
see Hewitt, Mary A.

Heaney, Mrs Maud   "Obituary"   Jul 18, 1901
see Kennedy, Geo. Thomas

Heaney, Mrs N.M.   "Local"   Nov 23, 1899
Died- Mrs Heaney, wife of N.M. Heaney.

Heaney, Mr and Mrs N.M.   "Obituary"   Apr 4, 1895
see Strickler, Clark

Heaney, Noble M.   "Obituary"   Apr 12, 1894
see Hewitt, Mary A.

Heaney, Mrs Noble M.   "Obituary"   Nov 23, 1899
    Died- Mrs Noble M. Heaney whose home is 2½ miles northwest of here died
    at Blessings hospital in Quincy last Sunday. Services at the home of
    S.W. Heaney Quincy Monday P.M. before bringing the remains to Mendon.
    Alice Sproat was born Jan 25, 1851 died November 19th. Age 48 yrs 9 mo's
    24 days. Married Mr H. January 22, 1874. Had 5 children, 2 dying in
    infancy. Leaves 3 children and her husband. Was member of St John's
    cathedral church in Quincy. Services at the Cong'l church Mendon by Rev
    Dean Moore of Quincy. Buried Mendon cemetery.

Heaney, Mrs S.W.   "Loraine"   Feb 21, 1901
    Mrs S.W. Heaney of Quincy rec'd word Wednesday that her brother E.W.
    Sproat of Holister, Calif was killed in an iron works. Mr S. was a
    fromer resident of Mendon twp. Leaves a wife and 3 children.

Heaney, Mr and Mrs S.W.   "Obituary"   Apr 4, 1895
    see Strickler, Clark

Heaney, Samuel   "Local"   Apr 6, 1904
    The will of Samue; Heaney was filed for probate last week. 5000.00
    is given to the 4 children of Edward Heaney, deceased and the rest of the
    estate between N.M. and S.W. the 2 sons.

Heaney, Samuel   "Obituary"   Apr 12, 1894
    see Hewitt, Mary A.

Heaney, Mrs Samuel   "Obituary"   Sep 19, 1889
    see Hewitt, John

Heaney, Mrs Samuel   "Local"   Apr 5, 1894
    Mrs Samuel Heaney of Quincy died at 2 A.M. Funeral will be here at
    2 P.M. Friday.

Heaney, Samuel   "Probate Notice"   Jul 20, 1904
    1st Monday of September 1904   Noble M. and Samuel W. Heaney, Ex's
    David P. Strickler, Atty.

Heaney, Samuel   "Obituary"   Aug 24, 1904
    see Foster, Mrs Eliza Ann

Heaney, Samuel W.   "Obituary"   Apr 12, 1894
    see Hewitt, Mary A.

Heaney, Samuel W.   "Died"   Mar 30, 1904
    Mr Samuel W. Heaney died at home of his son, Samuel W. Jr. in Quincy at
    2 P.M. Friday of old age and complications. Age 79 yrs 5 mo's 27 days.
    Born Sept. 28, 1824 in County Cavin, Ireland. Married in Ireland to Miss
    Mray Ann Hewitt and they came to U.S. in 1849. Settled on a farm near
    Mendon where he lived till he retired and moved to Quincy with his son.
    Member of Zion Episcopal church and in Quincy the St John's Cathedral
    Services at the zion church Sunday P.M. at 2:30 by Rev Robert W. Hewitt,
    a nephew. Buried in family plot in Mendon cemetery. Leaves 2 brothers,
    Richard of tihs village and Edward of Mendon, Mo. 2 sons, N.M. and S.W.,
    9 grandchildren and 5 gr grandchildren. Relatives from a distance were,
    N.M. Heaney, daugh

                              - cont-

180

Continued-
Heaney, Samuel W.

    Relatives from a distance were, N. M. Heaney, daughter Emma and son Arthur
Mr and Mrs S.W. Heaney Jr., and sons Sproat and Ross, Mr and Mrs Rolla
Henderson all of Quincy. Edward Heaney of Mendon , Mo. a brother, Samuel
Heaney of Mt Vernon, Ill. a grandson, Charles Heaney of Palmyra. Mo.

Heaney, Walter   "Obituary"   Aug 24, 1904
    see Foster, Mrs Eliza Ann

Heath, Alfred   "Estate Suit"   Oct 11, 1883
    see Jacobs, Alexander

Heath, Mary   "Estate Suit"   Oct 11, 1883
    see Jacobs, Alexander

Heaton, Mrs   "Local"   Dec 28, 1893
    Mr J.S. Wallace, our banker went to Camp Point yesterday to attend the
funeral of Mrs Heaton, mother of Mrs Rd Wallace.

Heaton, Meridith   "Ursa"   Jun 27, 1895
    Died- Meridith Heaton Saturday A.M. Funeral P.M. Sunday at the house.

Heaton, Mrs R.   "Death"   Jan 5, 1882
    see Pearson, Sarah

Heaton, Mr Vandever   "Local"   Aug 24, 1887
    Mr Charles Nixdoff writes from Augusta under date of August 16th that
Mr Vandever Heaton died yesterday at 6 A.M. Buried today.

Heberling, Mrs   "Marcelline"   Mar 10, 1886
    Old Mrs Heberling of Quincy was buried yesterday. She was the mother of
Mrs Campbell and Mrs G. Beatty.

Heckerman, Miss Catherine Marie Engel   "Death"   Jul 19, 1905
    see Lucking, F.W.

Heckerman, Geo.   Sep 1, 1881
    Died, August 30th Geo. Heckerman age 75 yrs at the residence of his
son, Fred.

Hecox, Mrs Mary Ann   "News"   Oct 8, 1885
    Died- September 29th at her home in Clark Co. Mo. Mrs Mary Ann Hecox
in her 65 th yr. She was one of the earliest settlers of Mendon,
arriving here in 1834. Was mother of 14 children, 6 still living. Also
leaves 1 brother and 1 sister. Her brother lives in Mendon and is Mr
Daniel Nutt.

Hedge, Mr John   "Ellington"   Jul 17, 1884
    A new tombstone has been placed at Mr John Hedges grave.

Hedges, Charles   "Death"   Feb 8, 1905
    Charles Hedges died at St Mary's hospital Monday afternoon from typhoid
    fever. He was broght to Quincy a few days ago from his home in Hannibal.
    Remains shipped to Seehorn on early train Tuesday A.M. A brother, R.L.
    Hedges of Palmyra, Mo. accompanied them. He was employed at the cement
    plant at Hannibal. Leaves wife and 2 boys who are in Hannibal. 38 yrs old
    "Quincy Journal"   Deaceased was a cousin of the Nutt brothers here
    William, Walter and Charles.

Hedges, Elizabeth   "Petition #1689   May 18, 1904
    see Moore, Annice S.

Hedges, Elizabeth   "Estate sale and Suit"   May 3, 1894
    see Johnson, John H.

Hedges, Mrs Fannie   "Death"   Apr 17, 1902
    Mrs Fannie Hedges, widow of the late Thomas Hedges, of Mendon died
    suddenly last Thursday P.M. at the home of her grandaughter, Nrs George
    Robbins at 620 N. 20th Street Quincy. She had stayed for sometime with
    her son, Rufus Hedges at Seehorn. Last Monday she came to Quincy to the
    grandaughters. She was suffering from Asthma. 76 yrs old. Husband has
    been dead several yrs. Leaves 3 sons and 1 daughter, Charles, Rufus,
    Mate and Mrs Sam Mc Clelland who lives in Riverside twp, besides one
    stepson, Thaddeus at Fairweather. She was a sister of the late Daniel
    Nutt.

Hedges, Mrs James   "Death"   Feb 13, 1890
    See Brown, Mrs

Hedges, Mrs Mary   Nov 3, 1881
    Died- Mrs Mary Hedges, age 31 yrs. Wife of M.J. Hedges. She was the
    daughter of John Crawford. Services by Rev Lloyd.

Hedges, Mary E.   "Death"   Aug 23, 1894
    see Colvin, Davis P.

Hedges, Rufus M.   "Died"   Aug 12, 1880
    "Whitehall Michigan Forum"
    Died- in Whitehall Tuesday A.M. June 29th of old age. Mr Rufus M.
    Hedges age 71 yrs 7 mo's 29 days. Born in Exeter, Otsego, Co. N.Y. and
    moved in an early day to Adams Co. Ill.. Moved from Adams Co. to this
    place about 15 yrs ago in the company with his brother, Mr Wheeler
    Hedges, built what of late yrs was known as the A.B. Brown saw mill.

Hedges, Thaddeus S.   "Estate Sale and Suit"   May 3, 1894
    see Johnson, John H.

Hedges, Thomas   "Death"   Jun 8, 1887
    see Ingram, Mrs Lottie

Hedges, Thomas S.   "Obituary"   Feb 16, 1893
     Died- Thomas S. Hedges, formerly of Mendon twp at his home near Seehorn,
     Illinois Feb 8th. Born in New York September 2, 1817. Came to Adams Co.
     when he was about 17 yrs old. Married 2 times and the father of a large
     family. Most are dead. Leaves a wife and 5 children, His wife is a sister
     of Mrs Daniel Nutt of Mendon.

Heidbreder, Mrs H.   "Quincy"   Mar 9, 1899
     Died- Mrs H. Heidbreder at St Mary's hospital Sunday. Age 38 yrs.

Heidbreder, John   "Fowler"   Sept 20, 1888
     Died- John Heidbreder in Quincy last Thursday of typhoid fever.

Heilamn, George   "Burton"   Apr 10, 1879
     We attended the funeral of Mr George Heilman who resided near Mr Tandy's
     schoolhouse. Was 45 yrs old. The mother and sons have our sympathy.

Heilwagon, Otto   "Local"   Apr 28, 1886
     The body of Otto Heilwagon who was drowned March 15th has been found
     in a slough near Fall Creek.

Heine, Elizabeth A.   "Death"   Jan 4, 1888
     see Fleming, Mrs Elizabeth A.

Heinecke, John   Jul 3, 1890
     John Heinecke, 21 yr old son of a farmer near Tioga was killed Saturday
     morning.

Heintz, Miss Minnie   "Death"   Jul 23, 1903
     see Lubbe, Mr Clemens A.

Heitland, Miss Minnie   "Death"   Dec 4, 1902
     see Holstein, George

Helm, Wm P.   "Died"   Jan 4, 1878
     Died- Wm P. Helm who was fromerly assistant teacher in our school
     died on January 1st.

Henderson, Mrs   "Paloma"   Jun 22, 1899
     George and Albert Thompson came from Chicago to attend the funeral of
     thier sister, Mrs Henderson.

Henderson, Alfred   "Local"   Nov 2, 1893
     Alfred, the 23 yr old son of Mr and Mrs G.H. Henderson died at 5:30 P.M.
     Wednesday. Funeral today at 4 P.M. from the house. Died from quick
     consumption.

Henderson, Alfred   "Local"   Nov 9, 1893
     Funeral of Alfred Henderson was last Thursday afternoon. Services at the
     house by Rev Reed, pastor of the M.E. church.

Henderson, Mrs G.H.   "Death"   Feb 8, 1883
     see Haskins, Mrs Emily

183

Henderson, Harry   "Obituary"   Jan 25, 1883
    see Gunn, Miss Sarah

Henderson, Henry R.   Jul 14, 1881
    Died- Henry R. Henderson, Commited suicide July 9th. Leaving letters to
    relatives in New York, Philadaphia and Brunswick, N.J.

Henderson, John   Jun 5, 1902
    Included in list of Civil War soldiers buried in Mendon.

Henderson, Martin Luther (Lute) "Local"   Jun 20, 1889
    Harlan, Ind. "Independent of June 6th"
    Died- Martin Luther (Lute) Henderson, formerly of Mendon died at his
    residence in Springfield twp Allen Co. Indiana on May 27th 1889. Age
    43 yrs 5 mo's 14 days. Leaves a wife, 3 daughters, 3 brothers and 2
    sisters.

Henderson, Ned   "Quincy News"   Feb 20, 1879
    Died- Ned Henderson, an inmate of the County poor house. Age 105 yrs

Henderson, Mr and Mrs Rolla   "Death"   Mar 30, 1904
    see Heaney, Samuel W.

Hendricks, Mildred Emma   "Obituary"   Feb 17, 1904
    See Hastings, Thomas Gilbert

Hendricks, Mr S.   "Death"   Aug 19, 1880
    see Alphine, Mrs M.J.

Hendrickson, Mrs   "Local"   Jan 7, 1892
    Mrs J.C. Casley rec'd word from Breckenridge, Mo. that her mother,
    Mrs Hendrickson was dying. Before she could leave she rec'd word of her
    death. Mrs C. and little son Clarence left on the night train.

Hendrickson, Alice E.   Nov 23, 1882
    Died- Alice E. Hendrickson, daughter of Hon Jas. H. Hendrickson of
    Breckenridge, Mo. age 14 yrs.

Hendrickson, Mrs Elizabeth   "Obituary"   Dec 31, 1891
    Elizabeth Hendrickson was born Feb 11, 1823 in Monmouth, N.J. where she
    grew up. Married Henry Van Dien in New York city and came to Illinois with
    her husband. They were married 19 yrs when he died in Adams Co. She
    had lived in Quincy where she had a millinery Est. and 15 yrs in Mendon.
    Buried Stones Church burying ground near Ursa on Friday December 25th.
    Services by pastor Rev A.A. White at the M.E. church at Mendon. Those
    present for the funeral were Wm and John Robbins of Kansas City and their
    wives, her sister Mrs Mary Robbins of Sedalia, Mo. and her son Prof C.W.
    Robbins of the same place, her sister Mrs Rebecca Robbins of Ursa with her
    daughter Miss Addie, her nieces, Mrs Ferree and Mrs Sarah Whitbread of
    Quincy and her brother Mr Garrett Hendrickson. Geo. Bryson her old and
    faithful colored friend was also among the chief mourners at the church.

Hendrickson, Mr Garrett   "Local"   Oct 6, 1886
  died- 11 month old daughter of Mr Garrett Hendrickson Saturday night
  at the home of her aunt, Mrs Van Dien. Buried in the old Stone church
  burial ground near Ursa.

Hendrickson, Garrett   Jan 7, 1892
  see Vandien, Elizabeth

Hendrickson, Mr Garrett   "Obituary"   Dec 24, 1891
  see Van Dien, Mrs

Hendrickson, Mrs Garrett   "Obituary"   Oct 28, 1897
  see Swan, Mrs Mary Ann

Hendrickson, Mr and Mrs Henry   Oct 13, 1881
  Died- last week at the age of 4 yrs, the son of Mr and Mrs Henry Hendrickson
  of Breckenridge, Mo.

Hendrickson, Jas. H.   "Local"   Feb 14, 1889
  The Hon. Jas. H. Hendrickson, of Breckenridge, Mo. came over to attend
  the funeral of his brother in law, D.H. Darby.

Hendrickson, Mrs Jas.   "Obituary"   Feb 5, 1891
  see McVay, Mr Charles

Hendrickson, John   "Death"   Dec 14, 1882
  John Hendrickson died Sunday December 10th at the home of his son,
  James H. Hendrickson in Breckenridge, Mo. Burial in Mendon cemetery
  Funeral in M.E. church by Rev McKown. Was 81 yrs old. Born in New
  Jersey and at an early age moved to Middletown, Butler Co. Ohio. Some
  40 yrs ago he settled in Illinois. He was considered one of the old
  settlers of Adams Co.

Hendrickson, John   Jun 1, 1899
  included in list of soldiers buried in Mendon cemetery.

Hendrickson, John and Mary   "Obituary"   Jan 3, 1895
  see Darby, Mrs D.H. (Danl)

Hendrickson, Lieut   Jun 4, 1885
  included in list of those buried in Mendon cemetery.

Hendrickson, Mamie   "Obituary"   Jan 10, 1895
  see Scranton, Mary

Hendrickson, Mary A.   "Obituary"   Feb 14, 1889
  see Darby, Daniel H.

Hendrickson, Mary A.   "Obituary"   Jan 3, 1895
  see Darby, Mrs D.H. (Dan'l)

Hendrickson, Miss Mina   "Obituary"   Jan 17, 1895
  see Scranton, Mary

185

Hendrickson, Mrs Phebe   "Died"   May 1, 1879
   In Kansas City, Mo. on the 24th inst, Mrs Phebe Hendrickson died in her
   32nd yr. She was the daughter of Amos Sranton of this vicinity. Had been
   sick several months. Mrs S. left for Kansas City and arrived only shortly
   before her daughter's death. Remains brought here for burial Friday P.M.
   Services by Rev A.B. Campbell in the Cong'l church. She leaves her
   husband and 4 children.

Hendrickson, Walter   "Whig"   Feb 22, 1900
   Died- Walter Hendrickson, the 7 month old son of Mr and Mrs Wm Hendrickson of Ursa died yesterday morning from pneumonia and spinal meningitis.

Hendry, Mrs Catherine   "Obituary"   Jan 29, 1891
   see Nichols, James

Henerhoff, Fred   "Ellington"   Nov 29, 1888
   Died- Mr Fred Henerhoff after a wagon accident on his way home from
   Quincy. Buried in Quincy Tuesday November 20th.

Henning, Mrs   "Death"   Feb 16, 1899
   see Hagmeyer, Mrs

Henning, Mrs   "Fowler"   Jun 22, 1893
   Funeral of Mrs Henning was Monday P.M. She had suffered a long time
   with a tumor.

Henry, Mr   "Paloma"   Aug 1, 1895
   Several from here went to Camp Point Friday to attend the funeral of
   Mr Henry.

Henry, Mrs Clara   "Obituary"   Dec 29, 1898
   see Tharpe, John W.

Herbin, Mr and Mrs   "Camp Point"   May 17, 1900
   The infant child of Mr and Mrs Herbin died last week of whooping cough.
   The child was a twin, the other died a few weeks ago. This is the 5th
   in this colored family within 4 months. 4 children from whooping cough
   and an older person from consumption.

Herndon, James   "Local"   Oct 5, 1905
   James Herndon of Camp Point was instantly killed last Friday eve by
   being caught under a traction engine which he was running when it
   precipatated into a deep ravine from a bridge he was crossing near the
   farm of Louis Leaferinghouse, 3 miles northwest of Camp Point. Leaves
   a wife 1 son and a daughter. Was about 65 yrs old.

Henrici, C.H.   "Local"   Nov 30, 1887
   C.H. Henrici, of Chicago, formerly editor of the Quincy Tribune (now
   the Germania) died Monday. Age 47 yrs. He was the son in law of Dr
   Rittler of Quincy. Leaves a wife and 3 children.

Herring, Salona   "Named in Will"   Jul 5, 1894
    see Witt, Samuel R.

Herron, Glenn   "Local"   Sep 27, 1905
    Samuel Willard rec'd word Monday of the death of his wife's nephew,
    Glenn Herron, of York Nebr. They attended the funeral at LaPrairie
    Tuesday.

Heron, Harry   "Local"   Jul 13, 1893
    One of Goldens old settlers "Old Harry Heron" committed suicide
    Tuesday A.M. by shooting homself in the temple while standing on the
    Wasbash tracks. Herron was peculiar and a crank and the act may be
    assigned to insanity in the absence of any known motive.

Herzog, Mrs Carl   "Coatsburg"   Aug 16, 1894
    Died- Saturday August 11th, wife of Carl Herzog of heart trouble. Born
    and raised in Germany. Came to U.S. with her husband 25 yrs ago. Leaves
    husband and 9 children. Services at the Lutheran church by the Lutheran
    minister Monday A.M. Buried in the village cemetery. ·

Herzog, Mr and Mrs John   "Tioga"
    Died- Mr and Mrs John Herzog are mourning the loss of 3 children which
    died recently of diptheritic sore throat.
    (So sorry, I missed getting a date on this item)

Herzog, Rudolph and Ernest   "Coatsburg"   Aug 16, 1894
    Rudoplh Herzog, of Montpelier, Ohio and Ernest Herzog of Silvah Springs,
    Ark. returned to attend the funeral of their mother.

Hess, Mrs Roxie   "Death"   Jan 4, 1905
    see VanDyke, Mrs P.C.

Hewes, Grandma   "Payson"   Jul 27, 1887
    Grandma Hewes, the mother of our supervisor S.E. Hewes died yesterday
    A.M. Funeral will be at the M.E. church Tuesday at 10.

Hewes, Mrs Etta   "Death"   Jan 24, 1901
    see Sinnock, George

Hewes, Rev M.A.   "Local"   Mar 23, 1904
    Rev M.A. Hewes of Quincy, a retired Methodist minister died last Sat.
    Services at the Vernon St M.E. church Monday P.M. Taken to Jacksonville
    for burial. He was pastor here during the war and often visited Mendon.
    He preached the sermon at Conrad Quig's funeral.

Hewes, Samuel E.   "Local"   Mar 15, 1905
    Died- Samuel E. Hewes of Quincy suddenly Thursday A.M. of paralysis
    of the heart. Formerly lived at Payson. Leaves a wife and daughter, Mrs
    Clarence A. Wells, 2 brothers, Dr C.T. Hewes of Quincy and George Hewes
    of Preston, Kansas, 2 sisters, Mrs C.W. Kay of Pasadena, Calif and Mrs
    W.M. Gooding of Weedman, Illinois.

187

Hewitt, Mrs Bessie   "Obituary"   Aug 13, 1891
    see Kells, Richard

Hewitt, Mr and Mrs E.   "Deaths"   May 14, 1903
    see Fitzgerald, Mrs Millie

Hewitt, Elijah   "Death"   Nov 28, 1878
    see Downing, Mrs Martha

Hewitt, Miss Elizabeth   "Obituary"   Aug 8, 1901
    see Lunn, John

Hewitt, Mrs Elizabeth   "Obituary"   Jan 8, 1903
    see Shupe, Mrs Mary

Hewitt, Mrs Elizabeth   "Obituary"   Oct 27, 1886
    see Mealiff, Mrs Jane

Hewitt, Georgia   "Death"   May 14, 1903
    see Fitzgerald, Mrs Millie

Hewitt, Mrs Harriet (Hattie)   "Obituary"   Apr 4, 1901
    see Spencer, Miss Elmira

Hewitt, Mrs Harriet   "Obituary"   Aug 8, 1901
    see Lunn, John

Hewitt, Mrs Harriet E.   "Obituary"   May 12, 1886
    see Betts, Coley E.

Hewitt, Mrs Hattie   "Obituary"   Nov 7, 1901
    see Betts, James A.

Hewitt, Miss Jane   "Obituary"   Dec 22, 1898
    see Wilcox, Mrs Jane

Hewitt, John   Sep 19, 1889
    Died- News rec'd Tuesday from Mrs Robert Stark of Chicago of the death
    of her father, Mr John Hewitt, at Peterboro, Canada on Septmeber 8th.
    Was 84 yrs old. He was a brother of Mr Thomas Hewitt, Mrs Samuel Heaney
    and Mrs Thomas Wilcox all living among us and now the sole survivers
    of 8 children. All born in the North of Irealnd.

Hewitt, John J.   "Local"   Oct 18, 1900
    Died- John J. Hewitt at his home in Riverside, Calif. Tuesday morning
    Sept 11th from congestion of the lungs. Was a Proprietor of the Pearl
    Mills yrs ago.

Hewitt, Martha J.   "Death"   Aug 12, 1880
    see Downing, Wm M.

Hewitt, Mary A.   "Obituary"   Apr 12, 1894
    see Heaney, Mrs Mary A.

Hewitt, Mary A.   "In Memoriam"   Apr 12, 1894
    Died- Mrs Mary A. Heaney at 2 A.M.last Thursday at the home of her
    son, S.W. Heaney, 931 Hampshire St. Quincy at age 82 yrs.
    Mary A. Hewitt was born in the parish of Killishandra, county Cavan,
    Ireland. Married Samuel Heaney Decmeber 2, 1844 and came to this
    country with her husband in the spring of 1849 and after a delay of about
    2 months in St Louis where Mr H's mother was stricken with cholera they
    arrived at Mendon where they lived until 2½ yrs ago when they moved to
    Quincy to live with 2 sons slready settled there. Leaves husband and 2
    sons, Samuel W. and Noble M. Heaney of Quincy, 1 sister, Mrs Thos. Wilcox
    of Loraine and a brother, Mr Thomas Hewitt of Mendon besides nieces and
    nephews and grandchildren. Was a life long member of the Episcopal church.
    Buried in Mendon cemetery Friday after services in the Zion church by
    Rev R.W. Hewitt, a nephew of the deceased.

Hewitt, Millie   "Deaths"   May 14, 1903
    see Fitzgerald, Mrs Millie

Hewitt, Rev R.W.   "Deaths"   Apr 12, 1894
    see Heaney, Mrs Mary A.

Hewitt, Mr Robert   "Local"   Feb 15, 1894
    Sad news of the death of Mr Robert Hewitt of Chelan, Washington was
    rec'd here Monday. His remains are expected here on Saturday.

Hewitt, Mrs Robert   "Obituary"   Feb 27, 1890
    see Lunn, Dr

Hewitt, Robert E.   "In Memoriam"   Feb 22, 1894
    Last Saturday A.M. Mrs Hewitt and her daughter and Mr John Hewitt
    arrived from Chelan, Washington with the remains of Robert E. Hewitt.
    Corspe was taken to the old home in Honey Creek and brought back to
    Mendon next day for burial in Mendon cemetery. Services in the Zion
    Episcoplal church by Rev Savage assisted by Rev R.W. Hewitt of Kewanee.
    Born in county Cavan, Ireland October 24, 1846. Died Feb 9, 1894 at
    age 47 yrs 3 mo's 15 days. 14 yrs ago he married Miss Harriet Lunn, of
    this place and went to Fremont. Nebr. to reside. 4 yrs ago he moved to
    Chelan.

Hewitt, Rev Robert W.   "Death"   Mar 30, 1904
    see Heaney, Samuel W.

Hewitt, Mrs Sarah   "Obituary"   Aug 13, 1891
    see Kells, Richard

Hewitt, Thomas   "Obituary"   Dec 29, 1898
    Died- Mr Thomas Hewitt of Mendon on Xmas day from old age. Born county
    Cavan, Ireland 1811 and came to this country in 1849. Settled Mendon
    July of same yr. Married Sarah Kells March of 1852 who survives him
    along with 6 children, 4 girls and 2 boys, 5 survive him, Anna E. wife of
    Wm Mealiff of Honey Creek, Rev R.W. of Moline, Martha J. wife of G.H.
    Baldwin of Honey Creek, Sarah L. (Sadie) at home and Mary E. wife of Geo.
    T. Chant of Stronghurst. Thomas D. the eldest son was drowned in Bear
    Creek May of 1872. Funeral in Zion church. Services by Rev T.A. Waterman.
    Buried in village cemetery.

189

Hewitt, Thomas   "Died"   Feb 16, 1899
Died- Mr Thomas Hewitt, December 26th at age 87 yrs. Son Robert W. is
rector of Christ church at Moline, daughter Sadie and Annie who married
Wm Mealiff, Martha married a son of the late Henry Baldwin, Lizzie another
daughter married Hon. G.T. Chant mayor of Stronghurst. Buried from the
Zion Episcopal church December 28th. Services by Rev T.A. Waterman.

Hewitt, Thomas   "Obituary"   Dec 22, 1898
see Wilcox, Mrs Jane

Hewitt, Thomas   "Obituary"   Apr 12, 1894
see Heaney, Mrs Mary A.

Hewitt, Mrs Thos.   "Death"   Jul 20, 1904
see Butler, Hannah

Hewitt, William   Jan 10, 1884
Died- January 10th, Mr Wm Hewitt, age 72 or 3 yrs at his residence
in Honey Creek. Services in Zion Episcopal church by Dean Irvine

Hewitt, Mrs Wm   "Obituary"   Aug 13, 1891
see Kells, Richard

Hewitt, Wm   "Obituary"   Dec 22, 1898
see Wilcox, Mrs Jane

Hewitt, Mrs Wm   "Death"   Jul 20, 1904
see Butler, Hannah

Hewitt, Mr and Mrs Wm   "Obituary"   Oct 27, 1886
see Mealiff, Mrs Jane

Hicks, Mrs   May 3, 1883
A child of Mrs Hicks of Colchester fell into a bucket of hot water
last week and died.

Higbee, Judge   "Quincy News"   Dec 11, 1884
Death of Judge Higbee at Pittsfield. He had been on the bench since
1861 and 40 yrs in the legal profession. Age 66 yrs.

Higbie, Squire   "Death"   Oct 4, 1888
see Poling, Mr Wykoff

Higbie, Mrs   Mar 21, 1889
50th wedding anniversary for Squire Poling and wife on Monday, the
day of Mrs Higbie's death

Higbie, Edmund   Jun 22, 1893
Included in list of graves decorated in Mendon on Decoration Day.

Higbie, Squire Edmund   "Obituary"   Dec 7, 1893
    Died- Squire Edmund Higbie, one of Mendon's early settlers Saturday at
    8 A.M. December 2nd. Buried Sunday P.M. in the Mendon cemetery. Services
    by Rev Wm Burgess at the grave. He was Caption in the 118th Ill. Inf.
    during the war. In 1844 he was county assessor, was notory public 25 yrs
    and J.P. nearly that long. Born in Queens Co. New York January 4, 1819
    Was nearly 75 yrs old. Came to Mendon in July 1842 and lived there since.
    Married July 31, 1842 to Mary Ann Poling, who died about 3 yrs ago.
    They had 9 children, only 3 are living, Mrs E. Anderson and Charles Higbie
    of Mendon and Mrs Warren Munroe of Beverly. Borne to the grave by
    members of the local G.A.R. post.

Higbie, Mrs Edmund   "Obituary"   Mar 21, 1889
    Died- Mrs Edmund Higbie at 2 A.M. Monday morning. Mary Ann Poling was
    born in Brooklyn N.Y. August 15, 1821. Was 68 yrs old at her death. She
    was the only daughter of the late Charles Poling by his first marriage.
    Came to Illinois with her father in 1839 and lived around Mendon since.
    Joined Baptist church in 1840. Married July 31, 1842 at the parental
    home of Edmund Higbie. Had 9 children, 8 daughters and 1 son.
    5 daughters died in infancy and 1 (Mrs W.J. Nutt) about 17 yrs ago.
    Other children are, Mrs W.T. Munroe of Beverly and Charles Higbie at
    home. She leaves also several brothers and sisters, grandchildren and
    other relatives. Services at her home Tuesday P.M. by Rev S.D. Peet, her
    Pastor of the Cong'l church. Buried Mendon cemetery. Those present were
    her brother Charles of Hamilton, Hancock Co., her niece Mrs Kelley from
    West Point, and Mr and Mrs Munroe and their niece Katie Anderson from
    Beverly with their oldest son Eddied, from Chaddock college and other
    relatives.

Higgins, Mrs   "Obituary"   Aug 25, 1886
    see Logan, Mrs Mary H.

Higgins, Joseph   "Death"   Sep 1, 1881
    A son of Joseph Higgins was killed in a R.R. accident at Camp Point
    August 24th.

Higgins, Joseph N.   Sep 1, 1881
    Died- August 23rd Joseph N. Higgins, Esq. He was born Penn. in 1823
    and moved to Wheeling, Va. in early boyhood, moved to Adams Co. at age
    22 yrs. Married 1858 to Mrs Wilhelmina Runyon (widow of a Methodist
    minister) Survived by his wife and 4 children, 2 girls and 2 boys,
    oldest son Charles, youngest daughter Anna. Moved from Mendon to Carthage
    in 1877. Buried by Rev Prof. Richard on August 25th at the Wesley
    Chapel in Mendon.

Hightower, Mrs   "Death"   May 11, 1893
    see Johnson, Miss Lizzie

Hightower, Wm   "Local"   Dec 25, 1890
    Died Mr Wm Hightower, postmaster at Marcelline.

Hild, Miss Amelia M.   "Death in Adams Co."   Mar 2, 1899
    Died- Miss Amelia M. Hild, only daughter of Adam Hild Wednesday
    Feb 22 nd. Age 22 yrs.

Hildebrand, Mrs   "Loraine"   Feb 7, 1901
Death, Saturday eve at the home of Mrs Darby Wilson. It being Mrs
Hildebrand, who was 83 yrs old and had been living with Mrs Wilson.
Buried Ebenezer cemetery Sunday.

Hill, Charles   "Lima"   Dec 28, 1887
Died- Mr Charles Hill a former resident of Lima twp died at his home
near Warsaw last Thursday. Buried in Lima cemetery. Services at the M.P.
church.

Hill, Mrs DeWitt   "Ursa"   Apr 13, 1899
Died- last Sunday at her home in Quincy, Mrs DeWitt Hill of spinal
meningitis. Brought here for burial Tuesday at 11 A.M. from the Christian
church. Services by Rev E.A. Ince of Quincy. 25 yrs old. Before her
marriage she was Miss Lela McAdams and was the daughter of Mrs Anderson
of this place. Mr H. is engaged in the mail service and was principal
of our school 4 yrs ago. Leaves husband and 2 little girls, mother ,
2 brothers and 2 sisters.

Hill, Mrs E.S.   "Local"   Apr 24, 1884
Mrs E.S. Hill died. She was 71 yrs old. Her niece was Mrs D.H. Darby of
Mendon. She lived Carthage.

Hill, Lem   Sep 24, 1891
Lem Hill of Carthage died September 21st.

Hill, Martha   Jan 9, 1890
Martha Hill was buried at Warsaw on January 7th. She was the niece of
Mrs Harris and Mr Pres. Hill.

Hill, Mrs Wm   "Loraine"   Dec 10, 1903
Remains of Mrs Wm Hill was shipped here Friday eve from Galesburg and
buried Saturday December 5th at the Brenneman cemetery.

Hill, Old Mother   "Lima"   July 8, 1880
Old mother Hill died today.

Hillman, Joseph   "Death"   Jun 26, 1902
Mr Jospeh Hillman, born Worchestershire, England January 31, 1834 died
June 21, 1902. Age 68 yrs 4 months 20 days. Married Francis Elizabeth
Bedale April 9, 1858 in Dudley England. Had 9 children, 3 died when
small. Surviving is Mrs Frank Evans of near Mendon, Mrs Geo. Hughes of
Kellerville, Ill., Frances E., John, Mrs Jane Bedale and Rose A. all of
Mendon. All at funeral. Mr H. was a moulder by trade and worked at it
till he came to U.S. He sailed from Liverpool March 1, 1869 and settled
on a small place 1½ miles southwest of Mendon where he stayed since. He
was a member of Ancient order of United Workman for almost 20 yrs.
Funeral at the Zion Episcopal church Sunday afternoon by pastor Mr
Alexander of Warsaw. Buried Mendon cemetery. Leaves a wife and children.
Pallbearers were- Geo. Steiner, Cyrus Overbay, Rufus McCune of Loraine,
Wm Thompson, D.W. Worman and E.H. Wilkins of Mendon.

192

Hillman, Mary Ann   "Obituary"   Mar 29, 1894
    see Donichan, James

Hillman, Willie   Sep 1, 1881
    Willie, son of Jos. Hillman died August 26th.

Hilton, Rev T.B.   "Obituary"   Aug 16, 1894
    "Supplement fron Sunday School"
    Rev T. B. Hilton, late pastor of the Vermont St M.E. church of Quincy
    died March 25, 1894

Hinchback, Mr   "Coatsburg"   Apr 16, 1891
    Died- at his residence Mr Hinchback, age 70 yrs. Buried village cemetery.

Hinnes, Mr   "Death"   Mar 17, 1881
    see Hall, Mr

Hire, Mrs Charles   "Paloma"   Aug 2, 1888
    Died- Mrs Charles Hire living 1½ miles west of here died Monday July 23rd
    Leaves a husband and 3 children, the youngest about 1 yr old.

Hiron, Mr and Mrs James   "Fowler"   Oct 12, 1887
    Mr and Mrs James Hiron buried their oldest daughter last Friday. She
    was 13 yrs old.

Hirths, Jacob   "Burton"   Jan 2, 1879
    Died- the youngest daughter of Jacob Hirths, age 12 yrs.

Hobbs, Mrs Mary   "Obituary"   Jul 18, 1901
    see Kennedy, Geo. Thomas

Hobby, Oliver   "Local"   Sep 21, 1887
    Died- Oliver Hobby, only son of Mr Wm Hobby of Honey Creek September
    19th. Age 29 yrs 7 months 7 days. Born July 12, 1858. Buried in Mendon
    Cemetery. Services at the Cong'l church by Rev S.D. Peet.

Hobby, Mr Wm   "Local"   Oct 23, 1884
    Died- October 15th at the home of her son, Mr Wm Hobby, Mrs Ellen Oliver,
    76 yrs old. Services by Rev E.C. Crane. She was an old resident of Mendon.

Hobby, William   "Probate Notice"   Nov 5, 1903
    1st Monday of January 1904   David P. Strickler, Adm.

Hobby, William   "Death"   Oct 8, 1903
    William Hobby living about 5 miles northeast of Mendon died Tuesday
    noon from heart disease. 74 yrs old and had lived on the farm where he
    died over 50 yrs. Survived by his wife and daughters, Mrs John Shepherd
    and Mrs W. McArthur. Deceased was born in Connecticut and served in the
    U.S. Navy during the civil war.

Hobby, Willaim Henry   "Obituary"   Oct 15, 1903
William Henry Hobby was born May 6, 1830 and died at his home in Honey
Creek October 6th. Was 73 yrs 5 months old. Born State of Conn. Came to
Illinois 1851 and settled on the place where he died. Married Martha
O"Dear in November 1853. They had 6 children, 4 girls and 2 boys, Susan,
Ellen, Oliver, William, Nancy and Hattie. Only Nancy and Hattie survive
him. He was in the naval services in the 60's for 6 months and on the
ocean from the age of 12 to 18 yrs. Was at one tome a member of the
Christian church. Leaves a wife, 2 daughters, 14 grandchildren. Services
by Rev S.R. Reno at the home. Buried Mendon cemetery.

Hodge, Sid   "Payson"   Mar 20, 1884
Sid Hodge brought one of his children to Quincy March 16th for burial.

Hoener, Henry   "Tioga"   Oct 6, 1898
Died- October 1st at his home Mr Henry Hoener, 75 yrs old. Leaves 9
children. His wife and 2 children preceded him in death. Buried
in German cemetery in Tioga Monday. Services by Rev. Ott.

Hofer, Aletha C.H.   "Local"   Aug 11, 1892
Died- Miss Aletha C.H. Hofer, 2nd daughter of Prof John E. Hofer
537 Locust St. Quincy. She died on Friday afternoon. Age 21 yrs 8 months
17 days.

Hoffman, Mrs   "Local"   Oct 4, 1894
An old colored lady of Honey Creek named Hoffman, grandmother of
Alex Scott, was found dead in bed Sunday morning. Died from old age.
Was over 90 yrs old. Buried Mendon cemetery on Monday.

Hoffman, Mrs C.H.   "Obituary"   Feb 23, 1887
   see Boyer, Mrs Hannah C.

Hoffman, Mrs C.H.   "Obituary"   Aug 11, 1881
   see Cooke, Mrs Julia

Hoffman, Mrs C.H.   "Obituary"   May 17, 1900
   see Cooke, Dudley Benton

Hoffman, Charles H.   "Probate Notice"   Apr 17, 1902
   1st Monday of June 1902   William W. Benton Adm.

Hoffman, Charles Henry   "Death"   Jan 23, 1902
Died- January 18th Charles Henry Hoffman of apolplexy. 77 yrs 8 mo's
25 days old. Born in New York City April 24, 1824. Married Miss Elizabeth
A. Cooke daughter of the late A.D. Cooke of Mendon June 1856. She
survives him. Member of the Episcopal church over 50 yrs. Services at his
home Monday P.M. Left N.Y. 1834 for N. Carolina and attended school till
1840 moved to Boston, Mass to learn daguerretype business under John
Plumb and went to N.Y. City and opened up rooms and made the 1st picture
in the city according to those principals. Went to Philadelphia and
opened rooms for a short time and on to Baltimore and had a lumber business
in N. Carolina 1848. 1846 he moved to Quincy and went farming next fall
on the Mound farm in Ellington till 1849, went to California and assisted
building 1st frame house in Scramento for B.P. Cornwall. returned to Ill.
1855 and lived here since. Had a hardware and grocery store in Mendon till
recently. Was P.M. at Mendon for nearly 25 yrs.

Hoffman, Edith Carlton   Feb 14, 1884
    Died- in Quincy Feb 6th of diptheria, Edith Carlton youngest daughter
    of Wm B. and Ellen Hoffman. Age 6 yrs 10 months 8 days.

Hoffman, Elizabeth   "Obituary"   Apr 11, 1889
    see Ingersoll, Ralph A.

Hoffman, Dr Geo. C.   "Local"   Jan 15, 1888
    Died- Dr Geo. C. Hoffman at his home in Quincy on Wednesday A.M. Born
    in Bamberg, Bavaria October 22, 1839. Came to America 1870. Leaves a
    wife and 4 children. The oldest being 15 yrs and the youngest 5 yrs.
    Mass from the St Boniface church and buried in Catholic cemetery.

Hoffman, H.H.   "Local"   Dec 23, 1885
    The remains of the late H.H. Hoffman who died at the insane asylum at
    Jacksonville was buried in Woodland cemetery Quincy Sunday afternoon.
    Services from the Epiacopalian church. Funeral in charge of the Masons
    #439.

Hoffnickle, Mr   "Coatsburg"   Sep 12, 1889
    The family of Mr Hoffnickle near Columbus has typhoid fever. A son and
    daughter were buried last week. Another son is very low.

Hofmeister, Mrs Conrad   "Local"   Sep 15, 1898
    Suicide- Mrs Conrad Hofmeister, age 65 yrs committed suicide by hanging
    early Monday A.M. at her home 3 or 4 miles south of Kellerville while
    temperarily insane.

Hogan, Ed   "Local"   Mar 10, 1886
    Murdered- Ed Hogan of Cameron, Mo. in Big Slough, south of Quincy.

Hogan, Mrs Frank   "Death"   Mar 30, 1899
    see Ausmus, Mrs Ann

Hoig, Annie F.   "Will Suit"   Apr 12, 1894
    see McAdams, Clifton

Hoke, Evertt   "Camp Point"   Dec 14, 1882
    Evertt Hoke died at the home of George W. Omer Sunday eve December 10th
    Burial Kentucky.

Holden, Mr   "West Point"   Jul 13, 1893
    Died- Mr Holden age 67 yrs died July 8th at his home about 5 miles west
    of town. Buried at Cook's graveyard.

Holden, Mrs J.P.   "Death"   Apr 5, 1900
    see Michael, James

Holden, Mrs   "West Point"   Jun 16, 1892
    Mrs Holden died Saturday. Buried Sunday 2 P.M.

Holden, Daniel   "Loraine"   Mar 8, 1905
    Several from here attended the funeral of Daniel Holden west of town
    Saturday.

Holeman, Edwin Charles   "Local"   Nov 1, 1900
Died- Little Edwin Charles Holeman, youngest child of William and the late
Margaret Holeman at his home in Payson of membranous croup Friday A.M.
October 26th. 10 yrs old. Edwin was a nephew of Mr and Mrs J.R. Urech.
Funeral Sunday A.M.

Holeman, Margaret L.   "Local"   Jan 17, 1895
Died- Margaret L., wife of Wm Holeman at her home in Payson, Illinois
Friday A.M. January 11th of pneumonia. 43 yrs old. She was a sister
of Mrs J.R. Urech. Funeral Sunday.

Holiday, Albert   Jun 4, 1885
Included in list of Soldiers graves decorated on Memorial Day in Mendon
cemetery.

Hollenstein, Henry   "Quincy"   Mar 16, 1899
Died- Henry Hollenstein, age 69 yrs Monday night of general debility.
Leaves an aged wife and 2 sons.

Hollingsworth, J.T.   "Local"   Apr 13, 1899
Comrade J.T. Hollingsworth, of the 28th Ill. Inf. was found drowned
in the pond at the Soldiers home Quarry Monday A.M.
Verdict; Suicide.

Hollister, Miss Anna   "Obituary"   Mar 16, 1882
see Campbell, Rev A.B.

Holmes, Jos.   "Fowler"   Feb 2, 1888
Jos. Holmes of Chiola was buried in the Chase cemetery Wednesday. Services
by Rev Wolfarth of Quincy.

Holmes, Wm   "Quincy Whig"   Aug 17, 1879
An old man named Wm Holmes nearly 70 yrs old jumped into the river last
night. He was in the business as a picture maker. Was married the 2nd
time. Left a note he was going to take his own life.

Holstein, Arthur   "Obituary"   Mar 15, 1900
Died- Arthur Holstein of typhoid fever at Blessing hospital Quincy
Mar 9th at 4 P.M. Born Mendon twp Jan 18, 1868 Was 32 yrs old. Mother
was Miss Olive Sproat, 2nd daughter of the late Percy Sproat. She died
1873 and after her death the family moved to Oklahoma and returned to
Ill. Father died at Carthage a few yrs ago. Brothers Geo. and Arthur
settled in Mendon. Arthur was a school teacher and school master at
Coffield, Prairie and Bealty schools, Principal of the Fowler school 2 yrs
and later taught near Columbus. Married September 17, 1892 to Miss Lulu
Snider of Marcelline who survives him. They had 1 son and 1 daughter.
Was a member of the Mendon Cong'l church. Had 1 brother, Geo Holstein of
Fall City, Iowa and a half sister, Miss Ollie Holstein of Bolivar, Mo. who
also survives hime. Services by Rev J.S. Bayne at the Cong'l church
Saturday at 2 P.M. Buried in family lot in Mendon cemetery.
Pallbearers were- Rolla Henderson, Walter Baldwin, Lee Siple, Frank
Morrison, C.W. Pepple and J.B. Frisbie Jr.

Holstein, David   Oct 30, 1890
Mr David Holstein of Bolivar died October 10th at age 84 yrs. He was
the grandfather of Arthur and George Holstein.

196

Holstein, George   "Local"   Dec 4, 1902
    Died- Mr George Holstein at his home in Falls City, Nebr. November 20th of
    catarrh of the stomach. Married Miss Minnie Heitland of Tioga some yrs ago
    and is survived by her and 4 daughters. Was formerly a resident of
    Mendon and worked at Zimmerman's mill for a time. Was a cousin of Orville
    Strickler.

Holstein, Muriel   "Died"   Jul 26, 1905
    Muriel, 8 yr old son of Mrs Arthur Holstein died Friday July 21st. at
    Camp Point. Buried Mendon beside his father.

Holstein, Mr Thomas   "Local"   Dec 20, 1894
    Died= at his home in Carthage at age 53 yrs, Mr Thomas Holstein. Remains
    brought here for burial and buried in family lot Friday A.M. Services by
    Rev W. Burgess. Leaves 2 sons, Arthur and George and 1 daughter.

Holtschlag, Mrs Elizabeth   "Death in Adams Co."   Mar 30, 1899
    Died- Mrs Elizabeth Holtschlag Sunday at the home of her father, Herman
    Bockenfeld 4 miles east of Quincy at age 27 yrs.

Homan, Mrs Mary   "Local"   Aug 31, 1899
    Died- Mrs Mary Homan and Mrs Anna L. Parker, 2 old residents of
    Quincy died this week.

Homer, Mr and Mrs Herman   "Tioga"   Dec 22, 1898
    Died- the infant child of Mr and Mrs Herman Homer last week. Buried
    German cemetery, Tioga last Thursday.

Honer, Mr and Mrs   "Tioga"   Apr 5, 1894
    Died- on March 26th the little infant son of Mr and Mrs Honer. Buried
    in Lutheran cemetery on the following Wednesday.

Hood, Miss Aralita Hooh (Darley) "Payson"   Feb 19, 1880
    Died- on Feb. 12th, Miss Aralita Hood (Darley) of consumption. Services
    by Rev Wallace at the Cong'l church. 6 young ladies were pallbearers.

Hood, Joseph   "Local"   Jun 22, 1893
    Mr Joseph Hood, an old resident of Payson fell from the top of a ladder
    Monday while picking cherries fracturing his skull. Death resulted in
    a few minutes.

Hooten, Prof J.E.   "Suicide"   Jun 19, 1902
    Prof J.E. Hooten committed suicide at Joliet, Ill Friday eve at the
    Duncan Hotel in his room. Had been Supt of schools at Lockport 7 yrs. Was
    a principal of Mendon High school from 1892 to 95. Was about 36 yrs old.
    Leaves a wife and 1 child.

Hooten, Joseph E.   "Death"   Jun 26, 1902
    "Morton Advocate"   Joseph E. Hooten took his own life in his
    room at the Duncan Hotel at Joliet. Leaves a wife and 7 yr old son.
    Remains were brought back to Lockport. Services Sunday afternoon at the
    church and taken to Mortin, Mrs H.'s home for burial.

Hooker, Judge C.E.   "Local"   Jul 25, 1901
    Judge C.E. Hooker died Tuesday at his home in Carthage. 30 yrs old. Was
    elected County judge of Hancock Co. in 1898.

Hoover, Mr Henry   "Payson"   Nov 11, 1885
   Mr Henry Hoover, while chopping wood, fell off the log he was chopping
   falling across the log, killing himself. Dr said he fractured his spleen.
   Mr H. was an old resident of Fall Creek. Leaves a wife and several children.
   Buried at Fall Creek church.

Hopkins, Mrs Elizabeth   "Tioga"   Aug 9, 1888
   Died- August 2nd in Tioga, Mrs Elizabeth Hopkins age 64 yrs 8 mo's 23
   days. Born in Bracken Co. Ky. in 1823 and married R.T. Hopkins on
   March 24, 1842. Settles Tioga in 1861. Mr H. died Feb 26, 1878. She was a
   member of the Baptist Methodist church for about 40 yrs.

Hopkins, Jimmie   "Lima"   Apr 8, 1880
   A young man named Jimmie Hopkins age 9 yrs living with his parents
   west of Tioga was drug by his horse and lived only a short time.

Hopson, Mr and Mrs Alex   "Loraine"   Sep 13, 1894
   A 18 month old child of Mr and Mrs Alex Hopson, living northwest of here
   fell into a boiler of water Saturday and was drown.

Hopson, Mrs Bradley   "Loraine"   Feb 7, 1889
   Mrs Bradley Hopson, of Breckenridge was buried here Saturday.

Hopson, Mrs Nathan   "Loraine"   Aug 3, 1904
   Funeral of Mrs Nathan Hopson was held here at the Christian church
   Saturday A.M. and was buried Loraine cemetery.

Horn, Mrs A.E.   "Death"   Mar 2, 1882
   see Thompson, Mrs

Horn, Adam   "Death"   Nov 3, 1881
   see Stahl, Mrs Mary

Horn, Mr Adam   "Died"   Aug 17, 1882
   Mr Adam Horn of Fowler died August 14th. He was a native of Westmoreland
   Co. Penn. He was the father of our well known citizen Peter G. Horn and
   A.E. Horn and also Mrs Brinton of Ellington and the late Mrs Stahl of
   Fowler. He was 77 yrs old. Services by Rev John Stahl of Augusta.

Horn, Adam   "Probate Notice"   Feb 1, 1883
   3rd Monday of March 1883   A.E. Horn Adm.

Horn, Adam E.   "Death"   Feb 19, 1903
   Died- Mr Adam E. Horn a few days ago in Chicago. He was formerly a
   resident of Mendon twp, was a Republican. 1876 was elected to assessor
   and re-elected 1877 served 2 yrs. elected supervisor 1879.

Horn, Mr C.S.   "Death"   Feb 9, 1888
   see Foltz, Mrs Mary

Horn, Mr and Mrs C.S.   "Local"   Nov 16, 1887
   Mr and Mrs C.S. Horn are at home again after an absence caused by the
   sickness and death of Mr Horn's father.

Horn, Mrs Charles   "Death"   Mar 2, 1899
   see Judy, Mrs. Nancy

Horn, Mrs. Martha E.   "Local"   Feb 1, 1900
   Died-Mrs Martha E. Horn, wife of Adam E. Horn, formerly a resident of
Mendon twp died at her home in Chicago Thursday night. Buried there
Saturday. Was the daughter of Rev Naylor of Macomb and the mother of
Frank C., Joseph E., Adam N. and Margaret E. Horn.

Horn, Mary   "Probate Notice"   Mar 6, 1884
   3rd Monday of April 1884   P.C. Horn, Adm.

Horn, Mr. Peter G.   "Obituary"   Oct 26, 1887
   Mr. Peter G. Horn died at his home near Fowler on Sunday P.M. in his
63rd yr. Born Westmoreland Co. Penn on July 14, 1825. Married April 19,
1853 to Desilla Stahl. They came west in April 1857 and settled near
Fowler where they lived since. Leaves a wife, 3 daughters and 1 son.
Daughters are all unmarried and live at home. Son is married and lives
in Mendon. Also leaves a brother, A.E. Horn of Chicago and a sister,
Mrs. Brinton of Quincy. Services at the Fowler cemetery by Rev King
following services at the Horn home. Rev King is of Lomax, Ill.
Mr. Horn belonged to the U.B. Church.
CORRECTION: "Local"   Nov 1887
The late Mr. P.G. Horn left 2 daughters and 1 son. 3 children in all.

Horn, Peter G.   "Probate Notice"   Jan. 19, 1888
   1st Monday of March 1888   C.S. Horn and Mary J. Horn, Adms.

Hornecker, J.G.   "Camp Point"   Sep 12, 1901
   Funeral of J.G. Hornecker was at the Methodist Church last Thursday P.M.
by C.F. Stecher assisted by Rev McNabb. Buried in Village cemetery.

Hornecker, Mrs Kate   "York Neck"   Dec 8, 1898
   Died-at her home in Camp Point twp., Mrs. Kate Hornecker, wife of Geo.
Hornecker. Leaves her husband, 6 boys and 8 girls.

Horner, Anna Elizabeth   "Death"   Dec. 23, 1897
   see Simpson, Benjamin Franklin

Hoskins, Mr. Alex   "Northwest end"   Aug. 3, 1899
   Died-a little child of Mr. Alex Hoskins was buried at Keith cemetery on
Saturday eve.

Houdyshell, Miss Eliza   "Died"   Oct 15, 1891
   Miss Eliza Houdyshell was born November 10, 1825 and died at the
residence of Mr. Jacob Casley near Mendon October 10th 1891 at the age of
65 yrs 11 months. She came to Illinois 30 yrs ago and has lived in Adams
Co. since. She leaves 1 sister and 2 brothers. Funeral services in the
Lutheran church by pastor Rev M.L. Schmucker on October 11th.

Houdyshell, Eliza   Dec 14, 1893
    Will sell 2 promissory notes of Eliza Houdyshell, deceased on Dec 26,
    1893   Jacob Casley, Adm.

Houdyshell, Eliza   "Probate Notice"   Oct. 22, 1891
    1st Monday of December 1891   Jacob Casley, Adm.

Houdyshell, Mrs. Harry   "Death"   Jun 26, 1890
    see Zoe, Miss Isora

Houdyshell, Mrs. Mary E. (Jacob)"Obituary"   Jun 27, 1889
    Died-Mrs. Mary E. Houdyshell was born near Mendon, Illinois May 18, 1854
    and died at Ursa July 1, 1889 at age 56 yrs 1 month 13 days. Was the
    daughter of J.H. and Martha Johnson. Married Jacob Houdyshell October 10,
    1888. Leaves a father, brothers, sisters, husband and an infant child.
    Funeral in Mendon cemetery by Rev J.W. Thomas of the Lutheran Church.

Houdyshell, John   "Local"   Feb 21, 1895
    Died-Mr. John Houdyshell's infant child of brain fever Saturday. Buried
    Monday.

Houdyshell, Mr. and Mrs. John "Local"   Sep 17, 1903
    The 1 yr old child of Mr. and Mrs. John Houdyshell died of dysentery
    Saturday A.M. Buried in the P.M.

Houghes, Miss Hattie   "Big Neck"   Nov 5, 1891
    Miss Hattie Houghes died of congestion of the lungs October 21st.

Houghton, Mrs.   "Cyclopian Gleamings"   Oct 12, 1887
    The remains of Mrs. Houghton of Quincy was buried in the cemetery at
    the Stone's church last Tuesday.

Householder, A.J.   "Tioga"   Mar 8, 1900
    A.J. Householder fell dead in Weiler and Otts store last Friday from
    heart disease. 77 yrs old. Leaves a wife and 5 children., buried in our
    cemetery Monday.

Howard, Mrs.   "Stillwell"   Dec 9, 1897
    Died-wife of Mr. Howard, the section foreman. Funeral at the M.E.
    church November 30th at 10 A.M. Remains taken to Woodville for burial.
    Orville Wade of Loraine had charge of the funeral.

Howard, Abe   "Payson"   Aug 16, 1883
    A daughter of Abe Howard was buried August 9th.

Howard, Alice   Apr 27, 1882
    Alice Howard, daughter of our former townsman, George Howard, died at
    Loraine April 21st of scarlet fever in her 16th year. She was buried
    beside her mother and father in Frazier cemetery.

Howard, Hartson P.   "Local"   May 3, 1905
    Hartson P. Howard of Quincy, an employee of A.J. Clark, the well driller
    dropped dead yesterday while working near Ursa. Mr. Clark came home this
    A.M. bringing the body in a spring wagon and turned it over to the
    Soldiers Home officials. "Quincy Hearald of April 26th"

Howard, Mrs. Sarah   "Stillwell"   Sep 4, 1884
    Mrs. Sarah Howard, one of our oldest citizens died August 29th. Funeral
    by Rev C.F. McKown of Mendon. Buried Woodville cemetery.

Howard, Tilmon   "Loraine"   Mar 11, 1880
    Died-Tilmon Howard of the southeast part of Walker twp died March 12th
    of consumption. Age 35 yrs. Leaves a wife and several children.

Howell, Emma   "Honey Creek"   Dec 1, 1886
    Died--at her home in Coatsburg Sunday morning November 28th, Emma Howell
    of typhoid fever. Buried Village cemetery.

Howell, Miss Emma and Hattie   "Coatsburg"   Dec 8, 1886
    Funeral services for Misses Emma and Hattie Howell were held at the
    Baptist church Sunday A.M. by Rev T.B. Ausmus.

Howell, Mr. and Mrs. Harry   "Big Neck"   Oct 16, 1890
    Died-October 9th a small child of Mr. and Mrs. Harry Howell.

Howell, Miss Hattie   "Local"   Nov 3, 1886
    Died-Miss Hattie Howell, daughter of Wm. Howell, Esq. of Coatsburg.
    Age 16 yrs. Died from typhoid fever Sunday a.m. Her sister Emma is
    very ill from the same disease.

Howell, Hattie M.   "Honey Creek"   Nov 3, 1886
    Died-at the residence of her parents in Coatsburg October 31st, Hattie
    M. Howell in her 16th year of typhoid fever. Buried in village cemetery.

Howell, Wm.   "Coatsburg   Dec. 21, 1893
    Died-at his home Saturday of congestion of the lungs, Mr. Wm. Howell,
    He was an old citizen.

Hoys, George Fletcher   "Obituary"   Dec 15, 1886
    Died-of croup Dec. 11th at 12 P.M. Age 2 yrs less 9 days George Fletcher,
    son of Thomas and Mary Ellen Hoys of HoneyCreek. Buried Mendon cemetery
    Monday.

Hoys, Thomas   "Local"   Feb 23, 1888
    Died-the 5 yr old daughter of Mr. and Mrs. Thomas Hoys of Honey Creek
    twp of typhoid fever on Feb. 18th. Buried Mendon cemetery.

Hoys, Mr. and Mrs. Thomas   "Local"   Dec. 15, 1885
    Mr. and Mrs. Thomas Hoys' 2 year old child died of croup late Saturday.
    Was buried in Mendon cemetery.

Hoys, Wm C.
Dec 18, 1890
Wm C. Hoys died December 11th at LaGrange, Mo. Services in the Catholic church. He was 25 yrs old. He had a brother, Thomas Hoys.

Huhbard, Melinda   "Death"   Dec 1, 1898
see Baldwin, Harry D.

Hubert, Mrs Dorothy   "Will"   Jan 27, 1904
see Frike, Mrs Anna

Hubert, Fred   "Fowler"   Feb 3, 1904
Remains of Fred Hubert was brought here from Kansas City, Mo. last Monday. Funeral at the M.E. Church Tuesday P.M. by Rev Rose of Paloma. Burial in the Chase cemetery. Leaves a wife, 1 daughter, mother and father.

Huddleston, David   "Local"   Nov 24, 1892
The little 4 yr old daughter of David Huddleston of Liberty was playing with matches and her clothes caught fire. She was fatally burned.

Hudnall, Mrs W.T.   "News"   Jul 16, 1885
Mrs W.T. Hudnall, mother of Walt Hudnall died at the home of her daughter Mrs M.M. Gilbert at Astoria, Ill. July 12th in her 80th yr. Mr Hudnall left for Astoria the same morning.

Hudson, Mrs   "Local"   Sep 12, 1895
The death of Mrs Hudson of Big Neck is reported this week. We are without particulars.

Hudson, Miss Belle   "Loraine"   Dec 29, 1881
Died- Miss Belle Hudson on December 22nd.

Hudson, Cleveland   "Loraine"   Feb 16, 1887
Cleveland Hudson died at his home 2½ miles northeast of Loraine of complications of diseases. Son of T.S. Hudson, pioneer settler and the oldest man now living in the twp.

Hudson, Elizabeth Anne   "Death"   Jun 9, 1898
see Adair, Mrs Elizabeth

Hudson, George   "Loraine"   Oct 19, 1899
Died- George, the little son of Mrs Joseph Hudson Tuesday eve from a gathering on his side. Buried in the cemetery here Wednesday.

Hudson, Mrs Huse   "Big Neck"   Nov 5, 1891
Died- Mrs Huse Hudson, formerly of Big Neck, but late of York Neck died of consumption October 21st. Leaves a husband and 2 little boys. Funeral by Rev I.M. Johnson of LaPrairie. Buried in Ebenezer cemetery.

Hudson, Mrs Phebe   "Loraine"   May 18, 1904
see Payne, Miss Catherine Ann

Hudson, Mrs Catherine   "Loraine"   Nov 17, 1886
Died- Wednesday morning, Mrs Susanna Hudson, wife of T.S. Hudson. She was nearly 79 yrs old. Came with her companion to this country in an early day. Lived in Keene twp 49 yrs. Leaves a great number of children
-cont-

grandchildren and great grandchildren and her husband. Services by
Elder Atcheson at the Dunkard church and buried in our cemetery.

Hudson, Thomas   "Bear Creek"   Apr 28, 1898
    Died- Sunday, Thomas Hudson, age 90 yrs.

Hudson, Mrs Thomas   "Death"   Apr 5, 1905
    see Rust, Charles W.

Hudson, Tommy   "Death"   Aug 31, 1887
    see Hains, Thomas

Hues, Mrs Eliza   "Ursa"   Jan 21, 1892
    Died- Mrs Eliza Hues of Ursa twp on Sunday January 10th. Buried in
    Denson cemetery Tuesday January 12th. She leaves husband, son and 2
    daughters.

Hufendick, Bertha   "Tioga"   Nov 10, 1898
    Died- Bertha Hufendick, daughter of Mr and Mrs Wm Hufendick a few days
    ago of croup. Age 4 yrs. Buried in German cemetery at Tioga. Services by
    Rev Ott.

Hufendick, Mr and Mrs W.   "Lima"   Nov 3, 1898
    Died- Little girl of Mr and Mrs W. Hufendick from croup.

Huffman, Mrs Isabella   "Payson"   May 5, 1881
    Mrs Isabella Huffman, widow of David Huffman died April 29th.

Hughes, Mrs   "Payson"   May 27, 1880
    Mrs Hughes, of Melrose twp died May 22nd.

Hughes, Mrs   "Obituary"   Dec 4, 1890
    see Jennings, Thomas W.

Hughes, Albert   "Ursa"   Jul 26, 1905
    Died- Albert Hughes at his home in Ursa last Saturday afternoon of old
    age. Born January 10, 1810 in Jefferson Co. Ky. Came to Adams Co 1835
    Next yr he married Sarah Ann Taylor and they lived togather 53 yrs.
    She died 20 yrs ago. 3 children survive him, Miss Elizabeth J. and
    Robert C. of Ursa and Mrs Minerva Johnson of Carthage.

Hughes, Mrs Albert   "Death"   Jan 23, 1890
    see McFarland, Catherine

Hughes, Miss Emma   "Local"   Oct 9, 1884
    Miss Emma Hughes, niece of Dr Young who visited in his home a few yrs
    ago died at Altoona, Florida September 23rd.

Hughes, Mrs Geo.   "Obituary"   Jun 26, 1902
    see Hillman, Joseph

Hughes, Mrs Sarah E. (Wm)   "Local"   Mar 16, 1893
    Died- on March 10th, Mrs Sarah E. Hughes. She was the daughter of John
    and Catherine Spears and was born July 18, 1842. Was 1 of 10 children
    2 brothers and 3 sisters survive her. Married Wm Hughes July 4, 1869.
    Leaves husband and 2 children. Services at the Christian church Sunday
    by Rev Whalton. Buried in Stone church cemetery.

Hughes, Zach   "Local"   Oct 4, 1900
    "Bayliss Guide" Died- Zach Hughes, who several weeks ago was pardoned
    by President McKinley for robbing Uncle Sam while he was carrying the
    mails on the Beverly Quincy route died at Beverly last week from
    consumption.

Hulburd, Mrs Anna   "Local"   Jul 3, 1902
    Mrs Anna Hulburd, a ½ sister to Samuel Tallcott, died at her home in
    Otho, Iowa on June 17th of pneumonia. Was 55 yrs old.

Hulendick, Mrs   "Tioga"   Jul 14, 1898
    Died- Saturday July 2nd old Mrs Hulendick. Age 84 yrs at the home of her
    son Henry. Funeral Tuesday. Buried in German cemetery at Tioga.

Hull, Mrs H.C.   "Death"   Jun 15, 1904
    see Leeper, Thomas Fletcher

Hull, Sarah A.   "Obituary"   Mar 21, 1901
    see Nutt, Daniel

Humphrey, Rev C.C.   "Local"   Jan 11, 1894
    Rev Wm Burgess was called on Friday to preach the funeral of Rev C.C.
    Humphrey, last pastor of the Cong'l church, Wythe. Services Saturday
    P.M. He had also been a pastor of the Cong'l church at Summerhill, but
    his best yrs were spent in the home mission field of Nebraska.

Humphrey, Mrs Ira   "Local"   May 12, 1898
    Dr Knapp was in Quincy Tuesday to make out a death claim of Mrs Ira
    Humphrey who died recently in the city.

Humphrey, Col. J.G.   "Death"   Mar 11, 1880
    see Shepherd, Dr

Humphrey, Mary E.   "Death"   Mar 11, 1880
    see Shepherd, Dr

Humphrey, Mrs Wm   "Payson"   Mar 5, 1885
    Died- February 26th, Mrs Humphrey, wife of Wm Humphrey who died about
    2 yrs ago. Mrs H. was 57 yrs old. Leaves 8 grown children.

Humphrey, Wm V.   "Payson"   Aug 29, 1883
    Wm V. Humphrey our deputy sheriff was buried at Burton August 24th.

Hunkey, Louis   "Local"   Dec 18, 1884
    Louis Hunkey committed suicide Dec 11th at the Windsor Hotel. He was a
    well known saleman. Leaves a wife and 4 children.

Hunsaker, Mrs Alexander   "Death in Adams Co."   Mar 9, 1899
    Died- Mrs Alexander Hunsaker at the home of her daughter, Mrs Chris
    Rump, in Payson twp Friday night. Was 69 yrs old.

Hunt, Sarah L.   Adm. Sale"   Apr 12, 1894
    see McAdams, Clifton

Hunter, Mrs   "estate"   Aug 31, 1887
    see Dean, Miss

Hunter, Mrs Ella   "coatsburg"   Sep 24, 1885
    Mrs Ella Hunter, iwfe of Hugh Hunter died Saturday night and was buried
    Sunday in Coatsburg cemetery. Services by Rev Weir.

Hunter, Mr Hugh   "Local"   Jul 7, 1886
    Died- Mr Hugh Hunter of Honey Creek. Age 69 yrs. Buried in Mendon cemetery
    from the M.E. Church.

Hunter, Mrs Hugh Jr.   "Local"   Sep 24, 1885
    Died- September 19th at her late residence in Houston twp, Mrs Hugh
    Hunter Jr. formerly known as Ella Turner. Leaves a husband and a baby
    3 weeks old to be cared for by Mrs H. Hunter Sr. Buried in Coatsburg
    cemetery.

Hunter, Mr John   "Local"   Feb 19, 1903
    Died- Mr John Hunter, who has been suffering from cancer of the stomach
    for some time died at his home near Adrian, Thursday last. Buried
    Saturday in Carthage cemetery. His brothers, Hugh, George and Joseph, his
    sisters, Mrs C.H. White and Miss Elizabeth all attended the funeral.

Hunter, John   "Obituary"   Feb 26, 1903
    John Hunter, son of Hugh and Jane Hunter was born in Catasuqua, Lehigh
    Co. Penn December 16, 1847 and died at his home near Burnside Feb 12,
    1903 being 55 yrs 1 mo. 26 days old. Came with parents to Adams Co. in
    1854 and married Martha A. Eckles Feb 25, 1880. They had 4 children, 3
    survives him. They are Ada, Willie and Grace. Also leaves his loving
    wife 4 brothers and 2 sisters. Services at the M.E. church Saturday
    by Rev T.E. Newland. 4 brithers, a cousin and a brother in law were
    pall-bearers. Burial rites at Moss Ridge. "Burnside Cor. for Carthage
    Gazette"

Hunter, Mrs Rachel   "Local"   Nov 16, 1904
    Mrs Rachel Hunter died Saturday eve. at the family home in Quincy of
    cancer. They moved to the city about a yr ago from the vicinity of
    Loraine where Mrs H. lived nearly all her life. Born in Adams Co. 57 yrs
    ago. Buried in Loraine.

Hunter, Mrs Thomas   "Death"   Mar 21, 1895
    see Patterson, Old lady

Hupert, George E.   "Local"   Aug 20, 1903
    George E. Hupert, of Payson twp, this Co. died suddenly of heart trouble
    at 2 a.m. Sunday. Was about 66 yrs old. Leaves a wife, 4 sons and 3
    daughters.

Huston, Mr and Mrs   "Coatsburg"   Feb 13, 1890
    Buried February 10th at Coatsburg an infant child of Mr and Mrs Huston.

Huston, Mrs   "Death"   Jan 8, 1891
    see McClelland, Mrs Margaret Smiley

Huston, Mrs   "Death"   Apr 14, 1886
    see Felgar, Gracie

Huston, Mrs   "Death"   Aug 25, 1892
    see Jaffers, Mrs

Huston, Annie J.   "Obituary"   Dec 4, 1902
    see Felgar, Simon S.

Huston, Mrs James   "Local"   Mar 2, 1904
    Died- Mrs James Huston at St Mary's hospital Rochester, Minn. Remains
    will probably reach here tomorrow A.M.

Huston, Mrs James   "Died"   Mar 9, 1904
    Funeral of Mrs James Huston was Friday P.M. March 4th from the Lutheran
    church by Rev A.M. Reitzel. Attending were, J.M. Andrew of Denver, Colo
    a brother etc   Euphemia Virginia Andrew was born April 29, 1860 and
    died March 1st. was 43 yrs 10 mo's 2 days old. Married James Huston
    Feb 19, 1885. They had 4 children, Milo, Willie, Grace and Susie who all
    survive her. Joined the Lutheran church Jan 31, 1875 and remained active.
    Also leaves her husband.

Huston, Mrs Susan   "Death"   May 10, 1900
    Died- Mrs Susan Huston at 4 P.M. Friday at the home of her daughter, Mrs
    S.S. Felgar with whom she lived the past yr. Services at the house by Rev
    J.S. Bayne. Buried village cemetery. Susan Jane McClelland was born of
    Scotch parentage at Articlave, County Derry, in the north of Ireland
    Feb 22, 1823. Married James Huston 1846. Came to America 1848 to Lehigh
    Valley of Penn. Family moved to Mendon Oct 1859. United with Prssbyterian
    church in her native place at an early age and with her husband joined the
    Cong'l church of Mendon soon after coming west. Husband died Sept 21, 1871
    leaving her with 6 children. All survive her. She died May 4th at age
    77 yrs 2 mo's 11 days Lived Mendon 41 yrs. Children are- Mrs David Felgar
    of Newton, Kansas, Mrs S.S. Felgar, Miss Sarah and James Huston of Mendon,
    Mrs J.C. Grover of Ellington and Wm Huston of Los Angles, Calif. Pallbearer-
    were, R.B. Starr, D.L. Dickerman, F.F. Dudley, C.B. Garrett, J.R. Urech
    and G.H. Baldwin.

206

Huston, William   "Died"   Mar 12, 1903
    Miss Sarah Huston rec'd word Friday last of the death of her brother,
    William at his home in Los Angles, Calif. Born in Catasauqa, Penn
    Feb 19, 1853 and died of pneumonia Feb 27, 1903. He was the eldest son
    of Mr and Mrs James Huston, deceased. Leaves wife, 1 son and 4 sisters.
    Mrs David Felgar of Newton, Kan., Miss Sarah, Mrs Anna J. Felgar of
    Mendon and Mrs J.C. Grover of Ellington and 1 brother James.

Hutcheons, Miss Amanda Caroline "Obituary"   Dec 14, 1893
    see Nixdorff, Rev Charles Alexander

Hutchison, Mrs   "Payson"   Nov 16, 1882
    Buried last Week, the youngest daughter of Mrs Hutchison.

Hutmacher, Frank   Aug 4, 1881
    Drowned Frank Hutmacher (a boy) Friday July 21st. He lived Quincy.

Hutton, Esq.   May 17, 1883
    Esq. Hutton of Quincy died May 14th. resident of Quincy 45 yrs. Was
    Justice of Peace 20 yrs.

Hyatt, Mrs   "Coatsburg"   May 1, 1890
    Mrs Hyatt was buried here April 23rd.

Hyatt, Miss Elizabeth C.   "Obituary"   May 3, 1900
    see Brown, Capt William J.

Hyatt, Mrs Mary Elizabeth   "Obituary"   Sep 8, 1892
    Mrs Mary Elizabeth Hyatt (Bills) died on Saturday A.M. Sept 3rd of
    dysentery at the home of her son in law, Capt Wm Brown. Born Baton
    Rouge, La. January 1, 1814. Was 78 yrs 8 mo's 2 days old. Came to Mendon
    in October of 1867 to live with her daughter and did until her death.
    She leaves one other daughter, Mrs Fearson of New Orleans, La. Funeral
    at the house by Rev Grantham, priest in charge of the Zion church and
    last rites said at the graveside.

Hybarker, Mrs   "Obituary"   Jan 28, 1892
    see Fletcher, Mrs Wm

Hynes, Mr   "Lima"   Jan 12, 1893
    Died- old Mr Hynes who has been living with his sister, Mrs Workman,
    on Saturday A.M.

Hynes, Mrs Lydia J.   Mar 6, 1884
    Friday Feb 29th was the death of Mrs Lydia J. Hynes in Quincy, wife of
    Mr Charles J. Hynes Pro and editor of the Quincy Herald.

Hyre, Mrs Charles   "Fowler"   Auf 2, 1888
    Died- Wife of Mr Charles Hyre on July 22nd. Leaves husband and 3 children.

Inamn, Lavina J.   "Obituary"   Nov 19, 1903
    Lavina J. Inamn was born Feb 18, 1827 and died at her home in Mendon twp
    Saturday November 14th 1903 at age 76 yrs 8 mo's 26 days. Came to Illinois
    from East Tennessee with her parents in 1832 having lived on this farm
    over 71 yrs. Married October 9, 1853 to John Wilcox who was wounded at
the battle of Pittsburg Landing April 6, 1862 and died Quincy same spring.
    Married 2nd to James O. Baker October 3, 1865, he died December 23, 1873
    Married 3rd to Levi Wright on Sept 7, 1876 who is still living in Mo.
    She also leaves 1 brother out of a family of 12 children. Services at the
    house Monday P.M. by Rev A.M. Reitzel pastor of the Lutheran church.
    Buried Mendon cemetery.

Ippensen, August   "local"   Dec 6, 1888
    Died- youngest child of Mr and Mrs August Ippensen yesterday about noon.
    Buried in Quincy tomorrow.

Ippensen, Mrs Nellie   "Death"   Oct 5, 1904
    Sudden death of Mrs Nellie Ippensen, wife of senior member of the firm
    of Ippensen Bros. Died at her home in Mendon Friday noon. September 30th
    1904 of peritonitis. Born Lima Twp December 8, 1876. She was eldest
    child of Mr and Mrs William Selby. Married Henry Ippensen August 7, 1901
    Had 2 sons who with her husband and parents, 1 sister, Mrs Joseph
    Whitefield of Marcelline and 1 brother, James Ringland survive her. Services at
    the house Sunday afternoon by Rev Thos. Ringland of Weldon, Ill. formerly
    of Ursa. Buried in Stone church cemetery north of Ursa.

Ippersen, Mr Chris   "Local"   Mar 3, 1892
    Died- Mr Chris Ippersen, a grocer and saloon keeper of 339 Cedar St,
    Quincy died Saturday. Age 42 yrs. Leaves a wife and 3 children. Funeral
    Tuesday from Salem church. He was a younger brother of August and Henry
    Ippersen, both of this twp.

Irvin, Elmer   "York Neck"   May 18, 1899
    Died- Little Elmer, son of John and Catherine Irvin on Wednesday May 11th
    of spinal meningitis. Born February 22, 1890. Was 9 yrs 2 mo's 18 days old.
    Services by Rev Wehrman of Golden at York Neck cemetery. Buried in York
    Neck cemtery.

Irvin, J.F.   Funeral   Feb 9, 1899
    see Coffield, Dr James

Irvin, Ora May   "Local"   Apr 21, 1898
    Died- Ora May, infant daughter of Mr and Mrs J.T. Irvin of York Neck.
    Died yesterday at age 1 yr 8 mo's 11 days. Funeral this A.M.

Isixison, Mr   "Marcelline"   Dec 11, 1879
    A man named Isixison, living on the bottoms died of pneumonia and was
    buried at the Keath graveyard last Sunday.

Iltner, Gus   "Local"   Aug 10, 1899
    Drowned, Gus Iltner of Quincy was drowned Saturday in the Big Slough
    about 3 miles south of that city. Leaves a wife and 6 children.

Imel, Mrs Catherine   "Death"   Jan 11, 1900
    see Cramer, Capt H.P.W. Cramer

Ingersoll, R.A.   Jun 22, 1899
    Included in list of graves to be decorated in Mendon cemetery on
    Memorial Day.

Ingersoll, Ralph A.   "Obituary"   Apr 11, 1889
    Died- Ralph A. Ingersoll on April 9th at 12 P.M. Was the eldest son of
    the late Hon Ralph I. and Margaret E. Ingersoll of New Haven, Conn.
    Age 72 yrs. Was born March 4, 1817 and came to Quincy in 1849. Married
    Elizabeth Hoffman of Quincy, Ill. December 12, 1850. Leaves 2 brothers
    and 1 sister, Colin M., Charles R. and Grace Ingersoll of New Haven, Conn.
    Also his wife and 5 children Maggie, Bessie, Mrs Grace Duffy, Fannie
    and Harry B. Ingersoll. Services held in Zion church Wednesday afternoon.

Inghram, Miss Berdie   "Local"   Apr 19, 1900
    Died- Miss Berdie Inghram, daughter of Robert Inghram and niece of
    Fred Borgholthaus, died in Chicago Sunday A.M. Buried in Fowler cemetery
    Tuesday. 22 yrs old. Formerly lived at Fowler.

Ingraham, Thomas   Jun 8, 1887
    Died- Mr Thomas Ingraham of Ellington last Wednesday in his 78th yr.
    Buried at Wesley Chapel 2 days later. His wife died about 4 yrs ago. He
    leaves 1 son, Robert Ingham who is one of the largest farmers of the
    county.

Ingram, Mr   "Indian Grave"   Jul 11, 1895
    Mr Ingram was buried here on the 4th.

Ingram, Mrs Lottie   "Local"   Jun 8, 1887
    News rec'd of the death of Mrs Lottie Ingram of Pike Co. Mo. , a
    daughter of Mr and Mrs Thomas Hedges, formerly of this twp, now of Mo.

Inman, Mrs Adeline   "Obituary"   Nov 8, 1900
    see Wright, Mrs Phebe

Inman, Daniel   "Local"   Mar 9, 1887
    Died- Mr Daniel Inamn, a former resident of Fall Creek, Adams Co. Ill.
    where his son Wm Inman still lives. He died of cancer near St Anne in
    St Angles Co. California on February 27th at age 66 yrs. His sister,
    Mrs Lavina Wright of this twp and his son left to go see him before he
    died. They arrived on Saturday night and he died Monday, but he was not
    conscious. Another brother of Mrs W's, Mr Huston Inman died in Oregon
    of cancer December 6th 1886 and her only remaining brother is sick
    with pneunomia in Scotland Co. Mo.

Jackson,   "Death"   Mar 3, 1886
    see Porter, Mrs Sanford

Jackson, Martha   "Camp Point"   Oct 18, 1900
    The funeral of Prof. Jackson's little daughter, Martha was at the
    Ebenezer church last Sunday P.M. by Rev R.L. McNabb. The little girl had
    had scarlet fever last winter and had never recovered.

Jacobs, Alexander   "Ursa"   Oct 27, 1881
    Died- October 18th, Alexander Jacobs. Buried October 20th.

Jacobs, Alexander   "November Term"   Oct 11, 1883
    Henry S. Loucks, Adm. of the estate of Alexander Jacobs deceased vs.
    Sarah J. Jacobs, James H. Jacobs, Wm Jacobs, Alice Jacobs, Mary Jacobs,
    Mary Heath and Alfred Heath.   Wm Haselwood, Clerk of said court.

Jacobs, Mrs Frank   "Obituary"   Nov 29, 1894
    see Crenshaw, Mrs Martha

Jacobs, Mrs Fred   "Tioga"   Apr 9, 1903
    Wm Muegge was called last Monday near West Point to direct the funeral
    of Mrs Fred Jacobs.

Jacobs, Mrs Jas.   "Camp Point"   Jun 27, 1901
    see Bayne, Dr

Jacobs, James C.   Sep 7, 1904
    Mrs Kate Dexter of Denver, daughter of the late James C. Jacobs
will rec 250.00 of the 2000.00 insurance carried by her father in the A.O.U.W.
    The rest will be paid to ½ brother of the deceased and the nephew,
    both residents of Lima twp to whom it was all left.

Jacobs, Samuel   "Columbus"   Oct 1, 1885
    An infant son of Samuel Jacobs was buried in Columbus cemetery last
    week. Mr Jacobs formerly lived in Columbus, but now lives in Kingston.

Jaffers, Mrs   "Local"   Aug 25, 1892
    The remains of Mrs Jaffers, a sister of Mrs Huston, a former resident
    of this vicinity were brought here from Tabor, Iowa for burial
    accompanied by her brother Robert McClelland and her 2 daughters.
    Services at the Cong'l church. Buried in Mendon cemetery.

James, Mrs E.B.   "Obituary"   Apr 25, 1889
    Franklin, Nebraska "Republican"
    Died- on April 17th of congestive chills, Mrs E.B. James age 36yrs
    8 mo's 15 days. She and her husband were among the earlist settlers of
    Franklin. She leaves her husband and 4 children. Mrs James was a sister
    of Mrs Harry Chittenden of Mendon, Illinois.

James, Mr and Mrs Ed   "Ursa"   Nov 10, 1892
    Infant child of Mr and Mrs Ed James of Quincy was buried at the Stone
    church cemetery Saturday P.M.

James, Lindsey   "Marcelline"   Oct 26, 1893
    Lindsey James died near Kansas city. His remains are expected here today.
    Funeral by the Odd Fellows.

James, Mrs M.   "Obituary"   Mar 11, 1880
    see Adair, Jas. F.

James, Mrs Mary   "Obituary"   Jan 27, 1881
    Mrs Mary James died at Fowler, Adams Co. Ill January 21st at the age of
    80 yrs. She was born in Madison Co. Ky. Moved to Missouri in 1829 and to
    near Mendon in 1847. Buried in Keaths cemetery from the Baptist church
    by Rev P.S. Slagle.

James, Mary F.   "Obituary"   Mar 2, 1893
    Died- Mary F. James born in Pittsfield, New Hampshire August 29, 1830
    Came to Illinois with her parents in 1842. Married Willaim B. Witt in
    1851 and died February 19, 1893. Was mother of 8 of which 3 died in
    infancy, the other 5(2 sons and 3 daughters) are Jennie S. Bagley resides
    in California, Lizzie Eckles in Mo. and Mary A. at home, sons Joel and
    Phillip live in Big Neck. She was a member of the M.E. church 40 yrs.
    Services by Rev A.A. White and buried in York Neck cemetery.

Jameson, Colonel   "Ellington"   Jul 10, 1884
    Mr Samuel and Alexander Jameson executors of the estate of Colonel
    Jameson will have a public sale July 17th.

Janes, Mr George   "Obituary"   Mar 17, 1892
    see Packard, Mrs T.

Janes, Mr P.S.   "Obituary"   Mar 17, 1892
    see Packard, Mrs T.

Jansen, Capt Matthew   "Local"   Oct 25, 1900
    Died- Capt Matthew Jansen the well known insurance agent at his home
    in Quincy Sunday night.

Jarand, Fritz C.   "Quincy"   Apr 6, 1882
    Suicide of Fritz C. Jarand Monday morning.

Jarrett, Mr Jas.   "Local"   Aug 11, 1892
    Died- Mr Jas. Jarrett of Quincy Sunday afternoon. Age 55 yrs. Born in
    Bonhill, Dumbartonshire, Scotland and came to America in 1843 settling
    at St Louis. Came to Quincy 1857 and was engaged in the Wood and Ice
    business.

Jasper, Mrs Alvina   "Local"   Mar 24, 1892
    Died- at 1 O.M. Tuesday at her home on the Coffield farm in York Neck
    of blood poisioning following child birth, Mrs Alvina Jasper. Age 29 yrs
    Funeral in Quincy her former home on Wednesday P.M. according to the
    rites of the catholic church. Corrected in March 31st paper to the
    St Peters Evang. Lutheran church in Quincy
    SEE MRS ALVINA HARRY for another correction.

Jasper, Geo. F.   "Local"   Jan 30, 1902
    Geo. F. Jasper who last week suffered a stroke of apoplexy died
    Thursday night. He was buried with Masonic honors Sunday.

Jeffery, Miss   "Obituary"   Dec 13, 1888
     see Booth, Mrs Wm

Jellison, Beulah   "Payson"   Aug 5, 1880
     Died- on August 6th, Beulah, infant child of Mr and Mrs Wm (Dora)
     Jellison. Age 12 days.

Jenkins, Mrs   "Marcelline"   Jun 1, 1901
     Funeral of Mrs Jenkins who died suddenly Sunday eve will be today at
     10 A.M.

Jenkins, B.H.   "Loraine"   Dec 26, 1878
     Died- Mr B.H. Jenkins, an old settler of this County at his home south
     of here Monday A.M.

Jenkins, Belle   "Estate Suit"   Jul 10, 1884
     see Owings, Howard W.

Jenkins, Mr and Mrs Ed   "Indian Grave"   Sep 26, 1895
     Died- baby of Mr and Mrs Ed Jenkins of Ursa last Sunday night. Buried
     Monday P.M.

Jenkins, Mr and Mrs Ed   "Ursa"   Sep 19, 1895
     Died- a little child of Mr and Mrs Ed Jenkins last Sunday night at
     midnight of summer complaint. Buried Denson Cemetery Monday P.M. at 3

Jenkins, Edward   "Estate Suit"   Jul 10, 1884
     see Owings, Howard W.

Jenkins, Ella   "Death"   Sep 14, 1899
     see Mitchell, Mrs Estella

Jenkins, H.C.   "Local"   Jul 27, 1899
     Died- 8 yr old son of H.C. Jenkins, living 4½ miles northeast of
     Mendon Saturday. Buried Sunday P.M. in the Reece cemetery.

Jenkins, Mr and Mrs H.C.   "Loraine"   Jul 27, 1899
     Died- the 8 yr old son of Mr and Mrs H.C. Jenkins of complication of
     diseases Saturday eve. Buried Sunday at Big Neck cemetery.

Jenkins, Mr and Mrs J.M.   "Loraine"   Feb 8, 1894
     Died- a 2 week old baby girl of Mr and Mrs J.M. Jenkins of whooping
     cough. Buried in Curless cemetery.

Jenkins, Katie   "Estate Suit"   Jul 10, 1884
     see Owings, Howard W.

Jenkins, Mrs Lillie   "Death"   Sep 12, 1901
     see Seals, Joseph

Jenkins, Margaret   "Estate Suit"   Jul 10, 1884
     see Owings, Howard W.

Jenkins, Matilda   "estate Suit"   Jul 10, 1884
     see Owings, Howard W.

Jenkins, Mr and Mrs W.   "Bowen"   Feb 2, 1882
     Died- Golda, only child of Mr and Mrs W. Jenkins on   January 20th.

Jenkins, W.B.   "Indian Grave"   May 2, 1895
     W.B. Jenkins rec'd the sad news last week of the death of a sister and
     her daughter. Both died within 3 or 4 weeks of one another.

Jenkins, Wm B.   "Estate Suit"   Jul 10, 1884
     see Owings, Howard W.

Jenkins, Wm H.   "Estate Suit"   Jul 10, 1884
     see Owings, Howard W.

Jenners, Mrs   Apr 28, 1886
     Mrs Jenners, the mother of Mrs W. Habighorst, died very suddenly at
     her home in Hannibal a few days ago.

Jennifer, Miss Minnie   "Mallard, Ill."   Feb 16, 1887
     Died- Miss Minnie Jennifer, age 17 yrs.

Jennings, Miss Clementine   "Death"   Jun 9, 1886
     see Shaffer, Jacob

Jennings, Miss Susan A.   "Death"   Jul 15, 1900
     see Chant, Joseph

Jennings, Thomas W.   "Died"   Dec 4, 1890
     Died- November 30th and buried in Mendon cemetery December 2nd from
     the Methodist church by Rev F.C. Read. Mr Thomas W. Jennings was born
     in Pittsylvania Co. Va. December 22, 1805. Was 84 yrs 11 mo's 8 days
     old. Married 3 times. 1st on March 17, 1825   2nd on April 27, 1840
     3rd on January 25, 1866. Had 12 children. Those named were, Mrs Joseph
     Chant, Mrs Jacob Shafer of Mendon, Mrs Hughes of Lewistown, Mo., Ben and
     D.K. in Mo. and Tom in Kansas. He lived Virginia, Iowa and Illinois.
     Lived 30 yrs in Mendon. Was a member of Methodist church.

Jewell, C.C.   "Obituary"   Jan 4, 1900
     see Roth, Mrs John W.

Jewell, Miss Gertie   "Obituary"   Jan 4, 1900
     see Roth, Mrs John W.

Jewell, Henry   "Obituary"   Jan 4, 1900
     see Roth, Mrs John W.

Jimison, Supt.   "Death"   Jun 8, 1893
     "Death of Supt Jimison - Quincy Herald"
     Died- Supt Jimison on Saturday eve at 6:30 at Liberty of typhoid
     pneumonia. Dr's Spence and Enlow of Liberty, Dr Parker of Clayton and
     Dr Crocker of Payson all attended him. His sister of Clayton took care
     of him. Was 47 yrs old (or 48) and unmarried. Leaves 1 brother and 3
     sisters, Edward Jimison, Mrs Lierie of Kansas, Miss Angeline Jimison
     and Mrs Sarah Davis of Clayton, wife of his partner in the drug business
     and with whom he lived. Buried at Clayton. Services from the Christian
     church by Elder H.G. Dervoort.

213

Jobe, Mrs   "Marcelline"   Mar 1, 1883
    Mrs Jobe, a widow lady living on the bottoms was buried at the old
    Stone church Feb 23rd.

Johnson, Mr   "Marcelline"   Mar 16, 1904
    Mr Johnson of Augusta, father in law of David Welling was brought here
    last week and buried in Keath cemetery.

Johnson, Rev.   "Lima"   Jul 19, 1888
    Died- Rev Jofnson's youngest daughter Wednesday July 14th and was buried
    in Lima cemetery Thursday.

Johnson, Mr A.   "Local"   Sep 4, 1884
    A colored man named A. Johnson died Sunday in Quincy. Cause, Heart disease

Johnson, Mrs Celia   "Local"   Dec 13, 1888
    News rec'd this A.M. of the death of Mrs Celia Johnson of Marcelline
    on Sunday A.M. of paralysis. She was a daughter of the late Mr McCormick
    Miller and a niece of John Miller of this twp.

Johnson, Charles   "Ursa"   May 23, 1895
    A little girl about 6 yrs old who was staying with Charles Johnson in
    the bottoms fell from a wagon and a wheel ran over her. Funeral this
    P.M. in the cemetery north of town.

Johnson, Charles W.   Partition #1689"   May 18, 1904
    see Moore, Annice S.

Johnson, Miss Ella   "Obituary"   Jan 29, 1899
    see Devore, Mr Andrew

Johnson, Eva   Jan 12, 1890
    Died- January 3rd, Eva Johnson age 22 yrs, and wife of E.H. Johnson.
    also leaves 2 children (2yrs and an infant)

Johnson, Mrs Fannie A.   "Local"   Feb 3, 1898
    Died- Mrs Fannie A. Johnson of Corvallis, Oregon from pneumonia. She was
    oldest child of John and Lucy Ray. She died January 23rd. Born Mendon
    July 30, 1852. Leaves husband and 3 daughters.

Johnson, G.W.   "Local"   Jul 27, 1887
    Mr G.W. Johnson's youngest child (a girl) died last night of cholera
    infantum and was buried this P.M. in the Mendon cemetery.

Johnson, Geo.   "Death"   Oct 28, 1897
    see Lewis, Mr and Mrs

214

Johnson, George W.   "Obituary"   Mar 16, 1904
    Died- at his home in Ursa Tuesday March 8th at 8:40 P.M. George W.
    Johnson of pneumonia at age 62 yrs 2 mo's 21 days. Born Mendon twp Dec
    18, 1841 and lived Adams Co. all his life. Married Miss Sarah J. Lewis
    of Mendon September 1, 1870, had 8 children, 1 son and 7 daughters,
    one daughter, Lizzie died in infancy. Leaves a wife 7 children, 8 grand-
    children, 2 brothers and 3 sisters. Children are Charles, Nettie, Georgia,
    Mrs B.F. Garmer, Mrs Charles Lawber of Ursa, Mrs Fred McReynolds of
    Mendon and Mrs B.F. Green of Burnside, Illinois all home for the funeral.
    Joined M.E. church as a young man and was a member of A.O.U.W. at one time
    Funeral at the house Thursday at 10 A.M. by Rev A.C. Ament. Buried Stone
    church cemetery.

Johnson, Georgia   "Partition #1689"   May 18, 1904
    see Moore, Annice S.

Johnson, J.H.   "Death"   Jan 27, 1881
    see Reeder, Mrs Francis

Johnson, Mrs J.H.   "Local"   Apr 20, 1887
    Monument was erected in the Mendon cemetery in honor of the late Mrs
    J.H. Johnson, by her family.

Johnson, J.H. and Martha   "Death"   Jun 27, 1889
    see Houdyshell, Mrs Mary E. (Jacob)

Johnson, James W.   "Partition #1689"   May 18, 1904
    see Moore, Annis S.

Johnson, John   "Payson"   Feb 6, 1879
    Mr John Johnson, south of Payson took sick on Monday. Died Tuesday.
    Buried Wednesday.

Johnson, John H.   "Probate Notice"   Apr 20, 1894
    1st Monday of June 1894   Daniel Nutt, Ex.

Johnson, John H.   "Real Estate Sale"   May 3, 1894
    By virtue of a decree rendered on the 27th of April 1894 at the March term
    by the circuit court of Adams Co. ill in a certain cause wherein Thomas M.
    Johnson is complainant, and James W. Johnson, George W. Johnson,
    Elizabeth Hedges, Thaddeus S. Hedges, Paulina Ann Wright, Sarah J.
    Johnson, Letitia R. Johnson, Margaret Francis Johnson, Lucy Jane
    Johnson, Geo. D. Riddle, Wm H. Fisher, Rowland Persels and Daniel Nutt
    as the executor of the last will and testament of John H. Johnson,
    Deceased. Quincy, Ill. May 3, 1894   Samuel Woods, Special Commissioner.

Johnson, Miss Lizzie   "Obituary"   May 11, 1893
    Died- Miss Lizzie Johnson at the home of Mrs Hightower in Marcelline on
    Monday May 8th of inflammation of the stomach. Age 53 yrs. Born
    Marcelline and was a member of the Christian church. Her father was a
    minister there. Leaves 1 sister, Mrs Sabrie Sartoria, of Springfield,
    Missouri and 2 brothers, Wm Johnson of Augusta, Ill. and Smith Johnson
    of Buffalo, Missouri. Buried Tuesday eve in the Keith cemetery after
    services in the Christian church.

215

Johnson, Miss Lucy J.   "Died"   Jul 26, 1894
    Died- Miss Lucy J. Johnson was taken to Blessings hospital to be
    operated on for a tumor. The operation was very long and the patient could
    not stand it. Died 6 hours later (Thursday Eve) Buried Mendon after
    services at the Methodist church in Mendon by Rev Burgess (Wm). She was
    the daughter of the late J.H. Johnson. Born near Mendon September 30, 1845
    being 48 yrs 9 mo's 19 days old at the time of her death. Joined the
    Christian church as a girl and remained in it.

Johnson, Miss Malissa   "Payson"   Jan 15, 1880
    Died- Miss Malissa, daughter of Christopher Johnson January 8th at
the home of her sister, Mrs Bennet's. Age about 20 yrs.

Johnson, Margaret Frances   "Partition # 1689"   May 18, 1904
    see Moore, Annice S.

Johnson, Martha   "Local"   Feb 9, 1887
    Died- on Sunday Feb 6th at 9:15 A.M. Martha, wife of Mr J.H. Johnson
    of this twp age 74 yrs 3 mo's 5 days. Buried Mendon cmeetery. Services
    by Elder Mayfield of the Christian church Quincy.

Johnson, Mattie   "Lima"   Nov 1, 1883
    Died- October 26th, Miss Mattie Johnson in her 18th year. Died in Quincy.
    Leaves parents and 1 brother.

Johnson, Mrs Minerva   "Death"   Jul 26, 1905
    see Hughes, Albert

Johnson, Nettie   "Columbus"   Apr 13, 1887
    Aunt Nellie Johnson died Sunday P.M.

Johnson, Nettie   "Partition # 1689"   May 18, 1904
    see Moore, Annice S.

Johnson, Mr and Mrs R.M.   "Bowensburg"   Dec 22, 1881
    Died, the son of Mr and Mrs R.M. Johnson.

Johnson, Ruth   "Local"   Oct 24, 1889
    Ruth, the eldest daughter of Rev. Johnson died Monday A.M.

Johnson, Sarah J.   "Partition # 1689"   May 18, 1904
    see Moore, Annice S.

Johnson, Thomas M.   "Local"   Sep 21, 1887
    Mr and Mrs Thomas M. Johnson's infant child died Monday night. Buried
    next day at Ursa.

Jones, Mrs Alice   "Funeral"   Mar 16, 1904
    see Wright, Henry

Jones, Miss Eleanor   "Obituary"   Jan 29, 1899
    see Devore, Mr Andrew

Jones, Mrs Emma   "Death"   Dec 21, 1893
    see Leach, Mr A.H.

Jones, Mrs Fannie   "Center"   Jan 31, 1889
    Mrs Sophie Jones went to Marblrhead to attend the funeral of her
    daughter in law, Mrs Fannie Jones.

Jones, Homer Henry   "Local"   Dec 21, 1904
    Died- Homer Henry Jones, age 26 yrs early this A.M. at his home on 10th
    Street between Vermont and Broadway from consumption. Leaves a wife,
    mother, the latter being Mrs Alice Jones of Mendon.
    Tuesday's Quincy Herald-- He will be buried in Quincy Thursday 2 P.M.

Jones, John   Jun 5, 1902
    includee in list of Civil war soldiers graves decorated in Mendon
    on Memorial Day.

Jones, John   "Loraine"   Mar 1, 1888
    Mr John Jones died Friday a.m. of lung fever at the home of the late
    Richard Adair. Age 69 yrs. He had not seen any of his relatives for 54
    yrs. Left Conn. when he was 15 yrs old. Was in the U.S. navy for some 15
    yrs. Buried in our cemetery Saturday. Had lived with different families
    in Lima and Keene twps.

Jones, Mr K.K.   "Local"   Aug 25, 1886
    Died- Mr K.K. Jones of Quincy Friday afternoon of paralysis of the
    brain. Buried Chicago.

Jones, Mrs Mary (P.W.)   "Died"   May 13, 1880
    Died- at Milano, Milan Co. Texas on May 4th, Mrs Mary, wife of P.W.
    Jones, late of Fowler, Illinois. Been in Texas only a few months.
    Leaves 2 sisters in the north and an aged mother and loving husband
    and a son.

Jordan, James   "Local"   Oct 31, 1889
    Died- James Jordan in Quincy yesterday morning.

Jordan, James W.   "Local"   Jan 30, 1890
    The widow of James W. Jordan has rec'd an increase to the pension of
    her husband.

Jordan, Mrs Mary Virginia   "Obituary"   Sep 27, 1894
    Died- Mrs Mary Virginia Jordan at her home in Marcelline September
    21st at age 46 yrs 8 mo's. Born January 21, 1848 in West Virginia and
    came to Adams Co. with her parents in 1863. Married Wm J. Jordan
    July 16, 1864, they had 2 sons and 4 daughters, i daughter died in
    infancy. 5 children survive her. The husband died March 26, 1876. All the
    living children were with her in her last hours except 1 stepson and a
    son in Washington. Services by Rev Cline of Canton, Mo. at her house.
    Buried in Keath burying ground. She was a member of the Christian church
    at Marcelline.

Jordan, Wm   "Local"   Jan 18, 1900
    Killed in a silver mining blast, Wm Jordan a former resident of
    Marcelline and Ursa, now of Washington. Leaves a wife and 2 children in
    Washington and 1 brother and 3 sisters here.

Joseph, Mrs A.C.   "Obituary"   Mar 3, 1886
    see Owens, Mrs T.S.

Joseph, J.F.   "Obituary"   May 11, 1887
    see Brown, Lizzie Lunn

Joseph, Wolf   "Death"   Apr 11, 1901
    Died- Wolf Joseph, a member of Joseph Bros and Davidson died at his home
    in Quincy Monday P.M. Was sick 3 weeks. Had been in business in Quincy
    40 yrs. Born Hanover, Germany 1824 and when 24 yrs old came to U.S.
    landed at Bangor, Maine where he stayed till 1860 when he moved to Quincy
    with his brother. (the first name of the firm was Joseph & Nelke)

Joslin, Mrs Alice   "Death"   Mar 22, 1905
    Died- Mrs Alice Joslin, nee Walter, died about 2 A.M. Friday at her home
    at 118 N. 12th St. from an abdominal cancer. Born 1860. Was 45 yrs old.
    Native of Mendon moving to Quincy about 6 months ago. Leaves 5 children
    2 sons and 3 daughters, Harry, Martin, Effie, Ada and Jennie, all at
    home except Martin who went to Wisconsin about 2 weeks ago. She was widow
    of James Joslin who died 8 yrs ago and is buried at Mendon. Also leaves
    1 brother, William H. Walter and a sister, Mrs Reuben Kellogg, both of
    Quincy.
    "Quincy Herald" Remains brought to Mendon on Saturday evening passenger
    train and taken to cemetery. Services at the grave by Rev. A.M. Reitzel.

Judd, Mrs George   "Local"   Sep 12, 1889
    Mrs George Judd (Kate Slack) of Quincy lost her 10 weeks old son from
    cholera infantum on Tuesday.

Judd, Mrs George W.   "Obituary"   Nov 19, 1903
    see Wall, Mrs Joseph W.

Judson, Calista   "Obituary"   May 15, 1902
    see Whelden, Mary Crane

Judy,   "Died"   May 6, 1880
    Judy, Died at his residence in Gilmer twp on Thursday April 29th.

Judy, Mrs Nancy   "Quincy"   Mar 2, 1899
    Died - Mrs Nancy Judy, widow of the late Paris T. Judy Sunday A.M. of lung
    and throat infection. resident of Quincy since 1881. her husband died
    about 20 yrs ago. Born Flemingsburg, Ky. July 31, 1815. Married Mr J.
    October 11, 1851 had 7 children, James M. of Camp Point, Mrs W. Finley of
    Gilmer, Mrs M.B. Taylor of Maywood, Mo., Mrs Xamtippe Finley, widow of
    Lycurgus E. Finley of Gilmer, Mrs Wm Criswell of Quincy, Mrs Charles Horn
    of Chicago and Mrs Frederick Rush of Quincy.

Judy, W.H.   "Local"   Jan 18, 1905
    Died- W.H. Judy of Coatsburg, a prominent grain buyer died Monday A.M.
    57 yrs old. Leaves a wife and 4 children.

Judy, Wm Winepark   "Columbus & Gilmer"   Jan 22, 1891
Wm Winepark Judy, oldest son of Philip and Elizabeth V. Judy was born
October 24, 1855 in Gilmer twp and died at Jacksonville, Illinois
January 14th at the age of 35 yrs 2 mo's 21 days. Married Rovilla Corder
December 25, 1880. They had 1 son. In spring of1881 he had jaundice
which caused insanity and on May 15, 1881 he was taken to Jacksonville.
Leaves a wife , 1 son, father and mother, Mr and Mrs Philip S. Judy who
were blessed with 7 children and 19 grandchildren, Son wm was the 1st
in the family. Buried Columbus cemetery. Services by Bro. Staker, pastor
of the German M.E. church.

Julian, Hannah   "Death"   May 5, 1892
see Willaims, Mrs Dr.

Kaltenbach, Charley   "Local"   Apr 21, 1886
    The bodies of Charley and Eddy Klusmeyer and Charley Kaltenbach were
    found on the river front. The 3 little boys had been missing since
    last September. Doubtless they had been digging in the bank when it
    caved in on them burying them alive.

Kammarre, Gottlier   "Lima"   Nov 29, 1883
    Gottlieb Kammarre died last Monday A.M.. Mr K. was a widower. Buried
    at Tioga.

Kamphaus, Mrs Barbara   "Death in Adams Co."   Apr 6, 1899
    Died- Mrs Barbara Kamphaus of influenza and grip Thursday March 30th
    4 miles east of Quincy. Was 40 yrs old. Leaves husband and 3 children.

Karns, Mr and Mrs W.   "Death"   Mar 1, 1894
    see Dix, Mrs Viola

Kauder, Mrs   "Correction"   Apr 17, 1890
    Mrs Kauder was the grandaughter not the stepmother of Mrs Ertel. Mrs
    Kauder would have been 83 yrs old in a few days.

Kauder, Conrad   Aug 7, 1890
    Conrad Kauder died in Quincy at his residence July 31st. He was born
    Newburgh, Bavaria. Came to Quincy as a boy. He was a butcher. Leaves a
    wife and 2 children, Mrs F.G.Ertel of Mendon and Edward. He lived at
    609 Washington St. Quincy. Paper said he lost his eyesight in 1782

Kauder, Mrs Katherine   "Local"   Apr 10, 1890
    Mrs Katherine Kauder of Quincy died April 9th. Was the daughter of Elsie
    of Mendon.

Kay, Mrs C.W.   "Death"   Mar 15, 1905
    see Hewes, Samuel E.

Kay, Mrs Gabriel   "Payson"   Apr 5, 1883
    Mrs Gabriel Kay was buried April 3rd. She was one of the oldest
    citizens here.

Kay, Miss Sarah Ann   "Death   Jan 24, 1901
    see Sinnock, George

Kaylor, W.   "Loraine"   Jan 8, 1891
    Mr Herman Wenning has been appointed Adm. of the estate of W. Kaylor,
    deceased.

Kaylor, Wm   "Big Neck"   Dec 25, 1890
    Wm Kaylor died December 25th. He was born in Ohio in 1822 and moved to
    Illinois in 1850. Was a member of the M.E. church. Leaves 1 sister and
    7 brothers.

Keal, Mrs   "Death"   Aug 5, 1880
   see Scattergood, Mrs

Kearney, Mrs John   "Local"   May 31, 1900
   Mrs John Kearney last week rec'd 1000.00 from a policy held by her
   recently deceased husband who died 3 weeks ago.

Keath, Mrs U.H.   "Death"   Mar 25, 1880
   see Turner, Mrs

Keath, Clarence   "Local"   Apr 19, 1894
   Clarence Keath, son of Capt U. Keath of Quincy committed suicide at
   Dayton Ohio last week by taking Laudamum. Brought to Quincy for burial.
   It is thought he did this because he could not break the drinking habit.

Keath, Mrs Lucinda   "Died"   Jun 17, 1880
   Died- in Mexico, Missouri June 8th at age 77 yrs, Mrs Lucinda Keath,
   relict of Gabriel Keath and mother of U.H. Keath Esq. of Quincy. She
   came to Adams Co. with her husband from Kentucky in 1832 and lived here
   until after the death of her husband and all her children, but one who
   moved to Missouri.

Keisling, Susan   "Obituary"   Oct 29, 1885
   see Wieser, Susan

Keith, Mrs Eliza C.   "Obituary"   May 12, 1886
   Died- at the residence of her son in Lima on Friday May 7th, Mrs Eliza
   C. Keith after an illness of 2 yrs. She was born in Harrison Co. Ky.
   September 16, 1??1 where her father was a prominet Dr. Married Adam
   Keith January 15, 1844 and came with him to Adams Co. in the fall of
   1847. Was a member of the M.E. church 30 yrs. Services by Rev A.T. Stodgel
   of the M.E. church. Leaves 7 grown children.

Keith, Effie   "Lima"   Jan 27, 1886
   Effie, infant daughter of J.L. and Sallie Keith died Wednesday eve
   January 20th of pneumonia.

Keith, Miss Jannette   "Local"   Jan 15, 1885
   Died- January 14th with typhoid fever complicated with inflamation of
   the brain, Miss Jannette Keith, daughter of Richard Keith of Mendon.

Keith, Maggie   "Lima"   Mar 31, 1881
   Died, Maggie the youngest daughter of John and Sallie Keith.

Keith, Richard and Nancy   Jul 22, 1882
   Died Sunday July 23rd James A. infant son of Richard and Nancy Keith.

Keith, Mrs Richard   "Lima"   Jan 11, 1894
   Died- Mrs Richard Keith at her home here January 6th.

Keithly, Mrs Angie   "Obituary"   Jul 18, 1901
   see Kennedy, Geo. Thomas

221

Kelley, Aaron   "Estate Sale"   May 13, 1880
    see Hartman, Alexander

Kelley, Armilda   "Obituary"   Apr 13, 1899
    see Tittle. Mr A.J.

Kellogg, Lucy   "Carthage"   May 1, 1879
    Mrs Dr. Kellogg's little Lucy, 3 yrs old fell into a well yesterday and
    drowned.

Kellogg, Mr Reuben   "Death"   Sep 1, 1892
    see Walters, Mrs Daniel

Kellogg, Mrs Reuben   "Death"   Mar 22, 1905
    see Joslin, Mrs Alice

Kells, Mr Richard   Aug 13, 1891
    Mr Richard Kells died August 7th at his home in Honey Creek twp at
    age 62 yrs1 Buried Mendon cemetery. Services by Rev Mr Mayo of Quincy in
    the Zion Episcopal church. He was born at Ballyheady county Cavan, Ireland
    August 12, 1829 and came to this country in 1870 and settled in Adams Co..
    he was married twice. 1st in Ireland in 1869 to Fannie Kells who died
    March 31, 1872. They had 2 children, one of whom is Miss Pet Kells who was
    brought up by an aunt, Mrs Wm Hewitt. His second wife was Martha Clair
    They had 1 daughter. He leaves a widow and 2 daughters, 2 brothers, Robert
    living in Honey Creek and David in Ireland, 5 sisters, Mrs Ann Sewell
    in Ireland, Mrs Bessie Hewitt, Mrs Sarah Hewitt and Mrs Hanna Butler all
    of Mendon. NOTE: paper says 5 sisters but only 4 are named.

Kells, Robert   "Obituary"   Feb 9, 1899
    Died- Mr Robert Kells. Born County Cavan, Ireland February 2, 1838 and
    died at his home in Honey Creek twp Thursday night February 2nd at age
    61 yrs. Came to U.S. may 18, 1859 and settled on a farm east of town where
    he lived since. Married Mrs Martha Wible May 1862, they had 4 children
    (2 sons and 2 daughters) William, Mrs Joseph McGinley, of Rogers Ark.
    Robert and Minnie. His wife died January 7, 1896. Funeral at the Zion
    Episcopal church by Rev W.F. Mayo. Buried in Mendon cemetery.

Kells, Robert   "Probate Notice"   Mar 2, 1899
    1st Monday of May 1899   R.B. Starr, Adm.

Kells, Mrs Robert   "Obituary"   Mar 23, 1887
    see McClung, Mrs Ella Jane

Kells, Sarah   "Obituary"   Dec 29, 1898
    see Hewitt, Thomas

Kells, Mrs Wm   "Dead"   May 19, 1892
    Mrs Wm Kells, youngest daughter of Dr & Mrs Fletcher of Honey Creek twp
    died on Friday A.M. Sarah Elizabeth Kells(Fletcher) was born March 17,
    1863 and married December 2, 1885, died May 13, 1892 at age 29 yrs 1 mo
    16 days. Leaves husband, 4 yr old boy and infant 8 wks old, father,
    mother, 2 brothers, 1 sister and other relatives. Services at the house by
    Rev M.L. Schmucker Saturday P.M. Buried Mendon cemetery.

Kelly, John S.   "Quincy"   Mar 2, 1899
    Died- Mr John S. Kelly of cancer of the stomach Tuesday A.M. Born Erie
    Co. Penn January 27, 1827. Lived Quincy 16 yrs. Leaves 1 son John of
    East St Louis and 3 daughters, Mrs M. Damesell of Walnut, Kansas, Mrs E.Y.
    Downing of Camp Point and Mrs Chas. Schrag of Quincy.

Kelly, Mrs Eleanor B.   Dec   1882
    Mrs Eleanor B. Kelly, the only daughter of Thomas Bailey died December
    10th. Leaves parents and husband.

Kemp, Mrs Henry   "Ellington"   Apr 21, 1892
    Mrs Henry Kemp was buried today at the farm home near Eubanks. Deceased
    had lived in Quincy several yrs.

Kemp, Mr Henry S.   May 3, 1883
    Mr Henry S. Kemp died in Ellington twp on April 28th at age 70 yrs.

Kemp, Rhoda C.   "Camp Point"   Nov 10, 1881
    Died- Rhoda C. Kamp November 5th. Leaving a grown son and daughter.
    Services by Rev W.W. Whipple.

Kemper, Mrs Z.T.   "Death"   Mar 5, 1903
    see Platt, Rev H.D.

Kendall, Adam   "Fowler"   May 9, 1889
    Died- Adam Kendall May 1st at age 83 yrs and 26 days. Born in Landen
    Co. Virginia in 1806. Moved to Illinois in 1846. Married twice and
    father of 9 children. All presnet for his funeral. Buried in Chase cemetery
    (no names of wives given)

Kendall, Mrs E.   "Death"   Sep 12, 1901
    see Shipley, Mrs

Kendall, Mrs Fanny C.   "Death"   May 31, 1894
    see Collins, Miss Fanny C.

Kendall, Frank C.   "Quincy"   Apr 20, 1899
    Died- Frank C. Kendall of pneumonia Saturday A.M. Born Blueball, Ohio
    Feb 14, 1834. Leaves 3 sons, 2 daughters. W.E. Kendall the alderman and
    C.B.& Q. baggagemaster is a son of the deceased

Kendall, Dr H.W.   "Death"   May 31, 1894
    see Collins, Miss Fanny C.

Kendall, J.F.   "Local"   Jun 14, 1905
    Died- J.F. Kendall, an employee of the Quincy telephone Co. was stricken
    with apoplexy Monday while at work at the top of a 50 foot pole and fell
    across the wires where he was rescued and taken to Blessings hospital.
    Died 6:15 P.M. the same evening. Body taken to Fowler for burial.

Kendall, Joshua   "Fowler and Oakland"   Jan 11, 1900
    Funeral of Joshua Kendall who died of pneumonia was held last Monday.

Kendall, L.W.   "Death"   May 31, 1894
    see Collins, Miss Fanny C.

Kendrick, Mr Wm   "Obituary"   Aug 16, 1894
    "Sunday School Supplement"
    Died- Mr Wm Kendrick, late of Clayton was loyal to the Prssbyterian
    church at Calyton.
    Other deaths in Clayton twp were, Eli Thomas- Feb 2, 1894 Mrs Margaret Park-
    er, Wm B. Smith and Mrs Alma Curry

Kennedy, Mr   "Local"   Jan 5, 1893
    Died- Mr Kennedy, C.B. & Q. agent at Loraine last Thursday eve of
    congestive chills.

Kennedy, Mrs Elizabeth   "Local"   May 2, 1889
    Died- Mrs Elizabeth Kennedy early Monday morning. Buried in Mendon
    cemetery yesterday morning.

Kennedy, Rev J.C.   "Local"   ·   Mar 16, 1899
    Died- Rev J.C. Kennedy, pastor of the Baptist church, Payson yesterday
    from consumption.

Kennedy, Neal   "Loraine"   Oct 11, 1905
    Funeral of Neal Kennedy was held Monday afternoon at Chili.

Kennedy, Geo. Thomas   "Obituary"   Jul 18, 1901
    Died- Geo. Thomas Kennedy July 14th at 5 P.M. He was born March 3,
    1836 in Kentucky. In 1852 he went to Knox Co. Missouri where 5 yrs later
    he was converted and joined Southern M.E. church. Married October 6, 1858
    to Irene Franses Thompson also of Knox Co. Mo. at approx the end of
    the civil war they moved to McDonough Co. Illinois where they lived
    till they followed theri only son to Loraine Nov 1889. They had 8
    children. 1st born, a girl died in infancy 2nd Walter P. died in Loraine
    December 29, 1892. Wife and 6 daughters survive him, Mrs Angie Keithly and
    Mrs Mattie Sly of Blandenville, Ill, Mrs Maud Heaney and Mrs Lou Yenter
    of LaBelle, Mo., Mrs Florense Everbay of Loraine and Miss Edna Moon of
    Macomb, Illinois, his son's wife, Mrs Retta Kennedy lives in Macomb, Ill.
    3 brothers and 1 sister also survive him, Harve and James K. of Chili, Ill
    Mrs Mary Hobbs of LaBelle, Mo., Will K. of Randall, Kansas. Oldest brother
    is 77 yrs old and youngest is 63 yrs. , 15 grandchildren also survive him.
    He was 65 yrs 4 mo's 8 days old. Funeral by Rev Bonnefon of the M.E.
    church at 4:30 P.M. July 15th. His 6 son in laws were pallbearers.
    Buried Loraine cemetery.

Kennedy, Walter P.   "Loraine"   Jan 5, 1893
    Died- Walter P. Kennedy Thursday eve. Was born in Plymouth, Illinois
    in 1863. Raised on a farm where he remained until 4 yrs ago he went to
    study telegraphy. He was first in Colusa and then at Loraine. Member of
    Baptist church. Services by Elder McComb of Plymouth, his first pastor.
    also by whom he was married in 1890. Buried in our cemetery. Leaves a
    wife and 1 child, mother, father and 6 sisters.

224

Kenstler, Miss Clara   "Obituary"   Feb 5, 1903
  see Loynd, Harry William

Kent, Mr Henry   "News"   Aug 24, 1879
  Mr Henry Kent who resides some 5 miles this side od Quincy died Wednesday
  A.M. of last week, was 84 yrs old.

Keppell, Leah   "Obituary"   Jun 28, 1894
  see McCormick, John

Kepler, Mrs   "Indian Grave"   Feb 1, 1900
  Died- Mrs Kepler yesterday morning. Leaves a husband, 1 son and 1
  daughter.

Kepple, Leah   "Obituary"   Jan 3, 1895
  see McCormick, Mrs Leah

Keppler, Mrs Albert   "Ursa"   Jan 25, 1900
  Died- near Indian grave Saturday, Mrs Albert Keppler. Buried Sunday ay
  2 P.M. at the Denson burying ground.

Kerkering, Mrs Anna E.   "Quincy"   Mar 23, 1899
  Died- Mrs Anna E. Kerkering of pneumonia Tuesday A.M. Was 61 yrs old
  Leaves a husband, 2 sons and 2 daughters.

Kern, Catherine   "Obituary"   Nov 29, 1894
  see Strickler, Wesley

Kerr, Rev Father   "Death"   May 10, 1894
  see McGirr, Mrs Mary Ann

Kerr, Rev Dr Robert   Jul 10, 1890
  Rev Dr Robert Kerr died at Wakefield, Kansas last Sunday night, age 61
  yrs. He was the father of Mrs A.P. Stacy of Minneapolis. He was pastor of
  the Cong'l church of Tomah, Wisc. He was a native of Scotland.

Kerrick, Dr   "Lima"   Jan 27, 1886
  Mrs Dr Kerrick is settling up the estate of Dr Kerrick and will move
  to Missouri.

Kespohl, Mr Henry A.   "Local"   Nov 20, 1884
  see Schnarr, Mrs Ida (John)

Ketchum, Cassie   "Death"   Apr 18, 1895
  see Roberts, Mrs E.L.

Ketchum, Mrs Clara (S.A.)   "Loraine"   Nov 30, 1893
  died- Mrs Clara Ketchum, wife of S.A. Ketchum at her home in Hamilton,
  Illinois on Thursday A.M. Buried our cemetery Friday. She was formerly
  the late wife of Alonzo Guymon and daughter of Mr J.J. Banks now of
  Kansas City.

225

Ketchum, Elizabeth Josephine   "Death"   Jan 4, 1905
    see Rust, George Washington

Ketchum, Mrs Rebecca   "Obituary"   Jun 20, 1901
    see Seals, Dennis

Ketchum, S.A.   "Death"   Jan 19, 1899
    see Guymon, Carl

Ketchum, Mr and Mrs Washington "Obituary"   Apr 18, 1895
    see Roberts, Mrs E.L.

Keturah, Mrs   "Ursa"   Dec 23, 1885
    Mrs Keturah died Saturday night at the home of Mr Wm Grimes, she was
    a loving mother and wife. Services in Mr G's home by the Christian
    minister.

Key, Francis S.   "Death"   Jun 9, 1886
    see Pendleton, Mrs

Kidder, John   "Death"   Mar 20, 1879
    see Estus, Mr

Killam, Carl   "Lima"   Aug 9, 1894
    Died- Little Carl Killam, 8 mo's old died July 26th. He was the only
    child of Harry Killam. Carl's mother died when he was just a few hours
    old.

Killam, Mary E.   "Lima"   Dec 21, 1893
    Supplement Dispatch-- Died at her home here December 16th, Mrs Mary E.
    Killam, daughter of Mr and Mrs Geo. Snyder and beloved wife of Harry
    E. Killam. Was member of the M.E. church since the age of 15 yrs.
    Married Harry E. Killam October 26, 1892 when about 21 yrs old. Leaves
    father, mother, 4 sisters, 3 brothers and an almost broken hearted husband,
    a babe a few hours old. Services by Rev Hathaway. Buried in our cemetery.

Kimball, Mrs   "Obituary"   Dec 1, 1892
    see Arnold, Mrs Elizabeth A.

Kimball, Mrs Josephine (E.S.)   "Obituary"   Aug 2, 1905
    see Bradley, Daniel A.

Kincaid, Mrs John   "Death"   Jun 21, 1905
    see Clair, John

Kincaid, Mrs Mina   "Obituary"   Nov 17, 1898
    see Berrier, Mrs Hannah Mason

Kincheloe, Hon. C.F.   "Death"   Aug 11, 1898
    see Michaels, Mrs Jas.

Kincholoe, Mrs E.L.   "Local"   May 15, 1902
    Funeral services of Mrs E.L. Kincheloe, youngest daughter of Mr and Mrs
    Cornelius Van Blair was held at the M.E. church Tuesday A.M. Burial in
    Stone burial ground S.W. of town. Survived by Husband and 3 small children

Kincheloe, Mrs E.L.   "Loraine"   May 15, 1902
    Remains of Mrs E.L. Kincheloe were brought back from Hart, Michigan
    and buried in Frank Stone cemetery near Ursa last Tuesday. She was the
    youngest daughter of Mr and Mrs Cornelius Van Blair and grew up here.
    Leaves 3 small children, youngest a little over a yr old and a husband.

Kincheloe, Mrs I.N.   "Obituary"   Apr 11, 1889
    see Prather, Mrs

Kincheloe, I.N.   "Local"   Oct 25, 1900
    I.N. Kincheloe, postmaster at Loraine died very suddenly yesterday
    afternoon of heart failure.

Kincheloe, Isaac N.   "Probate Notice"   Dec 13, 1900
    1st Monday of February 1901   Cyrena C. Kincheloe, Adm.

Kincheloe, Isaac Newton   "Obituary"   Nov 1, 1900
    Died- Isaac Newton Kincheloe was born Washington Co. Tenn. August 11,
    1837 and came to Adams Co. when 12 yrs old. Married June 12, 1862 to
    C yrene C. Guseman who came with her parents from the state of Virginia
    to Illinois in 1858. They had 5 children, Mary J. now the wife of Jas. A.
    Wilcox of Loraine, Charles F. of Washington D.C., Edwin L. of Hart, Mich.
    Herman E. now dead and Herbert E. of Loraine. Mr K. died at his home
    in Loraine October 24th in the P.M. Services by Rev S.N. Wakefield of
    Mendon M.E. church October 26th in the A.M. Buried in Woodville
    cemetery. Relatives from afar were, D.E. Guseman of Aurora, Ill.,
    Jno. Cain of LaPrairie, Ill. C.F. Kincheloe of Washington D.C.

King, Miss Ada   "Camp Point"   Mar 28, 1901
    Miss Ada King went to Huntsville last week to attend the funeral of
    her niece who committed suicide.

King, Eddie   "Local"   May 22, 1902
    Miss Allie, Bert Jr. and Chalres Leckbie Jr. left Thursday A.M. for
    Edina, Mo. to attend the funeral of Eddie King.

King, Joseph W.   "Local"   May 29, 1884
    The death of Joseph W. King of Jacksonville was May 24th. Was 76 yrs old
    He and his wife celebrated their 50th wedding anniversary recently.

King, Miss Mary   "Obituary"   Jun 9, 1886
    see Shaffer, Jacob

King, Mrs R.   Fowler"   Jan 17, 1895
    Funeral services of Mrs R. King was in the Christian church Sunday
    January 11th. She lived with a daughter near Ursa.

King, Mrs Ruth   "Died"   Jan 24, 1895
    Died- Mrs Ruth King January 12th. Was sick 4 days with pneumonia. 81 yrs
    old. Had lived with her daughter, Mrs Morton 2 yrs. Leaves 4 daughters.

King, Wm Sr.   "Ursa"   Nov 20, 1879
    Died- Wm King Sr. at his residence near this place on November 14th of
    typhoid fever. Leaves a family.

King, Wm   "Personal"   Nov 20, 1879
    Died- Wm King, an old citizen of Ursa died Friday A.M. Age 68 yrs. He
    was an early settler of Quincy, having settled there in 1831. Buried
    at the Woodland cemetery.

King, Mrs Wm   "Died"   Feb 20, 1879
    Died on February 16th, the wife of Wm King Sr. of Ursa twp age 59 yrs.

King, Mrs Wm   "Ursa"   Feb 27, 1879
    Mrs Wm King died on the 16th of February.

Kingsbury, Mr A.B.   "Local"   May 19, 1886
    Mr A.B. Kingsbury died yesterday in his 57th yr. Lived Quincy.

Kingsbury, Mrs A.B.   "Obituary"   May 9, 1895
    see Berry, Col. W.W.

Kinney, Mrs Joseph   "West Point"   Feb 16, 1893
    Died- at her home 3 miles northwest of town, Mrs Joseph Kinney (Graham)
    age 65 yrs 7 mo's 4 days. Leaves 2 sons and 2 daughters. Was a member
    of the Baptist church. Services by Rev McDonald at the M.E. church.
    Buried in Chili cemetery.

Kirchner, Jacob F.   "Death in Adams Co."   Feb 16, 1899
    Died- Jacob F. Kirchner at his home in Ellington twp of Catarrh of the
    stomach Saturday A.M. Was a native of Germany. Born September 25, 1819.

Kirk, Mit   Jun 20, 1895
    Died-
            (Forgot to copy the complete item, Sorry)

Kirkpatrick, Caroline   "Obituary"   Aug 23, 1894
    see Colvin, Davis P.

Kirkpatrick, Mrs Jack   "Lima"   Dec 28, 1887
    Mrs Jack Kirkpatrick of Elvaston was here to attend the funeral of her
    brother Grayson Orr last week.

Kirkpatrick, Wm M.   "Died"   Nov 28, 1878
    Died- Wm M. Kirkpatrick at the home of Micajah Stone of this two on the
    night of November 22nd. He had stopped to spend the night with Mr S.
    Services held at the home of Mr Stone by Rev V.C. Randolph of Mendon.
    He had been a school teacher many yrs. Leaves a wife and several children
    living in Camp Point.

Kirkman, Mrs   "Burton"   Mar 6, 1879
    Died- Mrs Kirkman at the residence of her son in law, Mr Volrath.
    Age 85 yrs. She was the mother of Rev Kirkman, minister of the German
    Methodist Conference.

Klatt, Martin   "Loraine"   Oct 2, 1879
    Mr Klatt's youngest child died last evening.

Klatt, Mr and Mrs Martin   "Obituary"   Nov 23, 1893
    see Crays, Mrs Julia

Kling, Mrs Adam   "Fowler"   Jan 12, 1893
    Died- Mrs Adam Kling January 4th. 43 yrs old. Leaves husband and daughter.
    Funeral Saturday by Rev A.B. Peck.

Klingingsmith, Mr Sol   "Burton"   Jan 1, 1880
    Died- Mr Sol Klingingsmith at noon Friday. Age 57 yrs.

Kluseman, Harry   "Marcelline"   Feb 8, 1905
    Mrs Joseph VanDyke and son John attended the funeral of Harry Kluseman
    here Thursday.

Kluseman, Harry   "Marcelline"   Feb 8, 1905
    On account of the cold weather there were not many attended the funeral
    of little Harry Kluseman.

Klusman, Walter   "Local"   Feb 1, 1905
    Walter Klusman, an orphan about 9 yrs old, who Wm Walbring had taken
    to raise, died of lung trouble Tuesday at 4 P.M.

Klusmeyer, Charley   "Died"   Apr 21, 1886
    see Kaltenbach, Charley

Klusmeyer, Eddy   "Died"   Apr 21, 1886
    see Kaltenbach, Charley

Kneis, John   May 7, 1891
    Died- Tuesday May 5th of inflammation of the lungs at the home of his
    son in law, Hy Weichman, Mr John Kneis at the age of 79 yrs 4 mo's
    9 days. He was a native of Rothausen, Germany. Buried Mendon cemetery.
    Services at the house by Rev M.L. Schmucker of the Lutheran church.

Knowell, Uncle Jimmy   "Payson"   Feb 26, 1885
    Uncle Jimmy Knowell died February 11th. Resident about 40 yrs. Leaves
    wife and 6 grown children and a number of grandchildren. Born 1811.

Knox, James   "Fowler"   Feb 26, 1902
    Several from here attended the funeral of the late James Knox, near
    Chiola Sunday afternoon.

Kobel, Mr Jacob   "Camp Point"   Aug 9, 1900
    The funeral of Mr Jacob Kobel was at the home of his daughter, Mrs
    Fred Boger. He was 85 yrs old.

Koch, Charles G.   Feb 26, 1891
    Charles G. Koch, age 59 yrs 9 mo's died February 19th at Mendon.
    Resident of Adams Co. 44 yrs. He was born at Mulhausen, Germany and
    came to this country at age 16 with his parents in 1846. Leaves a wife
    and 4 children. Buried Greenmount cemetery Quincy. Services from the
    Salem German Lutheran church at Quincy. He lived in St Loius 1 yr and then
    moved to Adams Co. settling in Melrose twp about 7 miles east of Quincy
    and from there moving to Mendon twp in the spring of 1874 where he
    remained till now.

Koch, Chalres G.   "Probate Notice"   Mar 5, 1891
    1st Monday of May 1891   Eva E. Koch, Ex.

Koch, Charles H.   "Suicide"   Jul 10, 1879
    "Whig" Charles H. Koch, resident at 628 State St was found dead in
    the basement of his home. Was 78 yrs old. He had had trouble with a
    daughter, Mrs Landes. Inquest by coroner Seehorn.

Koch, Edward M.   "Estate Suit"   Sep 26, 1894
    see Robertson, Andrew

Koch, Dr John W.   "Local"   Nov 16, 1887
    Died- last week in Quincy, Dr John W. Koch.

Koch, Mrs Susie (Dr C.L.)   "Quincy"   Mar 30, 1899
    Died- Mrs Susie Koch, wife of Dr C.L. Koch at age 29 yrs Tuesday of
    heart disease. Born Canton, Mo. May 13, 1870. She was a cousin of
    Mayor Harrison of Chicago.

Krauss, Frankie   "Payson"   Nov 20, 1879
    Death of Mr Krauss's little son in Payson at Mrs Warton's on Wednesday
    November 14th His father was at home in St Loius when the boy died, but
    was here for the funeral on the 15th. Boy was 10 yrs old.
    Died at the residence of Mrs A.S. Wharton in Payson on Thursday A.M.
    Nov 13th Frankie, son of Frank and Catherine Krauss of St Louis.
    Age 10 yrs.

Krauth, Mr   "West Point"   Dec 1, 1892
    An old citizen, Mr Krauth died last week. Buried next day.

Krieger, Jennie S.   "Death"   Mar 22, 1905
    see Baldwin, George Dutton

Kropp, Amelia   "Obituary"   May 12, 1898
    see Steiner, Mrs Anna C.

Kropp, Mrs Eva   "Tioga"   Oct 19, 1887
    Died- Near this place October 11th, Mrs Eva Kropp age 81 yrs. Born in
    Germany and came to this twp 36 yrs ago and resided here since. Leaves
    a husband, 3 sons and 1 daughter. Buried in Tioga cemetery. Services by
    Rev Kern's.

Kuhn, Gertrude M.   "In Memoriam"   Aug 28, 1884
Gertrude M. Kuhn was born January 30, 1865 and died August 23, 1884
(not married) She was the youngest of 6 children and the 1st to go.
Services from the M.E. church by Reb McKown August 25th.

Kuhn, Isaac   "A Sad Accident"   Nov 9, 1887
Mr Isaac Kuhn, at Bowen last Wednesday. He and his brother in law, Harry
Walker and 6 other employes of the flouring mill were engaged in moving
an open wagon shed, when the whole thing collapsed and caught Mr Kuhn.
His family except 2 sons in Kansas have arrived here. His dauhgter, Miss
Emma Kuhn who is teaching in the Clayton high school was the 1st home,
followed by her sister, Mrs Ben Duffy of West Burlington, Iowa and her
2 children. Mr Phillip Kuhn, a brother and his 2 sisters, Mrs Nancy
Boyce and Mrs Ellen Colt drove over from Rushville a distance of 60 miles
Mr and Mrs John Walker, Mrs K's parents came from Joliet where they were
visiting their daughter, Mrs George Walker.

Kuhn, Isaac   "Obituary"   Nov 23, 1887
Died- Mr Isaac Kuhn died Friday at 5 A.M. on November 17th. Services held
at the M.E. church of which he was a member by Rev E.P. Droke, the pastor.
After which the remains were taken to the cemetery. Born in Lancaster Co.
Penn. April 6, 1827 and moved to Westmorland Co. Penn where he married
March 29, 1849 Mary M. Walker who survives him. In 1851 they moved to
Iowa and on to Mendon in 1855 where they have since resided. He leaves
a wife, 2 sons and 3 daughters, Mr John B. living at Trego, Kansas,
R.L. living at Anderson, Kansas, Mrs B.F. Duffy of West Burlington, Iowa,
Mrs G.B. McClellan of Ellington and Miss Emma, a teacher at Clayton high
school.

Kuhn, Mr and Mrs Robert   Nov 5, 1885
Died- Monday October 19th at Mineral Point, Kansas, Lillie, infant
daughter of Mr and Mrs Robert Kuhn.

Kunkel, Mrs   Sep 11, 1884
Death of Mrs Kunkel of Macon, Mo. She was grandaughter of Mrs McGibbons
and formerly Miss Lottie Ward. Leaves 2 children.

Kunkel, Mrs Martha A.   "Quincy"   Apr 6, 1899
Died- Mrs Martha A. Kunkel age 81 yrs. She died Wednesday March 29th
from grip and old age.

Kunz, Mr and Mrs H.   "Tioga"   Aug 17, 1893
Mr and Mrs H. Kunz are mourning the loss of their infant child which
died on Monday July 14th.

Kurk, Geo.   "Quincy"   Mar 16, 1899
Died- Geo. Kurk age 57 yrs died Tuesday A.M. of grip. Lived Quincy
all his life. Leaves wife, 7 children, 1 brotherand 1 sister.

Lading, Charles   "Local"   Jul 27, 1887
    Chalres Lading, age 13 yrs of Tioga was accidently shot through the
    head Sunday while playing with a 38 caliber revolver. Lived 22 hrs.

Laffey, Timothy   "West Point"   Mar 11, 1880
    Died- Timothy Laffey, an old citizen of the west side of thie twp on
    March 2nd of chronic dysentery. Services at St Peters church at Keokuk by
    Rev H.A. O'Kelly of Carthage. Was about 63 yrs old. Born in Ireland.
    Leaves a large family.

Lambert, Mrs Dr   "Obituary"   Jul 28, 1898
    see Carlin, Mr

Lambert, Dr and Mrs J.R.   "Local"   Sep 20, 1900
    Died- The infant daughter of Dr and Mrs J.R. Lambert, age 9 days.
    (of Coatsburg) Died Wednesday eve September 12th.

Lambur, Mrs Louise   "Obituary"   Mar 23, 1899
    see Goodapple, Mrs Geo.

LaMonte, Mr W.H.   Jul 21, 1892
    "Exchanges from the Carthage Republican"
    Died- Mr W.H. LaMonte, a well known young attorney of Hamilton committed
    suicide Friday A.M. July 8th by hanging himself in his barn. Leaves a wife
    who found him.

Lampe, John   "Local"   Apr 11, 1889
    John Lampe, a Quincy saloon keeper committed suicide Sunday eve by
    shooting himself in the head with a revolver.

Lampton, Elder   "Payson"   Aug 10, 1882
    Elder Lampton lost a child last Saturday night.

Lancaster, W. Emery   "Partition # 1689"   May 18, 1904
    see Moore, Annice S.

Landers, Artha   "Loraine"   Feb 26, 1880
    Died- Artha Landers, one of the oldest settlers of Keene twp died.
    Age 66 yrs. Died Thursday A.M.

Landes, Mrs   "Suicide"   Jul 10, 1879
    see Koch, Charles H.

Landon, Mrs   "Burton"   Oct 9, 1879
    Mrs Landon, mother of Dr W.M. Landon died Sunday eve. She was an old
    lady and a resident of the county 30 yrs. Leaves a large family of
    grown children and grandchildren.

Landon, Mrs Ellen   "Fowler"   Jan 27, 1904
    Mrs Ellen Landon, who lived with her father till last October died
    at the county farm January 15th. 46 yrs old. Funeral at the M.E. church.
    Burial at the Chase cemetery.

Lane, Alice M.   "Obituary"   May 15, 1902
    see Whelden, Mary Crane

Lang, Mrs Caroline   "Quincy"   Mar 2, 1899
    Died- Mrs Caroline Lang Saturday. Was a native of Germany and 69 yrs old.
    Resident of Quincy 51 yrs. Member of the Salem church. Leaves several
    children. She had been an invalid for some time.

Langdon, Mr A.L.   "News"   Oct 22, 1885
    The mother of Mr A.L. Langdon, editor and prop. of the Quincy Saturday
    Review died Sunday morning at the age of 85 yrs. Died october 25th.

Lange, Henry   "Quincy"   Mar 2, 1899
    Died- Mr Henry Lange, a resident of Quincy for 28 yrs died there
    Saturday A.M. Born Staffordshire, England April 5, 1837. Leaves a wife
    3 sons and 2 daughters.

Lanoix, Dr F.W.   "Local"   Dec 18, 1902
    Dr F.W. Lanoix died in the Cook Co. hospital in Chicago Thursday A.M.
    last. It will be remembered that for a short time he was a resident of
    Mendon.

Large, Mr John   "Payson"   Feb 22, 1883
    A child of Mr John Large died on the 16th.

Larimore, Fred   "Local"   Oct 30, 1902
    Mr Fred Larimore, a prominent young man of Plainville, this Co. was
    found murdered near the home of his parents Thursday eve last week.

Lasley, Joseph P.   "Local"   May 21, 1885
    Joseph P. Lasley of Camp Point died on the 13th in his 40th yr. He
    enlisted in Co. 50th Ill. in Feb 1864 and served to the end of the war.
    He was at one time commander of the Co. of state guards in Camp Point.

Laughery, Mrs Lucinda   "Obituary"   Dec 16, 1897
    see Simmons, Elias

Laugherty, Mr Wm   "Local"   Aug 25, 1892
    Died- Mr Wm Laugherty died on Friday of consumption and buried next day.
    Services at the Lutheran church. Leaves a wife and 1 child, a young boy.

Laughery, Mrs Wm   "Personal"   Nov 6, 1879
    Died- on Thursday October 30th 1879, Mrs Laughery, wife of Wm Laughery
    of this village.

Laughery, Mrs Wm   "News"   Nov 6, 1879
    Funeral sermon of Mrs Wm Laughery will be at the M.E. church next
    Sunday at 11 A.M. by Rev Bruner.

Laughlin, Benjamin F.   "Obituary"   Feb 23, 1888
    Mr Benjamin F. Laughlin of this twp died at his home 4½ miles northwest of
    Mendon on Saturday afternoon February 18th, age 81 yrs 11 mo's 14 days.
    Buried following afternoon in the Franklin cemetery near Marcelline.
    Services by Rev Ausmus. Had been an invalid the past 4 to 5 yrs. Mr L.
    was a member and trustee and one of the founders of the Franklin Free Will
    Baptist church. A colleague of the late Mr F.N. Thayer whom he rests near
    in death. Born in Harrison Co. Ky. March 4, 1806 and married March 1, 1832
    to Miss Sarah Robeson. Came to this Co. in spring of 1832 and settled
    near Quincy. a yr later they moved to their present home. He leaves a
    widow and 4 sons.

Laughlin, Mr Bolivar   "Tioga"   Jan 12, 1888
    Died- January 6th, Mr Bolivar Laughlin in his 61 st yr. Born Kentucky
    and came to Illinois about 30 yrs ago. Had few relatives here, a brother
    near Breckenridge and some cousins near Marcelline.

Laughlin, Boswell P.   "Local"   Feb 15, 1900
    Died- Boswell P. Laughlin formerly a resident of Mendon and a brother of
    Mrs C.W.S. Miller died at the home of his mother on N. 5th St Quincy
    Monday from congestive chills. Services in Quincy yesterday A.M. Buried
    in Franklin cemetery. Was 46 yrs old. Leaves his aged mother, a sister and
    brother

Laughlin, Mrs D.C.   "Death"   Mar 15, 1905
    see Shepherd, Mrs Susan

Laughlin, Mrs George   "Death"   Mar 15, 1905
    see Shepherd, Mrs Susan

Laughlin, Mrs Eliza Ann   "death"   Nov 23, 1904
    Funeral of Mrs Eliza Ann Laughlin was at the Baptist church 4 miles
    northwest of Mendon Monday 10:30 A.M. by Rev A.M. Reitzel of the Lutheran
    church. Eliza Ann Randolph was born January 5, 1843 and died Nov 19th at
    the age of 61 yrs 10 mo's 24 days. Married John R. Laughlin Dec 19, 1861
    Leaves husband, son and daughter, a brother and a sister.

Laughlin, Heddessa   Nov 29, 1894
    see Smith, Cyrus

Laughlin, Mrs Hedissa   "Obituary"   Oct 2, 1879
    Died- September 23rd at the age of 78 yrs of pleuro- pneumonia, Mrs
    Hedissa Laughlin, wife of the late Wm Laughlin Esq. Born in Pendleton Co.
    Ky. and came to Mendon Prairie with her husband about 1832 and were one of
    the first settlers of Adams Co. Had 8 children, 1 son and 3 daughters
    survive her. Joined the Presbyterian church in Ky. and became a member
    of the Lutheran church after moving to Mendon. Services by pastor of the
    Lutheran church. Buried beside her husband in the Mendon cemetery.

Laughlin, John W.   "Local"   Feb 26, 1903
    Word was rec'd from W.W. Laughlin of the death of his father, John W.
    Laughlin at his home in Sweet Springs, Mo. He formerly lived in Mendon
    twp. He was a brother of Mrs H.F. McNay and Miss Lizzie Laughlin.

Laughlin, Mary E.   "Obituary"   May 2, 1889
    see Rogers, Clark E.

Laughlin. Mrs Sarah   "Local"   Oct 20, 1898
    Died- Mrs Sarah Laughlin, widow of the late Daniel Laughlin at the home
    of her son Robert about 3½ miles northeast of Mendon Saturday eve. Was
    90 yrs old. Buried next day in Franklin cemetery.

Laughlin, Wm   "Marcelline"   Apr 19, 1894
    Bob Laughlin rec'd a telegram Saturday that his brother Wm, of Mendon
    Missouri was dead. The Laughlin brothers started Sunday at attend the
    funeral.

Laughlin, Wm   Jun 22, 1899
    Included in lists of graves decorated on Memorial Day by Rebeckas in
    Mendon cemetery.

Laughrey, Mrs Jane   "Obituary"   Nov 17, 1898
    see Berrier, Mrs Hannah Mason

Launing, Mr and Mrs James   "Local"   Jul 25, 1895
    Died- Mrs Jas. Launing at her home in Honey Creek twp last Friday at the
    age of 60 yrs. She was 2nd wife of James Launing who came to Adams Co. in 1849
    from Tenn. Leaves 5 daughters, 4 sons and 4 stepchildren.

Lawber, Mrs Charles   Partition #1689   May 18, 1904
    see Moore, Annice S.

Lawber, Mrs Charles   "Obituary"   Mar 16, 1904
    see Johnson, George W.

Lawber, Mr Geo.   "Indian Grave"   Aug 15, 1895
    Died- Mr Geo. Lawber, of Mill Creek. Leaves a wife and several children,
    3 sisters, 2 brothers, Jerry Lawber and Mike his twin brother, Mrs Barnett
    and Mrs Doty of Quincy and Mrs Ben Blyler of this place.

Lawrence, Miss   "Payson"   Jan 3, 1884
    Miss Lawrence was buried Xmas day 1883

Lawrence, Mr Bluford   "Payson"   Jan 29, 1880
    Died- a daughter of Mr Bluford Lawrence, age 14 yrs on January 22nd.
    Funeral at the house by Prof. McClure.

Lawrence, Mr C.   "Payson"   Dec 25, 1879
    Died- on Saturday A.M. a child of Mr C. Lawrence, 2 yrs old from diptheria

Lawrence, Jas.   "Ursa"   Jul 20, 1887
    Died- Jas. Lawrence on Saturday night. Funeral at 10 A.M. Monday by the
    minister who only 3 yrs ago married he and Miss Nora Campbell. He was only
    29 yrs old. Leaves his wife Nora and 2 babies.

Lawrence, Rebecca   "Payson"   Dec 30, 1880
    Buried, Miss Rebecca Lawrence, oldest daughter of Alfred Lawrence on
    December 26th 1880

Lawrence, Richard J.   Nov 29, 1883
    Richard J. Lawrence, deputy county clerk and corner of McDonough Co.
    was killed a few days ago. was 50 yrs old. Leaves a wife and several child-
    ren. Was a resident of the county 30 yrs.

Lawrence, Richard J.   "News"   Nov 29, 1883
    Richard J. Lawrence, deputy co. clerk and coroner of McDonough co. was
    killed by the cars a few days ago. He was drunk and it is supposed he
    lay down on the tracks to sleep. 50 yrs old. Leaves wife and several
    children. Resident of that Co. 30 yrs.

Lawrence, Wm   "Center"   Jan 13, 1881
    Wm Lawrence died January 7th 1881

Lawrence, Mr Wm   "Center"   Jan 26, 1899
    Died- Mr Wm Lawrence, an old pioneer resident, living near Rock Creek
    died last Thursday and was buried at Wesley Chapel on Friday.

Lawrence, Mr Woodford   "Payson"   Jan 1, 1880
    Died- on December 28th 1879 at 7 a.m., Mr Woodford Lawrence of pneumonia.
    Born in Farquier Co. Virginia January 8, 1800, went to Kentucky with his
    parents in 1810 and lived there until 1823 when he returned to his native
    state and spent 3 yrs there teaching school. He taught the 1st school in
    Payson twp. Funeral December 29th at 1 p.m.

Lawson, Mrs Victor F.   "Death"   Feb 19, 1903
    see Bradley, Mrs William H.

Lay, Sarah A.   "Death"   Nov 2, 1904
    see Frisbie, Sarah A. (Lay)

Lay, Willoughby Lynde   "Death"   Nov 2, 1904
    see Frisbie, Mrs Sarah A. (Lay)

Leach, Rev.   "Payson"   Jan 26, 1887
    Funeral sermon of Rev. Mr Leach was held in the Cong'l church last week.
    Some yrs ago Rev Leach was pastor here for 10 yrs. He died in Missouri and
    his remains brought here for burial. Age 64 yrs.

Leach, Mr A.H.   "Coatsburg"   Dec 21, 1893
    Mrs Emma Jones of Chicago was called home to attend the funeral of her
    father, Mr A.H. Leach.

Leach, Mr and Mrs Charles   "Death"   Jun 8, 1899
    see Leckbee, Julia Anne Rhodes

Leach, Delia   "Death"   Dec 24, 1904
    see Carpenter, Mrs Sarah

Leach, Emma   "Death"   Dec 24, 1904
    see Carpenter, Mrs Sarah

Leach, Mrs Nancy   "Coatsburg"   Mar 8, 1894
    Died- Thursday March 1st, Mrs Nancy Leach, age 73 yrs. Leaves 8 children
    Services Friday P.M. by Elder Dilly. Buried in the villagr cemetery
    beside her husband who died 3 months before her.

Leach, Orren Lee   "Death"   Jun 8, 1899
    see Leckbee, Julia Anne Rhodes

Leach, Miss Sarah   "Death"   Dec 28, 1904
    see Carpenter, Mrs Sarah

Leachman, Mrs Elizabeth   "Ursa"   Sep 3, 1891
     Mrs Elizabeth (Betsy) Leachamn, a resident of Ursa died at her home
     August 21st. Age 78 yrs. Services by Rev Lampton at the Christian church.

Leachman, James   "Marcelline"   Feb 14, 1901
     Quite a number of Woodmen of Lima and this place attended the funeral of
     James Leachman, at Ursa Sunday at 2 P.M.

Leachman, Mrs James   "Ursa   Dec 27, 1900
     Mrs James Leachamn died Wednesday abiut 1 P.M. Buried Friday at the
     Stone church cemetery.

Leachman, Mrs James   "Death"   Jan 7, 1892
     see Selby, Mr and Mrs Milton

Leachman, Mrs James   "Death"   Jan 14, 1892
     see Selby, Mrs Emily

Leachman, Mrs Lucy   "Death"   .   Jan 14, 1892
     see Selby, Mrs Emily

Leachman, Mrs Lucy   "Death"   Jan 7, 1892
     see Selby, Mr and Mrs Milton

Leachamn, Mrs Maria   "Death"   Mar 23, 1893
     see Dalby, Joseph

Leachman, Mrs Thos.   "Death"   Mar 2, 1899
     see Taylor, Mrs Barbara

Leachman, Mrs W. C.   "Death"   Jan 7, 1892
     see Selby, Mr and Mrs Milton

Leachman, Mrs W.C.   "Death"   Jan 14, 1892
     see Selby, Mrs Emily

Leachamn, Mrs Walter   "Death"   Jan 14, 1892
     see Selby, Mrs Emily

Leachman, Mrs Walter   "Death"   Jan 7, 1892
     see Selby, Mr and Mrs Milton

Leachman, Wm   "Ursa"   Jan 26, 1882
     Mr Wm Leachman died this morning.

Leachamn, Wm   "News"   Feb 2, 1882
     The personal property of the estate of Wm Leachman is est. at 17,000.00
     Esq. Geo. H. Walker of Marcelline , Adm.

Leak, Wm   "Personal"   Oct 9, 1879
     Wm Leak died at his residence in Lebanon, Missouri Saturday September 27th
     Burial Mason's fraternity last Sunday.

237

Lear, Frank   "Local"   Dec 7, 1899
    Liveryman Frank Lear, of Camp Point committed suicide Tuesday by taking
    a dose of strychnine.

Leckbee, Mrs   "Local"   Jun 8, 1899
    Mr and Mrs Ira Rockwell of Clayton came to attend the funeral of their
    grandmother, Mrs Leckbee. Mrs R. will remain with her parents, Mr and Mrs
    Charles Leckbee for a time.

Leckbee, Mrs Ellen   "Obituary"   Sep 7, 1904
    see Woodruff, Charles Edwin

Leckbee, Julia Anne Rhodes   "Obituary"   Jun 8, 1899
    Died- Julia Anne Rhodes Leckbee. She was born Ola twp Redner Co. Penn.
    April 15, 1808 and died at the home of her son Albert in Mendon June 2nd.
    She was 91 yrs 17 days old. Married Richard Leckbee in Schuylkill twp
    Chester Co. 1834. They had 10 children, Wm, Harriet, Mary, Joseph, Albert,
    John, Charles, Alonzo, Ann Matilda and Frank. (5 are dead), Wm Harriet,
    Alonzo and Anne Matilda. Joseph, Albert and Chalres live in Mendon, Mrs
    Mary Frick in Phoenixville, Penn., and Frank in Knox City, Mo. The family
    moved to Mo. in 1861 where Mr L. died August 27, 1878 and since that time
    she has lived with her son Albert. She was a member of the Baptist church.
    Liked to read her German bible. Leaves 45 grandchildren and 24 gr grand-
    children and 1 gr gr grandchild, Orren Lee Leach, son of Mr and Mrs Charles
    Leach of Mendon. Services by Rev E.K. Crews at the house at 2:30 P.M.
    Buried in Mendon cemetery.

Leckbie, Mrs John(Amanda)   "Local"   Jan 31, 1889
    Mrs Amanda Leckbie of Novelty, Mo. widow of the late John Leckbie has been
    visiting her brother "Jake" Rice.

Leckbie, Joseph Griffith   "Obituary"   Aug 1, 1901
    Died- Joseph Griffith Leckbie died July 27, 1901 at Mendon, Ill. Was
    born Phoenixville, Chester Co. Penn February 14, 1839. His father was a
    native of England and came to U.S. as a boy. On February 23, 1867 her
    married Mary Elizabeth Chambers of Philadelphia, Penn. They had 9 children,
    8 are still living who with a mother and 3 brothers, Frank, Charles and
    Albert survive him. He and his wife came to Ill. December 13, 1868 and
    since May 1869 have lived in Mendon. He joined the M.E. church 27 yrs ago
    under Rev O.H.P. Ash. He was caretaker and sexton of the Mendon cemetery.
    Services from the M.E. church Monday P.M. by Rev S.N. Wakfield. Buried
    in Mendon cemetery. Pallbearers were- S.H. Bardley, C.W. Pepple, C.A.
    Chittenden, F.O. Dickerman, J.H. Nichols and Wm Thompson.

Lee, Dr A.F.   "Local"   Aug 25, 1892
    Dr A.F. Lee of Quincy who had a sudden attack of insanity June 7th died
    at Jacksonville asylum on Friday. Buried in Quincy in Woodland cemetery
    on Sunday.

Lee, Mrs Charlotte   "Quincy"   Mar 16, 1899
    Died- Mrs Charlotte E. Lee Sunday morning. Had lived Quincy 10 yrs.

Lee, Mrs Chas.(Sarah Jane)   "Quincy"   Mar 30, 1899
     Died- Mrs Sarah Jane Lee, Wife of Chas. Lee died Friday from grip and
     winter cholera. 82 yrs old.

Lee, Mrs Francis   "Obituary"   Oct 5, 1899
     Died- Mrs Francis Lee, (nee Washburne) was born Harrison Co. Ky. August 5,
     1816 and died in Quincy September 27. Was 83 yrs 1 mo 22 days old. This
     is the 3rd sister to died within a yr. Services by Rev E.K. Crews at the
     Franklin Church. Buried in nearby cemetery.

Lee, Sarah   "Indian Grave"   Dec 27, 1894
     Died- Sarah Lee, age about 4 yrs died of diptheria on December 13th.

Lees, Thomas   "Death"   Apr 20, 1887
     see McNulty, Mrs Samuel

Leeper, Mrs   "Local"   Jan 4, 1883
     Mr and Mrs Henry Ott rec'd word of the illness of Mrs O's mother, Mrs
     Leeper at Lima. They arrived there only a short time before her death.

Leeper, Thomas Fletcher   "Death"   Jun 15, 1904
     T.F. Leeper of Lima twp died at noon yesterday at his home 2 miles
     southeast of the village of Lima. 3 yrs ago he suffered a paralylic stroke
     and never fully recovered. Thomas Fletcher Leeper was born in Ohio.
     Came to Adams Co. 41 yrs ago. Leaves a widow, 2 children, Burton Leeper
     of Lima is a son and Mrs Eva Leeper the daughter, 2 sisters, Mrs H.C. Hull
     of Lima and Mrs Belle Ott of Denver.   "Whig"

Leeper, Mr and Mrs T.F.   "Lima"   Jun 29, 1893
     Mr and Mrs T.F. Leeper buried their young dhild, age 9 yrs last Thursday
     at the Lima cemetery. He had been sick since Xmas.

Legatt, Mrs John A.   Sep 8, 1881
     Died September 8th at Butte, Montana Mrs John A. Legatt formerly of
     Mendon. Husband survives.

Leggatt, A.J.   Feb 17, 1886
     Message was rec'd Thursday eve from St Louis by Mr A. Benton telling of
     the death of his son in law, Mr A.J. Leggatt from cancer of the stomach at
     the age of 51 yrs. Leaves a wife and 4 children.

Leggatt, Mrs John A.(Jack)   "News"   Sep 15, 1881
     We learn that John A. Leggatt formerly of this vicinity lost his wife
     September 3rd. Jack has been a resident of Butte, Montana for several yrs.

Leighty, George   Feb 3, 1886
     George Leighty died Thursday and was buried in Gilliland (his mother's)
     family burying ground. Services by Rev Howard Miller of the M.E. Church.
     Was 18 yrs old.

Leighty, John   "Obituary"   Jul 6, 1899
Died- John Leighty was born Westmoreland Co. Penn February 4, 1830 and died July 3rd. Was 69 yrs 4 mo's 29 days old. Came to Adams Co. 1851 and settled in Mendon twp. Married Mildred Ann Gilliland September 15, 1853. She died June 11, 1891. They had 6 children, John W., Geo. S.have preceded her in death. others are Wm P., R. Thomas, Letitia A. and Edward G.. Mr L. has a sister, Mrs Ann Tinnsman living in Penn, a brother Peter in Ohio and two ½ sisters, Mrs Fanny Vance and Mrs Betty Spears in Iowa. Services held Tuesday at 3 P.M. by Rev E.K. Crews. Buried beside his wife in the Gilliland cemetery.

Leighty, John   "Probate Notice"   Aug 24, 1899
1st Monday of October 1899   W.P. Leighty, Adm.

Leighty, Mrs John(Mildred)   Jun 18, 1891
Mrs John Leighty died June 11th at her home 1½ miles southeast of Mendon of heart complication. Leaves her husband, 3 sons, 1 daughter, an aged father and 4 brothers. She was born Mildren Ann Gilliland in Morgan Co. Ill. Feb 22, 1835. Was 56 yrs 3 mo's 19 days old. Came to Adams Co. in 1841 and married Mr John Leighty September 15, 1853. Services at the home by Rev F.C. Read. Buried in Gilliland family burying ground.

Leighty, Wm P.   "Obituary"   Aug 9, 1905
Wm P. Leighty was born in Mendon twp August 15, 1862 and died in Citronelle, Ala. August 2nd. Was 42 yrs 11 mo's 17 days old. Lived all his life in Mendon twp until last December when he and wife and 2 daughters moved to Citronelle, Ala. Was taken sick August 31st with an obstruction of the bowels and a rupture of a blood vessel on the brain, died Wednesday Aug 2nd. He was oldest of 6 children of the late John and Mildred A. Leighty. Leaves wife, 2 daughters, 1 sister and 2 brothers. The sister Letitia lives in New Haven, Conn. Brothers, Thomas in LaHarpe, Kansas and Edward in Iola, Kan He was a member of M.W.A. of Mendon, also Charter member of I.O.O.F. lodge of Mendon, having attained the highest office in the subordinate lodge that of Deputy Grand Master of the Mendon lodge #877 Funeral at Citronelle, Ala. Friday August 4th and conducted by I.O.O.F. of that place.

Lemmon, Mrs Alice   "Obituary"   Mar 30, 1899
see Brown, Mrs Lillie

Lemmon, Mrs Amanda   "Obituary"   Mar 14, 1901
see Rawlings, John H.

Lemmon, Mrs Ashel   "Loraine"   Nov 28, 1901
Sudden death of Mrs Ashel Lemmon after a torturing illness of 4 days. She was the oldest daughter of Mr and Mrs John Crabby and grown up among us. Born May 23, 1875 and married Wm A. Lemmon June 10, 1900 died November 24th 1901. Funeral by Rev Bennett the Christian minister from Marcelline at the Methodist church November 25th at 11 A.M. Buried Loraine cemetery. Leaves husband, father, mother, 3 sisters and 2 brothers.

Lemmon, Mrs Laura J.   "Obituary"   May 17, 1900
    Died- Mrs Laura J. Lemmon, wife of C.B. Lemmon of Suter, Hancock Co. at
St Mary's hospital Sunday May 13th. Was born this Co. October 1, 1846.
Lived here till 2 yrs ago when the family moved to Hancock Co. Leaves husban-
5 sons and 3 daughters. Was a member of the Christian church. She was a
sister of O.W. Thompson of Ursa and W.S. Thompson of Campbell, Minn.
Buried in Keith cemetery Tuesday P.M.

Lemmon, Mrs W.D.   "Died"   Mar 8, 1883
    Mrs W.D. Lemmons died March 1st. Was 40 yrs old. Born Adams Co. Maiden name
was Elizabeth F. Tout. She married 1865. Leaves husband, 4 daughters and
1 son. Was a member of the Christian church.

Lemmon, William Daniel   "Obituary"   Jan 18, 1905
    William Daniel Lemmon was born February 17, 1838 and died January 15th
at age 66 yrs 10 mo's 28 days. Born about 6 miles northwest of Mendon and
lived most of his life in Hancock Co. and Adams Co. Married Elizabeth Francis
Tout October 25, 1864 near Marcelline in this Co. Had 6 children, 1 son
5 daughters. Wife and 3 daughter died before him. Wife 22 yrs ago and
Sarah Elizabth when almost 2 yrs old and Mamie at age 14 yrs and Eldora,
wife of James McClelland when she was 18 yrs old. He is survived by 1 son
Sterling P. of Augusta, Ill. and 2 daughters, Mrs J.W. Cunningham of Mendon
and Mrs F.W. Hart of West Point. Services held at the home of his daughter
Mrs J.W. Cunningham Tuesday A.M. by Rev Joseph F. Bacon. Buried beside his
wife in Keath cemetery.

Lemmons, Mrs Anna   "Marcelline"   Nov 28, 1901
    Some attended the funeral of Mrs Anna Lemmons of Loraine from here.

Lemmons, Mrs Calvin   "Ursa"   May 17, 1900
    The funeral of Mrs Calvin Lemmons of Sutter, Ill was at the Christian
church at 1 P.M. She was brought from the St Mary's hospital where she was
suffering intensely from the removal of a cancer.

Lemmons, Mamie   "Ursa"   Aug 13, 1891
    Mamie, youngest child of Mr Lemmons who died at their home in Loriane
was brought to Keaths cemetery Ursa for burial August 7th.

Lemons, Mrs Sarah   "Ursa"   Aug 11, 1892
    Died- Mrs Sarah Lemons died Saturday August 6th at 10 P.M. Was 84 yrs old
Leaves 6 children. Buried in Keith cemetery Sunday. Services by Rev Ward.

Lennon, Anthony   "Death"   Sep 11, 1879
    see Rowney, Mrs

Lennox, Mrs John   "Obituary"   May 19, 1886
    see Ellis, Horatio T.

Lenzey, Mrs John   "Lima"   Nov 24, 1886
    Mrs John Lenzey of Missouri, one of our old neighbors died in Quincy a few
days ago.

241

Lesen, Isaac "Local" Aug 31, 1899
 Died- Isaac Lesem, formerly in the wholesale dry goods business in Quincy
 died in Wildbad, Germany last Wednesday of heart disease.

Leslie, Elizabeth Ann "Obituary" Apr 2, 1903
 see Long, Mrs Elizabeth Ann

Leslie, William C. "Obituary" Apr 2, 1903
 see Long, Mrs Elizabeth Ann

Lessman, Henry F. "Local" Jan 27, 1886
 Henry F. Lessman of Columbus twp hanged himself Wednesday the 20th inst.
 He was a member of the Lutheran church.

Levi, Mr Henry Apr 24, 1884
 On April 21st Mr Henry Levi, aged 72 yrs died suddenly at his home due
 to the shock caused by the sudden intelligence that his youngest daughter
 had that afternoon been married at the Fremont House to a man named Wm
 Miller, not of their faith and a gambler. He leaves a wife.

Levy, Joe "Local" Mar 23, 1887
 Joe Levy of St Louis, a saleman well known in the Jewish section shot
 himself in Quincy last Monday. Died Tuesday.

Lewis, Mr and Mrs "Local" Oct 28, 1897
 Dead- - Mr Geo. Johnson of Ellington twp informed us this A.M. that both
 his wife's parents are dead. Mrs Lewis died January 25, 1897 and her
 husband died March 4, 1897. They lived at Key West, Canton Co. Ky.

Lewis, Mrs J.W. "Ursa" Jul 5, 1900
 Mrs J.W. Lewis (Bud) rec'd word of the death of her brother, Dan Aydelotte
 at St Mary's hospital Saturday night.

Lewis, Miss Sarah J. "Death" Mar 16, 1904
 see Johnson, George W.

Lewis, Dr H. N. "Local" Dec 11, 1884
 Dr H.N. Lewis of Quincy died December 5th at age 76 yrs.

Libbet, Christ "Quincy Advance " Dec 11, 1884
 Christ Libbet, an employe of Matthew Dick committed suicide December 4th
 by hanging himself to a apple tree. (to much liquor)

Lichteberger, Alexander May 26, 1881
 Alexander Lichteberger died May 23rd 1881. Lived Quincy and was formerly
 of Mendon twp. His son in law is Mr William Miller of Mendon.

Licke, Miss Louise "Ursa" May 7, 1885
 Miss Louise Licke died April 26th. Her father died a yr ago.

Lierly, Mrs Daniel Feb 16, 1882
 Mrs Daniel Lierly was buried at Hannibal last Sunday.

242

Lindsay, Mrs Mary   "Death"   Aug 3, 1904
    Died- Mrs Mary Lindsay at her home, 1½ miles north of Lima last Wednesday
    A.M. Was sick several yrs. 76 yrs old and had lived in this state several
    yrs. Leaves husband, 3 sons and 4 daughters.

Linenburger, Bertha   "Tioga"   Jul 18, 1895
    Died- Tuesday night July 9th at 9 from brain fever, Bertha Linenburger
    age 5 yrs. Funeral at the family home at 3 P.M. July 12th. Buried in the
    German cemetery after services by Rev P. Ott.

Lingham, Jimmy   "local"   Jan 19, 1893
    Died- Jimmy Lingham at his home in Quincy. Brought to Mendon for burial.
    Services at the M.E. colored church in Quincy near the deceased home at
    814 N. 8th St. Jimmy was acting as stable boy for the Chittenden Bros.
    His parents were Mr and Mrs Wm Lingham.

Lingham, William   "Local"   Mar 1, 1905
    Died- William Lingham who formerly lived in Mendon, but the last 13 yrs
    had lived in Quincy died in that city Friday night. Age 85 yrs. Buried
    Mendon cemetery. We knew him as "Uncle Billy"

Lingham, Mr and Mrs Wm   "Burial"   Oct 26, 1904
    see McGill, Mrs Mary

Linn, Mrs Kate   "Loraine"   Jan 31, 1901
    Died- Mrs Kate Linn (Blackman) died of consumption at her sister's at
    Stillwell last Wednesday. Buried Loriane cemetery Friday P.M.

Linn, Mrs Nancy   "Local"   May 11, 1904
    Mrs Nancy Linn died last Wednesday at her home in Camp Point of old age.
    She was a pioneer of this county and was 95 yrs old.

Linnenburger, Mrs Henry   "Obituary"   Mar 15, 1894
    see Ensminger, Mrs

Linnenburger, Herman   Tioga"   Apr 14, 1886
    The sale of the residence of the late Herman Linnenburger, deceased.
    (between here and Mendon) was largely attended.

Lint, Catherine   "Obituary"   Jul 11, 1901
    Died- Catherine Lint, born in Williams Co. Ohio June 4, 1845, married
    Jacob Roth 1861 and had 1 child William. She was left a widow by the civil
    war and married 2nd to Uriah Dumbauld December 22, 1867. They had Janie
    who died, Arthur, Lennie and Eldon all residents of this village. She joined
    the M.E. church at Mendon 1892 and died July 6th 1901 at the age of 56 yrs
    1 mo 2 days. Was sick 3 yrs. Funeral at the family home by her pastor
    Rev S.N. Wakefield Sunday July 7th. Buried in Mendon cemetery.

Lint, Charles F.   "Obituary"   Mar 1, 1905
    Charles F. Lint, son of Conrad and Lydia Lint born September 26, 1872 in
    Powershiek Co. Iowa died February 10, 1905 in Cripple Creek, Colorado of
    pneumonia. Was sick 3 days. Married Sylvia L. Wicoff November 1, 1900
    and they had 1 son and 1 daughter, the former died in infancy, the daughter
    Natalie is 16 mo's old and with his wife survives him. When 2 yrs old
    he and parents left Iowa and settled in Fremont, Indiana where he was
    raised (except for the time he worked for Mr J. Huston here) up to 10 mo's
    ago when he went to Cripple Creek Colo. at the age of 19 yrs he joined the
    M.E. church. Remains were taken to Fremont, funeral at the M.E. church by
    Rev Reicheldorfer and Rev Ranner. Buried in a vault and will later be
    placed in the Jamestown cemetery.

Lippincott, Mrs Emma   "Local"   May 23, 1895
    Died- Mrs Emma Lippincott, the respected matron of the Soldiers Home died
    Tuesday A.M. in her room in the headquarters bldg. of pneumonia. Was 62 yrs
    old and the widow of General Chas. Ellot Lippincott, the 1st superintendent
    of the Home. Buried in Springfield.

Lippincott, Lillie Dale   "Fowler & Oakland"   Dec 29, 1898
    Died- Lillie Dale Lippincott, wife of Oliver Lippincott, living near
    Oakland died Friday A.M.. She gave birth to a male child a week ago. Buried
    in Byler cemetery Sunday A.M. Infant survives.

Littleton, Mr and Mrs Hugh   "Local"   Dec 31, 1903
    Died- the 4 yr old son of Mr and Mrs Hugh Littleton, living on part of
    the Jeff Finley farm, 3 miles east of Loraine was burned to death Thursday
    P.M. His father had gone to Quincy and his mother had gone to the buggy
    shed to make arrangements to attend Xmas excercises at thier church in
    Loraine. On returning she found him lying on the floor, nearly all his
    clothing burned from his body. A number of burned matches were on the
    floor by the body.

Littleton, Hugh Sr.   "Loraine"   Jun 1, 1901
    Train hit the buggy Thursday carrying Hugh Littleton Sr. and 2 grand-
    children, Mr L. was killed and Miss Laura Brownlee 16 yrs old was hurt
    with little hope of recovery. Ed Littleton, son of Wm Littleton Sr. was
    also hurt badly. The 2 were taken to the home of her uncle, Mr Frank Little-
    ton from the Dr's office, Mr Hugh L. Sr. was buried in the Reece cemetery
    Friday P.M.

Livingston, Thomas   "Camp Point"   Aug 7, 1879
    Thomas Livingston, age 74 yrs, father of Benj. Livingston of this town
    died at Bardolph Saturday. Remains were brought here and buried Monday.

Livingstone, Jas.   "Camp Point"   Mar 30, 1882
    Died- Saturday night a little daughter of Jas. Livingstone.

Lloyd, Dr Walter Frederick   Jun 16, 1892
    "Death of Dr Lloyd, Iowa State Reporter" (Waterloo)
    Died- Dr Walter Frederick Lloyd Tuesday at 9 A.M.. His wife died 6 yrs ago
    this coming September. His only child, a daughter lives in Colorado. Services
    at the Church of Christ Saturday at 11:30 A.M. by Rev Thomas E. Green of
    Cedar Rapids and Rev W.B. Walker of Dubuque.

244

Lock, Mr Newton   "Payson"   Aug 19, 1880
    Mr Newton Lock, son of Turner Lock who moved from here to California a
    few yrs ago. Since moving there Newton has lost his wife, mother, sister and
    a brother by death.

Lockner, Mr Jacob   "Tioga"   Mar 7, 1901
    Died- last Sunday morning February 24th, Mr Jacob Lockner of apoplexy,
    in his field.About 11:30 as the Wolf Lockner was returning from Elvaston
    where he works he found the body of his father. Leaves a wife and 3 sons.
    Buried in the Catholic cemetery at Warsaw Tuesday A.M.

Logan, George   Jan 15, 1903
    George Logan, a boy 15 yrs old was shot and killed by Floyd Stahl near
    Fowler Saturday. Stahl then tried to kill himself with a gun taken from
    Frank Logan. Shooting was the result of carelessness. Geo. Logan 15 yrs,
    Frank Logan 18 yrs and Floyd Stahl 18 yrs all were hunting. Funeral at the
    Methodist church at Fowler Tuesday P.M. George was born Quincy June 19, 1889
    was the youngest of 6 children of Mr and Mrs Thomas Logan. For past several
    yrs he had lived with his grandmother in Fowler.

Logan, George   "Fowler"   Jan 22, 1903
    Died- George Logan on January 10th. Born Quincy June 19, 1889 and was the
    youngest of 6 children of Mr and Mrs Thos. Logan. 4 of whom survive him.
    Funeral at the M.E. church Tuesday by Rev F.P. Bonnefon of Rushville.

Logan, Mrs Mary H.   "Fowler"   Aug 25, 1886
    Mrs Higgins was called to Topeka to attend the funeral of her daughter,
    Mrs Mary H. Logan last week. Mrs L. died from typhoid fever.

Lohr, Mr and Mrs   "Local"   Mar 14, 1895
    Died- the infant child of Mr and Mrs Lohr on Friday A.M. of tonsilitis
    and was taken to West Point fro burial.

Lohr, Mr and Mrs G.G.   "Funeral"   Mar 8, 1894
    see Hart, Grace

Lohr, G.G.   "Local"   Oct 11, 1900
    G.G.Lohr is at the bedside of his aged father at Columbus who is 84 yrs
    old. LATER- Mr Lohr died about noon yesterday.

Lohr, Mary E.   "Obituary"   Feb 17, 1904
    see Hastings, Thomas Gilbert

Long, Dr   "Local"   May 12, 1898
    Died- Dr Long, the dentist formerly of Mendon at his home in Woodhull,
    Henry Co. on Friday A.M. of heart failure. Buried Mount Morris Monday.
    Leaves a wife (a sister of Mrs Geo. Lyle) and 1 child, also 3 children
    by a former marriage. Howard living in Penn., Ray at college in Missouri
    and Blanche at home.

Long, Mrs   "Death"   Sep 12, 1900
    see Shipley, Mrs

Long, Mrs A.G.   "Local"   May 4, 1899
    Mrs A.G. Long attended the funeral of her brother in Quincy. Returned
    Monday eve.

Long, Adolphus R.   "Local"   May 19, 1898
    We learn from a clipping of the Woodhull paper that the late Adolphus R.
    Long, the dentist,died. Was a little over 50 yrs old. His son Ramon has taken
    charge of the business

Long, Mr and Mrs Andrew   "Elm Grove"   Dec 25, 1884
    Mr Andrew Long with his son Walter and daughter, Annie went to Chili for
    the funeral of Mrs Long's cousin who died December 17th.

Long, C.   "Carthage"   Apr 3, 1884
    March 20th a young child of C. Long was buried.

Long, D.W.   Jun 1, 1899
    Included in list of graves decorated in Mendon Memorial day. (Soldiers)

Long, Daniel W.   "Probate Notice"   Apr 30, 1891
    1st Monday of July 1891   John Pratt, Adm.

Long, Mrs Elizabeth Ann   "Died"   Apr 2, 1903
    Died- Mrs Elizabeth Ann Long, wife of Andrrw G. Long died at her home 2½
    miles southeast of Mendon Friday eve March 27th from cancer of the liver.
    Age 64 yrs 8 mo's 4 days. Born Ellington twp July 23, 1838 and married
    Andrew G. Long December 29, 1859. They had 7 children, 6 still living.
    One died in infancy. Also leaves husband. Children are- Mary, Annie, Walter,
    William, David, Emily -1 brother, William C. Leslie of Columbus, Ill and
    1 sister, Mrs Margaret Pollock of Martinsburg, Iowa. Funeral Monday at
    1:30 at the house and at 2:30 at the church by Rev J.S. Bayne.

Long, George and Sarah   Feb 27, 1890
    Infant child of George and Sarah Long died February 20th. Buried Feb. 21st.
    in the Coatsburg cemetery.

Long, Henry   "Bowensberg"   Jan 19, 1882
    Died- January 15th Henry Long, one of our oldest citizens. Leaves his
    wife and children.

Long, John   Jun 5, 1902
    Included in list of Soldiers graves decorated in Mendon for Memorial Day.

Long, Mrs John A.   "Local"   Jul 30, 1903
    Died- Mrs Margaret Long yesterday afternoon at 1 at her home at Fowler
    from a form of brain trouble. She was the wife of John A. Long. Born and
    raised in vicinivty of Fowler. Was 50 yrs old. Leaves husband and several
    children. funeral Monday at Fowler. "Sunday's Whig"

Long, Mr Robert   "Local"   Jan 24, 1889
    Died- Mr Robert Long, senior member of the firm of Long Bros. produce
    merchants of Quincy and a brother of A.G. Long died Saturday P.M. of typhoid
    fever. Was 42 yrs old. Leaves a wife and 2 children. Services held at the
    family residence at 818 Oak St on Monday at 2 P.M.

Long, Mrs Sarah   "Coatsburg"   Mar 24, 1886
    Died- Mrs Sarah Long on Friday. Funeral at the Christian church Saturday
    P.M. by Rev Wilson of Camp Point. Buried in the village cemetery. Leaves
    husband and 3 small children, the youngest only 1 week old.

Longbaugh, Eliza   "Death"   Mar 17, 1898
    see Nedrow, Mrs Eliza

Lose, Mrs Barbara   "Coatsburg"   Dec 25, 1884
    Mrs Barbara Lose will be buried on December 16th.

Loucks, H.S.   "Ursa"   Jan 27, 1898
    H.S. Loucks was called to Missouri last week to attend the funeral of his
    brother.

Loucks, Mrs H.S.   "Local"   Oct 18, 1886
    Died- Mrs H.S. Loucks of Ursa. Was 45 yrs old died Tuesday at 2:30 P.M.
    Services from the Lutheran church of Mendon at 10 A.M.

Loucks, Mrs H.S.   "Local"   Oct 20, 1886
    Funeral of the late Mrs H.S. Loucks, of Ursa took place Thursday morning.
    Services at the Lutheran church by Rev E.W. Souders. Buried in Mendon
    cemetery.

Loucks, Henry S.   "Adm. Suit"   Oct 11, 1883
    see Jacobs, Alexander

Lowary, Mr   "Loraine"   Jun 1, 1877
    Mr Lowary lost a year old child from whooping cough.

Lowary, Dan'l P.   "Loraine"   Dec 9, 1880
    Died- Dan'l P. Lowary on December 5th at the age of 35 yrs.

Lowary, Daniel P.   "Probate Notice"   Dec 23, 1880
    Wm D. Lowary, Adm.

Lowary, Daniel P.   Adm. Sale   Feb 24, 1881
    Administrator's sale of the estate of Daniel P. Lowary   Wm D. Lowary, Adm.

Lowary, Grover   "Loraine"   Sep 4, 1890
    Grover Lowary an orphan boy living with Mr Henry Theitten for the past
    year died Friday night. Buried beside his mother in Stone cemetery near
    Ursa.

Lowary, Tom   "Loraine"   Mar 21, 1895
    Uncle Tom Lowary who lived 5 miles east of here was buried yesterday.

Lowe, Mrs   "Camp Point"   Aug 29, 1901
    The funeral of Mrs Lowe who died in Kansas was here at the Christian church
    last Wednesday by Elder Webb. Buried in village cemetery.

Lowery, John   "Local"   Jun 21, 1888
    Tragedy near West Point last Thursday A.M. by which 3 died.
    John Lowery, a well to do farmer in a fit of jealousy murdered his wife
    and a hired man, Abraham P. Clark. Mrs L? was the daughter of the late John
    Hardy of this twp and she was buried Saturday in the Stone church cemetery
    north of Ursa. Lowery and Clark were buried at West Point on Sunday. Left
    3 young children.

Lowery, John   Apr 11, 1889
    Sold land as guardian of Jhon Lowery's Heirs. see Pratt, John

Lowery, John   "Estate Sale"   Jul 10, 1884
    see Owings, Howard W.

Lowery, Nancy F.   "Estate Sale"   Jul 10, 1884
    see Owings, Howard W.

Lowry, David   "Local"   Oct 18, 1888
    Died- Mr David Lowry, for many yrs a resident of Keene twp died at the
    home of his son, Jacob F. Lowry in Clayton on October 4th at the age of 80 yr
    Mr L. was one of the early settlers of the county.

Lowry, Thomas   "Big Neck"   Mar 21, 1895
    Died- Thomas Lowry, "Uncle Tom Lowry" March 15th after a short illness
    age 78 yrs. Was a member of the Presbyterian church. Funeral by Rev
    McDonald of the Ebenezer church

Lowry, Thomas   "Death"   Aug 1, 1889
    see Adair, John

Loynd, Cora   "Will"   Mar 28, 1901
    see Nutt, Daniel

Loynd, Geo.   "Will"   Mar 28, 1901
    see Nutt, Daniel

Loynd, Geo.   "Local"   Jun 14, 1900
    Geo. Loynd of Quincy attended the funeral of his aunt, Mrs Rhine last
    Saturday.

Loynd, Gilbert   "Will"   Mar 28, 1901
    see Nutt, Daniel

Loynd, Giles   Oct 18, 1883
    Mr Giles Loynd died on June 17th at Lucas Iowa at the age of 83 yrs
    Born England and came to America in the 1850's and to Lucas Co. 1868
    settleing in Otter creek twp.

Loynd, James   "Obituary"   Mar 21, 1901
    see Nutt, Daniel

Loynd, Harry   "Obituary"   Mar 21, 1901
    see Nutt, Daniel

Loynd, Harry   "Will"   Mar 28, 1901
    see Nutt, Daniel

Loynd, Harry William   "Obituary"   Feb 5, 1903
Harry William Loynd was born in Mendon, Ill February 20, 1876 and died
Albuquerque New Mexico January 25, 1903. He was 26 yrs 11 mo's 5 days old
Was oldest son of a family of 4 children of Mr and Mrs James Loynd. Up
till his mother's death February 7, 1890 he lived at home, afterwards with
his maternal grandfather, Daniel Nutt in Mendon, Ill. Fall of 1899 he
started work for the C.B. & Q. railroad at Galesburg, Ill as fireman.
Health failed him more than a yr ago. Married Miss Clara Kenstler, of
Galesburg October 1, 1901. Leaves father, 1 sister, (Miss Cora), 2 brothers
(George and Gilbert) and a wife. Funeral at the M.E. church by pastor
Rev S.R. Reno. Buried Mendon cemetery by the side of his mother.

Loynd, Harry   Obituary"   Jan 29, 1903
Died- Harry Loynd at Albuquerque, New Mexico Sunday January 25th from
tuberculosis. Leaves a wife and brother George of Chicago. Was brought
back to Mendon for burial beside his mother. Services to be at the M.E.
church Friday 2 P.M. He was born Mendon Feb 20, 1876. Was the oldest son
of James Loynd of Carthage.

Loynd, Mrs Julia   Feb 13, 1890
Died- Mrs Julia Loynd (nee Nutt) February 7th at the age of 33 yrs 9 mo's
26 days. Was youngest daughter of Daniel and Sarah A. Nutt of Mendon. Born
Mendon April 11, 1856 Married James Loynd May 20, 1875 had 3 sons and
1 daughter, 3 brothers and 1 sister. Was the first in the family to die.
Funeral February 9th at the M.E. church. Buried Mendon.

Lubbe, Mr Clemens A.   "Local"   Jul 23, 1903
Died- Mr Clemens A. Lubbe, head clerk and advers. manager at J. Stern and
Sons, at the home of his mother in Quincy Saturday night last from
intestinal obstruction. Was born in Quincy August 1858. Married Miss Minnie
Heintz about 15 yrs ago. She died about a yr after marriage leaving him with
a child which died the next yr. Leaves his mother, 4 brothers and 3 sisters.

Lucas, Mr and Mrs W.H.   "Local"   Aug 24, 1899
The 9 yr old son of Mr and Mrs W.H. Lucas was killed by a C.B. & Q.
passenger engine at the foot of Locust St Quincy last Wednesday.

Lucking, F.W.   "Died"   Jul 19, 1905
F.W. Lucking of Fowler died July 11th at 11 or 12 P.M. at the age of 74 yrs
10 mo's 18 days. Born in Mindon, Germany August 22, 1830. Married December
13, 1830 to Miss Catherine Marie Engel Heckerman. Had 10 children, 8 died
early in childhood. Leaves wife, son Henry and daughter, Mrs Henry Reichert
and 5 grandchildren. Came to U.S. in 1852 and worked as a famr hand at
Coatsburg and Ellington, then bought a farm 2 miles south of Mendon where
he lived till wife's health failed. Services at Fowler Lutheran church
Friday at 10 A.M. Buried in Gilliland cemetery.

Lummis, Mrs John   "Paloma"   Jan 22, 1891
Mrs John Lummis (nee McNeal) died January 18th, leaves a child of 1 week.

Lunbeck, Mrs Gertrude   "Death"   Sep 13, 1905
see Bray, John Henry

Lunn, Dr   Feb 27, 1890
     Died- Dr Lunn on February 20th at his home in Fremont, Nebr. Buried
at Mendon by his daughter Mrs Robert Hewitt. Services at the Zion church
by Rev W. Michael Hicks. He came to Adams Co. from England more than 40
years ago.

Lunn, Miss Harriet   "Obituary"   Feb 22, 1894
     see Hewitt, Robert E.

Lunn, Jas. H. and wife   "Death"   May 11, 1887
     see Brown, Lizzie Lunn

Lunn, John   "Obituary"   Aug 8, 1901
     Died- John Lunn at 3:15 A.M. Thursday July 25th in his apartments on
2nd St., this city of heart trouble. Leaves parents and a sister, Mrs
Harriet Hewitt and his niece, Miss Elizabeth Hewitt of Fremont, Nebr.
He was born September 17, 1843 in Parish of Fordan, Montgomershire, N.
Wales. His father was an english physican and came to U.S. with his family
of 7 children when John was 7 yrs old. Family settled in Mendon, a town
16 miles from Quincy, Ill. When war broke out he was appointed enrolling
officer, but after 3 mo's was discharged because of stomach trouble. While
living in Quincy he met and married Mrs Catherine R. Bull, a widow with
1 child, a boy and they were married June 5, 1875. In 1885 he moved to
Minnesota where he lived in Albert Lea from 1885 to 1895, then Mankato
until last fall when they made their home here with their son's John D.
and Ralph M. Lunn, their only children. Was a member of the Episcopal
church. Leaves wife and 2 sons.

Lunn, John   "Local"   Aug 1, 1901
     Died- Mr John Lunn's daughter at his home at Redwood Falls, Minnesota
Thursday July 25th.

Lunn, R.S.   Jun 22, 1899
     Included in list of graves decorated in Mendon on Memorial day by the
I.O.O.F and the Rebekahas

Lunt, Benjamin   Jun 8, 1887
     News rec'd of the death of Mr Benjamin Lunt at Stillwell. Formerly of
Honey Creek.

Lunt, Joseph   "Loraine"   Jun 8, 1887
     Mr Jacob Lunt was buried at Woodville cemetery yesterday. Approx 1000
people were there.

Lunt, Matilda   Jan 10, 1884
     Died- at the residence of her parents in Hiney Creek twp 2½ miles east
of Mendon, Mrs Matilda Lunt. Was 24 yrs old. Born January 9, 1860 and
died Jan 3, 1884. Her 2 little babies preceeded her but a short time ago.
Leaves 1 girl 5 yrs old. She was also the only child of her parents.

Lyle, Mrs Geo.   "Obituary"   May 14, 1898
    see Long, Dr

Lyle, John   "Fowler"   Nov 13, 1884
    Mr John Lyle an old and respected citizen died November 7th. Was 60 yrs
    old.

Lynch, A.B.   "Death"   Sep 15, 1886
    see Mecum, Nettie May

Lynch, Patrick   "Probate Notice"   Sep 26, 1889
    1st Monday of December 1889   Ann Lynch, Adm.

Lynum, Clyde   "Local"   Aug 23, 1905
    Clyde Lynum, of Canton, Missouri, the young man who drowned Thursday of
    last week was a grnadson of Mrs Tillie Gallimore.

Lyon, Frank   "Local"   Aug 17, 1887
    An accident which probably will prove fatal to Frank Lyon, 18 yr old son
    of Dr Lyon, Postmaster of Camp Point. He fell while attempting to board
    a moving train at Coatsburg and missed his footing and fell between the
    cars and the platform.

Lyon, Dr T.A.   "Camp Point"   Jul 28, 1881
    Death of an infant son of Dr T.A. Lyon. Buried July 17th.

Macfall, Thos. W.   "Local"   Aug 31, 1899
        Died- Thos. W. Macfall of Quincy died Monday A.M. He was Supt of schools
        27 yrs.

Macfall, Mrs Catherine   "Local"   Jul 4, 1901
        Died- Mrs Catherine Macfall, widow of the late Thos. W. Macfall at her
        home in Quincy Tuesday eve.

Machesney, Mrs James   "Funeral"   Mar 8, 1905
        see Frisbie, Mrs Caroline

Mallinson, Mrs   "Fowler"   Feb 3, 1904
        Geo. Evans and wife attended the funeral of Mrs Mallinson.
        The remains of Mrs Mallinson of Quincy, a former resident of this place
        was brought here for burial at Stahl cemetery. Funeral at the M.E. church
        Saturday P.M.

Mallinson, Mr Theodore   Mar 16, 1882
        Mr Theodore Mallinson, a Fowler painter died last week in the fire in the
        Elmore House at Trenton, Mo. He leaves a wife and 3 children. One almost
        a young man.

Maloau, R.M.   "Death in Adams Co."   Apr 20, 1899
        Died- R.M. Maloau, a wealthy farmer of Newton. Age 87 yrs. He cut his
        throat Monday eve. His death is looked for at any moment.

Maloney, Martin   Mar 13, 1884
        Martin Maloney, the noted horse shoer of Quincy died March 8th.

Manaly, James   "Big Neck"   Oct 15, 1891
        James Manaly's youngest child died October 12th of brain fever.

Manly, James   Aug 21, 1890
        The youngest child of James Manly of Big Neck died August 13th. Age 1 yr
        11 mo's 20 days. Services by F.C. Read in the Union church and buried in
        Ebenezer cemetery.

Mann, Mrs   Feb 6, 1890
        Mrs Mann died in Reeders Mills, Iowa. She was the mother of Mrs Wm Quig.

Mann, Mrs   "Funeral"   May 12, 1886
        see Sturgiss, Dr

Mann, Mr Abijah   "Payson"   May 12, 1886
        Mr Abijah Mann and 2 daughters were here to attend the funeral of his
        mother.

Mann, Mrs Abijah   "Payson"   Mar 20, 1884
        Mrs Abijah Mann and family are here to attend the funeral of her mother.

Mann, Isabella   Feb 27, 1890
    Died- Mrs Isabella (Dickson) Mann on February 4th at her home in
    Harrison Co. Iowa. Was wife of Wilford Mann formerly of Mendon. She was
    born November 6, 1826 in Augusta Co. virginia. Her parents moved to
    Kentucky when she was a child where she married Wilford Mann. 1885 she
    moved to Harrieson Co. Iowa. Was a member of the Methodist church. Has
    3 sons and 6 daughters, Mrs Wm Quig of Mendon, Mrs Nora Wasson of
    Montezuma, Iowa and Mrs Wm Fulton of Montezuma, Iowa. Was 63 yrs 2 mo's 28
    days old.

Mann, Mrs J.   "Funeral"   Dec 20, 1883
    see Barrow, Levia

Mann, Mrs Jimmy   "Payson"   May 12, 1886
    Friday eve Mrs Mann died, Was wife of Uncle Jimmy Mann. Services at
    the Cong'l church by Rev Allaber. She was 71 yrs old. Leaves husband.

Marcy, Mr F.V.   "Local"   Jul 17, 1884
    While in Quincy we heard of the death of Mr F.V. Marcy, the eminest
    attorney. He was a member of Wheat and Marcy. Was a native of Vermont
    and came west shortly before the war. He was a bachalor. Had no relatives
    in the city. Was 50 yrs old.

Markley, Uncle Wm   "Loraine"   Aug 25, 1886
    Uncle Wm Markley, of Woodville died on Wednesday of Paralysis.

Marlett, Mr and Mrs F.   "West Point"   Aug 24, 1893
    Mr and Mrs F. Marlett are called to mourn the death of their infant
    child, Fred, which occured at 10 P.M. last Sunday. Services on Monday
    at the M.E. church by Rev McDonald.

Marrett, Mrs L.C.   "Clayton"   Nov 29, 1883
    Mrs L.C. Marrett died November 23rd.

Marsh, Miss Cara   "Local"   May 11, 1904
    The body of Miss Cara Marsh of Warsaw who so mysteriously disappeared
    2 weeks ago Sunday A.M. and was supposed to have thrown herself in the
    river, was found floating in the river at Meyer, Ill. Saturday A.M.
    Taken to Warsaw for burial.

Marsh, Judge Wm   "Local"   Apr 19, 1894
    Judge Wm Marsh, one of Quincy's most prominent and honored citizens died
    Saturday night in his 72 nd year.

Marston, Mrs Addie   "Obituary"   May 15, 1902
    see Whelden, Mary Crane

Martin, Mrs Albert   "West Point"   Dec 11, 1879
    Died- Mrs Abert Martin died yesterday of typhoid fever. It is but a few
    weeks ago that Albert led her to the alter. She was, we think, the 5th
    or 6th member of her family to die of the same disease within a few mo's.

253

Martin, Edward   "Local"   Jan 10, 1901
    The body of Edward Martin of Quincy age 24 yrs was found cut in half
    by the side of the R.R. tracks a short distance south of La Grange, Mo.
    Sunday morning. Leaves a wife and mother.

Martin, Miss Famria   "Obituary"   Oct 17, 1895
    see Stone, Mr Micajah

Martin, Gaylord   "Camp Point"   Jan 27, 1881
    Gaylord Martin died of complication of diseases last week. Was 71 yrs
    old. He was the father of E.G. Martin prop. of the Pottery here.

Martin, John   "Payson"   Nov 18, 1885
    Mr John Martin formerly a resident of this twp, but now of Hannibal, Mo.
    was buried at Fall Creek last Monday. He leaves a wife and 4 children.

Martin, Lucien A.   "Local"   Jan 27, 1886
    Lucien A. Martin at one time a well known teacher at Columbus twp and
    formerly connected with the Whig, died in San Francisco, California
    on the 9th inst. at the age of 43 yrs.

Martin, Miss Susie   "Local"   Jan 16, 1902
    B.A. Van Dyke rec'd telegram Saturday A.M. telling of the death of Miss
    Susie Martin of Malta Bend, Mo. She was the daughter of J.K. Martin
    for many yrs a former citizen of this twp. She was in the prime of life.

Martine, John   "Local"   Feb 26, 1903
    John Martine, of Port Jarvis, N.Y. was shot and killed by a man named
    Koepping who had been boarding ay his home. Mr Martine is an old friend
    and shopmate of Chas. Chant, having worked together for 9 yrs.

Marvin, Fred   Dec 20, 1883
    One of Fred Marvin's children living 3 miles from Plymouth was poisoned
    a few days ago from eating wild turnips. He was buried December 18th.

Marvin, Mrs George   "Local"   Sep 15, 1898
    Ben McCrellis of Quincy rec'd word Sunday of the death of his sister, Mrs
    George Marvin at Davenport. Leaves no children.

Mason, Father   "Loraine"   Jun 5, 1879
    Father Mason died on May 25th. He was among the 1st settlers on the Creek.

Mason, Andrew   "Probate Notice"   Jul 31, 1879
    3rd Monday of August 1879   Kesiah Mason, Adm.

Mason, Dr David H.   "Local"   Sep 25, 1884
    Died August 17th at McPherson, Kansas, Dr David H. Mason age 61 yrs.
    Born WestfordOtsego Co. New York July 21, 1824. Graduted at the Baltimore
    medical college 1848 and in May 1850 came to Mendon where he stayed 8 yrs.

Mason, Miss Hannah   "Obituary"   Nov 17, 1898
    see Berrier, Mrs Hannah Mason

Mason, Mr W.E.   "Local"   Jun 9, 1886
    Mr W.E. Mason, a prominent lawyer of Carthage and for 8 yrs prosecuting
    attorney of Hancock Co. died of heart disease last Wednesday at age 34 yrs.
    Leaves a wife and 3 children.

Masquerier, Louis   "Local"   Jan 26, 1888
    "Quincy Journal" A frenchman named Louis Masquerier died at his home at
    Greenpoint, N.Y. at age 89 yrs. He was the 1st settler in Carthage, Ill.
    having built in 1830 a cabin and lived there until 1835 when he moved
    to New York City. Born in Paris, Kentucky. Studied law.

Maston, Mrs   "Payson"   Nov 10, 1881
    Mrs Maston was buried November 7th at age 93 yrs. Was one of the county's
    earliest settlers.

Matticks, David   "Loraine"   Sep 4, 1902
    Died- David Matticks at his home Tuesday of last week. Buried Loraine
    cemetery Wednesday P.M. Leaves a wife, daughter and 3 sons.

Mayfield, Edna   "Loraine"   Jul 10, 1902
    July 4th about 7:30 P.M. Edna, 1 yr old daughter of Mr and Mrs Lamont
    Mayfield drowned. Mrs M. had come here to visit his brother Irvin and
    family. Funeral Saturday at 10 A.M. by Rev Haskill at the home of it's
    uncle. Buried in Keith cemetery near Marcelline.

Mayfield, Edna   "Loraine"   Jul 10, 1902
    Drowned at the home of Irvin Mayfield on the eve of the 4th Edna, the
    little daughter of Mr Mayfield of Marcelline. Services Saturday A.M. and
    was buried near Marcelline.

Mayfield, James W.   "Obituary"   Dec 15, 1886
    Died- James W. Mayfield at his residence in Ursa at 6:30 A.M. December
    10, 1886. Was born near the place of his death June 21, 1840. In the
    fall of 62 he enlisted in Co. B. 78 th Ill. Vol. Inf. Married Miss Era
    Melteberger November 18, 1873. Leaves a wife, 2 girls and 2 boys.

Mayfield, James W.   "Probate Notice"   Jan 12, 1887
    3rd Monday of March 1887   Eva S. Mayfield, Adm.

Mayfield, Mary   "Ursa"   Mar 28, 1901
    Died- Aunt Mary Mayfield Monday eve at 8. Funeral Wednesday.

Mayo, Mrs Nettie   Dec 29, 1881
    Died- last week, Mrs Nettie Mayo age 32 yrs, second daughter of Mr and
    Mar Amos Scranton. Married 8 yrs ago and moved to Bellevue, Michigan.
    Leaves husband and 2 children. a 6 yr old and an infant. Died in Bellevue.

Mayor, Mr Jas.   "Local"   Aug 8, 1889
    Died- Mr Jas. Mayor of Carthage.

Mealiff, Mrs Anna   "Will"   Jul 27, 1904
    see Butler, Mrs Hannah

Mealiff, Mrs Anna E.   "Obituary's"   Dec 29, 1898
   see Hewitt, Thomas   Feb 16, 1899

Mealiff, Mrs Anna   "Will"   Jul 27, 1904
   see Butler, Mrs Hannah

Mealiff, Bessie   "Local"   Feb 3, 1886
Bessie, 10 yr old daughter of Mr and Mrs James Mealiff, of Honey Creek died on Saturday A.M. and was buried in Mendon cemetery on Sunday P.M. Services by Rev Mr Holst in the Zion church.

Mealiff, James   "Death"   Apr 12, 1905
   see Dickerman, Sarah J.

Mealiff, Mrs Jane   "Local"   Oct 27, 1886
Died- at her home in Honey Creek twp Saturday afternoon October 23rd Mrs Jane Mealiff, wife of James Mealiff and daughter of Mrs Elizabeth and the late Wm Hewitt. Age 37 yrs 3 mo's 13 days. Born in county Cavan, Ireland on August 10, 1849. Came to America with her parents in 1850. Leaves husband and 4 children (3 boys and 1 girl) Services in Zion church by Rev Colton of Carthage on Monday afternoon. Buried in Mendon cemetery.

Mealiff, Sarah J.   "death"   Apr 12, 1905
   see Dickerman, Sarah J.

Mealiff, Sarah Letitia   "News"   Sep 3, 1885
Sarah Letitia, infant daughter of Mr and Mrs Wm Mealiff, one of the twins died August 30th. Buried Mendon cemetery. Services by Rev Holst.

Mealiff, Mrs Wm   "Obituary's"   Dec 29, 1898
   see Hewitt, Thomas   Feb 16, 1899

Mecum, James A.   Feb 16, 1882
Died Friday evening February 3rd James A. Mecum, 21 yrs old.

Mecum, Nettie May   "Local"   Sep 15, 1886
Died- at the residence of her uncle's, A.B. Lynch of near Ellingwood, Kansas, Nettie May, only daughter of Mrs Margaret Mecum on September 3rd of consumption. Age 16 yrs 3 mo's 16 days. Leaves only her mother.

Meek, Mrs   "Local"   Jun 16, 1892
Died- Mr Louis C. Meek's mother, Mrs Meek at Hillsborough Saturday at 10:30 A.M. Was 67 yrs old. died from dropsy of the heart.

Meek, Edna   "Local"   Sep 1, 1892
Died- Saturday August 27th of dysentry, Edna, youngest child of Mr and Mrs L.C. Meek at age 2 yrs 10 mo's 19 days. Services at the house by Rev M.L. Schmucker of the Lutheran church. Remains taken to Waresgrove, near Hillsborough for burial.

Meek, Mr and Mrs L.C.   "Local"   Feb 9, 1893
The infant child of Mr and Mrs L.C. Meek died last week and taken to Hillsboro for burial.

Meek, Miss Sarah   "Obituary"   Nov 21, 1901
   see Fletcher, Mr E.S.

256

Meise, Mrs Fred   "Obituary"   Feb 3, 1904
     see Slack, Benjamin Franklin

Meise, Mrs Fred G.   "Obituary"   Nov 19, 1903
     see Wall, Mrs Joseph W.

Meltabarger, Jane Alice   "Obituary"   Sep 3, 1903
     see Harness, Mrs Jane Alice Meltabarger

Melteberger, Miss Era   Dec 15, 1886
     see Mayfield, James W.

Menn, Charles   "Quincy"   Mar 16, 1899
     Died- Charles Menn on Friday of Asthma. Was 69 yrs old. Lived Quincy
     47 yrs. Leaves a wife and 2 sons and a daughter.

Merril, Mrs Nathaniel   "Payson"   Jan 1, 1880
     Died- Mrs Merril, widow of Nathaniel Merril died Friday night. Services
     by Rev Huntley at the Baptist church at 2 P.M. Saturday.. Was 65 yrs old.

Metcalf, Mrs Sarah   "Local"   Jan 22, 1903
     Died- Mrs Sarah Metcalf on December 24th at her home in Salimas, Calif.
     She was the wife of Arch Metcalf formerly of Ursa and almost 80 yrs old.
     Leaves husband and 4 children, 2 sons and 2 daughters all living in
     California. She was aunt of Mrs H.M. Frisbie of Mendon and a sister of
     Miss Martha Forsythe of Ursa. 2 other sisters survive her, 1 in Missouri
     and 1 in California.

Metcalf, Mrs Susan Riddle   "Quincy"   Mar 23, 1899
     Died- Mrs Susan Riddle Metcalf an old pioneer of Quincy Wednesday A.M.
     March 15th at the home of her daughter, Mrs S.F. McKeeby where she lived
     the last few yrs. Was 88 yrs old Born Falmouth Kentucky January 27, 1811
     Married Mr Western Metcalf August 1830 and a few yrs later came to Illinois
     by boat down the Ohio river from Cincinnati (took 3 weeks) Settled on a
     farm near Mendon where Mr Metcalf died 1863. She leaves 1 son and 1
     daughter. Son James Metcalf who is in livestock commission business in
     St Louis.

Metz, Mr Joe   "Coatsburg"   Sep 21, 1887
     Mr Joe Metz's 8 yr old son was kicked by a horse and died almost instantly.
     Mrs M. was a Miss Felsman of this place.

Metzger, Geo. J.   "Obituary"   Jun 14, 1888
     Mr Geo. J. Metzger of Quincy died at his home in Quincy Saturday A.M.
     in his 43rd yr of consumption. He was married twice. By his first wife he
     leaves 1 son and by the 2nd, who survives him 2 children. Funeral on
     Tuesday A.M. at the St Boniface church.

Mewmaws, Mr   "Payson"   Apr 15, 1880
     A child of Mr Mewmaws was buried Friday south of here.

Mewmaw, Grandma   "Payson"   Feb 2, 1888
     Buried- Grandma Mewmaw was buried yesterday. She was an old settler in this
     country and was nearly 76 yrs old. Services by Rev Edwards at the
     Christian church.

Mewmaw, Charles   "Payson"   May 4, 1882
    Chalres Mewmaw, son of John Mewmaw was buried April 30th.

Mewmaw, Mr John   "Payson"   Jan 29, 1880
    A child of Mr John Mewmaw died January 22nd and buried January 23rd.

Mewmaw, John   "Payson"   May 5, 1881
    John Mewmaw was buried in Payson April 28th.

Meyer, Miss Carrie   "Local"   Feb 26, 1903
    Miss Carrie Meyer, daughter of Mr and Mrs August F. Meyer of Quincy died
Tuesday night at St Mary's hospital from injuries rec'd in jumping from
an outgoing train. Her sister Emma and cousin Miss Lena Vaughn also
jumped from same car, but was not hurt. They were at the depot seeing a
friend off and were not aware the train had started until the porter told
them. They rushed to the platform and jumped with the above results.

Meyer, F.W.   "Death"   Aug 17, 1899
    Died- F.W. Meyer, of Quincy died Saturday night. Was in the wholesale
grocery business for yrs. Leaves a widow and 3 daughters.

Meyers, F.C.   "Coatsburg"   Dec 12, 1889
    Died- At his home east of Coatsburg November 30th F.C. Meyers of lung
fever. Buried in village cemetery from the Lutheran church. Leaves a wife
and 5 small children.

Michael, James   "Loraine"   Apr 5, 1900
    Died- James Michael died suddenly at the home of his daughter, Mrs J.P.
Holden Sunday A.M. Services at the Christian church on Wednesday.
Buried in Loraine cemetery beside his wife who died a yr ago last August.

Michael, Mrs Nancy   "Loraine"   Aug 18, 1898
    Died- Mrs Nancy Michael, wife of James Michael of this place. She was
the daughter of Thos. Stillwell who was one of the pioneers of Adams Co.
Leaves a husband, 2 sons and 5 daughters.

Michaels, Mrs Jas.   "Local"   Aug 11, 1898
    Died- Mrs Jas. Michaels of Loraine, mother in law of Hon. C.F. Kincheloe
died Sunday at 2 A.M. and was buried next day in the Loraine cemetery.

Michels, Miss Ada   "Fowler"   Nov 5, 1903
    Miss Ada Michels passed away at the home of her sister, Mrs Haxel Friday
A.M. from typhoid fever and spinal meninitis. Buried in Quincy.

Mileham, Dr   "Local"   Nov 10, 1892
    Died- Dr Mileham died at 2 last Thursday of heart disease at his home in
Camp Point. Was about 55 yrs old.

Miller, Miss   "Payson"   Oct 5, 1887
    A funeral procession passed thru here yesterday from Hannibal with the
body of Miss Miller, going to the grave yard east of here.

Miller, Mrs   "Obituary"   Dec 1, 1898
   see Baldwin, Harry D.

Miller, Mrs   "Tioga"   Mar 21, 1889
   Died- at her home 1½ miles south of Tioga, Friday A.M. March 15th, Mrs
Miller in her 65th yr. Buried in German cemetery on Saturday P.M. Leaves 6
children, 3 sons and 3 daughters.

Miller, Mrs   "Local"   Nov 1, 1888
   Died- Mrs Miller, an elderly widow lady of Marcelline died Tuesday morning
while washing the breakfast things. She told her daughter of a strange pain
in her head before her death. Buried next day.

Miller, Mrs   "Marcelline"   Nov 8, 1888
   Mrs Miller died last Thursday morning.

Miller, Mrs   "Ursa"   Nov 11, 1897
   Died- Mrs Miller of Marcelline died very suddenly yesterday of heart
trouble at her home.

Miller, Mrs A.B.   "Death"   Jul 6, 1899
   see Watson, Geo. W.

Miller, Mrs Alf.   "Ursa"   May 24, 1900
   The funeral of Mrs Alf Miller was preached at Marcelline Sunday.

Miller, Anna   "News"   Sep 9, 1880
   Anna Miller, 14 yrs old who lived at 11th and Maine St Quincy was burned to
death Sunday when her clothes caught fire while she was cooking.

Miller, Mr August   "Tioga"   Aug 16, 1894
   Died- Mr August Miller, Friday August 10th. Was 69 yrs old. Leaves 5
children. Services by Rev Pessel, of Sutter. Buried in the Tioga Lutheran
cemetery Sunday afternoon.

Miller, Mrs C.W.S.   "Death"   Feb 15, 1900
   see Laughlin, Boswell P.

Miller, Mrs Catherine   Feb 1, 1883
   Mrs Catherine Miller died January 20th at the age of 73 yrs. She was
born Westmoreland Co. Penn. Lived Adams Co. 25 yrs. Member of the M.E.
church. Services by Rev McKown and buried Fowler. Leaves husband 81 yrs
old and 8 children.

Miller, Chester   Aug 7, 1890
   July 30th, Chester Miller, son of Uriah K. and Ella Miller died at the
age of 3 yrs. Buried Keath cemetery. Uncle Johnny Ruddell officiated.

Miller, D.B. "Tuck"   "Marcelline"   Nov 14, 1901
   The home of "Tuck" D.B. Miller burned and 2 children didn't make it out.
one boy named Dewitt age 8 and Pearl age 12 yrs. Leaves parents, 6 brothers
and 2 sisters. Article dated Nov 12, 1901

Miller, Mrs E.R.   "Death"   Mar 8, 1905
   see Odear, Joshua

Miller, Mrs Eliza   "Death"   Jun 23, 1898
  see Burns, James

Miller, Mrs Elizabeth   "Quincy"   Mar 16, 1899
  Died- Mrs Elizabeth Miller, age 86 yrs died suddenly Thursday A.M.
March 9th. Had lived Quincy 53 yrs. Survived by 1 son and 2 daughters.

Miller, Emma J.   "Obituary"   May 5, 1898
  see Wright, Albert

Miller, Frank   "Loraine"   Feb 28, 1901
  Frank Miller, formerly of this place died at his home in Quincy Saturday
and brought here by train and buried in the Loraine cemetery.

Miller, Frank   "Local"   Feb 28, 1901
  Frank Miller, eldest son of Mr and Mrs Aaron Miller of Quincy was buried
in Loraine cemetery today.

Miller, Gabe   "Local"   Feb 23, 1888
  News reached here of the death of Mr Gabe Miller of Marcelline.

Miller, Garrett   "Loacl"   May 7, 1885
  Garrett Miller, son of John W. Miller formerly of this vicinity now
living at Graham, Mo. was struck by lightning and killed instantly
April 20th.

Miller, Mrs Rev. Howard "Local"   May 26, 1892
  Died- Mrs Ellen H. Miller, wife of Rev. Howard Miller, a former resident
of this place and pastor of our M.E. church died of ulceration of the
stomach at Griggsville, Pike Co. Ill. on May 21st.

Miller, Henry   "Local"   May 17, 1905
  Henry Miller of north of Tioga who lost a little boy a few days ago with
diptheria, lost another son 9 yrs old Saturday night with same disease.
The 3 daughters are affected with same now. "Journal"

Miller, Henry   "Local"   Sep 15, 1886
  Died- Henry Miller, a youth of 15 yrs was fatally hurt on the premises
of Robert McMahan, a wealthy farmer of Wythe twp, about 5 miles east of
Warsaw.

Miller, John   "Death"   Dec 13, 1888
  see Johnson, Mrs Celia

Miller, John   "Local"   Oct 24, 1895
  Died- Mr John Miller Sunday eve at the home of his daughter, Mrs Dr Young
in his 87th yr from pure exhaustion of natural powers. Services at the
home Tuesday at 1 P.M. Buried in Woodville.

Miller, Mrs Louisa   "Obituary"   Mar 24, 1883
  see McGibbons, John

Miller, Mrs Lucy   "Quincy"   Mar 23, 1899
     Died- Mrs Lucy Miller Friday afternoon after an illness of 5 yrs.

Miller, Mrs Lydia   "Payson"   Apr 28, 1881
     Mrs Lydia Miller died April 24th 1881

Miller, Maggie   "Deadly Revolver"   Feb 2, 1888
     Died- Little daughter of Rev and Mrs Howard Miller at Delavan, Tazewell Co.
Illinois died January 21st, Maggie and her small brother went to the
neighbors and they played with an old revolver and Maggie was shot.
Buried at Griggsville on Tuesday. Services by Rev G.B. Wolfe at the grave.

Miller, Mrs Maria   "Local"   Sep 27, 1900
     News reached here of the death last Thursday of Mrs Maria Miller in
France. She was the owner of the Tremont House in Quincy. Mrs Miller went
on a visit to France last April. Was 64 yrs old.

Miller, Mrs Mary Jane   "Sudden Death"   Nov 11, 1897
     Died- Mrs Mary Jane Miller, widow of the late Eliazer Miller. Was sick
about 30 <u>minutes</u> Services at her home at 11 A.M. Buried in Keath
cemetery. Leaves 2 children, Mrs Minnie Potter of Marcelline and Shepherd
Miller of Ursa, 2 sisters, 2 brothers. Her maiden name was Cox. Born in
Ursa twp November 23, 1842

Miller, McCormick   "Death"   Dec 13, 1888
     see Johnson, Mrs Celia

Miller, Nathan   "Camp Point"   Nov 5, 1877
     Nathan Miller was found hanging from a tree last Friday morning. Was
over 60 yrs old.

Miller, Nettie   "Local"   Sep 21, 1887
     Died- Monday September 19th of typhoid pneumonia at age 10 yrs 7 mo's
Nettie, daughter of Mr and Mrs C.W.S. Miller. Services at the house by
Rev E.W. Souders.

Miller, Mr and Mrs Robert   "Local"   Aug 15, 1895
     Died- the infant child of Mr and Mrs Robert Miller, living on L.D.
Nichols place died last week and was buried at Ursa Thursday.

Miller, Col. Rufus   Jul 14, 1881
     Died- Col. Rufus Miller, lawyer of Quincy died on July 10th.

Miller, Mrs Sallie   "Marcelline"   Oct 10, 1901
     Mrs Sallie Miller who recently died in Quincy was brought up Thursday eve
and buried here Friday at the Keith cemetery.

Miller, Mr T.M.   "Local"   Jul 21, 1898
     Died- Mr T.M. Miller of Loraine died last Saturday after a long illness
of lung trouble.

Miller, W.E.   "Death"   Nov 8, 1888
     see McNay, Mr and Mrs Charles

261

Miller, Wm   "Death"   Apr 24, 1884
    see Levi, Henry

Miller, Mr and Mrs Wm   "Died"   Feb 8, 1883
    Mr Wm Miller died February 1st at the age of 81 yrs. His wife died just
    a few days before this. He was a native of Westmoreland Co. Penn.

Miller, William   "Death"   May 26, 1881
    see Lichteberger, Alexander

Mills, Charles   "Local"   Sep 10, 1885
    Charles Mills died Saturday night September 5th and was buried in Mendon
    cemetery the next day. Leaves a wife and 2 children.

Mills, Mrs George   "Death"   Nov 28, 1889
    see Wood, John

Mills, Mrs Herbert   "Death"   Jan 17, 1901
    see Green, Mrs Susan F.

Miner, Mrs S.J.   "Death"   Oct 29, 1891
    see Ross, Mrs Caroline

Minton, Mrs Nancy   "Loraine"   Jun 29, 1899
    Died- Mrs Nancy Minton at her home Monday A.M. Services at the Christian
    church Tuesday at 11 A.M. by Rev Hall of Canton. Buried at Ebenezer.
    Leaves 2 sons and 1 daughter.

Mirgel, Mr C.   "Tioga"   Jun 14, 1900
    Died- Thursday morning June 7th, Mr C. Mirgel at the age of 71 yrs.
    Funeral from the residence Saturday P.M. at 2 by Rev Gotto of Sutter.
    Buried in German cemetery.

Mitchel, Mrs   "Payson"   Mar 16, 1882
    Mrs Mitchel, mother of Wm Mitchel died March 13th. Mr Mitchel has
    lost 2 children and his mother in a yr.

Mitchell, Dr   "Ursa"   Sept 8, 1898
    Died- youngest son of Dr Mitchell died September 1st at the age of 10 mo's

Mitchell, Christopher   "Local"   Nov 1, 1888
    Died- Mr Christopher Mitchell, a well known and wealthy farmer of Columbus
    twp died of heart disease on Monday A.M. while attneding to his horses
    in the barn.

Mitchell, David   "Obituary"   Mar 1, 1901
    Died- at the home of his son James, in Lima twp, David Mitchell, an old
    citizen of Adams Co. Born in County Tyrone, Ireland February 26, 1826
    Came to Marietta, Ohio 1842 at the age of 24 yrs he married Rebecca
    Wakefield of Bridgeport, Ohio, she died 1871, they had 4 children, 3
    survive him., Mrs Seth M. Baker of Hickory Ridge, John and James of Lima
    twp. He came to Lima twp in 1865. Was a member of the Methodist church in
    Illinois. The Presbyterian in Ohio. Services by Rev Whistnant of Tioga.
    Buried in Hunter cemetery.

Mitchell, David   "Probate Notice"   Apr 11, 1901
    1st Monday of June 1901   John D. Mitchell, Ex.   Bennett and James
    Attorneys.

Mitchell, Mrs Estella   "Obituary"   Sep 14, 1899
    Died- Mrs Estella Mitchell, (nee White) Born Monmouth, Warren Co. Ill.
    July 30, 1861 and died Mendon September 13th at age 38 yrs 1 mo 13 days.
    Married William Mitchell February 24, 1881. Had 9 children- Earl, Nellie,
    Cora, Boyd, Ross, Zue, Eugene, Willie and the baby boy born Friday Sept 8th
    7 children living- Eugene and Ross deceased. Her mother died several yrs ago.
    Her father is living in Missouri. Has 3 sisters and 1 brother living,
    Nellie White living at Circleville, Ohio, Delia Echert at St Louis, Ella
    Jenkins in Quincy and Homer White in Montana. Was a member of the Methodist
    church, Ursa and then Mendon. Services at the Methodist church by Rev
    E.K. Crews. Buried Fowler.

Mitchell, Julia   "Payson"   Dec 30, 1880
    Died- December 25th, Miss Julia Mitchell, 2nd daughter of Wm Mitchell at
    the age of 15 yrs.

Mitchell, Ross   Apr 4, 1895
    Died- Ross, the little 5 yr old son of Mr and Mrs Wm Mitchell on Sunday
    of membraneous croup. Buried family lot at Fowler Monday P.M. This is the
    2nd child they have lost in 10 days. Rev Wm Burgess and R.A. Hartrick
    collected enough money from benevolent people to defray expenses of the
    funeral and leave some cash in hand for their immediate necessities.

Mitchell, Mrs Wm   "Fowler & Oakland"   Sep 21, 1899
    The remains of Mrs Wm Mitchell of Mendon was brought here and buried in
    Stahl cemetery.

Mitchell, Dr and Mrs   "Ursa"   Sep 3, 1891
    August 21st the infant daughter of Dr and Mrs Mitchell died. Was 7 months
    old.

Mitchell, Wm   "Payson"   Mar 16, 1882
    Mrs Mitchell, the mother of Wm Mitchell died March 13th. Mr Mitchell
    has lost 2 children and his mother in a yr.

Mitchell, Wm   "Payson"   Feb 9, 1882
    Died, a child of Wm Mitchell.

Mitchell, Wm and Catherine   Mar 20, 1884
    Infant son of Wm and Catherine Mitchell was found dead Monday morning,
    March 17th.

Mitchell, Mr and Mrs Wm   "Local"   Mar 21, 1895
    Died-the infant son of Mr and Mrs Wm Mitchell this A.M. Funeral tomorrow
    at Fowler.

Mock, Wilson   Aug 14, 1884
    "Exchange from the Camp Point Journal" Wilson Mock, 14 yr old son of
    Joseph Mock living 4 miles northwest of here was accidently hung while
    playing in the barn Monday night.

Moecker, Herman   "Local"   Mar 23, 1893
    Died- Mr Herman Moecker, the prop of the Pacific House, Quincy died at his
    home on North 5th St. Saturday A.M. and at 5 P.M. the same day his eldest
    daughter, Miss Amelia died at the Pacific House of consumption. She was
    32 yrs old.

Moellering, Mrs   "Paloma"   Jul 13, 1899
    Died- Mrs Moellering living ½ mile south of Paloma last Wednesday A.M.
    Services at the Lutheran church at Fowler. Buried in Chase graveyard ½
    mile south of Fowler.

Moffit, Pete   "Payson"   Sep 25, 1879
    Pete Moffit a young man raised by Mr Joe Severe, formerly of Payson
    killed a man named Greenwood at Hannibal last week. He is in Jail.

Mollenhauer, Mrs John   "Death"   Mar 9, 1899
    Died- Mrs John Mollenhauer at her home in Burton Tuesday night of spinal
    meningitis. Born Adams Co February 27, 1868. Leaves husband, 1 son and
    1 daughter.

Mollering, Mr Ernest   "Ursa"   Apr 20, 1899
    Funeral services for Mr Ernest Mollering were held at his late home last
    Friday. Buried Quincy.

Monnet, Dr C.S.   "Death"   Jan 4, 1900
    see Roth, Mrs John W.

Montgomery, Mrs Estella "Payson"   Feb 16, 1887
    Mrs Estella Montgomery, daughter of R.F. Edmonds died last Thursday.
    Funeral at the M.E. church by Rev McFadden.

Montgomery, Margaret   "Obituary"   Apr 13, 1899
    see Tittle, Mr A.J.

Montgomery, Marshall   "Payson"   Dec 29, 1886
    An infant son of Marshall Montgomery was buried last week.

Montgomery, Marshal   "Payson"   Jun 2, 1886
    A child of Marshal Montgomery's about 6 mo's old was buried here last week.

Montgomery, Mrs Mary   "Quincy"   Mar 23, 1899
    Died- Mrs Mary Montgomery, a old resident of Quincy died at St Mary's
    hospital Monday. Age 89 yrs.

Moon, Mrs Edna   "Obituary"   Jul 18, 1901
    see Kennedy, Geo. Thomas

Moon, Eugene W.   Aug 28, 1884
    "Clips from the Carthage Gazette" Triplets, all boys born to Mr and Mrs
    Eugene W. Moon. Lost one shortly after birth.

264

Moore, Col.   "Indian Grave"   Jun 13, 1895
    Died- Col. Moore of Canton, Mo. was found hanging from a tree near the
    locks about 3 miles north of here Tuesday night where he committed suicide
    about 2 weeks ago.

Moore, Annice S.   May 18, 1904
    "Partition # 1689   May term of circuit court"
    Annice S. Moore vs,
    James W. Johnson, Pauline Ann Wright, Elizabeth Hedges, Margaret Frances
    Johnson, W. Emery Lancaster as Conservator of Margaret Frances Johnson,
    C.B. Garrett as Adm. with the will ennexed of the estate of Jeannette
    Fowler, deceased, Mary J. Bray Frances A. Garrett, Estella I. Dickerman,
    Charles W. Johnson, Georgia Johnson, Nettie Johnson, Mrs Ben Garner, Mrs
    Charles Lawber, Mrs B.F. Green, Fred McReynolds and Sarah J. Johnson.
    James W. Johnson lives out of state of Illinois.
    Hiram R. Wheat, clerk
    David P. Strickler, Solicitor for complainant.

Moore, Artha   "Loraine"   Mar 25, 1880
    Died- Artha Moore yesterday of consumption in the prime of life. This
    makes the 4th of the children leaving the mother to mourn.

Moore, Arthur   "Local"   Feb 28, 1884
    Arthur Moore, little son of Dr Moore of Quincy died. Dr Moore also has
    a son Freddie.

Moore, Miss Evaline   "Obituary"   Apr 24, 1902
    see Fletcher, Chas, Wolvertine

Moore, Dr Fred P.   "Loacl"   Jan 24, 1889
    "Quincy Paper" Dr Fred P. Moore, the well known dentist died in his 36th
    yr. Funeral at the Unitarian church yesterday P.M. after which ElAksa
    commandery #55 K.T. took charge of the remainder. Dr Moore was the 1st
    member of the commendery that has died since its organization in 1882

Moore, Miss Minnie   "Payson"   Oct 19, 1887
    Miss Minnie Moore died last night at 8 P.M.

Moore, Sam   "Local"   May 24, 1888
    Sunday afternoon Sam Moore and Geo. Hardy went out into the flood waters
    and their boat overturned. Sam Moore drowned. Body was recovered Monday
    night.

Moore, Sam   "Ursa"   May 24, 1888
    Sunday eve at the head of Indian Grave lake Sam Moore drowned. He was out
    in a boat with his little son and daughter and his brother in law, Geo.
    Hardy when the boat overturned. (only Sam drowned) Leaves a wife and 4
    children.

Morehead, Mr   "Death"   Apr 15, 1883
    see George, Henry

Morehead, Miss Belle   "Death"   Sept 26, 1895
    see Smith, Mrs Rodney

Morehead, Mrs Cordelia   Oct 15, 1891
    Mrs Cordelia Morehead, widow of the late Daniel Morehead died at her home
    in Quincy October 9th. She was 77 yrs old. Had 6 children, Thomas M.,
    Ella, Mrs C.T. Reynolds of Quincy, Mrs D.B. Cooke of Mendon, Mrs Rodney
    Smith of St Joseph, Mo. and Breckenridge Morehead of St Louis. Burial in
    Woodlawn cemetery. She was a Baptist.

Morehead, Mr Daniel   "Local"   May 18, 1887
    Died- Mr Daniel Morehead, one of the oldest inhabitants of Quincy died at
    his home on Vermont St Quincy last week. Buried Sunday. Leaves a widow,
    and 7 children, T.M. Morehead, Mrs D.B. Cooke of Mendon, Napoleon Morehead
    of California, Mrs Rodney Smith of Atchison, Kansas, Mrs C.T. Reynolds and
    Miss Ella Morehead of Quincy. 3 children, J.W. Morehead, Charles Morehead
    and Mrs Anna Bebee are dead. Funeral was delayed for N. Morehead to return
    from California.

Morehead, Napoleen   "Local"   Apr 24, 1890
    Funeral of Napoleen Morehead took place at Wichita, Kansas April 17th.

Morehead, Parthenia   "Obituary"   May 17, 1900
    see Cooke, Dudley Benton

Morehead, Thomas M.   "Local"   Mar 9, 1904
    Justice of the peace Thomas M. Morehead of Quincy suffered a stroke of
    paralysis Tuesday P.M. and died of apoplexy Wednesday night. He was a
    brother of Mrs D.B. Cooke.

Morehouse, Mrs Louisa   "Local"   Jun 15, 1887
    Mrs Louisa Morehouse, wife of E.B. Morehouse died in Brooklyn, N.Y. last
    Wednesday. Body was brought to Quincy by her husband, son and her cousin
    Miss Kate Prest. Services by Rev Dana of the Cong'l church. Burial in
    Woodland cemetery. (Mr Morehouse reacher his wife before her death and
    was at her side.)

Morely, Miss Molita   "Lima"   Mar 1, 1883
    Miss Molita Morely died February 16th at her home near Lima. 16 yrs old.
    Services by Rev Madison.

Morey, Mrs S.J.   "Clayton"   Nov 29, 1883
    Mrs S.J. Morey, one of the earliest settlers died November 24th. Her
    husband died several yrs ago.

Morgan, Mrs George   "Payson"   Jul 21, 1881
    Died- Mrs George Morgan of Richfield on July 16th.

Morgan, Mrs J.H.   "Local"   Nov 9, 1904
    Principal Chas. M. Gash was called home Monday eve to attend the funeral of
    the wife of Rev. J.H. Morgan, held at Industry.

Morgan, Joseph L.   "Local"   Dec 14, 1904
    Died- Major Joseph L. Morgan, formerly of the firm of Clark and Morgan,
    Quincy was found dead in bed by his wife Thursday A.M. last. Born March
    8, 1843 at Alton, Ill. Leaves his wife and daughter, Mrs Jessie Goetz.

Morley, Wm   "Camp Point"   Oct 26, 1882
    Died- a little son of Wm Morley October 21st from cerobro spinal
    meningitis.

Morris, Mrs Charles   "Local"   Dec 26, 1901
    Died- Mrs Charles Morris, nee Alice Gunn at her home 4 miles southwest
of Mendon on Saturday eve December 21st of consumption. Buried Tuesday A.M.
in Bloomfield cemetery. Leaves husband and 2 children. (1 boy 1 girl)

Morris, Hon. I.N.   "News"   Oct 30, 1879
    Hon. I.N. Morris died at his residence on E. Broadway in Quincy yesterday
    at 2 P.M. 67 yrs old. Funeral at 2:30 tomorrow.

Morris, Israel Floyd   "Obituary"   Mar 6, 1879
Died on Monday March 3rd, little Israel Floyd, age 3 yrs 6 mo's. Was son
    of John T. and Jane M. Morris. Left his sorrowing friends and relatives
here to join his papa in a better land.

Morris, Mrs W.G.   "Obituary"   Jan 29, 1899
    see Mary Edmonds

Morris, Mrs W.G.   "Death"   Feb 9, 1899
    see Mrs Mary Daugherty

Morrison, Miss Belle   "Death"   Dec 7, 1893
    see Thomas Rippetoe

Morrison, Walter   "Fatal Accident"   Nov 8, 1894
    A fatal accident befell Walter, 6 yr old son of Mr and Mrs Frank
Morrison living 1½ miles northwest of town Saturday P.M. Services at
the M.E. church Sunday. Buried in Mendon cemetery.

Morton, Mrs   "Death"   Jan 24, 1895
    see Mrs Ruth King

Morton, Mrs   "Burton"   Apr 29, 1880
    Mrs Morton, a very old lady died at Newtown last Friday and was buried
Saturday.
                      "Payson"   Apr 29, 1880
    Mother Morton was buried at Newtown last Saturday. Cause of death was
cancer.

Morton, Mrs Almira   "Local"   Aug 31, 1904
    Mrs Almira Morton, widow of Col. Chas. H. Morton, died in Blessing
hospital Quincy Friday eve from progressive paralysis.

Morton, Charles   "Suicide"   May 27, 1880
    We learn from Thos. Morehead of Quincy that Charles Morton of Quincy
was found dead in his bed at 7 A.M. yesterday. A pistol was by his side.
Mrs M. did not hear the shot.

Morton, Albert   "Fowler and Oakland"   Jan 11, 1900
    Albert, little son of Horace Morton was buried at the Presby church.

Morton, Freddie   "Fatal Accident"   Jan 25, 1900
Died- Freddie, the little 5 yr old son and only child of Mr and Mrs Wm
Morton residing 1 mile north of Mendon Monday eve of last week. Services
at the house by Rev Bayne. Buried in Mendon Cemetery.

Muegge, Tillie   "Tioga"   Oct 5, 1893
Died- Tillie Muegge Monday morning at 5 of typhoid fever. Age 18 yrs.
Buried from the Brethern church Tuesday P.M.

Mueller, Mrs Wilhelmina   "Quincy"   Apr 20, 1899
Died- Mrs Wilhelmina Mueller Tuesday afternoon April 11th. Born Germany
1817 and camt to Quincy 1846. Leaves husband and 2 sons.

Mulch, Conrad   "Tioga"   Dec 14, 1899
Died- Conrad Mulch, son of Mr and Mrs Wm Mulch who lives near Lewistown,
Mo. Friday A.M. December 8th at the age of 6 yrs. Funeral Sunday after-
noon. Buried in the German cemetery at Tioga.

Mulherin, Charles   "Local"   Apr 27, 1887
Charles Mulherin, an old soldier, formerly of Cole Valley, Ill. died at
the home in Quincy from comsumption.

Mull, Mr   "Camp Point"   Sep 13, 1900
The funeral of Mrs J.J. Earle's father, Mr Mull is this afternoon
(Tuesday) at the home of Mr Earle. Mr Mull came here to visit his daughter
about a week ago and died very suddenly.

Mullen, Mrs A.M.   "Obituary"   Jan 29, 1899
see Edmonds, Mary

Mulligan, Mrs Jas.   "Ursa"   Dec 28, 1882
Mrs Jas. Mulligan an old resident of Ursa died December 19th.

Mulligan, James   "Local"   Oct 20, 1886
Died- Friday night, Mr James Mulligan of Rock Creek. Was a well known
farmer.

Mullins, Mrs Pierce   "Lima"   "Lima"
Mrs Pierce Mullins was called to Ursa Sat. by the death of her father,
Mr Burress.

Mulqueeney, Patrick   "Probate"   Nov 17, 1898
Probate notice- Patrick Mulqueeney, deceased 1st Mon. of Jan. 1899
Elisha B. Hamilton, Conservator and Ex. officio Adm. Hamilton and Woods
attorneys.

Mund, Mrs Lizzie   "Tioga"   June 20, 1901
Died- Mrs Lizzie Mund, wife of Henry Mund on Sat. June 8th. Funeral
Monday. Buried in German cemetery.

Mund, Mr and Mrs Gus   "Tioga"   Aug 4, 1898
Buried Saturday of last week, the 18 month old son of Mr and Mrs Gus
Mund in the German cemetery.

Munroe, Mrs W.T.   "Obituary"   Mar 21, 1889
    see Higbie, Mrs Edmond

Murphy, Mrs Albert   "Death"   May 18, 1904
    see Frye, Charles J.

Murphy, Mrs Iva   "Local"   Sep 20, 1894
    Mrs Iva Murphy (nee Tarr) of Tamaroa, Perry Co. losr her oldest child
    (obout 3 yrs old) last Friday A.M. of typhoid fever.

Murphy, John   "Death"   Sep 17, 1903
    Died- lineman John Murphy was killed by an electric shock while at work
    on an electric pole Friday P.M. at Hannibal. He was a brother of Albert
    Murphy, the barber of our town and brother in law of Mrs Claude Brown of
    Hannibal. Mother, Mrs Emeline Murphy, mother of John and Albert lives
    on North 4th St., a sister, Mrs Ida Coonlives at Peoria. Body will probably
    be taken to New Canton, his former home for burial today.

Murray, Con   "Marcelline"   Oct 24, 1895
    Died- October 21st at the home of Con Murray, of typhoid fever, a nephew
    of Mr M's. He was about 12 yrs old.

Murray, Capt Wm   "Local"   Jul 4, 1901
    Died- Capt Wm Murray, adjutant of Soldiers home in Quincy Sunday A.M.
    Age nearly 60 years.

Musgrave, Miss Elizabeth   "Obituary"   Jan 24, 1895
    see Walker, John C.

Myer, Mrs   "Obituary"   Jan 14, 1892
    see Roberts, Mrs Jas.

Myer, John   "Quincy"   Mar 23, 1899
    Died- John Myer Monday eve of consumption. Was 51 years old. Leaves a
    wife and 1 child.

Myers, Mrs Anna Tinsman   "Obituary"   Apr 20, 1899
    Died- Mrs Anna Tinsman Myers at 6 P.M. Wednesday April 12th at the old
    homestead near Elm Grove. Her youngest son L.C. has been living there
with her. Born Greensburg, Westmoreland Co. Penn May 31, 1811. Married Henry
    Myers Jan 3, 1828 and they came with their family to Illinois 1851 and
    settled Mendon twp where she died. Mr Myers died July 20, 1869. They had
    14 children (8 girls and 6 boys) all living except 2 sons and 1 daughter.
    Namely C.C. and Jesse and Mrs Polly Worman. Living are- Mrs Dr Gilliland
    of Coatsburg, Mrs Frank Ogle of Paloma, Mrs Nancy Worman, Mrs F.F. Dudley,
    Mrs James Evans of Mendon, Mrs Wm Osborn of Quincy and Mrs Simon Young of
    Oklahoma. Jacob and Lee of Columbus, John and L.C. of Mendon. All present
    for her funeral except Mrs Young. Leaves 60 grandchildren and 78 great
    grandchildren. Was member of the U.B. church 72 years. Buriea Myers
    cemetery Saturday A.M. Services by Elder A. Rigney of Prairie City, Ill.

Myers, C.C.   "Local"   Dec 11, 1902
    At the regular meeting of Mendon Camp #751, December 9th officers were
    elected. They have 110 members. It was organized Feb 6, 1889. 5 deaths
has occured since that time, C.C. Myers, John W. Schaffer, James Joshua Havens,
    James Coffield and Simon S. Felgar.

Myers, Mrs C.C.   "Obituary"   Nov 19, 1891
   see Dudley, Mrs E.B.

Myers, Mrs Dudley   "Obituary"   Sep 11, 1902
   see Fowler, Mrs Jeanette

Myers, Mr and Mrs Dudley   "Local"   Mar 15, 1905
Mr and Mrs Dudley Myers mourns the death of their infant daughter from
lagrippe. She was 3 weeks old. Sick only a few hours. Funeral last
Thursday at 2:30 P.M. by Rev J.F. Bacon.

Myers, Homer   "Obituary"   Oct 17, 1895
Died- Homer Myers October 10, 1895 at 9:30 P.M. Born October 28, 1875
was 18 days short of being 20 years old. Member of the Cong'l church 2
years. Also a member of Y.P.S.C.E. (sic) Services at the house by
Rev Burgess at 1 P.M.

Myers, Dr Irving   "Local"   Sep 12, 1901
Dr Irving Myers of Marshall, Wisc. and Walter Myers of Galesburg are
here to attend the funeral of their grandfather, Mr Jas. H. Dudley.

Myers, Jacob   "Death"   Oct 29, 1903
   see Osborn, William

Myers, John   "Death"   Oct 29, 1903
   see Osborn, William

Myers, Lee   "Death"   Oct 29, 1903
   see Osborn, William

Myers, Jesse J.   Sep 3, 1891
Jesse J. Myers born Westmoreland Co. Penn Nov 9, 1842 and died August
28, 1891. Moved with his parents Mr and Mrs Henry Myers to Illinois in
1851. Married Anna Potter Nov. 15, 1866. They had 8 children, 7 of
whom are still living. (4 girls and 3 girls) All but 2 yrs of his
married life was spent in the neighborhood of Fowler and Paloma. He
was one of a large family, there being 5 brothers and 7 sisters living
and having families. One sister, Mrs Young living in Kansas, another
sister, Mrs Evans living in Mendon. Mother still living at this date and
attended the funeral. Funeral from Paloma M.E. Church by Rev C.F. McKown.
After which he was laid to rest in the Myers cemetery in Mendon twp.

Myers, John   "Local"   Nov 2, 1887
John Myers, infant child, a little boy age 10 months 5 days died on
Sunday and was buried next day in the family burying ground.

Myers, Mrs Mary   "Obituary"   Sep 11, 1902
   see Daugherty, Mrs Jane

Myers, Mrs Mary A.   "Died"   Nov 23, 1904
Funeral of Mrs Mary A. Myers, wife of Frank A. Myers was at their home
4 miles south of Mendon, Monday at 2 P.M. by Rev A.M. Reitzel. Buried
Fowler cemetery. Mary A. Daugherty was born December 8, 1873 and died
November 19, 1904 at the age of 30 yrs 11 mo's 19 days. Married to Frank
A. Myers March 22, 1899. Leaves husband, 4 brothers, James, George,
Thomas and William Daugherty and 1 sister, Mrs Henry Shriver.

Myers, Mrs Sarah   "Obituary"   Sep 12, 1901
   see Dudley, James H.

Myers, Mrs Sarah   "Funeral"   Sep 12, 1901
   see Dudley, James

McAdams, Mrs Anna E.   "Local"   Jan 19, 1899
   Died- Mrs Anna E. McAdams, wife of senator John McAdams at her home
   229 North 8th St. Friday. Buried Rock church cemetery 2 miles north of
   Ursa Monday.

McAdams, Miss Catherine   "Obituary"   Dec 28, 1899
   see Thompson, Mrs Lewis

McAdams, Charles   "Ursa"   Jun 30, 1898
   Died- Charles McAdams at 12:45 P.M. Sunday. He was the eldest son of
   Mrs T.B. Anderson by a former marriage. Sick 7 weeks. "Whig"

McAdams, Mr and Mrs Charles   "Local"   Dec 9, 1885
   Little Bessie, infant daughter of Mr and Mrs Charles McAdams of Ursa
   died Thursday morning at 5.

McAdmas, Charley   "Ursa"   Jun 30, 1898
   Died- Charley McAdams Sunday. Was 21 yrs old. Funeral today at Christian
   church by Rev Roe of Shelbina, Mo. Buried in Denson cemetery. Leaves
   many relatives.

McAdams, Clifton   "Local"   Apr 14, 1892
   died- by his own hand, Clifton McAdams of Lima.

McAdams, Clifton   Apr 12, 1894
   State of Illinois county of Adams. In the co. court thereof to the May
   term 1894 in the matter of the application of James F. McAdams Adm. of
   the estate of Clifton McAdams, deceased. vs; Adm's petition to sell
   real estate to pay debts-- Nathan McAdams, Nettie V. Hansen, Lee H.
   Carlock, Wm W. Carlock, Archie B. Carlock, Wm P. McAdams, Joseph E.
   McAdams, Edward B. McAdams, Sarah L. Hunt defendents
   Annie F. Hoig, Julia F. Fisher, Nettie V. Hansen, Lee H. Carlock,
   Wm W. Carlock, Archie B. Carlock. Joseph E. McAdams and Charles L. McAdams
   all reside out of state.

McAdams, Geo.   "Obituary"   Dec 28, 1899
   see Thompson, Mrs Lewis

McAdams, Jas.   "Local"   Aug 28, 1890
   Jas. McAdams of Ursa died Friday on his porch while talking to his wife.
   He was about 68 yrs old. Leaves wife, but no children.

McAdams, John   "Obituary"   Dec 28, 1899
   see Thompson, Mrs Lewis

McAdams, John   "Probate"   Jan 15, 1880
   see Williams, Mary F.

McAdams, Mrs John   "Obituary"   Jan 15, 1880
   see Williams, Mrs Joel

271

McAdams, John W.   "News"   Sep 18, 1879
    John W. McAdams, a young man living near Lima died last Wednesday from
    hemorrhage of the lungs. Buried at Lima on Thursday. He was about 28 yrs
    old.

McAdams, Miss Lela   "Obituary"   Apr 13, 1899
    see Hill, Mrs Dewitt

McAdams, Mamie   "Loraine"   Dec 16, 1885
    Miss Mamie, only daughter of Mr and Mrs John McAdams of Quincy was buried
    in the family vault at the Stone Church yesterday.

McAdams, Mary Jane   "Obituary"   May 17, 1883
    see Rockwell, Mrs C.B.

McAdams, Mrs Mattie   "Obituary"   Jul 9, 1903
    see Anderson, Thos. B.

McAdams, Mr and Mrs Nathan   "Ursa"   Apr 14, 1892
    Youngest son of Mr and Mrs Nathan McAdams who committed suicide last
    Thursday was buried Saturday afternoon at the Stone church.

McAdams, Samuel   "Local"   May 17, 1900
    Died- Mrs Ellen C. Abrams of Hanford, Calif. writes that Mr Samuel
    McAdams died at Hanford, Kings Co. Calif. age 82 yrs. He was a resident
    of Lima twp nearly 60 yrs.

McAdams, Theo   "Local"   Jan 17, 1889
    Died- Mr Theo McAdams at Ursa on Monday night at 8 o'clock. Funeral
    yesterday morning at the Denson burying ground.

McAdams, Theodore   "Ursa"   Jan 24, 1889
    Died- Thoedore McAdams Monday January 14th at 8 P.M. from consumption.
    Joined the M.E. church at Lima at age 19 yrs. He was 33 yrs 3 mo's old
    when he died. Services by Rev Ades of the Christian church at 10 A.M.
    Wednesday. Buried in the Denson cemetery. Leaves a wife and 2 little
    girls. He had been sickly since childhood.

McAdams, Thomas   "Ursa"   May 26, 1881
    Mr Thomas McAdams died May 18th.

McAdams, Wm   "Obituary"   Dec 28, 1899
    see Thompson, Mrs Lewis

McAdams, Mr W.   "Local"   Jan 21, 1892
    Died- Mr W. McAdams an old resident of Ursa. Leaves a widow and family.

McAdams, William   "Ursa"   Jan 21, 1892
    Died- Mr William McAdams Sunday Jan 17th, Born in Logan Co. Ky.in 1816
    Moved to Ill. in 1835 and married Elizabeth Taylor 1838 who died. 2nd
he married Mrs Martha Archer 1880. He leaves a wife 2 sons, John of Quincy and
    George of Ursa, 2 daughters, Mrs Lewsi Thompson of Mt Hebron and Mrs
    John Bittleson of Mendon. He was a resident of Ursa twp. Services at the
    Christian church by Rev. Sam Jones, state evangelist of the Christian
    church. Buried in Denson cemetery.

McAdams, Mrs Wm   "Ursa"   Jan 8, 1880
Died at her residence near here Dec. 31st, Mrs Wm McAdams.

McAnulty, Mrs Margaret   "Ursa"   Apr 20, 1887
Mrs Margaret McAnulty of Camp Point, formerly an old resident of Honey
Creek died of typhoid fever and was buried in Byler cemetery Friday.

McArthur, Ray   "White Oak Ridge"   Dec 6, 1894
Died- Ray, 10 yr old son of Benjamin McArthur of pneumonia on November
25th. Buried in Loraine cemetery.

McArthur, Mrs W.   "Death"   Oct 8, 1903
see Hobby, William

McBride, Arthur Andrew   "Loraine"   Jan 8, 1903
Died- last Friday at 8 P.M., Arthur Andrew McBride. Born in Pike Co. Ill.
near Fall Creek, but lived most of his life in Liberty, Ill. Last March
they moved to Loraine. Arthur their oldest child died Jan 2nd 1903.
He was 16 yrs 10 mo's 26 days old. Leaves father, mother, 4 sisters and
1 brother. Services at Christian church by Rev Haskell Sunday at 11 A.M.
Buried in cemetery here. Died from typhoid fever.

McCabe, Mrs Kate Roth   Jan 25, 1883
Mrs Kate Roth McCabe died January 19th at the home of her mother, Mrs Roth
in her 36th yr. Services from Christian church.

McCarl, Mrs   "Death"   Dec 14, 1893
see Dick, Mrs

McCarl, Mr and Mrs   Jul 18, 1895
Mrs Ida Comer, of Kansas is here visiting her parents Mr and Mrs McCarl.
She came to attend the funeral of her nephew, Emmett.

McCarl, Carlton   "Fatal Shooting"   Dec 2, 1885
see Brown, Willie

McCarl, D.M.   "Obituary"   Aug 29, 1901
see Cromer, Ida J.

McCarl, David   "Death"   Apr 21, 1886
see Patterson, Mrs

McCarl, Emmet Beard   "Fatal Accident"   Jul 18, 1895
A sad accident, resulting in death 2 days later, Emmet Beard McCarl
eldest son of Mr and Mrs J.B. McCarl last Wednesday eve. He had been
hauling hay for his employer to Mr Waite's, who lives on the old Forsythe
place and was unharnessing the horses when he was kicked in the stomach
by a colt.He was eldest of 3 boys. Born May 10, 1882. Buried Sayurdat A.M.
in the Denson cemetery north of Ursa after services at the house by Rev.
R.A. Hartrick of the Methodist church. His brother Frankie died from
diptheria 5 yrs ago.

McCarl, Franklin   Dec 26, 1889
Franklin McCarl, son of John McCarl died December 25th.

McClean, Mrs   "West Point"   Oct 27, 1892
     Died- at the residence of her daughter October 12th of old age, Mrs
     McClean. She was over 90 yrs old. Lived with her daughter, Mrs Millard
     Spence for the past 40 yrs. Services by Rev Finley. Buried in the Graham
     graveyard.

McClellan, Mrs G.B.   "Obituary"
     see Kuhn, Isaac   Nov 23, 1887

McClelland, Dr Cochran   "Obituary"   Feb 26, 1903
     Dr Cochran McClelland, a leadong specialist in gynaecalogy died Monday
     A.M. Feb. 16th at his home in Philadelphia, Penn from double pneumonia.
     Born Ireland 1844 and came to U.S. 5 yrs later with his parents who stayed
     in Catasauqua, Penn and after 10 yrs in Penn the boy came to Ill. and then
     back to Philadelphia in 1871 graduated from Jefferson Medical College 1873.
     Married Mary Carlisle of Philadelphia in 1886. She is of a Virginian
     family and is a niece of Stonewall Jackson. Wife survives him. No children.
     His 3 brothers live in Illinois and Nebraska. "Philadelphia Evening
     Bulleton"

McClelland, Dr Cochran   "Funeral"   Feb 26, 1903
     Funeral of Dr Cochran McClelland was at the Cong'l church Friday. He was
     a successful physycian in Philadelphia. He was brought back and buried
     by the side of his mother, father, brother and sisters in the old church
     yard. Leaves a wife and 2 brothers, Dr Thomas McClelland, Pres. of Knox
     College and Robert of Omaha, Nebr.

McClelland, Dr Cochran   "Death"   Feb 19, 1903
     Miss Sarah Huston rec'd word of the death of her uncle, Dr Cochran
     McClelland at his home in Philadelphia, Penn. on Monday of pneumonia.
     He is brother of William, Robert and Thomas McClelland. Funeral in the
     Cong'l church Dec. 20th at 10 A.M. and buried in Mendon cemetery.

McClelland, Mrs Dora   "Ursa"   Mar 28, 1889
     A number of people from here attended the funeral of Mrs Dora McClelland
     which took place at the Keath cemetery yesterday. She formerly resided
     here.

McClelland, Mrs Dora   "Local"   Mar 28, 1889
     Died- Mrs Dora McClelland at her home in Loraine Saturday at 4 A.M. of
     neuralgis of the stomach. She was the daughter (2nd) of W.D. Lemmon, of
     this place and married about 1 yr ago to Mr J. T. McClelland. Was 18 yrs old.
     Services in the Methodist church by Rev. Thomas and buried in the Keith
     cemetery. Leaves a baby 4 weeks old, a father, brother and 3 sisters.

McClelland, Mr and Mrs George   "Local"   Sep 19, 1889
     Buried, the infant child of Mr and Mrs George McClelland. Will be buried
     today.

McClelland, Mr and Mrs J.T.   "Local"   Oct 26, 1893
     Born, to Mr and Mrs J. T. McClelland, a son on Saturday. It lived only
     a short time. Buried Sunday. Mr McClelland Sr. was present for the funeral.

McClean, Mrs   "West Point"   Oct 27, 1892
Died- at the residence of her daughter October 12th of old age, Mrs
McClean. She was over 90 yrs old. Lived with her daughter, Mrs Millard
Spence for the past 40 yrs. Services by Rev Finley. Buried in the Graham
graveyard.

McClellan, Mrs G.B.   "Obituary"
see Kuhn, Isaac   Nov 23, 1887

McClelland, Dr Cochran   "Obituary"   Feb 26, 1903
Dr Cochran McClelland, a leadong specialist in gynaecalogy died Monday
A.M. Feb. 16th at his home in Philadelphia, Penn from double pneumonia.
Born Ireland 1844 and came to U.S. 5 yrs later with his parents who stayed
in Catasauqua, Penn and after 10 yrs in Penn the boy came to Ill. and then
back to Philadelphia in 1871 graduated from Jefferson Medical College 1873.
Married Mary Carlisle of Philadelphia in 1886. She is of a Virginian
family and is a niece of Stonewall Jackson. Wife survives him. No children.
His 3 brothers live in Illinois and Nebraska. "Philadelphia Evening
Bulleton"

McClelland, Dr Cochran   "Funeral"   Feb 26, 1903
Funeral of Dr Cochran McClelland was at the Cong'l church Friday. He was
a successful physycian in Philadelphia. He was brought back and buried
by the side of his mother, father, brother and sisters in the old church
yard. Leaves a wife and 2 brothers, Dr Thomas McClelland, Pres. of Knox
College and Robert of Omaha, Nebr.

McClelland, Dr Cochran   "Death"   Feb 19, 1903
Miss Sarah Huston rec'd word of the death of her uncle, Dr Cochran
McClelland at his home in Philadelphia, Penn. on Monday of pneumonia.
He is brother of William, Robert and Thomas McClelland. Funeral in the
Cong'l church Dec. 20th at 10 A.M. and buried in Mendon cemetery.

McClelland, Mrs Dora   "Ursa"   Mar 28, 1889
A number of people from here attended the funeral of Mrs Dora McClelland
which took place at the Keath cemetery yesterday. She formerly resided
here.

McClelland, Mrs Dora   "Local"   Mar 28, 1889
Died- Mrs Dora McClelland at her home in Loraine Saturday at 4 A.M. of
neuralgis of the stomach. She was the daughter (2nd) of W.D. Lemmon, of
this place and married about 1 yr ago to Mr J. T. McClelland. Was 18 yrs old.
Services in the Methodist church by Rev. Thomas and buried in the Keith
cemetery. Leaves a baby 4 weeks old, a father, brother and 3 sisters.

McClelland, Mr and Mrs George   "Local"   Sep 19, 1889
Buried, the infant child of Mr and Mrs George McClelland. Will be buried
today.

McClelland, Mr and Mrs J.T.   "Local"   Oct 26, 1893
Born, to Mr and Mrs J. T. McClelland, a son on Saturday. It lived only
a short time. Buried Sunday. Mr McClelland Sr. was present for the funeral.

McClelland, Mrs Susie   "Local"   Mar 24, 1886
   Died- of heart disease at her home in Brunswick, Mo. Wednesday March 17th
   Susie, the beloved wife of Wm McClelland and the oldest daughter of Mr
   and Mrs Jacob Funk of this twp. Married December 25, 1880. Moved with her
   husband to Missouri. Buried here at the Wesley Chapel Friday.

McClelland, Thomas   "Probate"   Oct 15, 1885
   Probate Notice of Thomas McClelland, deceased- 3rd Monday of December 1885
   James A. McClelland, Ex.

McClelland, Mr Thomas   "News"   Aug 27, 1885
   Mr Thomas McClelland died August 26th in Ursa twp. Services by Rev Weir
   Burial in cemetery at Wesley Chapel..

McClelland, Mrs Thomas   "Local"   Mar 28, 1889
   Died- Mrs McClelland, widow of the late Thomas McClelland Saturday A.M.
   at her home in Ellington twp. Age 73 yrs. Services held at the family
   residence Monday A.M. and buried at Wesley Chapel cemetery. She had been
   a resident of Adams Co. 38 yrs. Leaves 2 sons, John in business in Quincy
   and Thomas on the farm, 1 daughter Miss Jennie McClelland, the artist.

McClelland, William   "Loraine"   Sep 14, 1899
   Died- William McClelland and daughter Margaret died last week. Margaret
   Wednesday night and the father on Saturday night.

McClelland, William   "Probate"   Oct 19, 1899
   Probate Notice- William McClelland, deceased   1st Monday of December 1899
   J.T. McClelland, Adm.

McClelland, Mrs Wm   "Fowler"   Nov 23, 1887
   News rec'd of the death of Mrs Wm McClelland of Bloomington, Nebr.
   She had lived here many yrs.

McClintock, Mary Ann   "Camp Point"   Mar 17, 1881
   Mary Ann McClintock, an old settler of Clayton twp died Sunday March 13th
   Buried Hebron cemtery.

McClintock, Shannon   "Camp Point"   Dec 14, 1882
   Shannon McClintock died December 9th. He leaves a wife and 3 children.

McClintock, Thomas   "Camp Point"   Mar 13, 1884
   Thomas McClintock died Friday morning March 7th at the age of 82 yrs.
   He was of Scotch Irish ancestry. Leaves a wife.

McClintock, W.R.   Death list"   Oct 10, 1901
   W. R. McClintock's name was in a list of veteran's deaths.

McCloud, Mrs   "Loraine"   Jul 17, 1879
   Mrs McCloud of Big Neck died last week and was a rather old lady. Buried
   Curless cemetery.

McClung, Cascandria   "Obituary"   Nov 30, 1899
 see Hardy, Joseph Patterson

McClung, Charity H.   "Death"   Mar 9, 1904
 see Blazer, Rachel Louise

McClung, Clara Belle   "Death"   Mar 9, 1904
 see Blazer, Rachel Louise

McClung, Mrs Elizabeth   "Local"   Jul 24, 1884
 Died July 11th at Gratis, Ohio, Mrs Elizabeth McClung. 89 yrs old. Mother
 of Wm L. McClung, Mrs J.P. Hardy and a widowed daughter in Gratis, Ohio.
 She had been a widow more than 50 yrs.

McClung, Mrs Ella Jane   "Local"   Mar 23, 1887
 Died- Thursday afternoon March 17th at the hospital in Quincy, Mrs Ella
 Jane McClung, wife of Mr S.H. McClung of Mendon twp and the daughter of
 the late Joseph Wible. Born July 21, 1855. Was 32 yrs old. Leaves a
 husband and 4 young children, one of them a mere infant. Buried Mendon
 cemetery. Services from the home of the mother, Mrs Robert Kells and the
 Lutheran church to which she belonged by Rev E.W. Souders, pastor.

McClung, James Brooks   "Death"   Mar 9, 1904
 see Blazer, Rachel Louise

McClung, Louis Cass   "Death"   Mar 9, 1904
 see Blazer, Rachel Louise

McClung, Rachel   "Probate"   Mar 16, 1904
 Probate Notice of Rachel McClung, deceased 1st Monday of May 1904
 Samuel H. McClung, Adm.

McClung, Rachel Louise   Death"   Mar 9, 1904
 see Blazer, Rachel Louise

McClung, Mrs S.H.   "Obituary"   Dec 22, 1898
 see Wilcox, Mrs Jane

McClung, Mrs S.H.   "Death"   May 17, 1905
 see Wilcox, Morton Robert

McClung, Samuel H.   "Death"   Mar 9, 1904
 see Blazer, Rachel Louise

McClung, William Allen   "Death"   Mar 9, 1904
 see Blazer, Rachel Louise

McClung, Mrs Wm L.   "Obituary"   Dec 27, 1888
 see Blazer, Hannah

McClung, William L.   "Obituary"   Mar 9, 1904
 see Blazer, Rachel Louise

277

McClyment, William H.   "Local"   Dec 27, 1900
     Died- Willaim H. McClyment at his home in Wyoming, Ill. December 18th
     in the A.M. Born Camden, Deleware May 23, 1813. When a boy the family
     moved to Philadelphia where he attended school and learned the trade of
     tailor. 1836 he came to Illinois, locating in Mendon, Adams Co. later he
     moved to Warsaw and a short time later lived Ursa where he was in the
     merchandising business and was post master. May 15, 1839 he married Miss
     Mary Crooks of Mendon who survives him. They had 3 sons and 1 daughter.
     Only Alexander survives him.

McColm, Mrs Arvilla   "Obituary"   Mar 30, 1899
     see Brown, Mrs Lillie

McColm, Chas.   "Funeral"   Mar 30, 1899
     see Brown, Mrs F.

McConnell, Elizabeth   "Obituary"   Jan 22, 1891
     see Thompson, Samuel Sr.

McCormack, Emma   "Obituary"   Mar 8, 1905
     see Rust, Mrs M.N.

McCormack, Mrs Maggie   "Lima"   Aug 21, 1890
     Died- Mrs Maggie McCormack at the home of her father August 14th. Buried
     Marcelline. Her father was Wm Beatty.

McCormack, Wm   "Edgings"   Jan 4, 1878
     Died, Mr Wm McCormack of Ursa Wednesday.

McCormick, Mr   "Ellington"   Jun 4, 1885
     Mr McCormick died recently and was buried in the cemetery of the
     Presbyterian church May 22nd.

McCormick, Mrs   "Ellington"   Jan 13, 1886
     Mrs McCormick who recently died was buried in the Presbyterian cemtery
     Jan 6th.

McCormick, John   "Obituary"   Jun 28, 1894
     Died- Mr John McCormick at 11 P.M. Thursday June 21st at the age of 73
     yrs from consumption and heart trouble. Born in Indiana Co. Penn. in
     1821. In 1839 he married Leah Keppell of Greensburg, Westmoreland Co.
     Penn. where they had 5 children born to them, 2 boys and 3 girls. The
     boys died young, the daughters are Mrs D.W. Dickerman and Mrs S.F.
     Chittenden of this place and Mrs Mike Rust of Mendon, Mo. In the spring
     of 1859 or 60 the family came to Mendon where they lived since. He was a
     carpenter by trade. Member of the Lutheran church. Leaves a wife and 3
     daughters. Services at the house Friday at 5 P.M. by Rev Burgess. Buried
     in Mendon cemetery.

McCormick, John   "Whig"   Aug 23, 1894
    The will of the late John McCormick of Mendon who died June 15th last was
    admitted to the probate yesterday. (Friday) He leaves all his property
    to his wife Leah. The will was made June 13, 1894 and wittnessed by S.H.
    Bradley and Wm McFarland. The wife and Benjamin Simpson are named executrix
    and executor.

McCormick, John   "Probate"   Aug 23, 1894
    Probate Notice John McCormick, deceased 1st Monday of October 1894
    B. Simpson, Ex.

McCormick, Mrs Leah   "Obituary"   Jan 3, 1895
    Died- Mrs Leah McCormick at her home in Mendon of pneumonia Monday P.M.
    December 31st. 75 yrs old. Leah Kepple was born April 1, 1819 at Greens-
    burg, Westmoreland Co. Penn. Came to Mendon spring of 1860. Married John
    McCormick of this town who died last August. They had 5 children (2 dead)
    Mrs DeWitt Dickerman, Mrs M. Rust, Mrs S.F. Chittenden survive their parents
    Funeral yesterday P.M. in the village cemetery after services at the house
    by Rev Wm Burgess.

McCormick, Miss Lizzie   "Local"   Mar 10, 1892
    Death of Miss Lizzie McCormick, daughter of Mr and Mrs John W. McCormick,
    of Edmunds, Hancock Co. Wednesday eve March 2nd of paralysis. 23 yrs old.

McCormick, Mrs M.   "Loraine"   Jul 28, 1881
    Death of a daughter of Mrs M. McCormick.

McCormick, Mr W.C.   Aug 17, 1882
    A late number of the Eureka, Kansas "Herald" notes the death of a few
    days since of an infant son of Mr W.C. McCormick, formerly of Mendon.

McCormick, Wm   "Loraine"   Dec 29, 1881
    Died- Wm McCormick. Leaves a wife and a few small children.

McCormick, Willie   "Loraine"   Apr 29, 1880
    Willie McCormick, son of Michael McCormick, age 10 yrs was drowned in
    a small creek north of their home Sunday eve.

McCoy, Mrs Robert   "Obituary"   Jan 31, 1889
    Mrs Robert McCoy died at her home in Quincy Sunday. Born West Virginia.
    Came with her husband to Adams Co. in 1864. Leaves husband and 4 children
    being, Mrs T. Dwight Ives, Mrs James B. Gardner, Mrs G.B. Raburg, all of
    Quincy and Mr William McCoy of Hicksville, Arkansas.

McCrellis, Ben   "Death"   Sep 15, 1898
    see Marvin, Mrs George

McCullough, Mrs George   "Obituary"   May 2, 1889
    see Rogers, Clark E.

McCullough, Mrs Margaret   "Obituary"   Nov 18, 1897
    see Rogers, Amelia May

McCullough, Miss Melissa   Aug 29, 1883
    Died at Lima on August 25th of typhoid fever Miss Melissa McCullough.
    Services at the M.E. church in Lima by Rev J.W. Buried Rocky Run cemetery.

McCully, Mr Henderson   "Accident"   Aug 30, 1888
    News rec'd by Mrs Wynn from her daughter, Mrs Arthur P. McCully of the
    death of her father in law, Mr Henderson McCully from falling on a saw.

McCune, Mr Everett   "Loraine"   Jul 12, 1900
    Died- Mr Everett McCune at the home of his father last Saturday A.M.
    Services at the Christian church on Sunday at 11 A.M. 21 yrs old.

McDade, Mamie   "Local"   May 8, 1888
    Death in Wichita of Mamie McDade, wife of J.B. Fox who left Quincy a
    bride just 1 yr ago.

McDivitt, Harry   "Indian Grave"   Nov 23, 1899
    Harry McDivitt was killed in Arkansas November 2nd. He served thru the
    Cuban war. Remains brought here for burial Monday.

McDonal, Mrs Samuel   "Payson"   Oct 14, 1880
    Mrs Danley and daughter of Springfield, Ill. and Miss Clara H. Keenan of
    Quincy, both sisters of Mrs Samuel McDonal, deceased. There was a family
    reunion at the McDonal home Saturday.

McDonald, Old Auntie   "Death"   Apr 13, 1899
    Died- Old Auntie McDonald at the poor house near Carthage the 1st of the
    week. Buried in the Oak Valley cemetery near Mallard, Hancock Co. on
    Tuesday. Was an old resident of Rocky Run in the early days. She was
    not a county charge as her support was wholly or in part provided for.

McDonald, Rose   "Local"   Mar 30, 1904
    Rose McDonald and Nettie Broniski both lost their lives in the fire at
    the Newbomb hotel annex in Quincy Saturday night.

McDonald, Miss Sallie   "Loraine"   Mar 22, 1883
    Miss Sallie McDonald is absent from her position as post mistress this
    week owing to the death of her grandpa, Mr Benson.

McDonald, Mrs Samuel   "Payson"   Aug 14, 1879
    Died on August 7th Mrs Samuel McDonald of this place. Services at the
    home by Rev G.W. Huntley. Member of Baptist church.

McDonnal, Grandpa   "Payson"   Mar 3, 1886
    Grandpa McDonnal was buried Saturday.

McDonnal, Wm   "Patson"   Mar 3, 1886
    Wm McDonnal of Denver, Colo was here for the funeral of his father.

McElmoyle, Mrs Wm   "Obituary"   Jan 29, 1899
    see Edmonds, Mary

McFadden, ____   Dec 26, 1878
    see Scott, Winfield

McFarland, Adam   "Obituary"   Feb 16, 1882
    Adam McFarland died Sunday night Feb. 12th at the age of 34 yrs. He leaves
    a wife and 4 children. Services by Rev Kunkleman.

McFarland, Mrs Adam   "Death"   Jan 25, 1883
    see Ely, Mrs Ralph

McFarland, Catherine   Jan 23, 1890
    Died- Mrs Catherine McFarland (nee Taylor) Mrs John, January 24th at
    7:45 P.M. Buried January 26th 1890 at Mendon cemetery. Services by Rev.
    F.C. Read at the M.E. church assisted by Rev's S.D. Peet and M.L.
    Schmucker. She was born April 16, 1818 in Shelby Co. Ky. Came to Mendon
    about the same time as her husband. Only surviving sister is Mrs Albert
    Hughes of Ursa.

McFarland, Deborah   "Probate"   Dec 22, 1898
    Probate notice of Deborah McFarland, deceased 1st Monday of March 1899
    Leonidas Thompson, Adm.

McFarland, Mrs Deborah   "Obituary"   Dec 8, 1898
    Died- Mrs Deborah McFarland on Friday December the 8th of pneumonia.
    Funeral Monday A.M. in the Methodist church by Rev E.K. Crews.
    Mrs Debora Ely McFarland was born June 18, 1847 in Mendon and died June
    2nd 1898 at age 51 yrs 5 mo's 14 days. Married 1871 to Adam McFarland
    and they had 5 children, Ray, deceased, Fred Orville, Herman Earl,
    deceased, John Ralph and Malcolm Floyd. Mr McFarland died in 1882. She
    also leaves 2 sisters, Mrs Phaebe Austin and Mrs Emma Thompson. Joined
    the M.E. church in 1886.

McFarland, Herman   Jun 5, 1902
    Included in list of Spanish and Philippine war soldiers buried in Mendon
    Cemetery, Herman McFarland.

McFarland, Herman Earl   Sep 29, 1898
    Mendon's 1st offering at Camp Cuba Libre, Jacksonville, Florida- News
    of the death of Herman McFarland reached Mendon last Friday. Cause,
    typhoid fever. Died- Herman Earl McFarland, born March 2, 1877 in Mendon
    Illinois died at Camp Cuba Libra September 23, 1898. Joined Cong'l
    church 1891 when Rev. S.D. Peet was pastor. Graduated from Mendon school
    in 1896. Enrolled in Co. M. of the state Militia and was sent with the
    4th Ill. Reg. to Jacksonville Florida (of which Co M. was a part)
    Body arrived here at 10 A.M. Tuesday. Services at 11 A.M. at the Cong'l
    church by Rev Parker Shields, pastor of the M.E. church at Hoopeston, Ill
    Buried Mendon.

McFarland, John   "Probate"   Feb 19, 1891
    Probate Notice of John McFarland, deceased 1st Monday of April 1891
    William McFarland, Adm.

McFarland, John   "Obituary"   Jan 23, 1890
    Died- January 24, 1890, John McFarland at 1:20 A.M. Buried January 26th
    in Mendon cemetery. Services by Rev F.C. Read in the M.E. church assisted
    by Rev S.D. Peet and M.L. Schmucker. He was born in Clermont Co. Ohio
    April 22, 1815 and came to Adams Co. about 1842. Married Catherine Taylor
    July 14, 1845, they had 1 son and 3 daughters. By a previous marriage
    he had 2 sons and 2 daughters and by her previous marriage she had 1 dau.
    Making a total of 9 children for them. 4 lived in the Mendon area, Son
    William lived with them and 3 daughters. Other children attending the
    funeral was Mrs Bristol of Omaha, Nebr., Mr and Mrs Thomas McFarland of
    Carthage, Mrs Dr Akins and Mrs Warren Fletcher, John's brother Ephraim
    McFarland of West Point. A married sister now living in Ohio and Mrs
    McFarland's only surviving sister, Mrs Albert Hughes of Ursa were unable
    to attend.

McFarland, Lew   "Local"   Jan 24, 1895
    Poor Lew McFarland will trouble us no more. He had been leading a kind
    of vagabond life since being forced by the terrors of the law to leave
    Mendon was taken with pneumonia Friday and died the next day 1 mile West
    of Golden. Buried without ceremony Sunday. It is a sad ending of an
    erratic life.

McFarland, Sarah   "Obituary"   Aug 10, 1893
    see Ely, Jared

McFarland, William   "Local"   Jul 2, 1903
    The deaths of William McFarland, George Davis and H.C. Walker may be
    referred to as a coincidence as all three were Cooper's by trade, all
    worked for S.H. Bradley at one time, each died on Sunday and within
    3 weeks.

McFarland, William   "Died"   Jun 4, 1903
    William McFarland died Sunday night. Born in Ursa 1846, parents moved to
    Mendon 1863 where he lived since. Learned the trade of cooper in his
    fathers shop and worked at this trade till about 1878. Services Wednesday
    A.M. at the house by Rev J.S. Bayne. Buried Mendon cemetery in charge of
    Mendon Lodge A.F.&A.M. Buried beside his father and mother. Mr Thos.
    McFarland a ½ brother of deceased and wife of Carthage attended the
    funeral. Owing to the late arrival of the train Ralph McFarland of St
    Louis and Floyd of Quincy, nephews of the deceased did not reach here in
    time to attend the funeral.

McFarland, William   "Probate"   Feb 10, 1904
    Probate Notice of William McFarland, deceased 1st Monday April 1904
    Charles A. Chittenden, Adm.

McGibbons, Mrs   "Death"   Sep 11, 1884
    see Kunkel, Mrs

McGibbons, Mrs   "Death"   Apr 22, 1880
    see Barclay, Mrs Foster

McGibbons, Mrs Elizabeth   "Birthday"   Oct 19, 1904
    Mrs Elizabeth McGibbons celebrated her 94th birthday at the home of her son
    Furman McGibbons in Sioux City, Iowa. She has 6 children, 30 grandchildren,
    30 great grandchildren. Living children are, George, Furman, Mrs George
    Wilson and Mrs Louise Miller all of Sioux City, Mrs John Gibbs of Fresno,
    Calif. 2 children are dead, One was Jacob McGibbons who died in Anderson
    prison during the Civil War. She was born Somerset Co. Penn July 1, 1810
    and July 1, 1835 married John McGibbons who died 20 yrs ago in Sioux City,
    Iowa Mr and Mrs McGibbons and 4 children moved to Mendon 5 yrs after their
    marriage. She is only remaining person out of 12 brothers and sisters.
    Her father died at the age of 56 yrs and mother at the age of 62 yrs,
    both of consumption. Note: The Sioux City, Iowa Journal of Oct 2, 1904
    carried a picture of Mrs McGibbons and her 6 living children.

McGibbons, John   May 24, 1883
    Died, May 24th John McGibbons. He was born in Westmoreland Co. Penn.
    in March 1810 Took up residence in Sioux City, Iowa in March 1868. Had 4
    daughters and 2 sons, Mrs Mary Ann Ward and Mrs Elizabeth Gibbs of
    Chariton County Missouri, George of Minneapolis, Mrs Malinda Wilson of
    San Francisco, Mrs Louise Miller of Mendon and Furman of Sioux City.
    Funeral from the home on Pearl Street in charge of Mr C.T. Wescott. Was of
    Catholic faith.

McGill, Mrs Mary   "Local"   Oct 26, 1904
    Remains of Mrs Mary McGill (colored), oldest daughter of Mr and Mrs
    William Lingham, formerly a resident of Mendon was brought here for burial
    last week in the Mendon cemetery.

McGinley, Annie Amelia   "Obituary"   Feb 28, 1901
    Died, Mrs W.H. McGinley, nee Annie Amelia Tittle, born Mendon, Ill
    Adams Co. Feb 5, 1868 died at her home in LaBelle Feb. 18, 1901 at the
    age of 33 yrs 13 days. Married Wm McGinley Oct 19, 1886. They had 4
    children, 2 sons and 2 daughters. Boys are both dead, the girls are Edna
    and Edith, twins survive her. In 1894 she was baptized in the 1st Baptist
    church of LaBelle, Mo. Services at her home by Elder G.C. Kell and Elder
    J.H. Coil. Buried in LaBelle cemetery beside her little darlings.

McGinley, Mr and Mrs John   "York Neck"   Oct 11, 1894
    Died- the youngest child of Mr and Mrs John McGinley, of summer compaint
    on Friday. Buried Coatsburg cemetery on Saturday.

McGinley, Mrs Joseph   "Obituary"   Feb 9, 1899
    see Kells, Robert

McGinley, Mrs Wm   "Obituary"   Apr 13, 1899
    see Tittle, Mr A.J.

McGinley, Mr and Mrs Wm   "Local"   Nov 23, 1893
    The infant child of Mr and Mrs Wm McGinley of LaBelle, Mo was brought here
    and buried in Mendon cemetery last week.

McGinnis, Mrs Martha   "Big Neck"   Jan 23, 1890
  Mrs Martha McGinnis died at her home in Big Neck Jan 14th. Funeral
  services by Elder Valentine of the U.B. church of York Neck.

McGinnis, Smith   "Camp Point"   May 26, 1881
  Smith McGinnis died in Quincy last week. He was an old settler of Houston,
  Ill. and was living in Missouri.

McGirr, Grandma   "Fowler & Oakland"   Feb 16, 1899
  Died- Grandma McGirr, an aged lady living 1½ miles northeast of Fowler
  last Saturday Feb. 4th. Funeral at the Catholic church in Bloomfield on
  Monday. Buried in the adjoining cemetery.

McGirr, Edward   "Local"   Feb 14, 1889
  Died- Mr Edward McGirr, a well known farmer at his home near Bloomfield
  on Monday eve. Age 75 yrs. Born in Ireland and was one of the oldest
  settlers in this part of the country. He was brother of the Rev Father
  Peter McGirr of Quincy. Leaves a widow, 2 daughters and 3 sons. Funeral
  at Bloomfield catholic church.

McGirr, Mrs John   May 1, 1890
  Died- Mrs John McGirr of Bloomfield, age 54 yrs. Died April 26th. Funeral
  by Rev Father McGirr of Quincy and Rev Father Gesenhues of Bloomfield.
  Only 2 weeks before, Joseph McGirr, son of the above died. Age 18 yrs.
  Buried St Joseph's cemetery.

McGirr, Mrs Mary Ann   "Whig"   May 10, 1894
  Died- Mary Ann, wife of Mr Owen McGirr at her home in Bloomfield, this
  Co. Monday afternoon about 10:30 Suffered from consumption for 2 yrs.
  Age 44 yrs. Lived Adams Co. 16 yrs. Leaves husband and 1 brother, Rev
  Father Kerr of the St Peters Catholic church.

McGirr, Peter   "Elm Grove"   May 11, 1899
  Died- Peter McGirr of consumption last Thursday. Buried Bloomfield
  cemetery Saturday. He was a nice young man.

McGovern, Patrick   "Augusta Review"   Oct 1, 1885
  Patrick McGovern of Mendon who died recently willed his property to
  Andrew Carolin.

McGrew, Mrs Hannah C.   "Local"   Feb 23, 1893
  Died- Mrs Hannah C. McGrew, a former resident of Mendon died at the home of
  her daughter, Mrs John Fifer in Lincoln, Nebr. Feb 10th. Age 79 yrs.
  Had been a widow about 2 yrs. She and her husband had lived in Mendon from
  1876 to 1881 and were members of the M.E. church
                                        John Fifer
                                        Lincoln, Nebr. Feb 20th

McGrew, Mr and Mrs P.R.   "Death"   Oct 30, 1890
  see Combs, Lydia

McGrew, Paul R,   Sep 4, 1890
    Paul R. McGrew died August 25th at the home of his son, Mr John Fifer
    in Lincoln, Nebr. Age 73 yrs 11 mo's 27 days. Buried Fairview cemetery
    near Raymond, Nebr.

McIntyre, Mrs   "Payson"   Jan 25, 1883
    Mrs McIntyre, daughter of Samuel Bradfield was buried Jan 18th.

McIntyre, Mrs   "Local"   Apr 13, 1887
    Mrs McIntyre had a monument erected on the family plot in the Mendon
    cemetery to the memory of her husband and 2 children,Mrs McIntyres
    mother and her own parents, Mr and Mrs Ray.

McIntyre, Mrs Alice   "Death"   Sep 14, 1882
    see Ray, Mrs Francis

McIntyre, B.   "Obituary"   Mar 18, 1880
    see Tressler, Rev Prof D.L.

McIntyre, Miss Ida J.   "Obituary"   Mar 18, 1880
    see Tressler, Rev Prof D.L.

McIntyre, Mrs James   "Obituary"   Feb 23, 1899
    see Tringle, Mrs Mary

McIntyre, John   "Graves"   Jun 22, 1899
    Grave of John McIntyre decorated during Memorial services of the IooF
    and Rebeccas.

McIntyre, John   "Obituary"   Feb 9, 1893
    see Gibson, Miss Mary (McIntyre)

McIntyre, Mrs Mary   "Died"   Feb 14, 1884
    Died at Mendon Feb. 9th at the age of 82 yrs, Mrs Mary McIntyre. Mother
    of Mr W.H. McIntyre of the Dispatch. She died in her sleep probably of
    paralsis of the heart. Born Ulverstone, Lancashire, England May 26, 1802
    After death of her husband in the Isle of Man she was brought to this
    country by her oldest son, the late John McIntyre. She settled in Mendon
    the spring of 1855. John had 4 children. Mrs Mary McIntyre leaves
    children W.H. and a daughter. Burial services in Zion Episcopal church
    by Rev Stuart Crockett.

McIntyre, Mr and Mrs R.R.   "Obituary"   Feb 24, 1904
    see Copelin, Mrs Eunice Atheda

McIntyre, Mrs R.I.   "Obituary"   Mar 16, 1899
    see Chatten, Mrs W.I.

McIntyre, Mrs William   "Death"   Jun 21, 1905
    see Clair, John

McKee, Mrs Mary   "Obituary"   May 9, 1895
    see Berry, Col. W.W.

McKeeby, Mrs S.F.   "Obituary"   Mar 23, 1899
    see Metcalf, Mrs Susan Riddle

McKinney, J.W.   "Ursa"   May 3, 1905
    Died- Mr J.W. McKinney of Adams Co. at the home of his daughter, Mrs
    C.A. Randolph of this place Thursday of last week. 74 yrs old. Born and
    raised and lived in Adams Co. Most of the time in Lima Twp Mr and Mrs
    McKinney went to live with their only daughter last fall because of old
    age. Married 1856 to Miss Lunda Workman and had 2 children, 1 died in
    infancy. Leaves 3 brothers, 3 sisters, wife and daughter. Was member of
    Masonic Fraternity since 1852. Services at the Methodist church of which
    he was a member by Rev W.O. Livingstone.

McKinney, J.W.   "Ursa"   May 3, 1905
    G.W. McKinney of Baxter, Iowa and J.A. McKinney of Valley Junction, Iowa
    also Mrs Martha Adair of Camp Point, Ill attended the funeral of their
    brother J.W. McKinney last week.

McKinney, Miss Laura   "Local"   Mar 22, 1894
    Miss Laura McKinney who formerly lived here with Mr and Mrs Simmons was
    buried at Wesley chapel last Friday. We understand she died in Missouri.

McKinney, Wseley   "Ursa"   May 3, 1905
    Died- Friday the 28th, Mr Wesley McKinney at the home of his daughter,
    Mrs C.A. Randolph. 75 yrs old Services by Rev W.O. Livingston at the M.P.
    church. Buried Denson burying ground north of town.

McKinzie, Mart   "Payson"   Mar 20, 1884
    March 16th death of Mart McKinzie.

McKown, Mrs   "Obituary"   Feb 10, 1886
    see Simpson, Mrs Sarah

McLaughlin, Mrs   "Loraine"   Nov 30, 1899
    Died- Mrs McLaughlin at her home here last Thursday at 8 P.M. Services
    at the M.E. church Friday at 3 P.M. Buried Loraine cemetery beside her
    husband. Leaves 8 children. 4 boys 4 girls.

McLaughlin, Edna Leonora   "Local"   Jul 17, 1884
    Died July 16th Edna Leonora McLaughlin. Age 2 yrs 8 mo's 2 days. Daughter
    of Mr and Mrs McLaughlin. Buried Loraine. Services by Rev McKown.

McLaughlin, Mrs Minnie   "Obituary"   Mar 17, 1892
    see Bolt, John

McLaughlin, Samuel   "Ursa"   Feb 21, 1889
    Died- Mr Samuel McLaughlin, an old resident of this twp yesterday A.M.
    He was nearly 80 yrs old. Buried in Denson burying ground today.

McLaughlin, W.   "Farm for Sale"   Sep 19, 1889
  Farm of the late W. McLaughlin, deceased situated 5 miles northwest of
  Mendon and 3 miles northeast of Ursa, Adams Co. Illinois Saturday Sept.
  28th 1889   at the house at 10 A.M.   by the heirs.

McLaughlin, Wm   "Marcelline"   Jul 13, 1887
  Mr Wm McLaughlin died July 9th. His oldest son who lives in Texas arrived
  home on the 6th. He leaves a wife and ?

McLaughlin, Wm   "Ursa"   July 13, 1887
  Wm McLaughlin, of Marcelline died Saturday A.M. Buried Denson cemetery
  near Ursa on Sunday by Masonic order. Procession 2 miles long.

McLaughlin, Wm   "Obituary"   March 7, 1889
  Died- Wm McLaughlin was born in Penn. November 9, 1829 and moved to Ill.
  in his childhood. Married Jennie Springer in Missouri Jan 22, 1866. Died
  March 1, 1889 at the age of 59 yrs 3 mo's 22 days. Leaves a wife and 3
  children- 2 boys preceeded him. He enlisted in 1861 for 3 yrs in the war
  of the Rebellion in Co. C. 3rd Iowa Cavalry. Resident of this community
  18 yrs. Was admitted to the soldiers home in Quincy Sept. Buried Saturday
  P.M. at the Sweet Home cemetery north of Fowler. Services by Rev R.P. Droke
  at the M.E. church at Fowler.

McMeachem, Mr   "Lima"   Jun 29, 1893
  Mr McMeachem died last Tuesday eve and was taken to Burton on Thursday
  for burial in the Burton cemetery.

McMillen, Caroline   "Obituary"   May 16, 1901
  see Frisbie, Morris E.

McMillen, Caroline   "Funeral"   Mar 8, 1905
  see Frisbie, Mrs Caroline

McMurray, Mr Aaron   "Local"   Oct 26, 1887
  Died- Mr Aaron McMurray, an attorney at Quincy at 7:30 Tuesday. Born
  near Clayton September 24, 1840. When 21 he enlisted in the 3rd Mo.
  Cavalry Vol. and served 3 yrs. Leaves a wife and 2 children.

McNay, Andrew   "Obituary"   Feb 5, 1903
  Andrew McNay was born in Scotland January 12, 1812 and came to the U.S.
  with his parents when 5 yrs old. Married Mary A. Webb October 14, 1841 and
  they had 5 children, namely Sarah J.(Shepherd), Samuel B., Mary A. (Hughes)
  Albert W. and Viola F. (Pride) all living in Adams Co. Illinois except
  Samuel who lives Mendon, Mo. He died at his daughter, Sarah J. Shepherd,
  Marcelline, Ill Feb. 1, 1903. He was 91 yrs 19 days old. Was a charter
  member of Franklin Freewill Baptist church (Member 48 yrs). Funeral
  by Rev S.R. Reno of Mendon from the home of his daughter, Mrs Sarah J.
  Shepherd. Buried Franklin cemetery.

McNay, Mrs Andrew   "Death"   Dec 1, 1898
    Died- Mrs Andrew McNay at her home northwest of Mendon Tuesday A.M.
    Buried Wednesday in the Franklin cemetery after services at the house by
    Rev E.K. Crews of this place. Mary Webb was born August 18, 1822 and died
    November 29th 1898 at the age of 76 yrs 3 mo's 21 days. Married Andrew
    McNay October 14, 1841, he survives her along with 2 sons and 3 daughters
    Member of the Free Will Baptist church since 1853.

McNay, Mr and Mrs Andrew   "Obituary"   Nov 14, 1889
    see Webb, Mrs

McNay, Mrs Charles   "Local"   Nov 8, 1888
    Died- at her home in Marcelline of typhoid malaria at 7 P.M. Sunday, Mrs
    McNay, wife of Charles McNay and daughter of Mr and Mrs W.E. Miller. Was
    26 yrs old. Born Feb 7, 1863. Married Dec 19, 1882. Leaves husband and
    1 small boy. Buried in Baptist burying ground east of Marcelline. Services
    by Elder Wilson of Camp Point. She was a member of the Christian church.

McNay, Mrs D.F.   "Death"   Mar 15, 1905
    see Shepherd, Mrs Susan

McNay, Gertie   "Obituary"   May 21, 1885
    Gertie McNay died suddenly while on a visit to her cousin, Josie Copelin
    May 19th. She was 16 yrs 10 mo's 15 days old. Services held in Lutheran
    church Wednesday May 20th. Born July 4th 1868 and died May 19, 1885.
    Services by Rev E.W. Souders.

McNay, Mrs H.F.   "Death"   Feb 26, 1903
    see Laughlin, John W.

McNay, Herschell   Jan 19, 1882
    Died- Herschell McNay, Sacremento, Calif, brother of Wm McNay of Ursa and
    son of Mrs McNay of Mendon.

McNay, John C.   Jan 30, 1890
    John C. McNay, only child of Mr and Mrs D.F. McNay died January 25th
    age 11 yrs 1 mo. 13 days. Funeral January 26th at the Franklin burying
    ground. Services by Rev Schmucker of the Lutheran church.

McNay, Myrtle Mary   "Obituary"   Nov 22, 1894
    Died- Myrtle Mary, daughter of Andrew and Heddessa McNay born in Marion Co.
    Mo. July 23, 1880 and died at her home near Mt Hebron, this twp Nov 18,
    1894 at the age of 14 yrs. Sick 3 days. Services at her church at 2 P.M.
    by Elder W.S. Lowe. Buried in the Free Will Baptist church cemetery.
    Leaves her mother and 3 brothers. Member of the Christ worshipping at
    Mt Hebron under the preaching of Elder W.S. Lowe.

McNay, Mrs Ollie   Nov 8, 1888
    Mrs Ollie McNay died Sunday eve.

McNeal, Miss____   "Obituary"   Jan 22, 1891
    see Lummis, Mrs John

McNulty, Mr and Mrs Edward   "Fowler"   Aug 22, 1889
    Buried Wednesday, the only child of Mr and Mrs Edward McNulty.

McNulty, Mrs Samuel   "Big Neck"   Apr 20, 1887
    Thomas Lees went to Camp Point Thursday to attend his mothers funeral,
    Mrs Samuel McNulty.

McReynolds, Fred   "Estate Contest"   May 18, 1904
    Partition #1689
    see Moore, Annis S.

McReynolds, Mrs Fred   "Obituary"   Mar 16, 1904
    see Johnson, George W.

McReynolds, Mrs Martha A.   "Local"   Sep 1, 1892
    Died- Mrs Martha A. McReynolds at the home of her son, J. McReynolds
    in Camp Point on August 17th in her 69 th yr. The remains were taken to
    Abingdon, Iowa for burial. Mr McReynolds was fromer station agent at
    Mendon.

McVay, Mrs Anna C.   "Local"   Jan 19, 1899
    Died- Mrs Anna C. McVay, widow of the late Michael McVay at her home
    532 S. 4th St. Quincy January 11th at the age of 76 yrs. Leaves a
    daughter, Mary F. and a son William. Funeral Friday.

McVay, Charles   "Probate"   Mar 19, 1891
    Probate notice of Charles McVay, deceased 1st Monday April 1891
    Mary A. McVay, Adm.

McVay, Charles   Feb 5, 1891
    Died- Feb 2nd, Mr Charles McVay. Born in Ireland. Came to U.S. with his
    parents. Had 1 brother Michael. In 1836 Michale came to Quincy and was
    followed 1 yr later by Charles. They were both plasterers by trade. In
    1845 he married Miss Adeline Dewey in Quincy. He had 1 sister, Mrs Jas.
    Hendrickson of Missouri. Also 2 sons and 1 daighter, sons are Charles and
    George, daughter is Mrs Charles French of Mendon. Services from the M.E.
    church by Rev F.C. Read Buried Mendon cemetery.

McVay, Geo.   "Local"   Dec 14, 1893
    Mr Geo. McVay went to Mayville, Pike Co. last week to attend the funeral
    of his brother in law, Rev Chas. A. Nixdorff.

McVay, Sam   "Payson"   Mar 5, 1885
    Buried Feb 28th, Mr Sam McVay.

Naderhoff,A.H.　　　　　　"Coatsburg"　　　　　　Oct 11, 1894
　　Died- A.H. Naderhoff at the home of his father October 3rd. Born near
　　Coatsburg. 22 yrs old. Died from typhiod fever. He was attending school
　　at Bushnell when stricken. Bert was a boy highly respected by all. Leaves
　　father, mother, 1 sister and 5 brothers. Services by Elder Dilly at the
　　Christian church October 4th.

Naderhoff, Albert D.　　　　　"York Neck"　　　　　　Oct 11, 1894
　　Died- Albert D. Naderhoff October 3rd of typhoid fever. Born near
　　Coatsburg March 27, 1872. Leaves a father, sister, 5 brothers and a step
　　mother. Buried in Coatsburg cemetery besdie his mother who died some time
　　ago.

Naegelin, Mr and Mrs　　　　　"Death"　　　　　　Mar 16, 1887
　　see Tanner, Franklin

Nagel, Jacob　　　　　　　　　　　　　May 4, 1882
　　Jacob Nagel, a German laborer was instantly killed by a caving of a bank
　　near the corner of Front and Maine Sts. Quincy.

Nash, Mrs Melvina Lucinda　　　"Quincy"　　　　　　Mar 2, 1899
　　Died- Mrs Melvina Lucinda Nash, age 46 yrs died Monday A.M.

Nayler, Richard　　　　　　"Camp Point"　　　　　　Nov 8, 1883
　　Richard Nayler of Columbus twp dropped dead in his field one day last
　　week. Was about 55 yrs old.

Naylor, Rev.　　　　　　　"Obituary"　　　　　　Feb 1, 1900
　　see Horn, Mrs Martha E.

Naylor, George　　　　　　"Coatsburg"　　　　　　Feb 2, 1888
　　An infant of Mr and Mrs George Naylor was buried in the cemetery here
　　last Tuesday.

Neal, Mr and Mrs James　　　"Big Neck"　　　　　　Nov 24, 1892
　　Born, to Mr and Mrs James Neal, Nov 17th, a boy
　　Died, this A.M. Nov 21st　cause deformity and erruption of the spinal
　　column.

Neal, Thomas　　　　　　　"Local"　　　　　　Oct 9, 1902
　　Thomas Neal, the hotel man at Lima died Sunday of Consumption. Buried
　　Monday.

Neaterour, Mr and Mrs Andy　"Tioga"　　　　　　Mar 24, 1898
　　Died- the infant son of Mr and Mrs Andy Neaterour last week.

Neaterour, Frank　　　　　"Tioga"　　　　　　Oct 10, 1901
　　A child of Frank Neaterour's age about 2 yrs was buried in our village
　　cemetery last week.

Nedick, Mr and Mrs Louis　　"Ursa"　　　　　　Aug 14, 1902
　　The 5 month old child of Mr and Mrs Louis Nedick died Saturday of
　　cholera infantum and was buried Sunday.

Nedrow, Mrs Adela (Andrews)   "Sudden Death"   Dec 22, 1898
    Died- Mrs Adela (Andrews) Nedrow, wife of John H. Nedrow from paralysis
    last Friday. Buried in village cemetery Sunday P.M. Services by Rev.
    Bayne. Adela Drusilla Andrews was born Brantford, Conn. May 30, 1839
    Came to Illinois with fathers family when she was 7 yrs old. Married
    August 6, 1859 to John H. Nedrow. Had 5 children, Charles, Mrs Wm Chant,
    Miss Etta of Mendon, Mrs Patrick O'Brien and Mrs Frank Binson of Quincy.
    Joined Episcopal church at age 12 yrs.

Nedrow, Eli   Apr 10, 1902
    As we go to press we learn that Eli Nedrow, for years mail carrier from
    the post office to the depot died last night. Had been in feeble health
    for several mo's/ He carried the mail day before yesterday for the last
    time.

Nedrow, Eli   "Obituary"   Apr 17, 1902
    Eli Nedrow an old citizen of Mendon died at his home Thursday A.M.
    April 10th at 2:30. 75 yrs 4 days old. Born April 5, 1827 Somerset, Penn
    When a boy his parents moved to Mt Pleasant, Penn where he married Miss
    Margaret A. Bingeman in 1850. They had 4 children, Samuel and his twin
    brother who died at birth, Mary C. who died at age 2 yrs and John D.
    Came to Mendon 1851. Worked in Wm Battell plow factory, the 1st plow
    factory west of the Allegheny mountains, then Blacksmithing in Mendon and
    Bloomfield and 10 yrs ago started as a mail carrier. His wife kept a
    hotel, the Nedrow House for nearly 35 yrs until forced to retire because
    of old age. Leaves his widow, who is over 80 yrs old, 2 sons, Samuel and
    John D. and several brothers and sisters. United with the Lutheran
    church of Mendon under Rev Jos. Harkey. Services at his home Saturday
    A.M. by Rev J.F. Booker. Buried Mendon cemetery. William Walters, a
    relative of deceased and his wife of Quincy attended the funeral.

Nedrow, Mrs Eliza   "Obituary"   Mar 17, 1898
    Died- Mrs Nedrow, widow of the late John Nedrow Tuesday P.M. Eliza
    Longbaugh was born in Somerset Co. Penn January 15, 1811. Married Samuel
    Nedrow in Somerset Co. Penn. May 12, 1828. They came to Mendon March 1851
    Joined Methodist church 16 yrs ago. Died March 15th 1898 at 2 P.M.
    87 yrs 2 mo's ols. Leaves 6 children, Eli, John and Samuel, Mrs T.J. Quinn,
    Mrs Annie Winn, all of Mendon and Mrs Elizabeth Allison of Beattie, Kansas.
    Services by Rev E.K. Crews of the M.E. church at 2 P.M.. Buried village
    cemetery beside her husband who died a little over a yr ago.
    NOTE: John one place Samuel another.

Nedrow, Lutha May   "Obituary"   Jul 2, 1903
    Lutha May, daughter of Mr and Mrs J.H. Nedrwo was born in Mendon, Ill.
    August 3, 1876 and married Joseph B. Somerville, Nov. 3, 1901 in St Louis
    Missouri. Died Mendon Ill. June 27, 1903 at age 26 yrs 10 mo's 24 days.
    Leaves husband, father, 3 sisters and 1 brother. Services held at the
    father's home Monday P.M. Buried Mendon cemetery. Mr J.H. Nedrow and
    family thanks friends for kindness.

Nedrow, Mrs Margaret A.   "Obituary"   Feb 3, 1904
    Mrs Margaret A. Nedrow, nee Bingaman, an old lady died at her home in
    Mendon January 30th at the age of 82 yrs 5 mo's 4 days. Born near
    Gettisburg, Penn August 26, 1821. Married Eli Nedrow at Mt Pleasant, Penn
    in 1850 and came to Mendon, Ill 1851. Leaves 2 sons, 9 grandchildren, and
    2 great grandchildren, 3 sisters and 1 brother. Was charter member of
    the Lutheran church at Mendon. Services at the house Monday P.M. by Rev
    Reitzel, her pastor. Buried Mendon cemetery beside her husband who died
    a few yrs ago.

Nedrow, Samuel C.   "Local"   Mar 2, 1904
    Died- Samuel C. Nedrow, the barber of kidney trouble Tuesday night.
    Funeral tomorrow at 3 P.M.

Nedrow, Samuel C.   "Obituary"   Mar 9, 1904
    Died- Samuel C. Nedrow at his home in this village March 2nd 1904 at
    age 56 yrs 10 mo's 1 day. Born Mt Pleasant, Westmoreland Co. penn.
    May 1, 1847. Came with parents to Mendon 1851. Married Miss May Luella
    Featheringill of Marcelline, Ill. March 14, 1880 by Rev Frank C. Bruner
    pastor of the M.E. church, Marcelline. Leaves wife, daughter, 3 sisters
    and 1 brother. Funeral at 3 P.M. last Thursday at his home on Church Street
    by Rev Joseph F. Bacon, pastor of the Cong'l church. Buried Mendon cemetery

Nedrow, Mrs Sam   "Death"   Jul 16, 1885
    see Dixon, Mrs H.

Nedrow, Mrs Samuel   "Death"   Jun 18, 1903
    see Featheringill, Mrs Louisa

Neidick, John   "Ursa"   Jun 21, 1900
    John Neidick, of Ellington died Friday and buried today.

Neil, Miss Sarah   "West Point"   Feb 19, 1880
    Died- Miss Sarah Neil, 18 yrs old. She told her sister she never
    expected to leave her sick bed alive. Died at 11 P.M. Saturday. Leaves
    father and his only two children. Mother and 4 children died several
    yrs ago.

Nelson, Mrs   "Local"   Sep 4, 1884
    Died August 28th the infant child of Mrs Nelson (lucy Forsyth).

Nelson, Mr and Mrs   "Local"   Jun 16, 1898
    Mr and Mrs John Wyatt went to Big Neck Sunday to attend the funeral
    of Mr and Mrs Nelson's infant child.

Nelson, Mr Basil   Oct 26, 1882
    Mr Basil Nelson, one of the oldest and most respected citizens of Big
    Neck died October 19th from heart disease.

Nelson, Mrs Douglas   "Local"   Aug 15, 1889
    Died, Mrs Douglas Nelson of Woodville.

Nelson, Mrs J.B.   "Loraine"   Aug 22, 1899
    Died- Mrs J.B. Nelson at her home near Woodville Uuesday night Aug. 13th
    of consumption. Buried in Woodville cemetery Thursday.

Nelson, James   Mar 3, 1881
    James Nelson of near Woodville died last week.

Nelson, James D.   "Adm. Sale"   Mar 6, 1902
    Adm's sale of real estate of James D. Nelson. March term of court.
    Baptist Will, Adm of estate of James D. Nelson, deceased was and is
    petitioner, and Ardena E. Nelson, Goldie A. Nelson, Apollos W. O'Harra
    and Timothy A. Scofield defendents. E.C. Peter, Quincy, Ill. Attorney
    for petitioner.

Melson, Mary   "Obituary"   Jan 28, 1892
    see Swan, Sarah

Nelson, Robert Sr.   "Big Neck"   Jan 15, 1891
    Robert Nelson Sr. living near Meadville, Mo. died last week. Formerly
    of Big Neck.

Nelson, Robert Sr.   "Big Neck"   Jan 15, 1891
    Robert Nelson Sr., who had been living near Meadville, Mo. died last
    week. He was found dead in his timber with one foot badly cut. His team
    had also run off and broken the wagon.

Nelson, Sadie   "Big Neck"   Nov 19, 1891
    Died- of cholera infantum Saturday November 14th, little Sadie, only
    daughter of Wm and Carrie Nelson. Age 1 yr 6 mo's 13 days. Services
    at Union church by Rev Jasper Miller of Loraine. Buried in Curless
    cemetery.

Nelson, Mrs Sadie   "Woodville"   Nov 7, 1889
    A beautiful tombstone has been set up at the grave of Mrs Sadie, wife of
    Mr J. D. Nelson.

Nelson, Wm   "Big Neck"   Dec 29, 1892
    Wm Nelson died at his home near Grand Pasa, Saline Co. Mo. December 12th.
    He was one of the early settlers of Big Neck. Had lived in Saline Co. for
    25 or 30 yrs.

Nesbitt, Agnes   "Estate law suit"   Jun 15, 1893
    see Snodgrass, T.C.

Nesbit, Jerry   "Lima"   Mar 31, 1886
    Jerry Nesbit whose mind has been reranged for a number of yrs died
    Thursday eve at 5 P.M.

Nevins, Mrs Joseph   "Obituary"   Jan 29, 1899
    see Edmonds, Mary

Nevins, Miss Nancy   "Death"   Jan 11, 1905
    see Cochran, Thomas W.

Nevins, Miss Nancy   "Obituary"   Mar 2, 1899
    see Cochran, Mrs Nancy Nevins

Newall, Alice   "Obituary"   Jul 27, 1887
    see Boscow, Mrs Alice

Newhall, Mrs   "Obituary"   Dec 1, 1898
    see Stone, Elbridge K.

Newhouse, Mrs W.R.   "Death"   Jul 27, 1904
    see Raling, Theodore

Newlan, Mrs Mary   "Obituary"   Jun 20, 1901
    see Seals, Dennis

Newman, Mrs Albert   "West Point"   Apr 20, 1893
    Mrs Albert Newman, who lived 2½ miles west of town died last Tuesday
    at 4. Leaves husband and 2 children, a father and mother.

Newmyer, Mrs   "Death"   Feb 25, 1892
    see Shrader, Mrs Hiram

Newton, Bro.   "Burton"   Mar 6, 1879
    A number of IOOF and Knights of Pythias attended the funeral of Bro.
    Newton who was buried in Quincy on the 23rd.

Newton, Mrs M.W.   "Personal"   Mar 13, 1879
    Mrs M.W. Newton has rec'd 2.000 insurance on one of the policies the
    deceased had been carrying.

Nicely, B.W.   "Lima"   Oct 4, 1883
    Infant child of B.W. Nicely died September 26th. Buried Tioga. Services
    by Rev. Madison.

Nichols, Annie   "Heir in Estate"   Jun 28, 1905
    see French, Matilda

Nichols, Mrs Catherine   "Obituary"   Jun 23, 1886
    Died- at her home 2½ miles northeast of Ursa, Ill , Mrs Catherine
    Nichols, wife of James Nichols Sr. "Aunt Kitty" as she was called was
    born in Burbon Co. Ky. September 28, 1814- came to Adams Co. with her
    parents in the fall of 1817. She was a good mother and step mother. Leaves
    3 children and 9 step children, (the latter who loved her as their own
    mother), 2 brothers and 3 sisters. Buried in Stone church cemetery.
    Obituary dated June 15, 1886 Ursa, Ill by Josie B. Pearson.

Nichols, Charley   "Died"   Sep 21, 1882
    died on September 19th, Charley, son of L.D. and E.N. Nichols of
    spinal affection in his 5th yr of age.

Nichols, Mr G.M.   "Ursa"   Mar 28, 1889
    Mr G.M. Nichols, who died last week was born in Ursa twp April 20, 1851
    and married to Miss Mary Pearson in 1873. Was a member of the Christian
    church 11 yrs. Leaves a wife and 3 little girls.

Nichols, Geo. M.   "Probate"   Apr 18, 1889
    Probate Notice of Geo. M. Nichols, deceased- 1st Monday of June 1889
    Lewis W. Nichols, Adm.

Nichols, George   "Local"   Mar 21, 1889
    Died- Mr George Nichols, of Ursa, died last night at 9 P.M. Buried this
    afternoon at 3.

Nichols, Mrs H.C.   "Funeral"   Dec 8, 1886
    see French, Mrs Jos.

Nichols, Mr J.P.   Jun 4, 1885
    Mr J.P. Nichols of Ursa was called to Abingdon, Ill. May 20th on acct
    of the death of his aunt, Mrs Elizabeth Campbell, age 90 yrs.

Nichols, James   "Obituary"   Jan 29, 1891
    James Nichols died at his home near Ursa January 18th in his 92nd yr.
    Buried at the Stone church north of the village on the 20th. Born Bourbon
    Co. Ky. September 11, 1799. Came to Adasm Co. 1833 and settled in
    Ellington twp where he lived about 3 yrs and moved to Ursa. He was
    educated in Bryan Station, Fayette Co. Ky. Married October 21, 1824
    to Miss Margaret Wallace,a native of the same Co. as her husband. She died
    June 20, 1834. They had 5 children, 4 sons 1 daughter. 2 of whom are still
    living. On December 22, 1834 he married 2nd time to Miss Mourning Bowles,
    a niece of Mr Jesse Bowles a pioneer minister of the Christian church of
    Ursa and a native of Bourbon Co. Ky. She died May 29, 1849, to them were
    born 8 children. 6 daughters and 2 sons. 5 still living. On September 23,
    1849 he married his 3rd wife, Mrs Catherine Hendry (Formerly Ruddle)
    also a native of Bourbon Co. Ky. and the daughter of Mr Stephens one of
    the pioneer ministers of the Christian church of Ursa. She died June 12,
    1886 leaving him 1 son who preceeded his father to the spirit land.

Nichols, James   Jan 22, 1891
    James Nichols of Ursa twp died January 18th. He was 92 yrs old. Buried
    from the Stone church north of the village of Ursa.

Nichols, James   "Probate"   Feb 12, 1891
    Probate Notice of James Nichols, deceased- 1st Monday of April 1891
    F. Woodruff, Adm.

Nichols, James   "Obituary"   Oct 10, 1895
    see Riddle, Orville E.

Nichols, Mrs Jane   "Obituary"   Sep 15, 1898
    Mrs Jane Nichols, wife of L.W. Nichols of Ursa twp died Saturday A.M.
    between 8 and 9. Born Francis J. Wood, daughter of Henry and Sarah Wood in
    Rolls Co. Mo. July 15, 1829. Came to Ill. with parents 1833. Married
    Lewis W. Nichols October 14, 1849 and died September 10th at the age of
    69 yrs, 1 mo and 20 days. Leaves husband and 2 sons, L.D. and J.H. both
    residents of this village. Services by Rev W.M. Roe of Shelbine, Mo.
    at the house Tuesday P.M. Buried in the old Stone church burying ground,
    north of Ursa.

Nichols, Mr Joseph W.   "Obituary"   Dec 22, 1886
    Died- Mr Joseph W. Nichols age 52 yrs. Was a resident of Mendon, Mo.
    Sunday eve from an overdose of morphine at the Sherman House, Quincy. He
    was a brother of J.P. and L.W. Nichols of Ursa twp. Mr Nichols was a
    former resident of Ursa. Leaves wife and 7 children. Corspe was removed
    to his late home for burial.

Nichols, Mr Joseph W.   "Mendon, Mo."   Dec 29, 1886
    Death of Mr Joseph W. Nichols who died at Quincy.

Nichols, Lewis W.   "Local"   Dec 12, 1901
    Inventory of the estate of Lewis W. Nichols shows real estate worth
    20, 475 and notes and accts 17, 834.45. "Whig"

Nichols, Lewis W.   "Probate"   Nov 14, 1901
    Probate Notice of Lewis W. Nichols, deceased- 1st Monday of Jan 1902
    Lorenzo H. Nichols and John H. Nichols, Adms.
    Bennett and James, Attorneys

Nichols, Mrs Wm   "Ursa"   Jan 13, 1886
    see Reuck, Mrs

Nicholson, Essie   "Mt Pleasant"   Mar 29, 1888
    Mr Wm Nicholson's little twin daughter, Essie, died Wednesday at age 4 yrs
    8 mo's from scarlet fever. Leaves mother and father. Essie was buried in
    family burying ground Wednesday eve.

Nicholson, Geo.   "Mt Pleasant"   Apr 5, 1888
    The infant daughter of Mr Geo. Nicholson died last Tuesday A.M. the
    victim of scarlet fever. Buried same day in the graveyard near where her
    little cousin was laid some time ago.

Nicholson, Mrs John   "Payson"   Jan 29, 1880
    Mrs Nicholson, wife of Mr John Nicholson was buried last Thursday.

Nicholson, John   "Mt Pleasant"   Mar 13, 1890
    Death of John Nicholson March 3rd at the age of 79 yrs. Services held
    at son John's house by Rev Anthony of Ursa. Buried at Frazier burying
    ground. He was born Pendleton Co. Ky. in 1811 and came to Adams Co. 11 yrs
    later. In 1834 he married Miss Lucetta Fletcher who lived only one yr
    after their marriage. They had one child who is now dead. In 1845 he
    married Hester Orr who died in 1886. They had 9 children. 4 in this
    district and 5 away.

Nicholson, Wm   "Local"   Apr 19, 1888
    Mr Wm Nicholson, of Ursa twp lost a second child by scarlet fever on
    Friday night.

Nicolai, Mrs   "Coatsburg"   Aug 17, 1887
    Mrs Nicolai was buried in the cemtery here last Thursday A.M.

Nixdorff, Rev Chas. A.   "Funeral"   Dec 14, 1893
    see McVay, Geo

Nixdorff, Rev Charles Alexander   Dec 14, 1893
    "Maysville, Pike Co. December 2, 1893
    Rev Charles Alexander Nixdorff died. Born in Germany November 20, 1842
    left Germany Dec 21, 1867 and landed in New York Jan 5, 1868. Married
    Miss Amanda Caroline Hutcheons Feb 20, 1872. Was in Ministry 7 yrs.
    Member of Masonic order. Leaves wife and 4 children.

Noddler, Mr and Mrs   "Local"   Aug 15, 1895
    Thursday of last week the infant child of Mr and Mrs Noddler living on
    the widow Austin's place was buried at Bloomfield.

Noe, Mr Jasper   "Loraine"   May 22, 1890
    Mr Jasper Noe died Wednesday night May 21st. No age given.

Nolan, Ed   "Obituary"   Mar 16, 1899
    see Dempsey, Jimmy

Nolan, Miles   "Local"   Nov 4, 1897
    Died- Miles Nolan an inmate of the Co. farm was killed in a team run-
    away accident at Paloma yesterday.

Nolan, Patrick   "Local"   Feb 28, 1895
    Died- Patrick Nolan, an insane pauper and old resident of Bloomfield
    at the poor farm of which he had been an inmate for nearly 15 yrs, on
    Tuesday A.M.

Norman, Mrs   "Local"   Jan 27, 1886
    Mrs Norman, an old lady of 70 yrs died on Tuesday night. Her remains
    were taken to Philo, Champaign Co. for interment. Mrs Norman was the
    mother of Mrs Bud Spicer and Mrs Howard Watson.

Norris, Mrs Nellie   "Obituary"   May 9, 1901
    Died- Thursday A.M., Mrs Nellie Norris, Nee Chittenden, Services
    Friday May 3rd at 2 P.M. at the home of her parents, Mr and Mrs Harry
    Chittenden. Less than a yr ago she married Mr James G. Norris of Bowen.
    Born November 28, 1877- married July 25, 1900- died May 2, 1901. United
    with the Cong'l church of Mendon at age 16 yrs Pallbearers were-
    Henry Evans, Adelbert Austin, Charley Evans, John Dickerman, Wm Hardy
    and Walter Baldwin.

Northcraft, S.D.   "Local"   Aug 24, 1899
    S.D. Northcraft was run over by an electric street car Monday afternoon
    and was killed. He was employed by the Electric Street Car Co. and was
    working at the time.

Norton, Mrs Mary A.   "Death"   Jun 12, 1884
    see Pierson, Frank

Norton, Mrs Mary A.   "Mt Pleasant"   Jun 12, 1884
    Mrs Mary A. Norton rec'd telegram from Idaho that her son, Frank Pearson
    had died Tuesday June 3rd.

Nowell, Mr Charles   "Payson"   May 4, 1887
    Mr Charles Nowell died about 2 A.M. today.

Noyes, Ella M.   "Local"   Feb 7, 1895
    Died- at Waubaunsee, Kansas of consumption January 21st, Ella M. Noyes,
    daughter of the late James and Mary Noyes, fromerly of Mendon.

Noyes, Miss Mary J.   "Obituary"   Apr 16, 1891
    see Bray, David C.

Noyes, Susie A.and Mary E.   "Local"   Dec 27, 1894
    Died at Wabaunsee, Kansas November 13th Susie A. Noyes, daughter and on
    December 13th Mary E. Noyes, wife of the late James Noyes formerly a
    resident of this twp. Mr Noyes died a yr ago last June. The family was
    well known here 30 yrs ago.

Nutt, Mrs C.H.   "Death"   Mar 5, 1903
    see Strickler, Frank

Nutt, Chas. A.   "Obituary"   Apr 10, 1902
    see Dickerman, I.R.

Nutt, Mr Cyrus   "Loraine"   Nov 2, 1893
    Died- Mr Cyrus Nutt at his home Tuesday at 3 A.M. Also his 2 sons are
    sick with typhoid fever. Leaves a wife and 7 children.

Nutt, Mrs Cyrus H.   "Local"   Nov 23, 1893
    Mrs Cyrus H. Nutt whose husband was buried on November 1st is very low
    with typhoid fever.

Nutt, Daniel   "Obituary"   Oct 8, 1885
    see Hecox, Mrs Mary Ann

Nutt, Daniel   "Obituary"   Feb 13, 1890
    see Loynd, Julia

Nutt, Daniel   "Obituary"   Oct 4, 1888
    see Wright, Abraham

Nutt, Daniel   "Obituary"   Nov 8, 1900
    see Wright, Mrs Phoebe

Nutt, Mrs Dan'l   "Obituary"   Feb 16, 1893
    see Hedges, Thomas S.

Nutt, Daniel   "Obituary"   Mar 21, 1901
    Daniel Nutt died at his home at 6:15 A.M. Mon. March 18th. Funeral from
    the house by Rev Wakefield of the M.E. church. Born Nov. 5, 1817 in Oxford
    Co. England. Came to U.S. 1837 with his mother and sister. 1st lived at
    Salem, Ohio and came to Mendon 1839 and same yr married Miss Sarah A. Hull
    She died July 17, 1896. Mr Nutt was one of a family of 9 children, all of
    whom he outlived. His sister, Mrs Wright of Mendon, age 86 and his brother
    of England both died recently.Daniel and Sarah had 5 children, Elizabeth,
    Wm T., Walter J., Julia, and Charles H. only the sons are living. Mr Nutt
    was a carpenter and farmer. Buried Mendon cemetery. Relatives from afar
    were Mr & Mrs W.J. Nutt and son Chester of Benboro, Mo. William and James
                            -continued-

Nutt, Daniel   Continued
of West Point, James Loynd of Carthage and Harry Loynd of Galesburg.
Pallbearers were; S.H. Bradley, Wm Thompson, C.A. Chittenden, D.L.
Dickerman. Honorary bearers were; Andrew Long, Conrad Quig, W.P. Poling,
Wm Pepple, J.M. Bortz and C.H. Hoffman.

Nutt, Daniel   "Will"   Mar 28, 1901
Will of Daniel Nutt was filed for probate last Friday. Dated December 22,
1900 and witnessed by D.L. Dickerman and A.D. Nutt, both of Mendon.
Leaves 100 acres of land in 3 parcels to his son William T. Nutt, 95
acres in Mendon and Honey Creek and Lot 2 in Mendon to his son Walter J.
Nutt. Lot 3 in Mendon and hearse and all undertaking stock on hand to
son Charles H. Nutt. 800.00 cash to grandson, Harry Loynd, 800.00
cash to grandson Geo. Loynd, the Blacksmith shop with ground and 400.00
in cash to grandson Gilbert Loynd. Lot 27 in Mendon and 1200.00 cash
to grandaughter Cora Loynd. Homestead not to be sold for 2 yrs. Walter J.
Nutt and Charles H. nemaed Excutors, but Walter being a resident of Marion
Co. Mo. formerly disclaimed and relinquished and renounced his right.
Charles H. may act alone.

Nutt, Daniel   "Probate"   May 2, 1901
Probate Notice of Daniel Nutt, deceased- 1st Monday of July 1901
Charles H. Nutt, Ex.   Govert Pape and Govert, attorneys.

Nutt, Daniel   "Obituary"   Apr 17, 1902
see Hedges, Mrs Fannie

Nutt, Daniel   "Obituary"   Feb 5, 1903
see Loynd, Harry William

Nutt, Elizabeth   "Obituary"   Jun 14, 1900
Died- Elizabeth Nutt, daughter of Daniel and Sarah Ann Nutt, born
October 6, 1840 at Mendon, Ill. She was the oldest of 5 children. Three
of whom with her father are still living. Her mother died July 17, 1896
In the spring of 1860 she married Daniel Rhine who died December 4, 1896
After her husband died she took charge of her father's home where she
remained until her death June 7th. She was 59yrs 8 mo's 1 day old. Had no
children. Services Saturday at 4 P.M. from her father's home by Rev.
S.N. Wakefield. Buried in the family plot in Mendon cemetery.

Nutt, Mr and Mrs Jas.   "Local"   Jun 27, 1895
Killed, a daughter of Mr and Mrs Jas. Nutt, Tuesday night. Lived 1½
miles west of Loraine. Was killed by lightning in the harvest field
during the storm.

Nutt, Lucy   "Loraine"   Jun 27, 1895
Died- Lucy Nutt, age 14 yrs, the youngest daughter of Squire J.R. Nutt
was killed by lightning yesterday eve. She had been driving a binder for
her father and had just quit and stepped a few rods from the binder. Her
father was within a few feet of her. Lived 1 3/4 miles west of Loraine.
Funeral at the Christian church at 5 P.M. today.

Nutt, Miss Mary   "Local"   May 3, 1888
    Died- April 12th in England, Miss Mary Nutt, sister of Mr Dan'd Nutt,
    of this place. Age 78 yrs. Miss Nutt was a former resident of this twp.

Nutt, Miriam   "Obituary"   Oct 4, 1888
    see Wright, Abraham

Nutt, Mrs Sarah   "Obituary"   Jul 5, 1905
    see Smith, Hamilton

Nutt, Thomas   "Local"   Mar 15, 1900
    Died- last Saturday, Mr Thomas Nutt at Bobicot county of Oxford England.
    95 yrs old and an invalid many yrs. Word was rec'd of the death by his
    brother Daniel Nutt who had not seen Thomas for 24 yrs that was when
    Daniel visited his old home in England.

Nutt, Walter   "Death"   Feb 8, 1905
    see Hedges, Charles

Nutt, Mr and Mrs Walter   "Died"   Aug 23, 1883
    Infant son of Walter and Mrs Nutt was born June 16, 1883 and died
    August 21, 1883.

Nutt, William   "Death"   Feb 8, 1905
    see Hedges, Charles

Nutt, Mrs Wm   "Obituary"   Jun 9, 1886
    see Shaffer, Jacob

300

O'Brien, James   Deaths"   Feb 16, 1899
    Died- James O'Brien of Quincy died Tuesday afternoon from consumption.
    age 29 yrs

O'Brien, John   "Local"   Nov 7, 1901
    John O'Brien of Mattoon, this state died last week. Age 108 yrs.
    Born Ireland and served in Nelson's fleet in the battle of Trafalgar.

O'Brien, Mrs Patrick   "Obituary"   Dec 22, 1898
    see Nedrow, Mrs Adela (Andrews)

O'Brien, Wm   "Local"   Jan 22, 1885
    Wm O'Brien, the well known criminal lawyer of Peoria, Ill died in
    Chicago last week.

O'Brien,Wm   "Local"   Feb 3, 1904
    Chas. O'Brien has been in Quincy since last Wednesday at the bedside of
    his father, Wm O'Brien. Later; Mr O'Brien died Tuesday A.M.

O'Conner, Mrs Kate   "Obituary"   Nov 23, 1899
    see Wilkinson, Martha

O'Daniels, Louzettie   "Loraine"   Feb 16, 1893
    Died- Louzettie, daughter of Mr and Mrs John O'Daniels, February 7th
    of typhoid fever. Age 18 yrs 10 mo's 2 days. Joined Christian church and
    was baptized January 11, 1891. Services by Elder Hollawell of Canton, Mo.
    at the Christian church. Buried in our cmeetery. Leaves her father, mother,
    4 sisters and 2 brothers.

Odear, Mrs Elizabeth   "Local"   Feb 24, 1904
    Died- Mrs Elizabeth Odear, living northeast of Mendon Sunday A.M.
    February 21st. Was 31 yrs 11 mo's old and the eldest daughter of Mr and
    Mrs Oliver Hastings. Leaves husband, 3 children, 5 brothers and 3 sisters.
    She had been ailing for yrs. Funeral Monday P.M. Buried Mendon cemtery

Odear, Joshua   "Obituary"   Mar 8, 1905
    Died- Joshua, son of Mr and Mrs John Odear at his home near Paloma
    February 19th. 23 yrs 10 days old. Joined Catholic church about a year
    ago. Leaves father, mother, 8 brothers and 3 sisters. Sisters are,
    Mrs J.W. Slonigar, Mrs O.C. Hastings and Mrs E.R. Miller. Funeral at
    the house Tuesday at 12 by Rev Rose of Paloma. Buried Coatsburg cemetery.

O'Dear, Mrs Lizzie   "Local"   Oct 13, 1892
    Died- Mrs Lizzie O'Dear fromerly Lizzie Clair, died at the home of her
    sister, Mrs Wm Roberts Tuesday A.M. Buried in Mendon cemetery Wednesday
    P.M. Services by Rev A.B. Peck, pastor of the M.E. church. Leaves husband
    and a 4 week old baby.

O'Dear, Martha   "Obituary"   Oct 15, 1903
    see Hobby, William Henry

Ogle, F.E.   "Paloma"   May 17, 1888
     F.E. Ogle and wife attended his brother-in-law's funeral, Moses Worman,
     Sunday near Elm Grove.

Ogle, Mrs Frank   "Obituary"   Apr 20, 1899
     see Myers, Mrs Anna Tinsman

Ogle, Joseph   "Columbus"   Aug 17, 1887
     Mr Joseph Ogle, of Paloma died August 10th. Burial here Sunday afternoon.

Ogle, Mrs Nancy   "Local"   Aug 3, 1899
     Died- Mrs Nancy Ogle of Prairie City, Ill. Age 73 yrs. Buried at
     Franklin cemetery Thursday eve of last week.

Ogle, W.H.   "Paloma"   Aug 15, 1889
     W.H. Ogle, of Godfrey, Ill. arrived to superintend the selling of his
     deceased fathers property Saturday.

Ogilive, Miss Lida   "Local"   Jun 16, 1892
     Died- Miss Lida Ogilive was one of the graduating class of Plymouth
     high school. In Saturday's Plymouth Enterprise is a copy of her graduation
     essay and her death notice. Died from brain fever. 16 yrs old.

O'Hara, J.   "Quincy News"   Sep 11, 1884
     A strange death of the 15 yr old son of J. O'Hara of Bowen while he
     was running a foot race.

O'Harra, Apollos   "Estate"   Mar 6, 1902
     see Nelson, James D.

O'Hare, Patrick   "Death"   Feb 16, 1899
     Died- Patrick O'Hare of Burton twp Saturday A.M. of pneumonia. Born
     March 17, 1818 in the city of Belfast, Ireland. Leaves 4 sons and 2
     daughters. Wife died 2 yrs ago.

Olbrenshaw, Rev.   "Burton"   Aug 21, 1879
     Died- the only child of Rev Olbrenshaw (an adopted daughter) died.
     She was 3 yrs old. Remains taken to Prairie City for burial.

Oliver, Mrs Ellen   "Local"   Oct 23, 1884
     Died- October 15th at the home of her son, Mr Wm Hobby, Mrs Ellen Oliver,
     76 yrs old. Services by Rev E.C. Crane. She was an old resident of Mendon.

Olsen, Mr and Mrs J.L.   "Loraine"   Aug 13, 1891
     An infant of Mr and Mrs J.L. Olsen was buried August 12th.

Olson, Miss Jessie   "Obituary"   Jul 14, 1898
     died- Miss Jessie Olson, daughter of Mr and Mrs John Olson of
     615 Spruce St. Quincy died July 8th at 11:30 A.M. 21 yrs old. Left
     a mother and sister.

Olson, Ole   "Local"   Feb 7, 1901
Ole Olson, son of John Olson of Honey Creek who was killed while at
work as a brakman on the Southern Pacific R.R. was buried in Mendon
cemetery Sunday.

Olson, Mrs John   "Death"   Jan 27, 1904
see Bixby, Mrs

Omer, Mrs C.   "Tioga"   Apr 13, 1893
Died- Mrs C. Omer Monday March 27th at 5 P.M.. 66 yrs old. Leaves 3
children. Services by Rev Ott. Buried in the Lutheran cemetery Wed. P.M.

Omer, Geo. W.   "Camp Point"   Mar 30, 1882
Geo. W. Omer lost a son Friday night with typhoid fever.

Omer, Elder R.A.   "Obituary"   Nov 8, 1888
see Dewey, Lorenzo D.

Oolery, Mr P.   "Payson"   Jul 24, 1879
Mr P. Oolery, living northeast of here died on July 16th of consumption.
Also a child of Mr Ferris died on July 18th.

Opplt, Mrs Charles   "Obituary"   Jul 4, 1889
see Pepple, Catherine Sophia

Orr, Grayson   "Lima"   Dec 28, 1887
Grayson Orr, an old and respected citizen of Lima twp died at his home
December 14th. He was an old settler here. Born in Bourbon Co. Ky. in
1810 and came here in 1829. Leaves a wife, 3 sons and 1 daughter. Remains
buried in the Orr graveyard.

Orr, Hester   "Obituary"   Mar 13, 1890
see Nicholson, John

Orr, Miss Milly   "Death"   Jan 18, 1905
see Selby, Lewis V.

Orr, Morris   "Lima"   Feb 2, 1893
Died- on Sunday eve at 11 P.M. Morris, eldest son of Elizabeth Orr in
his 23rd yr from consumption. Services at the Christian church at
Marcelline by Elder Branic, of Canton, Mo.

Orr, Mr Savil   "Death"   Mar 23, 1882
see Eshorn, Mrs Sallie

Orr, Mr Savill   "Local"   Dec 7, 1887
Died- Mr Savill Orr, an old settler at his home in Lima twp about ¼
mile north of the Eshom school house Wednesday eve. Buried at the Stone
church cemetery near Ursa on Friday.

Orr, Mrs Wm   "Ursa"   Jan 16, 1902
Remains of Mrs Wm Orr of Quincy passed through here to Tioga for burial.

Osborn, Mrs Wm   "Obituary"   Apr 20, 1899
    see Myers, Mrs Anna Tinsman

Osborn, William   "Local"   Oct 29, 1903
    Died- William Osborn, the well known Quincy grocer Saturday A.M. from
    heart failure at his place of business at 615 Hampshire St. while
    talking to a friend. His wife is sister of Jacob T. and Lee Myers of
    Columbus, Mrs Frank Ogle of Paloma, John H. L.C., and the late C.C.
    Myers, Mrs F.F. Dudley and Mrs Jas. Evans of Mendon.

Osteman, Peter   "Local"   May 21, 1885
    10 yr old son of Peter Osteman of Golden was run over and killed May 15th
    while attempting to cross the line in front of a moving train.

Ott, Mrs   "Death"   Feb 9, 1899
    see Daugherty, Mrs Mary

Ott, Mrs Belle   "Death"   Jun 15, 1904
    see Leeper, Thomas Fletcher

Ott, Mr and Mrs Henry   "Death"   Jan 4, 1883
    see Leeper, Mrs

Ott, Henry   "Personal"   Jun 19, 1879
    Mr Henry Ott was called to St Louis last Saturday by the death of his
    mother.

Ott, Henry   "Local"   Jan 8, 1903
    Died- Mr Henry Ott, formerly a resident of this village at his home in
    Denver, Colo. December 24th. Leaves a wife and 2 sons.

Ott, Mrs Lizzie (Rev. P.)   "Tioga"   Jan 31, 1901
    Died- Mrs Lizzie Ott, wife of Rev. P. Ott suddenly at her home here
    Saturday January 19th. 37 yrs old. Fell down the cellar fracturing her
    skull and dide within 30 minutes. Services at the Evangelical church
    Monday P.M.   Rev Ott accompanied by his brother left Tuesday A.M. with
    the remains for burial at Kankakee, Ill her former home where she was
    buried beside her father.

Ottenstein, Barbara   "Estate"   May 13, 1880
    see Hartman, Alexander

Overbay, Mrs Anna   "Loraine"   Jun 9, 1892
    Died- on Sunday morning June 5th of consumption, Mrs Anna Overbay, age
    36 yrs. Leaves husband and a little girl, an aged mother and father, 2
    sisters and 3 brothers. Services by Rev Miller. Buried in our cemetery.

Overbay, Mrs Forence   "Obituary"   Jul 18, 1901
    see Kennedy, Geo. Thomas

Owen, Mrs Nellie   "Camp Point"   Jun 5, 1884
    Mrs Nellie Owen, wife of C.J. Owen of the railway mail service died
    May 29th. She was the daughter of the late Wm Farlow. She leaves husband
    and 2 small boys and her mother.

Owen, W.R.   "Local"   Sep 13, 1888
    Mr and Mrs Jacob Slonigar left for Quincy to attend the funeral of his old
    army comrade, Mr W.R. Owen's today.

Owens, Archibald   "Big Neck"   Jun 4, 1891
    Archibald Owens of Huston twp died May 27th.

Owens, Mrs T.S.   "Local"   Mar 3, 1886
    Mr and Mrs B.F. Slack were called to Quincy Monday for the funeral of
    Mr Slack's sister, Mrs T.S. Owens, who died in St Louis of heart disease on
    Saturday. She was 57 yrs old. Funeral was a the home of her daughter,
    Mrs A.C. Joseph at 168 North 3rd Street.

Owings, Howard W.   "Comm. Sale"   Jul 10, 1884
    Howard W. Owings, Thomas J.C. Owings, Samuel A. Owings, James R. Owings,
    and Margaret C. Baker, Complainants, vs Wm B. Jenkins, Wm H. Jenkins,
    Katie Jenkins, Belle Jenkins, Margaret Jenkins, Matilda Jenkins, Edward
    Jenkins, Nancy F. Lowery, Calphurnia E. Hardy, Geo. Harford, Sophia
    Moener, S.L. Waide, H.C. Nichols, Adm of Mathias Weidner, deceased.
    Howard W. Owings Adm. of Margaret Owings, deceased and the unkown heirs
    of Mathias Weidner, deceased' Partition #3504

Owings, Mr J.R.   "Local"   Apr 5, 1888
    Mr J.R. Owings, a former resident of this prairie died on Saturday at
    the home of Widow Baker's west of Mendon where he had gone to recover
    from injuries rec'd on the railroad at Quincy. Buried Monday at the
    Franklin church graveyard.
    CORRECTION-- J.R. Owings was born in Ohio 1844 and moved to this Co.
    with his father, Dr Owings in 1850 and died at his sisters, Mrs Baker
    in Quincy, Ill March 31st. Buried in Franklin cemetery April 2nd.
    signed Charles Tarr.

Owrey, Mrs A.   "Tioga"   Jan 11, 1900
    Died- a few miles southeast of Tioga at her home Saturday, Mrs A. Owrey
    Services by Rev Whisnant. Buried in our village cemetery Sunday afternoon.

Owrey, Thomas   "Killed"   Sep 15, 1892
    see Zopf, Adam

Owrie, Mr   "Lima"   Sep 15, 1892
    Mr Owrie, a farmer living south of Lima was killed by a train last
    Thursday night. Leaves wife and 4 children.

Packard, Mrs T.   "Local"   Mar 17, 1892
  Died- Mrs T. Packard, formerly of Quincy and Mendon at Pasadena, Calif.
  March 5th of consumption. Leavibg husband and 4 children. She was a
  sister of George M. and P.S. Janes of this city. "Quincy Herald"

Page, Mr_____   "Payson"   Apr 7, 1881
  Died a man named Page, who lived about 4 miles north of here. Was buried
  here last Saturday.

Palmer, J.C.   Feb 27, 1890
  Died- Mr J.C. Palmer of Quincy at the home of his daughter, Mrs Weems.
  Was 81 yrs old. Mr Palmer was brother-in-law to Mr Henry Baldwin of
  Mendon. Buried at Woodland cemetery.

Palmer, Mrs J.C.   Nov 21, 1889
  Mrs J.C. Palmer died at the home of her daughter at 1641 Hampshire St.
  on November 19th at the age of 81 yrs. She left 2 children, Mrs J.E. Weems
  at whose home she died and Mrs W.W. Barr of Buffalo, N.Y. Mrs Palmer was
  a sister of H.B. Baldwin of Mendon and of New England origin.

Pape, Mrs Mary Ann   "Quincy"   Mar 16, 1899
  Died- Mrs Mary Ann Pape Sunday of old age. Over 80 yrs old.

Paramore, Mr Geo.   "Loraine"   Aug 25, 1892
  Mr Geo. Paramore and his sister Lizzie were called to Fairfield, Iowa
  last Saturday to attend the funeral of their father's brother. He was 75
  yrs old and the last survivor of a family of 9 children.

Paramore, Mr and Mrs George   "Loraine"   Mar 17, 1892
  20 month old child of Mr and Mrs George Paramore died last Friday of
  brain fever. Buried Sunday P.M.

Paramore, Mr J.O.   "Loraine"   Jun 6, 1889
  Died- Mr J.O. Paramore at his residence Thursday May 30th. His brother
  died at his residence May 15th. Services at the M.E. church by Rev.
  Biggs. Buried Loraine cemetery. Was nearly 65 yrs òld. Leaves a wife,
  2 sons and 2 daughters. Youngest son lives in California and was not
  present for funeral.

Paramore, J.O.   "Loraine"   May 23, 1889
  Died- brother of J.O. Paramore here. He had just arrived here from the
  west to visit J.O. and died within a week from lung fever. Buried in
  Fort Madison Thursday. Was about 75 yrs old.

Parish, Mr J.B.   "Local"   Dec 8, 1886
  Died- Mr J.B. Parish, formerly known in Quincy in the insurance business
  Friday in Jacksonville. Leaves a wife and 2 daughters, Mrs Bane, wife of
  General Bane and Miss Lizzie K. Parish.

Parish, Mrs Jeanette   "Obituary"   Jun 20, 1901
  see Seals, Dennis

Parker, Mrs Anna L.   "Local"   Aug 31, 1899
    Died- Mrs Anna L. Parker and Mrs Mary Homan, two old residents of Quincy
    died this week.

Parker, Mrs E.J.   "News"   Oct 22, 1885
    Quincy suffered a great loss last week in the death of Mrs E.J. Parker.

Parker, Mrs Emma   "Columbus"   Oct 19, 1887
    Mrs Emma Parker died last Friday eve. Leaves a husband.

Parker, Henry(Rev.)   "Local"   Oct 29, 1891
    Rev. Henry Parker of Honolulu, Sandwich Islands, pastor of the native
    church there made a short visit to relatives in Mendon. His mother who
    is 85 yrs old is a sister of the late Mrs Lyman Frisbie. Mr Parker was
    born in the Marquesas Islands in 1832. Mr Parker Sr. has been dead
    several yrs.

Parker, Mrs Margaret   "Death"   Aug 16, 1894
    see Kendrick, Wm

Parker, Wm   "Columbus"   Feb 10, 1886
    The infant child of Wm Parker was buried Saturday. It was found dead
    in bed.

Parkhurst, Jonathan   "Local"   Sep 20, 1905
    Jonathan Parkhurst, one of Quincy's clothier's died Sunday A.M. Had been
    ailing for some time.

Parks, Mrs   "Ursa"   Nov 19, 1891
    Funeral of Mrs Parks of Quincy passed thru here yesterday. Deceased
    was buried in the Stone church cemetery.

Parson, Mr Charles   "Payson"   Jan 22, 1880
    Mr Charles Parson, living south of here lost a child last Wednesday.
    It was a grandchild of Eli Seehorn, deceased.

Parson, Flin   "Big Neck"   Oct 2, 1890
    Flin Parson's died this morning of typhoid fever.

Paton, Mr   "Ursa"   Apr 30, 1885
    Mr Paton of Marcelline died April 25th. Buried Ursa.

Paton, Mr   "Marcelline"   Apr 30, 1885
    Mr Paton of Marcelline died Saturday night and was buried Ursa cemetery
    Sunday afternoon.

Patterson, Mrs   "Local"   Apr 21, 1886
    Mr David McCarl rec'd a message on Saturday night of the death by
    drowning of his sister, Mrs Patterson and her grandson, about 2 miles
    from Ossawattomie, Kansas.

Patterson, Old Lady   "Local"   Mar 21, 1895
    Died- "Old Lady" Patterson of Marcelline Monday at 9 A.M. Age 76 yrs.
    Buried next day. Her son-in-law, Sam Gerard and her daughter, Mrs Thomas
    Hunter of Stronghurst was in Mendon Monday to purchase the casket.

Patterson, W.A.   "Local"   Jul 27, 1887
    The Carthage paper contained the obituary notice last week for W.A.
    Patterson, a pioneer farmer, merchant and hotel keeper of Hancock Co.
    77 yrs old. He was of English puritan and Revolitionary linage.

Patterson, Wm C.   "Sudden Death"   Dec 14, 1882
    Wm C. Patterson, cousin of John W. Richards of Ursa twp died December
    11th. He was 45 yrs old and had lived at Clay Co. Mo. Leaves no family.

Patton, Dr Ella   "Quincy"   Feb 23, 1899
    Died- Dr Ella Patton, one of Quincy's leading Dr's in St Lukes hospital
    St Louis Thursday A.M. 38 yrs old. Was visiting friends in St Louis.

Paye, Gracy   "Big Neck"   Jan 12, 1882
    Died- Gracy, daughter of Mrs Paye.

Payne, Miss Catherine Ann   "Obituary"   May 18, 1904
    Miss Catherine Ann Payne was born May 6, 1829 and died at the home of her
    sister, Mrs Mary Thietten May 14th 1904. Was 75 yrs 8 days old. Early in
    life she met with an accident which caused her to lose her eyesight.
    Leaves 4 sisters, Mrs Mary Thietten of Loraine, Mrs Barbary Woods of
    Woodville, Mrs Phebe Hudson of Cassville, Mo. and Mrs Nancy Thurman of
    Shelbyville, Ind. Funeral at the house Sunday 10 A.M. by Rev C.S.
    Baughman. Buried in Woodville cemetery.

Payne, Mrs Mary   Feb 14, 1884
    Died- Feb. 10th, Mrs Mary Payne, wife of Thos. Payne of Quincy. Aged
    50 yrs. Daughter of Mr and Mrs John Denson of Ursa.

Payne, Thomas   "Local"   Aug 31, 1899
    Daniel Nutt's hearse was sent to Ursa Friday to meet the train to
    convey the body of Thomas Payne, deceased, to the Stone cemetery where it
    was placed in the family vault. He died at Eureka Springs, Ark. Wednesday
    August 23rd. Age 85 yrs and was an old pioneer of this Co.

Pearce, Mr   "Burial"   Jul 27, 1893
    see Donley, Henry

Pearce, Augustus F.   "Local"   Jan 25, 1905
    Augustus F. Pearce, father of Co. clerk Pearce died Monday A.M. at the
    home of his son of old age. 80 yrs old.

Pearce, Mrs Augustus F.   "Local"   Sep 7, 1904
    Died- Mrs Augustus F. Pearce, mother of Co. clerk J.R. Pearce suddenly
    at the latters home in Quincy Monday eve. Leaves husband, 4 children and a
    brother, Samuel Woods, attorney and 7 sisters.

Pearce, David   "Obituary"   Dec 28, 1877
    Gilmer- December 20, 1877 Died- David Pearce at his residence in Gilmer
    twpof cancer of the liver on Sunday eve December 16th. Born Baltimore Co.
    Maryland March 18, 1807. Married Elizabeth Stabler February 27, 1829.
    They moved to Butler Co. Ohio in 1835 and bought a farm where they lived
    until 1848 when they moved to Adams Co. and settled in Gilmer twp. He
    was a life long democrat. Joined the M.E. church as a young man. All his
    children were with him at his death. Leaves wife and __ children.

Pearson, Mrs Clara   "Ursa"   Jan 26, 1888
    Died- Mrs Clara Pearson of Hannibal, wife of John Pearson, formerly a
    resident here died. Buried here Saturday at the family cemetery on the
    farm of R.F. Stone.

Pearson, Clara S.   "Probate"   Mar 22, 1888
    Probate notice of Clara S. Pearson, deceased 1st Monday of May 1888
    A.M. Castle, Adm.

Pearson, Frank   "Death"   Jun 12, 1884
    see Norton, Mrs Mary A.

Pearson, Sister J.B.   "Local"   Jan 5, 1887
    Sister J.B. Pearson was buried December 29th 1886. May her children be
    comforted. A.A. Berry, Pastor

Pearson, John C.   "Probate"   Nov 16, 1882
    Probate Notice of John C. Pearson, deceased 3rd Monday of January 1883
    Josephine B. Pearson, Adm.

Pearson, Dr John C.   "Died"   Oct 26, 1882
    Dr John C. Pearson was born November 25, 1825 in Norfork, Va. and died
    in Ursa October 22nd 1882 in his 57th yr. He started studying for his
    profession about 1847 under Dr M.W. Hall of Mo. Came to Illinois and
    began practice in 1855. Leaves wife and 5 children.

Pearson, Mrs Josie   "Ursa"   Dec 29, 1886
    Died- Mrs Josie Pearson at her home Decmeber 27th. Funeral 11 A.M.
    at the Christian church.

Pearson, Josephine B.   "Adm Sale"   Mar 2, 1887
    Adminstrator's sale March 29th personal property belonging to the late
    Josephine B. Pearson. M.C. Varnier, Adm.

Pearson, Miss Mary   "Death"   Mar 28, 1889
    see Nichols, G.M.

Pearson, S.D.   Aug 18, 1881
    Died- August 14th 1881 S.D. Pearson at age 81 yrs. Born New Jersey.

Pearson, Sarah   "Stillwell"   Jan 5, 1882
    Mrs R. Heaton attended the funeral of her sister, Sarah Pearson of
    Ursa last Saturday.

Pecare, Ike   "Personal"   Aug 26, 1880
    Rec'd a card from Ike Pecare of Peabody, Kansas saying that Mrs Bodine,
    his mother in law died a few days ago of apoplexy.

Peet, Joseph B.   "Local"   Apr 2, 1891
    Rev Dr Peet was called to Beloit, Wisc. last Thursday to the sick bed of
    his brother who died before he arrived. Joseph B. Peet, a pioneer
    resident and business man of Beloit died this A.M. from spinal meningitis
    at the age of 60 yrs. He had been in business in Beloit 37 yrs. Was sick
    only a few days.'

Pence, Wm   "Camp Point"   Mar 11, 1880
    Died- Wm Pence, an old resident of this twp last week of consumption.
    Leaves a wife and a grown son and daughter in comfortable circumstances.

Pendleton, Mrs   "Stringtown"   Jun 9, 1886
    Mrs Clara Clyne of this place is a niece of Francis S. Key, the author
    of the Star Spangled Banner and a cousin of Mrs Pendleton who was
    killed a few days ago in N.Y.

Penfield, Sylvester G.   "Camp Point"   Jul 10, 1879
    Died- Sylvester G. Penfield, one time bookeeper for the W.L. Oliver Co.
    and later the Alden Co. at Fowler died Monday eve from consumption.
    Leaves an aged mother.

Penick, Mr D.   "Tioga"   Mar 30, 1893
    Died- at his home in Hamilton March 20th Mr D. Penick, age 54 yrs.
    Services by Rev Wheeler. Buried in Tioga cemetery Wednesday P.M. Leaves
    a wife and 3 children.

Pepple, Mr   "Local"   Jul 27, 1893
    James, Ella and Pheme Pepple arrived from Elgin to see their sick father.
    Mr ___ Pepple died yesterday at 3 P.M. Buried this P.M. in the Mendon
    cemetery. Services at the Lutheran church by Rev Wm Burgess. Age 71 yrs.

Pepple, Mrs C.W.   "Obituary"   May 5, 1898
    see Wright, Albert

Pepple, Catherine Sophia   "Obituary"   Jul 4, 1889
    Died- Catherine Sophia Pepple, wife of John H. Pepple of heart disease
    Wednesday eve June 26th Born Emmettsburg, Frederick Co. Maryland
    February 19, 1830. Married June 8, 1848. Came with her husband in October
    1858 to Mendon where she has lived since. 14 children were born to them.
    11 still living and all except Mrs Armor of Farmington, Kansas were present
    for the funeral. The others are, Mrs Senior of Cleveland, Ohio, Mrs
    Charles Opplt of Venton, Benton Co. Iowa, Mrs Ed Sheldon of Traer, Tama Co.
    Iowa, Mrs Vandenburg, Ella, Edward and James from Elgin, Ill., Wm C.
    John H. Jr. and Pheme all of Mendon. Services at the Lutheran church
    Saturday by Rev J.W. Thomas assisted by Rev R.P. Droke. Buried in Mendon
    cemetery.

310

Pepple, Eldon   "Obituary"   Mar 30, 1899
    Eldon, the eldest son of Mr and Mrs J.H. Pepple died Monday night at 8
    of spinal meningitis. Born Mendon March 25, 1876. Member of the M.E.
    church. Buried village cemetery.

Pepple, Mrs J.H.   "Obituary"   Jan 4, 1904
    see Strickler, David W.

Pepple, John   Soldier list   Jun 1, 1899
    John Pepple listed in list of Soldiers graves decorated Memorial day.

Pepple, John H.   "Obituary"   Aug 3, 1893
    Died- John H. Pepple born December 28, 1822 at Emmettsburg, Frederick Co.
    Maryland and married Catherine Sophia Dyler June 8, 1848 at Millerstown,
    Penn. Moved to Mendon in 1857 and died at Mendon, Ill. July 25, 1893. He
    has 11 children surviving him, of these Wm C. and family of Mendon and
    Ella, Phemia and Alonzo of Elgin attended the funeral. Other girls live
    to far away to come.

Pepple, Mrs John   "Local"   Jun 27, 1889
    Died- Mrs John Pepple last night of heart disease.

Pepple, Mrs Mary   "Died"   Apr 24, 1879
    Died- Sunday April 20th Mrs Mary, wife of Wm Pepple of Mendon in her 61st
    yr. Been sick for some time and was operated on in Quincy last winter by
    Dr Curtis. Returned home 2 weeks ago. Services by Rev A.B. Campbell at
    4 P.M. Monday. She had lived in Mendon a quarter of a century. Member of
    Christian church. Leaves husband and children.

Pepple, Vinetta   "Died"   Nov 20, 1879
    Died on Tuesday morning November 18th of diptheritic croup, Vinetta,
    youngest child of John and Catherine Pepple. Age 4 yrs 7 mo's. Services
    at the house and at the Lutheran church by Rev G.F. Behringer.

Perine, Miss Phebe   "Obituary"   May 10, 1888
    see Barclay, Daniel

Perry, Meredith   "Lima"   Jun 22, 1893
    Meredith Perry's 6 yr old child was scalded to death a few days ago by
    falling into boiling water where it's mother was washing.

Perry, James   "Marcelline"   Nov 2, 1893
    Funeral of James Perry, an old resident of this place was last Saturday
    afternoon at Oak Ridge cemetery. Services by the Marcelline lodge #114
    A.F. & A.M. of which he was a member since 1859. Leaves a wife.

Perry, James   "Lima"   Nov 2, 1893
    Mr and Mrs Geo. Davis attended the funeral of their uncle, Mr James Perry
    at the Beatly cemetery last Saturday.
    NOTE: different cemteries listed on James.

Persels, Rowland   "Real estate sale"   May 3, 1894
    see Johnson, John H.

311

Peter, Joseph   "Payson"   Feb 20, 1879
    A child of Mr Joseph Peter's west of Payson died February 15th of
    membranous.

Peters, Mr   "Payson"   Apr 28, 1881
    Two men by the names of Rederick and Peters of the Sny Bottoms had some
    trouble yesterday which ended in the former killing the latter with a
    club, the two men were brother-in-laws.

Peyton, Mrs Delia   "Loraine"   Nov 21, 1901
    J.C. Rogers rec'd telegram November 19th which told him of the death of
    his sister, Mrs Delia Peyton of Louisburgh, Kansas. She had been unable to
    leave her bed for almost a year.

Peyton, John   "Camp Point"   Jan 12, 1882
    Died- John Peyton, medical student at Keokuk while homw here, Jan. 6th

Peyton, Mr Wm   "Marcelline"   Apr 30, 1885
    Died- at his home in Marcelline on Saturday night, Mr Wm Peyton, age 94
    years.

Pfanschmidt, H.   "Columbus and Gilmer" Feb 19, 1891
    Mr's Geo. Norris, Wm Hair, L.E. Finley, A. Lohse, James Skirvin, D.L.
    Wilhoit, James Arhcraft, Stacy Furgeson, G. Haley of Columbus lodge of
    IOOF's attended the funeral of brother H. Pfanschmidt of Burton who was
    buried at Burton by the order of the Odd Fellows.

Pfanschmidt, H.C.   "Quincy"   Apr 20, 1899
    Died- H.C. Pfanschmidt was found dead in his barn Tuesday A.M. Born
    Prussia March 8, 1825. Leaves 6 children.

Pfanschmidt, Hemry E.   Feb 5, 1891
    Mr Henry E. Pfanschmidt of Newtown, Ill. died February 2nd. He was
    32 yrs old and was born in Ellington twp. Is the son of C.C. Pfanschmidt
    Leaves wife and 4 small children.

Pfeiffer, Phillip   "Local"   May 17, 1894
    Phillip Pfeiffer, of Melrose twp drowned at Kate's lake, 4 miles below
    Quincy on Monday afternoon by falling from a skiff while running a
    trot line.

Phelps, Mark   "Local"   Apr 24, 1884
    A man named Mark Phelps was drowned in the river north of Quincy on
    Thursday.

Philips, Mrs   "Fowler"   Jan 17, 1895
    Mrs Philips who has been sick some time died Monday A.M. Services at
    the M.E. church Thursday January 10th at 2 P.M. by Rev Hartick.

Phirman, Mrs   "Obituary"   Jun 5, 1884
    see Grigsby, Mrs Irene

Pickens, Charles E.   "Local"   Aug 1, 1901
    Died- Charles E. Pickens Tuesday at 11:30 P.M. Leaves parents and an only
    sister. Funeral at the M.E. church at 2 P.M. today.

Pickens, Charles Henry   "Obituary"   Aug 8, 1901
    Died- Charles Henry Pickens, only son of Mr and Mrs Edward Pickens.
    Born Augusta, Ill. January 11, 1882 died July 30th 1901 age 19 yrs
    6 mo's 19 days. Services at the M.E. church Thursday P.M. by Rev S.N.
    Wakefield. Buried Mendon cemetery. Leaves parents and a sister. Pallbearer
    were, Abe Baldwin, Charles and Henry Evans, Joseph Dickerman, Adelbert
    Austin and Charles McIntyre. Attending from a distance were, Mr Geo.
    Pickens and daughter Abbie Lois Pickens, Mrs Ed Gorden of Augusta, Mr and
    Mrs Grant Stewart of Camden, Mr and Mrs Henry Sterwart and daughter of
    Plymouth, Mr and Mrs Frank Morrison of Marcelline and Mr and Mrs Al White,
    of Rock Creek.

Pieper, Jos   "Death"   Nov 11, 1880
    Died- Jos. Pieper, a well known citizen of Quincy was drowned accidentally
    near the mouth of North River, Marion Co. Mo. one day last week.

Pierce,   Dec 8, 1881
    The body of Pierce was found drowned November 25th 1881. No fowl play
    It had been in the water 25 days.

Pierce, E.O. and N.M.   "Obituary"   May 31, 1900
    see Foltz, Martha C.

Pierce, Mrs James   "Payson"   Jan 11, 1883
    Died- January 4th, Mrs James Pierce of heart disease.

Pierce, Martha C.   "Obituary"   May 31, 1900
    see Foltz, Martha C.

Pierce, Mrs Nancy A.   "Payson"   Apr 3, 1879
    Died- March 26th at the residence of her son, Mrs Nancy A., wife of
    James Pierce, Sr. Deceased was in her 69th yr. Born Garrett Co. Ky.
    Was converted in 1848, united with the Baptist church. Services by Rev
    Huntly of the Baptist church.

Pierce, Mrs Will   "Obituary"   Aug 24, 1904
    see Foster, Mrs Eliza Ann

Pierson, Dr   Nov 28, 1878
    Murdered- Dr Pierson, an old resident of Augusta was found dead with his
    head crushed beside the road near Augusta, Hancock Co. last Saturday eve.

Pierson, Frank   "Mt Pleasant"   Jun 12, 1884
    Frank Pierson died May 29th in Idaho. He was the son of Mrs Mary A. Norton.

Pierson, Robert Franklin   Jun 19, 1884
    Died at the Palace Hotel in Ketchum, Idaho June 3rd, Robert Franklin
    Pierson age 22 yrs 1 mo. of typhoid pneumonia. Born Mendon, Ill. Adams Co.
    where his mother and grandmother now reside. Lived Ketchum 2 yrs.
    Butied from the M.E. church in _____

Piggott, John   "Quincy"   Mar 9, 1899
    Died- Mr John Piggott, a native of Ireland, an employe of the Wabash R.R.
    Died Saturday eve of congestion of the lungs. Born 1839 and came to
    Quincy 1856. Leaves a wife, son and daughter.

Pilcher, Eliza A.   "Obituary"   Dec 28, 1893
   Died- Eliza A. Pilcher. Born in Athens Co. Ohio May 10, 1822. Came to
   Green Co. Ill. in 1828 and from there to this Co. where she married
   Daniel crow February 6, 1842. They had 5 children, 2 daughters and 3 sons.
   1 daughter and her husband preceeded her in death. She was a member of the
   M.E. church. She died December 12th at the age of 71 yrs 7 mo's 2 days.
   Leaves 2 sons and 1 daughter and 7 grandchildren. Services from the
   residence and was buried beside her husband in Stahl cemetery.

Pilcher, Miss Rachel   "Obituary"   Sep 9, 1880
   see Thompson, Wm

Piles, Mrs Lucinda   "Tioga"   Mar 1, 1888
   Died- February 17th, Mrs Lucinda Piles in her 41st yr. Leaves husband,
   son, daughter, sister and mother.

Pippitt, Mrs A.R.   "Obituary"   May 19, 1886
   see Ellis, Horatio T.

Pitman, Johnny   "Loraine"   Mar 7, 1889
   Died- Little Johnny, second son of Lewis and Phebe Pitman died Saturday
   A.M. and was buried in Curless cemetery Monday P.M. Funeral at Reece
   schoolhouse by Rev Lierly, of Liberty. He was always kind to his brothers
   ans sisters. He was 8 yrs 6 days old.

Pitney, Warren F.   "Estate Sale"   May 13, 1880
   see Hartman, Alexander

Pittman, Mr and Mrs Henry "Death"   Jan   1891
   see Hardy, Mrs Ben

Platt, Mr Enoch   Apr 30, 1891
   Mr Enoch Platt died April 12th at Westminster, Calif. Age 66 yrs. He was
   the second son of Deacon Jirch Platt of Mendon. He left Mendon 30 yrs ago
   to go to Wabannsee, Kansas where he lived until spring when he moved to
   Westminster.

Platt, George   "Died"   Jan 2, 1879
   Mr George Platt, son of Prof. J.E. Platt of Manhatten, Kansas died Dec 27th
   1878 at Oberlin, Ohio of typhoid fever. He had just entered college.

Platt, Rev H.D.   "Obituary"   Mar 5, 1903
   Died- Rev H.D. Platt who for 2 yrs was an invalid ,at his home in Franklin
   Nebr. Tuesday February 3rd about 9 P.M. He was 79 yrs 6 mo's 21 days old.
   Harry Dutton Platt was eldest of 8 children of which only 1 survive him.
   Born in Plymouth, Conn. July 13, 1823. Family came west in 1833 and settled
   on a farm near Mendon, Ill. Converted at age 12 yrs and joined Mendon
   Cong'l church. Married Sarah E. Stratton Feb. 5, 1852 and they had seven
   children, only 3 lived to grow up. Mrs Z.T. Kemper, whose buried in our
   cemetery, Mrs W.A. Harshbarger of Topeka, Kansas and Herman Platt of
   Franklin. Services at Franklin, Nebr. Cong'l church.

Plunkett, Miss Julia   "Obituary"   Jul 26, 1888
    see Potter, Dr J.W.

Poetsch, Miss Della   "Quincy"   Apr 6, 1899
    Died- Miss Della Poetsch of typhoid fever Tuesday March 28th. Had been
    employed as a typewriter at the Tremont House.

Poland, Minnie   "Local"   Nov 1, 1894
    A sad tragedy occured near Clayton last Thursday, Leonard Poland, a
    cripple was amusing himself shooting at a target while his sister Minnie
    Age 18 yrs, kept score when his gun went off entering her brain and
    killing her.

Poling, Mrs   Jun 2, 1881
    Mrs Poling died May 27th. She leaves a large family. She was an early
    settler.

Poling, Charles   "Obituary"   Apr 20, 1899
    "Hamilton Press" Died- Charles Poling March 25th 1899 at his residence
    in Hamilton. Born Brooklyn, N.Y. Feb 4, 1823. Was 76 yrs 1 mo and 19 days
    old. Joined Brooklyn Missionary Baptist church at 19 yrs. Was a member of
    the Masonic and Odd Fellows. Buried in Hamilton cemetery Monday March 27th
    Services by Rev Joseph Hart. In 1838 he with his family moved to Mendon,
    Adams Co. Ill. remaining a resident of that Co. until 1856 when he moved
    to Hancock Co. and located in Wythe twp. Married October 5, 1843 at Mendon
    to Ann Lakin who survives him. They had 8 children (2 are dead) Mr Poling
    is a borther to W.P. Poling of Mendon.

Poling, Charles   "Obituary"   Mar 21, 1889
    see Higbie, Mrs Edmund

Poling, Charles   "Personal"   Feb 12, 1880
    Mr Charles Poling, formerly of Mendon twp, but late of Quincy arrived
    here Saturday afternoon bringing the body of his little son for burial.
    Services were held Sunday A.M.

Poling, Mr E.   "Coatsburg"   Jun 24, 1880
    Mr E. Poling's babe was buried last Thursday.

Poling, Elijah   "News"   Oct 20, 1886
    see Wilcox, Mrs Ducilla

Poling, Eugene   "Died"   Sep 30, 1880
    Died- on Tuesday morning September 28th, Eugene, youngest son of Mr and
    Mrs T.C. Poling of diptheria. Age 7 yrs.

Poling, Geo.   "Graves"   Jun 4, 1885
    Soldiers graves decorated Memorial day included Geo. Poling in Mendon
    cemetery.

Poling, Geo.   "Obituary"   Mar 21, 1889
    see Higbie, Mrs Edmund

Poling, Hannah (Wm)   Mar 26, 1891
    Hannah (Battell) Poling died March 19th. She was married August 22, 1872 to
    Wm A. Poling and they had 9 children. Services at Methodist church by
    Rev F.C. Read. Buried Mendon cemetery.

Poling, Hannah M.   "Adm Sale"   Jun 17, 1880
    see Battell, Richard

Poling, James   "Graves"   Jun 4, 1885
    Soldiers graves decorated in Mendon cemetery Decoration day included
    James Poling.

Poling, Lulu   "Local"   Dec 22, 1886
    Lulu, 4 yr old daughter of Wm and Hannah Poling died Thursday at noon
    of typhoid fever. Buried Saturday afternoon in Mendon cemetery. Services
    by Rev R.P. Droke of the M.E. church.

Poling, Mrs Luscius   "Loraine"   Sep 7, 1904
    Funeral of Mrs Luscius Poling of West Point was preached here Thursday
    A.M. and buried Loraine cemetery.

Poling, Mrs Lydia Ann   Jul 9, 1891
    Death of Mrs Lydia Ann Poling, wife of W.P. Poling Esqr. July 2nd.
    Services at the house by Rev. F.C. Read assisted by Rev White. She was
    born Lydia Ann Powell May 30, 1818 in Queens Co. Long Island, New York
    She married March 18th 1839 to Wm P. Poling and on June 5 of that same
    year they moved to Illinois. Was mother of 9 children. 5 boys and 4 girls.
    4 preceeded her in death.

Poling, Mary Ann   "Obituary"   Dec 7, 1893
    see Higbie, Squire Edmund

Poling, Mary Ann   "Obituary"   Mar 21, 1889
    see Higbie, Mrs Edmund

Poling, Mrs Rachel (C.D.)   "Loraine"   Dec 9, 1880
    Died- December 5th 1880, Mrs Rachel Poling, wife of C.D. Poling at age
    36 yrs. Leaves husband and 2 children. Funeral services at the M.E. church
    by Rev Stagle.

Poling, Mr and Mrs Sam   "Loraine"   Mar 1, 1905
    An infant child of Mr and Mrs Sam Poling was buried here last week.

Poling, Mrs Wm   "Graves"   Jun 22, 1899
    Graves decorated in Mendon cemetery included Mrs Wm Poling.

Poling, Mrs Wm A.   Mar 26, 1891
    Mrs Swain Gibbs of Fall Creek came to attend the funeral of her sister,
    Mrs Wm A. Poling, but arrived to late for it.

Poling, Wykoff   "Local"   Oct 4, 1888
    News rec'd by Squire Higbie Monday night of the death of his brother-in-
    law, Mr Wykoff Poling.

316

Pollock, Mr and Mrs   "Local"   Oct 23, 1890
    The three yr old son of Mr and Mrs Pollock died October 21st. He fell
    into a pan of scalding water.

Pollock, John   "Probate"   Apr 20, 1882
    Probate Notice of John Pollock, deceased 1st Monday of June 1882
    Joseph Pollock, Adm.

Pollock, Mrs Joseph   "Local"   Sep 1, 1898
    Died- Mrs Pollock, relict of the late Joseph Pollock of Honey Creek twp
    died Tuesday A.M. Buried today in Mendon cemetery.

Pollock, Mrs Margaret   "Obituary"   Apr 2, 1903
    see Long, Mrs Elizabeth Ann

Pomroy, Caleb M.   "Local"   Mar 30, 1887
    Death of Caleb M. Pomroy last week. Age 77 yrs. Quincy loses one of her
    best citizens who was identified with her early history.

Pond, Dr   "Camp Point"   Sep 5, 1901
    The funeral of Dr Pond was held Sunday by the Masons. He was 92 yrs old
    and had lost his mind and become nearly blind. Buried village cemetery.

Pond, Mr Geo. P.   "Local"   Dec 15, 1898
    Rev W.J. Spire was called to Liberty last Thursday to conduct the funeral
    services of Mr Geo. P. Pond, uncle of Prof. Collins.

Pope, Thomas   "Local"   Apr 26, 1900
    Died- Thomas Pope an old citizen of Quincy Saturday. He came to Quincy
    in 1837. Owned the flouring mill in that city and for 25 yrs was in the
    agricultural implement business. Leaves a wife and 2 children.

Porter, Mrs Ellen (Sanford) "Died"   Jun 17, 1880
    Died- Tuesday June 15th, Mrs Ellen Porter, wife of Sanford Porter of
    Honey Creek. Age 40 yrs.

Porter, Mrs Sanford   "Local"   Mar 3, 1886
    Mrs Sanford Porter's little boy died on Sunday night. He had attended
    school on Friday. Cause of death was pneumonia, bilious colic and
    injury to the spine. Funeral was yesterday.
    In same paper later. The name of the little colored boy whose death was
    noticed in another column was Jackson, being a son of Mrs Porter by a
    former husband. He was in the 1st primary dept. Services by Rev Howard
    Miller of the M.E. church.

Potter, Mrs Charles   "Payson"   May 6, 1880
    Rumor says that Mrs Charles Potter, formerly Miss Effie Grissom, who
    married some time ago and living in Kansas is dead.

Potter, Emma   "Obituary"   Apr 25, 1895
    see Hardy, Mrs Emma

Potter, Dr J.W.   "Obituary"   Jul 26, 1888
    Died- lat week at his home in Quincy on Tuesday July 17th, Dr J.W.
    Potter from disease of the kidneys of long standing.
    "Quincy Herald" Dr Potter was born in New Brunswick in May 1821 and
    spent his early yrs in Eastport, Maine and in Mass. In 1851 he settled in
    Mendon. In Camden, Schuyler Co. Ill. he married Miss Julia Plunkett.
    They had 2 sons, Edgar S. and J.W. Potter. He leaves wife and 2 sons. He
    was a private in Co. B. 3rd Missouri Cavalary and out June 1865. Was
    member of the Christian church. Services held under the IOOF and GAR

Potter, John   "Local"   Sep 4, 1884
    Death of John Potter of Quincy September 1st. Age 72 yrs. Born in New
    Hampshire. Settled in Quincy 1840. Leaves a wife and 2 children.

Potter, Mrs John   "News"   Sep 23, 1880
    Died- Mrs John Potter who lived 2½ miles north of Fowler of consumption
    last Sunday morning. She was an old resident of the twp.

Potter, Mrs Minnie   "Obituary"   Nov 11, 1897
    see Miller, Mrs Mary Jane

Potter, Mrs Rebecca Jane   "Tioga"   Sep 15, 1886
    Died- September 9th in Lima twp Mrs Rebecca Jane Potter at age 41 yrs
    1 mo. 15 days. Born in Martinsville, Ind. and married to Sylvester Potter
    December 12, 1862. Lived in Illinois 24 yrs. Joined Christian church about
    18 yrs ago. Leaves husband and 4 children. Buried Tioga cemetery September
    10th Services by Elder Michaels.

Potter, S.M.   "Obituary"   Apr 25, 1895
    see Hardy, Mrs Emma

Potter, Mrs Sarah   "Loraine"   Dec 24, 1903
    Article dated December 14th-- Mrs Sarah Potter was buried here Tuesday
    Leaves 5 children, 2 boys and 3 girls. She was daughter of Mr and Mrs Jas.
    Dearwester. Also leaves parents and 4 sisters and 2 brothers.

Poulter, Mr R.   "Ursa"   Feb 21, 1895
    Died- Remains of Mr R. Poulter passed thru town Monday eve on the way to
    Lima for burial. Deceased was the father of John Poulter.

Powel, Miss Nancy   "Obituary"   Oct 5, 1899
    see Rue, Rev. Jonathan

Powell, Mrs   "Honey Creek"   Apr 6, 1887
    4 funerals at Coatsburg last week. Mrs Jasper White, Mrs Schlipmannn,
    Mrs Rittler and Mrs Powell. The services for Mrs Powell were conducted
    at Paloma and brought here for burial.

Powell, Geo. W.   "Herald"   Mar 1, 1900
    Died- Geo. W. Powell, one of the oldest and earliest residents of this Co.
    died at his home at Fowler at 2 A.M. Tuesday. He came here in 1832 and
    was over 90 yrs old. He was a well to do farmer. Had 1 son who resided
    with him on the farm. another in Ellington and the 3rd at Bentley. 2
    daughters, Mrs John C. Pearce of Bowen and another married daughter
    living in Missouri.

Powell, John Thomas   "Obituary"   Feb 14, 1889
     Died- John Thomas Powell was born August 14,1843 in Clark Co. Mo.
     and died February 5th 1889 near Bowen, Ill. of congestion of the lungs.
     Came to Illinois with his people and settled in Adams Co. Married Miss
     Louise Booth of Adams Co. February 17, 1870 where they lived until spring
     of 1881 when they moved to a farm near Bowen. A few weeks after Mrs Powell
     died on April 7, 1881. They had one son living. He married 2nd to Mrs
     Mary C. Wisner of near Bowen January 31, 1883. To them 1 daughter was born
     and yet living. Leaves wife. He was a member of the Methodist church
for almost 8 yrs. Buried near Fowler, Ill his old home.

Powell, Mrs L.M.   "Obituary"   Apr 14, 1881
     Mrs L.M. Powell died Wednesday April 6th at 2 P.M. leaves husband and
     1 child. -- Notice sent in by her cousin, Wm P. Aron of Bowensburg, Ill.

Powell, Miss Lydia   "Obituary"   Jul 9, 1891
     see Poling, Mrs Lydia Ann

Powell, Mrs Rosa   "Loraine"   Dec 6, 1900
     Mrs Rosa Powell (nee Cates) drank carbolic acid yesterday thru mistake
     or otherwise.

Powell, Mrs T.   "Mendon"   Apr 7, 1881
     Died- wife of Mr T. Powell late of Mendon. Funeral at Fowler on Friday at 2

Powell, Wm   "Bloomfiled"   Jul 4, 1901
     Wm Powell rec'd news informing him of the death of his sister at
     LaPriarie last week.

Powers, A.D.   "Search for Heirs"   Sep 26, 1895
     see Edwards, Wm

Powers, John   "Quincy"   Apr 20, 1899
     Died- John Powers at St Mary's hospital Wednesday April 12th of quick
     consumption. He was a former clerk at the U.K. Miller's store at Marcelline.

Prather, Mrs   "Loraine"   Apr 11, 1889
     Died- Mrs Prather at her home in Loraine Saturday at 1 A.M. Buried in
     Woodville cmeetery Sunday P.M. She was a sister of Mrs I.N. Kincheloe
     and Messrs W.A. and D.E. Guseman. Member of the M.E. church.

Prather, Sarah J.   "Probate"   Jun 20, 1889
     Probate notice of Sarah J. Prather, deceased   1st Monday of August 1889
     C.F. Kincheloe, Adm.

Pratt, Mrs   "Loraine"   Dec 28, 1893
     Died- last wednesday, Mrs Pratt in our village from lung trouble.
     Buried Thursday in the cemetery near the Co. line by the side of her father
     2 of the children left are sick with lung fever. Leaves husband and __
     children.

Pratt, Edward E.   Jan 23, 1890
    Died- January 26th Edward E. Pratt at the age of 39 yrs in Home hospital
    Was in the floral dept of the Soldiers Home, more recently Superintendent
    of the farm.

Pratt, John   "Obituary"   May 12, 1898
    see Steiner, Mrs Anna C.

Pratt, John   "Mt Hebron"   Apr 11, 1889
    Mr John Pratt, guardian for the heirs of the late John Lowery sold at
    auction Saturday- 40 acres of land belonging to hte heirs to Mr E.J.
    Shepherd for 1625.00

Pratt, Mrs Sarah   "Camp Point"   Feb 26, 1880
    Died- Mrs Sarah Pratt, mother of Z.S. Pratt at the latters home of
    pneumonia. Buried in Quincy Woodland cemetery.

Pratt, Mrs Z.S.   "Obituary"   Mar 16, 1899
    see Chatten, Mrs W.I.

Prepots, Edward   "Tioga"   Sep 22, 1898
    Buried, a little child of Edward Prepot's was buried here last week.

Prest, Kate   "Death"   Jun 15, 1887
    see Morehouse, E.B.

Prettyman, Miss Effie   "Gleamings"   Sep 21, 1893
    Miss Effie Prettyman died Monday. Age 25 yrs from quick consumption,
    caused by excessive eating of candy.

Price, Mr John   "News"   Nov 27, 1879
    Mr John Price, an old citizen of Canton, Mo. was found dead with a bullet
    hole in his head.

Pride, Viola F.   "Obituary"   Feb 5, 1903
    see McNay, Andrew

Proctor, Annie (George)   Aug 18, 1881
    Died in Quincy August 18th 1881, Mrs Annie Proctor wife of George
    Proctor, daughter of Wm Pepple.

Procter, Mr and Mrs Harry   "Ursa"   Feb 15, 1905
    Infant son of Mr and Mrs Harry Procter died on Thursday eve. Buried in
    New Providence cemetery on Friday P.M. Services by Rev W.O. Livingstone.

Prunt, Gale   "Local"   Jun 26, 1890
    Mrs Prunt, grandmother of Gale Prunt was run over by the Wabash pay car
    at Paloma Monday and killed.

Pryor, Grandma   "Loraine"   Aug 31, 1887
    Grandma Pryor died Tuesday and buried Thursday near Ursa. She was nearly
    80 yrs old. Her aged husband still lives and has lived on the farm
    where she died for 47 yrs. Leaves husband, children, grandchildren and
    great grandchildren.

Pryor, Billy   "Loraine"   Sep 20, 1888
     Died- Uncle Billy Pryor at his home in Keene twp on Monday September 10th.
     He was an old settler of this part of the Co. 80 yrs old. His wife died a
     little over a yr ago. Buried Tuesday in the Woodruff cemetery near Ursa
     by the side of his wife.

Pryor, Freman   Aug 21, 1890
     Infant child of Mr and Mrs Freman Pryor died Monday

Pryor, Freeman   "Loraine"   Aug 28, 1890
     A little child of Mr and Mrs Freeman Pryor was buried in our cemetery.

Pryor, Freeman   "Loraine"   Oct 4, 1888
     Died- Mr and Mrs Freeman Pryor's little girl who was kicked by a horse
     died this A.M. -- Item dated October 2nd.

Pryor, Tim   "Local"   Feb 14, 1895
     News reached us yesterday that Tim Pryor, living west of Loraine was
     killed when a log fell upon him crushing his skull.

Pryor, Timothy and widow   "Adm Sale"   May 9, 1895
     Adm's Sale of real estate-- May 30th 1895 in the interest of Timothy
     Pryor, deceased, and widow of Timothy Pryor, deceased. N. 20 acres
     of N.E. ¼ of the S.W. ¼ of Section 12 in twp 2 N. Range 8 W. and S.W. ¼ of
     the N.W.¼ of the N.W. ¼ of Section 18 in twp 2N. Range 7 W.
     John Oatman, Adm. of Timothy Pryor, deceased. W.H. Keath, Attorney for
     Adm.

Pryor, Mrs Timothy   "Loraine"   May 5, 1881
     Mrs Timothy Pryor died April 31st. Buried Loraine cemetery Monday.

Pryor, Wm   "Probate"   Nov 22, 1888
     Probate notice of Wm Pryor, deceased 1st Monday of January 1889
     H.W. Strickler, Adm.

Pryor, Wilson   "Loraine"   Dec 1, 1886
     Wilson Pryor was buried in our cemetery Wednesday.

Puling, Charles   "Local"   Jan 15, 1891
     Charles Puling died January 8th. Was son of Luther Puling. Buried in
     Franklin cemetery.

Pullman, Fannie   Feb 16, 1882
     Miss Fannie Pullman died last week.

Purnell, Riley E.   "Local"   Mar 21, 1895
     Died- Riley E. Purnell, a colored resident of Quincy died the other day
     at the age of 100 yrs.

Pushner, Mr   "Payson"   Jun 30, 1886
     Mr Pushner, of Fall Creek was buried last Sunday.

321

Pyles, Josh   "Tioga"   Jun 21, 1905
      Suicide at Tioga-- Josh Pyles, a middle aged man went out into the woods
   west of his house and blew the top of his head off rather than be taken
   by the sheriff who was going to arrest him for shooting Dick Baker
   Tuesday night. Baker had been paying attention to Pyles stepdaughter, Miss
   Effie Glance and Pyle didn't like it so he shot him in the thigh.
   "Quincy Journal"

Quigg, Charley   "Local"   Sep 6, 1905
 Died- Charley Quigg yesterday A.M. at 9 at his home 2½ miles northwest
 of Mendon. He was 2nd son of Mr and Mrs W.B. Quigg and several months had
 lived at Montezuma, Iowa, returning home about 3 weeks ago and while
 playing ball run into another player rec'ing internal injuries. Leaves
 parents, 1 sister, Miss Nettie and 3 brothers, Will, Arthur and Harry all
 of here except for Will who is in Iowa. Services at the home 2 P.M.
 today by Rev S.R. Reno. Buried Mendon cemetery.

Quigg, Charles Burtis   "Died"   Sep 13, 1905
 Charles Burtis Quigg was born September 26, 1878 and died at parents home
 2½ miles northwest of Mendon at 9 A.M. September 5, 1905. He was 26 yrs 11
 mo's 9 days old. Had lived past 5 yrs with relatives at Montezuma, Iowa
 Accident happened September 3rd. Leaves parents, sister and 3 brothers.
 Services at family home by Rev S.R. Reno. Buried Mendon cemetery.

Quig, Conrad   Death"   Apr 17, 1902
 Died, Conrad Quig another pioneer at 1:30 P.M. Sunday at the age of
 83 yrs 11 mo's 17 days. Born Somerset Co. Penn April 26, 1818 and when
 9 yrs old he was bound out to a farmer and stayed with him till he was
 17 yrs old when he served 3 yrs learning the carpenters trade. Came to
 Ursa twp 1843 settling near Wesley Chapel. In 1845 he married Miss
 Margaret Shupe who with her 2 sons, W.B. and M.P. survive him. Moved to
 Mendon twp 1846 settling on the farm where he died. 1849 he and 6 others
 walked all the way to the gold rush in California, but not having good
 health returned to Mendon 1851. Built the house where his son William
 lives, going to the woods and felling the trees himself. Services at the
 M.E. church Tuesday afternoon by his former pastor, Rev Avis Hewes of
 Quincy assisted by Rev S.N. Wakefield. Buried Mendon cemetery. Pallbearers
 were; Ed Pickens, Wm Thompson, Wesley Clair, Wm Nutt and D.W. Dickerman.

Quigg, Conrad   "Death"   Feb 18, 1892
 see Shupe, Christopher

Quig, Conrad   "Probate"   May 22, 1902
 Probate notice of Conrad Quig, deceased 1st Monday of July 1902
 William B. Quig, Adm.

Quig, Mr and Mrs Mike   Jun 18, 1885
 Mr and Mrs Mike Quig's infant child died June 15th.

Quig, Mrs Wm   "Obituary"   Feb 27, 1890
 see Mann, Isabella

Quig, Mrs Wm   "Death"   Feb 6, 1890
 See Mann, Mrs

Quimby, Rev Jesse   "Carthage"   Dec 12, 1878
 Rev Jesse Quimby died some days ago. He stepped on a nail and lockjaw
 set in.

Quinn, Mrs T.J.   "Obituary"   Mar 17, 1898
 see Nedrow, Mrs Eliza

Rae, Mr   "Local"   Dec 29, 1886
    Mr and Mrs S.R. Chittenden and son John have returned from St Louis and
    Mr Rae's funeral. George will stay to help his aunt arrange his late
    uncle's affairs. Miss Lina Chittenden will also stay with her aunt. Mrs
    R's mother, Mrs E. P. Chittenden is also staying for a short time.

Railsback, Mrs W.P.   "Obituary"   Apr 15, 1894
    see Smith, Jos.

Raisch, Mrs Sarah Jane   "Quincy"   Mar 23, 1899
    Died- Mrs Sarah Jane Raisch of pneumonia. Sick 2 days. Was 51 yrs old.

Raling, Theodore   "Death"   Jul 27, 1904
    Theodore Raling about 38 yrs old and employed by Joseph VanDyke died
    very suddenly yesterday of apoplexy. Leaves sister, Mrs W.R. Newhouse of
    Quincy who made arrangments for funeral. Services at the home of J.C.
    Vandyke this A.M. by Rev A.M. Reitzel of Mendon Lutheran church. Buried
    Keith cemetery.

Ralph, Charles   "News"   Jun 4, 1880
    An infant child of Charles Ralph died last night.

Ralph, Mrs Clem   "Loraine"   Aug 7, 1902
    Mrs Jennie Smith was called to Rock Creek Thursday A.M. to the bedside
    of her sister, Mrs Clem Ralph who died the same day.

Ralph, F.M.   "Obituary"   Apr 10, 1902
    see Dickerman, I.R. (Ira Rice)

Ralph, Mr and Mrs R.   "Obituary"   Apr 28, 1898
    see Stafford, Dora

Ralph, Mrs William   "Ellington"   Sep 4, 1884
    Died- at her.home August 20th, Mrs William Ralph. 51 yrs old, funeral
    by Rev Goodwin of Quincy

Ralph, Mrs Wm   "Ursa"   Aug 28, 1884
    Died- August 20th, Mrs Wm Ralph. She had been an invalid several months.

Randles, Mrs I.W.   "Obituary"   Jan 24, 1889
    see Grosh, Mrs A.R.

Randolph, Mrs   "Loraine"   Sep 21, 1904
    Remains of Mrs Randolph were shipped here last week from Kansas and buried
    at Woodville cemetery.

Randolph, Mrs C.A.   "Death"   May 3, 1905
    see McKinney, Wesley

Randolph, Mrs C.A.   "Death"   May 3, 1905
    see McKinney, J.W.

Randolph, Eliza Ann   "Death"   Nov 23, 1904
    see Laughlin, Mrs Eliza Ann

Randolph, F.M.   "Obituary"   Nov 24, 1898
 see Adair, Horatio Thomas

Randolph, Jas.   "News"   Mar 11, 1880
 Body of Jas. Randolph reported missing by our Marcelline correspondent
 last week was found Friday. Verdict of coroners jury was accidential
 death. His money was found on the body.

Randolph. Lazure   "Loraine"   Feb 3, 1881
 Lazure Randolph of Woodville died this week.

Randolph, Wm E.   "Probate"   Feb 10, 1881
 Probate notice of Wm E. Randolph, deceased Tobitha Randolph Adm.

Rankin, Mrs   "White Oak Ridge"   Mar 7, 1895
 Died- Mrs Rankin, near Breckenridge last week. 85 yrs old.

Rankin, Curtis   "Payson"   Feb 26, 1880
 Died- on February 17th Curtis Rankin. Only 2 of a large family left.
 2 persons died in less than a month. Both young. Curtis's funeral was at
 Fall Creek on the 18th by Dr Murphy of Payson.

Rankin, James   "Death"   Nov 29, 1894
 see Smith, Cyrus

Rankin, James S. and Sarah   "Obituary"   Oct 11, 1888
 see Clark, Sarah O.

Rankin, Mrs Sarah O.   "Obituary"   Oct 11, 1888
 see Clark, Mrs Sarah O.

Rankin, Miss Sophronia   "Death"   Nov 29, 1894
 see Smith, Cyrus

Rankin, Robert   "Payson"   Dec 19, 1878
 Died- Mr Robert Rankin, an old citizen of Fall Creek died on the night
 of December 11th at the age of 52 yrs. He was a kind husband and father.
 Buried in the midst of a snowstorm Friday the 13th. Services by Rev H.C.
 Adams.

Rankins, Mary   "Payson"   Dec 25, 1884
 Mary Rankin, daughter of Jesse Rankin was buried Monday.

Rawlings, E.J.   "Obituary"   Aug 27, 1903
 see Stackhouse, Safrona Isabelle Rawlings

Rawlings, Ezekiel J.   "Obituary"   Dec 20, 1900
 see Shupe, Catherine

325

Rawlings, John H.   "Obituary"   Mar 14, 1901
    Died- John H. Rawlings, born in Harrison Co. Ky, 1837. died in Springfield
    Ill. March 1, 1901. Came with parents to Illinois 1851 and settled Lima
    Twp 1861. He went to Pikes Peak and on to California where he lived for
    a number of yrs. Next he went to Central America where he worked as a
    machinist and engineer on a coffee plantation for 35 yrs. In 1899 he
    came back to Illinois, but soon went to Georgia and joined a cooperative
    colony. Last October he came back to Springfield where he lived with a
    sister until his death. Buried with IOOF honors in Stone church cemetery
    1 mile north of Ursa Saturday P.M. March 2nd. Leaves 3 sisters, Mrs Ellen C.
    Abrams of Lima, Mrs N.K. Rawlings of Springfield and Mrs Amanda Lemmon of
    Loraine, 1 brother, Geo. S. Rawlings of San Jose, California.

Rawlings, M.   "Death"   Nov 29, 1894
    see Smith, Cyrus

Rawlings, Margaret L.   "Death"   Jan 4, 1905
    see Rust, George Washington

Rawlings, Michael   "Obituary"   May 26, 1898
    see Woodburn, Mrs Mary

Rawlings, Sarah Jane   "Obituary"   Feb 10, 1898
    Died- Sarah Jane, daughter of Michael and Margaret Rawlings. Born Sept
    13, 1839 near Mendon, Ill. and died Feb. 4th in Quincy. Married Wm U.
    Sprinkle June 5, 1866 by Rev Joel G. Williams. Leaves 4 sisters 1 brother,
    Mrs Agnes Tyndall, Mayville, Mo., Mrs Margaret Rust, Mendon, Ill, Mrs Mary
    Woodbury, Denison, Ohio, Mrs Isabel Stackhouse, Kansas city, Mo. and
    Mr Ezekiel Rawlings of Mendon, Mo. Was a member of the Baptist church.
    Remains brought by train from Quincy to the old homestead, at present
    occupied by Mr and Mrs Geo. Rust Sr. Taken to the old Stone church
    north of Ursa on the Warsaw road where she was buried beside her mother
    and father. She was born, married and buried in the same house. Services
    by Rev Crews of the M.E. church.

Rawlings, Sarah J.   "Obituary"   Jul 14, 1898
    see Sprankle, Wm.

Rawlings, son of Mrs V.K. "Local"   Sep 22, 1898
    Mrs Ellen Abrams writes from Springfield that her sister, Mrs V.K.
    Rawlings had a son killed in or near Hotchkiss, Colo Sept 1st.

Ray, Mrs Johnny   "Payson"   Jan 31, 1884
    Mrs Ray, wife of Uncle Johnny Ray died in Hannibal, Mo. January 28th.
    Buried Payson.

Ray, Mr and Mrs   Apr 13, 1887
    see McIntyre, Mrs

Ray, Miss Fannie   "Obituary"   Feb 3, 1898
    see Johnson, Mrs Fannie A.

326

Ray, Mrs Francis   "Died"   Sep 14, 1882
   September 12th death of Mrs Francis Ray, Age 90 yrs at the residence
   of her daughter, Mrs Alice McIntyre.

Ray, James   "News"   Oct 29, 1885
   The fence being built by Mr John Ray and his late father, the late James
   Ray in front of Squire Chittendens home is being torn down and is to be
   sold.

Ray, John   "Payson"   Sep 7, 1887
   Died- Uncle John Ray was buried here Saturday. He was a citizen of this
   place some yrs ago. His wife died in Hannibal about 3 yrs ago and was
   brought here for burial. His funeral was held at the Cong'l church by
   Rev Alleben.

Ray, John   "Obituary"   Feb 3, 1898
   see Johnson, Mrs Fannie A.

Ray, Lucy   "Obituary"   Feb 3, 1898
   see Johnson, Mrs Fannie A.

Ray, Mrs Lucy A.   "Death"   Mar 22, 1905
   see Baldwin, George Dutton

Rea, Mrs Emeline Frisbie   "Obituary"   Feb 22, 1905
   Funeral of Mrs Emeline Frisbie Rea, 83 yr old widow of the late George H.
   Rea was buried Sunday P.M. from the old Cote Brilliante mansion, St Louis
   where she had lived for 43 yrs. Her brother, J.B. Frisbie 86 yrs old and
   her sister, Mrs E.P. Chittenden attended the funeral. Also Geo. R. and
   S.F. Chittenden, Miss Lizzie Chittenden, Mr and Mrs Chas. A. Chittenden,
   H.M. and J.B. Frisbie Jr and Samuel Chittenden all of Mendon. Miss Lucy
   Barker of N.Y. city, Mr and Mrs L.L. Allen and daughter of Pierce city
   Mo., Wm Chittenden of Springfield, Ill, Mrs Mary A. Barker, a sister living
   in New York was unable to attend because of old age. She was born in
   Connecticut and came with her parents to Mendon in 1837. Married Dec 16,
   1851 to Mr Rea of Boston and went to Tennessee for 18 yrs. Then to St
   Louis 1859 and moved into the mansion. They had no children. Mr Rea
   died Jan. 24, 1886.

Rea, Mrs Emeline Frisbie   "Estate"   Mar 15, 1905
   An inventory of the estate of Mrs Emeline Frisbie Rea, who died at her
   home in St Louis Feb. 16th filed in office of probate clerk shows
   estate valued at 411,423,32.00   "St Louis Dispatch"

Rea, Mrs Emeline F.   "Obituary"   May 16, 1901
   see Frisbie, Morris E.

Rea, George H.   "Local"   Dec 29, 1886
   Died- December 24th at his late residence in Cote Brilliante, St Louis,
   Mo. Hon George H. Rea at the age of 71 yrs.

Ready, Mike   "Payson"   Jan 27, 1881
   Mike Ready, a transit Irishman died at Nathan Cox home January 21st 1881

Rearick, Mr____   "Quincy"   Feb 22, 1883
Died- Feb. 19th ____ Rearick. He was the son of ex mayor Rearick of Quincy.

Reckmyer, Mr Fred   "Tioga"   Jan 24, 1895
Died- Tuesday January 15th, Mr Fred Reckmyer. Age 74 yrs. Buried in Lutheran cemetery Thursday afternoon.

Redmond, Thomas
Died- Mr Thomas Redmond, an old citizen of Quincy died a few days ago.

Reece, Grandma   "Loraine"   Sep 14, 1904
Mrs Rose Ruffcorn of Breckenridge attended the funeral of her aunt, Grandma Reece Sunday.

Reece, Dick   "Loraine"   Sep 14, 1904
Dick Reece of Chicago was called here by the death of his mother last Saturday.

Reece, Fraderick   "Local"   Sep 26, 1901
Mrs Polly Reece, ex of the late Frederick Reece will October 5th sell all his personal property at her residence 2½ miles northwest of Mendon.

Reece, Mrs John   "Death"   Mar 22, 1905
see Booker, George

Reece, Mrs Mary   "Death"   Mar 22, 1905
see Booker, George W.

Reece, Pearl   "Loraine"   Oct 26, 1904
Richard Reece was called here from Chicago to attend the funeral of his youngest daughter, Pearl. Remains shipped here from Los Angles, Calif. His 2 daughters from Chicago also were here.

Reece, Mrs R.M.   "Loraine   Apr 12, 1888
Died- Mrs R.M. Reece at Saturday at 7 P.M. Was 43 yrs old. Funeral at Dunkard church at 11 A.M. yesterday by Rev Thomas. Buried in Reece cemetery in Big Neck beside her 2 little babes. Leaves husband and 4 daughters. The youngest 6 yrs old.

Reece, S.S.   "Edgings"   Jul 27, 1877
Died- S.S. Reece of Keene twp Monday A.M.

Reece, Samuel   "Probate"   Sep 7, 1877
Probate notice of Samuel Reece, deceased 3rd Monday of 1877 Joseph S. Reece, Adm.

Reece, Mrs Wm   "Local"   Sep 3, 1903
Mrs Wm Reece returned Thursday last from her sad mission of attending the funeral of her father in Penn.

Reed, Mrs   "Died"   Jul 24, 1879
Died- Sunday July 20th at the residence of Mr Halsey of Keene twp, Mrs Reed, age 81 yrs.

Reed, Mr   "Coatsburg"   Sep 20, 1894
    Died- Mr Reed, of this place from an accident Wednesday eve September 12th.
    45 yrs old. He came here from Denver, Colo sometime in the spring.
    Leaves a wife and 4 children. Services by Rev Miner of Camp Point at
    the Christian church Saturday. Buried in our village cemetery.

Reed, F.   "Coatsburg"   Sep 20, 1894
    Mr F. Reed of Denver, Colo is here to attend the funeral of his brother.

Reed, Stella   "Payson"   Aug 4, 1881
    Stella, the 12 yr old daughter of John Reed was buried July 31st.

Reeder, Mr John   "Center"   Feb 26, 1880
    Died- Mr John Reeder, of Melrose who has many relatives and friends here
    will be buried tomorrow.

Reeder, Mrs Francis   "Center"   Jan 27, 1881
    Mrs Francis Reeder, a sister of J.H. Johnson died at her home in
    Melrose last Thursday.

Reese, Frederick   "Local"   May 23, 1901
    The will of Frederick Reese was presented for probate Monday. Leaves
    everything to his widow for her natural life and at death it goes to
    the children. Widow named Ex. of the estate.

Reese, Frederick   "Probate"   Jun 20, 1901
    Probate notice of Frederick Reese, deceased   1st Monday of August 1901
    Polly Reese, Ex.

Reese, Frederick   "Local"   Arp 18, 1901
    died- Frederick Reese an old citizen of Mendon twp died yesterday A.M.
    Services at the Lutheran church at 11 A.M. Buried village cemetery.

Reese, Frederick   "Obituary"   May 2, 1901
    Died- Frederick Reese, born Wurtemburg, Germany August 26, 1820 and
    died at his home in Mendon twp Wednesday April 24th at age 80 yrs
    7 mo's 28 days. Member of the Lutheran church. Learned trade of stocking
    weaving. Served 6 yrs in German army. Came to U.S. 1847, 1st stopping
    at St Louis, came to Quincy 1848 and on to Mendon twp in 1850. Married
    Miss Mary Shupe 1850. Had 5 children- 3 died when a few yrs old.
    2 survive him, William of Mendon and Mrs L.B. Frisbie of San Diego, Calif.
    his aged wife also survive him. Services at Lutheran church Friday A.M.
    by Rev J.F. Booher. Pallbearers were; C.H. White, J.H. Nichols, Wm
    Thompson, F.O. Dickerman, C.A. Koch and Quill Asher. Present from a
    distance were Mr and Mrs Benton Shupe of Paloma and N.M. Heaney of Quincy.

Reese, Lou   "Local"   Jan 25, 1894
    Double murder near Perry, Pike Co. Tuesday A.M. Lou Reese, a farmer
    killed his wife and child and escaped. Later shot himself. He had light
    brown hair and light moustache, weighed 150 lbs and was 5 ft 8 ot 10
    inches tall.

Reese, Mrs Mary   "Died"   Jul 24, 1879
    Died- on Sunday night July 20th, Mrs Mary Reese, wife of Wm Reese of
    Mendon twp in her 25th yr. Funeral Monday. Was member of Lutheran church.

Rettig, Isaac   "Loraine"   Jul 28, 1881
    Death of a child of Isaac Rettig's this week.

Rettig, Isaac   "Local"   Aug 30, 1900
    Died- Isaac Rettig at Loraine Monday eve and was buried Tuesday afternoon.

Renter, Mrs Mary   "Quincy"   Mar 16, 1899
    Died- Mrs Mary Renter Thursday March 9th of asthma. Born Germany.
    71 yrs old. Lived Quincy 45 yrs. Leaves 3 sons and 1 daughter. Husband
    died 15 yrs ago.

Reuck, Mrs   "Ursa"   Jan 13, 1886
    Mrs Wm Nichols and daughter attended the funeral of her sister, Mrs
    Reuck, near Carthage last week.

Reuschel, George   "Coatsburg"   Mar 27, 1890
    George Reuschel died March 27th and buried March 28th. He gave 100.00
    to the Lutheran church people to buy the bell with the understanding
    being not to toll it till his death. He also made a will lately leaving
    thousand dollars to the church.

Reuser, Louis   "local"   May 9, 1901
    Louis Reuser, father of our photographer died at his home in Quincy
    Friday A.M. Age 50 yrs. Leaves a widow and 7 children- 4 sons and
    3 daughters.

Reynolds, Mr   "Big Neck"   Dec 24, 1891
    Mr Reynolds of Quincy died last week. James Gibson, a nephew of the
    deceased attended the funeral.

Reynolds, Amos L.   "Local"   Nov 25, 1885
    Died- at the residence of George R. Reynolds, in York Neck Camp Point
    twp.,Amos L. Reynolds. He was born in Winchester, Litchfield Co. Conn.
    July 29, 1820 and died November 20, 1885

Reynolds, Annie   "Local"   Jan 8, 1885
    Died- January 4th at York Neck, Annie, relict of the late Horace
    Reynolds at age 92 yrs 1 mo. 4 days. Buried Houston cemetery.
    Her children - Lucius and Julia of Mendon twp, Charles and Horace of
    Houston twp, Amos, George and James of Camp Point, Hannah living in
    Dakota and Henry of Kansas.

Reynolds, Mrs C.T.   "Obituary"   Oct 15, 1891
    see Morehead, Mrs Cordelia

Reynolds, Mrs C.T.   "Obituary"   May 18, 1887
    see Morehead, Daniel

Reynolds, Miss Ella   "Indian Grave"   Jan 3, 1895
    News reached here Saturday about 4 P.M. of the sad accident of Miss Ella
    Reynolds who was spending the holidays in Quincy. While blackening a
    cook stove (gasoline) it caught fire and she was horribly burned about
    the face. Later- She died around 4:15 less than 2 hours after the
    accident.

Reese, Miss Mary   "Dead"   Jan 11, 1905
    Died- Miss Mary Reese at the home of her parents 2 miles southwest of
    this place Sunday at 6:30 A.M. Suffered a stroke of paralysis on
    December 29th at school and was taken to her home ¼ mile distant. She
    was the daughter of Mr and Mrs William Reese. 31 yrs 4 mo's old. Taught
    school 9 yrs. Leaves father, mother, 2 sisters and 1 brother. Buried in
    Reese cemetery.

Reese, Olivat   "Died"   Jan 24, 1884
    January 18th, Olivat infant daughter of W. and Anna Reese died. Age 5
    months. Buried Mendon. Services at Lutheran church by Rev M.L. Kunkelman.

Reese, Mrs Wm   "Local"   Aug 13, 1903
    Mrs Wm Reese was called to Latrobe. Penn. Friday by the serious and
    proved to be fatal illness of her father. She did not arrive in time to
    see him alive. He died Saturday A.M. and she arrived Sunday A.M.

Reichert, Mr and Mrs Henry   "Local"   Sep 18, 1902
    the 7 month old child of Mr and Mrs Henry Reichert, living on the Fred
    Lucking farm, south of here died Wednesday. Services at the house by
    German minister of Fowler and buried Friday at the Gilliland graveyard.

Reichert, Mrs Henry   "Death"   Jul 19, 1905
    see Lucking, F.W.

Relling, Barney   "Gleamings"   Oct 19, 1887
    Barney Relling, who formerly lived in Ursa Minor died of inflammatory
    rheumatism last week in Quincy.

Remp, Jacob   "Obituary"   May 4, 1877
    Died- Mr Jacob Remp of our village of pneumonia Wednesday at 7:30.
    He had been a resident of here several yrs.

Rempp, Mrs Catherine   "Obituary"   Jan 8, 1903
    see Shupe, Mrs Mary

Rempp, Joseph   "Obituary"   Jan 8, 1903
    see Shupe, Mrs Mary

Rempp, Samuel   "Obituary"   Jan 8, 1903
    see Shupe, Mrs Mary

Renshaw, Mrs   "Camp Point"   Apr 26, 1900
    The funeral of Mrs Renshaw was at the Christian church last Sunday P.M.
    by Rev Williams. Leaves husband and 6 small children.

Rettig, Mrs   "Obituary"   May 22, 1890
    see Shriver, Louis

Rettig, Mrs Francis   "Loraine"   Apr 17, 1884
    Mrs Francis Rettig, wife of Isaac Rettig died April 4th 1884. Leaves
    husband and 1 child.

Reynolds, Ella   "Indian Grave"   Jan 3, 1895
    Funeral of Ella Reynolds at the 4th and Jersey Baptist church , of which
    she was a member.

Reynolds, Horace   "Camp Point"   Feb 8, 1883
    Horace Reynolds of York Neck died Feb. 5th at the age of 93 yrs. Came
    to Illinois ans settled on the farm where he died in the spring of
    1835. He leaves a wife and several children.

Reynolds, Mr James   "Big Neck"   Sep 15, 1892
    Mr James Reynolds of Camp Point was killed by his threshing machine
    Friday night September 9th.

Reynolds, Mrs L.E.   "Local"   May 18, 1893
    News rec'd of the death at Washington D.C. of Mrs L.E. Reynolds,
    formerly of Mendon on Sunday May 7th at age 79 yrs.

Reynolds, Miss Lizzie   "Camp Point"   Nov 1, 1900
    Miss Lizzie Reynolds who just returned from visiting in Iowa rec'd
    word last week that her brother on Col. died.

Reynolds, Walter   "Died"   Nov 27, 1879
    Died- Mr Walter Reynolds, Sunday 23rd of November 1879 at the residence
    of his nephew, Mr George Reynolds at the age of 73 yrs.

Reynors, John   Mar 2, 1882
    A son of John Reynors and a grandson of H. Griffin was buried Feb.26th.

Rhine, Mrs   "Local"   Jun 14, 1900
    Geo. Loynd of Quincy attended the funeral of his aunt, Mrs Rhine,
    lat week.

Rhine, Daniel   "Obituary"   Jun 14, 1900
    see Nutt, Elizabeth

Rhine, Elizabeth   "Obituary"   Jun 14, 1900
    see Nutt, Elizabeth

Rhine, Elizabeth   "Probate"   Mar 28, 1901
    Probate notice of Elizabeth Rhine, deceased   1st Monday of June 1901
    W.T. Nutt, Adm

Rhodes, Charles   "Local"   May 12, 1886
    A young man, Charles Rhodes, but lately married was thrown from his
    horse Friday April 30th near Augusta and cracked his skull. Died the
    next day.

Rhodes, Julia Anne   "Obituary"   Jun 8, 1899
    see Leckbee, Julia Anne Rhodes

Rhoe, Henry Sr.   "Paloma"   Feb 8, 1900
    Died- Rec'd word that Henry Rhoe Sr. died last Friday night. Lived
    east of here.

Rhote, Mrs Celathia   "Local"   May 4, 1904
    Mrs Celathia Rhote, who had bad luck Monday eve of last week in Rocky
    Run Creek died Friday afternoon of pneumonia. Leaves husband and 4 sons
    in Idaho and 1 daughter who with her, parents, brothers and sisters

Rice, Jacob   "News"   Nov 13, 1879
    Died- a little son of Jacob Rice Thursday afternoon and was buried from
    the M.E. church the next day.

Rice, Jake   "Local"   Dec 13, 1888
    Died- infant child of Mr and Mrs Jake Rice this A.M.

Rice, Major Jas. M.   "News"   Dec 11, 1879
    Major Jas. M. Rice, well known in this county, died at Trinidad, Colo.
    on December 5th.

Rice, Peter   "Graves"   Jun 5, 1902
    Peter Rice was included in list of soldiers graves decorated in Mendon
    cemetery for Decoration Day.

Richards, Mrs J.W.   "Local"   May 23, 1889
    Announcement in the Carthage paper of the death of Mrs J.W. Richards
    at Harrisburg, Penn. on May 8th. She was the wife of Prof. Richards,
    formerly of the Carthage College and sister of the late President Tressler
    and Dr J.E. Tressler, formerly of Mendon and now of Peabody, Kansas. She
    had been an invalid many yrs.

Richards, John W.   "Burton"   Apr 28, 1881
    Mr John W. Richards died Friday April 22nd at the age of 63 yrs.

Richards, John W.   "Obituary"   Dec 14, 1882
    see Patterson, Wm C.

Richard, Miss Luella   "Local"   Dec 25, 1890
    Died- September 4th at the home of her mother near Rockport, Ind. Miss
    Luella Richard at age 27 yrs 11 mo's 20 days. Born Frederick Co. Va.
    When she was 4 months old her father was killed in the battle at
    Sharpsburg, Md. She attended Carthage College in Illinois in 1882.

Richards, Mrs Mary   "Loraine"   Oct 16, 1890
    Died at her home in Loraine October 11th, Mrs Mary Richards, wife of
    W.F. Richards. Was 35 yrs old. Funeral at the M.E. church by Rev M.L.
    Schmucker. Leaves husband and 4 small children. Youngest only a few
    months old and an aged mother and 3 brothers.

Richard, Mary   "Exchange"   Sep 25, 1884
    "Exchange from the Carthage Republican" Telegram was rec'd telling
    of the death of little Mary, only child of Prof. and Mrs J.W. Richard
    on the 15th in Penn.

Richards, Willis   Jun 9, 1881
    Mr Willis Richards died June 4th 1881 Buried Keaths cemetery. Leaves
    wife and 2 children. Question on the 2 children.

Richards, Willis E.   "Probate"   Jun 30, 1881
    Probate Notice of Willis E. Richards, deceased 3rd Monday of August 1881
    William Fletcher, Adm

Richardson, Frank and Ella   "Coatsburg"   Jul 18, 1889
    an infant of Frank and Ella Richardson of Quincy was buried here last wk.

Richardson, Mrs Frank   "Coatsburg"   Jan 1, 1891
    Died- in Freeman Kansas December 24th, Mrs Frank Richardson, only
    daughter of Mrs Julia Frost. Services at Paloma and buried at Coatsburg.

Richardson, Mr and Mrs Thomas "Coatsburg"   Jun 16, 1892
    Wednesday A.M. June 1st the 9 mo. old baby boy of Mr and Mrs Thomas
    Richardson of Paloma was buried here. Died from brain fever.

Richey, Mrs Maggie A.   "Death"   Jan 11, 1905
    see Cochran, Thomas W.

Richey, Miss Sarah A.   "Obituary"   Dec 1, 1886
    see Borgholthaus, George W.

Richney, Mrs Maggie E.   "Obituary"   Mar 2, 1899
    see Cochran, Mrs Nancy Nevins

Richter, Miss Kate   "Local"   Jen 12, 1899
    Suicide- Miss Kate Richter, who lived with Mr Louis Ebert, at Quincy.
    She had been broading over her mother being in the insane asylum. Left
    a note to her sister living at Alton, Ill.

Ricker, Henry F.J.   "Local"   Mar 9, 1904
    Henry F.J., the venerable banker of Quincy died Friday afternoon.
    Leaves wife and 5 children. Lived Quincy 64 yrs and said to be the
    largest indiyidual property owner in the city.

Ricker, Henry F.J.   "Local"   Apr 6, 1904
    There was not a single bequest in the will of the late banker, Henry
    F.J. Ricker, which was filed for probate Monday. Everything was left
    to the widow.

Riddle, Ebenzier   "Obituary"   Jan 17, 1901
    see Green, Mrs Susan F. (Mrs Amos)

Riddle, Mrs G.D.   "Obituary"   Apr 13, 1899
    see Tittle, Mr A.J.

Riddle, Mrs G.D.   "Local"   Feb 21, 1901
    Mrs G.D. Riddle and brother, A.J. Tittle were called to LaBelle, Mo.
    Monday morning by the serious illness of their sister, Mrs W. McGinley
    who died Tuesday morning.

Riddle, Homer   "Loraine"   Feb 7, 1901
    Died- at 10 P.M. Saturday, little Homer, son of Mr and Mrs M.V. Riddle.
    2 yrs 1 month old. Buried in Loraine cemetery beside the 2 little ones
    who died before him.

Riddle, Homer   "Loraine"   Feb 7, 1901
    Died- Little Homer, the infant son of Mr and Mrs Mace Riddle at the
    parental home northeast of town Friday night of spinal trouble. Funeral
    by Rev Lockhart at the Christian church Sunday at 11 A.M. Buried in
    Loraine cemetery.

Riddle, Orville E.   "Death"   Oct 10, 1895
    "Sudden death of Mr O.E. Riddle" Died- Monday A.M. at his home 2 miles
    west of town, Mr Orville E. Riddle. 65 yrs old. Born a mile from the
    farm where he died. Member of Christian church. Leaves his widow, (a
    daughter of the late James Nichols of Ursa) and 1 son, brother and 1
    sister, Mrs Amos Green of Quincy. Services at the house by Rev Wm Burgess
    of Mendon and Rev Hiram Van Kirk of Quincy. Buried in the family burying
    ground on the farm where he died.

Riddle, Orville Wade   "Obituary"   Jan 27, 1904
    Died- Orville Wade, infant son of M.V. and Florence Riddle, at his home
                            near Loraine January 17th. He had in his brief
    life of a yr seen pain and suffering. Services by Elder J.M. Rhodes at
    Christian church in Loraine January 18th.

Riddle, Orville Wade   "Loraine"   Jan 20, 1904
    Died- Orville Wade, youngest son of Mr and Mrs M.V. Riddle died Sunday.
    Leaves parents, 1 brother and 1 sister.

Riddle, Mr and Mrs M.V.   "Loraine"   Aug 1, 1889
    Died- a little child of Mr and Mrs M.V. Riddle died very suddenly
    Saturday P.M. of cholera infantum. Services at the M.E. church Sunday
    eve by Elder Biggs. Buried in our cemetery.

Riddle, Mr and Mrs M.W.   "Loraine"   Feb 14, 1895
    Died- a little babe of Mr and Mrs M.W. Riddle Feb. 3rd of congestion
    of the lungs.

Riddle, Susan   "Obituary"   Mar 23, 1899
    see Metcalf, Mrs Susan Riddle

Ridgel, Mrs Eliza Alice   "Local"   Jan 10, 1901
    Mrs Eliza Alice Ridgel living a few miles south of Columbus, this Co.
    while insane, committed suicide Saturday by shooting herself with a 22
    rifle. Leaves husband and 3 sons.

Ried, Minerva A.   "Obituary"   Feb 28, 1895
    Died- Minerva A. Ried, Feb. 20th. Born in Kentucky Feb. 7, 1840. Married
    Green B. Barry March 8, 1855 and they had 13 shildren. Services Feb. 22nd
    at Elm Grove. Buried Wesley Chapel. Signed Henry Worman.

Riedinger, Mrs Sophia   "Quincy"   Mar 9, 1899
    Died- Mrs Sophia Riedinger March 1st. Born Rappenau, Baden, Germany
    January 26, 1826. Leaves husband, 3 sons and 1 daughter.

Rigney, Elder   "Obituary"   Aug 3, 1899
    see Ogle, Mrs Nancy

Riley, Mrs   "Payson"   Apr 28, 1881
    Mrs Riley committed suicide last Saturday April 23rd. She leaves 2
    children. 1 five yr old and other 7 months old and her husband. She was
    the daughter of H. Wickenkemp.

Riley, Jas. A.   "Local"   Oct 10, 1901
    3 of our old army comrades have died within the past 10 days,
    Jas. A. Riley, W.R. McClintock and Joseph Straley.

Ringier, Mrs Mary   "Local"   Apr 10, 1902
    Funeral last Friday of Mrs Mary Ringier of 1259 Vermont St. Quincy
    who died Tuesday april 1st. Had been an invalid 15 yrs. Her daughter
    Miss Fannie had been with her the past 2 yrs. Buried in Woodland
    cemetery beside her husband and daughter who had preceded her.

Rippetoe, Thomas   "Quincy Whig"   Dec 7, 1893
    6 months ago young Thomas Rippetoe, of Colchester was assaulted and then
    he committed suicide. He was to have married Miss Belle Morrison.
    Recently Miss Belle became a mother and the father of the child as
    statded was young Rippetoe.

Ritchie, Mrs
    Mrs Ritchie mother of Rev Ritchie died last week in Peoria.

Rittler, Mrs   "Honey Creek"   Apr 6, 1887
    4 funerals at Coatsburg last week. Mrs Jasper White, Mrs Schlipmannn,
    Mrs Rittler and Mrs Powell.

Robbins, Deacon   "Payson"   Aug 16, 1888
    Deacon Robbins was buried yesterday. Came here in 1839 and resided here
    since. Was 75 yrs old. Leaves a wife and 4 children.

Robbins, Mrs Deacon   "Payson"   Dec 27, 1888
    Died- Mrs Deacon Robbins died. She was 68 yrs old. Buried in the cemetery
    here. Had lived Payson 53 yrs. Leaves 4 children, all married. Her
    husband Deacon Robbins died only a few months ago.

Robbins, Mrs   "Obituary"   Dec 24, 1891
    see Van Dien, Mrs

Robbins, Miss Addie   "Obituary"   Dec 31, 1891
    see Hendrickson, Elizabeth

Robbins, Prof C.W.   "Obituary"   Dec 31, 1891
    see Hendrickson, Elizabeth

336

Robbins, Furman   "Died"   Dec 26, 1878
    Died- Furman Robbins, age about 18 yrs, the youngest son of Mrs Robbins
    living just south of Rock Creek on the Warsaw Road died last Sunday of
    pneumonia.

Robbins, Mrs George   "Obituary"   Apr 17, 1902
    see Hedges, Mrs Fannie

Robbins, George   "Payson"   Dec 9, 1885
    Mr George Robbins died at his fathers house last Friday night. Leaves
    a wife and 1 child.

Robbins, John   "Obituary"   Dec 31, 1891
    see Hendrickson, Elizabeth

Robbins, Miss Lizzie   "Obituary"   Feb 16, 1888
    see Ferree, John E.

Robbins, Mrs Mary   "Obituary"   Dec 31, 1891
    see Hendrickson, Elizabeth

Robbins, Mrs Rebecca   "Obituary"   Dec 31, 1891
    see Hrndrickson, Elizabeth

Robbins, Wm   "Obituary"   Dec 31, 1891
    see Hendrickson, Elizabeth

Roberts, Bessie   "Local"   Apr 5, 1905
    Died- Wednesday March 29th, Bessie, the youngest daughter of Mr and
    Mrs James Roberts. Age 2 yrs. Services at the Christian church. Buried
    in Stone church burying ground.

Roberts, Mrs E.L.   "Local"   Apr 18, 1895
    Died- Mrs E.L. Roberts (Cassie) daughter of Mr and Mrs Washington
    Ketchum of typhoid pneumonia Monday at her home in Trinidad, Colo.
    30 yrs old. born December 28, 1865. Married about 3 yrs ago. Leaves
    1 child.

Roberts, George   "Obituary"   Jan 28, 1892
    see Swan, Sarah

Roberts, Horatio   "Obituary"   Jan 28, 1892
    see Swan, Sarah

Roberts, Mrs James   "Local"   Jan 14, 1892
    Died- Mrs Jas. Roberts last Thursday P.M. 72 yrs old. Buried in
    Woodruff family burying ground east of Ursa on Saturday. Her daughter,
    Mrs Myer of Quincy was present at the grave. Her sons, Cornelius and
    Wm thank all her neighbors for their kindness.

Roberts, Jas S.   "Local"   Dec 28, 1887
    December 16th burial at Big Neck for Jas. S. Roberts. Age 53 yrs.
    Member of Co. G. 23rd Ill. Reg. and member of Baptist church. Leaves wife
    and 5 children.(2 boys and 3 girls)

Roberts, Samuel   "Camp Point"   Dec 20, 1900
    Died- Samuel Roberts this morning (Monday) at 6 of consumption. Leaves
    wife and 2 children.

Roberts, Sarah   "Obituary"   May 8, 1902
    see VanBlair, Joseph

Roberts, Sarah   "Big Neck"   Jan 21, 1892
    Sarah Roberts died January 1st.

Roberts, Mrs Sarah   "Obituary"   Jan 28, 1892
    see Swan, Sarah

Roberts, Mr W.O.   "Local"   Mar 17, 1892
    "Peoples Press Cuba, Fulton Co."
    Died- Mr W.O. Roberts, formerly of this Co. by falling down a shaft of
    a coal mine.

Roberts, Wm   "Obituary"   Oct 28, 1892
    see Swan, Sarah

Roberts, Mrs Wm   "Obituary"   Oct 13, 1892
    see O'Dear, Mrs Lizzie

Robertson, Andrew   Sept 26, 1894
    State of Illinois Co. of Adams in the Adams circuit court to the Oct. term
    A.D. 1894 Maurice T. Moloney as the attorney general of the state of Ill.
    who sues, Etc, Complainant #208 vs in Chancery
    Edward M. Koch, Walter Robertson, Alfred Robertson and Elizabeth Smith,
    the unknown heirs and devises of Andrew Robertson, deceased, the unkown
    owners of the S.E.¼ of section 34 2N. range 8 west in Adams Co. Defendents
    Walter Robertson, Alfred Robertson and Elizabeth reside out of the state
    of Ill. Dated in Quincy August 30, 1894 Geo. Brophy, clerk per Hiram
    R. Wheat, deputy Hamilton and Woods, sol for complainant.

Robertson, Mrs Anna   Jan 9, 1890
    Mrs Anna Robertson died at the home of her parents, Fred and Anna
    Frike of Fowler. She was their youngest daughter. Funeral services by
    Rev McKown. Date of death January 7th.

Robertson, Annie   "Fowler"   Nov 20, 1902
    Died- Annie Robertson, 6 yr old daughter of Mr and Mrs Homer Robertson
    on November 6th. Funeral at Christian church Saturday.

Robertson, Mr C.E.   "Loraine"   Jan 26, 1887
    Died- Mr C.E. Robertson at his home 1 mile north and 2 miles west of
    here Friday at 2 P.M. of chrinic bronchitis. Buried Ursa at the cemetery
    at the Stone church.

Robertson, Cass   "Loraine"   Oct 16, 1884
    Found dead 2 miles north of here on the railroad by section men, Cass
    Robertson who lived in or near Webster, Ill. Hancock Co. Remains were
    sent to Carthage.

Robertson, Mr Cyrus   "York Neck"   Feb 2, 1887
    There has been no school at Mt Pleasant for 3 weeks on acct of the
    illness and death of the teachers father, Mr Cyrus Robertson of Loraine.
    School starts today.

Robertson, James   Sep 3, 1891
    James Robertson died at Camp Point last Saturday August 29th. He was a
    resident of Adams Co. 58 yrs. and 84 yrs old. A native of Indiana.

Robertson, James F.   "Obituary"   Jan 29, 1903
    Died- James F. Robertson Friday night at his home in Camp Point. Was 57
    yrs old. Son of James and Elizabeth Robertson who were among the real
    pioneers of Illinois. Married January 12, 1873 to Miss Sallie Francis,
    daughter of another pioneer family. Had 2 children, C.F. Robertson now of
    Chicago, and one time employed in Mendon bank and Miss Edith Robertson of
    Camp Point. 1st wife died August 30th 1884 and on December 5th 1889 he
    married Miss Lillian Workes who survives him. They had 3 children, Ruth,
    Esther and James F. all at home at Camp Point. He was post master at
    Camp Point during Clevelands term as president.

Robertson, Mrs Mary   "News"   Jul 29, 1880
    Mrs Robertson has been a resident of Mendon for 12 yrs died. She was a
    native of New Jersey and a sister of the late Edward Tyndall of Ursa.
    She leaves 3 grandsons, 2 live in Missouri and 1 living with his grand-
    mother. Same paper-- Died, Mrs Mary Robertson July 25th at age 67 yrs.
    from hemorrhage of the lungs.

Robertson, Mary   "Probate"   Feb 24, 1881
    Probate Notice of Mary Robertson, deceased   3rd Monday of April 1881
    Daniel H. Darby, Adm.

Robinson, Celia J.   "Will"   Jan 27, 1904
    see Frike, Mrs Anna

Robinson, Mrs Frank   "Obituary"   Aug 24, 1904
    see Foster, Mrs Eliza Ann

Robinson, Mrs Jas.   "Local"   Sep 4, 1884
    Mrs Jas. Robinson of Camp Point, wife of the agent of the Wasbash at
    Camp Point died September 1st. Leaves husband and 2 young children.

Robinson, Jimmy   "Eureka Notes"   Jan 26, 1888
    "Bible College" Uncle Jimmy Robinson of Secor, Ill . died January 19th
    age 92 yrs. He was known as the oldest preacher in Illinois. Had been a
    preacher 70 yrs. 10 yrs a Baptist and 60 yrs as a Christian preacher.
    Preached to the people of Illinois 50 yrs.

Robinson, Col. Samuel   "Obituary"   Jan 26, 1899
    see Chittenden, S.R.

Robinson, Sylvan   "Loraine"   Feb 10, 1881
    Died- Sylvan Robinson, eldest son of C. and P. Robinson in his 16th yr.
    of congestive chills last Friday afternoon Feb. 4th.

Rochinfield, Mrs John   "Quincy"   Apr 13, 1899
    Died- Mrs John Rochinfield Wednesday April 5th. 54 yrs old. leaves husband

339

Rockenfield, George   "Camp Point"   Aug 4, 1881
    George Rockenfield, an old resident died last week.

Rockwell, Mrs C.B.   "Ursa"   May 17, 1883
    Died- Mrs C.B. Rockwell of Ursa May 14th. Born Adams Co.. Maiden name
    was Mary Jane McAdams. Born March 1857. Leaves husband, 3 sons and 2
    daughters.

Rockwell, Charlie   "Ursa"   Sep 18, 1902
    Charlie Rockwell's remains were brought here last week from Kansas city
    Charlie died there September 10th and was buried here the 11th. He was
    a former Ursa boy, but of late yrs was interested with his brother in the
    drug business at Kansas city. 28 yrs old.

Rockwell, Mr and Mrs Ira   "Funeral"   Jun 8, 1899
    see Leckbee, Mrs

Rodden, Mrs Phillip   "Loraine"   Jul 8, 1880
    Died- Mrs Rodden, wife of Phillip Rodden of Big Neck on July 6th.
    Buried at Bloomfield yesterday.

Rodgers, Joel   "Loraine"   Nov 29, 1888
    Died- Uncle Joel Rodgers, an old settler of Adams Co. Tuesday night.
    Services at 10 A.M. Friday after the arrival of his daughter from the
    west. Services at the Dunkard church by Elder T.M. Johnson assisted by
    Elder Strickler. Buried in our cemetery. 69 yrs old. Was member of
    Christian church 25 yrs. Leaves an aged wife, 1 son and 3 daughters.

Roeschlaub, Dr   "Local"   Jun 18, 1885
    Dr Roeschlaub, an old practioner of Quincy died last Thursday June 11th
    Buried in Woodland cemetery on Sunday.

Rogers, Mayor   "Personal"   Apr 15, 1880
    Mayor Rogers of Quincy was buried yesterday.

Rogers, Amelia M.   "Probate"   Dec 9, 1897
    Probate Notice of Amelia M. Rogers, deceased 1st Monday of Feb. 1898
    Joseph S. Reese, Adm.

Rogers, Amelia M.   "Adm Sale"   Mar 17, 1898
    Adm Sale of real estate of Amelia M. Rogers, deceased against Mary E.
    Rogers and others Saturday April 16th at 2 P.M. N.22 acres of S. 44½
    acres of the following. the N.W. ¼ of section 22 and E. ½ of the N.E. ¼
    of section 21 twp 2 N. Range 8 W.   William H. Rogers in possession
of a portion of real estate. Joseph S. Reese, Adm. F.M. McCann, Solicitor.

Rogers, Amelia May   "Obituary"   Nov 18, 1897
    Died- Amelia May, daughter of Clark E. and Mary E. Rogers. Born January
    19, 1878. died at the home of her birth 6 miles N.W. of Mendon, Ill
    November 15th at the age of 19 yrs 9 mo's 26 days. Sick 7 mo's Became
    a member of the Church of Christ December 10, 1893 during meeting held
    by Bro. W.S. Lowe at the Mt Hebron church. Services at the home on Tuesday
    November 16th at 11 A.M. by Bro. Roe of Ursa and Bro. Knight. Buried
    in Franklin cemetery. Leaves her mother, 2 brothers, Johnson L. of
    Atlanta, Mo. and Wm H. and 3 sisters, Mrs Margaret F. McCullough of
    Bloomfield, Mrs Laura M. Thompson and Lottie E.

Rogers, C.E. and Mary   "Obituary"   Mar 20, 1890
   see Thompson, Mrs Lillie B.

Rogers, Clark E.   "Obituary"   May 2, 1889
   Died- Clark E. Rogers of Mendon twp died at his home last Saturday April
27th from nephritis. Born in Lyons, Lyons Co. N.Y. March 28, 1829, the
2nd of a family of 9 children. Came to Illinois in 1838 after tarrying
a short time near Carthage settled in the northern part of Adams Co.
Married Mary E. Laughlin in December 1860 and they had 3 children.
2 of whom are, Johnson Rogers of Carrollton, Mo. and Mrs George McCullough
of Camp Point, Ill. His wife died March 1868 and he married Mary E. Ward
in October 1870. Leaves his wife and their 5 children. Member of the
Christian church. Services at Franklin church and buried in Franklin
church yard.

Rogers, Clark E.   "Probate"   Jun 6, 1889
   Probate notice of Clark E. Rogers, deceased 1st Monday of August 1889
Mary E. Rogers, Adm. Gilmer and Moore, attorneys

Rogers, Edward   "Edgings"   Jun 29, 1877
   Died- Edward Rogers fell from the Quincy court house dome. Died
Wednesday morning. He resided at Altoona, Illinois.

Rogers, J.C.   "Obituary"   Nov 21, 1901
   see Peyton, Mrs Delia

Rogers, James W.   "Camp Point"   Mar 4, 1880
   Died- James W. Rogers, a brother of our plasterer, henry C. died
Tuesday A.M. with typhoid fever.

Rogers, Joel   "Local"   Nov 22, 1888
   Died- Mr Joel Rogers, an old settler of this Co. at his home near
Loraine Tuesday night. Funeral today (Thursday) at 1 P.M. in the
German Baptist church at Loraine. Services by T.M. Johnson.

Rogers, Joseph   Oct 11, 1883
   Joseph Rogers shot his wife and himself October 8th in Quincy. Graves
robbed on Tuesday night and bodies not found as yet.

Rogers, Margaret S.   "Obituary"   Mar 8, 1900
   see Hardy, Thomas

Rogers, Mrs Mary P.   "Local"   Nov 30, 1887
   Mrs Mary P. Rogers, widow of the late Dr Hiram Rogers died at her home
in Quincy on Friday morning.

Rogers, Miss Paisience M.   "Obituary"   Jan 1, 1880
   see Ward, W.J.

Rogers, Mr T.W.   "Obituary"   Oct 29, 1891
   see Ross, Mrs Caroline

Rogers, Thaddeus M.   "Whig"   Dec 8, 1898
   Died- Mr Thaddeus M. Rogers. Had lived in Quincy 60 yrs.

Rogers, Thomas   "Probate"   Nov 3, 1881
    Probate Notice of Thomas Rogers, deceased Clark E. Rogers Adm.

Rogers, Mr Timothy   "Herald"   Jan 10, 1889
    Died- Mr Timothy Rogers, one of the oldest citizens of Quincy and Adams
    Co. died at his residence, the Occidental Hotel on Hampshire St. at
    7:35 Sunday eve.

Rogers, Mrs Timothy   "Local"   Nov 17, 1892
    Died- Mrs Timothy Rogers, an old resident of Quincy died Saturday night
    at the Occidental Hotel, her home for 34 yrs in her 84th yr. Her husband
    died January 6th 1889. The Hon Thaddeus M. Rogers, E.A. Rogers their
    only surviving children were present for her death.

Rohl, Miss Pearl   "Local"   Aug 23, 1905
    Miss Pearl Rohl, of Peoria committed suicide Sunday afternoon by
    jumping from the deck of the steamer Silver Crescent into the river near
    Meyer, Ill. Was one of a party of 4 on an excursion on the boat from
    Keokuk to Quincy.

Rohr, Mrs   "Local"   May 21, 1885
    Mr and Mrs Joseph Frisbie paid the last sad tribute of affection to the
    memory of their daughter, Mrs Rohr, returning from Rockford Friday A.M.

Rohr, Mrs Dr   "Local"   Apr 30, 1885
    Mrs Dr Rohr, eldest daughter of Mr and Mrs Jos. Frisbie died Tuesday
    of typhoid pneumonia.

Rohrbaugh, Mrs Della   "Obituary"   Dec 4, 1902
    see Felgar, Simon S.

Roley, Bert   Feb 22, 1883
    Bert Roley's little son died on Feb. 20th. He was about 15 months old.

Roley, Mrs Henrietta   "Obituary"   Jun 25, 1903
    see Walker, Henry Clark

Roley, Joseph A.   "Obituary"   Jun 25, 1903
    see Walker, Henry Clark

Rolf, M.   "Local"   Aug 14, 1902
    M. Rolf, age 79 yrs died at his home in Coatsburg Tuesday night.

Rolf, Mrs Theresia   "Local"   Mar 30, 1904
    Died- Mrs Theresia Rolf Sunday A.M. at the home of her daughter, Mrs
    Pauline Dittmers 1½ miles northeast of Coatsburg. Was nearly 76 yrs old.
    Husband died about 1½ yrs ago. Leaves 1 son and 2 daughters.

Rose, Eliza   "Local"   Mar 31, 1892
    Eliza Rose, the old colored lady who was found in the timber last Monday
    died Friday night of exposure. 80 yrs old.

Rosenberger, Mrs Lizzie   "Death"   Apr 5, 1905
    see Rust, Charles W.

Rosenbrook, Mrs Caroline   Jan 31, 1884
    Died- in the home of her son Capt John Rosenbrook, Mrs Caroline
    Rosenbrook at the age of 81 yrs. Born March 1802 in city of New York, N.Y.
    Came to Adams Co. 1851. Services from the home by Rev E.C. Crane.

Rosenbrook, J.H.   "Graves"   Jun 22, 1899
    Graves decorated by I.O.O.F. and Rebaccas in Mendon cemtery Decoration Day

Rosenbrook, Mortimer   "Local"   Jul 20, 1887
    Mort (Mortimer) Rosenbrook, youngest son of Capt and Mrs John Rosenbrook
    of Mendon died Tuesday P.M. in Memphis, Tenn. Was 21 yrs old. Cause was
    typhoid fever.

Rosenburger, Dr Geo.   "Loraine"   Jun 21, 1894
    Dr Geo. Rosenburger died at his home Thursday eve at 8:30 Services by
    Rev Rose at the M.E. Church Saturday morning ay 9. Buried at Curless
    cemetery. Was 73 yrs old. Leaves a wife and 2 brothers, one of whom was
    present for the funeral. The other brother lives in Calif.

Roskamp, Gottlieb   "Tioga"   Aug 24, 1899
    Died- Thursday August 17th Gottlieb Roskamp. Was 48 yrs old. Funeral
    Sunday afternoon by Rev P. Ott.

Roskamp, Mrs Hanna   "Tioga"   Feb 9, 1887
    Died- January 27th Mrs Hanna Roslamp in her 68th yr. Born Germany and
    came to this country about 40 yrs ago. She and her husband settled 1½
    miles north of Tioga about 20 yrs ago and they had 8 children. 2 are
    still living. She was a member of Evangelical Lutheran church. Buried
    Tioga January 30th. Services by Rev Kerns. Leaves a husband and 2 sons,
    and 2 brothers.

Roskamp, Phillip   "Tioga"   Sep 10, 1891
    Phillip Roskamp died September 5th at age 76 yrs. Buried Tioga cemetery.

Ross, Deputy Sheriff   "Carthage"   Mar 20, 1879
    Deputy Sheriff Ross died recently. Taken to Plymouth for burial.

Ross, Mrs Caroline   "Died"   Oct 29, 1891
    Died- at her home in Hancock Co. October 17th of typhoid fever, Mrs
    Caroline Ross at age 51 yrs. She leaves 4 children, 3 boys and 1 girl from
    19 yrs to 12 yrs of age. 4 sisters and 1 brother, Mrs Thomas Hardy of
    Bently, Ill, Mrs E.A. Eddy of Loraine, Mrs A. Boyles of Osceola, Mo.,
    Mrs S.J. Miner of Ohio and Mt T.W. Rogers of Kansas.

Ross, Charley   "Shooting"   Aug 27, 1879
    Charley Ross, a bartender in Quincy was shot and killed.

Ross, Miss Jane   "Obituary"   Oct 27, 1886
    see Vickers, Thomas

Rossbach, Adam   "Suicide"   Nov 11, 1880
    Adam Rossbach residing near Cramers Distillery, Quincy committed
    suicide last Wednesday by taking strychnine.

Rossiter, Mrs Jane   "Obituary"   Sep 7, 1904
    see Woodruff, Charles Edwin

343

Roth, Mrs   "Obituary"   Jan 25, 1883
     see McCabe, Mrs Kate Roth

Roth, Jacob   "Obituary"   Jul 11, 1901
     see Lint, Catherine

Roth, John A.   "Funeral"   Aug 18, 1881
     see Francis, Mrs John T.

Roth, John W.   "Obituary"   Jul 28, 1881
     see Francis, Mrs John T.

Roth, Mrs John W.   "Death"   Jan 4, 1900
     Died- Mrs John W. Roth, wife of sheriff Roth Sunday at their home in
     the courthouse, Quincy. Daughter of Dr C.S. Monnet. Born Reno, Ind.
     May 16, 1856. Married twice. 1st to Henry Jewell, they had 2 children
     C.C.Jewel of Quincy and Mrs Gertie Boger of Camp Point. Married 2nd
     Mr Roth December 3, 1883. Was member of Vermont M.E. church. Services
     at the house Tuesday A.M. by Rev J.B. Wolfe. Buried Camp Point.

Roth, Wm   "Obituary"   Jul 11, 1901
     see Lint, Catherine

Rowbotham, Mr and Mrs John   "Local"   May 3, 1894
     Died- the adopted child of Mr and Mrs John Rowbotham last week and was
     buried in Stone cemetery between Ursa and Marcelline.

Rowney, Mrs   "Payson"   Sep 11, 1879
     Mrs Rowney died of cancer Tuesday September 2nd 1879. Her son Anthony
     Lennon of Chicago reached here shortly before the body was taken to the
     church. Services by Rev S.A. Wallace.

Roy, Mrs Joseph A.   "Local"   Jan 24, 1901
     Died- Mrs Joseph A. Roy, wife of the well known attorney Monday of
     peritonitis, age 33 yrs. Leaves husband, mother, 1 sister Mrs J.F. Walker
     and a ½ brother.

Ruddell, John   "Funeral"   Nov 21, 1889
     see Frazier, James Sr.

Rudden, Mrs   "Death"   Feb 26, 1903
     see Cubbage, William

Rudden, Phillip   "Loraine"   Nov 5, 1891
     "Uncle Phillip" Rudden died Friday October 23rd. Buried Sunday the 25th
     in cemetery at Bloomfield.

Rudder, James   "Ursa"   Oct 11, 1900
     The body of James Rudder was brought here for burial Wednesday. He died
     at Jacksonville of tumor on the brain.

Ruddle, Catherine   "Obituary"   Jan 29, 1891
     see Nichols, James

Rudolph, Fannie W.   "Obituary"   Jul 9, 1891
     see Denson, Mr and Mrs J.T.

Rue, Rev Jonathan   "Obituary"   Oct 5, 1899
Died- Rev Jonathan Rue. Born state of New Jersey November 1818 where he
lived till 10 yrs old- His mother died and he went to live with his
uncle in the state of Virginia. Married 1st Miss Nancy Powel, they had
3 children- 2 still living. His 1st wife died Jan 1895 and on June 3,
1897 he married Mrs Sarah Thayer who survives him. He died September 24th
at the age of 80 yrs 10 mo's. Organized the Baptist church at Franklin
and was pastor of the church several yrs. Services at the Lutheran church
September 27th by Rev J.W. Spire. Buried Mendon cemetery.

Ruff, Jacob   "Obituary"   Aug 1, 1889
   see Urech, Frederick J.

Ruff, Miss Lizzie   "Obituary"   Aug 1, 1889
   see Urech, Frederick J.

Ruffcorn, John   Sep 3, 1891
Died August 14th at his home in Loraine John Ruffcorn at the age of
83 yrs 9 mo's 4 days. He was born in Ohio November 10, 1808 and when
young he and parents moved to Penn. There they lived in Fayette and
Westmoreland Co's December 6, 1832 he married Eunice Smith in Westmoreland Co. She died Feb 13, 1858. They had 14 children, 8 of whom are still
living. May 16, 1861 he married Mrs Susan Dawson, eldest sister of
Elder H.W. Strickler of Loraine. In March 1867 they moved to Keene twp and
bought 160 acres of land. They lived there until March 1882 when they moved
to Loraine. Buried Big Neck cemetery. He leaves a wife and 8 children.

Ruffcorn, Hattie   "Loraine"   Apr 24, 1902
Hattie, eldest daughter of John Ruffcorn died at Buda and was brought
here Friday A.M. Funeral from the Christian church by Rev Haskill.
Buried in Curless graveyard. She was about 12 yrs old.

Rumbaugh, Anna C.   "Death"   Dec 7, 1904
   see Wible, Mrs Daniel

Rumbaugh, David   "Death"   Jan 12, 1888
   see Wible, Mrs K.

Rumbaugh, Mrs J.M.   "Death"   Mar 25, 1880
   see Turner, Mrs

Rumbaugh, W.H.   "Local"   May 18, 1887
The town of Blue Springs, Nebr. was struck by a cyclone Friday morning,
the school house, church and other bldgs were demolished. The janitor
of the school house W.H. Rumbaugh was buried beneath the ruins of the
bldgs. and rec'd fatal injuries. Mr Rumbaugh formerly lived at Loraine.

Rumbaugh, William   "Local"   Dec 16, 1897
Died- Mr William Rumbaugh, of Blue Springs, Nebr. a former resident of
here died at Lincoln Wednesday December 1st and buried the following
Saturday.

Rump, Mrs Chris   "Death"   Mar 9, 1899
   see Hunsaker, Mrs Alexander

345

Runyon, Wm   May 1, 1884
    Died- Wm Runyon at the age of 61 yrs. lived Mendon. Died April 24th 1884

Rush, Mrs Frederick   "Death"   Mar 2, 1899
    see Judy, Mrs Nancy

Rust, Mrs C.W.   "Loraine"   Mar 29, 1905
    Died- Mrs C.W. Rust Friday night. Buried Sunday. Services at Christian
    church by Rev H.D. Willaims. Buried Loraine cemetery.

Rust, Charles Jr.   "Loraine"   Aug 7, 1884
    Charles Rust Jr. buried a child here Sunday August 3rd.

Rust, Charles W.   "Obituary"   Apr 5, 1905
    Charles W. Rust, born Clearmont Co. Ohio Jan 30, 1833 and came to Ill.
    with parents overland when quite young and settled near Mendon, Ill.
    Married Eliza Benson August 27, 1853 and they had 6 children, 4 sons,
    2 daughters. 1 son dying in infancy. He enlisted in the army at Mendon,
    Ill. August 15, 1862 and mustered out October 1, 1865. Member of Co. K.
    118 Reg. Ill. Vol. Died at his home March 31st at the age of 72 yrs 2
    mo's 1 day. Joined Christian church about 40 yrs ago. Leaves 2 daughters,
    Mrs Josephine Smith of Tacoma Washington and Mrs Thomas Hudson of Indian
    Terr. 3 sons, Chad of Bowen, John and George of this place, 1 brother
    Samuel Rust of Kirksville, Mo. and 1 sister, Mrs Lizzie Rosenberger of
    Quincy. 28 grandchildren and 12 great grandchildren. Services Sunday
    April 2nd at 11 A.M. Buried Loraine cemetery.

Rust, Mrs Eliza Benson   "Obituary"   Mar 29, 1905
    Mrs Eliza Benson Rust was born in state of Indiana January 28, 1832 and
    died March 24th 1905. She was 73 yrs 1 mo. 26 days old. Married Chas. W.
    Rust August 27, 1853. they had 6 children, 4 sons and 2 daughters all
    survive her except 1 son who died in infancy. Had 28 grandchildren. 9
    great grandchildren. Joined Christian church about 40 yrs ago. leaves an
    aged husband, 2 sisters, 3 sons and 2 daughters. Funeral at Christian
    church Sunday March 26th at 11 A.M. by Rev H.D. Williams. Buried Loraine
    cemetery.

Rust, George   "Death"   Dec 19, 1878
    see Farner, Dr W.H.

Rust, Mrs George W.   "Death"   Aug 27, 1903
    see Stackhouse, Safrona Isabelle Rawlings

Rust, George Washington   "Died   Jan 4, 1905
    Died- George Washington Rust at his home 3 miles west of Mendon December
    28, 1904 at the age of 86 yrs 5 mo's 12 days. Settled in Quincy 1834
    Married Margaret L. Rawlings Feb 14, 1850 and had 3 children, Michael
    Newton, of Mendon Mo., Elizabeth Josephine Ketchum of Loraine and George
    Edward of Lima who with his wife survuve him. He was the last surviving
    veteran of the Mexican war. He enlisted in the 1st Ill. Cavalry under James D.
    Morgan. Made the trip to New Orleans on the 1st flat boat that left Quincy
    for that port with a cargo of provisions. Services at the house December
    30th by Rev A.M. Reitzel of the Lutheran church. Buried in Stone church
    cemetery.

Rust, Jacob   "Death"   Aug 21, 1890
    see Golden, Mrs Elizabeth

Rust, Mrs John   "Edgings"   Jun 1, 1877
    We learn the wife of John Rust died this A.M.

Rust, Mrs M.   "Obituary"   Jan 3, 1895
    see McCormick, Mrs Leah

Rust, Mrs M.N.   "Obituary"   Mar 8, 1905
    Died- Mrs M.N. Rust, wife of Mayor M.N. Rust on Sunday at 9:30 A.M.
    Feb. 26th, Mrs Emma McCormack Rust was born Greensburg, Penn October 31,
    1855 and married October 28, 1877 to M.N. Rust. Moved to Missouri and
    settled this community 14 yrs ago. Joined Lutheran church 1873. Leaves
    husband and 2 sisters. Funeral at the M.E. church Tuesday Feb. 27th at
    9:30 by Rev W.R. Enyeart. Buried in the cemetery at old Mendon.
    The Mendon Constitution.

Rust, Mrs Margaret   "Obituary"   Feb 10, 1898
    see Rawlings, Sarah Jane

Rust, Michael   "Local"   Jan 5, 1905
    Michael Rust of Mendon, Mo. came to attend the funeral of his father and
    is visiting relatives. Wife in poor health so was unable to come with him.

Rust, Mrs Michael   "Local"   Mar 1, 1905
    Died- Mrs Michael Rust at her home in Mendon, Mo. on Sunday Feb. 26th
    of dropsy of the heart. 49 yrs old. Leaves husband. She was sister of
    Mrs D.W. Dickerman and Mrs S.F. Chittenden. Buried at Mendon, Mo.
    yesterday A.M. Joseph Dickerman from here attended the funeral.

Rust, George   "Death"   Oct 23, 1890
    see Wright, Samuel R.

Rust, Elder W.H.   "Local"   Jul 27, 1899
    Elder W.H. Rust of Everly, Iowa is visiting his mother. His wife died
    2 weeks ago. The little babe was getting along fine on last report.

Ryan, Miss Mollie   "Quincy"   Mar 23, 1899
    Died- Miss Mollie Ryan at the home of her mother Sunday A.M. 29 yrs old.

Sabland, Henry   "Coatsburg"   Jan 1, 1891
   Died- at his home ½ mile south of Coatsburg December 24th, Henry Sabland
   in his 77th yr. Leaves a wife and 1 son. Will be buried in the village
   cemetery on Xmas day.

Safford, Elizabeth W.   "Died"   Sep 29, 1881
   Died- Mrs Elizabeth W. Safford Fletcher. Born May 19th 1819 and died
   Armada, Mich August 29th 1881. Married Adin H. Fletcher in 1845 a preacher
   who served Mendon nearly 27 yrs ago. 2 daughters and a sons wife preceeded
   her in death leaving 1 daughter and 5 sons. She was born in New Ipswich,
   N.H.

Sahland, Henry   "Coatsburg"   Sep 7, 1893
   Died- Tuesday night of last week, the 2nd son of Mr and Mrs A. Sahland.
   Henry was 19 yrs old.

Salmon, Mr I.N.   "Personal"   Nov 11, 1880
   Died- Mr I.N. Salmon a well known printer of Quincy Saturday. Been
   employed at the Whig office about 15 yrs.

Salone, Mr Sam   "Coatsburg"   Jun 4, 1885
   Mr Sam Salone was buried here a week ago Friday.

Sanderson, John   "Green Grove"   Aug 24, 1899
   John Sanderson's little child was brought here from Galesburg for
   burial Thursday. Buried same day at Brenneman cemetery.

Sartoria, Mrs Sabrie   "Obituary"   May 11, 1893
   see Johnson, Miss Lizzie

Sassenburg, Willie F.   "Died"   Jul 29, 1880
   Died- Monday A.M. July 26th, Willie F. , son of Ed Sassenburg at age
   2 yrs 22 days.

Sauble, George   "Probate"   Apr 19, 1890
   Probate of George Sauble, deceased   1st Monday of June 1890
   T.C. Poling, Attorney   Wm B. Sauble, Adm.

Sawyer, E.E.B.   "Camp Point"   Dec 23, 1880
   E.E.B. Sawyer read his obituary in the county news and said he was
   ashamed to ask people to insure ever since. But his courage will insure
   with time. He doesn't believe the story about his death even after he
   read it in so respectable a newspaper.

Scarborough, Mrs Deacon   "Payson"   May 15, 1879
   Died- May 8th at her residence in Payson, Mrs Deacon Scarborough. She
   has been a resident here many yrs. She was one of the original members of
   the Cong'l church at Payson. Services by Rev S.A. Wallace at the Cong'l
   church Friday May 9th.

348

Scarborough, Mrs Hattie   "Local"   Apr 23, 1903
    Died- Mrs Hattie Scarborough, wife of Joel K. Scarborough of Payson
    Saturday A.M. April 18th from effects of rheumatic heart trouble and
    advanced age. Was 83 yrs old Born in West Hartford, Conn. Jan 1, 1820
    Married Joel K. Scarborough 1856 who survives her and 1 son Henry F.,
    Niece and nephew, Miss Ellen Betts and William Betts attended funeral
    Monday at the Payson Cong'l church.

Scarborough, Henry   "Obituary"   Apr 4, 1901
    see Spencer, Miss Elmira

Scarborough, Mrs Mary   "Payson"   Apr 19, 1888
    Died- last Saturday, Mrs Mary Scarborough, one of our oldest citizens
    in her 73rd yr. Son William and Henry were called here for their mother's
    funeral.

Scattergood, Mrs   "Payson"   Aug 5, 1880
    Died- Mrs Scattergood, a sister of Mrs Keal at her home in Michigan
    July 29th.

Schafer, Mrs A.   "Obituary"   Dec 5, 1901
    see Zimmerman, Henry

Schaffer, J.   "Graves"   Jun 4, 1885
    J. Shaffer was included in list of graves decorated in Mendon cemetery
    Decoration Day.

Schaffer, John   "Lima"   Mar 28, 1901
    Died- John Shaffer, of Star was buried at 2 P.M. Sunday at the Rocky
    Run cemetery.

Schaffer, John W.   "Death List"   Dec 11, 1902
    John W. Schaffer was included in a death list.

Schardon, J.   "Death by drowning"   May 8, 1879
    see Steinbach, Mr A.

Schauf, Henry   "Death in Adams Co"   Mar 2, 1899
    Died- Mr Henry Schauf. Born Westphalia Prussia October 13, 1809 and
    died early Tuesday A.M. Resident of Quincy 60 yrs. Leaves 2 sons, John
    and Wm of Parkhurst Clothing Co. and 2 daughter, Annie and Mrs Joseph
    Gerber.

Schemerhorn, Mrs Martha   "Quincy"   Mar 16, 1899
    Died- Mrs Martha Schemerhorn Sunday. Born Warsaw, Illinois November 9,
    1865. Lived Quincy 17 yrs. Leaves husband and a 8 yr old son.

Schepp, Miss Lon   "Elm Grove"   Mar 31, 1898
    Died- Miss Lon Schepp of measles Sunday eve at 5 P.M. Buried Fowler
    Tuesday A.M. Her sister Tillie is sick with measles at Ed Crows. The
    2 sisters were the Crow boys housekeepers.

Scheutz, John and Pearl   "Tioga"   Jan 12, 1887
    Died- December 29th the infant child of John and Pearl Scheutz.

Schley, Henry   "Quincy"   Jan 6, 1881
    Died- December 30th 1880, Henry Schley. He was an old and respected citizen

Schlipmann, Mrs   "Honey Creek"   Apr 6, 1887
    4 funerals at Coatsburg last week, Mrs Jasper White, Mrs Schlipmann,
    Mrs Rittler and Mrs Powell.

Schlosser, John   "Tioga"   Nov 17, 1892
    Mr John Schlosser, a former resident, who about 8 yrs ago went to Dakota
    to live, died in New York November 2nd. Remains arrived here November 12
    th and buried in Tioga cemetery November 13th.

Schmitt, George   Jan 23, 1890
    Born to Mrs George Schmitt, a large male child on January 29th 1890
    He lived only a few minutes. Buried at Quincy. Dr Rooney of Quincy
    attended the mother.

Schnarr, Mrs Ida (John)   "Local"   Nov 20, 1884
    At a late hour last Thursday November 13th, Mr Henry A. Kespohl rec'd
    a telegram from John Schnarr at Wellington, Kansas, stating that his wife
    Mrs Ida Schnarr was killed by a sky rocket. Mrs Schnarr was the eldest
    daughter of Mr and Mrs Henry A. Kespohl's. She had lived in Kansas
    about 1 yr.

Schneider, Jacob   "Death in Adams Co"   Feb 16, 1899
    Died- Jacob Schneider, a resident of Quincy 40 yrs Friday afternoon of
    paralysis engaged many yrs in hotel and saloon business on Front St.
    Born March 17, 1834 at Korck,Grand Dochy of Baden. Leaves 4 sons and
    4 daughters.

Schneider, John   "Local"   Aug 17, 1893
    Died- a farmer named John Schneider living on the bottoms about 2½
    miles from Marcelline last Thursday. His body was found next day by his
    brother. Taken to Quincy for burial.

Schofield. Hon B.T.   "Carthage"   Mar 21, 1881
    Died Hon. B.T. Schofield March 18th 1881.

Schott, George   "News"   May 25, 1882
    Goerge Schott of Warsaw was found floating a few days ago near Hannibal.
    It is thought suicide.

Schrag, Mrs Chas.   "Obituary"   Mar 2, 1899
    see Kelly, John S.

Schuhardt, Mr   "Columbus"   Oct 15, 1885
    Infant son of Mr Schuhardt was buried October 7th.

Schulte, Solomon   "Death in Adams Co."   Apr 13, 1899
    Died- a son of Solomon Schulte, age 28 yrs on the Lemley farm in
    Indian Grave district Sundau night.

Schultz, Miss May   "Local"   Jun 22, 1904
    Died- Miss May Schultz of Ursa Tuesday A.M. Was 15 yrs old. Died from
    what seemed to be cholera morbus. Leaves parents and a brother.

Schultze, Wm   "Local"   Jul 4, 1895
    Drown-- 8 yr old son of Wm Schultze started to wade across Bear Creek
    and his little sister seeing him go down jumped in to help him and was
    also drown.

Schwartz, Mr Abram   "Loraine"   Feb 16, 1887
    Mr Abram Schwartz died yesterday 3 miles northeast of here of cramp colic.

Scott, Mrs   "Local"   Mar 24, 1892
    Mrs Scott, (colored) a former resident of Mendon who has for some time
    been an inmate of one of Quincy's hospitals, died on Monday at the home
    of her son-in-law, Wm Smith of Honey Creek and was buried Tuesday P.M.
    in the Mendon cemetery.

Scott, Mr and Mrs Alex   "Local"   Feb 23, 1899
    Died- the 8 month old baby boy of Mr and Mrs Alex Scott of Honey Creek
    Friday. Butied Sunday in Mendon cemetery. These same parents buried their
    oldest son a few months ago.

Scott, Alexander C. and Julia A.   Mar 12, 1885
    Died on March 7th the infant daughter of Alexander C. and Julia A. Scott
    of Honey Creek. Services by Rev E.C. Crane. She was 5 months 3 days old.

Scott, Mrs Mabel   "Quincy"   Mar 2, 1899
    Died- Mrs Mabel Scott, a colored woman, at St Mary's hospital Sunday
    A.M. of heart disease.

Scott, Mary Ellen   "Obituary"   May 10, 1900
    Died- Mary Ellen Scott born in Honey Creek twp November 10, 1876 and died
    May 8th 1900 at the age of 23 yrs 5 mo's 28 days. United with the U.B.
    church in 1895 Services by Rev Charles Gordon yesterday P.M. Buried
    in Mendon cemetery.

Scott, Nettie A.   "Death"   Mar 22, 1905
    see Baldwin, George Dutton

Scott, Mrs R.L.   "Obituary"   Dec 5, 1901
    see Zimmerman, Henry

Scott, Mrs Sarah   "Obituary"   Oct 28, 1897
    see Swan, Mrs Mary Ann

Scott, Miss Twila   "Payson"   Aug 26, 1880
    Died- at Clear Lake Iowa on August 16th of consumption, Miss Twila Scott.
    Leaves father and sister. She was a member of the Payson Baptist church
    where her funeral was held August 19th.

Scott, Walter   "Local"   Sep 22, 1898
    Died- at his home in Honey Creek Monday night of consumption, Walter, son
    of Mr and Mrs Alec Scott (colored) age 20 yrs. Services at the house
    Wednesday P.M. Buried in Mendon cemetery.

Scott, Walter Alexander   "Obituary"   Sep 29, 1898
Died- Walter Alexander Scott, eldest son of Alexander C. and Julia A.
Scott. Born Honey Creek twp Adams Co, October 31, 1878 and died in his
home same twp September 19th. He was 19 yrs 10 mo's 19 days old. On
December 29th 1895 he joined the U.B. church at Rigney Chapel. He was
sick several mo's.

Scott, Winfield   "Murder"   Dec 26, 1878
Murdered at Thorn's schoolhouse on the Mississippi bottoms a few miles
southwest of Marcelline Tuesday eve, Winfield Scott, formerly of Mendon.
He was shot by a young man named McFadden.

Scott, Wm   "Camp Point"   Jan 17, 1901
The funeral of Mr Wm Scott was at the Christian church last Sunday. He
was born in 1813. Was nearly 88 yrs old. Services by Orrin Dilley. Buried
in village cemetery.

Scott, Mr and Mrs Wm   "Local"   Apr 7, 1892
Mr and Mrs Wm Scott's infant child died on Monday A.M.

Scofield, Timothy A.   "Estate"   Mar 6, 1902
see Nelson, James D.

Scranton, Amos   Feb 6, 1879
Died- Mr Amos Scranton, who lived 1 mile east of Mendon. He fell from
a load of hay. His son Wm was with him and found his father senseless
and it appears that he scarcely breathed after he fell.

Scranton, Mr and Mrs Amos   "Death"   Dec 29, 1881
see Mayo, Mrs Nettie

Scranton, Amos   "Obituary"   Feb 13, 1879
The funeral of Mr Amos Scranton was Saturday at the Cong'l church.
7 of his children were present. Services by Rev A.B. Campbell. He was
born in Guilford, Conn in 1814. Came to Illinois in 1839 and we believe
he had been a resident of Mendon prairie since. 4 of his children are
already married. 1 lives in Michigan, 1 lives in Kansas and 2 live in
Missouri.

Scranton, Amos   "Probate"   Feb 27, 1879
Probate notice of Amos Scranton, deceased   3rd Monday of April 1879
Pheba Scranton, David C. Bray, Adms.

Scranton, Amos   "Funeral"   Jan 6, 1881
see Battell, Mr Sam L.

Scranton, Mrs Amos   "Death"   Aug 28, 1890
see Tallcott, Samuel

Scranton, Mrs Amos   "Obituary"   Apr 4, 1901
see Spencer, Miss Elmira

Scranton, Amos   "Death"   May 1, 1879
see Hendrickson, Mrs Phebe

352

Scranton, Edward   "Local"   Sep 25, 1902
    Edward Scranton, of Independence, Kansas, oldest son of Mr and Mrs George
    Scranton, died Sunday A.M. of typhoid fever. It is reported that Mrs
    Scranton is very sick with same disease.

Scranton, George   "Funeral"   Jan 6, 1881
    see Battell, Sam L.

Scranton, Hattie   Dec 7, 1882
    Died- Hattie, only daughter of Mr and Mrs Amos Scranton of Mendon, Mo.
    Age 6 yrs.

Scranton, Miss Kate   "Local"   Mar 3, 1892
    News rec'd of the death of Miss Kate Scranton at Northampton, Mass from
    LaGrippe. Buried at New Haven Saturday. Born in Mendon and was a sister
    of Susan Bushman and a daughter of Richard Scranton.

Scranton, Mrs Mary   "Obituary"   Apr 4, 1901
    see Spencer, Miss Elmira

Scranton, Mary   "Funeral"   Jan 17, 1895
    Funeral of Mary Scranton was held at the home on Hampshire St. yesterday.
    (Friday) P.M. by Rev Dana. "Whig"
    Brought here for burial Saturday A.M. Services at the Cong'l church and
    was buried village cemetery. Those attending from Quincy were- Rev Dana,
    Mrs Scranton and her 2 daughters, Miss Carrie and Miss Fanny, Miss Mina
    Hendrickson, sister of the deceased, Miss Annie Dills, niece of Mrs
    Scranton, Miss Leggatt and the 6 pallbearers and Miss Kate Shepherd of
    Ursa.

Scranton, Mary   "Local"   Jan 10, 1895
    News reached us yesterday of the death of Miss Mary Scranton, (Mary
    Henderickson) of brain fever. Brought to Mendon for burial. Services
    at the Cong'l church on Saturday at 11 A.M. Names per paper.

Scranton, Richard   Sep 6, 1883
    Died- Richard Scranton August 23rd at Minneapolis at the age of 36 yrs.
    Born Mendon. Buried Proria. Leaves wife and 2 children by a former marriage.

Seabrooks, Miss Elizabeth   "Obituary"   Dec 5, 1901
    see Zimmerman, Henry

Seabrooks, Miss Florence A.M. "Obituary"   Dec 5, 1901
    see Zimmerman, Henry

Seabrooks, Nancy M.   "Obituary"   Jul 14, 1898
    see Sprankle, Wm

Seals, Andrew   "Woodville"   Apr 4, 1889
    Born- about 2 weeks ago a son to Mr and Mrs Andrew Seals. It died
    last Monday night.

Seals, Dennis   "Loraine"   Jun 20, 1901
    Died- Dennis Seals, born Greene Co. Penn January 11, 1814. Married
    1837 to Mary Ann Farmer and had 5 sons and 3 daughters that survive him.
    His wife and 3 daughters are dead. Lived Illinois 64 yrs. Wife died 15
    yrs ago and he lived with son Frank since except 3 yrs when he lived with
    other children. After sleeping 96 hours he died June 14th at 11 A.M.
    Was 87 yrs 5 mo's 3 days old. Services by Rev F.P. Bonnefon at the house
    Saturday at 10 A.M. Buried Reece cemetery. 3 sons and 1 girl live to
    far away to attend the funeral. Mrs Mary Newlan, of Nickerson, Kansas
    Mrs Jeanette Parish of Knox City, Mo. Wm Seals of Quincy and Frank of
    Loraine were at home when he died. He was 2nd child of 11 brothers and
    sisters. 8 survive him. The oldest being 90 yrs old and the youngest
    65 yrs old. He had 35 grandchildren. All his brothers and sisters live
    close except for Mr Abe Seals of St Louis, Mo and Mrs Rebecca Ketchum on
    the Mendon prairie.

Seals, Mrs Dennis   "Loraine"   Mar 17, 1886
    Mrs Dennis Seals was buried at the Reece cemetery last Wednesday.
    Services by Elder Brunt at the M.E. church. Leaves husband and family.

Seals, Mrs Frank   "Local"   Feb 3, 1898
    Died- Mrs Frank Seals, she having lived just 3 weeks from the day the
    surgical operation was performed at Keokuk.

Seals, Mrs James M.   "Loraine"   Feb 8, 1894
    Died- Saturday at 2 A.M. of typhoid fever, Mrs James M. Seals in her
    58th yr. Services by Elder Rose at the M.E. church Sunday P.M. Buried
    in Curless cemetery in Big Neck. Leaves husband, 1 son and 2 daughters.
    She had been a member of the M.E. church for the last 3 yrs.

Seals, James N.   "Obituary"   Apr 14, 1892
    James N. Seals who lives 2½ miles southwest of here was killed April 7th
    when he came to Loraine for medicine for one of his children. His horse
    threw him and broke his neck. Born April 1, 1856. Was 36 yrs 7 days old.
    Leaves a wife and 4 children, father, mother and 2 sisters.

Seals, Joseph   "Loraine"   Sep 12, 1901
    Died- Joseph Seals living 1 mile south and 1½ miles east of Loraine died
    September 5th. Leaves a wife and 2 daughters, Mrs Ida Simpson of Quincy
    and Mrs Lillie Jenkins of Loraine. Buried in Reece cemetery on Friday
    September 6th. 3 brothers and 3 sisters also survive him.

Seals, Rachel   "Loraine"   Aug 15, 1901
    Died- Rachel Seals- born Feb. 22, 1829 in Clermont Co. Ohio. Married
    1846 to John Curless of same Co. In 1850 with their oldest daughter
    moved to Adams Co, Ill. Mr Curless died almost 13 yrs ago of heart
    failure. She joined the M.E. church at Union over 40 yrs ago, then the
    Loraine M.E. church. Died August 11th at the age of 72 yrs 5 mo's 20
    days. Had 9 children, 4 sons and 4 girls survive her. 1 daughter died in
    1866. Also leaves 4 brothers and 3 sisters, 32 grandchildren and 1 great
    grandchild. Funeral by Rev Wakefield of Mendon assisted by Rev Bonnefon of
    the M.E. church at 10:30 A.M. August 12th. Buried beside her husband in
    Reece cemetery.

Seals, Susie   "Loraine"   Feb 10, 1904
    Aunt Susie Seals died at her home southeast of here Saturday A.M.
    after a long illness. Leaves 1 daughter, Amanda and other relatives.
    Buried Sunday A.M. in the Curless cemetery.

Seals, Mr and Mrs Wm   "Obituary"   Aug 21, 1890
    see Garner, Miss Luetta

Searle, Deacon S.   "Local"   Apr 10, 1890
    Deacon S. Searle of Plymouth, Hancock Co. died April 3rd at the age of
    90 yrs. He was the uncle of Mrs Henry Baldwin of Mendon.

Seaton, G.K.   "West Point"   Aug 14, 1879
    A little child of G.K. Seaton died last Friday of some bowel complaint.

Secrese, Andrew J.   Jun 9, 1881
    Died- Andrew J. Secrese of Bowen, formerly of Columbus twp. He leaves
    5 children and was preceeded in death by his wife.

Seehorn, Alfred J.   "Local"   Aug 3, 1904
    Died- Alfred J. Seehorn of Fall Creek twp at his home Sunday A.M. at 6
    from paralysis, of old age and heart failure. Porn in Lincoln Co. Tenn
    June 30, 1822. Came with parents to Illinois 1832 and settled Fall Creek
    near where he died. Leaves wife and 7 children. Was a J.P. 30 yrs.
    Buried this P.M. at Payson. Lodge #379 A.F. & A.M. in charge.

Seehorn, Eli   "Death"   Jan 22, 1880
    see Parson, Charles

Seehorn, Elihu   "Local"   Nov 1, 1888
    Died- Elihu Seehorn, corner of this Co. died Saturday A.M. of heart
    discase at the age of 75 yrs. Buried in Woodland cemetery on Monday.

Seehorn, Rufus   "Payson"   Dec 9, 1885
    Died- Mr Rufus Seehorn last Saturday night. Funeral in Christian church.
    Mr Seehorn was raised in this Co. almost in the same neighborhood and was
    well known in this and adjoining twp's

Seehorn, Sherman   "News"   May 25, 1882
    A young man named Sherman Seehorn, a nephew of coroner Seehorn was
    thrown from a horse and thought fatally injured.

Seger, Mr S.E.   Mar 23, 1882
    Quincy paper reports the death of S.E. Seger. He was widely known
    wholesale grocer.

Seger, Charles E. Sr.   "Local"   Feb 6, 1902
    Chalres E. Seger, Sr member of the firm S.E. Seger's sons, Quincy was
    stricken with apoplexy in his office Friday afternoon and died almost
    immediately. Married Miss Mary Gilmer, who formerly lived 4 miles north-
    east of Mendon. Leaves wife, daughter, son, mother and 2 brothers.

Seifert, Daniel D.   "Obituary"   May 31, 1905
Daniel D. Seifert born in Cashtown, Adams Co. Penn. Feb 25, 1832 and
died at Mendon, Adams Co. Ill. May 28, 1905 at the age of 73 yrs 3 mo's
3 days. Married Anna M. Bingaman November 23, 1852 and had 4 children-
3 still living, Mary E. of Peoria, Ill., L. Belle of Mendon, Ill and
Marvin H. of Rockford, Ill. He came to Mendon in 1857 where he lost 1
child and his wife Feb 4, 1869. Married 2nd June 14th, 1874 to Mrs
Harriet Thompson. They had 2 children, 1 dead, the other is Walden D.
Seifert who is now the comfort of his widowed mother who is quite an
invalid. Services at his home 2 miles northwest of Mendon Tuesday at 10
A.M. by Rev A.M. Reitzel. Buried Mendon cemetery.

Seiple, Phillip   "Macomb Eagle"   Apr 20, 1887
Died- last Friday, Phillip Seiple, an old citizen of Hancock Co. Hancock
twp just over the line from McDonough Co. He was 69 yrs old. Killed in a
wagon accident in which his grandson was along but unhurt.

Selby, Mrs Emily   "Lima"   Jan 14, 1892
Died- Mrs Emily Selby in Ursa Saturday night. Husband was buried Saturday.
She was laid to rest by his side in the Stone church cemetery south of
Marcelline. Leaves daughters, Lucy Leachman of Ursa and Mrs Walter
Leachman of Lima.

Selby, Mr and Mrs Ernest   "Lima"   Jan 28, 1892
Mr and Mrs Ernest Selby and Mrs Lizzie Selby went to Kane, Green Co.
Ill. Wednesday to attend the funeral of their brother in law, Mr John
Finney.

Selby, James   "Lima"   May 23, 1895
Paul Smith, of Nevada is visiting relatives here and looking after
interests in the estate of his grandfather, James Selby.

Selby, James   "Death"   Oct 5, 1904
see Ippenson, Mrs Nellie

Selby, James   "Lima"   Aug 13, 1891
James Selby died August 6th. He was born Bourbon Co. Ky. October 26, 1816
He leaves a wife and 2 daughters, Mrs Fannie Wade and Nona Clark, both of
Lima. 2 aged brothers. Funeral at the M.E. church by Rev Puette of Quincy.

Selby, John Milton   "Local"   Jan 7, 1892
Died- Mr and Mrs John Milton Selby of Ursa.

Selby, Lewis V.   "Dead"   Jan 18, 1905
Died- Lewis V. Selby a pioneer farmer. He was 84 yrs old on the 1st day
of last August. Died Tuesday A.M. January 10th at 9 at the home of his
son Ernest Selby 2 miles southwest of here from old age. Born Bourbon
Co. Ky. and came to this county 1841. Married 3 times. 1st to Miss
Milly Dazey and they had a son and daughter. She died 1854. 2nd married
April 1, 1868 to Miss Annie Bolt and they also had a son and daughter.
She died Feb 1867 and on December 1, 1877 he married Miss Milly Orr who
was born in Bourbon Co. Ky. August 14, 1819. Survived by his wife, 2 sons
Ernest and William, who also live southwest of Lima and 1 daughter, Mrs
Laura Finney of Keokuk. Member of the M.E. church since he was 18 yrs old.
Services at the M.E. church Thursday at 2 P.M. at Lima by Rev Livingstone.

Selby, Mrs Louisa   "Lima"   Apr 4, 1895
Died- at her home here April 1st at 9, Mrs Louisa Selby at the age of
71 yrs. Was an invalid for a long time. Leaves 2 daughters, Mrs Fannie
Wade and Mrs Nona Clark. Buried beside her husband in Lima cemetery April
3rd. Services by Rev Richards of Canton, Mo.

Selby, Mr and Mrs Milton   "Ursa"   Jan 7, 1892
Died- Mr and Mrs Milton Selby. They had been married 55 yrs. He was born in
Bourbon Co. Ky. April 1811 and died December 31st 1891. Was nearly 81
yrs old. Came to Ill. in 1833 and married Emily Dazey in 1836. Mrs Selby
was born in Bourbon Co. Ky. also and died Jan 2, 1892 the same day he
was buried. She was 75 yrs old. Both buried in Stone church cemetery.
They leave 2 daughters, Mrs James Leachman and Mrs W.C. Leachman.

Selby, Nellie   "Death"   Oct 5, 1904
see Ippenson, Mrs Nellie

Selby, Wesley   "Obituary"   Dec 4, 1884
see Shaw, Mrs John E.

Sellers, Prof and Mrs E.W.   "Local"   Aug 10, 1904
We learn of the accidential drowning of the little son of Prof. and Mrs
E.W. Sellers of Liberty.

Sellick, Henry   "Loraine"   Jan 5, 1882
The remains of Henry, son of Mr and Mrs E.J. Sellick of Mendon, Mo.
was brought here for burial at Woodville.

Sells, Mrs Elijah   Jul 1, 1880
Mrs Sells, wife of Elijah Sells, died very suddenly last Wednesday eve
of congestive chills.

Sellwood, J.R.N.   Oct 17, 1901
"Sunday Oregonian Portland, Oregon" Died- J.R.N. Sellwood, a pioneer of
1856 died at his home, 41 East 31st St. October 5th. Born Mendon, Ill.
1841, with his father, Rev J.R.W. Sellwood and his uncle, John Sellwood
he started for Oregon 1856. They 1st settled at Salem and his father was
rector of the Salem Episcopal church for many yrs. J.R.W. and his
brother J.A. Sellwood graduated from the Williamette University 1866.
He leaves a wife, 2 daughters and 1 son, Mrs Fred S. West of Portland
Mrs A.W. Vosburg of DuBois, Penn and Charles Sellwood of Portland.

Sellwood, Rev Jas. R.W.   "Local"   Apr 19, 1894
"The Oregon Chruchman for April contains an acct of the death of Rev Jas.
R.W. Sellwood. Funeral at St Davids church, East Portland which he was
instrumental in founding, on Saturday March 24th. Buried in Lone Fir
cemetery beside his wife and only brother. The brothers were from
Cornwall, England and at one time lived here.

Senior, Mrs   "Obituary"   Jul 4, 1889
see Pepple, Catherine Sophia

Seward, Bud   "Local"   May 11, 1904
    News rec'd Monday of the death of Bud Seward in Sacramento, Calif,
    He is the brother of Timothy and Thomas Seward of this neighborhood.

Seward, Mr Byrum   "Local"   Jul 2, 1891
    Died- June 25th at his home 2½ miles southwest of Mendon, Mr Byrum
    Seward. 76 yrs old. resident of Mendon twp 40 yrs. Buried Woodruff
    burying grounds near Ursa.

Seward, Caroline   "Obituaru"   Feb 20, 1879
    see Fry, Jacob J.

Seward, Charlie   "Pryor"   Jul 31, 1884
    Died- July 27th, Charlie, the only son of Mr and Mrs C, Seward. Age
    22 months. Services by F.L. Wilson.

Seward, Gus   "Loraine"   Mar 15, 1888
    Gus Seward was buried in our cemetery Saturday.

Seward, Julia Ann   Feb 27, 1890
    Julia Ann Seward was born October 12th 1821 ans married Wm R. Conger
    May 10, 1838. Died Feb. 20th 1890. Buried Feb. 22nd from the Elm Grove
    U.B. church. Services by Rev D.L. Drake assisted by Rev W. Frost. Buried
    Wesley Chapel. Mother of 9 children. 1 girl and 8 boys.

Seward, Mr and Mrs Thomas   "News"   Jul 30, 1885
    Died- the 13 yr old daughter of Mr and Mrs Thomas Seward living west of
    town July 22nd from an accident at the home.

Sewell, Enoch   "Local"   Nov 30, 1887
    Mrs Sewell of Clarinda, Iowa has been staying with her brother Mr F.C.
    Turner and family since the funeral of her brother, Enoch, but will
    return home in a few days.

Sewell, Mrs Ann   "Obituary"   Aug 13, 1891
    see Kells, Richard

Seymore, Edward   "Local"   Jan 18, 1905
    The sum of 8,900.02 was paid to Frank Sonnett, County treas. Saturday.
    It was the amount of the inheritance from the estate of the late Edward
    Seymore minus the special appraisers fees.

Seymour, Edward   "Local"   Jul 20, 1904
    Died- Edward Seymour said to be the richest man in Adams Co. outside
    of Quincy died Friday night about 7:30 at his home in Fall Creek, about
    1 mile west of Payson from heart trouble. Lived Adams Co. nearly 70
    yrs. Born in West Hartford, Conn September 15, 1818. Never married.
    surviving him is 1 sister, Miss Eveline Seymour and nephews, Loren, Henry
    and Kay Seymour.

Seymour, Charles   "Death of a Pioneer"   Oct 13, 1898
    Died- Charles Seymour of Payson, one of the wealthest citizens of Adams
    Co. was found dead in the bed of Pigeon Creek, a small stream near the
    Adams Co. line on the Pike Co. side Tuesday A.M. He had fallen from the
    bridge, a short distance of 8 feet.

Seymour, Charles W.   "estate"   Mar 9, 1899
    Judge Epler yesterday finished his assessment of the inheritance tax
    of Chalres W. Seymour estate. Amts to over 240,000.00 After all
    deductions 222, 745.00 in clear market values and subject to taxation.
    Widows share 61,136.00 Each child 40,402.00

Shafer, Mrs Jacob   "Obituary"   Dec 4, 1890
    see Jennings, Thomas W.

Shaffer, Mrs H.K.   "Obituary"   Dec 5, 1901
    see Zimmerman, Henry

Shaffer, Mr and Mrs Henry   Nov 3, 1881
    Died- the 4 week old son of Mr and Mrs Henry Shaffer. Services by Rev
    Kunkleman.

Shaffer, Henry   "Ursa"   Apr 12, 1905
    Died- Henry Shaffer, age 89 yrs Friday A.M. at the home of his son,
    Alex Shaffer, living 2 miles west of here. Funeral was a the Catholic
    church in Ellington. Buried Catholic cemetery that place.

Shaffer, Jacob K.   Jun 2, 1881
    Jacob K. Shaffer died June 1st 1881 at the age of 32 yrs at West Point,
    Hancock Co.

Shaffer, Jacob   "Obituary"   Jun 9, 1886
    Died- in Melrose twp, Adams Co. Ill. June 3rd in his 69th yr of
    consumption, Mr Jacob Shaffer, formerly of this place. Born in Westmoreland
    Co. Penn. in 1817 and married Miss Mary King Feb. 14, 1840. Mrs died
    in 1858 and on March 3rd 1864 he married 2nd time to Miss Clementine
    Jennings. He joined the M.E. church of Mendon in 1875. He was previously
    a member of the United Brthern church for 19 yrs. He was an old settler
    of this part of Ill. Buried in Mendon cemetery June 5th from the M.E.
    church. Services by Rev Howard Miller. Leaves a wife and 6 children.
    (3 girls and 3 boys) besides 3 children by his 1st marriage. Mr Henry
    Shaffer, Mrs Wm Mutt and Miss Mary Shaffer, all of Mendon.

Shaffer, Jas. N.   "Graves"   Jun 1, 1899
    Jas. N. Shaffer included in list of soldiers graves decorated in Mendon
    cemetery on Decoration Day.

Shaffer, Mr and Mrs M.   "Local"   Sep 27, 1900
    Died- the infant daughter (1 week old) of Mr and Mrs M. Shaffer Saturday
    morning. Services at the house Sunday P.M. by Rev J.S. Bayne. Buried in
    Mendon cemetery.

Shaffer, Miss Mary C.   "Obituary"   Oct 20, 1886
   Died- Miss Mary C. Shaffer, born in Fayette Co. Penn January 20, 1856 and
   died in Melrose twp October 14th 1886 at the age of 30 yrs 8 mo's 24 days.
   Came to Ill. as a baby with her parents. Mother died when she was 3 yrs old
   Came to Mendon when she was 4 yrs old. Joined the M.E. church 7 yrs ago.
   Father died last spring. Buried Mendon cemetery near her brother Jim.

Shaffer, Mr Melvin   "Local"   Jun 22, 1904
   Mrs Melvin Shaffer and son of Quincy was visiting Mr and Mrs W.T. Mutt
   and was called home Tuesday A.M. on acct of the death of her husband.
   He was taken to insane asylum at Jacksonville for treatment recently and
   died there.

Shaffer, Mrs Melvin   "Local"   May 30, 1901
   Mrs Melvin Shaffer arrived home from Missouri where she was called to
   attend the funeral of her brother.

Shaffer, Mrs Wes   "Local"   Sep 15, 1898
   News rec'd from Missouri of the marriage of Wes Shaffer's widow.

Shambaugh, David P.   "Local"   May 19, 1892
   Surprise party for David P. Shambaugh last Friday night. It being his
   50th birthday. He was born May 14, 1842 at Carlisle, Cumberland Co. Penn.
   His father died August 1845 leaving a widow and 3 orphan children. He
   was put out among strangers until the age of 12 yrs. In 1854 his mother
   came to Rock Island Co. Ill. where he worked on a farm for strangers
   until August 1859 when he came to Mendon, Ill. to work for the late P.A.
   Ingersoll until January 1862 when he enlisted in the army for 3 yrs.
   He returned to Mendon May 1865. This being his 1st birthday party or
   present he ever rec'd.

Shambaugh, Mrs Emma J.   "Died"   Oct 7, 1880
   Died- Mrs Emma J. Shambaugh, at the residence of her father, Alex Gibbs
   in Mendon, Ill. October 4th at 5 P.M. She was born in Adams Co. Penn.
   December 22, 1848. Was 31 yrs 9 mo's 12 days old. Services by Rev Dr
   Hamilton at the Lutheran church.

Shanahan, Mr Wm   "Local"   Aug 18, 1892
   Died- Mr Wm Shanahan, an old irish American citizen of Quincy where he
   has lived since 1838. Died on Sunday at the age of 86 yrs. He was a
   devout Catholic.

Shanks, Mrs Orilla   "Loraine"   Sep 27, 1905
   Funeral of Mrs Orilla Shanks was at the Christian church Tuesday at 11 A.M.

Shannon, Mr J.H.   "Personal"   Sep 1, 1881
   Mr J.H. Shannon of Bishop's Creek Inyo Co. Calif. died. He os a former
   resident of Big Neck. While here he married Mrs Sue C. Anderson of
   Marcelline.

Shannon, Col W.M.   Jul 8, 1880
   Col. E.B.C. Chase of Chesterfield, S.C. killed Col. W.M. Shannon in a
   duel on the 5th.

Sharp, Mrs   "Personal"   Oct 16, 1879
   Mrs Sharp, wife of the editor of the Carthage Gazette died a few days ago.

Sharp, Mrs Judge   "Carthage"   Oct 23, 1879
    Mrs Judge Sharp, wife of editor of Carthage Gazette had one of the
    largest funeral processions ever seen in Carthage.

Shaw, Archibald   "Carthage"   Mar 17, 1881
    Died- Mr Archibald Shaw a few days ago on his 63rd birthday.

Shaw, Mr Ben   "Loraine"   Mar 8, 1894
    Died- Mr Ben Shaw, an old settler living near the Co. line some 7 miles
    northwest of here Sunday A.M. of lung fever.

Shaw, John and wife   Feb 22, 1905
    Tragedy 2½ miles east of Tioga at noon today (Friday) John Shaw, about
    35 yrs old shot and killed his wife and then himself because of legal
    and domestic troubles. Leaves 3 children, the oldest 5 yrs and the
    youngest 1 yr. They found them in a bedroom alive, but almost frozen.
    Lived here about 6 yrs. They were found by a brother of Mrs Shaw's
    named Moore.

Shaw, Mrs John E.   "Obituary"   Dec 4, 1884
    Kansas- Mrs John E. Shaw, wife of John E. Shaw died and soon after her
    small daughter Annie joined her. Also Wm Shaw preceeded her in death.
    Wm Shaw was 22 yrs old and son of Wesley Shaw now of Kansas. Mrs John
    Shaw was 24 yrs old and the daughter of Lewis Selby of Lima. Funeral
    held at Mendon by Rev Stodgel.

Shaw, Mrs Wesley   "Lima"   Sep 11, 1890
    Mrs Shaw, wife of the late deceased Wesley Shaw of Tioga has moved to
    Lima.

Shay, Wilheimina   "Obituary"   Feb 17, 1904
    see Hastings, Thomas Gilbert

Sheldon, Mrs Ed   "Obituary"   Jul 4, 1889
    see Pepple, Catherine Sophia

Shephard, George   "Payson"   Feb 6, 1879
    George Shephard's child fell into a tub of boiling water and died.

Shephard, P.B.   "Obituary"   Oct 31, 1889
    Died- at Barkhamsted, Conn Friday eve October 18th P.B. Shephard in his
    74th yr. "Notice from the Winsted, Conn. Herald"

Shepherd, Colonel   "Local"   Mar 30, 1887
    Died- Colonel Shepherd, Sec'y and Treas. of the Soldier's Home died on
    Thursday from a stroke of apoplexy. Remains were taken back to Spring-
    field for burial among his own folks.

Shepherd, Dr   "Payson"   Mar 11, 1880
    Mrs Dr Wood of Calif. arrived here March 6th to visit her father, Dr
    Shepherd who would call for Anna repeatedly. Later; Dr Spedherd died
    Monday A.M. Funeral Tuesday 2 P.M. March 9th. Father and daughter were
    always very close. Born December 28th 1814. Attended lectures at Louisville
    Medical Inst. Rec'd his degree of M.D. in 1845. In January 1843 he
    married Mary E., daughter of Col. J.G. Humphrey of Virginia. Mrs S.
    died in September of 1849.

361

Shepherd, Alonzo   "Local"   Jan 3, 1901
    Alonzo Shepherd, son of Mr and Mrs Frank Shepherd, formerly a resident
    of Mendon died at Hannibal, Missouri a few days ago.

Shepherd, Mrs B.F.   "Obituary"   Dec 28, 1899
    see Thompson, Mrs Lewis

Shepherd, Geo. W.   "Local"   Aug 25, 1892
    Died- on Monday August 15th of typhoid malaria at the age of 6 yrs
    7 mo's 19 days. Geo. W. only son of G.W. and Amanda Shepherd. Buried
    next day at 3 P.M. at the Free Will Baptist church near Marcelline.

Shepherd, Mr Jacob   "Mendon"   Jun 23, 1881
    Mr Jacob Shepherd died June 20th 1881

Shepherd, James M.   "Probate"   Aug 26, 1880
    Probate Notice of James M. Shepherd, deceased 3rd Monday of November 1880
    Mary A. Shepherd, Adm - Davis and Poling, attorneys.

Shepherd, James M.   "Loraine"   Jul 29, 1880
    Died- at his residence 3/4 mile north of town at 10 P.M. July 26th,
    James M. Shepherd. Age 40 yrs. Born in this vicinity and lived here all
    his life. Leaves a wife and 8 children. Buried Tuesday at the Baptist
    church near Marcelline.

Shepherd, John   "Probate"   Aug 24, 1893
    Probate notice of John Shepherd, deceased 1st Monday of October 1893
    A.L. Shepherd, Adm.

Shepherd, John   "Obituary"   Jul 27, 1893
    Died- John Shepherd July 16th 1893 of paralysis. Born in Sangamon Co.
    June 9, 1825. Was 68 yrs 1 mo 7 days old. Came to this twp as a young
    man with his father and lived here since. Married and raised 7 children
    2 sons and 5 daughters. 6 survive him besides his wife, 5 brothers and
    2 sisters. 1 sister lives in Texas, 1 brother in Missouri, 1 in Hancock,
    2' brothers and 1 sister in Ursa twp and 1 brother in Mendon twp. Buried
    Franklin church cemetery Monday P.M. the 16th. Services by Rev A.B. Peck.

Shepherd, Mrs John   "Death"   Oct 8, 1903
    see Hobby, William

Shepherd, L.D.   "Mt Hebron"   Feb 9, 1899
    L.D. Shepherd came up from Louisiana, Mo. to attend his mother's funeral.

Shepherd, Mrs Mary   "Mt Hebron"   Jun 30, 1886
    Mrs Mary Shepherd died June 24th at the age of 52 yrs. Leaves 3 sons and
    1 daughter. Buried in Franklin cemetery beside her husband who was buried
    some 25 yrs ago. Services by Elder C.S. Ballard.

Shepherd, Peter   "Probate"   Jul 5, 1883
    Probate Notice of Peter Shepherd deceased   3rd Monday of August 1883
    Joseph Shepherd, Adm.

Shepherd, Peter   Nov 21, 1878
    Died- on November 11th at his residence 5 miles northwest of Mendon,
    Peter Shepherd, in his 79th yr. Born in North Carolina January 1, 1800
    Came to Mendon twp over 40 yrs ago and raised a family of 9 sons and 2
    daughters.

Shepherd, Mrs Peter(Nancy)   "Obituary"   Jul 14, 1886
    Mrs Nancy Shepherd was born in 1801 and died July 2, 1886. She came from
    North Carolina to Madison Co. Ill. in 1819 and lived there 1 yr and moved
    to Sangamon Co. It was there that she married Mr Peter Shepherd, being the
    1st marriage in that Co. They moved to Adams Co. in 1835 and lived in
    Mendon twp until a yr ago when she moved to Marcelline. They had 11
    children (9 boys and 2 girls) 8 survive her. She has 50 living grand
    children. Baptized early in life in the Presbyterian church.

Shepherd, Samuel   "Death"   Nov 28, 1901
    Samuel Shepherd, who until recently had been a resident of Mendon twp
    died Monday at the home of his daughter, Mrs Adair at Lima at the age of
    71 yrs. Was father of 10 children (6sons 4 daughters) all living except
    2 sons. Living are the twins Elisha of Ursa and Elijah of Quincy, B.F. of
    Mexico, Mo., Samuel of St Louis, Mrs Adair of Lima, Mrs Robert McNay of
    Mendon, Mrs Brown of St Louis and Mrs Gerhard of Hancock Co. Also
    survived by 4 brothers and 1 sister. Member of Christian church 35 yrs.
    Funeral at Franklin church by M,E, minister of Lima Tuesday A.M. Buried
    Franklin cemetery by the side of his wife.

Shepherd, Samuel   "Obituary"   Feb 9, 1899
    see Crank, Mary Jane

Shepherd, Mrs Samuel(Jane)   "Mt Hebron"   Feb 9, 1899
    Died- Mrs Samuel Shepherd at her home Wednesday Feb. 1st, Jane Crank
    born Adams Co. 1833 and married Samuel Shepherd 1853. Had 10 children,
    9 survive her, Services by C.O. Crank on Feb. 3rd at the family home.
    Buried Franklin cemetery.

Shepherd, Sarah J.   "Obituary"   Feb 5, 1903
    see McNay, Andrew

Shepherd, Mrs Susan   "Death"   Mar 15, 1905
    Mrs Susan Shepherd, wife of the late John Shepherd died at her home in
    Marcelline Monday at 5 P.M. from a 2nd stroke of paralysis Sunday at noon.
    Mrs Shepherd (nee Webb) was 79 yrs old and born on a farm in Mendon twp
    where she lived most of her life. Was a member of Freewill Baptist church.
    Leaves 4 daughters and 2 sons, Mrs D.F. McNay of Quincy, Mrs George Groves,
    Mrs D.C. Laughlin, Mrs George Laughlin and A.L. and S.A. Shepherd all of
    this twp. She fell several yrs ago disabling her hip so was obliged to
    use crutches. Funeral at 10 A.M. today at Franklin church by Rev A.M.
    Reitzel. Buried beside her husband.

Shepherd, Mrs Susan   "Local"   Apr 12, 1905
    B.A. Van Dyke was Monday appointed Adm. of the estate of Mrs Sam Shepherd,
    deceased.   SUSAN

Sherlock, Mrs   "Obituary"   Feb 17, 1898
    see Forsythe, Berry

Sherlock, Mr and Mrs F.L.   "Local"   Jan 25, 1894
    Died- the 4 month old child of Mr and Mrs F.L. Sherlock, living on the
    VanDyke place Monday. Buried yesterday in the Catholic cemetery at
    Bloomfield. Servcies by Rev Father Dietrich.

Sherman, Mrs   "Camp Point"   Mar 7, 1901
    The funeral of Mrs Sherman will take place at the M.E. church Tuesday.
    Services by Rev McGaw, the Presbyterian pastor.

Sherman, J.D.   "Local"   Jan 19, 1888
    Died- Mr J.D. Sherman, of N.Y. who was visiting his wife at Mrs Doyle's
    last summer died about a week ago at Poughkeepsie on the Hudson, not
    having been able to reach home.

Shields, Dr M.   "Personal"   Oct 14, 1880
    Dr M. Shields, a noted physican of Mt Sterling, Ill. died on the morning
    of October 7th.

Shierman, Mr C.   "Tioga"   Mar 21, 1899
    Died- an infant child of Mr C. Shierman of Hickory Ridge. Buried here
    last Tuesday.

Shinn, G.W.   "Payson"   Mar 3, 1886
    The youngest child of G.W. Shinn died Saturday of lung fever.

Shinn, Isaac   "Payson"   Nov 2, 1882
    Died on October 28th Isaac Shinn, author of Shinn's Ready Advisor.

Shipe, Arthur W.   "Died"   Jan 17, 1895
    Died- at Table Rock, Nebr. on Friday A.M. January 4th of pleurisy,
    Arthur W. son of Jacob and Mary E. Shipe. Born in Lima, Ill. March 25th
    1878. His father died before he was 2 yrs old and in March 1890 his mother
    married Jas. A. Carlock of Table Rock. Leaves his mother and a sister.
    Services by Rev Wilson of the Presbyterian churchand was buried in Table
    Rock cemetery. He was converted 3 weeks ago.signed, A.C. Haig.

Shipe, Elizabeth   "Lima"   Jan 3, 1895
    Died- Aunt Lizzie, or Mrs Elizabeth Shipe on the eve of December 22nd.
    Left 1 son with whom she lived, 1 daughter, Mrs Geo. Brothers of
    California and a number of grandchildren and great grandchildren.

Shipe, Jacob   "Lima"   Dec 18, 1879
    Jacob Shipe, one of our best men, died last week.

Shipe, Jacob   "Probate"   Jan 29, 1880
    Probate Notice of Jacob Shipe, deceased   3rd Monday of March 1880
    James Michael, Adm.

Shipe, John H.   "Lima"   Feb 17, 1898
    Died- at his home some 2 miles northeast of Lima John H. Shipe. 63 yrs
    old. Born in Westmoreland Co. Penn. Came here when quite young and lived
    here since. Leaves 2 sons and 3 daughters and a wife. Services by Rev Hess
    of Tioga. Buried in Lima cametery beside his parents.

Shipe, Louis   "Local"   Jul 16, 1891
    Louis Shipe a young man from Lima died at the Franklin House in Quincy
    last Friday July 10th of Brights disease of the kidneys.

Shipley, Mrs   "Fowler"   Sep 12, 1901
    Died- last week, old Mrs Shipley, who made her home with her daughter,
    Mrs E. Kendall. At the time of her death she was visiting her daughter,
    Mrs Long, of Coatsburg.

Shippe, Daniel   "Lima"   Oct 16, 1890
    Daniel Shippe died October 5th at the poor farm. He was insane for 30 yrs.
    Buried October 6th.

Shippe, Isaac   Sep 1, 1881
    Died- August 21st, Isaac Shippe. Funeral August 22nd. He was a Mason.

Shoemaker, Charles   "News"   Feb 12, 1880
    Uncle Charley Shoemaker, probably the oldest colored man in this part of
    the country died last Saturday. Buried Sunday afternoon.- Thought to be
    about 90 yrs old.

Shoemaker, John   "Quincy"   Feb 23, 1899
    Died- Mr John Shoemaker, a native of Penn. Was 75 yrs old. Died Friday A.M
    Lived Quincy 65 yrs. Leaves a wife 5 sons and 2 daughters.

Short, Mrs   "Stillwell"   Dec 2, 1897
    Remains of Mrs Short who died Friday afternoon were sent to Virginia
    Saturady eve for burial.

Shourer, Nancy   "Obituary"   Aug 12, 1880
    see Downing, Wm M.

Shrader, George A.   "Big Neck"   Mar 19, 1891
    George A. Shrader, 5th child of John and Mary Shrader died March 11th
    at the age of 5 yrs 10 months. Funeral at the Union church by Rev F.C.
    Read after which the remains were buried in Curless cemetery.

Shrader, Mrs Hiram   "York Neck"   Feb 25, 1892
    Mrs Hiram Shrader was called to Macon City, Mo. by the death of her
    sister, Mrs Newmyer, and while there a daughter of the deceased died.

Shriver, Apollo   "Obituary"   Mar 1, 1900
    Died- Apollo Shriver, born Green Co. Penn. July 28, 1818. Married 1837
    to Miss Mary Haynes of same county. Had 10 children, 4 survive him.
    His wife died August 22nd 1869, children surviving are- B.F., J.A.,
    S.A.D. and Elizabeth. Mr Shriver died at the home of daughter Elizabeth
    Hardy near Greensburg, Mo. Feb. 21st Buried Mendon Feb. 24th Services
    by Rev Wakefield.

Shriver, Appollo   "Obituary"   Apr 21, 1886
    see Stilwell, Mrs Elijah

Shriver, B.F.   "Local"   Mar 1, 1900
    B.F. Shriver, of Big Neck was in town Saturday awaiting the arrival of
    the remains of his father.

Shriver, Mrs Hannah   "Obituary"   Apr 24, 1902
    see Fletcher, Chas. Wolvertine

Shriver, Mrs Henry   "Death"   Nov 23, 1904
    see Myers, Mrs Mary A.

Shriver, Louis   "Probate"   Jun 19, 1890
    Probate notice of Louis Shriver, deceased   1st Monday of August 1890
    Henry Shriver, Leonard Shriver, Ex's

Shriver, Louis   "Obituary"   May 22, 1890
    Louis Shriver died at his home 3½ miles south of Mendon May 13th. Born
    Guddelsheim, Waldeck, Germany in January 1816. Came to thie country in
    1854 and settled in Herman Mo. from there to St Louis and on to Quincy.
    There he married Miss Catherine Waggaman March 5, 1858 and shortly came
    to Mendon twp. He leaves a widow and 5 children, Henry, F.A., L.E., L.C.
    and Mrs Rettig. Buried in Gilliland family burying ground. Services by
    H.U. Rahn pastor of the German Lutheran church of Ursa,

Shriver, Louis and wife   "Obituary"   Aug 27, 1903
    see Bruggebos, Conrad Julius

Shriver, Mrs Martha   "Obituary"   Sep 11, 1902
    see Daughtery, Mrs Jane

Shuahart, Mrs   "Camp Point"   Oct 3, 1901
    Mrs Shuahart, living in Columbus twp was buried last Sunday.

Shultz, Mary   "Obituary"   Jan 8, 1903
    see Shupe, Mrs Mary

Shultz, Harve   "Lima"   Feb 16, 1888
    A little child of Mr and Mrs Harve Shultz, living south of this place
    died of membranous croup one day last week. Buried Keith cemetery near
    Marcelline.

Shultz, Harvey   "Marcelline"   Feb 16, 1888
    Died- Feb. 7th, the youngest and only daughter of Mr and Mrs Harvey
    Shultz, age 1 yr.

Shultz, Henry   "Ursa"   Feb 9, 1882
    Died- Feb. 1st the mother of Henry Shultz, age 93 yrs at Sparta, Ky.

Shultz, Jonas R.   Jan 11, 1878
    Died- Jonas R. Shultz at his parents home near Marcelline on Sunday eve
    December 30th 1877 at the age of 34 yrs 11 days. Buried December 31st
    Born Adams Co. near Marcelline and lived with his parents right up to
    the time of his death. Joined Christian church a few yrs ago. Joined the
    Marcelline Odd Fellows Lodge #127 on Feb. 13th 1875.

Shumate, Mrs   "Local"   May 2, 1889
Mr and Mrs Joseph Harrison were called on Friday to Burlington, Iowa
by the death of Mrs Shumate, wife of Mrs Harrison's brother,

Shupe, Mr and Mrs Benton   "Local"   Jan 7, 1892
Mr and Mrs Benton Shupe's infant child died Sunday P.M,

Shupe, Catherine   "Obituary"   Dec 20, 1900
Died- Catherine Shupe, born Stockdale, Westmoreland Co. Penn August 8,
1829 and died Mendon, Mo. December 7th 1900 at the age of 71 yrs 4 mo's
Married Ezekiel J. Rawlings at Mendon Ill May 21, 1848, had 1 child,
Mrs John Wilson of Ceres, Oklahoma. Leaves her husband, 1 daughter,
3 grandchildren, 1 great grandchild, 3 sisters. Member of the Mendon, Ill,
M.E. church since 1844. Services by Elder McNamara from the M.E. church
December 9th at 2:30 P.M. Buried in the old Mendon, Mo. cemetery.

Shupe, Mrs Charles   "Obituary"   Mar 2, 1904
see Althouse, Mrs Anna Isabelle

Shupe, Christopher   "Obituary"   Feb 25, 1892
Died- Christopher Shupe, born Westmoreland Co. Penn July 18, 1815.
Moved to Adams Co. Ill. in 1843 and died Feb. 16, 1892 at the age of
76 yrs 6 mo's 28 days. Funeral Friday A.M. at the Lutheran church by Rev.
M.L. Schmucker. Buried Mendon cemetery. Leaves a wife, 6 sons and 1
daughter. Some of them widely scattered but all here for the funeral.

Shupe, Mr Christopher   "Local"   Feb 18, 1892
Mr Christopher Shupe died at Jacksonville insane asylum Monday night.
Mr Conrad Quigg his brother in law went to the asylum to bring remains
back home. Funeral tomorrow A.M. at 11 in the Lutheran church.

Shupe, Mr David   "Local"   Apr 28, 1886
News have been rec'd that Mr David Shupe, of Mendon, Mo. died on the
previous Sunday and was buried on Tuesday. Mr Shupe was the oldest son of
Mr C. Shupe of this place and one of the founders of it's name sake in
Missouri.

Shupe, Mrs E.A. (Lew)   "Local"   Jul 27, 1887
Died- Mrs E.A. Shupe, wofe of Lewis Shupe of this place died Saturday
A.M. July 23rd. Buried Sunday P.M. in the Mendon cemetery. Services by
Rev E.W. Souders at her residence. Mr Shupe was in Maysville, Mo. when
his wife died. Leaves a husband and 2 children- 1 only a baby,

Shupe, Mrs Geo. W.   "Obituary"   Jun 1, 1904
see Chittenden, Abraham

Shupe, John   "Funeral"   Aug 23, 1905
The funeral services of John Shupe who died at the home of his brother,
Charles, north of town was Thursday P.M. by Rev E.P. Schueler of Quincy.
Brothers, Edward M. of Mendon, Mo. and Benton and family of Paloma were
present for services. He was born October 17, 1846 on the farm where he
died Tuesday eve August 15th 1905 at the age of 58 yrs 9 mo's 28 days.
Buried beside his parents in Mendon cemetery.Pallbearers were;
F.O. Dickerman, L.D. Nichols, J.P. Gilliland, S.H. McClung, Alvin Tripp,
W. Siple.

Shupe, Mrs Lewis   "Obituary"   Mar 24, 1886
   see Vandersall, Elizabeth

Shupe, Margaret   "Death"   Jun 21, 1905
   see Clair, John

Shupe, Miss Margaret   "Obituary"   Apr 17, 1902
   see Quig, Conrad

Shupe, Miss Mary   "Obituary"   May 21, 1901
   see Reese, Fredrick

Shupe, Mrs Mary   "Obituary"   Jan 8, 1903
Died, Mrs Mary Shupe at 9:45 A.M. New Years day at the age of 84 yrs
6 mo's 3 days. Mary Shultz was born in Westmoreland Co. Penn June 29, 1818
married Christopher Shupe November 19, 1841 and with him came to Adams
Co. 1843 and after a yr or 2 moved to their home where she died north
of Mendon. He died Feb. 16, 1892. had 10 children, 7 boys and 3 girls
all surviving but 2. Namely, Mrs Elizabeth Hewitt of Hutchinson, Kan.
Mrs Catherine Rempp, Montezuma, Iowa, Edward M. of Mendon Mo. John of
Mendon, Ill, Louis of Alexander, Ill, Geo. W., Benton of Paloma, Ill.
Charles of Mendon, 25 grandchildren, 33 great grandchildren, 4 great great
grandchildren and 1 sister living in Sioux City, Iowa. Was one of the
Charter members of Mendon Lutheran church of 50 yrs. Services by Rev E.P.
Schueler of Luther Memorial church,Quincy Saturday P.M. at the Lutheran
church. Buried Mendon cemetery beside her husband. All children were at
the funeral except George W. Her grandsons Joseph and Samuel Rempp of
Montezuma, Iowa attended the funeral.

Shupe, Mary   "Local"   Jan 22, 1903
Will of the late Mary Shupe was filed in Co. court last week and heard
Wednesday Feb. 4th. She leaves 1000.00 to son Charles- 300.00 to her
daughter Mrs Elizabeth Hewitt and 100.00 each to her sons George and
Louis. The residue of the estate to be devided between sons E.M., A.B.
and John Shupe. C.B. Garrett named Adm.

Shupe, Nellie May   "Local"   Aug 25, 1892
"Quincy Whig" Judge Berrian issued a decree yesterday granting the
petition of Charled Shupe and Anna I. Shupe to adopt Nellie May Shupe, a
8 yr old girl. Her mother is dead and her father, Lewis B. Shupe gave
his consent.

Sigebee, Mrs Baltis   "Local"   Mar 1, 1888
Dr Sigebee attended the funeral Tuesday of his brother Baltis' wife
at Woodland cemetery, Quincy

Sigsbee, Capt. Chas. D.   "Local"   Sep 28, 1899
Rec'd word of the death of the youngest daughter of Capt Chas. D.
Sigsbee, of the Maine fame, at Rehoboth, Deleware. Dr Sigsbee of Mendon
ia a relative.

Sigsbee, Edwin Eugene   "Burial"   Oct 24, 1901
    The body of Edwin Eugene Sigsbee reached here yesterday A.M. and was
    taken to Chas. H. Nutt's undertaking rooms for burial Thursday from
    the M.E. church. Born Mendon April 29, 1878 and died March 14th 1901 at
    the age of 22 yrs 11 mo's 15 days at Oroquita, Mindanoa P.I. Enlisted
    in the 40th Kan. Vol. September 6, 1899 and would have been mustered out
    June 1st, 1901 as private of Co. A. 40th Inf. U.S.A.

Sigsbee, Eugene   Jun 5, 1902
    Soldiers of Spanish and Philippine war buried in Mendon cemetery
    included Eugene Sigsbee.

Sigsbee, Eugene E. Pvt.   "Local"   May 9, 1901
    Dr Sigsbee rec'd word from Washington, D.C., Eugene E. Sigsbee Pvt.
    Co. A. 40th Inf U.S. Vol. Died March 14th 1901 at Oraquita, Mendanao,
    P.I. of cerbral imbolism. Buried in Grave #1 Northwest corner central
    yard. Same place. Signed Johnson, Ass't Adj't Gen.

Sigsbee, Nicholas   "Local"   Aug 14, 1890
    From the Rural Time of Otego, Otsego Co. N.Y. July 9th
    Death of Nicholas Sigsbee at the age of 74 yrs. Son of Nicholas Sigsbee,
    one of the early settlers of Deleware Co. and a cousin of Dr. Sigsbee of
    this place. He moved to Albany with his parents in 1832.

Sigsbee, Rosa Agnes   "Local"   Jul 7, 1898
    Miss Hattie Sigsbee arrived home from Chicago bringing her brother, Wm's
    orphaned daughter, Rosa Agnes with her to live with her grandparents,
    Dr and Mrs Sigsbee.

Sigsbee, Miss Rose (Agnes)   "Dead"   May 3, 1905
    Remains of Miss Rose Sigsbee were shipped to Quincy this A.M. from
    Chicago where she died Saturday of consumption. Body accompanied by an
    aunt, Miss Bessie Brapy, of Chicago. 29 yrs old and formerly lived
    Quincy. Parents are both dead. Survived by grandparents, Dr and Mrs
    William Sigsbee and a sister, Miss Lulu Sigsbee, all of Quincy. The
    latter since the death of her father has been staying at St Mary's
    hospital. Father was a mail carrier. Quincy Herald Monday.
    (Miss Sigsbee, Agnes, as hse was known to us at one time attended school
    here making her home with her grandparents)

Sigsbee, Miss Tillie   Dec 25, 1890
    Miss Tillie Sigsbee, daughter of Dr and Mrs Wm and A.E. Sigsbee of
    Mendon died of consumption at Jacksonville December 18th. Was 32 yrs old.
    Buried Mendon cemetery. Services at the home by Dr Peet and M.L.
    Schmucker.

Sigsbee, Mrs Wm   "Local"   Nov 19, 1891
    Mrs Wm Sigsbee died at her home at 707 Kentucky St. Quincy of
    rheumatic fever Tuesday A.M. Funeral this A.M. from St Peters Catholic
    church.

Sigsbee, William J.   "Local"   Sep 23, 1894
   The remains of William J. Sigsbee, 2nd oldest child of Dr and Mrs Sigsbee
of this village were brought from Quincy Monday eve and after a short
services at the parental home were laid to rest in Mendon cemetery,
Died from morphine poisoning under very painful circumstances. Was 37
yrs old. Leaves 2 children whose mother is dead. They are cared for in the
Aloyius Orphans home.

Sigbie, Dr   "Local"   Mar 10, 1886
   Dr Sigbie will go to New York to visit his father who is 89 yrs old. He
lives near Schenectady and not very many months ago lost his partner of
life at the age of 84 yrs.

Sigsworth, Mrs Sarah   "Quincy"   Mar 9, 1899
   Died- Mrs Sarah Sigsworth of ElDara, Ill who was on a visit to her
daughter, Mrs A.L. Brown of apoplexy Sunday noon. 71 yrs old.

Simmons, Mr E.   Aug 4, 1881
   Died- in Quincy, a son of Mr E. Simmons of Mendon.

Simmons, Edward   Aug 23, 1882
   Died- Mr Edward Simmons, son of Mr E. Simmons of Mendon, died in Quincy
November 15, 1882. Age 29 yrs.

Simmons, Elias   "Courthouse News"   Mar 17, 1898
   Will of Elias Simmons was admitted to probate. It as brought against the
legatees by Geo. Simmons, a son of the testator. Will dated 1895 when
Mr Simmons was 76 yrs old. It left 500.00 to Cordelia Wilson, a women
who lived at the Simmon home. 500.00 to his grandsons, Van R. and DeFay
Simmons, _____ to Geo. Simmons of Colo. the rest to his wife Lucinda
Simmons who was named Executox. The contestant is ruled out by the blank
before his name and inherits nothing. Attorneys, Chas. A. McColm.

Simmons, Elias   "Obituary"   Dec 16, 1897
   Died- Elias Simmons was born March 1, 1819 in Fairfax, Virginia. Left
early in life, went to Lafayette, Ind. where he married Caroline Circles
Had 5 children. (4 children and wife are dead) He had 2 brothers and 2
sisters (all dead) 1 brother was a Baptist minister, but his parents and
most of his relatives were Methodists. In 1840 he moved to Iowa where he
joined the Methodist church. Lived in Van Buren Co. for 24 yrs. then
moved to Warswa, Hancock Co. Ill. where he lived 12 yrs. From there he
moved in 1877. Here he married Mrs Lucinda Laughery who survives him.
He died December 8, 1897 - was 78 yrs 9 mo's 7 days old. Funeral at the
M.E. church Friday P.M. by Rev E.K. Crews. Buried in village cemetery.

Simmons, Mrs Eliza (Wm)   "Obituary"   Nov 16, 1899
   Died- Mrs Eliza Simmons, nee Gray, Born Pittsburg, Penn July 11, 1828
Died Mendon Tuesday A.M. at 12:30 Was 71 yrs 4 mo's 3 days old. Married
the late Wm Simmons Feb. 22, 1869. Services at the house yesterday A.M.
by Rev W.J. Spire of the Lutheran church. Buried beside her husband at
Wesley chapel.

Simmons, James   "Local"   Aug 28, 1902
    Mr and Mrs Richard Flack attended the funeral of James Simmons yesterday,
    who died at his home near Stillwell Tuesday A.M. He was buried at West
    Point. Mr Simmons was a brother in law of Mr Flack.

Simmons, John K.   Aug 11, 1881
    Died- John K. Simmons, son of E. Simmons of Mendon. Born 1842 near Memphis,
    Mo. Died August 2, 1881 at Quincy. Moved Memphis to Keoqua, Iowa at the
    age of 3 yrs. Studied law 1861 and graduated at Dayton, Ohio and joined
    his father in Warswa, Ill and practiced law, then moved to Quincy. Married
    Mary Cherry in Quincy 1872.

Simmons, Mrs Mary   "Death"   Jan 24, 1901
    see Duncan, Ferdinand M.

Simmons, Mr Wm   "Local"   Dec 1, 1892
    Mr Wm Simmons, living 3 miles south of Mendon died this A.M. Was 82 yrs
    old. Funeral at the house at 1 P.M. tomorrow. Burial at Wesley Chapel.

Simmons, William   "Probate'   Dec 8, 1892
    Probate notice of William Simmons, deceased   1st Monday of Feb. 1893
    Richard B. Starr, Ex.

Simpson, Benjamin   "Probate"   Feb 17, 1898
    Probate Notice of Benjamin Simpson, deceased   1st Monday of April 1898
    Elizabeth Ann Simpson, Ex.   Wilson and Wall Attorneys.

Simpson, Benjamin Franklin   "Obituary"   Dec 23, 1897
    Died- Mr Benjamin Franklin Simpson died last Friday of heart and kidney
    trouble and old age. Born at Greensburg, Penn. Was 81 yrs 2 mo's 1 day old.
    Came to Mendon in 1857 where he farmed, married Anna Elizabeth Horner
    March 30, 1859 who survives him. No children. Member of Lutheran church.
    Funeral Sunday afternoon from the Lutheran church by pastor Rev Scherer.
    Buried village cemetery.

Simpson, Bishop   Jun 26, 1884
    Bishop Simpson of the M.E. church died at his home in Philadelphia June
    18th.

Simpson, Mrs Ida   "Obituary"   Sep 12, 1901
    see Seals, Joseph

Simpson, Jesse   "Local"   Jul 27, 1887
    A saloon keeper of Quincy named Jesse Simpson committed suicide Sunday
    P.M. by shooting himself in the head. Buried in Decatur by the side of his
    mother as his last wish left in a note.

Simpson, Mrs Mollie   "York Neck"   Jan 21, 1892
    Mrs Mollie Simpson, widow of the late John Simpson was married to a
    druggist, of Colorado.

Simpson, Sam   "Ursa"   Jul 26, 1883
    A little child of Sam Simpson died July 19th.

Simpson, Mrs Sarah   "Clip from Augusta Eagle"   Feb 10, 1886
    Mrs McKown's older sister died, Mrs Sarah Simpson, consort of Wm
    Simpson of Butler, Bates Co. Mo. died January 23rd of pneumonia. Leaving
    a large family of children, 1 baby 2 months old. Mr Simpson is a former
    resident of this co. and is now a large land owner and cattle merchant
    of Bates Co.

Sinnock, Grandpa   "Payson"   Oct 13, 1886
    Died- last Friday Grandpa Sinnock was buried, He was 93 yrs old. Services
    by Rev Douglas at the Baptist church.

Sinnock, George   "Death"   Jan 24, 1901
    Died- George Sinnock, one of the pioneers of Adams Co. at 9·50 A.M.
    Tuesday at his home in Payson. Born in Battle, Sussex Co., England
    January 17, 1819. Came to America in 1837. 1st locating in Jamesville,
    Onondaga Co. N.Y. where he engaged in the shoe trade. In 1838 he moved
    to Detroit, Mich. and the same fall came to Quincy. In the spring of
    1840 he went tp Payson where he lived since. In October 1840 he married
    Miss Sarah Ann Kay. They had 8 children, 4 boys and 4 girls. They are,
    Mrs W.W. Eckman of Menphis, Mo., Mrs Richard Harris, Charles W. Sinnock of
    LaPlata, Mo. , J.W.Kay and Mrs Etta Hewes and George Sinnock of Quincy and
    Miss Carrie Sinnock of Payson.

Sinnock, Susie   "Quincy"   Mar 23, 1899
    Died- Susie, daughter of Mr and Mrs J.W. Sinnock. Age 5½ yrs Sunday A.M.

Siple, John   Jan 19, 1888
    Died- At Edina, Mo. Friday eve January 13th of pneumonia, John Siple,
    formerly of this place at the age of 40 yrs 4 mo's 11 days. Born at
    McDowell, Highland Co. Virginia September 2, 1847. Came west 20 yrs ago.
    Spent a yr in Ohio before coming to Illinois. Except for 2 yrs in Mo. he
    lived the rest of his life in Hancock and Adams Co's Here he married.
    Leaves a wife and 1 child (son) who lives in Mendon with his grandparents,
    Mr and Mrs Bortz. He has a married sister living in Hancock Co. and 2
    nephews, Lee.Siple and a younger brother are living in our midst.

Siple, Lizzie   "Estate"   Jun 28, 1905
    see French, Matilda

Sisley, Mrs Arthur   "Obituary"   Oct 28, 1897
    see Swan, Mrs Mary Ann

Sivertson, Mrs C.F.   "Paloma"   Jan 11, 1894
    Died- another old settler, Mrs C.F. Sivertson Sunday A.M. at the age of
    77 yrs 1 mo. Services by Rev Miner of Camp Point in the F.W.B. church
    of which she was a member. Remains taken to their narrow home in Coatsburg
    cemetery.

Skauts, James H.   "Camp Point"   Jan 23, 1879
    Died- James H. Skauts, an old citizen Monday night at the age of 60 yrs.

Skidmore, Mrs   "Paloma"   Jan 27, 1886
    Died- January 21st at Yates City, Mrs Skidmore. Her remains were brought
    here Saturday and laid to rest beside her husband.

Skidmore, Mr John L.   May 8, 1884
    Died- Mr John L. Skidmore, an old settler of Adams Co. at his home in
    Paloma last week.

Skinner, Josephine   "Obituary"   Nov 28, 1889
    see Wood, John

Skinner, Mary   "Obituary"   Nov 28, 1889
    see Wood, John

Skirvin, Hamilton   "Columbus"   Jul 14, 1886
    Died- in Gilmer twp, Hamilton Skirvin, at the age of 64 yrs. He came to
    Adams Co. in 1832. Services by Rev Ausmus and buried in Columbus cemetery.

Slack, Mrs B.F.   "Death"   Feb 2, 1882
    see Walker, Mr Harmon

Slack, Mrs B.F.   "Death"   Jul 20, 1882
    see Walker, Mrs Abigail

Slack, Mr and Mrs B.F.   "Obituary"   Mar 3, 1886
    see Owens, Mrs T.S.

Slack, B.F.   "Will"   Feb 24, 1904
    The will of the late B.F. Slack was filed for probate in Co. court
    Friday. All property left to the widow, Ann Eliza Slack who is also
    named executrix. He also carried a 2000.00 policy in the A.O.U.W.

Slack, Mr and Mrs Benjamin F. "Obituary"   Nov 19, 1903
    see Wall, Mrs Joseph W.

Slack, Benjamin Franklin   "Death"   Feb 3, 1904
    Benjamin Franklin Slack, another veteran of the civil war died at 10
    P.M. Saturday from pleural pneumonia. Born Lancaster Co. Penn December
    22, 1834. Was 69 yrs old. When young he came with parents to Illinois
    and located near Mendon where he lived till 9 yrs ago when he came to
    the city. He served in the 78th Vol. Reg't Ill. Inf. Leaves a widow,
    nee Elizabeth Walker), 2 daughters, Mrs George W. Judd and Mrs Fred Meise
    and 1 brother, Albin B. Slack. Also 5 grandchildren, Mrs J.W. Wall, who
    died about 2 mo's ago was a daughter of the deceased. Was a member of
    the Masons and A.O.U.W. at Mendon"Herald" Funeral at the home by
    Mendon Lodge #449 A.F. and A.M. Buried Woodland cemetery.

Slack, Charles C.   "Local"   Sep 22, 1886
    Died- Mr Charles C. Slack of Quincy Sunday afternoon from typhoid fever
    in his 51st yr. Mr Slack was a brother of Mr B.F. Slack of this place.
    Leaves a wife and 3 children. 2 boys and 1 girl. Funeral at the family
    home at 613 Vermont St.

Slack, Kate   "Death"   Sep 12, 1889
    see Judd, Mrs George

Slack, May   "Obituary"   Nov 19, 1903
    see Wall, Mrs Joseph W.

Sloan, Arthur   "Murder"   Oct 8, 1891
    see Baldwin, Benj.

Sloan, John   "Coatsburg"   Apr 5, 1894
    Died- at the home of his mother's in this vicinity March 24th 1894
John Sloan, at the age of 23 yrs. He had been a patient sufferer for
the past 5 weeks. He leaves a father, mother, 3 brothers and 3 sisters.
Funeral services by Elder Dilly at the Christian church after which
his remains were laid to rest in the village cemetery.

Sloan, Arthur D.   Pierre, S.D."   Jan 28, 1892
    Murderer Sloans fate- Pierre, S.D. January 22nd-- Arthur D. Sloan,
the Nebraska murderer, closely tracked by soldiers, sheriffs and indians
for the past 2 weeks is dead. He was found by B.C. Ash, sheriff of this
Co. with the help of an indian, about 17 miles from Pierre on the Brule
reservation. He apparently died Monday night from exhaustion and cold
weather. (Sloan, as readers will remember for some real or fancied
grievance killed his step father, Mr Ben Baldwin, formerly a resident of
Mendon and his step brother and badly wounded his mother. He was
captured in Iowa and taken back to Nebraska, but escaped from jail.

Slocum, Lewis   "Clayton Enterprise"   Oct 30, 1884
    Lewis Slocum a long time resident of Clayton died at Howard, Kansas
on Friday October 17th of consumption. Age 50 yrs.

Slonigar, Cora E.   "Obituary"   Feb 17, 1904
    see Hastings, Thomas Gilbert

Slonigar, Mrs Evelina (Joel)   Oct 27, 1881
    Died- Mrs Evelina Slonigar October 23rd, 1881. Wife of Joel Slonigar
of Honey Creek, Adams Co. She was born in Holmes Co. Ohio August 16,
1816. They came to this state 33 yrs ago.

Slonigar, Mrs J.W.   "Death"   Mar 8, 1905
    see Odear, Joshua

Slonigar, Mrs Jas.   "Local"   Oct 29, 1885
    Mrs Jas. Slonigar died Saturday A.M. Buried in Mendon cemetery.
Services by Rev E.C. Crane.

Slonigar, Jas. P.   "Obituary"   Feb 19, 1885
    see Wright, Mrs

Slonigar, Mrs James   "News"   Oct 29, 1885
    Mrs James Slonigar died October 24th. Buried Mendon cemetery.
Services by Rev. E.C. Crane.

Slonigar, Mr James   "Local"   May 21, 1885
    Infant child of Mr and Mrs James Slonigar died May 14th and buried
    Mendon May 17th. Services by Rev E.C. Crane at the home. The poor
    mother has been an invalid for a long time and is in a weak condition.

Slonigar, Joel   "Probate"   Feb 4, 1892
    Probate notice of Joel Slonigar, deceased   1st Monday of April 1892
    James P. Slonigar, Ex.

Slonigar, Joel   "Obituary"   Jan 28, 1892
    Died- Mr Joel Slonigar, an old resident of these parts at his home in
    Honey Creek twp Friday P.M. and buried Mendon cemetery Sunday P.M.
    Born in Mercer Co. Penn May 14, 1818. Moved with his parents to Ohio
    staying there until 1847 when he moved with his family to Adams Co.
    Ill. where he resided since.

Slonigar, Joshua   "Obituary"   Dec 6, 1900
    Died- Joshua Slonigar at his home 4 miles northeast of Mendon November
    26th. Born Mercer Co. Penn March 18, 1824. Came to Ill. from Ohio 1859
    with his wife who died in 1865. Married 2nd to Mrs G.A. Anderson who
    survives him. Leaves a son, James B. of Great Bend, Kan. and 2 brothers
    O.P. and J.W.. Services at the house on Thanksgiving A.M. by Rev Lambert
    of Mendon. Buried in the cemetery West of Byler's school house.

Sly, Mrs Mattie   "Obituary"   Jul 18, 1901
    see Kennedy, Geo. Thomas

Smallwood, Mrs A.A.   "Death'   Dec 28, 1904
    see Wible, Daniel

Smiley, Margaret   "Obituary"   Jan 8, 1891
    see McClelland, Mrs Margaret Smiley

Smith, Dr   "Obituary"   Dec 19, 1878
    see Farner, Dr W.H.

Smith, Mrs   "Death"   Jun 11, 1885
    Mr Benson was called to Elvaston on Saturday by the dangerous condition
    of his daughter, Mrs Smith. He was accompanied by his son Tom. News since
    have reached us that Mrs Smith died June 8th.

Smith, C.J. (Jap)   "Payson"   Mar 15, 1888
    Mr C.J. Smith, known in this community as Jap Smith, died in Hannibal,
    Mo. last Friday.

Smith, Caleb   Feb 8, 1883
    Caleb Smith bequested in his will to the following people:
    Francis A. Green, a step daughter- to his daughter's Carlotte and
    Nanette Smith- a son Alfred Smith and to his wife Mary Ann Smith.

Smith, Caleb   "Graves"   Jun 22, 1899
    Caleb Smith included in list of Soldiers graves decorated on Memorial
    Day in Mendon cemetery.

Smith, Caleb A.   Jan 25, 1883
    Caleb A. Smith died January 19, 1883. He was a Mason for 50 yrs. Was 78
    yrs old. Services from Cong'l church Resident of Adams co 48 yrs.

Smith, Caleb A.   "Probate"   Feb 22, 1883
   Probate Notice of Caleb A. Smith, deceased 3rd Monday of April 1883
   Clark Strickler, Ex.

Smith, Miss Caroline   "Death"   Jul 5, 1905
   see Smith, Hamilton

Smith, Charity H.   "Death"   Mar 9, 1904
   see Blazer, Rachel Louise

Smith, Cyrus   "Correction "   Nov 29, 1894
   To the editor of the Dispatch to correct Dispatch of November 15th--
   Mr Cyrus Smith was the 1st male child born in Quincy, Ill. He married
   Squire Laughlin's 4th daughter, Miss Heddessa Laughlin. He was a nephew
   of Mr James Rankin of Breckenridge, Hancock Co. Ill. His parents came
   to Quincy in 1832 or 33 if I'm not mistaken died of cholera andleft their
   son an orphan. Mr Geo. Pollard took the child and cared for him until his
   uncle came for him from Pendleton Co. Ky. and took him back. Then he
   came west and married. His mother was own cousin of M. Rawlings.
   Miss Sophronia Rankin was her maiden name. Their bones bleach in the lot
   where the courthouse stands today. Signed Mrs A.D. Tindall of Marysville,
   Missouri -dated November 22nd.
   THE ABOVE CLAIM IS DISPUTED IN November 15th paper.

Smith, Mrs Dennis   "Carthage"   Feb 19, 1880
   Mrs Dennis Smith died. She was wife of Judge Smith, better known as
   Uncle Tubby. He is sick and not expected to live.

Smith, Mr E.D.   "Murder"   Sep 25, 1890
   see Porter, Dan

Smith, Ed   "Obituary"   Mar 7, 1895
   see Williamson, John H.

Smith, Elizabeth   Mar 13, 1884
   Mrs Elizabeth Smith, wife of Hamilton Smith died March 7th. Age 60 yrs
   8 mo's 4 days. Born Stantsbury, N.Y. July 1, 1844. Had 12 children,
   8 still living. Husband still living too.

Smith, Elizabeth   "Chancery Suit"   Sep 26, 1894
   see Robertson, Andrew

Smith, Mr and Mrs Geo.   "Local"   Dec 6, 1894
   Died- 4 yr old son of Mr and Mrs Geo. Smith on Monday night of
   membraneous croup after a few days illness. Buried next day at Reese
   burying ground near Loraine. An older son (about 7) is down with pneumonia.

Smith, Gertie Elma   "Died"   Nov 4, 1880
   Died- Saturday October 23rd of malarial fever, Gertie Elma, youngest
   daughter of G.W. and Charity Smith. Age 1 yr 9 mo's 16 days.

Smith, Granville   Oct 13, 1881
   Died- Granville Smith from fractured skull due to a rock thrown by
   Simon Dyer October 5th 1881 in Pike Co. Ill.

Smith, Hamilton   "Death"   Jul 5, 1905
    Hamilton Smith of Adams Co. for over a ½ century lived in vicinity of
    Mendon died at his country home Saturday afternoon from an accident
    the day before when he fell from a ladder. 81 yrs old. Born Feb. 29, 1824
    at Brooklyn, N.Y. and died on wedding anniversary as he was married
    July 1, 1844 to Miss Elizabeth Conklin in New York City. Wife died 21 yrs
    ago on March 7, 1884. Had 12 children, 8 still living, Henry A. of Ferndale
    Washington, Hamilton Z. of Quincy, Mrs Mary Gillialnd, Mrs Caroline
    Gilliland, Mrs Julia Dickerman, Mrs Sarah Nutt, Miss Emma and Elmer E.
    all in or around Mendon. 2 daughters married Gilliland's, Mary is wife of
    Thomas Gilliland and Caroline is wife of J.P. Gilliland. 30 grandchildren
    17 great grandchildren also survive him. Services at hte Lutheran
    church by Rev A.M. Reitzel. Buried Mendon cemetery. 2 sisters, Mrs Sarah
    Dykes and Miss Caroline Smith both of Brooklyn died on his wedding
    anniversary and buried on his wife's birthday.

Smith, Hamilton   "Probate"   Aug 2, 1905
    Probate notice of Hamilton Smith, deceased 1st Monday of October 1905
    Thomas J. Gilliland, Adm.

Smith, Mrs Henry   "Obituary"   Nov 30, 1899
    see Heaney, Edward

Smith, Mrs Isadore   "Payson"   Apr 7, 1881
    Mrs Isadore Smith, widow of the late I.L. Smith of Hannibal is now a
    resident of our village.

Smith, Jas.   Oct 13, 1881
    Died- October 8, 1881, Jas. Smith's infant, of Ellington twp.

Smith, Mrs Jas.   "Death"   Oct 6, 1892
    see Donnelly, Mrs Jane

Smith, Mrs Jennie   "Death"   Aug 7, 1902
    see Ralph, Mrs Clem

Smith, Jim   "Local"   May 10, 1894
    When in Quincy we met our former fellow townsman "Jim" Smith, who we
    thought dead and buried in St Louis months ago.

Smith, John   "Ursa"   Jan 26, 1893
    Died- Mr John Smith who died of consumption was buried in Stones church
    cemetery on January 23rd. Mr Smith lived in the bottoms.

Smith, John L.   Dec 16, 1880
    John L. Smith living near Hannibal was buried December 12th.

Smith, Jos.   "Tioga"   Apr 5, 1894
    Died- in Peoria on Friday March 30th at the home of his daughter, Mrs
    W.P. Railsback, Mr Jos. Smith, age 65 yrs. Remains arrived here and laid
    to rest in the cemtery on Sunday. Leaves a wife and 3 children.

Smith, Mrs Josephine   "Death"   Apr 5, 1905
    see Rust, Charles W.

Smith, Miss Laura E.   "Obituary"   Apr 10, 1902
    see Dickerman, I.R. (Ira Rice)

Smith, Laura E.   "Death"   Mar 2, 1904
    see Dickerman, Mrs Laura

Smith, Lillie   "Estate"   Jun 28, 1905
    see French, Matilda

Smith, Deacon Lorin   "Obituary"   Apr 10, 1902
    see Dickerman, I.R. (Ira Rice)

Smith, Maria A.   "Death"   Mar 22, 1905
    see Baldwin, George Dutton

Smith, Mary Ann   "Obituary"   Mar 1, 1900
    see Clair, Benjamin

Smith, Mrs Mary Elizabeth   "Local"   Apr 7, 1886
    Died- at her home near Fowler, Adams Co. Ill. on Friday the 2nd inst
    in her 85th yr, Mrs Mary Elizabeth Smith. Born Westmoreland Co. Penn.
    October 4, 1801. Was member of the Lutheran church 45 yrs. Her husband
    died 15 yrs ago. Had 12 grandchildren and 6 great grandchildren
    Buried in Mendon cemetery. Services by Rev Howard Miller.
    NOTE: No mention of children.

Smith, Mr Nathaniel   "Obituary"   Dec 1, 1886
    Mr Nathaniel Smith died November 26th at the age of 93 yrs 4 mo's 19
    days. Born at Brattleborough, Vermont July 7, 1793 and married Hariett
    Wicoff in 1820. They had 12 children, 6 boys and 6 girls. 3 of whom are
    still living, Mrs Dyke of Brooklyn N.Y., Miss Carrie Smith of Quincy and
    Mr Hamilton Smith of Mendon twp. Mr Smith came to Illinois about 33 yrs
    ago. Services at the house Sunday afternoon by Rev E.W. Souders. Buried
    in Mendon cemetery.

Smith, Patrick   "Obituary"   Mar 7, 1895
    see Williamson, John H.

Smith, Patrick   "Elm Grove"   Feb 15, 1900
    James Smith and a daughter, Mrs Frank Bittner of St Louis were here to
    attend the funeral of Patrick Smith.

Smith, Patrick   "Elm Grove"   Jan 25, 1900
    Died- Patrick Smith who died Sunday in Quincy will be buried in Bloom-
    field cemetery.

Smith, Mrs Patrick   "Death"   Aug 10, 1893

Smith, Mrs Patrick   "Death"   Aug 10, 1893
    Died- Mrs Patrick Smith, wife of Patrick Smith, at her home in the south
    part of the twp Friday August 4th of inflammation of the bowels. Buried
    in Bloomfield cemetery Monday August 7th. Services by Rev Father John
    Dietrich. Margaret Carlin was born in the parish of Killincare, county
    Cavan Ireland some 60 yrs ago. Came to Adams Co. in 1850 after spending
    1 or 2 yrs in New York State. Married in Quincy to Patrick Smith in ____
    Leaves a husband and 8 children. 5 sons and 3 daughters. All of whom
    reside in the county. 2 boys and 1 girl still at home.

Smith, Mrs Rodney   "Obituary"   May 18, 1887
    see Morehead, Daniel

Smith, Mrs Rodney   "Obituary"   Oct 15, 1891
    see Morehead, Mrs Cordelia

Smith, Mrs Rodney   "Local"   Sep 26, 1895
    Died- Mrs Rodney Smith, formerly Miss Belle Morehead, a sister of Mrs D.B.
    Cooke, at Chicago Friday night from the effects of an operation performed
    at one of the hospitals. 48 yrs old. Had been an invalid several yrs.
    Buried Woodland cemetery, Quincy. Services by Rev Ince Monday P.M.

Smith, Mrs Susan   "Died"   Feb 21, 1884
    Feb. 18th at the residence of her son in law, Dr W.A. Byrd, Mrs Susan
    Smith died at the age of 53 yrs. She was buried on the 19th in the Smith
    cemetery at Ursa.

Smith, Mrs Tom B.   "Obituary"   Dec 11, 1902
    see Frazier, Mrs Eva J.

Smith, Thomas   "Ursa"   Jul 14, 1881
    Died- July 10th, a 1 yr old son of Thomas Smith.

Smith, Valley   Oct 6, 1881
    Died- October 2nd, Valley, daughter of Mr and Mrs Jas. Smith of
    Ellington. Age 3 yrs and 4 months.

Smith, Wm   "Obituary"   Mar 24, 1892
    see Scott, Mrs

Smith, Wm   "Local"   Jul 26, 1888
    A little daughter of Wm Smith of Honey Creek died on Monday A.M. of
    consumption. Age 10 yrs 4 mo's 16 days. Buried in Mendon cemetery Tuesday
    P.M. Services by Rev Peet.

Smith, Wm   "Local"   Sep 17, 1885
    Died- Wm Smith of Keene twp.

Smith, Wm B.   "Sunday School Supplement"   Aug 16, 1894
    Died- Wm B. Smith of Clayton twp.

Smith, Wm B.   Mar 30, 1882
    Died- Mr Wm B. Smith of Ursa died Sunday. He had lived in the twp for
    half a century. He was about 53 or 58 yrs old and is survived by a wife,
    2 sons and 2 daughters.

Smith, William   "News"   Oct 8, 1885
    News reached us last week of the death of Wm Smith of heart disease
    at the age of 63 yrs at his home in San Francisco, Calif. Mr Smith was
    the son of Nathaniel Smith and a brother of Wm Smith. Mr S. visited
    Mendon about 2 yrs ago.

Snider, Mrs   "Marcelline"   Mar 5, 1903
    Friends of Mrs Snider were shocked by hearing of her death. She was brought
    from her home in Camp Point to Lima for burial.

Snider, Miss Lulu   "Obituary"   Mar 15, 1900
    see Holstein, Arthur

Snodgrass, T.C.   "Estate"   Jun 15, 1893
    Quarrel over Estate. "Kansas City Star"
    The estate of T.C. Snodgrass of Kansas City, Mo, (former Mendon resident
    some 20 yrs ago) Mary U. Snodgrass, his widow claims her share of
    $1000,000, but the remaining heirs contend she has no right as they were
    divorced. (but the couple lived togeather all the time right up to his
    death) They had lived in K.C. 17 yrs at 1227 Troost Ave. They were married
    19 yrs. He died Feb. 28th leaving no will. Only survivers were his
    widow, Mary U., J.J. Snodgrass a brother, Agnes Nesbitt, Lizzie Elliot,
    Mary Gray, sisters and Eddie Snodgrass the 9 yr old nephew. He had gone
    to Guthrie, Oklahoma and obtained a divorce while living with her and
    had told her nothing about it.

Snyder, Mrs   "Local"   Mar 5, 1903
    Died- Mrs Snyder, Saturday at Camp Point. Sme yrs ago she lived on Geo.
    Lyle's farm.

Snyder, Daniel   "Camp Point"   Jul 4, 1901
    Died- Daniel Snyder Monday A.M. at the age of 82 yrs. He had been an
    invalid a couple of yrs.

Snyder, Edith Lillie   "Died"   Aug 12, 1880
    Died- on August 2nd Edith Lillie, eldest daughter of Mr and Mrs
    Phillip Snyder of Lima twp. 15 yrs 9 mo's 14 days old.

Snyder, Mr and Mrs Geo.   "Obituary"   Dec 21, 1893
    see Killam, Mary E.

Snyder, Miss Lulu   "Obituary"   Mar 15, 1900
    see Holstein, Arthur

Snyder, Mary   "Obituary"   Dec 21, 1893
    see Killam, Mary E.

Somerville, Joseph B.   "Obituary"   Jul 2, 1903
    see Nedrow, Lutha May

Souders, Rev E.W.   "Death"   Jun 22, 1899
    see Burnett, Mrs Frank T.

Southworth, Mrs   "Mallard"   Mar 28, 1889
    Died- Mrs Southworth, a lady 86 yrs old of typhiod pneumonia.

Soverns, Ed   "Ursa"   Jun 19, 1884
    Ed Soverns died last week. Buried June 10th.

Sparrow, Mr Jim   "Local"   Jan 14, 1892
    Mr Jas. Ruddell, adm announces a sale of personal property at the
    residence of Jim Sparrow, ½ mile south of Rock Creek school house
    Feb. 4th.

Spears, Mrs Betty   "Obituary"   Jul 6, 1899
    see Leighty, John

Spears, John and Catherine   "Obituary"   Mar 16, 1893
    see Hughes, Mrs Sarah (Wm)

Spears, John Sr.   "Mt Pleasant"   May 14, 1903
    Several from this vicinity attended the burial services of John Spears Sr.
    who died in the hospital last week. The Marcelline Masons had charge of
    the services.

Spears, Mr and Mrs John   "Ursa"   Mar 1, 1905
    Died- the infant child of Mr and Mrs John Spears of LaGrange, Mo. was
    brought here Saturday for burial in Keith cemetery.

Speckhart, Mrs Frederick   "Quincy"   Apr 6, 1899
    Died- Mrs Frederick Speckhart Saturday at noon. Sick 3 yrs. Leaves a
    husband and 6 children.

Speers, John   "Tioga"   Jun 1, 1901
    A child of John Speers age about 2 yrs was buried in our village
    cemetery last week.

Spence, Mrs Millard   "Obituary"   Oct 27, 1892
    see McClean, Mrs

Spencer, Grandma   "Local"   May 31, 1900
    Died- Grandma Spencer, living just north of Payson Tuesday. Age 91 yrs.

Spencer, Miss Almira   "Obituary"   May 12, 1886
    see Betts, Coley E.

Spencer, Mrs Eliza   "Quincy"   Mar 23, 1899
    Died- Mrs Eliza Spencer, a colored woman Monday night. 78 yrs old.

Spencer, Miss Elmira   "Death"   Apr 4, 1901
    Died- another of our old New England settlers, Miss Elmira Spencer,
    Born in West Hartford, Conn. July 20, 1816 and died in Mendon April 1, 1901
    Moved to Illinois with parents overland in November 1839 and married in
    Payson in May 1841 to Mr Coley B. Betts. Lived Mendon nearly 60 yrs.
    Mr Betts died nearly 15 yrs ago. Had 8 children, 3 died young. 3 daughter's
    and 2 sons survive her, James, William and Ellen Betts of Mendon, Mrs
    Harriet Hewitt of College Springs, Iowa and Mrs Mary Scranton of Payson,
    Ill. She was nearly 85 yrs old and member of the Cong'l church 60 yrs.
    Services at the Cong'l church by Rev J.S. Bayne. Buried Mendon cemetery
    beside her husband. Present from a distance were, Mr and Mrs Amos
    Scranton, Samuel Spencer, a brother of the deceased and his son, Henry
    Scarborough a nephew of the deceased and Mrs Hattie Hewitt of College
    Springs, Iowa.

Spencer, Mrs Annie E. (George)   "Local"   Oct 12, 1904
   Mrs John and Douglas Nicholson and H.A. Ippenson attended the funeral of
   Mrs Annie E. Spencer at Lima Sunday. She was the widow of George Spencer
   and formerly lived at Lima, but of late yrs had lived with her married
   daughter, Mina, at Chicago, where she died.

Spencer, Mr Flavel   "Payson"   Oct 2, 1879
   Mr Flavel Spencer died on the last day of September. Services at the
   Cong'l church on October 1st by Rev Wallace. He was an old citizen.

Spencer, Rev Geo. M.   "Obituary"   Feb 13, 1879
   Died Feb. 3rd 1879 Rev Geo. M. Spencer. Born in 1841 in Hancock Co. Ill.
   Joined the Ill. conference of the M.E. church in 1872. Died at his home in
   Lima. Leaves wife and 2 children.

Spencer, Mr George   "Payson"   Mar 26, 1885
   Buried on March 11th, Mr George Spencer, son of uncle Samuel Spencer.

Spencer, Mrs John   "Obituary"   .   Apr 16, 1891
   see Bray, David C.

Spencer, Mrs Perry   "Local"   Mar 8, 1905
   Died- Mrs Perry Spencer of Lima on Monday at 2 P.M. Funeral this A.M.
   at 10. Leaves husband and 3 daughters.

Spencer, Mrs Polly   "Tioga"   Sep 26, 1901
   Died- Mrs Polly Spencer at the age of 72 yrs. Buried Fletcher cemetery.

Spencer, S.M.   "Local"   Dec 17, 1903
   William Betts attended the funeral of his uncle, S.M. Spencer, at
   Payson last Friday.

Spencer, S.M.   Mar 17, 1881
   Died- the youngest daughter of S.M. Spencer.

Spencer, Samuel   "Payson"   Jul 13, 1887
   The daughter of Samuel Spencer who was here on a visit to her parents
   from Dakota buried 1 child last week.

Spencer, Rev Seymour   "Death"   Jul 7, 1898
   Died- Rev Seymour Spencer, a brother of Mrs Betts, of this place died
   May 6th at his home in New Zealand where he has been a missionary many
   yrs. 85 yrs old. Was a founder of the Zion Episcopal church when it was
   started here in 1838. A son of Mr Spencer, also a clergyman of the
   church of England visited here a few yrs ago.

Spicer, Mrs Bud   "Obituary"   Jan 27, 1886
   see Norman, Mrs

Spicer, Charles R.   "Adm Sale"   May 13, 1880
    Adm. sale of real estate-- Alexander Hartman, Adm of the estate of Charles
    R. Spicer, deceased vs Martha J. Spicer, Sarah Louisa Spicer, Warren F.
    Pitney, Barbara Ottenstein and Aaron Kelley. Alexander Hartman, Adm.
    Davis and Poling, Attorneys.

Spicer, Charles   "Probate"   Jan 30, 1879
    Probate notice of Charles R. Spicer, deceased 3rd Monday of March 1879
    Alexander Hartman, Adm.

Spicer, James   "Mt Hebron"   Sep 10, 1885
    Three orphaned children of the late James Spicer of Colorado, Texas
    arrived last Monday to make their home with their aunt, Mrs Riley Crank.

Spicer, Rawser   "Adm Sale"   Feb 10, 1881
    Adm. sale of real estate - County court of Hancock Co.-
    Estate of Rawser Spicer   Sarah A. Spicer, Adm.

Spillars, James   "Local"   Oct 9, 1890
    An ex-soldier living at the home of James Spillars fell from the bridge
    between the boiler house and the kitchen and died in less than an hr.
    Died October 2nd.

Spires, Mrs Samuel   "Local"   Jan 2, 1902
    Died- Mrs Samuel Spires, mother of Rev W.J. Spires, former pastor of
    the Mendon Lutheran church of heart disease in the Ante room of the 1st
    M.E. church in Elgin, Ill. while servcies were in progress. Was 54 yrs old
    Born in Clifton Park, N.Y. Leaves husband and 3 sons.

Sprague, W.J.   "Local"   Jul 6, 1899
    Died- W.J. Sprague, of Palmyra, Mo. dropped dead from heart disease
    last Thursday.

Sprankle, Wm   "Death"   Jul 14, 1898
    "June 23rd Bonaparte, Iowa Record" Death of Wm Sprankle
    Died- W.U. Sprankle of cancer of the stomach at his home in Bonaparte
    on Monday eve June 13th at the age oq 69 yrs 3 mo's 2 days. Born
    Hollidaysburg, Blair Co. Penn March 11, 1829. Married Nancy M. Seabrooks
    at Fairfield, Penn March 14, 1852. Had 2 children. Moved to Mendon 1855
    where his wife died July 8, 1865. He married 2nd Sarah J. Rawlings,
    June 9, 1866 and moved to Bonaparte in 1869. They also had 2 children,
    1 son and 1 daughter, Sarah died Quincy, Ill. Feb. 14, 1898. Surviving
    children are Emma Beck, wife of John Q. Beck and Minnie and Geo. Sprankle.
    He also leaves 2 sisters and 1 brother.

Springer, Jennie   "Obituary"   Mar 7, 1889
    see McLaughlin, Wm

Sprinkle, Ella M.   "Obituary"   Apr 8, 1881
    Ella M. Sprinkle died March 30th at the age of 20 yrs 8 mo's 10 days.
    Buried Keith cemetery April 1st. This was the third death in Mr Sprinkle's
    family since last August. Was daughter of Henry and Mary Sprinkle.

Sprinkle, Henry   "Ursa"   May 2, 1889
Died- Mr Henry Sprinkle, living southwest of Ursa about noon Friday of
paralysis of the heart. Buried Saturday afternoon at the Keith cemetery.

Sprinkle, Mabel   "Died"   Aug 12, 1880
Died- on August 7th of flux, Mabel, daughter of H. and M, Sprinkle.
Age 2 yrs 7 mo's. living 4 miles northwest of Mendon.

Sprinkle, Rosa   "Died"   Aug 12, 1880
Died- on August 6th of inflamation of the brain, Rosa, daughter of
Martha Sprinkle, age 1 yr 3 months.

Sprinkle, Mrs Sarah Jane   "Obituary"   Feb 10, 1898
see Rawlings, Sarah Jane

Sprinkle, Wm U.   "Obituary"   Feb 10, 1898
see Rawlings, Sarah Jane
see Sprankle

Sproat, Alice   "Obituary"   Nov 23, 1899
see Heaney, Mrs Noble M.

Sproat, Mr and Mrs E.W.   "Local"   Feb 2, 1887
Infant daughter of Mr and Mrs E.W. Sproat of Hollister, Calif. died
January 26th at the age of 3 mo's 13 days.

Sproat, E.W.   "Loraine"   Feb 21, 1901
Mrs S.W. Heaney of Quincy rec'd word Wednesday that her brother E.W.
Sproat of Holister, Calif. was killed in an iron works. Mr Sproat was a
former resident of Mendon twp. Leaves a wife and 3 children.

Sproat, Edward   "Obituary"   Feb 28, 1901
Died- Edward Sproat in an accident Wednesday noon Feb. 20th in the
Union Iron Works. He was struck by a 1,000 pound steel plate in the chest
and crushed against a brick wall. He was a machinist labored. Roomed at
1996 Golden Gate Ave. Leaves a wife and 2 children in Hollister, Calif.
Moved from Mendon to Hollister about 18 yrs ago. Married Elizabeth, the
eldest daughter of Mr and Mrs David Furry, deceased.

Sproat, Mrs Edward   "Obituary"   Feb 12, 1891
see Furry, David

Sproat, Miss Julia A.   "Obituary"   Apr 4, 1895
see Strickler, Clark

Sproat, Miss Olive   "Obituary"   Mar 15, 1900
see Holstein, Arthur

Sproat, Percy   "Obituary"   Mar 15, 1900
see Holstein, Arthur

Sproat, Percy   "Local"   Mar 8, 1888
Telegram rec'd from Edward Sproat Hollister, Calif Feb. 29th
Father died at 1:30 P.M. (Percy sproat was known to most of our readers
from his long residence in this locality. Leaves a widow and children.

Sproat, Mrs Percy   "Whig"   Apr 4, 1901
   Mrs Percy Sproat, formerly of Mendon died in Hollister, Calif. last
   Friday.

Sproat, Mr and Mrs Percy   "Obituary"   Feb 28, 1884
   see Strickler, Mrs Clark

Staaf, Mr Andrew   "Tioga"   Feb 21, 1895
   Died- Mr Andrew Staaf, Friday eve at the age of 63 yrs. Leaves a wife
   and 7 children. Services by Rev Ott. Buried in Lutheran cemetery Sunday P.M.

Stackhouse, Mrs Isabel   "Obituary"   Feb 10, 1898
   see Rawlings, Sarah Jane

Stackhouse, Safrona Isabelle Rawlings (John)   Aug 27, 1903
   Safrona Isabelle Rawlings Stackhouse was born December 27th 1842 and
   died August 22nd 1903 at the age of 60 yrs 8 mo's 25 days. Married John
   Stackhouse 1867 and he died 1867. No children born to them. Leaves
   2 sisters, Mrs G.W. Rust and Mrs A. Tindell and 1 brother, E.J. Rawlings
   of Mendon, Mo. Services by Rev S.R. Reno of Mendon from the home of
   Mr George W. Rust 8 miles west of Mendon. Buried in Stone cemetery, near
   Marcelline.

Staffey, Mrs Susan   "Obituary"   Oct 18, 1894
   see Funk, Samuel

Stafford, Dora   "Ursa"   Apr 28, 1898
   Died- Sunday A.M. at 12, Dora Stafford at the age of 11 yrs after an
   illness of 2 days. She made her home with Mr and Mrs R. Ralph of this
   place since a mere child.

Stafford, Dora F.   "Obituary"   Apr 28, 1898
   Died- Dora F. Stafford, born October 21, 1885 and died April 24th 1898
   at hte age of 12 yrs 6 mo's 3 days. Leaves a loving father. Her mother
   died October 26, 1885 leaving her to her father's care when only 5 days
   old. She was baptized in the M.P. church in the winter of 1893

Stafford, Mrs Wm   "Lima"   Nov 11, 1885
   Mrs Wm Stafford of thie village died a few days since, leaving an infant
   8 days old. Mrs Stafford was the daughter of A. Goodwin Esq. whose death
   was mentioned in our last paper.

Stafford, Mr and Mrs Wm   "Lima"   Jun 21, 1883
   Died- an infant son of Wm Stafford on June 17th.

Stahl, Mr   "Tioga"   Apr 12, 1900
   A 4 mo. old daughter of Mr Stahl of Hickory Ridge was buried in the
   German cemetery Sunday afternoon.

Stahl, Mrs   "Obituary"   Aug 17, 1882
   see Horn, Adam

Stahl, Desilla   "Obituary"   Oct 26, 1887
   see Horn, Mr Peter G.

Stahl, Miss Ida   "Fowler & Oakland"   Mar 1, 1900
Died- Friday Feb 23rd at the home of her parents, Miss Ida Stahl, She was the oldest child of Mr and Mrs Hanby Stahl. Leaves father, mother, sister and 2 brothers. Buried in Stahl cemtery Saturday.

Stahl, Mr and Mrs John   "Fowler"   Nov 14, 1901
Mr and Mrs John Stahl of Augusta came down Sunday eve and with Mr and Mrs Hanby Stahl drove to Mendon Monday to the funeral of the late Michael Worman. Mr Worman was a brother of Mrs John Stahl.

Stahl, Mrs Mary   Nov 3, 1881
Died- Mrs Mary Stahl, wife of Noah Stahl October 30th 1881 at the age of 55 yrs. She was the daughter of Adam Horn of Fowler and sister of Peter G. and A.E. Horn.

Stahl, Solomon   "Local"   Mar 29, 1900
Died- Solomon Stahl, an old resident of Quincy at his home Saturday afternoon of dropsy. Was nearly 70 yrs old. Leaves wife and 3 sons and 1 daughter.

Stalf, Leonard   "Quincy"   Apr 20, 1899
Died- The body of Leonard Stalf who has been missing since March 9th was found Sunday in the Big Slough, 2 miles south of Quincy. Was 53 yrs old. Leaves wife, 1 daughter and 1 son.

Standhart, Miss Edna   "Local"   Apr 27, 1899
Died- Miss Edna Standhart of Quincy fell from the 4th story in the Newcomb bldg. corner of 4th and Maine March 10th and died last Friday A.M. from the injuries rec'd at that time.

Stanley, Pat   "Green Grove"   Mar 16, 1899
Dead- Pat Stanley was found dead in his bed at the home of Ervin Lunts last Thursday A.M. from heart failure. No relatives in vicinity.

Stansbury, Old Mother   "Lima"   Jan 12, 1882
Old Mother Stansbury died Christmas morning.

Stark, Mrs Robert   "Death"   Sep 19, 1889
see Hewitt, John

Starr, Mrs Sarah R.   "Died"   Nov 20, 1879
Died- at the residence of her son, R.B. Starr, Esq. on Tuesday November 18th, Mrs Sarah R. Starr. 68 yrs old. Funeral will be at the Cong'l church at 10:30 A.M. Friday.

Starr, Willis Fitch   "Local"   Feb 19, 1885
Died- Saturday morning of typhoid pneumonia, Willis Fitch Starr youngest child of Mr and Mrs R.B. Starr at the age of 3½ yrs. Buried Mendon cemetery. Services by Rev E.C. Crane.

Starrett, Old Father   "Payson"   Mar 17, 1881
Died- Old Father Starrett, an old settler March 11th 1881.

St Clair, Elizabeth   "Obituary"   Sep 6, 1888
   see Golden, J.W. Sr.

St Clair, Harry   "Death"   Dec 4, 1902
   see Golden, Stephen M.

Stearns, Mrs   "News"   Oct 21, 1880
   Mrs Stearn of Ellington who was very sick a few weeks ago when her husband
   died, died a couple of days after him. Buried side by side.

Steffin, Mr   "Ellington"   Jan 27, 1886
   Mr Steffin who has been sick for months died January 19th.

Steinagel, Mrs Mary   "Local"   May 12, 1898
   Died- Mrs Mary Steinagel, of Fowler Saturday A.M, of brain fever.
   60 yrs old.

Steinbach, Mr A.   "Personal"   May 8, 1879
   Drowned- two young men, named A. Steinbach and J. Schardon were drowned
   by upsetting a skiff near the ferry landing at Quincy last Sunday about
   1 P.M.

Steinback, Mrs Wm   "Lima"   Jan 8, 1880
   Died- Mrs Wm Steinback, who died near Ursa a few days ago was buried
   at the Lima cemetery December 25th.

Steinback, Mrs Louisa Margaret   "Obituary"   Apr 17, 1902
   Died- Saturday at 8:25 A.M, Mrs Louisa Margaret Steinback. Born
   Wuertemberg, Germany October 20, 1815. Came to U.S. when 1 yr old with
   parents and settled in Baltimore, Md. for 15 yrs. then to Cincinnati,
   Ohio. On June 17, 1834 she married John Steinback and in 1836 they came
   west settling near Bloomfield for about 2 yrs and on to Ursa to the old
   homestead. On March 14th 1878 she was left a widow. Had 10 children, 6 boys
   and 4 girls. 4 boys and 4 girls survive her. Baptized and confirmed in
   Lutheran church. Services at Ursa M.E. church Monday P.M. by Rev Thos
   Ringland and Rev E.E. Read. Buried Denson cemetery. Funeral in charge of
   undertaker Chas. H. Nutt and A.D. Nutt.

Steiner, Mrs Anna C.   "Local"   May 12, 1898
   Died- Mrs Anna C. Steiner Friday P.M. at the home of her daughter, Mrs
   Monroe Hartman, near Woodville. Her maiden name was Goebel. Married in
   Quincy to Michael Steiner in 1840. In 1842 they moved to Keene twp. He
   died 5 yrs ago. Leaves 5 children, Nancy E. Hartman of Woodville, Hiram
   Steiner of Stillwell, Geo. Steiner of Loraine, Amelia Kropp of Mountain
   Grove, Mo. and D.D. Steiner of Quincy. Supervisor John Pratt of Keene twp
   is a son in law of the deceased.

Steiner, Mr Hiram   "Obituary"   Dec 6, 1894
   see Woods, Mrs Laurie

Steiner, John   "Woodville"   Mar 14, 1889
   Died- John Steiner- 32 yrs old. Leaves a widow and 2 little children,
   mother and father, sister and brothers and other relatives.

Steiner, Michael   "Probate"   July 14, 1892
   Probate Notice of Michale Steiner 1st Monday of September 1892
   John Pratt and Geo. Steiner, Ex's

Steiner, Mr Michael   "Local"   May 26, 1892
     Died- Mr Michael Steiner, an old resident of Keene twp last Thursday at
     the age of 82 yrs. Funeral Sunday.

Steiner, Paul   "Loraine"   Jun 19, 1890
     Died- June 13th the infant son of Dr D.D. and Emma Steiner from scarlet
     rash. Paul was 22 months old.

Steinman, Maud   "Local"   Jun 12, 1884
     Died- Maud Steinman lately of Mendon died at Phillipsburg, Penn.
     on May 27th.

Steinwedell, Mrs Wm   "Local"   Nov 28, 1901
     Mrs Wm Steinwedell, wife of Capt Steinwedell died at their home in Quincy
     last Monday at the age of 60 yrs. Leaves husband and 5 children.

Stephens, Mr Amzi   "Obituary"   Apr 27, 1882
     Mr Amzi Stephens, formerly a resident of Mendon died at his home at
     Durham, Hancock Co.. Buried Mendon beside his 1st wife who died several
     yrs ago. Services at the M.E. church by Rev T.P. Henry of Burnside. Mr
     Stephens settled in Mendon on 1834 or 35. He was 69 yrs old.

Stern, Frank   "Mendon"   Jul 14, 1881
     Died- July 9th, Frank Stern, son of William Stern an old settler of
     Ellington.

Stern, Joseph   "Local"   Jan 31, 1901
     Died- Joseph Stern, senior member of the large clothing house of J.
     Stern and sons of Quincy. Died Sunday evening at his home in New York
     City. 77 yrs old. Leaves 2 sons and 1 daughter. His wife died a few yrs ago

Stern, Joseph Sr.   "Obituary"   Feb 7, 1901
     Died- Joseph Stern Sr, member of the Quincy clothing firm of J. Stern
     and Sons. Born in Berlichingen, Wurtemburg, Germany December 7, 1823 and
     died at his home in New York City Januray 27, 1901. Came to U.S. when he
     was 17 yrs old and located 1st at Richmond, Va. He was a poor lad, but
     worked hard. Married 1n 1849, she died July 30, 1862 from typhoid fever.
     He never remarried again, but devoted his life to his daughter, who was
     an invalid at her 12th yr caused by rheumatism. After the war he went
     to New York City and started a wholesale mfg business, Stern and Steighity.
     In 1867 he started his son Charles in business in Quincy and in 1870
     sent his other son David west to join him.

Stern, Charles   "Gleamings"   Sep 21, 1893
     Funeral of the little daughter of Mr and Mrs Charles Stern, who died in
     the last several months was attended this afternoon. Services held at the
     Temple B. nai Shalom by Rabbi Eppstein.

Sterns, John   "Personal"   Oct 14, 1880
     John Sterns, one of the oldest settlers of this co. died at his home
     in Ellington twp last Sunday.

Stevens, A.B.   "Graves"   Jun 22, 1899
     A.B. Stevens included in list of graves decorated in Mendon cemetery
     on Decoration Day.

Stevens, Mrs Dr A.F.   "Obituary"   Aug 16, 1894
   "Sunday School Supplement" -- Mrs Dr A.F. Stevens, a member of the
   Presbyterian church at Camp Point died in Feb. of 1894. Over 75 yrs old.

Stevens, John   "Local"   Apr 26, 1900
   Hyram Stevens, employed by Ed Flack rec'd word Monday A.M. that his
   brother, John, of LaGrange, Mo. was dying. He and wife left on the
   morning train.

Stevenson, Mrs Rev William   "Obituary"   Feb 13, 1879
   Died- Feb 2nd, wife of Rev William Stevenson, pastor of the Methodist
   church at Rushville, Ill. Services by Rev P. Wallace.

Stevenson, Prof   Oct 22, 1891
   Prof. Stevenson of Quincy High School died by his own hand.

Steward, Mrs Leve   "Lima"   Oct 6, 1881
   Mrs Leve Steward, formerly Mrs Conover died September 28th.

Steward, Miss Keziah   "Died-   Feb 6, 1879
   Died- on Feb 3rd of consumption, Miss Keziah, daughter of Abijah Steward
   Esq. of Mendon twp.

Steward, Miss Kezia   "Obituary"   Feb 13, 1879
   Miss Kezia Steward, born August 1862 near Mendon, Ill. and died Feb. 3rd
   1879. Services Wednesday at the house by V.C.Randolph, burial at Woodruff's
   cemetery.

Stewart, grandmother   "Payson"   Feb 22, 1883
   Grandmother Stewart died Feb 13th. She was in her 75th yr. Came to Payson
   in 1835..

Stewart, Mrs   "Payson"   Jan 3, 1884
   Mrs Stewart, John Wingfield's mother-in-law, was buried Xmas day 1883

Stewart, Miss Alice   "Fowler"   Jan 4, 1888
   Miss Alice Stewart was called to the home of her mother in Camp Point
   where her mother died at 5 A.M. this morning.

Stewart, Cyrus   "Payson"   Aug 18, 1881
   Died- the 5 yr old son of Cyrus Stewart. Buried August 15th.

Stewart, Cyrus   "Payson"   Sep 15, 1881
   Cyrus Stewart lost another child by death last week.

Stewart, Cyrus   "Payson"   May 27, 1880
   Mr Cyrus Stewart's youngest child, a girl, age 10 months died May 22nd.

Stewart, Ella   "Local"   Jul 6, 1887
   Died- at Denver, Col. June 28th of cholera infantum, Ella, the infant
   daughter of V.V. and Eva Stewart at the age of 3 mo's 14 days. Services
   by Rev P.A. Heilman of the Lutheran church.

Stewart, Frank   "Payson"   May 20, 1880
   Died- on May 13th, Mr Frank Stewart, son of Mr Charles Stewart, of
   Payson. age 24 yrs.

Stewart, Marie DeCorsey   "Death"   Jan 4, 1905
   Word rec'd last Saturday by Mrs Benj. Stewart of Shreveport, La. Body
   was returned by frieght Tuesday by father and brother, Mark. Funeral
   at the Lutheran church Wednesday at 2:30 P.M. by Rev A.M. Reitzel.
   Marie DeCorsey Stewart, daughter of Vinet V. and Eva Stewart was born
   Denver, Colo. July 9, 1888. Baptized Mendon by Rev Mayo November 1897
   Died Shreveport, La. December 31st 1904 at the age of 16 yrs 5 mo's 22 days
   7 yrs ago she and brother Mark came to Mendon to live with grandparents, Mr
   and Mrs Benj. Gilmer and attend school. 2 yrs ago last May they returned
   to their home in Louisania. Cause of death was a malignant form of typhoid.

Stewart, Mr and Mrs Robert   "Local"   Jun 12, 1890
   Mr Robert Stewart and daughter, Mrs Stratton of Atlantia, Ill. are visiting
   the family of Mr Jos. Hardy and other friends. Mrs S. was a sister of Mrs
   Hardy and died in Ohio, Mr S's home.

Stewart, Gladys   Feb 5, 1891
   Died- at Denver, Colo. January 27th, Gladys, the infant daughter of
   Mr and Mrs V.V. Stewart. Was 3 mo's 14 days old. Services by Rev C.J.
   Keifer of St Pauls Lutheran church.

Stewart, Mr and Mrs Vinet   "Local"   Nov 11, 1885
   Death of the infant son of Mr and Mrs Vinet Stewart of Pilot Grove, Mo,

Stewart, Mrs Vinet   "Death"   Dec 2, 1897
   see Gilmer, Frederick A.

Stewart, Mrs Eva   "Obituary"   Jan 11, 1905
   see Gilmer, Benjamin

Stickney, Mr and Mrs O.   "Loraine"   May 17, 1900
   An 8 yr old daughter of Mr and Mrs O. Stickney of Quincy was buried at
   this place Friday evening.

Still, Henry   "Deaths in Adams Co"   Apr 13, 1899
   Died- Henry Still, Friday April 7th at Marblehead. 65 yrs old. Leaves
   a wife and 1 daughter.

Stillman, Henry S.   Feb 12, 1891
   "Taken from Honolulu paper" Henry S. Stillman died Feb. 6th. He was a
   native of Connecticut. Was almost 69 yrs old. Lived in Illinois 35 yrs.

Stillman, Samuel Osgood   "Death"   Mar 29, 1905
   S.O. Stillman died shortly after 1 A.M. at his home on Bench St, this city,
   of acute bronchitis on March 16th 1905. Samuel Osgood Stillman was born
   New Haven, Conn. July 28, 1824. Came west with father's family in 1834
   and settled on a farm in Mendon, Ill at which place he married Miss
   Charlotte C. Clark in 1849. After a few yrs he went to Galena in 1856 and
   was in the boot and shoe business with his brother-in-law Charles Blackman
   in 1860 he bought out the interest to Mr Trego of Trego and Woodruff hdwe
   merchants and 2 yrs later became sole owner until 1894 when he retired.
   Was a active Mason, a member of Miners Lodge #273 Jo Daviss chapter and
   Galena Commandary. Member of South Presbyterian church. Leaves wife and
   5 children and 8 grandchildren. Galena, Ill Gazette March 16th

390

Stillwell, Thos.   "Obituary"   Aug 18, 1898
    see Michael, Mrs Nancy

Stilwell, Mrs Elijah   "Loraine"   Apr 21, 1886
    Mr Elijah Stilwell of Carroll Co. Mo. arrived with the corspe of his
    wife. Her funeral will be in the Dunkard church by Elder T.M. Johnson
    at 10 A.M. today. Buried in our cemetery. She was the youngest daughter of
    our old friend Appollo Shriver, of Stillwell, Ill. Leaves husband and
    3 small children.

Stilwell, Michael   "Loraine"   Oct 6, 1886
    Young Stilwell, son of Michael Stilwell, was buried in our cemetery
    last Tuesday.

Stipe, William   "Local"   May 11, 1904
    William Stipe of Lima died Thursday A.M. last of a complication of
    diseases after a lingering illness. 35 yrs old. Leaves wife and 2 sons,
    mother, 2 brothers and 3 sisters.

St John, Frank   "Lima"   Mar 5, 1885
    Frank St John died Feb. 23rd of inflammatory rheumatism at the age of
    21 yrs. Services by Rev Knock. Buried Lima.

Stockton, Miss Rosa Ann   "Death"   Jan 4, 1905
    see VanDyke, Mrs P.C.

Stockwell, W.W.   "Camp Point"   Jul 28, 1881
    Died- W.W. Stockwell of Quincy July 23rd.

Stokes, Mrs Elizabeth   "Obituary"   Oct 29, 1903
    see Tomlinson, Alice Jane

Stokes, Eva E.   "Local"   Sep 1, 1892
    A young lady of Carthage, Eva E.,3rd daughter of Mr and Mrs T.J. Stokes
    at the age of 26 yrs. Met her death last week by an explosion of
    gasoline vapors.

Stone, Daniel   "Lima"   Jan 12, 1893
    Died- Infant babe of Mr Daniel Stone died last Thursday.

Stone, Mrs E.K.   "Death"   Jan 19, 1887
    see Wood, Mrs Governor

Stone, Elbridge K.   "Local"   Dec 1, 1898
    Died- Elbridge K. Stone at his home at 1245 Maine St Friday November 25th
    from the effects of an operation from strangulated hernia. 80 yrs old.
    Was one of Quincy's earliest settlers. Was of that New England Puritan
    stock. Wife was a sister of the 2nd wife of the late Gov. Wood. Died just
    11yrs to a day before Mr S. 2 children survive, Elbridge K. Stone Jr and
    Mrs Newhall of Boston.

Stone, Mrs Euphemia   Feb 9, 1882
Died- Mrs Euphemia Stone. 58 yrs old. Wife Micajaw Stone. Born in
Lawrence Co. Ill. Leaves husband and 3 daughters.

Stone, Mr J.R.   "Local"   Jun 6, 1889
Died- Mr J.R. Stone died on Thursday at his home east of 36th St and
Broadway. Born in Penn September 12, 1822. Came to Adams Co. about 1859.
Lived at Mendon several yrs where he worked ar blacksmithing. (his shop
was about 2½ miles southeast of Mendon on the right hand side of the road
going to Fowler.)

Stone, Mrs M.   "Ursa"   Feb 9, 1882
Mrs Stone, wife of M. Stone was buried today.

Stone, Mrs M.   "Ursa"   Feb 9, 1882
Mrs Stone, wife of M. Stone was buried Feb. 5th.

Stone, Micajah   "Ursa"   Oct 17, 1895
Died- Mr Micajah Stone last Sunday at 10 A.M. of Brights disease. Born
in Pittis Co. Mo. September 13, 1819. In 1821 his parents moved to Tenn.
where they lived till 1831 when they moved to Adams Co., Ill. He married
Miss Famria Marin. They had 6 children, 3 still living. Wife is dead. In
1883 he married 2nd wife,Sallie Adair who survives him. He was a member of
the Christian church. Funeral Tuesday A.M. by Rev Roe. Buried in family
cemetery on the Mr Frank Stone's home place.

Stone, Mr R.F. or W.   "Ursa"   Feb 10, 1886
Mr R.F. Stone was called to Paris, Mo. where his grandson was very sick,
but the child died before he arrived there. W. Stone returned with his
father and laid the child to rest in the old family burying ground on his
farm near Ursa.

Stone, Mrs Sarah   "Ursa"   Nov 23, 1899
Died- Mrs Sarah Stone at this place Thursday at the age of 69 yrs.
Services by Rev Ringland at the Christian church Friday afternoon. Buried
Stone church cemetery. Leaves a son and daughter.

Stowe, Mr   "Loraine"   Feb 26, 1903
Joe Hardy attended the funeral of his grandfather, Mr Stowe at Adrain,
Wednesday.

Straley, Joseph   "3 deaths"   Oct 10, 1901
see Riley, Jas. A.

Strathoff, Annie   "Local"   Sep 1, 1886
Annie Strathoff, daughter of the late Bernard Strathoff, living in
Ellington twp committed suicide on last Sunday by shooting herself through
the heart with a pistol, cause - a quarrel with her lover.

Stratton, Mrs   Jun 12, 1890
see Stewart, Robert

Stratton, Sarah E.   "Death"   Mar 5, 1903
see Platt, Rev H.D.

Straub, Mrs   Fowler"   May 8, 1884
    Mrs Straub died May 1st. age 76 yrs.

Straub, J.D.   "Local"   Dec 21, 1904
    Died- J.D. Straub of Fowler of heart failure Monday afternoon. 70 yrs old.
    Leaves 4 sons and 2 daughters.

Straub, Mr J.D.   "Fowler"   Jun 4, 1880
    The grandchild (Baby) of Mt J.D. Straub was brought here from Colchester
    for burial.

Straub, Mrs J.D.   "Fowler and Oakland"   Dec 29, 1898
    Died- Mrs J.D. Straub, wife of one of Fowler's merchants Saturday at 2 P.M.

Straub, Isaac   "Fowler"   Jan 29, 1885
    Mr and Mrs J.D. Straub have been sorely afflicted in the death of Isaac,
    their youngest son.Cause was croup.

Straub, Mrs Nancy   "Fowler"   Nov 20, 1902
    Died- Mrs Nancy Straub, widow of the late Wm Straub last Tuesday. She
    was 89 yrs old. Services by Rev Meader at the Christian church Thursday.
    Leaves 9 sons and daughters and many other relatives. Mr and Mrs John
    Straub of Colchester, Mr and Mrs Wm Straub of Brookfield, Mo. and
    several relatives from Quincy attended the funeral of Mrs Nancy Straub.

Straub, Wm Sr.   "Fowler"   Apr 18, 1901
    Died- Wm Straub Sr. at his home in Fowler Monday night. Funeral Wednesday
    at the Christian church by Rev Hamilton of Meyer. Buried Chase Cemetery.

Strickinger, Charles   May 24, 1883
    Charles Strickinger a resident of Quincy committed suicide Saturday
    May 19th.

Strickler, Mrs B.H.   "Death"   Dec 14, 1899
    see Eddy, Miss

Strickler, Clark   "Death"   Apr 4, 1895
    Died- Clark Strickler March 28th from consumption. Funeral Sunday P.M.
    in the Cong'l church by Rev Wm Burgess and Pev R.A. Hartrick. Buried in
    cemetery beside his wife. Born Fayette Co. Penn November 15th 1833. Came
    to Ill. with parents 1837 and settled in Houston twp. Moved to Mendon twp
    30 yrs ago. Married Miss Julia A. Sproat of this two August 28, 1862. Mrs
    Strickler died at Hollister, Calif. Feb. 12, 1884 where she had gone for
    her health. They had 3 children, Orville, Minnie Myrtle and David Perry,
    All survive their parents. Relatives attending the funeral were- -
    Mr W.A. Thomas of Fairfax, Mo., Mr and Mrs Geo. W. Cyrus of Camp Point,
    Mr and Mrs Jerry Strickler of York Neck, Minnie and Elmer Thomas of
    Augusta, Mr and Mrs Wilbur Strickler of Big Neck, Mr and Mrs H.M. Heaney
    and Mr and Mrs S.W. Heaney of Quincy, Mr and Mrs Chas. Gay of Camp Point,
    Mrs Cora Wright of Skidmore, Mo.

Strickler, Clark   "Probate"   Apr 4, 1895
    Probate Notice of Clark Strickler, deceased 1st Monday of June 1895
    Orville Strickler, Adm -Hamilton and Woods attorneys.

Strickler, Mrs Clark   "Local"   Feb 28, 1884
    Mrs Clark Strickler died in Hollister Calif. Her body arrived in Mendon
    accompanied by her husband and youngest child. This was the 1st interment
    in the new extension of the Mendon cemetery. Services by Rev E.C. Crane
    pastor of the Cong'l church. She was the daughter of Mr and Mrs Percy
    Sproat. She died Feb. 12th at the home of her parents at the age of
    43 yrs 5 mo's 5 days. Married nearly ½ of this time. Leaves husband and
    3 children and both parents.

Strickler, David W.   "Obituary"   Jan 4, 1904
    Mr David W. Strickler, living 6 miles west of Bolchow, Mo. died October
    23rd. He was 39 yrs 9 mo's 23 days ols. Funeral at the house next day. His
    wife died March 5, 1903 leaving 4 little children, the oldest, a boy 12 yrs
    old and the youngest, a girl 7 yrs old. He was the youngest son of Louis L.
    Strickler and was born on the farm now owned by W.I. Felgar. Moved to
    Bolchow about 20 yrs ago. He was a brother of Mrs J.H. Pepple and Mrs
    Herman Dudley. His wife's name was Miss Mary Johnson. His mother, Mrs
    Catherine Strickler has been staying with him several yrs taking care of
    the children was present at the time of death. She is 71 yrs old.

Strickler, Miss Fannie   "Obituary"   Feb 26, 1902
    see Thompson, Mrs Fannie

Strickler, Frank   "Local"   Mar 5, 1903
    News rec'd here Saturday A.M. of the death Friday night of Frank
    Strickler, son of Mr and Mrs David Strickler, of Skidmore, Mo. He was
    a cousin of Mrs C.H. Nutt and Orville Strickler.

Strickler, Fred   "Loraine"   Mar 19, 1903
    Little Fred Strickler died Monday A.M. at 5 with complications of diseases
    Funeral by Rev C.D. Haskill at the Christian church at 2 P.M. Wednesday.
    He was 3 yrs old

Strickler, Mr and Mrs H.W.   "Obituary"   Feb 26, 1902
    see Thompson, Mrs Fannie

Strickler, John (Jack)   "Camp Point"   Jan 27, 1881
    John (Jack) Strickler died last week of typhoid fever.

Strickler, Lewis L.   "Probate"   Dec 11, 1879
    Probate Notice of Lewis L. Strickler, deceased 1st Monday of Feb. 1880
    Catherine Strickler, Adm.

Strickler, Mr L.L.   "Died"   Nov 27, 1879
    Died- Mr L.L. Strickler Sunday November 23rd at his residence 3½ miles
    northwest of Mendon at the age of 58 yrs. Burial Tuesday in Mendon.

Strickler, Mrs Nancy J.   "Death"   Nov 30, 1899
    see Hardy, Joseph Patterson

Strickler, Oliver   "Loraine"   Sep 14, 1887
    A child of Mr and Mrs Oliver Strickler was buried here Saturday.

Strickler, Orville   "Chancery Suit"   Jan 20, 1898
    see Worman, Geo. M.

Strickler, Orville   "Death"   Dec 4, 1902
    see Holstein, George

Strickler, Mr Wesley   "Local"   Nov 29, 1894
    Mr David Strickler of Maysville, Mo, came to attend the funeral of his
    brother, Wesley, at Camp Point and is expected here to visit the family
    of his brother Clark Strickler.

Strickler, Wesley   "Camp Point Journal"   Nov 29, 1894
    Died- Wesley Strickler Friday November 23rd in his 74th yr. Had been
    an invalid several yrs. Born in Penn and came to Illinois as a lad with his
    parents in 1837. They settled in Huston twp where most of his life was
    spent. In 1843 he married Catherine Kern, they had 4 sons and 2 daughters,
    Wife and 6 children survive him. Funeral Sunday P.M. Buried village cem.

Stringham, Harriet   "Obituary"   Jan 4, 1900
    see Talcott, Mrs Harriet

Strong, Mrs Elixa   "Obituary"   May 15, 1902
    see Wheldon, Mary Crane

Stuart, Georgie   "Lima"   Feb 24, 1886
    Died- on Thursday eve Feb. 18th, Georgie, son of George and Elizabeth
    Stuart.

Sturat, John   "Probate"   Feb 7, 1889
    Probate notice of John Stuart, deceased   1st Monday of March 1889
    Alonzo Jackson, Adm.

Stucke, Mrs Wm   "Ursa"   Jun 14, 1905
    Mrs Wm Stucke, who has been laying at death's door at St Mary's hospital
    for several weeks from wounds inflicted by her brutal husband died
    yesterday afternoon.

Stump, Mrs Hannah (F.M.)   "Obituary"   Apr 13, 1893
    Died- Hannah V. Stump, wife of F.M. Stump at her home in Big Neck April
    4th at the age of 53 yrs 17 days. Born in Bourbon Co. Ky. March 18, 1840
    Married F.M. Stump July 1, 1858 and had 2 sons. Burial from Ebenezer
    church, services by Rev J.B. King.

Sturgis, Dr   "Death"   Dec 21, 1887
    see Elliott, Mrs Joseph

Sturgiss, Dr   "Payson"   May 12, 1886
    Dr Sturgiss of Quincy attended the funeral of his sister, Mrs Mann,
    here yesterday.

Sturgiss, Dr S.M.   "Local"   Jul 25, 1889
    Dr S.M. Sturgiss, Dentist, died at his home in Quincy last Thursday
    July 18th. 61 yrs old. Buried Saturday.

Sullivan, Major H.V.   Oct 25, 1883
    Major H.V. Sullivan one of the oldest residents of Quincy died October 22nd
    at the age of 67 yrs. Resident of Quincy since 1836. He was the original
    proprietor of the Quincy Whig.

Sullivan, John   "Local"   Feb 22, 1894
    A tramp named John Sullivan, hailing from Petersboro, Ind, was killed
    on the farm of J.T. Nelson Saturdat P.M. in the Lima Lake levee district,
    Fell on a portable saw mill and his skull was cut thru to the brain.
    Lived only a few hours.

Sullivan, W.H. Jr.   "Quincy"   Mar 23, 1899
    Died- W.H. Sullivan Jr. at the age of 10 yrs. Was taken with convulsions
    Sunday night and died within 24 hours. Son of Patrolman H. Sullivan.

Summers, Mrs Cora (James)   "Local"   Feb 1, 1900
    Died- Mrs Cora Summers, wife of James Summers of Quincy. She was found
    dead on her babe's grave in Woodland cemetery Sunday night at 8. Baby
    had died 2 weeks before.

Summers, Mr Nathaniel   "Personal"   Jul 1, 1880
    Died- Mr Nathaniel Summers of Melrose twp last Monday. He settled in
    Quincy 50 yrs ago. He was a carpenter and builder, but a farmer for the
    past 30 yrs.

Summers, Wm A.   "Local"   Jul 19, 1900
    Died- Wm A. Summers (uncle Billy) of Quincy died in that city Monday eve.

Sutherland, W.P.   "Stillwell"   Jan 5, 1882
    Died- last week the baby of W.P. Sutherland's.

Swaim, Rachel   "Probate"   Oct 20, 1882
    Probate Notice of Rachel Swaim, deceased-- Wm L. McClung, Adm

Swan, Miss Flora   "Death"   Dec 6, 1900
    see Dressback, Mrs Frank

Swan, Mrs Mary Ann(Abner)   "Obituary"   Oct 28, 1897
    Died- Mrs Mary Ann Swan Saturday A.M. at the home of her son, Sanford, of
    congestion of the lungs. Mary Ann Daniels Swan was born Knox Co. Ohio
    May 17, 1820 and died October 23, 1897 at the age of 77 yrs 5 mo's 6 days.
    Married Abner Swan April 12, 1838 and had 9 children, 5 girls and 4 boys
    3 girls and 2 boys survive her, Mrs Sarah Scott, Sanford Swan of Mendon,
    Mrs Garrett Hendrickson of Ursa twp, Mrs Arthur Sisley of Keokuk and
    Wesley Swan of Buckhardt, Mo. Was a member of the Methodist church.
    Abner her husband died in 1882 and since that time she has lived with
    Sanford. Funeral Monday A.M. at the house by Rev E.K. Crews. Buried in
    Franklin cemetery.

Swan, Mr and Mrs Sanford   "Local"   Aug 8, 1889
    Died- an infant daughter of Mr and Mrs Sanford Swan's of cholera
    infantum. Buried Franklin church cemetery. Services by Rev R.P. Droke
    the next day.

Swan, Sarah   "Obituary"   Jan 28, 1892
    Sarah Swan was born October 22nd 1804 in Cumberland Co. Ky, and was
    married to Wm Roberts in 1823. Moved to Rushville, Ill in 1835, lived there
    2 yrs and on to Adams Co settling near Big Neck where they raised 8
    children. 6 sons and 2 daughters. Husband and 5 children are dead. Husband
    in 1863. the remaining children are, George who lives in Calif.. Horatio
    in Nebr. and Mary Nelson in Big Neck. Mrs Roberts lived with her daughter
    and died January 15th. Member of Baptist church. Her death erased a name
    from the pension list of the war of 1812.

Swaney, Mrs E.(W.W.)   "Local"   Oct 17, 1901
    Mrs J.F. Booher rec'd word of the death of her mother, Mrs E. Swaney,
    at Nokamis, Ill. She was 83 yrs old. Was the wife of Rev D.D.Swaney and
    had been a widow since 1876.

Swearington, Wm   "Columbus and Gilmer"   Apr 23, 1891
    Wm Swearington, a young man working for L.L. Myers was called to Quincy
    to attend the funeral of his father who died Thursday.

Sweat, Lilburn   "Coatsburg"   Jan 13, 1886
    Lilburn Sweat died of erysipelas January 4th. Services by Rev R.A. Omer
    at the Christian church.

Sweat, Mr Orson   "Coatsburg"   Jan 18, 1894
    Died- While at work Thursday January 11th, Mr Orson Sweat died of heart
    disease. He farmed and lived 2 miles east of town. Was 58 yrs old.
    Leaves 4 sons and 1 daighter. Services by Elder Dilly at the Christian
    church, buried beside his wife in our village cemetery.

Sweat, Lulu (Mrs W.T.)   "Coatsburg"   Oct 11, 1894
    Died- Lulu Sweat, nee Gray, wife of W.T. Sweat, died at this place
    October 1, 1894. She was 21 yrs old. Services by Elder Dilley at the
    Christian church, buried in our village cemetery. Leaves a husband and a
    daughter 5 months old.

Swope, Mr John   "Clip from Clayton Enterprise" Feb 12, 1885
    2 yr old child of Mr John Swopes died Wednesday.

Symonds, Mrs   "Obituary"   Mar 20, 1890
    see Fowler, Mrs E.H.

Symonds, Mr E.K.   "Local"   Jun 5, 1902
    Mr E.K. Symonds died at his home in Chicago, Saturday May 31st and
    buried in Rose Hill cemetery Sunday June 1st. He formerly lived Quincy
    and was in the insurance business.

Taft, Mrs A.H.   "Obituary"   Jan 11, 1900
    see Cramer, Capt H.P.W.

397

Taft, Mrs A.H.   "Obituary"   Jan 11, 1900
    see Cramer, Capt. H.P.W.

Taft, Mrs Samuel   "Obituary"   Jul 20, 1893
    Died- Mrs Samuel Taft, an old resident of Mendon died Monday afternoon
    at 3. Only 5 hours after an operation for umbitucal hernia. Funeral Tues.
    at the house by Rev Fitfield of Chicago a visiting clergyman. Born at
    Cherisbrook, Conn. May 30, 1833. Married Samuel Taft in 1857 and came to
    Illinois in spring of 1860 settling at Payson. That fall they moved to
    Mendon. Mr Taft survives her along with 1 son, Mr A.H. Taft of this place
    and 1 daughter by a former marriage, Miss Frances Chidsey.

Tailor, Mother   "Carthage"   Mar 20, 1879
    Mother Tailor died this morning. She was the mother of the Tailor Bros.
    our grocerymen.

Talcott, A.W.   "Funeral"   Jan 4, 1900
    A.W. Talcott of Hollenburg, Kansas arrived here Monday to attend his
    mother's funeral.

Talcott, Asa W.   "Death"   Mar 7, 1895
    see Clair, Mrs Wesley

Talcott, Mrs Harriet   "Obituary"   Jan 4, 1900
    Died- Mrs Hariett Talcott on January 1st at 10 A.M. She joins her
    husband and children gone before her. Hariett Stringham was born Broom Co.
    N.Y. April 21, 1821. Came to Illinois at the age of 10 yrs with her
    parents. While living at Jacksonville she met and married Chester H.
    Talcott December 1849. They came to Mendon soon after. Mr T. was born at
    Glastonberry, Conn. They had 7 children, 3 girls and 4 boys. Mary, Julia,
    Ella, William, Samuel, Elmer and Albert. The 2 youngest Elmer and Albert
    are deceased. Mr T. died 28 yrs ago. She was member of the Mondaon Cong'l
    church for almost 50 yrs. Services at 1:30 P.M. at the Cong'l church and
    a short service at the house by Rev J.S. Bayne. Buried Mendon.

Talcott, Mary H.   "Obituary"   Mar 7, 1895
    see Clair, Mrs Wesley

Talcott, Sarah Louise   "Funeral"   Mar 13, 1902
    Funeral services of Deacon and Mrs Samuel Talcott's youngest daughter,
    Sarah Louise was Monday at 2 P.M. at their home. Taken with pneumonia
    Tuesday night and died Sat. A.M.

Talcott, Wm   "Death"   Jan 4, 1900
    Wm Talcott of Rothville, Mo. arrived Sunday to see his sick mother who
    died the next morning.

Tallcott, Mrs A.W. (Phoebe) "Death"   Jan 18, 1886
    Died on the 4th inst at her home in Hollenberg, Kansas, Phoebe, wife
    of A.W. Tallcott.

Tallcott, Mary A.   "Death"   Mar 22, 1905
    see Baldwin, George Dutton

Tallcott, Samuel   "Death"   Jul 3, 1902
    see Hulburd, Mrs Anna

Tallcott, Samuel   "Death"   Aug 28, 1890
    Mr Samuel Tallcott and Miss Ella Tallcott were called to Mo. by the
    illness of Mrs Amos Scranton. News was rec'd of her death yesterday.

Tallis, Joseph   "Died"   Oct 25, 1900
    Joseph Tallis, of Tennessee, Ill. a newspaper correspondent was found
    dead in the alley west of the Occidental Hotel in Quincy Sunday A.M.
    It is supposed he fell from the 3rd story window of the hotel where he
    stopped.

Tanner, Dr   "Died"   Feb 11, 1892
    G.H. Baldwin shows us a card which tells its own brief sad tale.
                            Jacksinville, Ill Feb 18th
    Dear Father;
    Dr Tanner died at 7:45 A.M.   52 yrs old.
           E. G. Baldwin

Tanner, Franklin   "Death"   Mar 16, 1887
    Mr Naegelin has been attending the funeral of his father in law at Basco.
                     "Death"
    Mrs Naegelin was summoned to Basco on the death of her father, Mr Franklin
    Tanner.

Tarr, Mrs   "Death"   Mar 17, 1892
    see Adair, Mr Jas.

Tarr, Miss Iva   "Death"   Sep 20, 1894
    see Murphy, Mrs Iva

Tarr, Mary M.   "Probate"   Dec 3, 1891
    Probate notice of Mary M. Tarr, deceased   1st Monday of Feb. 1892
    Charles Tarr, Adm.

Tarr, Mrs Mary Mitchell Adair   "Obituary"   Oct 15, 1891
    Mary Mitchell Adair Tarr died October 8th. Born December 10, 1813, being
    77 yrs 9 mo's 28 days old. She married April 23, 1833 to Wm Tarr who died
    a few yrs ago. They had 11 children of whom 6 (4 boys and 2 girls)
    survive. These are, Mrs Mary Jane Shields of El Dorado, Mo., Mrs Martha
    Barnett of Mendon twp, Mrs Lucinda Mc Gibbons of Sioux City, Iowa, Miss
    Alice Tarr of Mendon, Mr James F. Tarr of Mo., Mr Charles Tarr of West
    Point. Was member of the Methodist church 40 yrs. Services from the M.E.
    church by Rev A.A. White. Burial in the burial ground of the Free Will
    Baptist church near her old home this side of Marcelline. Other relatives
    at the funeral were, her sister, Mrs Ellis of Kansas City and her grand-
    daughter, Mrs Iva Murphy of Peoria.

Tarr, Wm R.   "Death"   Dec 12, 1878
    Died- Tuesday Dec. 10th at his home in Mendon, Wm R. Tarr. 69 yrs old.
    Born in Bourbon co. Ky. Came to Adams co about 1830. Married and settled
    near Marcelline and lived there until about 3 yrs ago when he moved to our
    town. Member of the M.E. church and Masonic fraternity.
                     "Memoriam"   Dec 1878
    Wm R. Tarr died December 10th in his 69th yr.

Tarr, Wm R.   "Probate"   Jan 2, 1879
    Probate notice of Wm R. Tarr, deceased 3rd Monday of Feb. 1879
    Mary M. Tarr and Charles Tarr, Executors.

Tatmen, Elizabeth   "Obituary"   Jan 19, 1893
    see Tout, John S.

Tawson, Mrs Michael   "Death in Quincy"   Mar 2, 1899
    Died- Mrs Michael Tawson Sunday P.M. 73 yrs old from heart disease.
    Was a native of Ireland. Resident of Quincy 56 yrs. Leaves husband.

Taylor, Mrs   "Indian Grave"   Apr 4, 1895
    Died, Mrs Taylor at her daughters, Mrs Charley Hedges, last Wednesday
    about noon. Sick 1 week. Buried in Quincy. Leaves children.

Taylor, Annie M.   "Heirs"   Apr 14, 1892
    see Wible, Sarah

Taylor, Mrs Barbara   "Obituary"   Mar 2, 1899
    Died- Mrs Barbara Taylor living with the family of M.B. Frazier, about
    1 mile north of Ursa Friday A.M. 85 yrs old. Survived by 6 children, Mrs
    M.C. Varnier, Mrs Thos Leachman and Mrs M.B. Frazier of Ursa, Mrs Lewis
    Thornton and Clarence Taylor of Lima, William Taylor of Walla Walla, Wash.
    Buried Sat. P.M. in the Denson cemetery.

Taylor, Charles A.   "Heirs   Apr 14, 1892
    see Wible, Sarah

Taylor, Charley   "Died"
    Charley Taylor, 22yrs old died at his home in Columbus May 30th. His
    father in Coatsburg was sent for, but did not arrive in time. Buried
    Columbus cemetery.

Taylor, Daniel   "Obituary"   Oct 5, 1877
    Died- Daniel Taylor, an early settler of Adams Co. article dated Oct 1st

Taylor, David   "Heirs"   Apr 14, 1892
    see Wible, Sarah

Taylor, Edward   "Obituary"   Nov 23, 1899
    see Wilkinson, Martha

Taylor, Edward   "Obituary"   Jun 26, 1884
    Died- Edward Taylor June 22nd at 12:30 P.M. Buried in Mendon cemetery.
    Services in the Zion church by Dean Irvine. He was a native of Ireland.
    Came to this country with his father in spring of 1849. Settling near
    Philadelphia. Moved west in the fall of the same yr and settled in Mendon.
    71 yrs old. Leaves a widow and 5 children. (3 boys and 2 girls)

Taylor, Effie M.   "Heirs"   Apr 14, 1892
    see Wible, Sarah

Taylor, Elizabeth   "Obituary"   Nov 23, 1899
    see Wilkinson, Martha

Taylor, Mrs Elizabeth   "Death"   Apr 4, 1895
    Mrs Elizabeth Taylor, the widowed mother of Mr Fred Taylor, prop. of
    the Journal of Industry, died last week. 69 yrs old. Born England. Lived
    Quincy nearly 50 yrs.

Taylor, Mrs Elizabeth   "Death"   Dec 21, 1877
    Died- Mrs Elizabeth Taylor, wife of Christopher Taylor of Honey Creek
    December 12th. Services at the Centre school house by Rev V.C. Randolph.
    She was 53 yrs old last April. Joined the M.E. church as a girl.

Taylor, George   "Marcelline"   Aug 7, 1879
    George Taylor lost his youngest child last Friday.

Taylor, George   "Star District"   Feb 16, 1882
    Died- a child of George Taylor of near Franklin.

Taylor, George   "Star District"   Feb 23, 1882
    Mr George Taylor buried another child last Friday. The second in 2 weeks.
    Both died of scarlet fever.

Taylor, Herman G.   "Heirs"   Apr 14, 1892
    see Wible, Sarah

Taylor, James   "Obituary"   Jan 9, 1890
    James Taylor, the second son of the late Edward and Martha Taylor of
    Honey Creek, died at home 2 miles southeast of Mendon at 3 P.M. January 4th
    at the age of 47 yrs. He was born in Kildare, Ireland October 14, 1842
    Came to this country with his parents and 2 surviving brothers in 1849.
    The family remained in the neighborhood of Philadelphia, Penn a few mo's,
    but in the fall of the same yr found their way to Mendon. Funeral was
    in Zion Episcopal church by Rev W. Michael Hicks, the pastor.

Taylor, Mrs James   "Tioga"   May 11, 1899
    Mrs James Taylor who died Sunday at her home 4 miles southeast of town
    was buried in our village cemetery Monday.

Taylor, John A.   "Heirs"   Apr 14, 1892
    see Wible, Sarah

Taylor, Mrs M.B.   "Obituary"   Mar 2, 1899
    see Judy, Mrs Nancy

Taylor, Mrs Martha   "Obituary"   Nov 23, 1899
    see Wilkinson, Martha

Taylor, Nellie G.   "Heirs"   Apr 14, 1892
    see Wible, Sarah

Taylor, Rebecca   "Heirs"   Apr 14, 1892
    see Wible, Sarah

Taylor, Sarah   "Obituary"   Nov 23, 1899
    see Wilkinson, Martha

401

Taylor, Sarah Ann see Hughes, Albert	"Death"	Jul 26, 1905
Taylor, Sarah M. see Wible, Sarah	"Heirs"	Apr 14, 1892
Taylor, Thomas see Wilkinson, Martha	"Obituary"	Nov 23, 1899
Taylor, Mr W.C. see Cupp, Mrs George	"Death"	Apr 1, 1880
Taylor, Mrs W.G. see Wible, Andrew	"Obituary"	Jun 26, 1890
Taylor, Wm G. see Wible, Sarah	"Heirs"	Apr 14, 1892
Taylor, Wm H. see Wible, Sarah	"Heirs"	Apr 14, 1892
Taylor, William see Wilkinson, Martha	"Obituary"	Nov 23, 1899

Teas, Z.W.   "Funeral"   May 1, 1884
    Funeral April 27th of Z.W. Teas. Member of the Quincy Typographical
    Union. Buried Woodland cemetery. Age 32 yrs. Unmarried.

Tenford, John   "Local"   Nov 19, 1891
    Died- John Tenford of Honey Creek twp Monday night from typhoid fever.

Tennis, Mrs   "Payson"   Apr 15, 1880
    Mrs Tennis was buried Monday P.M. at Burton.

Tenvord, Mr   "Local"   Jan 14, 1892
    Death of old Mr Tenvord of Honey Creek.

Tenvord, John   "Paloma"   Nov 26, 1891
    John Tenvord died November 23rd. Was a young man in the prime of life.

Tenvorde, Mrs   "Local"   Mar 30, 1893
    Died- Mrs Tenvorde on Monday night at her home in Honey Creek. Funeral
    Wednesday A.M. at Bloomfield Catholic cemtery.

Tenvorde, Mrs George   "Bloomfield"   Mar 13, 1902
    Mrs George Tenvorde was buried in Bloomfield cemetery last week. Services
    by Father McVay.

Tenvorde, Mr and Mrs Geo.   "Fowler and Oakland"   Dec 28, 1899
    Died- The infant son of Mt and Mrs Geo. Tenvorde last Sat.

Tenvorde, Mrs Henry   "Local"   Apr 20, 1893
    Died- the wife of Henry Tenvorde, of Honey Creek Friday night April 14th
    Buried in Catholic cemetery at Bloomfield on Sunday. Henry has lost within
    a yr his father and mother, a brother, 2 children and now his wife.

Tenvorde, John Theodore   "Probate"   Mar 17, 1892
    Probate notice of John Theodore Tenvorde, deceased 1st Monday of May 1892
    Mary A. Tenvorde, Adm.

Tenvorde, Mary A.   "Probate"   Aug 24, 1893
    Probate notice of Mary A. Tenvorde, deceased 1st Monday of Oct 1893
    Alfred J. Brockschmidt, Ex.

Terrill, Mr George   "Payson"   Nov 27, 1879
    Mr Terrill of Newtown, Ill. died suddenly November 17th.
                                 "Burton"
    Death of Mr George Terrill who was found dead in bed November 17th from
    unknown causes.

Terry, John   "Camp Point"   Oct 10, 1901
    The death of John Terry was on last Friday at the home of his mother in
    this city from typhoid fever. Services by Rev O. Dilley Sunday P.M. after
    which the N.P.'s took charge of the funeral.

Terry, Mr Wm   "Camp Point"   ·   Aug 28, 1900
    The funeral of Mr Wm Terry was here last Monday. Was over 80 yrs old.
    Services at the house by O. Dilley. Buried in the cemetery.

Teufel, Mrs Mary A.   "Local"   Apr 12, 1905
    Geo. W. Teufel left last week for Springfield to attend the funeral of his
    mother, Mrs Mary A. Teufel, who died of old age at that place. He returned
    Sat.

Thacker, Allen E.   "Local   Apr 27, 1899
    Died- Allen E. Thacker, Born in Adams Co. 1877. In 1884 he was adopted
    into the family of Esther A. Eddy. Lived most of the last 4 yrs with
    Mrs Mary Rogers. Died April 20th. Services by Mr Hall of Canton, Mo.
    at the home of Mrs Rogers. His parents are believed to be dead and he has
    no brothers or sisters.

Tharp, Warren S.   "Local"   Dec 31, 1891
    Warren S. Tharp is dead. Not Mr J. W. Tharp of Edgewood, Ill. formerly
    of Loraine, Died November 13th and buried November 14th. Had he lived
    till Feb. 1st 1892 he would have been 40 yrs old.

Tharpe, John W.   "Obituary"   Dec 29, 1898
    Died- John W. Tharpe, born North Carolina 1823. He was 75 yrs old.
    Left his birthplace as a boy and went to Tenn., stayed there until grown
    when he went to Ohio. There he married Meriah Burtsell in 1857 and they
    came to Illinois and settled 1½ miles northeast of Loraine. Lived there
    until 1889 when they moved to Clay Co. Ill. Died December 24th of lung
    fever. Had 5 boys and 5 girls. 3 girls and 3 boys still living, Geo. the
    eldest living near Canton, Ill. Wm of near Edgewood, John Jr. still living
    with parents, Mrs Sarah Sellie of near Myer, Mrs Clara Henry of near Golden
    and Mrs Alice Batley of near Edgewood and his wife survive him.

Thayer, Rev   Apr 5, 1883
    Rev Thayer died March 29th. Buried Quincy. He was born Ipswitch, N.H.
    in 1848 Graduated at Dartmouth, spent 2 yrs at Bangor and 1 yr at
    Andover. His first pulpit was in Westboro, Mass. for 1½ yrs and then to
    quincy. Leaves a wife.

Thayer, Albina see Beal, Mrs Albina	"Obituary"	Jan 10, 1889
Thayer, Mrs Charles see Tomlinson, Mrs Sarah	"Obituary"	Apr 12, 1894
Thayer, Chas. see Tomlinson, Alice Jane	"Obituary"	Oct 29, 1903
Thayer, Charles	"Obituary"	Mar 16, 1904

Charles Thayer was born Dunkirk, Chatauqua Co. N.Y. May 4, 1832 and died March 7th 1904 of dropsy and other complications. Was 71 yrs 10 mo's 3 days old. At age 6 he came with his parents to Illinois and settled near Fowler where he stayed 62 yrs. Married Decmeber 10, 1854 to Alice Jane Tomblinson at Columbus, Ill. they had 5 children, 4 girls and 1 boy. An infant daughter and Mrs Tenie Frost died before him. Surviving him are- Henry E. Thayer of Hollywood, Miss., Mrs Ettie Worman, Troy, Kansas and Miss Lillie who is now in St Joseph hospital, St Joe and unable to attend funeral. 4 yrs ago his health failed and he quit farming and moved family to Macomb where his wife died Oct 22, 1903 after which he returned home with daughter, Mrs Worman who cared for him during his last illness. Joined Free Will Baptist church as a young man. Buried in Mount Olive cemetery, Troy, Kansas.

Thayer, Mr and Mrs F.M. see Beal, Mrs Albina	"Obituary"	Jan 10, 1889
Thayer, Mr F.N.	"Local"	Apr 6, 1887

Died- Mr F.N. Thayer on Friday afternoon at his farm near Ursa. Funeral from the house Monday P.M. Buried in the burying ground of the Franklin Free Will Baptist church of which he was a member. Services by Rev J.B. King of Lomax his long time friend. Those present for the burial was son Wm Thayer and wife of Carmen, Mr and Mrs Beal of Clarinda, Iowa son in law and daughter, a brother Mr Charles Thayer and family of Paloma, another brother Horace Thayer of Kansas could not get here in time. F.N. Thayer died April 1st 1887 at the age of 67 yrs 5. mo's 27 days. Born Chatauqua Co. N.Y. on October 24, 1891 and moved to Adams Co. in 1838. Married Sarah Burroes April 8, 1847. Joined the Free Will Baptist church in 1849 and was one of the original founders of the Franklin and Paloma Baptist church. Had 5 children (2 dead and 3 living) . Also leaves a wife.

Thayer, Miss Lillie A. see Tomlinson, Alice Jane	"Obituary"	Oct 29, 1903
Thayer, Henry E. see Tomlinson, Alice Jane	"Obituary"	Oct 29, 1903
Thayer, Miss Lillie Alice	"Obituary"	Mar 30, 1904

Died- Miss Lillie Alice Thayer, daughter of Charles and Alice J. Thayer, formerly of Macomb, Ill. was born in Adams Co. Ill. near Fowler Oct. 10, 1876 and died in St Joseph Mo. March 25, 1904 Of tuberculosis was 27 yrs 4 mo's 15 days old. Past 8 yrs she had taught school in Adams Co. Ill. Was member of Methodist church at Camp Point, Ill. and a member of Naoma Rebekeh Lodge #5 Surviving her are, Henry E. Thayer of Hollywood, Miss. and Mrs George Worman of Troy Kan. Services at the home of her sister, Mrs Geo. Worman of Troy, Kan at 2 P.M. Sunday March 27th by Rev Butler, pastor of the Methodist church of Troy. Buried Mt Olive cemetery.

Thayer, Mrs Sarah   "Obituary"   Oct 5, 1899
    see Rue, Rev Jonathan

Thele, Henry   "Local"   Oct 2, 1884
    A young man named Henry Thele while washing windows on the 2nd floor of
    the Herald office fell and was killed.

Thomas, Mrs   "Obituary"   Apr 23, 1885
    see Ford, Rhoda M.

Thomas, Benj. L.   "Died"   Mar 1, 1883
    Benj. L. Thomas was born in New Jersey October 10, 1800 and moved with
    parents to Ohio about 1807. Married Margaret Caterlin in his 24th yr. Moved
    to Adams Co. in fall of 1837. Since the death of his wife whom he lived
    with 49 yrs 11 mo's he lived with his daughter and son in Loraine until
    December 22nd of 1882 when he went to visit his daughter, Mrs J.
    Daughterty at Griswald, Iowa where he died Jan 31st. Leaves 6 children
    plus 2 that are dead. He was grandfather of 46 and great grandfather of
    44.

Thomas, Calista   "Obituary"   May 15, 1902
    see Whelden, Mary Crane

Thomas, Clarence   "Obituary"   May 15, 1902
    see Whelden, Mary Crane

Thomas, Mr E.F.   "Death"   Sep 25, 1890
    see Cain, Ellen

Thomas, Eli R.   "Obituary"   Aug 16, 1894
    "Sunday School Supplement" Died- Eli R. Thomas of the Hebron S.S.
    Camp Point died the past spring. He was an earnest worker for 25 yrs.

Thomas, Mrs Elizabeth   "Loraine"   Nov 9, 1887
    Died- November 1st, Mrs Elizabeth Thomas, wife of Benjamin Thomas in
    her 53rd yr. Died from lung trouble. Was a member of the Christian
    church 30 yrs. Leaves husband, 2 sons and 5 daughtersand several grand-
    children. Funeral at Dunkard church on November 2nd by Elder T.M.
    Johnson. Buried Loraine cemetery.

Thomas, Jefferson   "Obituary"   May 15, 1902
    see Whelden, Mary Crane

Thomas, Elmer   "Funeral   Apr 4, 1895
    see Strickler, Clark

Thomas, Minnie   "Funeral   Apr 4, 1895
    see Strickler, Clark

Thomas, J.   "Marblehead"   Aug 16, 1883
    Died August 8th, the youngest child of J. Thomas. Age 5 mo's.

405

Thomas, Mrs J.K.   "Marblehead"   Apr 12, 1883
    Rev Loff of Quincy was called to preach the funeral of Mrs J.K. Thomas.
    She leaves husband and children.

Thomas, Mary Jane   "Obituary"   May 15, 1902
    see Whelden, Mary Crane

Thomas, Peter   "Camp Point"   Mar 6, 1879
    Peter Thomas, a former resident of York Neck died in Augusta last week.
    Age 83 yrs.

Thomas, Mr W.A.   "Funeral"   Apr 4, 1895
    see Strickler, Clark

Thompson, Mrs   "Fowler"   Mar 2, 1882
    Mrs A.E. Horn was called away to attend the funeral of a sister, Mrs
    Thompson at Marseiles, Ill.

Thompson, Mrs and Mr   "Payson"   Apr 28, 1886
    One week ago today Mrs Thompson of Mexico, Mo. was buried here. Today her
    husband is to be brought here for burial. Mrs T. is the daughter of
    Squire Baker of this place.

Thompson, Albert   "Funeral"   Jun 22, 1899
    see Henderson, Mrs

Thompson, Mr and Mrs Arthur   "Mt Hebron"   Aug 8, 1895
    Died- the infant child of Mr and Mrs Arthur Thompson last Thursday.
    Buried in Franklin cemetery next day.

Thompson, Caswell   Nov 13, 1890
    October 24th Caswell Thompson a bridge man died in a train accident. He
    fell from a train car. Buried Basco. Leaves a wife and 3 children. He
    was about 34 yrs old.

Thompson, Daniel   "Soldiers"   Jun 5, 1902
    List of Civil war veterans buried in Mendon cemetery included Daniel
    Thompson.

Thompson, Edwin J.   "Local"   Aug 11, 1898
    Died Mr Edwin J. Thompson, the well known Quincy clothing merchant of
    heart disease Saturday at 5:30 A.M. Age 57 yrs Leaves a widow, 1 daugh-
    ter, Mrs A.B. Sibley of St Paul and 3 sons, Thomas E., Notely and Harry.

Thompson, Elmer   Mar 2, 1882
    Died- Elmer, only son of Mr and Mrs C.W. Thompson Feb. 21st 1882

Thompson, Mrs Emma   "Obituary"   Dec 8, 1898
    see McFarland, Mrs Debora

Thompson, Mrs Fannie   "Loraine"   Feb 26, 1902
    Mrs Emma Curless, Mrs B.H. Strickler, Miss Ella Baggerly and Mr and Mrs
    H.W. Strickler was called to the home of Mrs Fannie Thompson on account
    of Mrs T's serious i-lness. Mrs T. was the youngest daughter of Mr and
    Mrs H.W. Strickler. Saturday the news reached us that she died just before
    noon on Feb 22nd. Remains brought by train Monday A.M. here. Services
    held at Brethren church by Rev Nichols of Dallas. She married Feb. 21,
    1901. Buried Reece cemetery. Was 29 yrs 28 days old. Leaves husband,
    father, mother, 1 sister, 3 brothers and a baby boy 1 week old.

Thompson, George   "Funeral"   Jun 22, 1899
    see Henderson, Mrs

Thompson, Mr and Mrs Henry   "Local'   May 28, 1903
    The little babe of Mr and Mrs Henry Thompson (colored) died Thursday
    night last, age 4 days.

Thompson, Mrs Harriet   "Death"   May 31, 1905
    see Seifert, Daniel D.

Thompson, Uncle Hugh   "Marcelline"   Jun 30, 1886
    Uncle Hugh Thompson died last Monday (21st) at his son in laws, Hiram
    Houghton's and was buried next day in the Denson graveyard. He had passed
    his 3 score and 10 yrs. We don't know his exact age, but we do know
    he was old enough to vote for Jackson in 1828.

Thompson, Irene Frances   "Obituary"   Jul 18, 1901
    see Kennedy, Geo. Thomas

Thompson, Mr and Mrs James   "Local"   Apr 13, 1904
    The 3 yrs old child of Mr and Mrs James Thompson living north of Mendon
    was buried in Mendon cemetery Tuesday P.M. Services by Rev Bacon at
    the house.

Thompson, Miss Laura J.   "Obituary"   May 17, 1900
    see Lemmon, Mrs Laura J.

Thompson, Mrs Laura M.   "Obituary"   Nov 18, 1897
    see Rogers, Amelia May

Thompson, L.C.   "Local"   Jun 15, 1887
    "Camp Point Journal" L.C. Thompson residing 4 miles east of Golden was
    killed by a bolt of lightning while standing in his barn door last week.

Thompson, Lee   "Obituary"   May 17, 1900
    see Lemmon, Mrs Laura J.

Thompson, Mrs Lewis   "Obituary"   Jan 21, 1892
    see McAdams, William

Thompson, Mrs Lewis   "Sudden death"   Dec 28, 1899
    Died- Mrs Lewis Thompson yesterday. She was wife of a citizen of Ursa.
    61 yrs 10 mo's 15 days old. Leaves her husband, 4 daughters 2 sons, all
    married. 1 daughter, Mrs B.F. Shepherd lives in Mexico, Mo. All the
    rest live within a few miles of her home. She was born Miss Catherine
    McAdams and only surviving daughter of the late Wm McAdams, one of the
    early settlers of our village. Her sister, Mrs John Bittleston died only
    2 months ago. 2 brothers survive her. John and Geo. McAdams of Quincy.
    Funeral at the Christian church of which she was a member at 2 P.M. today.

Thompson, Lillie   "Probate"   Aug 7, 1890
    Probate notice of Lillie Thompson   1st Monday of October 1890
    L.F. Brown, Adm.

Thompson, Mrs Lillie B.   "Mt Hebron"   Mar 20, 1890
    Mrs Lillie B. Thompson died March 14th at the age of 18 yrs 7 mo's
    20 days. She was the oldest child of C.E. Rogers and Mary Rogers. Father
    died a yr ago. She leaves mother, husband, 3 sisters and 1 brother,
    also leaves one half brother and a half sister. Services by Rev J.B.
    Jeans of Canton, Mo. at the Franklin church.

Thompson, Margaret   Feb 23, 1882
    Died- Miss Margaret Thompson, for many yrs a member of the late
    President Tresslers family in Carthage. She was an aunt to Mrs Tressler.
    Taught for 15 yrs in North Carolina.

Thompson, Mrs Mark   "Payson"   Aug 17, 1882
    A brother of Mrs Mark Thompson died at her home last Wednesday night
    August 9th 1882

Thompson, Mrs Mary E.   "Died"   Mar 20, 1879
    Died- Sunday A.M. Mrs Mary E. Thompson, wife of Wm Thompson and the
    oldest daughter of Mr and Mrs Alex Gibbs. Funeral at the Lutheran church
    by Rev G.F. Behringer. She was a member of the Lutheran church.

Thompson, O.W.   "Obituary"   May 17, 1900
    see Lemmon, Mrs Laura J.

Thompson, Mrs O.W.   "Obituary"   Feb 19, 1903
    see Denson, William

Thompson, Samuel Sr.   "Columbus and Gilmer"   Jan 22, 1891
    Died- at his home in Gilmer twp on Jan 10th, Mr Samuel Thompson Sr. of
    pneumonia. Born Derry Co. Ireland September 18th 1821. Came to America
    in 1842. Lived 6 yrs in Philadelphia, Penn, then came west in 1848 and
    settled on a farm in Gilmer twp where he spent the rest of his days.
    Married Elizabeth McConnell in 1854. 6 children born to them. 3 boys
    and 3 girls. (5 still living) Member of the M.E. church. Was 69 yrs 3 mo's
    22 days. Buried at Mt Pleasant cemetery Services by Rev Staker, pastor
of the German M.E. church.

Thompson, W.S.   "Obituary"   May 17, 1900
    see Lemmon, Mrs Laura J.

Thompson, Mrs Wm   "Death"   Jun 21, 1905
   see Clair, John

Thompson, Mr William   "Payson"   Sep 9, 1830
   Died- August 24th Mr William Thompson, born in Green Co. Penn September
29, 1789. His father was one of the earliest Methodist preachers and
moved with his family to Athens Co. Ohio in 1796. Married in Ohio to Miss
   Rachel Pilcher July 28, 1813. She died in 1856. 2nd he married Mrs Eliza A.
   Graham who survives him. He came to Adams Co. Illinois and settled near
   Payson in 1833. Member of the M.E. church 72 yrs. Had been blind 20 yrs.
   Was 91 yrs old. Services by Rev Dr Wm Murphy at Mr T's home. Buried at
   the cemetery at Fall Creek church August 25th, 1880

Thorn, Mr R.R.   "Local"   Jan 5, 1893
   Died- at his home at Willow Springs, Howell Co. Mo. December 24th 1892
   R.R. Thorn. 70 yrs old. Was an old settler of Adams Co. having only
   4 yrs ago moved to Missouri. Leaves a son in California and 1 daughter.

Thornton, Mrs James   "Obituary"   Jul 16, 1891
   see Alexander, Perry

Thornton, John Mrs   "Local"   Aug 28, 1900
   Died, the wife of John Thornton of Lima last Saturday eve. Buried at the
   Stone church cemetery on Monday. Leaves husband, 2 children, 1 of these
   an infant 2 weeks old.

Thornton, Mrs Lewis   "Obituary"   Mar 2, 1899
   see Taylor, Mrs Barbara

Thrush, Geo.   "Local"   Oct 30, 1902
   Mr Geo. Thrush, of Quincy well known in grand army and secret society
   circles died suddenly from heart disease Tuesday A.M.

Thuman, Mrs Nancy   "Death"   May 18, 1904
   see Payne, Miss Catherine Ann

Tibbett, Gertie   Apr 26, 1900
   see Gibbs, Mrs A.

Tibbetts, Mrs America   "Lima"   Jun 20, 1895
   Died- Mrs America Tibbetts learned of the death of her brother, Mit Kirk,
   a Lima boy yrs ago, but now a long time resident of Missouri.

Tibbetts, Miss Albina   "Ursa"   Feb 28, 1901
   Died- Miss Albina Tibbetts of consumption last Saturday. Age 23 yrs.
   Buried Stone church cemetery Sunday P.M.

Tibbetts, Luella Elvina   "Obituary"   Feb 28, 1901
   Died- Luella Elvina Tibbetts. Born June 29, 1877 at Lima Illinois, the
   daughter of Henry and America Tibbets. Joined Episcopal church at Lima
   1894 and after moving to Ursa with her mother she became a charter member
   of the P.E. church 2 yrs ago. Died Feb 23, 1901 from consumption. Leaves
   mother, 2 sisters. 3 sisters are dead. Services by Rev Wakefield and
   buried in Stone church cemetery.

Tibbets, Mrs J.C.   "Obituary"   Jan 1, 1880
   see Bean, Mrs

Tibbetts, Miss Sophia   "Lima"   Apr 11, 1895
Died- Miss Sophia Tibbetts at her home. 27 yrs old. Services by Rev Rose of Loraine. Leaves mother and 4 sisters. Buried beside her father in the Lima cemetery.

Tibbitts,Henry   "Lima"   May 4, 1882
Henry Tibbitts died May 2nd. Leaves a large family.

Tieken, Mrs Fred Jr.   "Local"   Dec 3, 1891
Died- on Tuesday A.M. November 24th, Mrs Fred Tieken Jr. Leaves husband and 6 children. Youngest only 9 mo's old.

Tieken, Mrs Dr J.D.   "Local"   Nov 11, 1897
Died- Mrs Tieken, wife of Dr J.D. Tieken at Piper City, Illinois Monday A.M. of consumption. Age 41 yrs. She was sister of Mr F.G. Ertel. Leaves husband and daughter Katie 17 yrs old.

Tieken, Mr and Mrs W.   "Coatsburg"   Jan 31, 1895
Buried, infant babe of Mr and Mrs W. Tieken at the Coatsburg cemetery last Monday.

Tilton, Geo.   "Payson"   Sep 20, 1888
Buried- the 3 month old child of Mr Geo. Tilton here yesterday.

Tilton, John and Mary   Dec 7, 1877
Died- last Sunday A.M. the infant daughter of John and Mary Tilton. Age 2 weeks.

Tindell, Mrs A.   "Death"   Aug 27, 1903
see Stackhouse, Safrona Isabelle Rawlings

Tinnsman, Mrs Ann   "Obituary"   Jul 6, 1899
see Leighty, John

Tinsman, Anna   "Obituary"   Apr 20, 1899
see Myers, Mrs Anna Tinsman

Tippett, Cora Irena   "Died"   Feb 20, 1879
Died on Feb. 17th Cora Irena, infant daughter of Wm E. and Hattie L. Tippett. Age 6 mo's. Services at the house and at the grave Wednesday 2 P.M. by Rev Behringer.

Tippett, Mrs Harriet L.   "Died"   Feb 5, 1880
Died- on Feb 3rd Harriet L. Tippett, wife of Wm E. Tippett. Age 23 yrs.

Tippett, Mrs Hattie   "Personal"   Feb 5, 1880
Died- on Tuesday Feb 3rd of consumption, Mrs Hattie Tippett. Age 23 yrs. Funeral at 2 P.M. this afternoon at the Lutheran church.

Tittle, A.J.   "Funeral"   Feb 21, 1901
see Riddle, Mrs G.D.

Tittle, Mr A.J.   "Obituary"   Apr 13, 1899
    Died- Mr A.J. Tittle at his home in Honey Creek Saturday April 8th
    at 10 A.M. Services at his home Monday 1 P.M. Buried Curless cemetery
    by the side of his first wife, the mother of his 5 children. Andrew
    Johnston Tittle was born Westmoreland Co. Penn 1809. Married Margaret
    Montgomery of Kittanning, Armstrong Co. Penn 1855. Came to Illinois 1857
    settled where they live now in 1858. Had 2 sons and 2 daughters, William
    of LaBelle, Mo., A.J. at home, Mrs G.D. Riddle, of Oxford, Ind. and Mrs
    Wm McGinley of LaBelle, Mo. Mrs Tittle died August 29, 1870 and he married
    2nd to Armilda Kelley in 1879 who died in the Cong'l church March 15th
    1897. He was 89 yrs 5 mo's 5 days old. Member of the Cong'l church of
    Mendon.

Tittle, Annie Amelia   "Obituary"   Feb 28, 1901
    see McGinley, Annie Amelia

Tittle, Mrs Hamilton   Aug 20, 1891
    Mrs Tittle, widow of the late Hamilton Tittle died August 17th. Buried
    in Mendon cemetery from the Lutheran church.

Tittle, Mrs Hamilton   "Obituary"   Aug 20, 1891
    Mrs Tittle, releit of the late Hamilton Tittle died on Monday night
    of heart trouble from which she had suffered at intervals for many mo's.
    The funeral was delayed till this morning to allow time for the arrival
    of her daughters, Mrs Weideman of ElDorado and Mrs Chase of Hutchinson,
    Kansas. The remains will leave the house at 9 A.M. for the Lutheran
    church where the services are to be held.

Tittle, Mrs Mary   "Loraine"   Jan 26, 1899
    Died- Mrs Mary Tittle, a former resident of this place in Quincy last
    Thursday. Remains shipped here Friday morning. Services by Elder Bonnifon
    at the M.E. church at 2 P.M. Buried Curless cmeetery.

Todd, John D.   "Probate"   Dec 28, 1882
    Probate notice of John D. Todd, deceased 1st Monday of Feb 1883
    Wm T. Todd, Adm.

Toebble, Mrs Elizabeth   "Quincy Death"   Mar 23, 1899
    Died- Mrs Elizabeth Toebble at age 77 yrs Tuesday A.M. Born Germany
    Leaves 2 sons and 3 daughters.

Tolbert, Mrs Emma   "Obituary"   Nov 30, 1899
    see Hardy, Joseph Patterson

Tolbert, Lewis   "Loraine"   May 20, 1880
    Lewis Tolbert, a young man of 22 yrs died last week of measles.

Tomblinson, Alice Jane   "Obituaru"   Mar 16, 1904
    see Thayer, Charles

Tomlinson, Alice Jane   "Obituary"   Oct 29, 1903
    Alice Jane Tomlinson was born Munice, Wayne Co. Ind. January 21, 1837
    and died October 22nd 1903 at her home at Macomb of heart disease. Came
    to Illinois with her parents on 1838. Joined Christian church at Columbus
    at an early age. Married at age 19 yrs to Chas. Thayer of Fowler, Ill.
    after which she joined the Free Will Baptist church at Palona and remained
    till death.   -Cont-

Tomlinson, Alice Jane- continued
    She had 4 brothers and 3 sisters of whom James B. of Salt Lake City, Rev
    Addisn Bishop of Tempa, Arizona and Mrs Elizabeth Stokes of Valley City,
    Iowa are still living. Was mother of 5 children, 4 daughters and 1 son.
    An infant daughter and Mrs Tenie Frost had preceded her to a better
    land. Leaves her aged husband, 3 children 15 grandchildren. Children living
    are Mrs Ettie Worman of Troy, Kansas and Miss Lillie A. of Macomb, and
    Henry E. of Choctaw, Miss. Services Monday A.M. at Macomb and buried in
    afternoon at Camp Point.

Tomlinson, Mrs Sarah   "Paloma"   Apr 12, 1894
    Died- last week at the residence of her daughter, Mrs Charles Thayer,
    Mrs Sarah Tomlinson (nee Berry) 83 yrs old. Services by Rev A.A.
    White in the F.W.B. church here. Buried in Camp Point cemetery.

Torns, Geo.   "Marcelline"   Aug 25, 1892
    Port Torns of Oklahoma is very low with consumption. His brother Geo.
    died a few weeks ago with same disease.

Torrence, Dr John   "Quincy Deaths"   Apr 20, 1899
    Died- Dr John Torrence Sunday eve. Born Pittsburg, Penn. Leaves 3
    daughters and 1 son.

Tout, Elizabeth F.   "Obituary"   Mar 8, 1883
    see Lemmon, Mrs W.D.

Tout, Elizabeth Francis   "Death"   Jan 18, 1905
    see Lemmon, William Daniel

Tout, Mrs John   "Local"   Oct 26, 1887
    Mrs Tout, wife of old uncle John Tout, of Marcelline died yesterday.
    Age 84 yrs.

Tout, John S.   "Obituary"   Jan 19, 1893
    Died- John S. Tout (uncle John) was born at Flemingsburg, Ky. October
    18, 1806. Married 1826 to Elizabeth Tatman. They had 2 sons and 3 daughters
    He died at his sons home in Ursa Monday night Jan 8th from a cancerous
    affection of the face at age 86 yrs 3 mo's 21 days. Buried at the
    Marcelline cemetery, his home for so many yrs on Thursday Jan 12th. He
    was an old settler of Adams Co. and member of the M.E. church, & Marcelline
    Lodge of Masons. He was a personal friend of General U.S. Grant.

Towley, John   Jan 3, 1884
    Uncle John Towley was buried December 24th 1883.

Townsend, Mrs R.S.   "Obituary"   May 3, 1883
    see Francis, Sarah

Traxler, Mike   "Local"   Aug 18, 1892
    Died- Mike Traxler. His dead body was recovered from Long Lake about ½
    mile northwest of the bay bridge in Quincy on Saturday. He was employed
    by Tobe Thomas at Phillip Thomas and Son's Stave factory on the bay
    island.

Traylor, Mrs Adeline   "Obituary"   Mar 21, 1889
    Died- Thursday March 14th at her home in Mendon of heart trouble at the
    age of 65 yrs, Mrs Adeline Traylor.

Traylor, Mrs Adeline   "Obituary"   Mar 21, 1889
    Died- Thursday March 14th at her home in Mendon of heart trouble at
    the age of 65 yrs, Mrs Adeline Traylor. Services the next day at the
    house by Rev Thomas, pastor of the Lutheran church. Buried in Marcelline
    cemetery. Born in Ohio and raised in Ind. near Indianapolis. Moved to
    Lee Co. Iowa where she married John Traylor. They had 7 children. 4 still
    living. 3 dead.

Treach, Miss Amy   "Loraine"   Jun 25, 1885
    Miss Amy Treach died June 20th of paralysis and was buried in Woodville
    cemetery.

Treatch, old mother   "Loraine"   Dec 30, 1897
    Died- old mother Treatch died and was buried at Woodland cemetery last
    Thursday at 11 A.M.

Treatch, Mr and Mrs Geo. W.   "Loraine'   Dec 21, 1893
    Died- a little daughter of Mr and Mrs Geo. W. Treatch Sunday A.M. of
    some spinal disease. Buried in Woodville cemetery Monday at 12.

Treatch, George   "Probate"   Sep 22, 1898
    Probate notice of George Treatch, deceased 1st Monday of Dec 1898
    Frederick Treatch, Adm with will annexed.

Trent, Mr   "Marcelline"   Oct 12, 1904
    Mr Trent, who was taken from here to St Mary's hospital in Quincy for
    treatment 2 weeks ago died and was brought back last week and buried in
    Keath cemetery.

Tressler, Dr   Oct 20, 1881
    Died last week in Carthage, a nephew of Dr Tressler's.

Tressler, Mrs   "Death"   Feb 23, 1882
    see Thompson, Margaret

Tressler, President   "Carthage"   Feb 26, 1880
    President Tressler died. The great college ship has lost her caption.
    Services by Dr Rhoades of St Louis.

Tressler, Rev. Prof. D.L.   "New Port News"   Mar 18, 1880
    Rev Prof D.L. Tressler died at his home in Carthage, Illinois on Friday
    A.M. last week. His sister, Mrs W.H. Minick, of this place arrived
    shortly before he died. He was the 4th son of John and Elizabeth Tressler of
    Tyrona twp, this co. Born Feb 15, 1839. Studied in the academy founded at
    Loysville by his father. At 18 he entered Penn college at Gettsburg
    and graduated with honors June 1860, the same yr he married Miss Ida J.
    daughter of B. McIntyre. In 1869 ha and family moved to Mendota, Ill
    He had 4 sisters besides Mrs M.and 4 brothers. Leaves wife and 2 sons and
    2 daughters.

Tressler, Prof David L.   "Died"   Feb 26, 1880
    Died- Prof David L. Tressler, President of Carthage college Friday A.M.
    of pneumonia. Age 44 yrs.

Tressler, Dr J.E.   "Death"   May 23, 1889
    see Richards, Mrs J.W. (Mrs Prof)

413

Trimble, Arthur H.   "Probate"   Apr 28, 1881
    Probate notice of Arthur H. Trimble, deceased--Wm Fletcher, Adm

Trimble, Sophronia   "Obituary"   Jul 20, 1899
    Died- Sophronia Trimble (nee Washburn). Born Harrison Co. Ky.
    Aug 28, 1824 Died July 12th at age 74 yrs 10 mo's 14 days. Married Arthur H. Trimble
    July 12, 1845. Had 3 children- 2 survive her also 2 brothers and 1 sister.
    Services Thursday at 2:30 P.M. at the family home 4½ miles northwest of
    Mendon by Rev E.K. Crews. Buried Keith cemetery. Member of Baptist church,
    being a charter member of the Franklin Baptist church.

Tringle, Mrs Mary   Quincy Deaths"   Feb 23, 1899
    Died- Mrs Mary Tringle at the home of her daughter, Mrs James McIntyre
    Wednesday Feb. 15th at age 68 yrs.

Tripp, Mr   "Lima"   Oct 26, 1887
    Mr ___Tripp, an old citizen of Lima twp was buried at the Fletcher grave
    yard last Sunday.

Tripp, Mrs Almira   "Lima"   Apr 5, 1894
    Died- at the home of her daughter, Mrs Albert Vinson of this place,
    Mrs Almira Tripp in her 86th yr. Born in Oxford Co. Maine. Came to Adams
    Co. in 1844. Mother of 9 children of whom only 2 are living. Her husband
    died 6 yrs ago. Services by Rev Hathaway. Buried in Fletcher graveyard.

Tripp, John C.   "Lima"   Nov 23, 1893
    Died- at his home at this place on November 13th, Mr John C. Tripp.
    62 yrs old. Mr Tripp had been an invalid many years. Father of 12 children.
    6 of whom are dead. He was a soldier for a little more than a yr.
    3 weeks before he died he was baptized and united with the M.E. church.
    Services by Rev Hathaway. Buried in the cemetery at this place.

Tripp, Thomas   "Local"   May 19, 1886
    Mr Thomas Tripp died on Monday A.M. of congestion of the brain after
    several weeks sickness in his 57th year. Lived Quincy.

Trogden, Mrs Mary   "Ellington"   Nov 23, 1887
    Mrs Mary Trogden, of Ursa, wife of Royl Trogden, was buried at the Stone
    church in Ursa Friday November 18th. Services by Rev Hitchens.

Tucker, Mrs Katie   "Local"   Apr 5, 1905
    W.L. Worley rec'd a telegram telling him of the death of his sister,
    Mrs Katie Tucker of Eolia, Mo. Brought here for burial. Services at the
    Christian church Tuesday 11 A.M.

Tucker, Mrs Kate   "Ursa"   Apr 5, 1905
    Charley Worley was in town this week to attend the funeral of his sister,
    Mrs Kate Tucker.

Tucker, Mrs Miranda Hayes   "Local"   Nov 23, 1887
    Died- at Mendon early Monday morning November 21st in her 75 th yr.,
    Mrs Miranda Hayes Tucker. Buried same day at the charge of the county.
    Funeral in charge of Supervisor Urech. Services by Rev S.D. Peet Buried
    in Mendon cemetery. Born near Plattsburgh, New York August 17th 1813 and
    Married James Tucker April 1, 1835. Had no relatives in this part of the
    country that she knew of.

Tumbleson, Lucy A.   "Death"   Mar 22, 1905
    see Baldwin, George Dutton

Turner, Mrs   "Personal"   Mar 25, 1880
    Mrs Turner, mother of Mrs U.H. Keath and Mrs J.M. Rumbaugh died at her
    home in Ellington on Wednesday of last week.

Turner, Alfred K.   "Loraine"   Oct 26, 1904
    Died- Alfred K. Turner Saturday A.M. at his home of consumption. Leaves
    wife, 1 daughter, 2 sons, 1 brother and 2 sisters. Funeral at the home
    at 2 P.M. Sunday October 23rd by Rev Baaranger. Buried Woodville cemetery.

Turner, Mr A.K.   "Death"   Feb 13, 1890
    see Bailey, Rabecca

Turner, Charles   "Obituary"   Sep 17, 1885
    see Dazey, Ishmeal (Stacey)

Turner, Miss Etta   "Death"   Feb 13, 1890
    see Bailey, Rebecca

Turner, Miss Ella   "Obituary"   Sep 24, 1885
    see Hunter, Mrs Hugh Jr.

Turner, Mr E.B. (Enoch)   "Local"   Nov 16, 1887
    News was rec'd at Ursa of the death of MrE.B. Turner, of Columbus, Kansas
    Enoch Turner was born and grew up in Ellington twp. Served 3 yrs in
    the late war and was a comrade of D.H. Darby and James Betts. Married
    1873 to Miss Maggie Wible of Mendon. Buried near Wesley Chapel Sunday
    afternoon.

Turner, Enoch   "Funeral"   Nov 30, 1887
    see Sewell, Mrs

Turner, Miss Etta   "Obituary"   Jan 20, 1898
    see Geibert, John

Turner, F.C.   "Obituary"   Nov 24, 1886
    see Bradbury, Mrs Ann

Turner, Mr F.C.   "Obituary"   Apr 6, 1893
    Died- Mr F.C. Turner Friday eve. Funeral on Sunday P.M. at the Wesley
    church ground. Short services by Rev A.B. Peck, pastor of the M.E.
    church Mendon. Born in Ellington twp May 17, 1839. Was 53 yrs 10 mo's
    14 days old. Leaves wife and 7 children, (2 girls and 5 boys)

Turner, Fred   "Local"   May 1, 1902
    Youngest child of Mr and Mrs Fred Turner living 4 miles west of Mendon
    died Tuesday A.M. Funeral at the home yesterday afternoon by Rev S.N.
    Wakefield. Buried at Wesley Chapel cemetery.

Turner, Fred C.   "Probate"   Apr 13, 1893
    Probate notice of Fred C. Turner, deceased   1st Monday of June 1893
    Mary Elizabeth Turner, Adm.

Turner, Mrs Isabella   "York Neck"   Aug 30, 1900
    Died- Mrs Isabella Turner Wednesday morning at the home of her son,
    Mr Wm Turner. Funeral at her home in Columbus Thursday. Widow of the late
    Wm E. Turner.

Turner, John T.   "Obituary"   Nov 24, 1886
    see Bradbury, Mrs Ann

Turner, Mary H.   "Obituary"   Apr 27, 1887
    Mary H. Turner born county Cavan, Ireland September 1, 1812 and married
    George Harris July 11, 1835. Mr Harris died May 4, 1837 and 2nd she
    married Joseph Turner September 1, 1850. He died March 10th 1876. Mother
    of 2 children, 1 by her 1st husband lived till it was 4 yrs old and
    1 by her 2nd husband died at the age of 14 mo's. Member of the M. church.

Turner, Mrs Mary   "Local"   Jul 28, 1892
    The late Mrs Mary Turner's property on the north side of the public
    square is to be offered for sale at auction in Quincy Friday Aug 5th.

Turner, Mrs Mary H.   "Adm Sale"   Jul 17, 1890
    Adm sale of Mary H. Turner, deceased August 12th 1890 Property and
    Household goods. James F Carrott, Adm.

Turner, Mrs Mary E.   "Obituary"   Nov 22, 1900
    see Fletcher, Miss Louise

Turner, Col S.B.   Jul 21, 1881
    Died- Col S.B. Turner of Canton, Mo. brother of Dr Turner of Marcelline
    on July 17th 1881

Turner, Stacey   "Obituary"   Sep 17, 1885
    see Ishmeal, Mrs

Tuttle, Mr E.B.   "Stillwell"   May 26, 1881
    Mr E.B. Tuttle died May 22nd. Leaving a wife and child. Buried Loraine.

Tuttle, George   "Local"   Aug 22, 1889
    Buried an infant child of George Tuttle's in Mendon cemetery Monday A.M.

Tuxford, James   "Camp Point"   Jan 18, 1883
    Mr James Tuxford, formerly of Mendon died suddenly Jan 14th. He was 76
    yrs old. Born Lansachire, England. Came to America when he was 18 yrs old.
    Services at M.E. church Mendon. Buried beside his first wife in Mendon.

Tuxford, Rebecca   "Death"   Jun 12, 1884
    see Hatton, Nicholas Parker

Tyler, Miss Orena   "Obituary"   May 10, 1900
    see Cook, Chauncey

Tyndall, Ms   "Local"   Jul 17, 1890
    An elderly lady named Tyndall died of cancer at Marcelline Sunday July 13th
    Buried 14th at Stone church burying ground.

Tyndall, Mrs Agnes   "Obituary"   Feb 10, 1898
    see Rawlings, Sarah Jane

Underwood, Virgil   "Lima"   Dec 18, 1884
    Virgil, son of William and Mary Underwood died November 22nd. age 1 yr
    and 6 mo's.

Unglaube, Ida E.   "Obituary"   Jul 10, 1879
    Died- Buried Saturday 4 P.M.in the old Baptist church cemetery, Ida E.
    Unglaube, age 1 yr 2 days. The youngest child of John and Johanna
    Unglaube. Services at the house and at the grave by Rev G.F. Behringer.

Upchurch, Mrs   "Loraine"   Nov 3, 1886
    Mrs Upchurch, of Big Neck died Wednesday night of typhoid fever.

Urech, Mr F.   Feb 15, 1883
    Death of Mr F. Urech of Quincy, father of proprietor of the Mendon
    Dispatch Feb 14th. He was 80 yrs old.

Urech, Frederick J.   "Obituary"   Aug 1, 1889
    Died- Mr Frederick J. Urech, elder and only brother of Mr J.R. Urech
    of the Dispatch died Saturday July 27th at his home near LaPlata,
    Macon Co. Mo. Buried next day in LaPlata cemetery with Masonic honors.
    Services at the M.E. church by Rev Moffatt, pastor. About 10 yrs ago
    he was struck with paralysis of the right side and had never recovered
    from it.
    Quincy Herald" by Capt Tom J. Heirs of Co. H. 151st Regt Ill. Vol. Inf.
    Born in Niederhallwyl, Canton Aargon, Switzerland August 3, 1840. Came to
    America with his parents in 1854 and lived Quincy until 1868 when he
    moved to Payson and in 1871 to LaPlata, Mo. Married Quincy to Miss Lizzie
    daughter of Jacob Ruff.Leaves wife and 1 son.

Urton, Mrs   "Death"   Jun 11, 1885
    Mr Benson was called to Elvaston by the illness of his daughter,
    Mrs Smith. He was accompanied by his son, Tom. Mrs Smith died Monday eve.
                                                            Jun 18, 1885
    CORRECTION__ The name was Mrs Urton, NOT Smith.

Van Blair, Mrs   Feb 13, 1890
    Mrs Van Blair died Feb 7th at an advanced age. Buried Feb 9th at the
    Stone burying ground near Ursa.

Van Blair, Cornelius   "Obituary"   Nov 24, 1898
    Died- Mr Cornelius Van Blair. Born Ohio state August 6, 1835 and died
    at his home near Loraine, Adams Co. Ill. November 13th at the age of
    63 yrs 3 mo's 7 days. Leaves wife and 7 children. (4 sons 3 daughters)
    all live in Adams co. Funeral at Christian church, Loraine on November
    15th by Rev R. Crank. Buried Stone burying ground nearhis former home.

Van Blair, Mr Cornelius   "Local"   Nov 17, 1898
    Died- Mr Cornelius Van Blair, formerly of this twp on Sunday A.M.
    of consumption at his home northwest of Loraine. Age 66 yrs. Sick 2 yrs.
    Funeral at Christian church, Loraine the following A.M. Buried in
    Stone burying ground near his former home.

Van Blair, Cornelius   "Probate"   Dec 22, 1898
    Probate notice of Cornelius Van Blair 1st Monday of March 1899
    John Pratt, Adm with will annexed.

Van Blair, Cornelius   "Local"   Dec 1, 1898
    The will of Cornelius Van Blair leaves his widow a life interest in ½
    of his estate and at her death th be equally divided among his 7 children.

Van Blair, Floyd   "Local"   Dec 20, 1894
    Died- Wednesday night or Thursday morning of last week of pneumonia,
    Floyd, the infant son of Mr and Mrs Wm Van Blair. Age 6 mo's 14 days.
    Buried in Stone cemetery on Friday. Services by Rev Hartrick.

Van Blair, Joe   "Ursa"   Apr 21, 1881
    A child of Joe Van Blair's of Quincy was buried in Stones cemetery
    last Friday.

Van Blair, Joseph   "Obituary"   May 8, 1902
    Joseph Van Blair was born in Butler Co. Ohio Feb 5th 1847 and died at
    his home in this village Thursday eve May 1st. Came to Mendon when 8 yrs old
    and lived here since except for a few yrs spent in Quincy a few weeks ago
    he went to Kewanee and worked in a factory and was injured there and
    returned home. Married Sarah Roberts of Mendon, Ill October 15, 1868.
    They had 12 children (7 girls and 5 boys) 8 of whom survive him along
    with his wife. (3 boys and 5 girls) All with him except for Charlie and
    Harry who came as soon as possible. His only surviving brother, Cyrus,
    of Hamilton was also with him. Services at M.E. church by Rev S.N. Wakefield
    Saturday P.M. Buried in Stone burying ground southwest of Mendon.

Van Blair, Joseph   "Local"   Oct 20, 1886
    Died- the infant child Friday morning of Joseph Van Blair. Buried in
    Stone's cemetery next day. Services by Rev Doke of the M.E. church
    at the house.

Van Blair, W.F.   "Local"   Feb 6, 1902
    Mr W.F. Van Blair, brother of our townsman Joseph Van Blair died
    suddenly at his home in Quincy Friday eve of heart disease. Was 74 yrs old.
    Leaves wife and 1 son and 3 daughters.

Van Blair, Wm   "Ursa"   Feb 6, 1902
    Mr Wm Van Blair for many yrs a resident of Ursa Twp, died suddenly in
    Quincy Friday. Buried at Stone cemetery.

Vance, Mrs Fanny   "Obituary"   Jul 6, 1899
    see Leighty, John

Vance, Wm   "Lima"   Jun 21, 1883
    Death of a daughter (infant) of Wm Vance. Services by Rev Hamilton.

Vancil, Mr Wm   "Gleamings"   Sep 21, 1893
    Mr Wm Vancil, an old citizen of Liberty shot himself in the temple
    Saturday. Was 73 yrs old. Leaves a widow and 4 children. Oldest of whom
    is John W. Vancil, sheriff of this county.

Vandenboom, Mrs Mary   "Death in Adams Co."   Mar 2, 1899
    Died- Mrs Mary Vandenboom, age 86 yrs Friday A.M. Lived Quincy 18
    yrs. Leaves 2 sons and 5 daughters.

Vandenburg, Mrs   "Obituary"   Jul 4, 1889
    see Pepple, Catherine Sophia

Vandersall, Elizabeth   "Local"   Mar 24, 1886
    News from Parson, Missouri by Mrs Lewis Shupe of the death of her mother
    at that place on Saturday the 20th at the age of 77 yrs. She was buried the
    next day. Elizabeth Vandersall was married to Rev John Hamilton in August
    1828 and mother of 6 children. (3 boys and 3 girls) All of whom are
    still living.

Van Dien, Mrs   "Death"   Oct 6, 1886
    see Hendrickson, Mr Garrett

Van Dien, Mrs   "Obituary"   Feb 16, 1888
    see Ferree, John E.

Van Dien, Mrs   "Local"   Dec 24, 1891
    Died- Mrs Van Dien died at 1 A.M. She had been sick in her millinery
    rooms and not able to be moved for 2 weeks. Her sister, Mrs Robbins
    of Rock Creek and her oldest sister, Mrs Robbins of Missouri were
    with her. Also her brother, Mr Garrett Hendrickson.

Vandien, Elizabeth   "Probate"   Jan 7, 1892
    Probate notice of Elizabeth Vandien   1st Monday of March 1892
    Garrett Hendrickson, Adm.

Vandien, Miss Elizabeth "Obituary"   Dec 31, 1891
    see Hendrickson, Mrs Elizabeth

419

Van Dien, Henry   "Obituary"   Dec 31, 1891
    see Hendrickson, Elizabeth

Vandiver, Edward   "Lima"   Nov 11, 1885
    Two gentlemen named Vandiver of Knox Co. Mo. identified the effects
    of the man found west of the lake last winter as belonging to their
    brother, Edward Vandiver.

Van Dyke, Mrs P.C.   "Died"   Jan 4, 1905
    Died- Mrs P.C. Van Dyke at her home 4 miles northwest of Mendon of cancer
    of the stomach and liver December 29th 1904 at 12 o'clock. Was member of
    U.B. church. Miss Rosa Ann Stockton was born November 13th 1846. Her parents
    died when she was quite young. Her early life was spent in Indiana.
    Married P.C. Van Dyke September 5, 1872. Leaves husband and an adopted
    daughter, Mrs Roxie Hess. Services at Franklin church December 31st by
    Rev A.M. Reitzel, pastor of the Lutheran church.

Van Dyke, Rosa   Jan 11, 1905
    In Love and Remembrance of Rosa Van Dyke who died December 29th, 1904
    This is followed by a poem and signed - by Friends, Mrs Moss

Van Dyke, Wm   "Obituary"   Dec 15, 1892
    Died- Wm Van Dyke. Born in Westmoreland Co. Penn December 29, 1812 and
    died December 10, 1892 at the age of 79 yrs 11 mo's 10 days. Married
    Hester Cort January 20th 1842. Had 7 children. 3 sons and 2 daughters
    survive their parents. The wife and 2 daughters died a number of yrs ago.
    He moved with his family to Adams Co. in 1844 and settled 4 miles north-
    west of Mendon and lived there until a few yrs ago when he went to live
    with a daughter and son in Mendon. Member of Reformed Lutheran church and
    then united with the Lutheran church. Funeral at his residence by Rev M.L.
    Schmucker. Buried in Franklin cemetery beside his wife.
    SAME PAPER + Thanks for the help during their fathers illness, signed
    B.A. Van Dyke and Vesta Van Dyke.

Van Horn, Jesse May   "Loraine"   Jan 29, 1880
    Died- Friday Jesse May, daughter of George L. Van Horn, age 2 weeks.

Vantuil, John   "Death in Quincy"   Mar 16, 1899
    Died- John Vantuil at Blessing hospital Monday afternoon. Born Moline,
    Illinois. Age 29 yrs. Leaves a wife and 3 children.

Van Valer, Mrs George   "Obituary"   Apr 24, 1902
    see Fletcher, Chas. Wolvertine

Varnier, D.C.   "Local"   Feb 2, 1888
    Mr and Mrs D.C. Varnier's little daughter died Tuesday night of
    scarlet fever.

Varnier, Mr and Mrs David   "Died"   Aug 12, 1880
    Died- on August 8th of cholera infantum, the infant daughter of Mr and
    Mrs David Varnier, near Marcelline.

Varnier, M.C.   "Obituary"   Feb 14, 1889
    see Dunlap, David

420

Varnier, Mrs M.C.   "Obituary"   Mar 2, 1899
    see Taylor, Mrs Barbara

Varnier, Miss Vina   "Ursa"   Apr 18, 1895
    Funeral last Sunday of Miss Vina Varnier by Rev A.C. Ament at the house.
    Then the Daughters of Rebecca took charge. Miss Varnier was a member of the
    D.A.R. for 25 yrs.

Varnier, Miss Vinnie   "Quincy Herald"   Apr 18, 1895
    Died- Miss Vinnie Varnier, daughter of M.C. Varnier of Ursa at 7:28 P.M.
    April 12th at the home of Wm Denson at 214 Chestnut St. 24 yrs old.

Vaugh, Miss Lena   "Death"   Feb 26, 1903
    see Meyer, Miss Carrie

Venghaus, Mrs   "Loraine"   Sep 21, 1893
    Died- a little child of Mrs Venghaus Thursday morning. Buried in
    Quincy Friday.

Verner, L.C.   "Death"   Jan 15, 1885
    see Ellis, George

Vickers, Howard   "Payson"   Feb 19, 1880
    Died- on Feb. 10th a child of Mr Howard Vickers, north of here.

Vickers, Mrs Jane   Aug 14, 1890
    Died- Mrs Jane Vickers August 5th at the age of 63 yrs 4 mo's 17 days.
    Died nea Atlantic, Iowa.

Vickers, Thomas   "Local"   Oct 27, 1886
    Died- Wednesday October 20th at his home in Honey Creek twp . Age 62 yrs
    Mr Thomas Vickers born in Belmont Co. Ohio Feb 3,1824. Married May 7th
    1855 to Miss Jane Ross, by whom he had 1 son and 1 daughter. Moved to
    Illinois in 1866. Buried at Burton Friday October 22nd.

Vincent, Mr Wm   "Ellington"   Feb 11, 1892
    Mr Wm Vincent was buried at Wesley Chapel cemetery today. 70 yrs old.

Vining, Mr   "Payson"   Aug 22, 1882
    Mr Vining of Plainville died August 7th.

Vinson, E.J.   "Lima"   Jan 12, 1882
    Died- the infant child of E.J. Vinson's. This is the tenth one they have
    laid away.

Vinson, Mr and Mrs   "Lima"   July 31, 1879
    Mr and Mrs Vinson lost their babe this eve from cholera infantum,
    making the 9th child they have had died in the past few yrs.

Vinson, Mrs Alfred   "Obituary"   Apr 5, 1894
    see Tripp, Mrs Almira

Volrath, Mr   "Death"   Mar 6, 1879
    see Kirkman, Mrs

Vorndam, Katie   "Local"   Oct 26, 1887
    Katie Vorndam, 15 yr old daughter of Mr Casper Vorndam living at 6th
    and Adams St Quincy had her clothes catch on fire and she was severly
    burned. Died the next morning.

Vosburg, Mrs A.W.   "Obituary"   Oct 17, 1901
    see Sellwood, J.R.N.

Vowels, Mrs Dr   "Death"   Nov 1, 1894
    see Borgholthaus, Mrs

Vowels, Mrs Dr   "Death"   Dec 1, 1886
    see Borgholthaus, George W.

Vradenburg, Mr Erastus   "Lima"   Apr 15, 1880
    Mr Erastus Vradenburg's little boy, age 6 yrs, died on Friday eve.
    March 9th.

Vradenburg, Nora   "Tioga"   Mar 2, 1899
    Died- Nora Vradenburg, daughter of Mr and Mrs John Vradenburg Tuesday
    night Feb. 21st about 15 yrs old. Funeral Thursday.

Vredenburg, Mr Stratton   "Tioga"   Jul 14, 1886
    Died- July 7th at the home of John Snyder, Mr Stratton Vredenburg in
    his 82nd yr. Mr V. was one of Adams Co. oldest farmers, He came to Lima
    twp about 1830 and lived on his home farm over 50 yrs. His wife died
    about 5 yrs ago. Leaves several sons and daughters.

Wade, Amanda   Sep 6, 1883
    Died- Mrs Amanda Wade, wife of S.A. Wade and mother of 2 small children.
    Age 24 yrs. Born October 13th 1858 and died at the residence of her
    father, Darby Wilson on August 26th.

Wade, Berthie Gertrude   "Loraine"   May 29, 1879
    Died- Berthie Gertrude, daughter of Austin Wade on May 14th of
    pneumonia. Age 1 yr and 15 days.

Wade, Mrs Fannie   "Obituary"   Apr 4, 1895
    see Selby, Mrs Louisa

Wade, Mrs Fanny   "Obituary"   Aug 13, 1891
    see Selby, James

Wade, James A.   "Obituary"   Mar 14, 1889
    Died- at his home in Loraine of consumption on Monday eve March 11th,
    Mr James A. Wade in his 54th yr. He was married November 1860 and they
    had 5 children (1 girl and 4 boys) 2 of the boys and the wife and an
    aged mother survive him. He was member of the German Baptist church 8 yrs.
    Funeral held in the church at Loraine Wednesday A.M. by Rev R.P. Droke
    of Mendon. Buried in Keith cemetery near Marcelline.

Wade, Keziah   "Local"   Dec 27, 1888
    Death of Mrs Keziah Wade Monday A.M. at her home in Loraine.

Wade, Matthew Allen   "local"   Oct 5, 1905
    Matthew Allen Wade died at his home in Lima Saturday. Age 68 yrs 4 mo's
    28 days. Born in Lima and spent his life in or near there. Leaves a
    wife and 3 sons.

Wade, Nancy Jane   "Obituary"   Apr 27, 1904
    see Adair, Nancy Jane

Wade, W.H.   "Late Local"   Jun 29, 1899
    Died- W.H. Wade of Lima died yesterday A.M. Funeral to be Friday at
    10 A.M. in charge of Lima Lodge #135 A.F.& A.M.

Wade, Wm M   "Obituary"   Apr 27, 1904
    see Adair, Nancy Jane

Wade, Wm M. (Willie)   "Loraine"   Aug 14, 1890
    August 7th Wm M. Wade died of consumption at his home in Loraine.
    Age 26 yrs 4 days. Services by Elder H.W. Strickler at the Dunkard
    church August 9th. Buried Keath cemetery near Marcelline. Leaves 1
    brother. Father died about 18 months ago.

Waggaman, Catherine   "Obituary"   May 22, 1890
    see Shriver, Louis

Wagner, J.C.   "Payson"   Sep 11, 1879
    Died recently, a child of J.C. Wagner.

Wagy, Henry   "Payson"   Jun 12, 1879
     Died- Uncle Henry Wagy on June 5th at his home in Plainville,
     4 miles east of Payson. Age 79 yrs. Member of the M.E. church. Services
     by Rev H.C. Adams of Payson.

Wagy, Phillip   "Payson"   Mar 18, 1880
     Mr Phillip Wagy, living east of Payson buried his last child one day
     last week.

Wait, Mrs Lorett (Allen)   "Obituary"   May 16, 1889
     Died- Mrs Lorett Wait, wife of Allen Wait at her home in Yuba City,
     Calif. April 29th at 12:25 P.M. Born in New York state October 30th
     1818 and married in Ohio May 22nd 1838 and shortly after she and husband
     moved to Illinois. They had 8 children, 2 boys and 6 girls. 2 died.
     Services from the M.E. church South. Surviving children live in Illinois,
Missouri and California. Went to Yuba City in 1885. Buried in Yuba City cemetery

Wait, Eddie   "Lima"   May 4, 1893
     Died- Eddie Wait at 5 A.M. Friday.

Wait,John and Phebe   "Obituary"   Dec 14, 1887
     see Barnett, Mrs Minnie Bell Wait

Wait, Minnie Bell   "Obituary"   Dec 14, 1887
     see Barnett, Minnie Bell Wait

Wait, Orlin and Pearl   "Lima"   May 4, 1882
     Died- May 1st an infant child of Orlin and Pearl Wait.

Wait, Stephen   "Lima"   Mar 16, 1893
     One of Stephen Wait's children died March 2nd. The others are getting
     along nicely.

Wakefield, Rebecca   "Obituary"   Mar 1, 1901
     see Mitchell, David

Wakefield, Mrs S.N.   "Local"   Oct 31, 1901
     Mrs S.N. Wakefield was called to Cowden, Ill. by the illness of her
     father, but before she could get there he died.

Walbring, Frederick W.   "Probate"   Mar 30, 1904
     Probate notice of Frederick W. Walbring, deceased 1st Mon. of June 1904
     D.L. Dickerman, Adm.

Walbring, Wm   "Death"   Feb 1, 1905
     see Klusman, Walter

Walbring, Wm   "Local"   Mar 23, 1904
     Died- Wm Walbring of pneumonia Monday night. Age 55 yrs. Services at
     the house Thursday at 9 A.M. and taken to the Ursa church for services
     Buried Quincy cemetery.

Walker, Grandmother   "Payson"   Mar 5, 1885
     Buried Feb. 26th Grandmother Walker who has been blind and helpless
     for a number of yrs. Age 87 yrs.

Walker, Mrs   "Death"   Dec 21, 1893
   see Garner, Wm

Walker, Mrs Abigail   "Died"   Jul 20, 1882
   Died- July 16th Mrs Abigail Walker. 73 yrs old. Mother of Mrs B.F.
   Slack and had lived with her daughter many yrs.

Walker, Mrs Ed   "Ursa"   Feb 10, 1898
   Mrs Ed Walker died yesterday at 3 P.M. Funeral this P.M.

Walker, Mr Edwin   "Ursa"   Nov 13, 1884
   Mr Edwin Walker, a former resident of the twp, now living in St Louis
   arrived to attend the funeral of his father who had been residing in
   Quincy.

Walker, Miss Elizabeth   "Obituary"   Feb 3, 1904
   see Slack, Benjamin Franklin

Walker, Mrs Emma   "Obituaru"   Jul 7, 1898
   Died- June 27th, Mrs Emma Walker (Ward) at the home of her brother,
   P.C. Ward, in Mendon, Missouri. Age 50 yrs. Remains were brought to
   the home of Wm Reece near Loraine for services by Bro. E.L. Grosh at
   2 P.M. July 29th. Buried Reece cemetery beside her father. Leaves a
   husband, 2 brothers and 3 sisters. All present except 1 brother F.W. Ward
   of Partridge, Kansas. Member of Christian church 25 yrs.

Walker, Mrs G.H.   "Obituary"   Sep 6, 1888
   Died- Friday August 31st at 10 A.M. at her home in Quincy. Her only
   daughter and child Claudius was at her bedside. Funeral Sunday buried
   in Denson cemetery near where she spent the days of her childhood. She
   was the daughter of Mr Wm Leachman, deceased and was born ½ mile north
   of this village April 24, 1837. Married G.H. Walker in the latter part
   of 1857 and started housekeeping in Marcelline where hse lived until
   about 4 yrs ago when they moved to Quincy. Member of Christian church.
   Leaves husband and 1 daughter. Article dated Ursa Sept 4th.

Walker, Mr George   Mar 5, 1885
   Mr George Walker of Joliet was through here last week on the way to
   Payson to attend the funeral of his aged mother.

Walker, Mr Harmon   Feb 2, 1882
   Died- Mr Harmon Walker father of Mrs B.F. Slack at the residence of
   a son in Kinderhook. Mrs Slack and Lillie will attend.

Walker, Harmon   Feb 9, 1882
   Died, Mr Harmon Walker week before last at the age of 82 yrs at
   Kinderhook his sons residence.

Walker, Henry Clark   "Obituary"   Jun 25, 1903
   Henry Clark Walker born Westmoreland Co. Penn November 11, 1842, died in
   Galesburg, Ill. June 21, 1903. 60 yrs 7 mo's 10 days old. His parents
   came to Mendon 1854 where he lived till 18 mo's ago when he moved to
   Galesburg. Married 1871 to Mrs Henrietta Roley. Had 3 children, Charles H.
   George P. and Minnie May. A mother, 4 sisters and a stepson (Joseph A.
   Roley), a wife and 2 sons survive him. Had been an invalid past 2 yrs.
   Buried Mendon cemetery. Services by Rev S.R. Reno. Belonged to Masons and
   Woodman lodge. Buried in charge of Mendon lodge # 449 A.F.& A.M.

Walker, Mrs J.F.   "Obituary"   Jan 24, 1901
    see Roy, Mrs Joseph A.

Walker, J.   "Death"   Nov 20, 1890
    see Birch, Wm

Walker, John   "Ursa"   Jul 20, 1887
    Death of 6 month old infant of Mr and Mrs John Walker on last Thursday.

Walker, John C.   "Obituary"   Jan 24, 1895
    Died- John C. Walker in Mendon January 14th. Bron Greensburg, Westmoreland
    Co. Penn May 22nd 1812. Married Miss Elizabeth Musgrave September 15, 1832
    They were married 63 yrs. Had 11 children, 5 of whom and wife survive him.
    Came to Illinois 1852 and settled Mendon. Member of M.E. church of Mendon
    40 yrs. Had rheumatism and partial paralysis for the last few yrs.
    Services at the M.E. church January 16th by Pastor Rev R.A. Hartick.
    Buried Mendon cemetery.

Walker, Mr John C.   "Local"   Jan 17, 1895
    Died- Mr John C. Walker Tuesday A.M. at the age of 83 yrs. Funeral
    yesterday P.M. Buried in Village cemetery after services at the M.E.
    church. Among those from a distant attending were, Mrs Andrews (his
    daughter) from Kansas and Mr and Mrs B.F. Duffy of Albia, Iowa

Walker, John C. (Judge)   "Quincy Herald"   Mar 14, 1895
    The will of Judge John C. Walker of Mendon was admitted to probate
    today. He died January 15th and the will date is November 5, 1891. Most
    of the estate left to the widow and to be devided among the children on
    her death, except some he left for his burial expenses and a monument
    at the cemetery in Mendon.

Walker, John C.   "Probate"   Jul 4, 1895
    Probate notice of John C. Walker, deceased   1st Monday of Sept 1895
    Harry Walker, Ex.

Walker, Mrs Lizzie   "Card of Thanks"   May 16, 1901
    Thanking for the kindness during the illness and at the death of her
    mother. Signed, Mrs Lizzie Walker.

Walker, Mary M.   "Obituary"   Nov 23, 1887
    see Kuhn, Isaac

Wall, Mrs J.W.   "Obituary"   Feb 3, 1904
    see Slack, Benjamin Franklin

Wall, Mrs Joseph W.   "Death"   Nov 19, 1903
    Died- Mrs Joseph W. Wall at 5 P.M. Sunday at the family home 1235 Maine
    St. Always frail of body and lately in poor health, she fell an easy
    victim to pleura pneumonia about 4 wks ago. Lived most of her life in
    Adams Co.born Ursa May 11, 1868. Was 36 yrs old, nee May Slack, daughter
    of Mr and Mrs Benjamin F. Slack of 220 N. 12th St. Quincy. Her parents
    moved to Mendon shortly after her birth where she lived until her marriage
    to Mr W. Nov. 22, 1893. Leaves husband, 2 daughters, Mildred and Marian
    ages 8 yrs and 5 yrs. resp., parents and 2 siters, Mrs George W. Judd and
    Mrs Fred G. Meise. Funeral Tues. P.M. at family home by Pastor Smith of the
    Cong'l church. Buried Woodland cemetery. Mr W. is sec'y of the Gardner
    Governor Co. "Quincy Herald"

Wallace, A.R.   "Local"   Feb 17, 1904
    Died- A.R. Wallace of Camp Point at his home last Wednesday A.M. Born
    Point Lick, Ky December 27, 1823 and at the age of 12 yrs with his
    mother, with several teams of oxen came to this Co. settling on the
    farm which was his home at the time of his death.

Wallace, Mr J.S.   "Death"   Dec 28, 1893
    see Heaton, Mrs

Wallace, Mrs J.S.   "Death"   Sep 10, 1891
    see Whitford, Albert

Wallace, Jason S.   "Camp Point"   Feb 19, 1880
    Jason S. Wallace, living near Keokuk Junction died last week from
    pneumonia.

Wallace, Margaret   "Obituary"   Jan 29, 1891
    see Nichols, James

Wallace, Mrs Mary J.   "Lima"   Oct 10, 1895
    Died- at her home here on Saturday October 5th, Mrs Mary J. Wallace.
    46 yrs old. Lived here 30 yrs. 25 yrs a member of Christian church and
    Eastern Star. Leaves husband, 3 sons and 2 daughters.

Wallace, Mrs Rd   "Death"   Dec 28, 1893
    see Heaton, Mrs

Wallace, Will   "Lima"   Jan 31, 1884
    Will Wallace lost his youngest child January 25th. Buried Saturday.

Wallbring, Frederick W.   "Adm Sale"   Oct 5, 1904
    Adm's sale of real estate by D.L. Dickerman, Adm of the estate of
    Frederick W. Wallbring, deceased at the September term of court.
    Property for sale is listed in article, but not copied here.
    David P. Strickler, attorney for Adm.

Wallbring, Mrs Lula A.(F.A.) "Local"   Oct 12, 1904
    Mrs Lula A. Wallbring, widow of the late F.A. Wallbring bought the house
    and lot sold at Adm's sale in Quincy Saturday for 725.00

Wallenbrock, John Henry   "Death in Adams Co."   Mar 30, 1899
    Died- John Henry Wallenbrock Saturday. Born Germany May 5, 1830
    Leaves a wife and 3 daughters and 3 sons.

Wallin, Jim   Apr 30, 1891
    Jim Wallin died Sunday morning April 26th at Blessing hospital in his
    51st yr. He was raised around Good Hope an McDonough Co.

Walter, William H.   "Death"   Mar 22, 1905
    see Joslin, Mrs Alice

Walter, Miss Alice   "Death"   Mar 22, 1905
    see Joslin, Mrs Alice

Walters, Mrs Daniel   "Local"   Sep 1, 1892
    Died- Mrs Daniel Walters from heart disease at the home of her son in law
    Rueben Kellogg in Quincy Tuesday evening. Brought here for burial.

Walters, E.   "Quincy"   Jan 10, 1884
    W. Walters, a miner in Quincy Coal Co's shaft at Colchester committed
    suicide January 3rd. Leaves a wife.

Walters, William   "Obituary"   Apr 17, 1902
    see Nedrow, Eli

Ward, Emma   "Obituary"   Jul 7, 1898
    see Walker, Mrs Emma

Ward, F.W.   "Obituary"   Jul 7, 1898
    see Walker, Mrs Emma

Ward, Mrs Fred   Dec 14, 1877
    Drowned- 4 yr old child of Mrs Fred Ward was found drown in Bear Creek.
    They lived a few miles northwest of Mendon.

Ward, Miss Lottie   "Death"   Sep 11, 1884
    see Kunkel, Mrs

Ward, Mrs Mary Ann   "Death"   May 24, 1883
    see McGibbons, John

Ward, Mary E.   "Obituary"   May 2, 1889
    see Rogers, Clark E.

Ward, Michael   Mar 6, 1890
    Michael Ward died Quincy a few days ago. Was buried Bloomfield March 4th
    He was 84 yrs old and was an old settler of Adams Co.

Ward, Michael   "Local"   Jun 7, 1905
    The remains of Michael Ward who was killed in a fight Sunday May 28th
    near Goldfield Nevada arrived here Tuesday A.M. and buried Bloomfield
    cemetery today. He was a brother of Thomas, Frank, James and John Ward.
    Frank of Southwest Missouri came over for the funeral.

Ward, Mrs Michael   "Local"   Feb 15, 1894
    Died- Mrs Ward, widow of the late Michael Ward at her home in Honey
    Creek on Saturday night and buried in Catholic cemetery at Bloomfiled
    Tuesday.

Ward, P.C.   "Obituary"   Jul 7, 1898
    see Walker, Mrs Emma

Ward, W.J.   "Obituary"   Jan 1, 1880
    Died- at the home of Wm Reece southeast of Loraine Tuesday December 23rd
    at 5 A.M., W.J. Ward age 65 yrs. Born in Lichfield Co. Conn Came to
    Illinois as a young man and married Miss Paisience M. Rogers near Chili,
    Hancock Co. in 1837. Worked as a carpenter and joiner at Carthage until
    1845 when he moved back east to Scipio, Cayugo Co. N.Y. intil 1851 when
    he came back to Adams Co.. Wife died January 18, 1852 at the age of 33 yrs.
    They had 6 children (4 girls and 2 boys) who survives them. Buried in
    Curless cemetery December 24th 1879.

Ward, Wm J.   "Probate"   Sep 2, 1880
    Probate notice of William J. Ward, deceased 3rd Monday of Nov. 1880
    Joseph S. Reece, Adm.

Ware, Thomas   "Lima"   Feb 24, 1898
    a 2 yr old child of Thomas Ware was buried in Tioga cemetery yesterday.

Warfield, J.S.   "Ursa"   Sep 5, 1901
    Died- J.S. Warfield, died Saturday about 4 P.M. and was buried at 11 A.M.
    Monday at the Stone church. He belonged to the Odd Fellows and the Court
    of Honor.

Warfield, John   "Marcelline"   Sep 5, 1901
    A large crowd attended the funeral of Mr John Warfield, of Ursa Monday.

Warren, Ansel   Feb 7, 1884
    Ansel Warren, an old settler of this Co. died Saturday at the age of
    84 yrs. He was connected with the Quincy paper. Was the elder brother
    of the late Calvin A. Warren of Quincy. Services in the M.E. church.
    Leaves 2 daughters, Mrs Brayman of Chicago and Mrs Henry L. Warren
    of Santa Fe, N.M.

Warren, Mrs Calvin   "Mendon"   Feb 9, 1882
    Mrs Warren, widow of the late Calvin A. Warren died Sunday Feb. 5th and was
    buried Tuesdat.

Washburn, Mr   "Ursa"   Jan 8, 1903
    Funeral of Mr Washburn was at the M.P. church at 11 A.M. Tuesday.

Washburn, Mrs Harrison   "Ursa"   Aug 23, 1905
    Funeral of Mrs Harrison Washburn was at 2 P.M. Sunday at the M.P.
    church by Rev W.O. Livingston. Buried in New Providence burying ground
    north of town.

Washburn, Sophronia   "Obituary"   Jul 20, 1899
    see Trimble, Sophronia

Washburne, Miss Francis "Obituary"   Oct 5, 1899
    see Lee, Mrs Francis

Wartick, Catherine   "Obituary"   Dec 25, 1890
    see Hardy, Mrs Catherine

Wartick, Mr Simon   "York Neck"   Dec 9, 1897
    Died- on Monday at 1:10 Mr Simon Wartick after a protracted illness of
    over a yr. Deceased was a man loved by all who knew him, of a good moral
    character and a good citizen. He will be missed not only by his family
    and wife, but by all who knew him. Funeral at the house by Rev Henry
    Pittman of Loraine after which the remains were laid to rest in the
    Coatsburg cemetery.

Wasson, Mrs Nora   "Obituary"   Feb 27, 1890
    see Mann, Isabella

Waters, Thomas   "Local"   Jan 15, 1885
    Thomas Waters committed suicide by drowning himself in the Quincy Bay
    Saturday night.

Watson, Geo. W.   "Local"   Jul 6, 1899
    Died- Geo. W. Watson, shoe merchant of Quincy at Blessings hospital
    Friday eve from blood poisoning. Born Clayton, Ill January 1844. Came
    to Quincy when 14 mo's old with parents, Mr and Mrs George D. Watson
    and 2 sisters, Mrs A.W. Blakesly of Quincy and Mrs A.B. Miller of Denver,
    Colo.

Watson, Mrs Howard   "Obituary"   Jan 27, 1886
    see Norman, Mrs

Watson, Thomas   "Fowler"   Sep 14, 1882
    Thomas Watson, a former resident of this place was buried in the
    Home cemetery. During the last 7 yrs he lived at St Augustine. He was
    80 yrs old.

Watson, W.G.   "Local"   Nov 9, 1887
    W.G. Watson, a student in Gem City college was drowned in bay last week
    when his boat upset. Remains taken to Pike Co. for burial.

Wear, Tom   "Tioga"   Aug 10, 1899
    Died- a child of Tom Wear, age about 3 yrs was buried in our village
    cemetery Monday.

Wear, Charley   "Tioga"   Feb 24, 1898
    Died- Charley Wear, the little son of Mr and Mrs Thomas Wear on
    Friday Feb 18th of pneumonia. age about 2 yrs. Buried from the M.E.
    church Sunday A.M. Services by Rev C. Hess.

Weaver, A.J.   Jun 4, 1885
    Mr A.J. Weaver in list of those buried in Mendon cemetery and is on
    the roll of soldiers.

Weaver, Mrs Chas   "Local"   Sep 4, 1902
    Mrs Chas Weaver of Kewanee, daughter of Mr and Mrs W.H. Doyle was
    called here by the death of her brother in law, Mr N.D. Hadley.

Weaver, J.B.   "Lima"   Nov 13, 1879
    J.B. Weaver, ex supervisor died this morning at 5:30. Will be buried in
    the Leachman cemetery by the Masonic rites at 10 tomorrow.

Weaver, John   Jun 5, 1902
    John Weaver in list of soldiers from the civil war buried Mendon cemetery.

Webb, Mrs   Nov 14, 1889
    Mrs Webb of Franklin district died at the age of 85 yrs on the 13th of
    November 1889. Son in law and daughter are Mr and Mrs Andrew McNay.

Webb, Anna Belle   "Paloma"   Nov 8, 1894
    Died- Anna Belle, youngest child of Wm and Belle Webb. Born July 19,
    1893 and died November 1, 1894. Sick 1 week with congestion of the brain.

Webb, Mary   "Obituary"   Dec 1, 1898
    see McNay, Mrs Andrew

Webb, Mary A.   "Obituary"   Feb 5, 1903
    see McNay, Andrew

Webb, Miss Susan   "Death"   Mar 15, 1905
    see Shepherd, Mrs Susan

Webber, Mrs   "Obituary"   Apr 27, 1887
    see Weed, Deacon L.A.

Webber, Frederick   Jul 24, 1890
    Frederick Webber, age 60 yrs died Ursa on July 18th. Buried in Quincy.
    He had 2 sons and 2 daughters.

Weber, Ernest   "Indian Grave"   Oct 10, 1895
    Died- Ernest, the little boy of Mr and Mrs Charles Weber while they
    were at Palmyra, Mo. attending the Marion Co. fair. (sick 6 hrs)

Webster, Amelia R.   "Obituary"   Apr 16, 1891
    see Bray, David C.

Webster, J.K.   "News"   Oct 5, 1882
    J.K. Webster, ex mayor of Quincy died last Saturday September 30th at
    the insane asylum at Jacksonville.

Weed, Deacon L.A.   "Obituary"   Apr 27, 1887
    Died- Deacon L.A. Weed was a native of N.Y. state. born about 1814.
    died in San Diego, Calif April 10th 1887. Came west as a young boy, stopped
    a short time in Circleville, Ohio and on to Illinois in 1838 and settled
    in Plymouth, Hancock Co.. Married Miss Rebecca Burton in 1842. She
    died 1868. In 1843 he came to Mendon. In 1869 he married Mrs Webber
    who survives him. In 1880 they moved to Fowler from there to Macon City,
    Mo. and last yr to San Deigo. Leaves by his 1st wife 1 son, Nelson Weed
    at whose home he died.

Weems, Mrs   "Obituary"   Feb 27, 1890
    see Palmer, J.C.

Weems, Mrs J.E.   "Obituary"   Nov 21, 1889
    see Palmer, Mrs J.C.

Weever, Mrs Emma   "Local"   Dec 31, 1891
    Mrs Emma Weever was buried in Denson burying ground near Ursa.

Wehmhoner, Mr and Mrs Henry   "Tioga"   Dec 27, 1900
    the infant child of Mr and Mrs Hy Wehmhoner who died Wednesday was
    buried in the German cemetery.

Weichman, Hy   "Obituary"   May 7, 1891
    see Kneis, John

Weiderkher, John   "News"   Mar 25, 1880
    John Weiderkher, a well known citizen of Palmyra, Missouri committed
    suicide Monday by shooting himself in the head.

Weidenhamer, J.C.   "Fowler"   Aug 21, 1902
    J.D. Straub attended the funeral of J.C. Weidenhamer at Galesburg
    last week.

Weidner, Mathias   "Estate"   Jul 10, 1884
    see Owings, Howard W.

Weiler, J.L. Sr.   "Tioga"   Feb 1, 1900
    Died- on Tuesday January 23rd at his home northeast of Tioga, J.L.
    Weiler Sr. at the age of 74 yrs. Funeral Friday P.M. from the
    Evangelical church. Buried in the German cemetery.

Weiler Mrs J.L. Sr.   "Tioga"   Dec 16, 1897
    Died- on Sunday morning December 5th 1897, Mrs J.L. Weiler Sr.
    71 yrs old. Leaves husband and 6 children, 2 brothers and 1 sister.
    Funeral Monday. Buried in the German cemetery, Tioga.

Weinberger, Mrs Elmira   "Obituary"   Jan 29, 1899
    see Devore, Andrew

Weir, Miss Pearly   "Local"   Feb 16, 1887
    It is reported to us that Miss Pearly Weir, of Hardy's Ford died of
    pneumonia last week.

Weiser, George W.   "Local"   Jun 2, 1886
    Mr George W. Weiser bade adieu to Mendon yesterday taking his infant
    child with him. He has gone to Indiana, to the home of his sisters,
    where his little girl has been cared for since the death of her mother.

Weisman, Mrs   "Woodville"   Jan 24, 1889
    Mrs Weisman, of Ursa come up to spend Sunday with her mother, Mrs
    Frederick. Mother F. and her 4 children ate their 1st meal togather
    last Sunday for over 30 yrs since their father's death.

Weister, Mr Wm   "Local"   Dec 21, 1893
    Died- Mr Wm Weister, (husband of Nelie "Cornelia" Battell) at his home
    in Kearney, Nebr. last Sunday. Leaves widow and 4 children.

Welch, Misses Elizabeth and Mary   Jun 29, 1904
    Fire ruined the Tremont Hotel property in Quincy last week, the well
    known teachers Misses Elizabeth and Mary Welch lost their lives.

Welling, Joseph   "Marcelline"   Apr 12, 1888
    The youngest child of Joseph Welling's died on the 3rd and was buried at
    Keith graveyard next day.

Welling, Theodore   "Soldiers"   Jun 1, 1899
    Thoedore Welling's grave included in list of soliers graves decorated
    in Mendon cemetery.

Wells, Mr   "Clinton, Mo.   Apr 3, 1884
    Mr Wells was murdered at his home by 2 lads named Thomas Brownsfield and
    Frank Hopkirt.

Wells, Mrs Clarence A.   "Death"   Mar 15, 1905
     see Hewes, Samuel E.

Wells, Robert   "Local"   Aug 11, 1898
     Died- Robert Wells, formerly of Mendon, at his home at 914 Hampshire St
     Quincy last Friday night. Leaves a wife, 1 son and 1 daughter.

Welsh, Mrs J.T.   "Loraine"   May 31, 1894
     Died- J.T. Welsh's wife at Quincy Friday A.M.

Welshom, Mrs J. W.   "Death"   Jul 28, 1892
     Died- Mrs J.W. Welshom's at her home in Montaque, Sickiyou Co. Calif.
     July 14th. Born Fall Creek twp Adams Co. Ill. Was wife of well known
     Supt. and miller of the Montaque flour mill of that place. Funeral on
     Friday at Little Shasta where she formerly resided. 37 yrs old. (husband
     was formerly the head miller at the Pearl mills in Mendon)

Wensing, Henay   "Death in Adams Co."   Feb 16, 1899
     Died- Henay Wensing of Quincy died Monday night of spinal meningitis.
     31 yrs old.

Werner, Henry   "Fowler"   Aug 2, 1888
     Henry Werner buried a little girl 14 months old Saturday.

Werner, Mrs Henry   "Fowler"   Apr 26, 1888
     Died- Mrs Henry Werner. She leaves husband and 4 small children.

West, Mr and Mrs   Feb 26, 1891
     Died- Sunday Feb. 22nd, the youngest child of Mr and Mrs West.
     Age 8 months.

West, Amos   "Loraine"   Mar 21, 1895
     Mr Amos West of Big Neck died Sunday at 8 P.M. of liver trouble.
     62 yrs old. Lived Big Neck 2 yrs. He and his son have been engaged in a
     general store at that place. Buried Clayton today.

West, Mrs Fred S.   "Obituary"   Oct 17, 1901
     see Sellwood, J.R.N.

Westfall, Mrs   Oct 20, 1881
     Died- of arsenic poisoning. Rest of family recovered (husband and 3
     kids) in Hannibal last week. Colored woman suspected.

Westrook,   "Cathage"   Apr 17, 1879
     Died- an old and very respecter citizen by the name of Westrook died
     this week. Services by Rev Warner at the M.E. chuech of which the deceased
     was a menber of for more than 40 yrs.

Wetzel, Mr and Mrs   "Local'   Aug 25, 1892
     Died- infant child of Mr and Mrs Wetzel of Fowler last Thursday.
     Buried next day.

Wever, Alvin   "soldiers"   Jun 1, 1899
     Alvin Wever's name was included in list of soldiers graves
     decorated in Mendon cemetery.

Wharton, Mrs Amy S.   Jan 2, 1890
    Mrs Amy S. Wharton died at her home in Payson at 11:40 P.M. December
    29th 1889. Her maiden was Amy Smedley. Born West Chester, Penn July 27,
    1817. Married in 1838 to Benjamin B. Wharton who died Jan 5, 1859
    They had 7 girls and 1 boy. Funeral at Cong'l church at Payson on
    Dec 31st.

Wharton, Amy S.   "Probate"   Jan 9, 1890
    Probate notice of Amy S. Wharton 1st Monday of March 1890
    J.R. Urech, Ex.

Wharton, Tomy   "Payson"   Oct 30, 1879
    Died- suddenly of croup, Tomy, a child of Mr and Mrs Henry Wharton on
    Saturday October 25th. Services at the house Monday the 27th at 2 P.M.

Wheaton, Mr and Mrs   "Loraine"   Dec 4, 1902
    Mr and Mrs Wheaton were called to Chicago last week by the death of
    Mr W's mother.

Wheaton, Mrs Charles   "Loraine"   Nov 12, 1903
    Mrs Charles Wheaton attended the funeral of her uncle at Albany, Ill.
    last week.

Wheeler, Mrs   "Obituary"   Aug 16, 1894
    Mrs Wheeler of the Vermont St. M.E. church Quincy died.

Wheeler, Mrs J.H.   "Obituary"   May 31, 1894
    see Collins, Miss Fanny C.

Wheeler, Mrs Joel   "Local"   Oct 26, 1904
    Mrs Joel Wheeler of Camp Point took a dose of strychine Sunday A.M.
    and died 2:30 Sunday P.M. Was about 42 yrs old. Leaves husband and
    3 children.

Wheeler, Mrs Silas   "Fowler"   Nov 23, 1887
    Mrs Silas Wheeler died of consumption Sunday eve at 8.

Wheeler, Sylvester   "Quincy Clips"   Jun 5, 1884
    Death of Sylvester Wheeler at Clayton. He was on a visit to his affianced,
    Miss Ada Montgomery and was taken sick at Major Montgonery's residence.

Wheeler, Sylvester   Jun 5, 1884
    Death of Sylvester Wheeler at Clayton June 4th. He was known as Ves
    to his friends.

Wheeler, Taylor   "Deaths in Quincy"   Apr 20, 1899
    Died- Taylor Wheeler a member of Co. 1 8th Reg. Ill. Vol. Sunday.
    40 yrs old. Leaves 2 sisters and 2 brothers.

Wheeler, Wes   "Columbus"   Feb 23, 1888
    Wes Wheeler of Missouri buried his wife some time ago and brought his
    6 little children over to his brothers, Theo Wheeler and now wants a
    good home for them.

434

Whelden, Mary Crane   "Died"   May 15, 1902
    Mary Crane Whelden died at Hotel Phoenix, Hyde Park, Vermont Sunday
    at 7 May 4th. Body was taken to her former home, Ludlow on Tuesday
    for services in the Cong'l church at 4 P.M. by Rev A.V. Bliss. Buried
    Ludlow beside her 1st husband, the late Edward C. Crane, brother of
    C.H. Crane of Hyde Park. Her maiden name was Mary Jane Thomas. She was
    the oldest of several children of Jefferson Thomas and Calista Judson
    of Morristown. Born in Starksboro April 10, 1853. Married June 2, 1873
    to Edward C. Crane of Hyde Park. Had 5 children, youngest died at
    Manchester, N.H. at age 6 mo's. Mr Crane was Cong'l minister at Holden,
    Me., Waldoboro, Me. Mendon, Ill and Manchester, N.H. Family moved to
    Ludlow in 1890 where Mr C. bought the Vermont Tribune till his deaht in
    June 1893. She sold the paper to her oldest son,Elphrain H. Crane.
    Married 2nd May 31st 1899 to B.F. Wheldon of Ludlow who survives her.
    Leaves a daughter, Lizzie A. of Bugbee, Weymouth Heights, Mass., Alice M.
    Lane of Readsboro, Vt., Ephrain H. and Charles E. of Ludlow. Also leaves
    parents and sisters, Mrs Elixa Strong of Morristown, Mrs Addie Marston of
    Barton and brother Clarence Thomas of Morristown.

Whips, Mrs Mary Ellen   "Death"   Jun 15, 1904
    Funeral of Mrs Mary Ellen Whips was at hte home of the deceased in Ursa
    twp Friday June 10th at 3 P.M. by Rev A.M. Reitzel of the Lutheran
    church. Buried Ursa cemetery. Was 73 yrs 8 mo's 27 days old. Spent her
    long life in Adams Co.. Married Feb 19, 1950 to Mr B.F. Whips. Leaves
    4 children, 1 daughter and 3 sons.

Whitebread, Mrs Sarah   "Obituary"   Dec 31, 1891
    see Hendrickson, Mrs Elizabeth

Whitbred, George   "Camp Point"   Feb 21, 1884
    George Francis and wife were called to Quincy last week by the death of
    Mrs F's brother, George Whitbred.

Whitcomb, Firman   "Lima"   Oct 13, 1884
    Died- October 4th at his residence in Lima, Mr Firman Whitcomb.
    Leaves a wife and 2 small children. Services at the M.E. church by
    Rev Agnew.

Whitcomb, Jasper Esq.   "Payson"   Feb 26, 1885
    On Feb 12th Jasper Whitcomb Esq. died. He was kicked in the head by
    a horse which broke his skull. Born 1807. Lived this community 40 yrs.
    Leaves wife and several grown children.

Whitcombe. Mrs Rhoda   "Lima"   Sep 19, 1889
    Died- Mrs Rhoda Whitcombe of Idaho, formerly of this place.

White, Mr   "Local"   Sep 21, 1899
    Mr White of Hurdland, Mo. came to attend the funeral of his daughter,
    Mrs Wm Mitchell. Took the baby and 1 small child home with him.

White, Mrs Addie   "Obituary"   Apr 26, 1888
    see Gooding, Mrs Keziah

White, Mrs C.H.   "Death"   Feb 19, 1903
   see Hunter, Mr John

White, Miss Estella   "Obituary"   Sep 14, 1899
   see Mitchell, Mrs Estella

White, Homer   "Obituary"   Sep 14, 1899
   see Mitchell, Mrs Estella

White, J.J.   "Obituary"   Aug 24, 1899
   Funeral services for J.J. White at his mother's home on the E.H. Wilken's place Monday August 21st at 9 by Rev J.S. Bayne. Buried in Coatsburg cemetery.

White, Mrs Jasper   "Coatsburg"   Mar 30, 1887
   Died- Mrs Jasper White died March 27th at 10 A.M. Leaves husband and 5 children. Services held at Baptist church by Rev Walforth of Paloma. Buried in the village cemetery.

White, Joel   "Coatsburg"   Jan 15, 1885
   Joel White was called home by the death of his father.

White, Joel Justus   "Obituary"   Aug 24, 1899
   Funeral services for J.J. White at his mother's home on the E.H. Wilken's place Monday August 21st at 9 by Rev J.S. Bayne. Buried Coatsburg cem. Joel Justus White was born September 4th 1883 near Woodville, Macon Co. Missouri. With parents came to Adams Co. Ill at the age of 4 yrs. He had been sickly since the age of 4 yrs when he was stricken down with fits and has been helpless most of the time.

White, Mr John A.   "Coatsburg"   Jan 15, 1885
   Died- Mr John A. White January 7th. Age 62 yrs. Services by Rev J.E. Goodson of Macon Co. Mo. Buried Coatsburg cemetery. He was an old settler and much respected.

White, John A.   "Probate"   Feb 12, 1885
   Probate notice of John A. White, deceased   3rd Monday of April 1885 John A. White, Adm. (Sic)

White, Nellie   "Obituary"   Sep 14, 1899
   see Mitchell, Mrs Estella

White, Wm   "Columbus"   Mar 3, 1886
   Died-Feb. 23rd Mr Wm White. Age 35 yrs from consumption. Services by Rev Walfarth.

White, Wm Thos.   "Local"   Nov 3, 1898
   Wm Thos White and his sister Ida were called to Camp Point by their father's illness Tuesday.
   News rec'd later that he died the same night at 7 P.M.

Whitefield, Mrs Joseph   "Death"   Oct 5, 1904
   see Ippenson, Mrs Nellie

Whitefield, Mr Wm   "Marcelline"   Sep 26, 1895
Died- at his home northwest of Marcelline of typhoid fever September
19th, Mr Wm Whitefield. 44 yrs old. Services by Rev Green of the M.P.
church of Ursa at the Christian church here. Leaves a wife, 4 sons and
1 daughter. Buried in the Baptist cemetery.

Whitehill, Willie F.   Nov 10, 1881
Died- October 14th 1881 Willie F. Whitehill, oldest son of Mr and Mrs
Whitehill who moved with their son to Peabody, Kansas 4 yrs ago.

Whitford, Mr Albert   Sep 10, 1891
Death of Mr Albert Whitford in Denver, son of Mr H.S. Whitford of
Golden. He was a brother of Mrs J.S. Wallace.

Whitlock, Derrick   "Obituary"   Jan 29, 1891
Died- Derrick Whitlock at his home at Columbus January 21, 1891.
Born in Sussex Co. New Jersey April 2, 1817 and the next summer his
folks moved to Butler Co. Ohio where he lived and married Miss Elliot
December 18, 1839. She also was born in that Co. on March 13, 1818. They
are parents of 4 children, 2 sons and 2 daughters. Leaves a wife, 1 son
and 1 daughter. He came to Adams Co. in 1853 and was in the mercantile
business in Columbus from 1857 to 71 where he also filled the office
of town and police magistrate since 1859. About 4 yrs ago he fell out
of a wagon and injured his spine and since that time his health has been
failing. Services by Rev Donley of Jacksonville. Buried here in Columbus.

Whitmore, Mrs W.D.   "Carthage Republican"   Nov 5, 1885
Mrs W.D. Whitmore who died at Fairbury, Ill October 14th was the 1st
and only female member of the well known union league.

Whitney, Lucinda   "Obituary"   Mar 21, 1889
  see Bray, Mrs Lucinda

Whitney, Sarah Marie   "Obituary"   Mar 9, 1983
  see Dutton, Mrs Sarah Marie

Whitney, Miss Thankful   "Obituary"   Apr 26, 1894
  see Golden, Mrs Thankful

Whittelsey, Nancy A.   "Death"   Mar 22, 1905
  see Booker, George W.

Whittlesey, Mrs May   "Loraine"   Nov 9, 1899
Mrs May Whittlesey left for Topeka, Kansas to see her sister who is
dying of consumption.

Whray, Ralph   Aug 31, 1904
Died- Ralph Whray, youngest son of Dr and Mrs T.R. Whray of Golden,
Friday eve while being taken to St Mary's hospital. He was employed
as operator by Burlington R.R. at the Wabash Jct. in Quincy. Was going
to work Friday eve and coming to his office jumped off the train and
struck a telegraph pole and died.

Wible, Miss   "Death"   Dec 14, 1893
  see Dick, Mrs

Wible, Andrew   Jun 26, 1890
    Mr Andrew Wible died June 24th. 75 yrs old. His children are, Mrs W.G.
    Taylor, Mr J.A. Wible, Mr Robert Wible and Mrs Marai Gibson. Also
    surviving him is his wife. Buried from the Lutheran church at Mendon
    by Rev E.L. Schmucker.

Wible, Andrew   "Probate"   Jul 10, 1890
    Probate Notice of Andrew Wible, deceased   1st Monday of Sept. 1890
    Albert Wible, Adm with will annexed.

Wible, Mrs Albert   "Death"   Jun 21, 1905
    see Clair, John

Wible, Mrs Clara Alice   "Obituary"   May 31, 1888
    Died- of typhoid fever, Mrs Clara Alice Wible, wife of Mr John A. Wible
    of 315 Woodland Ave Kansas City, Mo. on Sunday May 27th. Services held
    at the house the next day and the remains brought to Mendon on Tuesday
    and taken to the home of Mr F.W. Battell where a short services was held
    by Rev J.W. Thomas. Burieal in Keith graveyard near Marcelline, where
    her mother and sister rest. Mrs Wible was the 3rd daughter of Mr Peter
    and the late Mrs Cort of this place. Born July 28, 1851. Leaves no family.

Wible, Mrs Daniel   "Died"   Dec 7, 1904
    Sudden death of Mrs Daniel Wible of this village 6 A.M. yesterday. Born
    Feb. 2, 1819 in Westmoreland Co. Penn. and died Mendon December 6th 1904
    Age 85 yrs 10 mo's 4 days. Maiden name was Anna C. Rumbaugh. Married
    Mr Wible December 6, 1838. Died on her 66th wedding anniversary. Family
    came to Adams Co. 1852 and settled on a farm in Ursa twp until 12 yrs
    ago they moved to Mendon. Leaves aged husband who was born Westmoreland
    co Penn also on April 7, 1814. they had 2 sons, Josiah of Chicago and
    Frank of Palmyra, Mo. and 1 daughter, Miss Anna at home. Was member of
    Mendon Lutheran church. Funeral at Lutheran church Thursday 2 P.M.

Wible, Miss Hannah   "Died"   Feb 5, 1880
    Died- on last Friday Jan. 30th of pneumonia, Miss Hannah Wible, age
    56 yrs at the home of her brother, Andrew Wible where she had lived
    several yrs. Born in Westmoreland Co. Penn. Came to Illinois in 1852.

Wible, John   "Obituary"   Nov 1, 1888
    Died- October 29th, Mr John Wible at the age of 77 yrs 7 mo's 18 days.
    Born in Westmoreland Co. Penn. Came to Mendon, Ill in 1852 where he lived
    since. Joined Lutheran church as a young man. Married October 24th 1839
    and had 11 children. Leaves wife and 10 children. Buried in Mendon
    cemetery according to the rites of the Mosonic brotherhood. Services at
    the Lutheran church by Rev J.W. Thomas.

Wible, John   "Local"   Mar 30, 1893
    Mr John Wible of Kansas City came to attend to his father's estate.

Wible, John   "Probate"   Nov 29, 1888
    Probate notice of John Wible, deceased 1st Monday of Feb. 1889
    Caroline E. Wible, Adm.

Wible, John   Jun 22, 1899
 John Wible included in list of Soldiers graves decorated in Mendon
 cemetery on Decoration Day.

Wible, John   Feb 19, 1885
 Mr John Wible of Kansas City is here to attend the funeral of his wife's
 sister, Miss Aggie Cort.

Wible, John A.   "Local"   Oct 18, 1888
 Mr John A. Wible of Kansas City has just had a monument erected in
 Keith cemetery near Marcelline in memory of his late wife.

Wible, Joseph   "Obituary"   Mar 23, 1887
 see McClung, Mrs Ella Jane

Wible, Mrs K.   "Mt Pleasant"   Jan 12, 1888
 Mrs K. Wible, wife of Daniel Wible is sick with typhoid fever. Added to
 her illness was the death of her brother, David Rumbaugh who resides in
 Penn.

Wible, Mrs Margaret J.   "Obituary"   May 2, 1889
 Died- Margaret J. Wible, wife of Charles A. Wible of Marcelline died
 April 27th at the age of 24 yrs 11 mo's 5 days. Daughter of Mr Bade of
 Lima and was married October 23rd 1887. Leaves husband and a son 4 mo's
 old. Buried in the cemetery at Stone's church near Ursa. Services by
 Rev Anthony of the M.P. church, assisted by Rev Ades of the Christian
 church, Ursa.

Wible, Miss Maggie   "Obituary"   Nov 16, 1887
 see Turner, Mr E.B. (Enoch)

Wible, Mrs Martha   "Obituary"   Feb 9, 1899
 see Kells, Robert

Wible, Peter   "Died"   Oct 15, 1891
 Kern Valley, Calif.- Died Peter Wible September 24th at 2 P.M. His
 death was due to old age. He was a native of Penn. About 1888 he moved to
 Kern Co. He leaves a wife and 5 children. Was a Democrat. Gave his 1st
 vote to Andrew Jackson for President.

Wible, Sarah   Apr 14, 1892
 In Adams Co Circuit court to the June term 1892
 Sarah Wible, Complainant vs. Bill for Dower and Homestead, Albert Wible,
 Nancy Wible, Albert Wible, Ex. of the last will and testament of Andrew
 Wible, deceased. Maria Gibson, Charles S. Gibson, Maria D. Gibson, John A.
 Wible, Mary Wible, Robert Wible, Clara Wible, Emma J. Wible, Charles Wible,
 Rebecca Taylor, Wm G. Taylor, John A. Taylor, Alice Taylor, Cora Bell
 Addis, Charles Addis, Wm H. Taylor, Sarah M. Taylor, Herman G. Taylor,
 Effie M. Taylor, Charles A. Taylor, Nellie G. Taylor, David L. Taylor,
 John Nedrow, Albert Rosenbrook, Joseph Chant, Elmer Smith, the unkown
 devises, legatees and heirs of Andrew Wible, deceased. The unkown owners
 of the premises described in said bill of complaint and persons unkown
 interested in the premises described in said bill of complaint.

-cont-

Wible, Sarah Continued--   Apr 14, 1892
    Defendants-- It appearing by affidavit on file in the office of the
    clerk of the circuit court in and for said county, that said defendants,
    Charles S. Gibson, Maria D. Gibson, John A. Wible, Mary Wible, Robert
    Wible, Clara Wible, Emma J. Wible, Charles Wible, Rebecca Taylor, Wm G.
    Taylor, John A. Taylor, Cora Bell Addis, Charles Addis, Wm H. Taylor,
    Sarah M. Taylor, Herman G. Taylor, Annie M. Taylor, Effie M. Taylor,
    Charles A. Taylor, Nellie G. Taylor and David Taylor reside out of state
    of Illinois and that there are unkown devises, legatees and heirs of
    Andrew Wible deceased.   Geo. Brophy, clerk per Hiram R. Wheat, deputy
    Hamilton and Woods, Solicitors for complainant.

Wible, Vernia A.   "Local"   Jul 14, 1886
    Died- July 6th Vernia A., infant daughter of Mr and Mrs J.A. Wible of
    Kansas City, Mo.

Wickenkemp, H.   "Death"   Apr 28, 1881
    see Riley, Mrs

Wicoff, Hariett   "Obituary"   Dec 1, 1886
    see Smith, Nathaniel

Wicoff, Sylvia L.   "Death"   Mar 1, 1905
    see Lint, Charles F.

Wiedemann, Mrs   "Death"   Aug 20, 1891
    see Tittle, Mrs Hamilton

Wier, Mr S.R.   "Personal"   Oct 19, 1882
    Rev McKown left Monday for Plymouth to attend the funeral of one of his
    friends, Mr S. R. Wier, who died at Riverside, Calif.

Wieser, Susan   "Died"   Oct 29, 1885
    Died- October 23rd 1885, Susan, wife of George W. Wieser age 25 yrs
    10 mon's. Buried Mendon cemetery. Services by Rev E.C. Crane. Maiden
    name was Keisling. Born New York state on Dec 23, 1859. Leaves husband
    and 2 small children, a little girl 5 yrs old and an infant boy.

Wigans, Mrs C.   "Local"   Sep 20, 1888
    News rec'd from Mrs M.E. Frisbie at Pleasant Unity, Westmoreland Co.
    Penn that her mother, Mrs C. Wigans died on Sept 8th at the age of 80 yrs.
    Buried on the 10th.

Wigle, Solomon   "West Point"   Oct 30, 1879
    Mr W.T. Hart rec'd word from Clayton of the death of Solomon, a brother
    of Mrs Hart.

Wilcox, Chester A. (Chet)   "Death"   Aug 3, 1899
    Died- Chester Allen Wilcox (Chet) post master of Quincy at his home
    Sunday A.M. of Bright's disease. Born Harford Mills, Courtland Co. N.Y.
    Nov 8, 1847. Moved with parents to Janesville, Wisc 1858. Father was the
    late Daniel Wilcox who died May 1878. His father bought the Quincy Whig
    Jan 1, 1874 and C.A. came to Quincy with him. Sold Whig in 1897. Leaves
    his mother, Mrs Angeline Wilcox, 1 brother D.F. Wilcox and 1 sister Mrs
    C.E. Carley. Services Tuesday P.M. by the Lambert Lodge of Masons.

Wilcox, Mrs G.W.   "Died"   Feb 1, 1883
    Mrs G.W. Wilcox died in Quincy January 21st. 53 yrs old.

Wilcox, George W.   "Death"   Sep 24, 1885
    see Furry, Lewis

Wilcox, Jas. A. Mrs   "Obituary"   Nov 1, 1900
    see Kincheloe, Isaac Newton

Wilcox, John   "Obituary"   Nov 19, 1903
    see Inman, Lavina J.

Wilcox, John   Jun 5, 1902
    John Wilcox included in list of soldiers graves decorated in Mendon
    cemetery Decoration Day.

Wilcox, Mr and Mrs Joseph A.   "Local"   May 29, 1890
    May 19th Roy Wilcox, son of Mr and Mrs Joseph A. Wilcox died. Age 2 yrs.
    They lived 1½ miles west of Loraine.

Wilcox, Mrs Lavina J.   "Obituary"   Nov 19, 1903
    see Inman, Lavina J.

Wilcox, Dr Luman H.   "Local"   Feb 2, 1887
    Dr Lumna H. Wilcox died at his home in Springfield where he has resided
    since 1874 on last Thursday night. Age 78 yrs. Lived Mendon 32 yrs.
    Leaves wife and 3 children, Mrs Dr Free of Kansas City, Dr G.O. Wilcox
    and Mrs Samuel Grubb.

Wilcox, Meshach   "Death"   Feb 19, 1880
    see Haley, Mrs Kate

Wilcox, Morton Robert   "Obituary"   May 17, 1905
    Morton Robert, son of Thomas and Jane Wilcox was born Feb 2, 1861 and died
    May 9th 1905. Age 44 yrs 3 mo's 7 days. Leaves father, 2 brothers and
    4 sisters. Brothers are, William H. of West Line, Mo. and Joseph A. of
    Loraine. Sisters are, Mrs S.H. McClung, Mrs William Austin and Mrs Wallace
    Wright all of Mendon and Miss Mattie of Loraine. Joined M.E. church at
    Loraine at age 18 yrs. Died at the home of his father at 9 P.M. Mother
    and 1 brother died before him several yrs. Services Thursday P.M. at
    Mendon M.E. church by Rev Barringer of Loraine and Rev S.R. Reno of
    Mendon. Buried Mendon cemetery.

Wilcox, Mrs Nancy   "Ursa"   Apr 12, 1905
Died- Mrs Nancy Wilcox, one of Adams Co.'s oldest pioneers at the home of
her son, James Wilcox of this place April 7th of old age. Bron Athens,
Ohio July 10, 1811. Married in 1830 and came to Illinois 10 yrs later
among the earlist settlers. always lived in Ursa twp. Had 14 children
all but 4 of whom died prior to reaching their majority and 1 of these
died soon after. 1 son and 2 daughters survive her. Several grandchildren
and several great grandchildren also survive her. Was member of the U.B.
or Methodist church since 14 yrs old. Funeral by Rev W.O. Livingstone of
the M.P. church.

Wilcox, Mrs Nancy   "Ursa"   Apr 12, 1905
Funeral Sunday A.M. from the M.P. church of Mrs Nancy Wilcox. Buried
New Providence cemetery. 95 yrs old. Services by Rev W.O. Livingston.

Wilcox, Scott   "Ursa"   Dec 6, 1883
Died at his home, Mr Scott Wilcox at a ripe old age.

Wilcox, Seben   "Local"   Apr 13, 1904
Died- Seben Wilcox at the home of Henry Swank, 2 miles west of Ursa
Sunday eve. Suffered paralysis about 2 yrs.

Wilcox, Mrs Jane   "Sudden Death"   Dec 22, 1898
Died- Mrs Jane Wilcox, (nee Hewitt) from heart failure Saturday at her
home 2 miles west of Loraine. Born Ireland 1828 and baptized in
Episcopal church in infancy. Came with parents to Adams Co. in 1849.
Married Thomas Wilcox 1850 an emigrant from England who survives her.
Had 8 children. (4 boys and 4 girls) 7 survive her they are, Wm of Cass
Co. Mo., Joseph, Mortimer and Mattie of Keene twp, Mrs S.H. McClung
and Mrs Wm B. Austin of Mendon and Mrs Wallace Wright of Ursa. John was
killed in Arkansas a few yrs ago. She was a sister of Thomas and the late
Wm Hewitt. Joined the M.E. church at Loraine in 1892. Buried Mendon
cemetery Monday afternoon. Services at the M.E. church by Rev F.B.
Bonnifan of Loraine.

Wilcox, Mrs Thos.   "Obituary"   Apr 12, 1894
see Hewitt, Mary A.

Wilcox, Mrs Thomas   "Obituary"   Sep 19, 1889
see Hewitt, John

Wilcox, Mrs Verna   "Local"   Sep 20, 1900
Died- Mrs Verna Wilcox of Indian Grave yesterday morning of malaria.
Funeral tomorrow at 9 A.M. Burial to be in the Stone church cemetery.

Wilcoxson, Prof   "Payson"   Jan 6, 1881
Prof Wilcoxson was called to his home in Mo. a few days before Xmas
on acct of sickness in his family. On December 25th 1880 he lost a
little daughter. He will be here again this week to fill his appointments.

Wilderman, Mrs Etta   "Obituary"   Dec 11, 1902
see Frazier, Mrs Eva J.

Wilhelm, Miss Leah D.   "Death"   Jan 11, 1905
see Gilmer, Benjamin

Wilkenbuch, John   "Quincy death"   Feb 29, 1899
    Died- Mr John Wilkenbuch at St Mary's hospital Friday A.M. Leaves a
    wife and several children.

Wilkes, Mrs   "Ursa"   Apr 28, 1881
    Mrs Wilkes of Camp Point was buried in Denson cemetery last Friday
    April 15th 1881

Wilkins, Mrs E.H.   "Local"   Feb 20, 1902
    Mrs E.H. Wilkins left Monday eve for Rose, Kansas after rec'ing word
    that her mother died on Saturday. She was 85 yrs old and only sick a
    few days before she died.

Wilkins, Mr and Mrs Eli   "Death"   May 15, 1884
    see Beatly, Alie

Wilkinson, Mr   "Coatsburg"   Feb 2, 1887
    Mr Wilkinson buried a pair of twin boys last week.

Wilkinson, Martha   "Obituary"   Nov 23, 1899
    Died- Martha Wilkinson- Born March 8th 1822 in Naas Co. Kildare, Ireland
    Died Friday P.M. Nov 17th at the age of 77 yrs 8 yrs 9 days. Married
    Edward Taylor November 22, 1840. They came to America 1849 and on to
    Mendon in November of that year. Moved to Honey Creek 1854 and lived
    there since. Her husband died 1884. They had 8 children, 1 daughter died
    in infancy and 3 sons after arriving to manhood. 2 sons, Thomas and
    William and 2 daughters, Sarah and Elizabeth survive her, besides 6
    grandchildren, 1 sister, Mrs Kate O'Conner. She was baptized, confirmed
    and married in the Episcopal church at Naas, Ireland. Services in Zion
    Episcopal church by Rev Savage. Buried beside her husband this A.M.

Wilks, Miss Maria   "Columbus"   Nov 5, 1885
    Miss Maria Wilks who lived 5 miles from town was buried near Camp
    Point Friday.

Willard, Freddie M.   "Big Neck"   Jan 1, 1891
    Died- December 23rd Freddie M. Willard aged 15 yrs 8 mo's 8 days.
    Freddie's father George Willard joined the majority 10 yrs ago the 8th
    of this month, and since that tome up to his deaht he had lived with
    his grandfather Samuel Willard Sr. and had become the star of the family
    and his death is a hard stroke to the whole family. His mother who
    is yet a widow is heart broken, but her loss is his gain.

Willard, Samuel   "Death"   Sep 27, 1905
    see Herron, Glenn

Willard, Wm   "Lima"   May 9, 1895
    Funerals of Mr Wm Willard and Mr Aspey were at Ebenezer. The former
    on Sunday and the later on Monday of last week. Mr A. was a resident of
    the Neck where he farmed until moving to Golden.

Willhoit, Mrs Delilah   "Coatsburg"   Dec 25, 1884
    Mrs Delilah Willhoit died this A.M.

Williams, Mrs Dr   "Local"   May 5, 1892
Died- Mrs Dr Williams at her home Saturday at 6 from atrophy of the
liver. Born Logansport, Ind. Her maiden name was Hannah Julian. Came
to Illinois as a girl and taught school near Chicago. Also taught a
private school at this place. Married Dr Williams in 1853. Was member
of Christian church at Ursa. Funeral at the home on Saturday P.M.
by Rev M.L. Schmucker of Mendon. Buried Keath cemetery.

Williams, Mrs Dr   "Local"   May 5, 1892
Died- Mrs Dr Williams of Marcelline.

Williams, Arthur   "Loraine"   May 6, 1880
Arthur Williams - 18 yrs old living near Chili, Illinois fell in front
of the knives and was killed Monday about 4 A.M.

Williams, Rev G.W.   "Plainsville Observer"   May 25, 1893
Rev G.W. Williams of Newtown, an old citizen died last Sunday. Services
at Newtown on Tuesday.

Williams, James   "Local"   Jul 20, 1887
James Williams, age 17 yrs, son of Arthur Williams, a business man
in Keokuk was drowned in the river near Hamilton while bathing.

Williams, Elder Joel G.   "Died"   Mar 6, 1879
Died- Elder Joel G. Williams- for many yrs a resident of Mendon twp
at his home Feb 26th 1879. Mr Williams had been a preacher of the old
Predestination Baptist church for over 40 yrs.

Williams, Mrs Joel   "Personal"   Jan 15, 1880
Mrs Joel Williams died Jan 8th in her 76th yr. Her remains were
entombed in Leachman's cemetery. Early settler and a member of the
Baptist church. Leaves 2 sons, living in Mo.and 1 daughter, the wife of
John McAdams Esq. of Ursa.

Williams, Kenneth   "Fowler"   Sep 12, 1901
Died- Kenneth Williams, the little son of Mr and Mrs Joe Williams Sunday
Funeral tomorrow.

Williams, Kenneth   "Fowler"   Sep 19, 1901
Funeral of little Kenneth Williams was held Tuesday. Services by Rev
Bonnefon. He was a pupil of the primary Dept. of school and the school
attended in a body.

Williams, Mary F.   "Probate"   Feb 19, 1880
Probate notice of Mary F. Williams, deceased   3rd Monday of April 1880
John McAdams, Adm.

Williams, Peter S.   "Death in Adams Co."   Apr 20, 1899
Died- Peter S. Williams at his home 4 miles S.E. of Clayton April 8th
from pneumonia. 51 yrs old. Leaves wife and 5 children.

Williams, Dr R.   "Obituary"   Apr 27, 1893
    Died- Dr R. Williams at his home in Marcelline last Thursday April 20th
    69 yrs old. cause; consumption. Wife died about a yr ago. Born Virginia
    September 1824. Came with his parents as a young boy to Macoupin Co.
    Illinois and in about 1853 to Adams Co. Settled at Marcelline where he
    married and lived since. Leaves 3 brothers, 1 in Missouri, 1 in Colorado
    and 1's where abouts unknown. Buried in Keith cemetery Sunday by the
    side of his wife. Services by Rev Tunnicliffe.

Williams, Mrs Wesley   "Local"   Mar 23, 1904
    Died- Mrs Wesly Williams of Loraine Friday afternoon at Blessings
    Hospital after an operation which was performed as a last resort in
    hopes of saving her life. Was about 45 yrs old.

Williamson, John H.   "Local"   Mar 7, 1895
    Died- Mr John H. Williamson, supervisor of Liberty twp Sunday night at
    his home 1½ miles southwest of the village of consumption. Leaves a
    wife and 3 children. His wife is a daughter of Patrick Smith and a
    sister of deputy sheriff, Ed Smith. Was 40 yrs old.

Willis, Mrs W.L.   "Obituary"   Aug 16, 1894
    "Sunday School Supplement" Died- Mrs W.L. Willis of Quincy in the early
    spring. She was a faithful worker in the 1st Cong'l church in Quincy.

Willoit, Mrs Delilah   "Coatsburg"   Dec 25, 1884
    Mrs Delilah Willoit died December 15th.

Wilson, Dr   "Local"   Apr 21, 1894
    Wednesday eve a gentleman returned from Quincy and informs us that
    Dr Wilson, the Veterinary surgeon poisoned himself this afternoon in
    his office.

Wilson, Mrs   "Death"   Mar 27, 1902
    see Dunbar, Pearly

Wilson, Mrs   "Death"   Apr 5, 1883
    see George, Henry

Wilson, Darby   "Obituary"   Jan 3, 1901
    "Quincy Whig" Darby Wilson died at his home in Loraine, Tuesday December
    25th at 1:30 Born Franklin Co. Ind. July 28, 1821. Moved to Loraine
    in the ealy 40's. Settled in Lima twp for 1 yr then moved on to Loraine
    twp where he stayed. Married Mary J. Fowwell January 27, 1842. She died
    November 2, 1895. They had 10 children. Mr Wilson married 2nd on Feb
    3, 1897 to Margaret Bishop. She and 5 children survive him. Member of the
    Christian church 20 yrs. Funeral at the Christian church Thursday at
    10 A.M. Buried in Loraine cemetery.

Wilson, Darby   "Death"   Sep 6, 1883
    see Wade, Amanda

Wilson, Mr G.N.   "Mt Hebron"   Aug 25, 1886
    Died- Mr G.N. Wilson of Brownsville, Mo. He was formerly an ols settler
    of Adams Co., but moved to Mo. several yrs ago. Death caused by falling
    from a tree 3 mo's ago.

Wilson, Geo. T.   "Local"   May 30, 1901
    Mrs V. Young attended the funeral of Mr Geo. T. Wilson at Carthage Sun.

Wilson, Mrs George   "Local"   Jan 13, 1904
    Mrs V.C. Young left by train for Carthage Saturday to attend the
    funeral of Mrs George Wilson, returning in the evening.

Wilson, Herbert   "Death"   Nov 10, 1892
    see Cort, Peter

Wilson, Dr I. T.   "Local"   Apr 27, 1904
    Died- Dr I.T. Wilson of Quincy, of acute pneumonia Sunday P.M.
    Had been a resident of Adams Co. over 50 yrs.

Wilson, Mrs John   "Obituary"   Dec 20, 1900
    see Shupe, Catherine

Wilson, Lucy   Aug 4, 1881
    Aunt Lucy Wilson, an old settler died last week.

Wilson, Mrs Lucy   "Fowler"   Aug 11, 1881
    Died- Mrs Lucy Wilson. Age 78 yrs on July 23rd.

Wilson, Mrs Margaret(James)   "Loraine   Mar 20, 1902
    Died- Mrs Margaret Wilson, widow of the late James Wilson of
    pneumonia last Saturday at 6 A.M. Taken to her old home in the
    Webster neighborhood on Sunday for burial. Funeral also held there.

Wilson, Mrs Mary S.   "Body moved"   Oct 29, 1891
    see Cort, Peter

Wilson, Mrs Milanda   "Obituary"   May 24, 1883
    see McGibbons, John

Wilson, Mrs Louisa   "Local"   Sep 19, 1895
    Died- at her home in Honey Creek twp, Wednesday September 11th of
    paralysis, Age 66 yrs Mrs Louisa Wilson (colored) highly respected by
    all who knew her. Came from Missouri, but had lived in Honey Creek twp
    many yrs. Member of Christian church. Buried Byler burying ground on
    Friday. Services by Rev T.A. Waterman of the Zion Episcopal church of
    Mendon. Leaves husband and 1 son.

Wilson, Rachel   Jan 6, 1881
    Miss Rachel Wilson died at Loraine, Illinois Monday January 3rd of
    asthma in her 67th yr.

Wilson, Mrs Sophia   "Died"   Mar 1, 1878
 Died- this morning March 1st at the home of her father, Mrs Sophia
 Wilson, daughter of Peter Cort near Mendon.

Wilson, Mrs Stephen   "Local"   Sep 12, 1895
 Died- last night, Mrs Stephen Wilson, an old and respected colored lady
 of Honey Creek.

Wilson, Wash   "Loraine"   Feb 14, 1901
 Last Monday the remains of Wash Wilson were buried in Loraine cemetery.
 Mr Wilson lived several miles west of town. He was an old soldier.

Wilson, William Henry   "Jottings from Hundes" Sep 22, 1881
 William Henry Wilson was born in Kentucky 1801 and moved near Fowler in
 spring of 1833 and died some 33 yrs ago.

Wimmer, Mrs Joe Hanna   Apr 13, 1877
 "Adrain, Ill April 10, 1877" Mrs Joe Hanna Wimmer, grandmother of
 Dr W.P. Wimmer, of this place died in Montgomery Co. Virginia a short
 time ago at the age of 114 yrs 11 mo's and 12 days.

Wingfield, Mr John   "Payson"   Jan 15, 1880
 Died- on January 7th, a child of Mr John Wingfield. Buried on the 8th.

Wingfield, John   "Death"   Jan 3, 1884
 see Stewart, Mrs

Winklejohann, August   "Death in Quincy"   Apr 20, 1899
 Died- August Winklejohann at his home Tuesday eve of la grippe.
 Leaves 3 sons and 1 daughter. Born Hanover, Germany 1836. Came to U.S.
 in 1853.

Winklemann, Robert   "Death in Quincy"   Mar 9, 1899
 Died- Mr Robert Winklemann March 1st. Not quite 25 yrs old. Survived
 by his wife, 5 brothers and 3 sisters.

Winn, Mrs Annie   "Obituary"   Mar 17, 1898
 see Nedrow, Mrs Eliza

Winn, Mrs Florence   "Death in Quincy"   Mar 23, 1899
 Died- Mrs Florence Winn, late of Center, Mo. at St Mary's hospital
 Monday. 30 yrs old.

Winters, Mr Sebastian   "Local"   Sep 21, 1887
 Mr Sebastian Winters a molder by trade had both legs cut off by a train
 in Quincy and died shortly. He was 50 yrs old. Leaves a wife and 8
 children.

Wipprecht, Mr and Mrs A. "Obituary"   Jun 27, 1889
 see Claypool. Mrs Amelia C.

Wipprecht, Amelia C.   "Obituary"   Jun 27, 1889
 see Claypool, Mrs Amelia C.

447

Wipprecht, Lillie   Dec 22, 1881
    Died- Lillie, age 7 yrs on December 19th. Was daughter of A. and S.
    Wipprecht.

Wire, Miss Sarah   "Death"   Jul 24, 1884
    see Bryant, Mrs Ike

Wise, T.J.   Jun 4, 1885
    T.J. Wise's grave decorated in Mendon cemetery Decoration Day.

Wise, Thomas   Jun 1, 1899
    Thomas Wise listed among civil war veterans graves decorated in
    Mendon cemetery Decoration Day.

Wise, Wm T.   "Local"   Nov 29, 1888
    Died- from a letter rec'd by Charles Nutt from Orlando Fletcher, of
    Wichita, the death of Wm T. Wise at 2 P.M. November 20th of typhoid
    fever and inflammation of the bowels. He was in the prime of manhood and
    his death comes as a shock to his many old time comrades in Mendon.

Wisehart, James   "Camp Point"   Feb 3, 1881
    James Wisehart, an old settler in Columbus twp died Saturday January
    29th. Age 69 yrs. His remains were interned Sunday in Pleasant View
    cemetery.

Wisner, Mrs Mary C.   "Obituary"   Feb 14, 1889
    see Powell, John Thomas

Witcomb, Jasper Esq.   "Payson"   Mar 26, 1885
    Jasper Witcomb Esq. died Feb 12th. He was kicked in the head by a horse
    which broke his skull. Resident of this community 40 yrs. Born 1807.
    Leaves wife and several children, all grown.

Witt, Billy   "Coatsburg"   Jan 22, 1885
    Uncle Billy Witt departed this life January 17th.

Witt, Mrs Geo.   "Local"   Mar 16, 1899
    Mrs Rachel McClung attended the funeral of Mrs Geo. Witt of Big Neck
    yesterday. March 23, 1899 correction, it was Mrs Sarah McClung NOT
    Rachel McClung.

Witt, Mrs Mary F.(Wm B.)   "Local"   Feb 23, 1893
    Died Mrs Mary F. Witt, of Big Neck, relict of the late Wm B. Witt died
    on Sunday morning after a long illness.

Witt, Philip W.   "Hangs Self"   Mar 9, 1904
    Philip W. Witt a farmer living about 4½ miles southeast of Loraine
    committed suicide Thursday afternoon by hanging himself in the barn
    about 4 P.M. Leaves wife and only daughter about 8 yrs old. Mr Witt was
    adjudged insane by his own request and sent to Jacksonville for a month
    and discharged as cured. He was a cousin of William ans Samuel Witt, live-
    stock dealers. also survived by 3 sons. All children living at home, also
    a brother Joel in Oklahoma and a sister, Mrs Eckels of Lewiston, Mo.
    Wife was the former Miss Buckingham of Burton. Funeral by Rev Haskell of
    Fort Madison, Iowa at York Neck church Saturday at 10:30 A.M. "Herald"

Witt, Mr Samuel   "Local"   Jul 5, 1894
    Mr Samuel Witt, a well known resident of Big Neck died Wednesday eve.

Witt, Samuel R.   "Local"   Jul 5, 1894
    The will of the late Samuel R. Witt of Keene twp who died June 27th
    was admitted to probate Saturday. He leaves all of his estate to his wife
    for her use for life. at her death 300.00 is to be given to Salena Herring-
    300.00 to Samuel Witt Jr.- 300.00 to Alpha Witt and 100.00 to Albert
    Downing. The rest divided between testator's brothers ans sisters. The
    will made March 28, 1893 with J.B. Thomas, W.E. Ellis and H.H. Emminga
    as witnesses.

Witt, Mrs Samuel   "Obituary"   Nov 30, 1899
    see Hardy, Joseph Patterson

Witt, Mrs Sarah   "Death"   Mar 16, 1899
    Died- Mrs Sarah Witt, widow of the late Geo. Witt of Big Neck
    Monday night of congestion of the brain. Was mother of the 2 boys known
    as the Witt Bros. the large stock buyers and dealers of Big Neck.
    70 yrs old. Survived by 3 sons and 1 daughter. 1 son is in the
    klondyke and Miss Della in California. Buried Ebenezer cemetery.

Witt, Willaim B.   "Obituary"   Mar 2, 1893
    see James, Mary F.

Witt, Wm   "York Neck"   Nov 25, 1885
    Mr Bagby, son-in-law of Wm Witt, deceased has returned to Big Neck to
    live.

Wittler, Frank and Mrs Minnie "Death in Adams Co."   Mar 16, 1899
    Died- Mrs Minnie Wittler Friday A.M. Son Frank age 23 yrs died day before
    her. Funeral of mother and son were held together. She was born
    Germany. Came to U.S. 1848 when she was 18 yrs old.

Witts, Wm   "Death"   Jul 24, 1879
    see Bagley, Charley

Wolbring, Mrs   "Local"   Feb 2, 1888
    Died- Mrs Wolbring, whose sickness we feferred to last week died on
    Saturday afternoon of pueperal fever. Age 41 yrs. Buried in Quincy in
    the new German cemetery on Tuesday. Leaves husband and 11 children.

Wolfe, Mrs Amanda   "Local"   Jan 10, 1901
    Mrs Amanda Wolfe age 79 yrs died at her home in Liberty twp Saturday
    night. Leaves a husband and 6 children. Resided in Adams Co. 67 yrs.

Wollert, Mrs Julia Ann   "Death in Quincy"   Mar 30, 1899
    Died- Mrs Julia Ann Wollert March 22nd of heart disease.

Wood, Mrs Dr   "Death"   Mar 11, 1880
    see Shepherd, Dr

Wood, Gov.   "Obituary"   Dec 1, 1898
    see Stone, Elbridge K.

Wood, Mrs Governor   "Local"   Jan 19, 1887
    Mrs Governor Wood is reported lying at the point of death at the home
    of her sister, Mrs E.K. Stone.

Wood, Benjamin Harrison   "Local"   Jan 10, 1889
    Died- Saturday January 5th Benjamin Harrison Wood, infant son of Mr and
    Mrs Charled Wood, of Ellington. Funeral at Wesley Chapel on Monday by
    Rev R.P. Droke.

Wood, Mrs C.H.   "Ursa"   Dec 30, 1885
    Mrs C.H. Wood died Sunday morning. Funeral services at Wesley Chapel
    Tuesday afternoon by Mr Woodworth. The death of Mr Wood occurung as it
    did so shortly after that of her son is peculiarly sad. Leaves a family
    of 5 children.

Wood, Charles   "Local"   Feb 10, 1898
    Died- Chalres Wood of Ellington, west of Bloomfield this A.M. of
    consumption.

Wood, Francis J.   "Obituary"   Sep 15, 1898
    see Nichols, Mrs Jane

Wood, Mr Henry   "Obituary"   Oct 2, 1879
    Died- at his home near Marcelline, Ill September 23, 1879. Born
    October 24, 1802 in the district of Spartensburg, S.C. Married in 1824
    to Miss Sarah Alverson. In 1827 they moved to Ralls Co. Mo. and in 1827
    to Adams Co., Illinois where they lived since. He was made an Odd Fellow
    August 29, 1853 in Marcelline Lodge #127 Buried in Keath cemetery
    on September 24th.

Wood, Henry and Sarah   "Obituary"   Sep 15, 1898
    see Nichols, Mrs Jane

Wood, James   "Lima"   Nov 9, 1893
    Died- a 1 yr old child of James Wood last week of pneumonia and
    whooping cough.

Wood, John   Nov 28, 1889
    John Wood, son of ex-goernor, John Wood, the founder of Quincy and
    59 yrs old was found near his wife's grave after shooting himself in the
    temple. He was married 1st in 1854 to Josephine Skinner and they had
    3 children, John Woods, Mrs George Mills and ? After his 1st wife's death
    he married her sister, Mary Skinner in 1885. He died November 23, 1889

Wood, Lewis E.   "Local"   Jan 23, 1902
    Louis E. Wood, attempted suicide at Quincy last Friday. He is a son of
    the late Charles Wood of Ellington twp. (2 miles west of Bloomfield)
    Graduated Mendon high school about 3 yrs ago and taught school for 2
    yrs at Rocky Rill school house 2 miles east of Mendon. Last May he went
    to Oklahoma. Returned about December 1st. Will recover.

Wood, Lewis E.   "Obituary"   Feb 6, 1902
  Died- Lewis E. Wood, born Ellington twp Feb 22, 1879 and died in
  St Mary's hospital at Quincy, Illinois January 31st 1902 at age 22 yrs
  11 mo's 9 days. Death from pneumonia caused by bullet wound infliced
  by his own hand. Leaves 4 brothers, Abe, Ed, Enoch and Isaac, a step-
  mother and a half brother, 2 half sisters. Went to Oklahoma for his
  health last May, but returned discouraged 2 weeks before Xmas. Services
  at his late home Sunday 2 P.M. by Rev Wakefield. Buried Wesley Chapel
  cemetery.

Wood, Lewis   "Local"   Feb 13, 1902
  Will of Lewis E. Wood was filed for probate today dated Jan 18th and
  wittnessed by Sam Woods, Dr John A. Koch and Frank Daughterty. Leaves
  100.00 each to brothers Samuel, Abraham and Enoch. Provides for the sale
  of property in Oklahoma with proceeds to go to Samuel and Enoch.
  Property in Dakota goes to Isaac Wood who is also named Executor.

Wood, Mrs Sarah   "Death"   Mar 22, 1905
  Mrs Sarah Wood, wife of Isaac Wood died about 1:30 A.M. Wednesday
  March 15th at her home 8½ miles northeast of the city in Mendon twp
  from pneumonia. Leaves 2 little children, a boy and a girl ages 3 and 1
  resp. She was daughter of Francis Daugherty of Bloomfield and a member
  of the Bloomfield Catholic church. Was born in Adams Co. where she always
  lived. Born in Bloomfield/ Would have been 28 yrs old On November 6th.
  Leaves husband, 2 children, father, 5 brothers, and 3 sisters. Brothers
  are Tom, James, Edward and Leo Daugherty of Adams Co. and Frank of Iowa.
  Sisters are Mrs Mary Furry of Mendon and Misses Annie and Maggie Daugherty
  of Bloomfield. "Quincy Journal"

Wood, Sarah   "Probate"   Aug 1, 1889
  Probate notice of Sarah Wood 1st Monday of October 1889
  Lewis W. Nichols, Adm.

Wood, U.U.   "News"   Oct 8, 1885
  Mr U.U. Wood committed suicide at the Way House September 30th. He
  was son of Charles Wood, a prominent and wealthy farmer of Ellington
  twp. Burial Ellington cemetery.

Woodburn, Mrs Mary   "Local"   May 26, 1898
  Died- Mrs Mary Woodburn at Dennison, Ohio Tuesday May 17th. 64 yrs old
  Was daughter of Michael Rawlings formerly of this neighborhood.

Woodbury, Jerome   "Fowler"   Jun 4, 1880
  Died- Jerome Woodbury.

Woodbury, Mrs Mary   "Obituary"   Feb 10, 1898
  see Rawlings, Sarah Jane

Woodruff, Mrs   "Local"   Aug 11, 1886
  Died- Mrs Woodruff of Honey Creek while on her way home with her son.
  Her remains are in Mendon at the home of her daughter, Mrs Alex Devore.

Woodruff, Charles Edwin   "Obituary"   Sep 7, 1904
    Charles Edwin Woodruff, born in Honey Creek twp August 13th 1860 and
    died September 3rd 1904. 44 yrs 21 days old. Leaves 3 sisters, Mrs Jane
    Rossiter of Missouri, Mrs Ellen Leckbee, of Mendon and Mrs Cordelia
    Devore of Honey Creek. His parents and 3 sisters died before him
    several yrs ago. Funeral by Rev S.R. Reno of the Mendon Methodist church
    at home of Alex Devore. Buried Mendon cemetery.

Woodruff, Freeman   "Ursa"   Jan 18, 1905
    Death has taken one of Ursa's oldest citizens, Freeman Woodruff.
    Served in our late war as Lieut. in the 78th Reg Ill. Inf. 84 yrs old.
    Leaves wife, 2 sons and 3 daughters.

Woodruff, James   "Local"   Jan 18, 1905
    Died- James Woodruff, a pioneer citizen of Quincy at his home Thursday
    night. He was provost marshall of the 4th congeessional district 1863
    and in 1867 In Company with F. Boyd founded the paper mill in Quincy.
    84 yrs old. Leaves wife and 3 sons.

Woodruff, William   "Ursa"   Dec 7, 1877
    William Woodruff, a young man of this place was accidently shot Wednesday.
    Died 2 days later. Remains were taken to the residence of his father,
    Freeman Woodruff and buried Sunday in the family graveyard. Services by
    Elder Tandy.

Woods, Mrs   "Local"   Feb 14, 1889
    News from Loraine of the death of Mrs Woods on Saturday. Buried on
    Monday. Her daughter, Mrs Clark Clair of Missouri returned in time to
    see her alive.

Woods, Grandma   "Loraine"   Feb 7, 1889
    Died- Grandma Woods Sunday of lung fever. Buried in Curless cemetery
    in Big Neck.

Woods, Mrs Barbary   "Death"   May 18, 1904
    see Payne, Miss Catherine Ann

Woods, Mr Harry   "Marcelline"   Sep 25, 1879
    Mr Harry Woods is very ill. LATER_ Mr Harry Woods died at 12 last night.
    He was one of the oldest citizens here. Came here 50 yrs ago and was a
    member of the fraternity IOOF. Services at his home tomorrow.

Woods, Mrs Ike   "Local"   Mar 22, 1905
    Frank Daugherty was called here by the death of his sister, Mrs Ike Woods.
    He returned to his home at Fort Madison, Iowa Monday.

Woods, Mrs James   "Loraine"   Jun 2, 1886
    Mrs James woods died last Sunday and was buried in Reece cemetery Mon.
    Mr Lee Woods is in critical condition.

452

Woods, Mrs Laurie (Alva)   "Loraine"   Dec 6, 1894
    Died- Wednesday morning at the home of her father, Hiram Steiner, Mrs
    Laurie Woods, of typhoid fever. Age 21 yrs. Sick 6 weeks. She married
    Mr Alva Woods only a few mo's ago. Funeral by Elder W.E. Rose at the
    Green Grove church Thursday at 11 A.M. Buried in the Brinnamon grave-
    yard near the Co. line. Mr and Mrs S. have another daughter who is sick with
    lung fever.

Woods, Edna A.   "Local"   Dec 4, 1890
    Died- November 26th, little Edna A. only child of Mr and Mrs Leander
    Woods of Keene twp. Mothers name was Lizzie Gibson. Age 5 mo's.
    Buried Reece cemetery.

Woods, Mrs Samuel   Oct 1, 1885
    "Clips from the Camp Point Journal" Mrs Samuel Woods died at her home
    in Houston twp. Had been confined to her bed since the death of her
    husband last July. She came to her present home with her husband 50 yrs
    ago and reared a large family. Funeral at Ebenezer church Wednesday.

Woods, Thomas   "Carman, Ill."   Jun 28, 1883
    Thomas Woods killed by lightning June 15th. Leaves widowed mother.

Woodworth, Mr and Mrs Charles   "Tioga"   Jun 11, 1891
    Died- May 30th the infant child of Mr and Mrs Chalres Woodworth.

Woodworth, Rev Richard   "Ellington"   Jul 31, 1890
    Rev Richard Woodworth died July 12th at his home in Salem, Mich.
    Age 65 yrs.

Wooters, Mr E.M.   "Personal"   Oct 23, 1879
    Mr E.M. Wooters died in Quincy last Sunday.

Workes, Miss Lillian   "Obituary"   Jan 29, 1903
    see Robertson, James F.

Workman, Mrs   "Death"   Jan 12, 1893
    see Hynes, Mr

Workman, Lewis   "Marcelline"   Jul 16, 1903
    Mr Lewis Workman died at his home north of town July 10th.

Workman, Lewis   "Death"   Oct 2, 1884
    see Hines, Archibald

Workman, Miss Lunda   "Death"   May 3, 1905
    see McKinney, J.W.

Workman, Aunt Phebe   "Local"   Jan 31, 1889
    Died- Aunt Phebe Workman, an aged lady who lived north of Bear Creek
    on the Warsaw road Sunday between 8 and 9 P.M. Buried in Workman cemetery
    on Tuesday.

Workman, Mr Thomas   "Marcelline"   Mar 20, 1902
     Sudden death of Mr Thomas Workman, one of our early settlers, last
     Thursday March 13th at his daughter's house, Mrs Georgiana Beatty. Leaves
     1 daughter and 2 sons. Funeral from Marcelline church Saturday. Buried
     Stone cemetery.

Worley, Dr   "Ursa"   Jan 24, 1901
     Died- Dr Worley at 7 A.M. today. Funeral tomorrow at 2 P.M.

Worley, Katie   "Death"   Apr 5, 1905
     see Tucker, Mrs Katie

Worley, Mr W.F.   "Died"   Jan 29, 1880
     Died- Mr W.F. Worley Esq. of Ursa Friday morning January 23rd of
     pneumonia. He was probably the oldest native citizen of the county.
     Born in what is now Ursa twp December 26th 1829. Joined the Christian
     church about 25 yrs ago. Was Justice of Peace at the time of his death.

Worley, W.L.   "Death"   Apr 5, 1905
     see Tucker, Mrs Katie

Worman, Mrs Ettie   "Obituary"   Mar 16, 1904
     see Thayer, Charles

Worman, Mrs Ettie   "Obituary"   Oct 29, 1903
     see Tomlinson, Alice Jane

Worman, Ida   "Obituary"   Jul 6, 1904
     see Green, Mary Ann

Worman, Jesse Clarence   "In Memoriam"   May 21, 1903
     Jesse Clarence Worman, 2nd son of Wm H. and Sarah E. Worman was born
     Keene twp Adams Co. Illinois September 15th 1878 in which place he lived
     until his death May 15th 1903. Age 24 yrs 8 mo's. Leaves father, mother,
     2 brothers and a sister. April 4th he took measles and week later
     pneumonia and then blood poison set in. Services by Rev S.R. Reno of Mendon
     M.E. church. Buried Mendon cemetery.

Worman, John   "Obituary"   Oct 13, 1894
     Capt John Worman died at Soldiers Home on Thursday afternoon October
     11th. Remains brought home next day and funeral Saturday P.M. at the house
     by Rev Wm Burgess after which the corspe was taken over by the Masons of
     which he was a member. John Worman bron in Westmoreland Co. Penn 1829.
     Came to Mendon __?__ Here he married Mary Ann Rice July 15, 1851.
     They had 9 children (4 boys and 5 girls) 6 are still living. (3 girls
     and 3 boys) 2 brothers also survive him, William who lives in Keene
     twp and Dan in Minnesota. He also leaves a wife. Mr Worman enlisted in
     Co. A. 50th Regt Ill. Vol. as a private on August 20, 1861. Made 2nd
     Sergt and in April 1862 orderly Sergt. In May 1863 he was elected 2nd
     Lieut. on September 1864 on Capt Cramer resigning from service he became
     Capt."On Sherman's march to the sea". He acted as quartermaster of the
     Regt until the 50th was mustered out at Louisville, Ky.

Worman, John S.   Jun 5, 1902
     John S. Worman includedin list of Soldiers buried Mendon cemetery.

Worman, Mrs John   "Fowler"   Apr 16, 1903
    Mrs John Worman was called to Tioga Thursday by the news of her father's
    illness. She could not reach his bedside in time to see him alive as he
    died Thursday night. Mr and Mrs Worman returned home Saturday.

Worman, Mrs Mary(John)   "Obituary"   Jul 13, 1899
    Died- Mrs Mary Worman, Born August 30th 1839 in Lancaster Co. Penn
    Came to Illinois with her parents 1847. Lived Adams Co. 49 yrs. Married
    John Worman better known as Capt Worman. Had 6 children (3 sons and
    3 daughters) Died at York Nebr. July 10th at 11 P.M. 59 yrs 11 mo's
    20 days old. Joined Salem Lutheran church at Mendon Nov 20th 1853. Was
    member of Eastern Star of Mendon. Mrs Stella Worman Gill accompanied
    the remains here for burial. She and her brother John of this twp were
    the only children present for the funeral. Services at the Lutheran
    church at 4 P.M. yesterday by Rev Spires. Buried beside her husband in
    Mendon cemetery.

Worman, Mrs Mary (Michael)   "Obituary"   Sep 12, 1901
    see Dudley, James H.

Worman, Mary E.   "Obituary"   Apr 25, 1889
    Died- Mary E. Worman April 20th at age 49 yrs 9 mo's 25 days after a
    lingering illness of 9 yrs during a part of which time she was quite
    hepless. All that could be done to alleviate her suffering was done by
    the devotion of her husband and daughter. Mrs Worman was eldest daughter of
    Mr and Mrs Jas. Dudley and was born near Mendon July 5, 1839. She
    married Michael Worman November 11th 1859 to whom she bore 2 children,
    1 son and 1 daughter. Her remains were laid to rest in Mendon cemetery
    Sunday afternoon. Services held at the home of the late deceased near
    Elm Grove, the Rev Noah Stahl, assisted by Rev King of Lomax, officating.

Worman, Michael   "Death"   Nov 14, 1901
    Died- Michael Worman of heart trouble last Saturday at 3 P.M. Funeral
    Monday the 11th at his home at 2 P.M. by Rev J.S. Bayne. Born Mt Pleasant,
    Westmoreland Co. Penn October 16, 1836 and died November 9th 1901.
    65 yrs 23 days old. Came with his family to Illinois in fall of 1851 and
    located 2½ miles south of Mendon where he lived till fall of 1900. Since
    then he has lived in Mendon. November 11, 1859 he married Mary E. Dudley,
    daughter of the late James H. Dudley. They had 2 children, Clifton and
    Flora. His wife and son preceeded him in death. In early life he was
    connected to the United Brethern in Christ. Buried in Mendon cemetery
    beside his beloved wife.

Worman, Michael   Nov 14, 1901
    see Stahl, Mr and Mrs John

Worman, Moses G.   "Local"   May 24, 1888
    In probate court Friday the last will of Moses G. Worman was filed and
    proved by John Stewart and John H. Meyers. The deceased left his wife the
    homestead, also 20 acres, and all personal property during her life time.
    At her death the homestead is to go to John Worman and all personal
    property to be devided among the children, DeWitt Worman and George H.
    Worman were appointed Executors. DeWitt Worman filed his bond as one of
    the Executors. "Herald"

Worman, Moses   "Obituary"   May 17, 1888
    Mr Moses Worman died on Friday May 11th shortly afternoon at his home
    in the southeast part of the twp, age 65 yrs 1 day old. Mr Worman had
    been failing for some time. About a yr ago he had an atteck of paralysis
    from which he never fully recovered, but his final illness was of short
    duration, lasting only 2 days. His remains were intened on Sunday after-
    noon in the Myers cemetery, on the Fowler road. Services by Rev King of
    Lomax. He came from Westmoreland Co. Penn about 43 yrs ago. to the twp
    where he continued to live ever since. Leaves widow and 10 children
    (3 girls and 7 Boys) All of whom except 2 sons living in Nebr were present
    at the funeral

Worman, Moses G.   "Elm Grove"   May 24, 1888
    Mrs Kate Frost of Southwest Missouri, Mrs Sabie Beerer , of Chicago
    and Henry Worman of El Dorado, Kansas attended the funeral of their father,
    Moses G. Worman.

Worman, Moses G.   "Elm Grove"   May 24, 1888
    Moses G. Worman died Friday afternoon May 11th at his home. Age 65 yrs
    6 mo's 1 day. Buried in Meyers cemetery. Mr Worman was well known and
    his funeral was the largest ever attended in this part of the country.

Worman, Mrs Nancy   "Elm Grove"   Nov 1, 1900
    Mrs Nancy Worman returned home Saturday from Chicago where she was for
    2 weeks at the bedside of her sick daughter, Mrs J.S. Berer.Mrs B.
    was the former Saba Worman. She died Sunday October 21st from Asthma and
    heart trouble. Leaves husband and 5 children.

Worman, Mrs Nancy   "Obituary"   Apr 20, 1899
    see Myers, Mrs Anna Tinsman

Worman, Mrs Polly   "Obituary"   Apr 20, 1899
    see Myers, Mrs Anna Tinsman

Worman, Saba   Nov 1, 1900
    see Worman, Mrs Nancy

Worrell, Lishia   Apr 27, 1882
    Old Lishia Worrell was found dead in bed April 16th.

Worrell, Maggie   "Bowen"   Jan 16, 1879
    The funeral of Miss Maggie Worrell was at the Cong'l church on Saturday
    January 4th by Rev McConnahue. She died of consumption January 3rd.

Wray, Miss Margaret   "Died"   Jan 11, 1905
    Died- Miss Margaret Wray, a high school student, the daughter of Mrs
    Margaret and the late Thomas Wray at 3 A.M. Saturday at the family home,
    2030 Hampshire St Quincy. Was 18 yrs old. Born Adams Co. Family lived
    on a farm near Ursa till a yr ago when the widowed mother and children
    moved to Quincy. Leaves mother and 2 sisters.   "Quincy Herald"

Wray, Mr Thomas   "Ellington"   Sep 3, 1885
    Mr Thomas Wray was buried August 27th at the Presby' church by Rev Weir.

Wren, Mr Nicholas   "Local"   Sep 26, 1901
   Died- Mr Nicholas Wren, an old citizen of Ursa Monday. Nearly 81 yrs old.
   Was charter member of the Marcelline Lodge I.O.O.F. Services at the
   Ursa Christian church yesterday A.M. Buried in the Stone church cemtery.
   Charles H. Nutt was undertaker.

Wright, Mrs   "Local"   Feb 19, 1885
   Mrs Wright of Honey Creek, mother in law of Jas. P. Slonigar died Sunday
   at the home of her son J.Q. Wright. Age 84 yrs. Buried at the Flack
   cemetery. We are told that Mrs Wright and her husband who died a few
   yrs ago were originally from England.

Wright, Mrs   "Obituary"   Mar 21, 1901
   see Nutt, Daniel

Wright, Abraham   "Obituary"   Oct 4, 1888
   Died- Thursday morning September 27th at the age of 80 yrs, Mr
   Abraham Wright of this twp. Born in Oxfordshire, England. Married there
   to Miss Miriam Nutt, a sister of Daniel Nutt of this place by whom he
   had 1 child. The late Daniel Nutt died in the fall of 1876 and Mrs Wright
   the following spring. Mr Wright's daughter in law Paulline Wright has taken
   care of his house since. Services at the Wright home Friday A.M. by Rev
   S.D. Peet. Buried Mendon cemetery. Mr and Mrs Wright came to America in
   1842 and 1st settled in Ohio. Came to Illinois 2 yrs later and bought
   80 acres of unclaimed land southwest of Mendon where they continued to
   live till now. He paid 1.25 per acre for the land.

Wright, Abram   "Probate"   Nov 1, 1888
   Probate notice of Abram Wright, deceased   1st Monday of January 1889
   Paulina A. Wright, Ex.

Wright, Albert   May 5, 1898
   Died- Albert Wright born November 27th 1825 in Prince William Co.
   Virginia and died in Argonia, Kansas Friday A.M. April 29th. Was the
   eldest of 14 children. 4 survive him. Came to Adams Co. in 1848 and
   1 yr later he married Emma J. Miller. They had 6 children all but 1
   living. Charles living in Arizona, 1 daughter in Parker, Kansas,
Charles W. Wright and Mrs C.W. Pepple living in Mendon. (2 Charles)

Wright, Alex   "Loraine"   May 5, 1886
   Alex Wright died Sunday A.M. April 26th. 22 yrs old. Son of John Q.
   Wright of Honey Creek. He had lung fever only 5 days. Uncle John Curless
   conducted the funeral Monday A.M. at the house of young Wright's uncle
   where he died. Buried beside his mother in our cemetery.

Wright, Miss Alice   Jan 18, 1878
   Died- Monday A.M. January 14th, Miss Alice, eldest daughter of John H.
   Wright. Age 18 yrs. Member of the M.E. church for 3 yrs. Services by Rev
   V.C. Randolph.

Wright, Mr and Mrs Charles   "Local"   Sep 14, 1887
   Infant child of Mr and Mrs Charles Wright died. Buried in Mendon cemetery.
   It was born on September 4th.
   CORRECTION   Sep 21, 1887
   Mr and Mrs Charles Wright's baby was buried in Keith graveyard near
   Marcelline and NOT Mendon cemetery as reported.

457

Wright, Mr and Mrs Charles   "Moved remains"   Oct 29, 1891
    see Cort, Peter

Wright, Dan'l   "Local"   Oct 20, 1892
    Dan'l Wright of Loraine was thrown off the train car near Stillwell
    Saturday night and killed. Buried Mendon cemetery on Monday. Leaves wife
    and 3 children.
    Paper says 3 children and Dan'l-- see David Wright also.

Wright, Mr David   "Loraine"   Oct 20, 1892
    Died- Mr David Wright last Sunday afternoon. Services at the M.E. church
    at 1:30 P.M. Monday after which the remains were taken to Mendon for
    burial. Leaves wife and 4 children.
    Paper says David and 4 children. see Dan'l Wright also.

Wright, David   "Payson"   Feb 6, 1879
    Last Tuesday Mr David Wright buried one of his children.

Wright, David   Jun 5, 1902
    David Wright included in list of soldiers buried in Mendon cemetery.

Wright, Mr Decatur   "Lima"   Mar 20, 1884
    Mr Decatur Wright is in town after an absence of 40 yrs to visit his
    mothers grave and erect a monument. Her grave was the second one in the
    Lima Cemetery.

Wright, Mr and Mrs Geo.   "Card of Thanks"   Sep 4, 1902
    We desire to express our heartfelt thanks to our neighbors and friends
    who so kindly assisted us during the sickness and burial of our youngest
    son. signed, Mr and Mrs Geo. Wright.

Wright, Henry   "Local"   Mar 9, 1904
    Fred Wright left Tuesday for Quincy to attend the funeral of his brother
    Henry, who died in that city from paralysis. Was 40 yrs old. Leaves wife
    3 sisters and brother Fred.

Wright, Henry   "Local"   Mar 16, 1904
    Mrs Alice Jones went to Quincy Thursday last to attend the funeral of
    her brother, Henry Wright.

Wright, J.C.   "Payson"   Apr 19, 1888
    Died- last week, Mr J.C. Wright an old citizen who helped lay out the
    town.

Wright, John   Jun 4, 1885
    John Wright included in list of soldiers buried Mendon.

Wright, John   "Local"   Nov 16, 1887
    News rec'd by Mr J.H. Bray Thursday A.M. of the death from typhoid fever
    at Leoti, Kansas of his son in law, Mr John Wright age 27 yrs 8 mo's 7 days
    John was a Mendon boy and the oldest son of Mr Nehemiah and Elizabeth
    Wright. Leaves wife and 2 infant children. Funeral Friday.

Wright, John F.   "Local"   Aug 23, 1905
    John F. Wright, the 14 yr old son of Matthew Wright, a Burlington
    engineer, was drowned Sunday afternoon in the Quincy Bay near the
    mouth of Cedar Creek.

Wright, Lavina L.   "Local"   Dec 31, 1903
    Bond was filed in the sum of 400.00 by J.M. Daughtery as Adm. of the
    estate of Lavina L. Wright.

Wright, Mrs Lavina   "Death"   Mar 9, 1887
    see Inman, Mr Daniel

Wright, Levi   "Obituary"   Nov 19, 1903
    see Inman, Lavina J.

Wright, Milton Cort   "Obituary"   Dec 28, 1899
    Died- Milton Cort Wright, youngest son of Mr and Mrs Charles Wright.
    Born July 7, 1897 and died December 21st 1899. Age 2 yrs 5 mo's 14 days.

Wright, Mr and Mrs Nehemiah   "Burial"   Mar 30, 1893
    see Gardner, Mrs Julia

Wright, Pauline Ann   May 18, 1904
    see Moore, Annice S.

Wright, Paulina Ann   "Executor Sale"   May 3, 1894
    see Johnson, John H.

Wright, Mrs Phebe   "Obituary"   Nov 8, 1900
    Died- Mrs Phebe Wright. Born October 5, 1815 at Milton, England in the
    Parish of Atterbury, Co. of Oxford and died at her home near Mendon
    November 3rd 1900 at the age of 85 yrs 28 days. Married John Wright in
    1837 at Salem Ohio. They had 6 children. 4 still living, David and Wm of
    Texas, Rufus living near Mendon and Mrs Adeline Inman of near Ursa. Susan
    and Edwin are both dead. She joined the Baptist church in Salem, Ohio
    in 1844. Was a sister of Mr Daniel Nutt of Mendon. Services at the house
    Monday A.M. by Rev N.W. Lilly. Buried Mendon cemetery. Pallbearers were;
    Jacob Funk, Richard Flack, D.W. Worman, Wm Rowbotham, T.J. Gilliland
    and Henry Shafer.

Wright, Rufus Mrs   "Death"   Jun 7, 1894
    Died- Mrs Rufus Wright Sunday at 12:30 P.M. at the age of 38 yrs 6 mo's
    Services Monday eve by Rev D.A. Shelter of Quincy in the Lutheran church.
    Buried in Mendon cemetery. She was the eldest daughter of Mr and Mrs
    Jesse Dick who for 40 yrs were a resident of this twp, but now of Knox
    City, Missouri. She leaves husband and 3 young daughters from 8 to 13 yrs.
    Her father and mother, 4 brothers and 1 sister also survive her. She was
    a member of the Lutheran church since 1890.

Wright, Mr and Mrs Rufus   "Local"   May 17, 1894
    Born, a child was born to Mr and Mrs Rufus Wright Saturday eve. Died and
    was buried in Mendon cemetery Sunday afternoon.

Wright, Samuel R.   Oct 23, 1890
    Samuel R. Wright died October 18th. He lived at LeBelle, Mo. Was the son
    in law of George Rust. Leaves wife and 1 child.

459

Wright, Miss Susan see Furry, Henry	"Obituary"	Feb 28, 1889
Wright, Wallace see Gardner, Mrs Julia	"Obituary"	Mar 30, 1893
Wright, Mrs Wallace see Wilcox, Mrs Jane	"Obituary"	Dec 22, 1898
Wright, Mrs Wallace see Wilcox, Morton Robert	"Death"	May 17, 1905
Wright, Mrs William see Brown, Dr George Lafayette	"Obituary"	Aug 24, 1904

Wyatt, Thomas   Jun 5, 1902
   Thomas Wyatt included in list of Civil War soldiers buried Mendon.

Wyatt, Thomas   "Obituary"   Sep 14, 1899
   Died- Thomas Wyatt. Born England September 1828 and died Mendon September
   9th 1899. Married Elizabeth Cherry March 1854 who died January 19, 1889.
   They had 5 children, Anna who died in her youth, Wm, Sarah, George and John
   all live here except Geo. who lives Muscatine, Iowa. Mr Wright came to
   U.S. 1855 and laways lived in or near Mendon.Enlisted in the 155th Ill.
   Reg. Member of the Cong'l church. Services at the home Sunday at 1:30
   by Rev J.S. Bayne, pastor of the Cong'l church. Buried in Mendon cemetery
   beside his wife.

Wyatt, Mrs Thomas   "Obituary"   Jan 24, 1889
   Died- Mrs Thomas Wyatt died Monday January 21st at 6:30 P.M. She had
   been an invalid for the past 10 or 11 yrs and bedfast 2 or 3 yrs. Was
   the daughter of the late Wm Cherry formerly of this twp and was born
   in Marstens, St Lawrence, Northamptonshire, England March 28, 1825 and
   died at the age of 63 yrs 9 mo's 23 days. Married March 1854 and came to
   this country the following yr and settled in Mendon. They had 5 children
   2 boys and 3 girls, all of whom except the 1st born survive her. Funeral
   on Wednesday the 23rd at the Cong'l church by Rev S.D. Peet, pastor.
   Buried in Mendon cemetery.

Wyatt, Wm   "Killed"   Sep 1, 1898
   see Young, John (both killed in train accident)

Wynn, Mrs   "Death"   Aug 30, 1888
   see McCully, Henderson

Yancey, Mr   Jul 14, 1881
   Died last week, Mr Yancey, of Hannibal, Mo. Father of Dr Yancey of Camp
   Point.

Yates, Mr   Jun 28, 1883
   Mr Yates of Hancock Co., one of it's oldest residents died June 25th.

Yates, Arthur   "Local"   May 3, 1888
   Died- Arthur Yates of Carthage, Ill. of hydrophobia Monday morning.

Yeargen, Steven   "Columbus"   Jul 14, 1886
   Died- Funeral services of Steven Yeargen were held at Mt Pleasant church
   Sunday. Mr Y. owned an orange grove in Florida, but had been traveling.
   remains forwarded to this place.

Yeargain, Mrs John P.   "Death"   Apr 20, 1899
   "Death in Adams Co., this twp." Died- Mrs John P Yeargain Saturday
   night at the old homestead in Gilmer twp. Was daughter of John Lawless.
   Born Grant Co. Ky. December 14th, 1825. Leaves 2 daughters and 2 sons.

Yeargain, Milton   "Paloma"   Feb 14, 1889
   Died- the youngest daughter of Milton yeargain Sunday of heart disease.

Yeargain, Milton M.   "Vital records"   Dec 20, 1900
   see Chittenden, Abraham

Yeargain, Mrs Milton   "Paloma"   Jan 18, 1900
   The funeral of Mrs Milton Yeargain was at the Mt Pleasant church south
   of here last Thursady afternoon by Rev A.M. Danley of Chaddock College.

Yengland, Old Mrs   "Payson"   May 26, 1881
   Old Mrs Yengland was buried at Craigtown May 22nd.

Yenter, George A.   "Loraine"   Jul 17, 1879
   George A. Yenter was called away by the death of his brother's wife at
   Bowen.

Yenter, Mrs Lou   "Obituary"   Jul 18, 1901
   see Kennedy, Geo. Thomas

Yoe, Everett   "Lima"   Mar 24, 1886
   Everett Yoe an old citizen of this twp died Saturday morning the 20th.
   Leaves a wife and 4 children.

Yoe, W.B.   "Tioga"   Jul 12, 1900
   Died- W.B. Yoe, one of Tioga's oldest citizens died Wednesday June 27th
   74 yrs old. Survived by his wife and 3 children. Services at the M.E.
   Church Friday P.M. by Rev Whisnant. Buried village cemetery.

York, Mr and Mrs A.D.   "West Point"   May 8, 1884
   Died April 28th the little son of Mr and Mrs A.D. York. Buried Cook's
   graveyard.

York, Miss Fannie   "Local"   Jan 28, 1892
   Miss Fannie York, teacher of West Point public school died about 2
   weeks ago.

York, Mr Wm   "Tioga"   Aug 27, 1891
   Mr Wm York was buried in Tioga Friday last.

Yost, Mrs Emily   "Death in Quincy"   Apr 20, 1899
   Died- Mrs Emily Yost at the home of her parents Saturday A.M. of
   heart failure. Leaves 2 children.

Young, Dr   "Obituary"   Oct 9, 1884
    see Hughes, Miss Emma

Young, Dr and Mrs   "Obituary"   Aug 9, 1888
    see Bradley, Daniel Young

Young, Mrs Dr   "Obituary"   Oct 24, 1895
    see Miller, John

Young, Grandpa   "Personal"   Jan 8, 1880
    Died- Grandpa Young on Friday afternoon. Age nearly 88 yrs. He was a native
    of New Jersey, but at an early age settled in Butler Co. Ohio. Has lived
    several yrs now with his son Dr P. Young. Funeral Sunday.

Young, George W.   Nov 3, 1892
    Died- George W. Young at 2 P.M. Thursday October 27th. 68 hours after he
    rec'd the fatal shot at Abilene. Remains were brought here on Saturday A.M.
    and services held at his mother's in the P.M. by Rev Wm Burgess. Buried
    in Mendon cemetery. Bron July 1, 1858

Young, John   "Local'   Sep 1, 1898
    John Young of Paloma age 21 yrs and Wm Wyatt of Quincy age 48 yrs were
    killed by the C.B. and Q. frieght train #70 about 1:30 A.M. Sunday
    about 1 mile west of Coatsburg.

Young, John   Jun 5, 1902
    John Young included in list of Civil War soldiers buried Mendon cemetery.

Young, Laura   "Obituary"   Aug 2, 1905
    see Bradley, Daniel A.

Young, Lieut   Jun 4, 1885
    Lieut Young included in list of Soldier's honored Decoration Day.

Young, Louis   "Local"   Jun 28, 1905
    Died- Louis Young, a watch maker at Basco . Had come to Quincy to visit
    his mother because of his ill health and dropped dead at the train from
    heart failure. 34 yrs old. Leaves mother and brother.

Young, Peter   Jun 1, 1904
    Peter Young included in list of Mexican war soldiers buried in Mendon
    cemetery.

Young, Peter   "Probate"   Feb 12, 1891
    Probate Notice of Peter Young, deceased   1st Monday of April 1891
    Virginia C. Young and Chas. A. Chittenden, Adms.

Young, Dr Peter and Virginia C. "Obituary"   Aug 2, 1905
    see Bradley, Daniel A.

Young, Dr Peter   Jan 8, 1891
    Dr Peter Young died January 6th. Had a son George and a daughter, Mrs
    D.A. Bradley of Abilene, Kansas

Young, Dr Peter   Jan 15, 1891
    Died- January 6th Dr Peter Young. age 67 yrs. Born in Butler Co. Ohio
    December 11th 1823. Served in Mexican American war. Settled near Woodville
    Adams Co. Narried Mrs V.C. Miller. Came to Mendon January 1860. Leaves
    widow and 1 son, George W. of Abilene, Kansas and 2 daughters, Mrs D.A.
    Bradley of Abilene, Kansas and Mrs C.A. Chittenden of Mendon. Had 2
    brothers and 2 sisters. J.R. Young of Iola, Kansas was at the funeral
    January 9th. Services by Dr Peet of Cong'l church. Buried Mendon.

Young, Mrs Simon   "Obituary"   Apr 20, 1899
    see Myers, Mrs Anna Tinsman

Zahn, Rev Louis   "Local"   May 30, 1901
    Died- Rev Louis Zahn of St Jacobs church Quincy dropped dead Sunday P.M.
    48 yrs old. Leaves wife, father and an adopted child 7 yrs old.

Zanger, Moritz E.   "Death"   Mar 9, 1899
    Died- Moritz E. Zanger of Burton twp. 72 yrs old at his home March 2nd
    Lived on the home farm 40 yrs. Born Baden, Germany August 28, 1826.
    Leaves a wife, 1 son and 3 daughters.

Zern, Clara Belle   "Death"   Mar 9, 1904
    see Blazer, Rachel Louise

Zimmerman, Henry   "Obituary"   Dec 5, 1901
    Died- Henry Zimmerman of Mendon Thursday eve at his home 3 miles south-
    west of Mendon. Services at Lutheran church Sunday A.M. by Pastor
    Rev Booker. Buried Mendon cemetery. Born October 26, 1822 in Adams Co.
    Penn. near Emmitsburg, Md. Was 9th child of Joseph and Mary Weikart
    Zimmerman. Lost his father at an early age. 1892 he left Emmittsburg and
    went to Greenford, O. where he stayed till 1849 when he came to Mendon,
    Ill. Married April 1, 1845 to Miss Elizabeth Seabrooks who died in 1853,
    leaving him alone. On July 20, 1854 he married Miss Florence A.M. Seabrooks
    who survives him. Was father of 7 children. 4 survive him, Mrs H.K. Shaffer
    of Mendon, Mrs A. Schafer of Rossville, Ill., Mrs R.L. Scott and Mr
    U.L. Zimmerman of Mendon. In ealry life learned carpentering, but in
    1855 he bought a sawmill. Died November 28th 1901 at the age of 79 yrs
    1 mo. 2 days. He came to Mendon 52 yrs ago on Thanksgiving day.

Zimmerman, Henry   "Probate"   Dec 12, 1901
    Probate notice of Henry Zimmerman   1st Monday of Feb 1902
    Florence Zimmerman, Adm.

Zinn, E.D.   "Loraine"   Oct 6, 1886
    E.D. Zinn lost a son, aged about 10 yrs, Monday of typhoid fever.

Zoe, Miss Isora   "Local"   Jun 26, 1890
    Miss Isora Zoe was killed by lightning about 2 weeks ago near Tioga. Was
    half sister of Mrs Harry Houdyshell of Mendon.

Zopf, Adam   "Local"   Sep 15, 1892
    Killed, Adam Zopf & Thomas Owery, 2 farmers from near Marcelline were hit
    by a train and killed Wednesday night.

APPENDIX

Bradley, Daniel Arthur   "Obituary"   Aug 2, 1905
    We rec'd word Monday A.M. of death of Daniel Arthur Bradley at his
    home in McPherson, Kansas. He spent his first 30 yrs in Adams Co., Ill.
    and his family lived this vicinity for almost 75 yrs. Word came to his
    brother, Samuel H. Bradley and brother in law, Charles A. Chittenden.
    He died at 5 A.M. Monday from probable heart failure. Mrs Bradley will
    arrive Wednesday A.M. with the remains. Funeral Thursday. His grand-
    father and grandmother, Samuel and Elizabeth Bradley were members of
    the 35 persons who come west overland from East Haven, Conn. in 1831
    and settled 2 miles W. of what is now the town of Mendon. Their son
    Daniel was about 21 yrs old when they settled Adams Co.. He married
    Josephine Brown of Quincy and they had 7 children, Daniel A. being
    the youngest was born Mendon Feb. 26, 1855. Left of this family is
    Samuel H. and Miss Ellen Bradley of Mendon and Mrs Josephine Bradley
    Kimball, wife of E.S. Kimball of Galesburg. Moved to Wichita Co. Kan.
    near Leoti and helped establish the town. Later moved to Abilene
    and Peabody and 9 yrs ago to McPherson, Kansas. Was Deacon of the
    Mendon Congregational church. Also leave wife of about 29 yrs, nee
    Laura Young, daughter of Dr Peter and Virginia C. Young of Mendon
    who he married November 29, 1876. They had 3 children, all died in
    infancy and are buried in Mendon cemetery. He was member of Masonic
    lodge and recently took his 32nd degree. Was also a member of A.O.U..W

Brinloetter, Fred   "Death"   Feb 16, 1899
    see Mrs Anna Hagerbaumer

Brinton, Anna S.   "Obituary"   Sep 28, 1904
    see J.R. Chittenden

Brown, Josephine   "Obituary"   Aug 2, 1905
    see Daniel Arthur Bradley

Brown, Willie   "Fatal Shooting"   Dec 2, 1885
    Carlton McCarl accidently shot Willie Brown, son of Capt. and Mrs
    Brown while the two were rabbit hunting. Buried in Family plot.
    Services from the Espiscopla church by Rev Holst.

Chittenden, C.A., Geo. R. and S.F. "Obituary"   Nov 2, 1904
    see Sarah A. Lay Frisbie

Cromer, Ida   "Local"   Aug 29, 1901
    Mrs C.F. Burnham left for Rantoul, Kansas to see her sister, Ida
    who died Friday night. Mrs Cromer has been bedfast several months.

Dudley, Mrs Herman   "Obituary"   Jan 4, 1904
    see David W. Strickler

2

Feldkamp, Herman   "Local"   Jul 4, 1895
Mr J.R. Urech was called to Chicago to attend the funeral of his old
friend, Mr Herman Feldkamp.

Filbuster, Peter   "Loraine"   Feb 1, 1883
Capt. Fred Ward and Col. R. Wiltz will erect a monument near Bear Creek
bridge. Sacred to the memory of Peter Filbuster.

Frederick, Mrs   "Death"   Jan 24, 1889
see Mrs Weisman

Frisbie, Sarah A. Lay   "Obituary"   Nov 2, 1904
Sarah A. Lay Frisbie was born in Branford, Conn January 29, 1823 and
died at her home near Mendon, Ill. October 27, 1904. She was 81 yrs
8 mo's 28 days old. Married Joseph R. Frisbie May 5, 1845 and they
came west the next month to Mendon where she lived since except 4 yrs
spent at Rockford, Ill to educate her children. Leaves husband and
5 children, Louise, Willoughby L., Mary P., Joseph J. Jr., and James G.
12 grandchildren and 1 great grand child, 1 sister, Mrs Cornelia
Parker of New Haven, Conn. She was daughter of New England Dr Willoughby
Lynde Lay. Forebearers settled in New England in Colonial times. On
maternal side she was descended from the Wilfords, Harrison's and
related to the Howe's and also to Cotton Mather of colonial time. On
paternal died she was descended from Oliver Wollcott, one of the
signers of the Declaration of Indelendence who was also governor of
Conn. 1796-1798. Through Gov Griswold of Conn. Her great grandfather
who married Maria, daughter of Oliver Wolcott. Her great grandfather,
Gov Mathew Griswold married Oliver Wollcott's sister, Ursula Wollcott
and by another link she was related in direct line from Governor
Roger Wollcott, father of Oliver. Her father Dr Lay was cousin to the
late Chief Justice White, whose father was Dr Lay's tutor when he was
a boy. Capt. James Lay, of the 3rd Ill Cavalry, formerly of Mendon
was her brother. Her grandfather Capt. Lee Lay was officer in Rev. War.
He was eldest of family of 15 children and when he emigrated to the
colonies brought the family coat of arms, as eldest he was entitled.
It was a single cannon, under which was the Kings seal and "By the
name of Lay" One of the Lay's was knighted by King Edward 111 for
gallantry at the battle of Crecy in 1346 for saving the life of the
Prince of Wales. She joined the Congregational church at age 12 yrs.
Funeral from the family home by Rev S.R. Reno of the Methodist
Episcopal church because of illnes of her pastor, Rev J.F. Bacon.
Buried Mendon cemetery. Present from a distance were; Mrs Mary A.
Barker of New York, Mrs Emaline Rea of St Louis, Mrs Elizabeth Ingersoll
and Mrs A.N. Duffy of Burlington. Pall-bearers were her 2 sons and
4 nephews- Willoughby L. and J.B. Frisbie Jr and S.F., Geo R.,
C.A. Chittenden and Harry Frisbie.

Frost, Mrs Ephriam   "Funeral"   Mar 29, 1900
see Edward Gooding

Greenwood, Mr   "Killed"   Sep 25, 1879
see Pete Moffit

Hatton, Harvey see Harvey W. Clair	"Death"	Jun 4, 1891
Johnson, Miss Mary see David W. Strickler	"Obituary"	Jan 4, 1904
Judd, Mrs George W. see Benjamin Franklin Slack	"Obituary"	Feb 3, 1904
Kimball, Mrs Josephine Bradley (Mrs E.S.) see Daniel Arthur Bradley		Aug 2, 1905
Lay, Capt. James see Sarah A. Lay Frisbie	"Obituary"	Nov 2, 1904
Lay, Capt. Lee see Sarah A. Lay Frisbie	"Obituary"	Nov 2, 1904
Lay, Sarah A. see Sarah A. Lay Frisbie	"Obituary"	Nov 2, 1904
Lay, Dr Willoughby Lynde see Sarah A. Lay Frisbie	"Obituary"	Nov 2, 1904
Parker, Mrs Cornelia see Sarah A. Lay Frisbie	"obituary"	Nov 2, 1904
Shriver, Mrs Emma see Mrs Braggebos	"Obituary"	Oct 5, 1893
Wollcott, Maria see Sarah A. Lay Frisbie	"Obituary"	Nov 2, 1904
Wollcott, Oliver see Sarah A. Lay Frisibe	"Obituary"	Nov 2, 1904

Worthem, Prof. Amos H.   May 10, 1888
    Prof. Amos H. Worthem, the state geologist died at the residence of
his son near Warsaw. He had been state geologist for the past 30 yrs.
Succeeded Dr Norwood in 1858. The office was created in 1851.

Young, Miss Laura see Daniel Arthur Bradley	"Obituary"	Aug 2, 1905
Young, Dr Peter and Virginia C. see Daniel Arthur Bradley	"Obituary"	Aug 2, 1905

Heritage Books by
Mrs. Joseph J. Beals, Sr. and Mrs. Sandra Kirchner:

Births and Related Items Abstracted from The Camp Point Journal
of Camp Point, Adams County, Illinois, 1873–1903

Deaths Abstracted from The Camp Point Journal, *1873–1882,
Camp Point, Adams County, Illinois*

Deaths Abstracted from The Camp Point Journal, *1883–1892,
Camp Point, Adams County, Illinois*

Deaths Abstracted from The Camp Point Journal, *1893–1903,
Camp Point, Adams County, Illinois*

*Marriages (1895–1905) and Deaths (1895–1900) and Related Items Abstracted
from the* Golden New Era *of Golden, Adams County, Illinois*

Marriages and Related Items Abstracted from Clayton Enterprise
Newspaper of Clayton, Adams County, Illinois, 1879–1900

Marriages and Related Items Abstracted from the Mendon Dispatch
of Mendon, Adams County, Illinois, 1877–1905

Obituaries and Death Related Items Abstracted from Clayton Enterprise
Newspaper of Clayton, Adams County Illinois, 1879–1900, Volume 1

Obituaries and Death Related Items Abstracted from the Hendon Dispatch
of Mendon, Adams County, Illinois, 1877–1905

CD: Births and Deaths Abstracted from The Camp Point Journal,
Camp Point, Adams County, Illinois, 1873–1903

CD: Marriages and Related Items Abstracts from the Golden New Era
Newspaper of Golden, Adam County, Illinois, 1895–1905

CD: Marriages and Related Items Abstracts from the Mendon Dispatch
of Mendon, Adams County, Illinois, 1877–1905

CD: Obituaries and Death Related Items Abstracts from the Golden New Era
Newspaper of Golden, Adam County, Illinois, 1895–1900

CD: Obituaries and Death Related Items Abstracts from the Mendon Dispatch
of Mendon, Adams County, Illinois, 1877–1905

www.ingramcontent.com/pod-product-compliance
Lightning Source LLC
Chambersburg PA
CBHW050448270326
41927CB00009B/1652